D0871251

Twenty Years of Silents 1908-1928

compiled by

JOHN T. WEAVER

The Scarecrow Press, Inc.
Metuchen, N.J. 1971

"The Library of Congress Cataloged the Original Printing of
This Title as:".

Weaver, John T

Twenty years of silents, 1908–1928. Compiled by John T. Weaver. Metuchen, N. J., Scarecrow Press, 1971.

514 p. port. 23 cm.

Bibliography: p. viii.

1. Moving-picture actors and actresses. 2. Moving-pictures, Silent—U. S. I. Title.

PN1998.A2W38 016.79143'5 73-157729
ISBN 0-8108-0401-8 MARC

Library of Congress 71 [60-2]

DEDICATED to those wonderful "SILENT" people never to be forgotten--names that bring a reflective look, a smile of recognition--who gave so much for so little. Time has changed, memories cannot! One can only hope the new will be as agreeable and memorable as the old, that motion pictures can still cast their spell today and tomorrow, as their magic was cast those yesteryears.

Table of Contents

PREFACE

THE AUTHOR'S INTENTION IS TO RECORD "THE SILENTS" FOR POSTERITY: THOSE UNSUNG PLAYERS WHO PROVIDED THE WEDNESDAY AND SATURDAY MATINEES WITH A NEW BILL WEEKLY--SOMETIMES TWO--AND VODVIL TOO. THE WRITER DRAWS ON THE MEMORIES OF HIS CHILDHOOD, WHICH WAS FILLED WITH A MELODRAMATIC FEATURE OR SAGEBRUSH SAGA, A GRIPPING SERIAL, A PIE-THROWING COMEDY, AND MAYBE A NEWSREEL TOSSED IN FOR GOOD MEASURE IF TIME WOULD ALLOW--ALL FOR A DIME (10¢).

Editor's Note

John T. Weaver died the week his previous book, Forty Years of Screen Credits, 1929-1969, was published in 1970, and never saw the finished product of his labors. He was just completing work on this new book at the time. If it has flaws, it is because his great knowledge of the movies was not available to us in the final stages of preparing the book for publication. We shall miss a valuable author who has contributed greatly to the historical record of the motion picture and its players.

Explanatory Notes

Some films released in 1928 and 1929, with the inception of sound, have the letter "T" following the credits. This indicates they are talking pictures. "PT" denotes a part-talking release, and "SSE" synchronized sound effects. No symbol following a title indicates the film had no sound.

Birth dates are given according to the earliest and most reliable source. The letter "c" before some dates means "circa," indicating questionable exactness; "d" indicates "demise" or "death."

The gap between each film credit in the player's column refers to the year the feature was released:

1909: Friends
The Chief's Blanket
The One She Loved
Brutality
11: Fighting Blood
12: The New York Hat
The God Within
My Hero
A Cry for Help

If a gap between the years occurs and a year is unlisted or skipped, as for example the above (1910 missing), either the player did not make a picture that year, or the writer was unable to find any credits for that particular period of time.

Every effort has been made to supply correct dates for all the films listed in this volume. Where the dates are uncertain the title appears at the end of each screen credit entry with the symbol ?? in place of the date. This serves to establish the individual's connection with the film even though the date of that production is undetermined.

Acknowledgments

Film Year Book (1926)

Film Daily Year Book (1928)

Motion Picture Studio Directory & Trade Annual (1920, 1923-1924)

Daniel Blum's Silent Screen

Classics of the Silent Screen - Joe Franklin

The Movies - Richard Griffith & Arthur Mayer

Filmlexico Degli Autori E Delle Opere I-VI, Edizioni di Bianeo e Nero, Roma

Kops and Custards - Kalton Lahue & Terry Brewer, U. Of Okla. Press

Bound and Gagged - Kalton Lahue, A. S. Barnes & Co., N. Y.

The Rise of the American Films, Lewis Jacobs, Teachers College Press, N. Y.

Best Moving Pictures of 1922-1923 - Robt. Sherwood, Small, Maynard & Co., Boston, Mass.

Motion Picture Almanac (1934)(1930)(1929)

Who's Who in the Film World (1914) - Fred C. Justice & Tom R. Smith, Los Angeles

World Film Encyclopedia (1933) - Amalgamated Press, London, England

Catalog of Copyright Entries, Motion Pictures (1912-1939). -- U. S. Copyright Office.

PART I: THE PLAYERS

"SHEIK OF THE SILENTS"
RUDOLPH VALENTINO

Alphabetical Index

Billy Bevan
Buffalo Bill, Jr.
Constance Binney
Faire Binney
Carlyle Blackwell
Sally Blane
Holbrook Blinn
Monte Blue
Betty Blythe
Eleanor Boardman
Eddie Boland
Mary Boland
John Boles
Priscilla Bonner
Olive Borden
Hobart Bosworth
Wade Boteler
Clara Bow
John Bowers
William (Bill) Boyd
Sidney Bracy
James Bradbury, Jr.
James Bradbury, Sr.
Alice Brady
Ed Brady
Sylvia Breamer
Edmund Breese
El Brendel
Walter Brennan
Evelyn Brent
Mary Brian
Gladys Brockwell
Anna Brody
Betty Bronson
Clive Brook
Tyler Brooke
Van Dyke Brooke
Louise Brooks
Robert Brower
Joe E. Brown
Johnny Mack Brown
Tom Brown
Kate Bruce
Fritzi Brunette
Charles Bryant
Winifred Bryson
John Bunny
Billie Burke
Edmund Burns
Neal Burns
Robert (Bobby) Burns
Clarence Burton
Mae Busch
Francis X. Bushman, Jr.
Francis X. Bushman, Sr.
David Butler
Fred Butler

C

Orville Caldwell
Alice Calhoun
Catherine Calvert
E. H. Calvert
Eric Campbell
Frank Campeau
Eddie Cantor
Yakima Canutt
June Caprice
Arthur Edmund Carew
Ora Carew
Edwin Carewe
Rita Carewe
Harry Carey
Richard Carle
Richard Carlyle
Jewel Carmen
Tulio Carminati
Sue Carol
Mary Carr
Nancy Carroll
Mrs. Leslie Carter
Enrico Caruso
Kathryn Carver
Louise Carver
Dolores Cassinelli
Irene Castle
Barbara Castleton
Line Cavalieri
Joseph Cawthorn
Nora Cecil
Cyril Chadwick
George Chandler
Lane Chandler
Lon Chaney
Charlie Chaplin
Sidney Chaplin
Edythe Chapman
Mary Charleson
Charley Chase
Emile Chautard
Jack Chefee
Virginia Cherrill
George Chesebro
Naomi Childers

Ann Christy
Ethlyne Clair
Gertrude Claire
Marguerite Clark
Ethel Clayton
Marguerite Clayton
Ruth Clifford
Elmer Clifton
Andy Clyde
Edmund Cobb
Joey Cobb
Lew Cody
Junior Coghlan
Nick Cogley
George M. Cohan
Constance Collier
William Collier, Jr.
June Collyer
Ronald Colman
Betty Compson
Jackie Condon
Charles "Heinie" Conklin
Chester Conklin
William Conklin
Edward Connelly
Albert Conti
Jackie Coogan
Clyde Cook
Al Cooke
Hallam Cooley
Gary Cooper
George Cooper
Miriam Cooper
Virginia Lee Corbin
Marcelle Corday
Anne Cornwall
Geno Corrado
James Corrigan
Ricardo Cortez
Dolores Costello
Helene Costello
Maurice Costello
Lucy Cotton
Marguerite Courtot
Blanche Craig
Nell Craig
Ward Crane
Joan Crawford
Donald Crisp
Josephine Crowell
Dorothy Cummings
Irving Cummings
Grace Cunard
Lester Cuneo
Frank Currier
Jack Curtis
Bob Custer

D

Lil Dagover
Sidney D'Albrook
Dorothy Dalton
Hazel Daly
Viola Dana
Karl Dane
Bebe Daniels
Roy D'Arcy
Grace Darling
Jean Darling
Grace Darmond
Frankie Darrow
Jane Darwell
Alice Davenport
Dorothy Davenport
Milla Davenport
John Davidson
Max Davidson
William B. Davidson
Marion Davies
Mildred Davis
Yola D'avril
Marjorie Daw
Hazel Dawn
Doris Dawson
Alice Day
Marceline Day
Julia Dean
Priscilla Dean
Hazel Deane
Nigel De Brulier
Pedro De Cordoba
Adele De Garde
Sam De Grasse
Mr. and Mrs. Carter De Haven
Phillipe De Lacey
Marguerite De la Motte
Charles Delaney
Dolores Del Rio
William Demarest
Carol Dempster
Reginald Denny
Vernon Dent
Lya de Putti
Ruby De Remer

Charles De Roche
Andres De Segurola
William Desmond
Andy Devine
Dorothy Devore
Elliott Dexter
Marlene Dietrich
Eddie Dillon
Rose Dione
Richard Dix
Billy Dooley
Johnny Dooley
Mlle. Doraldina
Marie Doro
Billie Dove
Joseph Dowling
Regina Doyle
Louise Dresser
Marie Dressler
Roland Drew
Mr. and Mrs. Sidney Drew
Nancy Drexel
Claire DuBrey
Jack Duffy
Tom Dugan
Helen Dunbar
Bud Duncan
William Duncan
Josephine Dunn
Miss Du Pont
Minta Durfee
George Duryea (Tom Keene)
Dorothy Dwan

E

Jeanne Eagels
Claire Eames
Edna Earle
Edward Earle
Reeves Eason
Helen Jerome Eddy
Robert Edeson
Neely Edwards
Snitz Edwards
Jack Egan
Sally Eilers
Maxine Elliott
Robert Elliott
Robert Ellis
Julian Eltinge
June Elvidge
Alphonz Ethier
Madge Evans
Bessie Eyton

F

Elinor Fair
Douglas Fairbanks, Jr.
Douglas Fairbanks, Sr.
William Fairbanks
Virginia Brown Faire
Dot Farley
James Farley
Dustin Farnum
Franklyn Farnum
William Farnum
Geraldine Farrar
Charles Farrell
William Faversham
George Fawcett
Julia Faye
Louise Fazenda
Fritz Feld
Rockliffe Fellowes
Leslie Fenton
Al Ferguson
Casson Ferguson
Elsie Ferguson
Helen Ferguson
Lew Fields
W. C. Fields
Romaine Fielding
Clyde Fillmore
Flora Finch
Jimmy Finlayson
Margarita Fisher
Cissy Fitzgerald
Emily Fitzroy
Paul Fix
Bess Flowers
Maurice Flynn
Courtenay Foote
Ralph Forbes
Francis Ford
Harrison Ford
Eugenie Forde
Tom Forman
Allan Forrest
Ann Forrest
Helen Foster
Earle Foxe
Alec B. Francis

Betty Francisco
Robert Frazer
George B. French
Pauline Frederick
Charles K. French
Blanche Frederici
Trixie Friganza
Dale Fuller
Mary Fuller
Olive Fuller

G

Ray Gallagher
Richard "Skeets" Gallagher
Tom Gallery
Greta Garbo
Mary Garden
Pauline Garon
Anita Garvin
Gene Gauntier
Janet Gaynor
Clarence Geldert
Gladys George
Maud George
Carmelita Geraghty
Neva Gerber
Charles Gerrard
Douglas Gerrard
Helen Gibson
Hoot Gibson
Billy Gilbert
Eugenia Gilbert
John Gilbert
William Gillespie
William Gillette
Claude Gillingwater
Joseph Girard
Dorothy Gish
Lillian Gish
Gaston Glass
Louise Glaum
James Gleason
Ernest Glendenning
J. Frank Glendon
Dagmar Godowsky
Harold Goodwin
Bruce Gordon
Huntley Gordon
Julia Swayne Gordon
Kitty Gordon
Maude Turner Gordon
Robert Gordon
Vera Gordon
Jetta Goudal
John Gough
Gibson Gowland
Ethel Grandin
Greta Granstedt
Lawrence Grant
Valentine Grant
Bertram Grassby
Ralph Graves
Cesare Gravina
Gilda Gray
Lawrence Gray
Kempton Greene
Winifred Greenwood
Edna Gregory
Ena Gregory
Eddie Gribbon
Harry Gribbon
Corinne Griffith
David Wark Griffith
Raymond Griffith
Sybil Grove
Kit Guard
Texas Guinan
Dorothy Gulliver

H

George Hackathorne
Albert Hackett
Frank Hagney
Rea Haines
Robert T. Haines
William Haines
Alan Hale
Creighton Hale
Georgia Hale
Charlie Hall
Ella Hall
Evelyn Hall
James Hall
Thurston Hall
Winter Hall
Ray Hallor
Harry Ham
Hale Hamilton
Lloyd Hamilton
Mahlon Hamilton
Neil Hamilton
Elaine Hammerstein

Virginia Hammond
Hope Hampton
Einar Hansen
Juanita Hansen
Lars Hanson
Oliver Hardy
Sam Hardy
Lumsden Hare
Kenneth Harlan
Otis Harlan
Jean Harlow
Pat Harman
Mildred Harris
Jimmy Harrison
John Harron
Robert Harron
Neal Hart
Sunshine Hart
William S. Hart
Gretchen Hartman
Pat Hartigan
Lillian Harvey
Olive Hasbrouck
Raymond Hatton
Ulrich Haupt
Phyllis Haver
Ormi Hawley
Wanda Hawley
Mary Hay
Sessue Hayakawa
Richard Headrick
Edward Hearne
O. P. Heggie
Violet Heming
Del Henderson
Gale Henry
Holmes Herbert
Aggie Herring
Jean Hersholt
Herbert Heyes
Ruth Hiatt
Howard Hickman
Walter Hiers
Doris Hill
Ernest Hilliard
Harry Hilliard
Johnny Hines
Raymond Hitchcock
Otto Hoffman
Thomas Holding
Allice Hollister
Carol Holloway
Helen Holmes
Stuart Holmes
Taylor Holmes
Jack Holt
Robert Homans
Gloria Hope
De Wolf Hopper
Hedda Hopper
Camilla Horn
Clara Horton
Edward Everett Horton
Harry Houdini
Arthur Housman
Alice Howell
Reed Howes
Jobyna Howland
Hart Hoxie
Jack Hoxie
Arthur Hoyt
Louise Huff
Gareth Hughes
Lloyd Hughes
Gladys Hulette
Henry Hull
Glen Hunter
Madeline Hurlock
Brandon Hurst
Paul Hurst
Charles Hutchinson
Leila Hyams
Peggy Hyland

I

Ralph Ince
George Irving
Boyd Irwin
May Irwin

J

Mary Ann Jackson
Peaches Jackson
Gardner James
Gladden James
William "Bud" Jamison
Dorothy Janis
Elsie Janis
Emil Jannings
Thomas Jefferson
DeWitt Jennings
Eulalie Jensen

George Jessel
Arthur Johnson
Edith Johnson
Martin Johnson Production
Noble Johnson
Julanne Johnston
Justine Johnstone
Rita Jolivet
Buck Jones
Johnny Jones
Leatrice Joy
Alice Joyce
Francis Joyner
Joyzelle
Rupert Julian

K

Armand Kaliz
Gail Kane
Boris Karloff
Roscoe Karns
Raymond Keane
Buster Keaton
Cornelius Keefe
Zeena Keefe
Frank Keenan
Tom Keene see Geo. Duryea
Donald Keith
Ian Keith
Annette Kellerman
Paul Kelly
Fred Kelsey
Mayme Kelso
Matty Kemp
Edgar Kennedy
Madge Kennedy
Merna Kennedy
Tom Kennedy
Barbara Kent
Charles Kent
Crawford Kent
Larry Kent
Doris Kenyon
J. Warren Kerrigan
Norman Kerry
Kathleen Key
Joseph Kilgour
Anita King
Charles King
Claude King
Emmett King
Molly King

Florida Kingsley
Muriel Kingston
Natalie Kingston
Winifred Kingston
Kathleen Kirkham
James Kirkwood
Kithou
Lydia Knott
Alice Knowland
Fred Kohler
Henry Kolker
Lee Kolmar
Tetsu Komai
Mary Kornman
Theodore Kosloff
Paul Kruger

L

Florence LaBadie
Frank Lackteen
Ruby Lafayette
Roy Laidlaw
Alice Lake
Arthur Lake
Barbara Lamarr
Cullen Landis
Charles Lane
Lupino Lane
Nora Lane
Harry Langdon
Lillian Langdon
Laura La Plante
George Larkin
Rod La Rocque
Francine Larrimore
Fontaine La Rue
Stan Laurel
Lucille LaVerne
Dakota Lawrence
Florence Lawrence
Rex Lease
Ivan Lebedeff
Gretchen Lederer
Otto Lederer
Dixie Lee
Frances Lee
Frankie Lee
Gwen Lee
Jane and Katherine Lee
Lila Lee
Anna Lehr

Fritz Leiber
Frank Leigh
Lillian Leighton
Marion Leonard
Gladys Leslie
Kate Lester
George Lewis
Ida Lewis
Mitchell Lewis
Ralph Lewis
Sheldon Lewis
Walter P. Lewis
Vera Lewis
E. K. Lincoln
Elmo Lincoln
Max Linder
Ivan Linow
Ann Little
Lucien Littlefield
Margaret Livingston
Doris Lloyd
Harold Lloyd
Harold Lockwood
Jeannette Loff
Jacqueline Logan
Carole Lombard
Babe London
Tom London
Walter Long
Margaret Loomis
Lillian Lorraine
Louise Lorraine
Frank Losee
Willard Louis
Bessie Love
Montagu Love
Louise Lovely
Edmund Lowe
Myrna Loy
Wilfred Lucas
Jack Luden
Bela Lugosi
Paul Lukas
Alfred Lunt
Anna Luther
Helen Lynch
Sharon Lynn
Ben Lyon
Eddie Lyons and Lee Moran
Bert Lytell
Wilfred Lytell

M

Marc MacDermott
J. Farrell MacDonald
Katherine MacDonald
Wallace MacDonald
Charles Emmett Mack
Hughie Mack
Marion Mack
Willard Mack
Dorothy Mackaill
Mary MacLaren
Douglas MacLean
Golda Madden
Cleo Madison
Charles Mailes
Fred Malatesta
Molly Malone
Leo Maloney
Hank Mann
Margaret Mann
Martha Mansfield
Edna Marion
George Marion
Enid Markey
June Marlowe
Percy Marmont
Mae Marsh
Marguerite Marsh
Tully Marshall
Vivian Martin
Edward Martindel
James Mason
Leroy Mason
Shirley Mason
Otto Matiesen
Martha Mattox
Cyril Maude
Edwin Maxwell
Doris May
Herschel Mayall
Ken Maynard
Tex Maynard
Edna Mayo
Frank Mayo
Mary McAllister
Paul McAllister
May McAvoy
Gladys McConnell
Clyde McCoy
Gertrude McCoy
Harry McCoy
Tim McCoy

Philo McCullough
Francis McDonald
Claire McDowell
J. P. McGowan
Walter McGrail
Malcolm McGregor
Kathryn McGuire
Mickey McGuire
Lafe McKee
Raymond McKee
Robert McKim
Victor McLaglen
George Meeker
Thomas Meighan
Adolphe Menjou
Charles Meredith
Violet Mesereau
Buddy Messenger
Gertrude Messenger
Harry Mestayer
Earl Metcalf
Adolph Milar
John Miljan
Patsy Ruth Miller
Walter Miller
Mary Miles Minter
Rhea Mitchell
Tom Mix
William V. Mong
Bull Montana
Baby Peggy Montgomery
Colleen Moore
Matt Moore
Owen Moore
Tom Moore
Victor Moore
Lee Moran with Eddie Lyons
Lois Moran
Polly Moran
Milton Morante
Antonio Moreno
Harry T. Morey
Frank Morgan
James Morrison
Charles Morton
Maria Mosquini
Edward Moulton
Jack Mower
Jack Mulhall
Ann Murdock
Edna Murphy
Charles Murray
James Murray
Mae Murray
Carmel Myers
Harry C. Myers

N

Conrad Nagel
Nita Naldi
Alla Nazimova
Pola Negri
James Neill
Jack Nelson
Evelyn Nesbitt
George Nichols
Paul Nicholson
Anna Q. Nilsson
Greta Nissen
Marion Nixon
Mary Nolan
Mabel Normand
Barry Norton
Hedda Nova
Eva Novak
Jane Novak
Ramon Novarro
Wedgewood Nowell
Edward Nugent
Carroll Nye

O

Jack Oakie
Vivien Oakland
Wheeler Oakman
Eugene O'Brien
George O'Brien
Pat O'Brien
Tom O'Brien
Robert Emmett O'Connor
Peggy O'Dare
Dawn O'Day (Anne Shirley)
Molly O'Day
Spec O'Donnell
Charles Ogle
Warner Oland
Edna May Oliver
Guy Oliver
Gertrude Olmstead
Pat O'Malley
Nance O'Neil
Sally O'Neil

William Orlamond
Louise Orth
Baby Marie Osborne
Miles "Bud" Osborne
Vivienne Osborne
Muriel Ostriche
"Our Gang" Kids

- Joey Cobb
- Mickey Daniels
- Jean Darling
- Johnny Downs
- Farina
- Mary Ann Jackson
- Mary Kornman
- "Pete" (the circle-eyed dog)
- Harry Spear
- Stymie
- Wheezer

Seena Owen

P

Charles Paddock
Anita Page
Alfred Paget
Eugene Pallette
Franklin Pangborn
Paul Panzer
Kalla Pasha
Elizabeth Patterson
Bill Patton
Doris Pawn
Virginia Pearson
Edward Peil
Jack Pennick
Ann Pennington
Eileen Percy
Derelys Perdue
George Periolat
Jack Perrin
Robert Perry
House Peters
Olga Petrova
Mary Philbin
Carmen Phillips
Dorothy Phillips
Eddie Phillips
Jack Pickford
Lottie Pickford
Mary Pickford
Walter Pidgeon
Tempe Piggott
Zasu Pitts
Wellington Playter
Lon Poff
Daphne Pollard
Harry "Snub" Pollard
Eddie Polo
Guy Bates Post
Victor Potel
David Powell
William Powell
Tyrone Power, Sr.
Tom Powers
Purnell Pratt
Arline Pretty
Marie Prevost
Kate Price
Aileen Pringle
Herbert Prior
Lucien Prival
Jed Prouty
Frank Puglia
Edna Purviance

Q

Nena Quartaro
Eddie Quillan
Margaret Quimby
Billie Quirk

R

Esther Ralston
Jobyna Ralston
Marjorie Rambeau
Natacha Rambova
Sally Rand
Anders Randolf
Arthur Rankin
Doris Rankin
E. J. Ratcliffe
Jules Raucourt
Herbert Rawlinson
Allene Ray
Charles Ray
Florence Reed
Frank Reicher
Wallace Reid
Rennie Renfro
Ruth Renick
James Rennie
Dorothy Revier
Rex (the Horse)

Vera Reynolds
Billie Rhodes
Frank Rice
Irene Rich
Lillian Rich
Viola Richard
Jack Richardson
Charles Richman
Warner Richmond
Tom Ricketts
Cleo Ridgely
Fritzie Ridgeway
Duncan Rinaldo (Renaldo)
Rin-Tin-Tin
Bert Roach
Jason Robards Sr.
Edith Roberts
Theodore Roberts
May Robson
John Roche
Earle Rodney
Charles "Buddy" Rogers
Will Rogers
Gilbert Roland
Ruth Roland
Buddy Roosevelt
Rosa Rosanova
Albert Roscoe
Bodil Rosing
Alma Rubens
Benny Rubin
William Russell

S

Al St. John
John Saint Polis
Marin Sais
Virginia Sale
Monroe Salisbury
Harry Salter
Teddy Sampson
Tom Santschi
Lewis Sargent
Jackie Saunders
Templer Saxe
Betty Schade
Joseph Schildkraut
Rudolph Schildkraut
Karla Schramm
Violet Schramm
Ferdinand Schumann-Heink
Harry Schumm
Mabel Julienne Scott
Allan Sears
Dorothy Sebastian
Rolfe Sedan
Eileen Sedgwick
Josie Sedgwick
George Seigmann
Evelyn Selbie
Charles Sellon
Clarissa Selwynne
Larry Semon
Mack Sennett
Clarine Seymour
Effie Shannon
Ethel Shannon
Montague Shaw
Norma Shearer
Reginald Sheffield
Lowell Sherman
J. Barney Sherry
Nell Shipman
Lynn Shores
Antrim Short
Gertrude Short
Hassard Short
Lew Short
Marie Shotwell
Lee Shumway
George Sidney
Bernard Siegel
Milton Sills
Russell Simpson
Vera Sisson
Otis Skinner
Martha Sleeper
Phillips Smalley
Marguerite Snow
Sojin
Eve Southern
Sam Southern
Ned Sparks
Harry Spear
Wyndham Standing
Forrest Stanley
Pauline Starke
Vera Steadman
Lincoln Stedman
Myrtle Stedman
Bob Steele
Larry Steers
Ford Sterling
Charles Stevens
Edwin Stevens

Hayden Stevenson
Anita Stewart
Lucille Lee Stewart
Roy Stewart
Carl Stockdale
Edith Stockton
Arthur Stone
Fred Stone
George E. Stone
Lewis Stone
Ruth Stonehouse
Edith Storey
William H. Strauss
Strongheart
Nipo Strongheart
Nick Stuart
Slim Summerville
Valeska Suratt
Eddie Sutherland
Mack Swain
Gloria Swanson
Blanche Sweet
Josef Swickard

T

Richard Taber
Edith Taliaferro
Mabel Taliaferro
Constance Talmadge
Natalie Talmadge
Norma Talmadge
Richard Talmadge
Rose Tapley
Lilyan Tashman
Estelle Taylor
Laurette Taylor
Conway Tearle
Alma Tell
Olive Tell
Lou Tellegen
Barbara Tennant
Alice Terry
Ethel Grey Terry
Rosemary Theby
Olive Thomas
Duane Thompson
Lotus Thompson
Fred Thomson
Kenneth Thomson
Edith Thornton
Mary Thurman
Zeffie Tilbury
Fay Tincher
Lydia Yeamans Titus
Lola Todd
Thelma Todd
Kate Toncray
William Tooker
David Torrence
Ernest Torrence
Raquel Torres
Wayland Trask
Madlaine Travers
Richard Travers
Hugh Trevor
Norman Trevor
Maude Truax
Youcca Trubetzskoy
Howard Truesdale
Ernest Truex
Glenn Tryon
Richard Tucker
Florence Turner
Ben Turpin
Tom Tyler

U

Lenore Ulric

V

Viola Vale
Grace Valentine
Rudolph Valentino
Virginia Valli
Mabel Van Buren
Truman Van Dyke
Harry Van Meter
Victor Varconi
Alberta Vaughn
Michael Vavitch
Conrad Veidt
Lupe Velez
Bobby Vernon
Florence Vidor
Michael Visaroff
Theodore Von Eltz
Carl Von Hartman
Gustav Von Seyffertitz
Erich Von Stroheim

Harold Vosburgh

W

Marie Walcamp
Ethel Wales
Wally Wales
Charlotte Walker
Johnnie Walker
Lillian Walker
Morgan Wallace
George Walsh
Raoul Walsh
Henry B. Walthall
Gladys Walton
Fannie Ward
Helen Ware
H. B. Warner
Robert Warwick
Bryant Washburn
Blue Washington
Paul Weigel
Niles Welch
Charles West
William H. West
Winifred Westover
Stanhope Wheatcroft
Wheezer
Alice White
Leo White
Pearl White
Lloyd Whitlock
Alfred Whitman
Gayne Whitman
Claire Whitney
Crane Wilbur
Earle Williams
Guinn "Big Boy" Williams
Kathlyn Williams
Ben Wilson
Lois Wilson
Margery Wilson
Tom Wilson
Claire Windsor
Dick Winslow
Laska Winters
Jane Winton
Grant Withers
Louis Wolheim
Anna May Wong
Bert Woodruff
Harry Woods
Barbara Worth
Helen Lee Worthing
William Worthington
Fay Wray

Y

Edith Yorke
Clara Kimball Young
Loretta Young
Polly Ann Young
Tammany Young

The Keystone Kops

Hank Mann
Slim Summerville
Edgar Kennedy
Mack Riley
Bobby Dunn
Charles Avery
George Jesky
"Fatty" Arbuckle
Al St. John
Buster Keaton
Ben Turpin
Ford Sterling
Eddie Gribbon
Harry Gribbon
Chester Conklin
Heinie Conklin
Eddie Cline
Charlie Murray
Jimmy Finlayson
Andy Clyde
Victor Potel
Kalla Pasha
Horace McCoy
Del Henderson
Glenn Cavender
Vernon Dant
Billy Gilbert
Charley Chase
Bobby Vernon
Pinto Colvig
Wesley Ruggles
Tom Kennedy
Joe J. Murphy
Eddie Sutherland
Ingram Pickett
Al Thompson
George "Fats" Lebeck
Rea M. Hunt
Bud Jamison
Kewpie Moran
Grover G. Ligen
Billy Hauber
Rube Miller
Billy Bletcher
George Gray
George Dillon

"Ben" (Sennett's dog)
"Cameo" "
"Teddy Keystone" "
"Fido" "
"Pepper" (cat)

Sennett Bathing Beauties

Marie Prevost
Phyllis Haver
Carole Lombard (Jane Peters)
Juanita Hansen
Virginia Fox
Sally Eilers
Madeline Hurlock
Natalie Kingston
Jacqueline Logan
Julia Faye
Vera Steadman
Dale Fuller
Claire Amthes Anderson
Evelyn Lynn
Cecile Evans
Lucille Miller
Fifi Banvard
Irene Lentz
Ivy Crosthwaite (Rice Barrett)
Harriet Hammond
Louise Fazenda
Violet Bird
Mary Thurman
Gloria Swanson wore a bathing suit but was not one of the Girls!

The Original "Our Gang" Kids

Mary Ann Jackson
Jean Darling
Joe Cobb
Harry Spear
Farina
Wheezer
Mickey Daniels
Mary Kornman
Johnny Downs
Spanky McFarland
"Pete" (the circle-eyed dog)

Wampas Babies

-1922-

Bessie Love, Marion Aye, Helen Ferguson, Lila Lee, Lois Wilson, Jacqueline Logan, Louise Lorraine, Katherine McGuire, Patsy Ruth Miller, Colleen Moore, Mary Philbin, Pauline Starke, Claire Windsor.

-1923-

Eleanor Boardman, Evelyn Brent, Dorothy Devore, Virginia Brown Faire, Betty Francisco, Pauline Garon, Kathleen Key, Laura La Plante, Margaret Leahy, Helen Lynch, Derelys Perdue, Jobyna Ralston, Ethel Shannon.

-1924-

Clara Bow, Eleanor Fair, Carmelita Geraghty, Gloria Grey, Ruth Hiatt, Julianne Johnston, Hazel Keener, Dorothy Mackaill, Blanche Mahaffey, Margaret Morris, Marian Nixon, Lucille Rickson, Alberta Vaughn.

-1925-

Betty Arlen, Violet Avon, Olive Borden, Ann Cornwall, Ena Gregory, Madeline Hurlock, Natalie Joyce, Joan Meredyth, June Marlowe, Evelyn Pierce, Dorothy Revier, Duane Thompson, Lola Todd.

-1926-

Mary Astor, Mary Brian, Joyce Compton, Dolores Costello, Joan Crawford, Marceline Day, Dolores Del Rio, Janet Gaynor, Sally Long, Edna Marion, Sally O'Neill, Vera Reynolds, Fay Wray.

-1927-

Priscilla Bonner, Rita Carewe, Helene Costello, Barbara Kent, Natalie Kingston, Gladys McConnell, Sally Phipps, Sally Rand, Ann Rork, Martha Sleeper, Anamae (Adama) Vaughn, Myrna Loy, Gwen Lee, Iris Stuart, Pauline Avery, Mary McAllister.

-1928-

Lena Basquette, Flora Bramley, Sue Carol, Ann Christy, June Collyer, Sally Eilers, Alice Day, Audrey Ferris, Dorothy Gulliver, Molly O'Day, Ruth Taylor, Lupe Velez.

Screen Credits

Jean Acker
1919: Checkers
Lombardi, Limited
20: The Round Up
The Arabian Knight
21: Brewster's Millions
Wealth
The Affairs of Anatol
See My Lawyer
The Scarlet Shawl
22: Her Own Money
23: Woman in Chains
26: Brave Heart

Art Acord (1890-1931)
1915: A Man Afraid of his Wardrobe
19: The Squaw Man
20: The Moon Riders (serial)
21: Winners of the West (serial)
22: In the Days of Buffalo Bill (serial)
23: Oregon Trail (serial)
White Horseman
25: The Scrappin' Kid
Call of Courage
Three in Exile
Circus Cyclone
26: Pursued
Rustler's Ranch
Lazy Lightning
Man from the West
The Terror
Riding Rascal
Sky High Corral
Set Up
Western Pluck
27: Loco Luck
Set Free
Hard Fists
Spurs and Saddles
Western Rover
28: Two Gun O'Brien
28: His Last Battle
White Outlaw

Claire Adams
1919: Key to Power
Spirit of the Red Cross
20: Riders of the Dawn
The Penalty
The Great Lover
The Money Changers
21: The Spenders
The Lure of Egypt
The Man of the Forest
A Certain Rich Man
The Mysterious Rider
21: Dwelling Place of Light
22: Just Tony
Do and Dare
In Arabia
23: Brass Commandments
The Scarlet Car
White Silence
24: The Fast Set
Oh, You Tony!
25: The Big Parade
26: The Sea Wolf
Yellow Fingers
27: Married Alive

Renee Adoree (1898-1933)
1920: Mystic Faces
The Strongest
21: Made in Heaven
22: Monte Cristo
West of Chicago
The Law Bringers
A Self Made Man
Honor First
Mixed Faces
23: The Eternal Struggle
Six Fifty
24: Bandolero
25: The Big Parade
26: Exquisite Sinner (or, Escape)

26: La Boheme
That Certain Young Man
Blarney
Tin Gods
The Flaming Forest
27: Mr. Wu
The Show
Heaven on Earth
On Ze Boulevard
Back to God's Country
28: Forbidden Hours
The Cossacks
The Michigan Kid
Mating Call
29: Hollywood Revue of 1929 T
Show People T
The Pagan SSE
Tide of Empire
30: The Spieler PT
Redemption T
Call of the Flesh T
Singer of Seville T

Robert Agnew (1899-)
1920: Sporting Duchess
Valley of Doubt
Sin that Was His
21: The Highest Law
Frisky Mrs. Johnson
The Sign on the Door
Passion Flower
Wonderful Thing WB
22: Dangerous Adventure (serial)
Clarence
23: Kick In
Only 38
24: Spanish Dancer
25: Tessie
26: Taxi Mystery
Dancing Days
Unknown Treasures
Wild Oats Lane
Racing Blood
27: Wandering Girls
Down the Stretch
Quarantined Rivals
Heart of Salome
She's My Baby
Prince of Headwaiters
Snowbound
Slightly Used
College Hero
28: Heart of Broadway
Midnight Taxi

Spottiswoode Aitken (d. 1933)
1914: The Old Maid
Home Sweet Home
Avenging Conscience
Liberty Bells
Big James' Heart
15: The Birth of a Nation
Captain Machlin
16: The Wharf Rat
17: Stage Struck
19: Who Cares?
The White Heather
Evangeline
Thunderbolt
A Woman of Pleasure
Jane Goes A-Wooing
Hay-Foot, Straw-Foot!
Fighting Through
Wicked Darling
Broken Commandments
Man of Courage
20: Nomads of the North
The White Circle
21: Unknown Wife
Reputation
At the End of the World
Dangerous Love
22: The Young Rajah
Monte Cristo
The Trap
23: Around the World in 18 days (U. serial)

Mary Alden
1914: Ghosts
The Second Mrs. Roebuck
The Little Country Mouse
Home Sweet Home
Another Glance
Big James' Heart
15: The Birth of a Nation
Her Mother's Daughter
Bred in the Bone
16: Intolerance
Acquitted
17: The Argyle Case
Land of Promise
By Right of Possession
18: Naulahka
The Straight Path

19: The Broken Butterfly
Common Clay
Erstwhile Susan
Unpardonable Sin
20: Inferior Sex
Nobody's Girl
Milestones
Honest Hutch
Silk Husbands and Calico Wives
21: Trust your Wife
Witching Hour
The Old Nest
Parted Curtain
22: Bond Boy
Man with Two Mothers
A Woman's Woman
Hidden Woman
Notoriety
23: Has the World Gone Mad?
The Eagle's Feather
Tents of Allah
25: Siege
Plastic Age
26: Earth Woman
Lovey Mary
April Fool
Brown of Harvard
27: The Potters
Joy Girl
28: Ladies of the Mob
Fools for Luck
The Sawdust Paradise SSE
Someone to Love
The Cossacks
29: Port of Dreams
Girl Overboard PT

Ben Alexander (1911-1969)
1917: The Little American
Each Pearl a Tear
1918: Hearts of the World
Heart of Rachel
19: Turn in the Road
Hushed Hour
White Heather
Better Wife
Battle of Youth
Tangled Threads
Joselyn's Wife
20: Triflers
Family Honor
21: Heart Line
22: In the Name of the Law
23: Penrod and Sam
Boy O'Mine
24: Self Made Failure
26: Highbinders
Scotty of the Scouts (serial)
27: Fighting for Fame (serial)
28: River Pirate SSE
29: Divine Lady SSE

Hugh Allan (1903-)
1924: Sally
Object-Alimony
27: Birds of Prey
What Happened to Father
Cruel Truth
Wild Beauty
Dress Parade
Good Time Charley
28: Beware of Married Men SSE
Hold 'em, Yale!
Plastered in Paris SSE
Annapolis SSE
Voice of the Storm
Sin Town
The Tiger's Shadow (serial)

Phyllis Allen
1914: Caught in a Cabaret
The Rounders
Dough and Dynamite
Gentleman of Nerve
His Trysting Place
Tillie's Punctured Romance
Getting Acquainted
The Property Man (or, The Roustabout)
Shot in the Excitement
Fatty's Jonah Day
15: Fickle Fatty's Fall
Giddy, Gay, and Ticklish (or, A Gay Lothario)
A Submarine Pirate
Gussie's Wayward Path
16: A Movie Star
The Judge
No One to Guide Him
22: Pay Day

May Allison (1895-)
1915: Shop Girls
Governor's Lady

16: The Secret Wire
River of Romance
The Last Card
17: The Promise
Big Tremaine
18: Winning of Beatrice
Social Hypocrites
Testing of Mildred Vane
A Successful Adventure
19: In For Thirty Days
Peggy Does her Darndest
Fair and Warmer
Her Inspiration
Almost Married
Isle of Intrigue
The Uplifters
Return of Mary
Castles in the Air
20: The Cheater
Held in Trust
The Walk-Offs
21: Marriage of William Ashe
Extravagance
Big Game
Are All Men Alike?
22: The Woman who Fooled Herself
25: The Viennese Medley
26: Men of Steel
The City
Mismates
27: One Increasing Purpose
Telephone Girl

Don Alvarado (1904-1967)

1927: Monkey Talks
Loves of Carmen
Breakfast at Sunrise
28: Drums of Love
No Other Woman
Scarlet Lady
Battle of the Sexes SSE
Driftwood
29: Apache
Bridge of San Luis Rey PT
Rio Rita T

"Bronco Billy" Anderson (1882-1970)

1903: Great Train Robbery
07: An Awful Skate
09: Heart of a Cowboy
The Indian Trailer
A Western Maid
09: The Ranchman's Rival
Spanish Girl
His Reformation
Judgment
Best Man Wins
A Tale of the West
The Black Sheep
A Mexican's Gratitude
10: Away Out West
The Cowboy and the Squaw
The Cowpuncher's Ward
The Flower of the Ranch
The Forest Ranger
The Mistaken Bandit
The Outlaw's Sacrifice
The Ranch Girl's Legacy
The Ranchman's Feud
The Sheriff's Sacrifice
The Bandit's Wife
Western Chivalry
Take Me Out to the Ball Game
The Unknown Claim
Trailed by the West
The Desperado
Under Western Skies
The Dumb Half-Breed's Defense
The Deputy's Love Affair
The Millionaire and the Girl
An Indian Girl's Love
The Pony Express Rider
The Tout's Remembrance
Patricia of the Plains
The Bearded Bandit
A Cowboy's Mother-in-Law
Pals of the Range
The Silent Message
A Westerner's Way
The Marked Trail
A Cowboy's Vindication
The Tenderfoot Messenger
A Gambler of the West
The Bad Man's Christmas
The Girl on Triple X
The Good-for-Nothing
Bronco Billy's Redemption
11: A Girl of the West
The Border Ranger
Two Reformations
The Bad Man's Downfall
On the Desert's Edge
Romance of Bar "O"

11: The Faithful Indian
A Thwarted Vengeance
Across the Plains
Carmencita the Faithful
The Sheriff's Chum
The Indian Maiden's Lesson
The Puncher's New Love
The Lucky Card
The Infant of Snakeville
The Tribe's Penalty
The Sheriff's Brother
The Hidden Mine
The Corporation and the Ranch Girl
Bronco Billy's Adventure
The Count and the Cowboy
The Outlaw and the Child

12: Bronco Billy Outwitted
The Shotgun Ranchman
The Outlaw's Sacrifice
Bronco Billy's Love Affair
Bronco Billy's Mexican Wife
The Tomboy on Bar Z
The Ranch Girl's Trail
The Mother of the Ranch
An Indian Friendship
Cutting California Redwoods
Bronco Billy's Heart
The Dance at Silver Gulch
The Boss of the Katy Mine
Western Girls
Bronco Billy's Promise
The Prospector
The Sheriff's Luck
The Sheriff's Inheritance
The Reward of Bronco Billy
The Smuggler's Daughter
Alkali Ike's Boarding House
Alkali Ike's Pants
Alkali Ike Plays the Devil
Alkali Ike Stung!
Love on the Luck Ranch
Alkali Ike's Close Shave
Alkali Ike's Motorcycle

1913: Why Bronco Billy Left Bear County
The Last Roundup

13: When Love and Honor Called
The Cowboy Coward
Shootin' Mad
Bronco Billy and the Maid
Bronco Billy and the Outlaw's Mother
Bronco Billy's Brother
Bronco Billy's Gunplay
The Sheriff's Child
The Sheriff's Story
Bronco Billy's Last Deed
Bronco Billy's Ward
Bronco Billy and the Sheriff's Kid
Influence on Bronco Billy
Bronco Billy and the Squatter's Daughter
Bronco Billy and the Step-Sisters
Bronco Billy's Sister
Bronco Billy's Gratefulness
Bronco Billy's Way
Bronco Billy's Secret
The Sheriff's Honeymoon
Bronco Billy's First Arrest
Bronco Billy's Squareness
Bronco Billy's Christmas Deed
The Three Gamblers
Alkali Ike in Jayville
Alkali Ike's Homecoming
Alkali Ike's Auto
Alkali Ike's Misfortune

14: Treachery of Bronco Billy's Pal
Bronco Billy and the Rattler
Bronco Billy's True Love
Bronco Billy - Gun Man
Bronco Billy's Close Call
Bronco Billy's Sermon
Bronco Billy's Leap
Bronco Billy's Cunning
Bronco Billy's Duty
Bronco Billy and the Mine Shark
Bronco Billy's Outlaw
Red Riding Hood of the Hills
Bronco Billy's Jealousy

14: Bronco Billy's Punishment
Bronco Billy and the Sheriff
Snakeville's New Doctor
Bronco Billy Guardian
Bronco Billy and the Bad Man
Bronco Billy and the Settler's Daughter
Bronco Billy and the Red Hand
Calling of Jim Barton
The Interference of Bronco Billy
Bronco Billy's Bible
Bronco Billy and the Claim Jumpers
Bronco Billy and the Escaped Bandit
15: Bronco Billy and the Land Grabber
Bronco Billy and the Lumber King
Bronco Billy and the Posse
Bronco Billy Evens Matters
Bronco Billy Misled
Bronco Billy Well Repaid
Bronco Billy's Marriage
Bronco Billy and the False Note
Bronco Billy and the Vigilante
Bronco Billy's Parents
Bronco Billy's Protege
Bronco Billy's Sentence
Bronco Billy's Teachings
Bronco Billy and the Baby
Bronco Billy and the Card Sharp
Bronco Billy Begins Life Anew
Bronco Billy Sheepman
Bronco Billy's Greaser Deputy
Bronco's Surrender
Bronco Billy's Word of Honor
Bronco Billy's Vengeance
Bronco Billy's Cowardly Brother
Bronco Billy Steps In
19: Red Blood and Yellow
22: Greater Duty

Tsuru Aoki (1892-1962)

1914: The Typhoon
16: Alien Souls
The Call of the East
18: The Bravest Way
The Curse of Iku
His Birthright
19: Bonds of Honor
Heart in Pawn
Gray Horizon
The Courageous Coward
The Dragon Painter
Ashes of Desire
20: Breath of the Gods
Locked Lips
A Tokio Siren
22: 5 Days to Live

Oscar Apfel (d. 1938)

1913: The Squaw Man
21: Brewster's Millions
28: Valley of Hunted Men
29: Romance of the Underworld

Macklyn Arbuckle (1866-1931)

1914: The County Chairman
21: Squire Phin
22: Mr. Potter of Texas
Mr. Bingle
The Prodigal Judge
Welcome to our City
Young Diana
24: Janice Meredith
No Laughing Matter
26: Gilded Highway
That Old Gang of Mine

Roscoe "Fatty" Arbuckle) (1887-1933)

1913: In the Clutches of a Gang
Fatty's Flirtation
Fatty's Affair of Honor
Fatty on the Job
Help! Help! Hydrophobia!
The Waiters' Picnic
A Bandit
For the Love of Mabel
The Telltale Right
A Noise from the Deep

13: Love and Courage
The Riot
Mabel's New Hero
The Faithful Taxicab
Mother's Boy
A Quiet Little Wedding
Fatty Joins the Force
The Woman Haters
14: The Rounders
Caught in a Cabaret
The Knockout
Bright Lights
Fatty and the Heiress
A Film Johnnie
Tango Tales
His Favorite Pastime
The Masquerade
Miss Fatty's Seaside Lovers
Leading Lizzie Astray
A Misplaced Foot
A Flirt's Mistake
Chicken Chaser
The Water Dog
A Suspended Ordeal
That Minstrel Man
Those Country Kids
Fatty's Gift
A Brand New Hero
Fatty Again (or Fatty the Four Flusher)
Their Ups and Downs
Zip the Dodger
Lovers Post Office
An Inconsistent Hero
Fatty's Jonah Day
Fatty's Wine Party
The Sea Nymphs
Shotguns That Kick
Fatty's Magic Pants (or Fatty's Suitless Day)
Fatty and Minnie Ha-Haw
Fatty's Debut (or Fatty Butts In)
Fatty's HooDoo Day
15: Rebecca's Wedding Day
Mabel and Fatty's Simple Life
Mabel and Fatty's Wash Day
The Little Teacher (or A Small Town Bully)
Fatty's Plucky Pup
15: The Village Scandal
Fatty and Mabel
When Love Took Wing
Fatty and Mabel's Married Life
That Little Band of Gold
16: Fatty and Mabel Adrift
Fatty's Sweetheart
Fatty and the Broadway Stars
Fickle Fatty's Fall
His Wedding Night
Fatty in Coney Island
He Did and He Didn't (or Love and Lobsters)
The Other Man
The Waiters' Ball
A Creampuff Romance
His Wife's Mistake
The Bright Lights (or The Lure of Broadway
17: Fatty's Feature Film
The Butcher Boy
18: The Bell Boy
The Sheriff
The Cook
Camping Out
19: The Garage
Love
A Desert Hero
Back Stage
20: Life of the Party
The Round Up
Brewster's Millions
Out West
21: The Dollar a Year Man
The Traveling Salesman
Gasoline Gus
Crazy to Marry
27: The Red Mill
Special Delivery
29: Windy Riley Goes to Hollywood
31: Smart Work T
32: Keep Laughing T
Moonlight and Cactus T
Anybody's Goat T
Bridge Wives T
Hollywood Luck T
Mother's Holiday T
It's a Cinch T

Richard Arlen (1899-)
1923: Vengeance of the Deep
25: Coast of Folly
In the Name of Love
26: Behind the Front
The Enchanted Hill
Padlocked
She's a Sheik
27: Rolled Stockings
Blood Ship
Figures Don't Lie
Wings
Sally of our Alley
28: Feel My Pulse
Under the Tonto Rim
Ladies of the Mob
Manhattan Cocktail
Beggars of Life S&PT
29: Four Feathers SSE
Dangerous Curves T
The Man I Love T
Thunderbolt T

George Arliss (1868-1946)
1921: The Devil
Disraeli
22: The Ruling Passion
The Man Who Played God
23: The Green Goddess
24: $20 a Week

Henry Armetta (1888-1945)
1928: The Love Song
The Street Angel
Alias Jimmy Valentine PT

Robert Armstrong (1896-)
1921: Boys Will be Boys
Shavings
Honey Girl
Sure Fire
24: The Man Who Came Back
25: New Brooms
Judy
27: Is Zat So?
War and Women
The Main Event
Silent Voice
28: Shady Lady
Square Crooks
The Cop
Baby Cyclone
Celebrity
28: A Girl in Every Port
The Leopard Lady
29: The Leatherneck PT
Ned McCobb's Daughter SSE
Woman from Hell
Big News
30: Oh Yeah! T
The Racketeer T

George K. Arthur (1899-)
1921: Kipps
22: Lamp in the Desert
A Dear Fool
Wheels of Chance
23: Paddy the Next Best Thing
Hollywood
Don't Marry for Money
25: Salvation Hunters
The Big Parade
Her Sister from Paris
26: Irene
Bardelys the Magnificent
The Exquisite Sinner
The Boob
Sunnyside Up
The Boy Friend
Almost a Lady
The Waning Sex
When the Wife's Away
27: Baby Mine
Spring Fever
Tillie the Toiler
Bookies
Lovers
Gingham Girl
28: Brotherly Love
Circus Rookies
All at Sea
In Old Heidelberg
Detectives
29: China Bound
Wickness Preferred

Jean Arthur (1905-)
1923: Cameo Kirby
24: Temple of Venus
Fast and Fearless
Spring Fever
Case Dismissed
The Powerful Eye
25: Drug Store Cowboy
Seven Chances

25: Tearin' Loose
A Man of Nerve
Travelin' Fast
Ridin' Rivals
26: Thundering Through
Born to Battle
Hurricane Horseman
Fighting Cheat
Cowboy Cop
Twisted Triggers
College Boob
The Block Signal
The Mad Racer
8 Cylinder Bull
Hello, Lafayette (or, Lafayette, Where are We?)
Lightnin' Bill
27: Bigger and Better Blondes
Galloping On
Roaring Rider
Husband Hunters
Broken Gates
Horse Shoes
Poor Nut
Flying Luck
The Masked Menace (serial)
Winners of the Wilderness
28: Wallflowers
Easy Come, Easy Go
Warming Up
Brotherly Love
29: Sins of the Fathers

Johnny Arthur
1923: Unknown Purple
24: Mlle. Midnight
25: The Monster
28: On Trial

Julia Arthur
1918: The Common Cause
The Woman the Germans Shot

Linda Arvidson (1884-1949)
1908: Adventures of Dolly
The Politician's Love Story
Test of Friendship
When Knights were Bold
Balked at the Altar
An Awful Moment
09: Pippa Passes
Edgar Allan Poe
09: Mills of the Gods
Cord of Life
The Converts
In a Hamper Bag
The Helping Hand
Cricket on the Hearth
The Drunkard's Reformation
10: The Rocky Road
The Day After
The Unchanging Sea
11: Enoch Arden
Fisher Folks
13: The Scarlet Letter
14: The Wife
A Fair Rebel
Mission Bells
House that Jack Built
16: Charity

Sylvia Ashton
1912: The Would-Be Shriner
A Dash Through the Clouds
16: For the Defense
17: The Nick of Time Baby
Her Fame and Shame
18: A Pair of Silk Stockings
We Can't Have Everything
19: Don't Change your Husband
For Better, For Worse
20: Why Change your Wife?
Jack Straw
Thou Art the Man
The City Sparrow
Jenny Be Good
Sweet Lavender
21: Love Special
Hold Your Horses
The Blushing Bride
Garments of Truth
The Snob
22: A Daughter of Luxury
Manslaughter
Youth to Youth
While Satan Sleeps
23: Souls for Sale
White Flower
27: Cheating Cheaters
28: Wrecking Boss
Leopard Lady
Ladies' Night in a Turkish Bath

28: The Head Man
The Crash
The Barker PT
A Bachelor's Paradise

Nils Asther (1901-)
1924: Wienersarnet
25: Sveket Nej Volontar
26: Die Drei Uhren
Der Goldene Schmetterling
27: Gaiuner Im Frack
Die Versunckene Flotte
Hotelratte
Wiener Herzen
Budden Geheimnisse
Sorrell and Son
Topsy and Eva
28: When Fleet Meets Fleet
The Blue Danube
Adventure Mad
The Cossack
Laugh, Clown, Laugh
Loves of an Actress SSE
Our Dancing Daughters
Adrienne Lecouvreur
The Cardboard Lover
29: Wild Orchids
Single Standard
Hollywood Revue of 1929 T
Wrath of the Sea

Gertrude Astor (1906-)
1917: Cheyenne's Pal
The Gray Ghost
18: The Lion's Claw
19: The Lion Man
20: Burning Daylight
The Branding Iron
The Great Lover
Occasionally Yours
21: The Concert
Who am I
The Spenders
Fascinating Widow
The Great Moment
Through the Back Door
22: The Impossible Mrs. Bellew
Wall Flower
23: Rupert of Hentzau
The Ne'er-Do-Well
Lorna Doone
Alice Adams
24: Secrets
25: Stage Struck
Kentucky Pride
26: The Boy Friend
Strong Man
Old Soak
Too Many Women
Dame Chance
Cheerful Fraud
Don Juan's 3 Nights
Kiki
Pursued
27: Cat and the Canary
Small Bachelor
Shanghaied
Taxi Dancer
Irresistible Lover
Pretty Clothes
Uncle Tom's Cabin
28: Ginsberg The Great
The Family Group
Stocks and Blondes
Hit of the Show PT
5 and 10¢ Annie SSE
The Butter and Egg Man
Naughty Duchess
The Cohens and the Kellys in Paris
Pay as You Enter SSE
29: She Goes to War
Chasing Husbands
Two Weeks Off PT
Twin Beds T
The Fall of Eve T

Mary Astor (1906-)
1920: Hope
21: The Beggar Maid
The Young Painter
22: John Smith
23: Success
The Bright Shawl
Second Fiddle
The Scarecrow
To the Ladies
Puritan Passions
24: Oh, Doctor!
Beau Brummel
Unguarded Women
25: Don Q.
Enticement
26: Don Juan
Wise Guy
Forever After
High Steppers

27: The Rough Riders
Two Arabian Knights
Dressed to Kill
Dry Martini
Sea Tiger
Rose of the Golden West
The Sunset Derby
No Place to Go
28: Three-Ring Marriage
Heart to Heart
Sailors' Wives
Dressed to Kill
29: New Year's Eve SSE
A Romance of the Underworld SSE
Woman from Hell

Jimmy Aubrey
Starlight Pathe Comedies
Heinie & Louie Comedies
A Merry Chase
Monkey Shines
1919: Mules and Mortgages
20: Dames and Dentists
Rah! Rah! Rah!
His Jonah Day
He Laughs Last
21: The Nuisance
The Blizzard
25: He Who Gets Crowned
27: The Gallant Fool
Pirates of the Sky
When Seconds Count
The Down Grade
The Tale of the Shirt
Call of the Klondike
28: Wilful Youth
The Look-Out Girl
Have a Heart
Keep Smiling
Too Many Wives
A Simple Sap
Little Wild Girl
Out with the Tide
Girl He Didn't Buy
29: China Slaves
??: Maid and Muslin
The Back Yard
The Trouble Hunter
Pugs and Pats

Florence Auer (1880-1962)
1908: The Snow Man
25: The Beautiful City
26: That Royale Girl

Mischa Auer (1905-1967)
1928: Something Always Happens
29: Marquis Preferred

Edwin August (1883-1964)
1908: From Out the Shadows
10: A Child's Impulse
12: The Smile of a Child
Hand that Rocked the Cradle
The Eternal Mother
One is Business, The Other is Crime
13: Primitive Man
14: The Romance of an Actor
15: Bondwoman
16: Yellow Passport
17: A Tale of Two Cities
18: City of Tears
The Lion's Claw
Broadway Scandal
Mortgaged Wife
19: Poison Pen
21: Idol of the North

William Austin
1923: Ruggles of Red Gap
25: What Happened to Jones?
26: The Flaming Forest
Her Big Night
27: It
The World at Her Feet
Swim, Girl, Swim
Honeymoon Hate
28: The Fifty-Fifty Girl
Red Hair
Someone to Love
Just Married
What a Night
29: Illusion T
Sweetie T
Mysterious Dr. Fu Manchu T

Agnes Ayres (d. 1940)
(an extra at ESSANAY Studios)
1917: O. Henry series (25)
Richard the Brazen
The Defeat of the City
The Girl and the Graft

17: The Enchanted Profile
The Purple Dress
18: Bottom of the Well
$1000
19: Sacred Silence
20: Forbidden Fruit
Held by the Enemy
The Inner Voice
The Furnace
21: The Love Special
Too Much Speed
Affairs of Anatol
Cappy Ricks
The Sheik
22: Bought and Paid For
Borderland
Clarence
The Ordeal
The Lane that had no Turning
23: Daughter of Luxury
Racing Hearts
Marriage Maker
Heart Raider
Ten Commandments
24: Story Without a Name
Bluff
Modern Salome
Go and Get it
25: Tomorrow's Love
Her Market Value
26: Son of the Sheik
28: Napoleon and Josephine
29: Lady of Victory
Donovan Affair T
Broken Hearted PT
Bye Bye Buddy PT
36: Souls at Sea

Olga Baclanova (1896-)
1927: Street of Sin
28: The Dove
The Man Who Laughs
3 Sinners
The Czarina's Secrets
Woman Disputed
Forgotten Faces
Docks of New York
Avalanche
29: Wolfe of Wall Street T
The Man I Love T
Dangerous Woman T

Irving Bacon (1893-1965)
1928: Head Man
Caught in the Kitchen
Button My Back
29: Side Street T
Two Sisters
Half Way to Heaven T

King Baggott (1880-1948)
1910: The Wishing Ring
11: The Scarlet Letter
12: Human Hearts
Lady Audley's Secret
13: Ivanhoe
Absinthe
Dr. Jekyll and Mr. Hyde
14: Across the Atlantic
15: City of Terrible Night
Crime's Triangle
The Corsican Brothers
18: Kildare of the Storm
An Eagle's Eye
19: The Man Who Stayed at Home
The Hawk's Trail (serial)
20: Dwelling Place of Light
13th Piece of Silver
Life's Twist
The Cheater
Forbidden Thing
21: Nobody's Fool
Moonlight Follies
Girl Who Knew all About Men
Cheated Love
Snowy Baker
Shadow of Lightning Ridge
Fighting Breed
22: Girl in the Taxi
Kentucky Derby
Lavender Bath Lady
Better Man
Shadows
23: Love Letter
Gossip
His Last Race
Cross Wires
Town Scandal
Darling of New York
24: Tornado
Gaiety Girl
25: Tumbleweeds (dir.)
Jane and the Stranger

25: Raffles
The Home Maker
26: Lovey Mary
27: Perch of the Devil
Down the Stretch
Notorious Lady
28: House of Scandal
Romance of a Rogue

Leah Baird (1887-)
1912: Chumps
Stenographers Wanted
When a Woman Wars
13: Ivanhoe
Absinthe
There's Music in the Hair
Souls in Bondage
14: Neptune's Daughter
15: Tried for His Own Murder
16: The People Vs. John Doe
17: Sunset
One Law for Both
18: Moral Suicide
Life of Honor
19: The Volcano
Hearts of the First Empire
Echo of Youth
As a Man Thinks
The Window Opposite
20: The Capitol
Cynthia of the Minute
21: Heart Line
22: When the Devil Drives
When Husbands Deceive
Don't Doubt Your Wife
The Bride's Confession
23: Destroying Angel
Is Divorce a Failure?
24: Barriers Burned Away
25: The Primrose Path
26: Spangles
Devil's Island
27: Return of Boston Blackie

William Bakewell (1908-)
1923: Gold Diggers
25: Last Edition
26: Mother
28: Battle of the Sexes
Annapolis
West Point
Harold Teen
Latest From Paris

28: Devil's Trade-Mark
29: Iron Mask PT
Hot Stuff T
On With the Show

Mabel Ballin (1885-1958)
1919: The White Heather
The Quickening Flame
Lord and Lady Algy
The Illustrious Prince
20: Pagan Love
Under Crimson Skies
21: East Lynne
Journey's End
22: Other Women's Clothes
Jane Eyre
Married People
23: Vanity Fair
Ave Maria

George Bancroft (1882-1956)
1922: Driven
25: Pony Express
26: Sea Horses
Runaway
Enchanted Hill
Paying the Penalty
Code of the West
Old Ironsides
27: Underworld
White Gold
Too Many Crooks
Tell it to Sweeney
Rough Riders
28: Showdown
Docks of New York
29: Wolf of Wall Street T
Thunderbolt T

Monty Banks (1897-1950)
1920: Poor Simp
25: Keep Smiling
26: Atta Boy!
27: Play Safe
Horse Shoes
Perfect Gentleman
The Flying Luck
29: Honeymoon Abroad
Week End Wives
Atlantic
??: The Flivver Wedding
His Dizzy Days
Bride and Groom
Peaceful Alley

Vilma Banky (1903-)

1924: The Eagle
25: Dark Angel
King of the Circus
26: Winning of Barbara Worth
Son of the Sheik
27: Magic Flame
Night of Love
28: The Awakening
The Lovers
29: This is Heaven PT
30: A Lady to Love T
33: The Rebel T

Theda Bara (1890-1955)

1914: A Fool There Was
Carmen
15: Two Orphans
The Clemenceau Case
Sin
The Devil's Daughter
Lady Audley's Secret
Galley Slave
Kreutzer Sonata
Caravan
16: Romeo and Juliet
Destruction
The Serpent
The Eternal Sapho
Gold and the Woman
Her Double Life
The Vixen
East Lynne
Under Two Flags
17: Price of Silence
Tiger Woman
Her Greatest Love
Heart and Soul
Eternal Sin
Darling of Paris
Madame Du Barry
Cleopatra
Camille
The Rose of Blood
18: Salome
Soul of Buddha
Forbidden Path
Under the Yoke
When a Woman Sins
Wolves of Kultur (serial)
19: She Devil
Siren's Song
When Men Desire
19: Message of the Lilies
Light
A Woman There Was
20: La Belle Russe
Kathleen Mavourneen
21: Lure of Ambition
25: Unchastened Woman
26: Madame Mystery

Ben Bard

1926: Sandy
27: Love Makes 'em Wild
Two Girls Wanted
Seventh Heaven
28: Come to my House
Arizona Wildcat
Dressed to Kill
No Other Woman
Fleet Wings
A Romance of the Underworld
29: Love and The Devil SSE

T. Roy Barnes (1880-1936)

1920: Scratch My Back
So Long Letty
21: A Kiss in Time
Her Face Value
See My Lawyer
22: Is Matrimony a Failure?
The Old Homestead
Adam and Eva
23: Go Getter
24: Great White Way
26: Dangerous Friends
Unknown Cavalier
Ladies of Leisure
27: Tender Hour
Smile, Brother, Smile
Body and Soul
Lone Eagle
28: Leave it to Me
Blonde for a Night
Gate Crasher
29: Dangerous Curves
Sally

Nigel Barrie (1889-)

1917: The Marionettes
18: Better Wife
19: Widow by Proxie
Charge it
20: Girl in the Web
Notorious Miss Lisle

21: Their Mutual Child
A Prince There Was
22: East is West
Little Fool
The Little Minister
Heroes and Husbands
White Shoulders
23: Peg o' my Heart
The Turning Point
The Stranger's Banquet
Bolted Door
25: Steel Preferred
26: The Amateur Gentleman
Traffic Cop
Sunshine of Paradise Alley
27: Shield of Honour
The Climbers
Home Struck
Lone Eagle
32: The Ringer T

Bessie Barriscale (d. 1965)
1913: Eileen of Erin
Brewster's Millions
14: Rose of the Rancho
Ready Money
15: The Painted Soul
A Cup of Life
16: Not My Sister
A Corner in Colleen's Home
Plain Jane
17: Wooden Shoes
18: Two Gun Betty
Within the Cup
Rose of Paradise
Those Who Pay
Blindfolded
Patriotism
Maid o' the Storm
Heart of Rachel
19: A Trick of Fate
Her Purchase Price
Beckoning Roads
Cast-Off
White Lie
The Woman Michael Married
Tangled Threads
Joselyn's Wife
Hearts Asleep
All of a Sudden Norma
20: Luck of Geraldine Laird
20: The Woman Who Understood
Notorious Mrs. Sands
Life's Twist
Broken Gates
Twin Beds
Kitty Kelly, M. D.
Green Swamp
21: The Breaking Point
The Skirts
28: Show Folks
33: Secrets

Wesley Barry (1907-)
1917: Rebecca of Sunnybrook Farm
19: Daddy-Long-Legs
The Unpardonable Sin
A Woman of Pleasure
Male and Female
Her Kingdom of Dreams
20: Don't Ever Marry
Dinty
Go and Get it
21: Bob Hampton of Placer
Stronger Than Fiction
Bits of Life
School Days
The Lotus Eater
22: Penrod
Rags to Riches
School Days
23: Heroes of the Street
The Country Kid
Printer's Devil
His Own Law
24: George Washington, Jr.
Battling Bunyon
25: The Midshipman
Fighting Cub
27: In Old Kentucky
Wild Geese
28: Top Sergeant Mulligan

Ethel Barrymore (1879-1959)
1914: The Nightingale
15: Final Judgment
16: Kiss of Hate
17: The Lifted Veil
An American Widow
Call of Her People
Awakening of Helena Ritchie
The White Raven
The Eternal Mother

18: Our Mrs. McChesney
Life's Whirlpool
19: Lady Frederick
Super Woman
Test of Honor
The Divorcee

John Barrymore (1882-1942)
1913: An American Citizen
14: Man from Mexico
15: Are You a Mason?
The Dictator
Incorrigible Dukane
16: Nearly a King
Lost Bridegroom
Red Widow
17: Raffles, Amateur Cracksman
18: On the Quiet
19: Here Comes the Bride
The Test of Honor
20: Dr. Jekyll and Mr. Hyde
21: The Lotus Eater
Forever (Peter Ibbetson)
22: Sherlock Holmes
24: Beau Brummel
26: The Sea Beast
Don Juan
27: When a Man Loves
Beloved Rogue
Third Degree
28: Tempest
King of the Bernina
Cardigan's Last Case
29: Eternal Love SSE

Lionel Barrymore (1878-1954)
1909: Friends
The Chief's Blanket
The One She Loved
Brutality
11: Fighting Blood
12: The New York Hat
The God Within
3 Friends
My Hero
A Cry for Help
Gold and Glitter
The Informer
The Burglar's Dilemma
So Near, Yet So Far
Great Green Eye
13: An Adventure in the Autumn Woods
13: Oil and Water
The Sheriff's Baby
The Wanderer
Yaqui Cur
A Timely Interception
Death's Marathon
Power of the Press
Judith of Bethulia
Classmates
House of Discord
Near to Earth
The Lady and the Mouse
Love in an Apartment Hotel
The Perfidy of Mary
Just Gold
The Vengeance of Galora
14: Yellow Streak
Strongheart
Men and Women
Face in the Fog
15: Exploits of Elaine (serial)
Romance of Elaine (serial)
16: Brand of Cowardice
17: Peter Ibbetson (Forever)
Life's Whirlpool
The Millionaire's Double
20: Seats of the Mighty
The Master Mind
Jim the Penman
The Copperhead
Devil's Garden
21: Great Adventure
Two Minutes to Go
22: West of Zanzibar
Boomerang Bill
23: Enemies of Women
The Eternal City
24: America
Meddling Women
Decameron Nights
I am the Man
25: Splendid Road
Iron Man
26: The Barrier
Temptress
The Bells
Brooding Eyes
Lucky Lady
27: The Show
13th Hour
Love
Women Love Diamonds
Body and Soul

28: Drums of Love
La Granga
Paris at Midnight
Sadie Thompson
The Lion and the Mouse
Roadhouse
29: West of Zanzibar
River Woman SSE
Alias Jimmy Valentine PT
Mysterious Island PT

Richard Barthelmess (1895-1963)
1916: War Brides
Gloria's Romance (serial)
17: 7 Swans
Bab's Burglar
Eternal Sin
Nearly Married
Bab's Diary
18: Hit the Trail Holiday
Rich Man, Poor Man
The Hope Chest
Boots
19: Peppy Polly
3 Men and a Girl
Broken Blossoms
The Girl Who Stayed at Home
Scarlet Days
I'll Get Him Yet
20: Way Down East
Idol Dancer
Love Flower
21: Tol'able David
Experience
22: 7th Day
Sonny (dual role)
Bond Bay
23: Bright Shawl
Fury
Fighting Blade
The Winning Through
Twenty-One
24: Classmates
Enchanted Cottage
25: Shore Leave
Soul Fire
The Beautiful City
New Toys
26: Amateur Gentleman
White Black Sheep
Just Suppose
Ransom's Folly
27: Drop Kick
28: Little Shepherd of Kingdom Come
The Noose
The Wheel of Chance
Out of the Ruins
Scarlet Seas
29: Synthetic Sin
Drag T

Buzz Barton
1927: Boy Rider
Slingshot Kid
28: Wizard of the Saddle
Pinto Kid
Little Buckaroo
Bantam Cowboy
Rough Ridin' Red
Orphan of the Sage
The Fighting Redhead
The Lariat Kid
29: The Vagabond Cub
The Freckled Rascal
The Little Savage
Pals of the Prairie

Lina Basquette (1907-)
1916: Shoes
Juvenile Dancer
Supreme
17: Prince for a Day
27: Serenade
Ranger of the North
28: The Noose
Show Folks T
Trapped
Wheel of Chance
29: Godless Girl PT
Celebrity
Come Across PT
Younger Generation PT
30: Dude Wrangler T
31: Mounted Fury T
Hard Hombre T
Arizona Terror T
Morals for Women T
Goldie T
32: Arm of the Law T
Phantom Express T
Hello Trouble T
Dream Mother T
Pleasure T
37: Ebb Tide T

37: The Buccaneer T
Four Men and a Prayer T
??: Brother Jim
A Romany Rose
Mysterious Egypt
The Lonely Little Prince
Little Marian's Triumph
The Caravan
Dream of Egypt
Amelita's Friend

Miriam Battista (1914-)

1916: Blazing Love
18: Eye for Eye
20: Humoresque
21: At the Stage Door
22: Good Provider
Smilin' Through
Boomerang Bill
Just Around the Corner
23: Custard Cup
25: Shining Adventure
27: King of Kings
The Man Who Played God

Warner Baxter (1893-1951)

1918: The Traitor
All Woman
21: Her Own Money
Sheltered Daughter
First Love
Love Charm
Cheated Hearts
22: If I were Queen
The Ninety and Nine
Girl in His Room
A Girl's Desire
23: Blow Your Own Horn
24: Alimony
Those Who Dance
Christine of the Hungry Heart
The Female
Garden of Weeds
25: The Golden Bed
Son of His Father
Air Mail
Happy Days
26: Runaway
Aloma of the South Seas
The Great Gatsby
Mannequin
Miss Brewster's Millions
Mismates
27: Telephone Girl
The Coward
Drums of the Desert
Singed
A Woman's Way
28: Tragedy of Youth
Ramona
Three Sinners
Craig's Wife
Danger Street
29: West of Zanzibar
Far Call SSE
Behind That Curtain
Linda SSE
In Old Arizona T

Beverly Bayne (1896-)

1912: A Good Catch
The Magic Wand
13: Of Conscience
The Snarl
14: Under Royal Patronage
One Wonderful Night
Blood Will Tell
The Loan Shark
15: Graustark
Billy the Bear Tamer
16: Romeo and Juliet
The Great Secret (serial)
17: Their Compact
Red White and Blue Blood
18: Social Quicksands
The Adopted Son
A Pair of Cupids
Poor Rich Man
The Brass Check
Under Suspicion
With Neatness and Dispatch
Cyclone Higgins D. F.
19: God's Outlaw
Daring Hearts
20: Smiling All the Way
22: Making the Grade
23: Modern Marriage
24: The Age of Innocence

Louise Beaudet (1861-1948)

1915: Love's Way
A Model Wife
Price for Folly
The Battle Cry of Peace

20: Slaves of Pride
21: Her Lord and Master

Lucy Beaumont (1873-1937)
1924: The Family Secret
25: As No Man has Loved (or The Man Without a Country)
26: The Greater Glory
The Old Soak
The Torrent
27: Resurrection
What Every Girl Knows
Youth Triumphant
Ashes of Vengeance
Fighting Failure
The Beloved Rogue
Closed Gates
Stranded
Hook and Ladder No. 9
Outcast Souls
28: The Crowd
Comrades
The Little Yellow House
A Bit of Heaven
The Branded Man
Butter and Egg Man
Horace Goes to Hollywood
The Stool Pigeon
29: Greyhound Limited
Hardboiled Rose
One Splended Hour
The Riding Demon
She Knew Men
30: Girl in the Show T
Sonny Boy T

George Beban (1873-1928)
1915: The Alien
The Italian
16: Pasquale and His Sweetheart
17; Lost in Transit
18: Jules of the Strong Heart
One More American
19: Hearts of Men
21: One Man in a Million
22: Sign of the Rose
24: The Greatest Love of All
26: The Loves of Ricardo

Barbara Bedford
1920: Last of the Mohicans
20: Cradle of Courage
21: Deep Waters
Big Punch
Face of the World
Cinderella of the Hills
22: Gleam o' Dawn
Man Under Cover
Arabian Love
Winning with the Wits
Step on it!
Alias Julius Caesar
Unfoldment
Out of the Silent North
Another Man's Shoes
23: Romance Land
Acquittal
The Tie That Binds
The Spoilers
24: The Mad Whirl
25: Tumbleweeds
Percy
26: Old Loves for New
The Devil's Dice
Sporting Lover
27: Mockery
A Man's Past
Sunshine of Paradise Alley
Notorious Lady
Back Stage
Girl from Gay Paree
28: The Haunted House SSE
Marry the Girl
Manhattan Knights
City of Purple Dreams
Bitter Sweets
And How!
Cavalier
Port of Missing Girls
Broken Mask
29: Smoke Bellew
Heroic Lover
30: Brothers T
Tol'able David T
34: Girl of the Limberlost
35: Keeper of the Bees T

Noah Beery (1884-1946)
1917: The Hostage
18: Believe Me, Xantippe
Less Than Kin
The Source
Whispering Chorus

19: Squaw Man
Red Lantern
Valley of the Giants
20: Sea Wolf
The Sagebrusher
Go and Get It
Dinty
Mark of Zorro
Fighting Shepherdess
Mutiny of the Elsinore
21: Bob Hampton of Placer
Bits of Life
22: Penrod
Wild Honey
I am the Law
Crossroads of New York
Youth to Youth
Good Men and True
Ebb Tide
Omar the Tentmaker
23: Stormswept
Quicksands
Soul of the Beast
Tipped Off
Spiker and the Rose
The Spoilers
To the Last Man
24: Wanderer of the Wasteland
Thundering Herd
North of '36
Female
25: Coming of Amos
The Spaniard
Don Q
Call of the Canyon
26: Beau Geste
The Vanishing American
Enchanted Hill
Crown of Lies
Padlocked
Paradise
27: Rough Riders
Evening Clothes
Old Shoes
Quicksands
Tol'able David
A Soldier's Plaything
28: Beau Sabreur
The Passion Song
Isle of Lost Ships
The Dove
Godless Girl
Two Lovers
28: Hellship Bronson
Love Mart
29: Four Feathers SSE
Noah's Ark PT
Careers PT
Linda SSE
Love in the Desert
False Feathers

Wallace Beery (1889-1949)
1914: Sweedie Comedies
17: The Clever Dummy
Maggie's First False Step
Teddy at the Throttle
Cactus Nell
A Clever Dummy
19: Victory
Romany Rye
Unpardonable Sin
20: Round Up
Last of the Mohicans
Behind the Door
Mollycoddle
21: The Golden Snare
Tale of Two Worlds
Four Horsemen of the Apocalypse
22: Wild Honey
Only a Shop Girl
Robin Hood
Hurricane's Gal
Alias Julius Caesar
23: Flame of Life
Spanish Dancer
Bava
White Tiger
Ashes of Vengeance
Strangers of the Night
24: Richard the Lion-Hearted
Red Lily
Adventure
The Sea Hawk
Signal Towers
Dynamite Smith
25: The Lost World
The Wanderer
The Great Divide
Devil's Cargo
So Big
Night Club
Pony Express
26: We're in the Navy Now
Behind the Front

26: Old Ironsides
Volcano
27: Fireman, Save My Child
Now We're in the Air
Casey at the Bat
28: Wife Savers
Partners in Crime
The Big Killing
Beggars of Life PT
29: Stairs of Sand
Chinatown Nights T
River of Romance T

Rex Bell (1907-1962)
1928: Wild West Romance
The Country Kid
Girl Shy Cowboy
Taking a Chance
29: Salute T
Joy Street SSE

Madge Bellamy (1903-)
1921: The Riddle Woman
Love Never Dies
Blind Hearts
Cup of Life
Lost
Tinsel Harvest
22: The Hottentot
Lorna Doone
Hail the Woman
23: Are You a Failure?
Soul of the Beast
No More Women
24: Iron Horse
Alimony
White Sin
25: Havoc
The Man in Blue
Parasite
The Dancers
Lightnin'
A Fool and His Money
26: Sandy
Summer Bachelors
Dixie Merchant
Black Paradise
27: Very Confidential
Bertha the Sewing Machine Girl
Telephone Girl
Colleen
28: Silk Legs
Play Girl
Soft Living
Mother Knows Best T
The Sport Girl
29: Fugitives SSE
Tonight at 12
32: White Zombies T
33: Gold Diggers of Paris T
Riot Squad T
Gordon of Ghost City (serial) T
34: Charlie Chan in London
35: Gigolette
37: Ankles Preferred T
46: Northwest Trail T

Cosmo Kyrle Bellew (1886-1948)
1927: Magic Flame
Man, Woman and Sin
French Dressing
28: Black Butterflies
Midnight Life
Hit of the Show PT
29: The Devil's Appletree
The Bellamy Trial PT

Lionel Belmore (1867-1953)
1920: Dub
Strange Boarder
Jes' Call Me Jim
Madame X
Milestones
The Great Lover
21: Godless Men
The Man Who Had Everything
Guile of Women
A Shocking Night
22: Oliver Twist
Barnstormer
Peg o' my Heart
Sea Hawk
Bardelys the Magnificent
World's Champion
23: Quicksands
25: Eve's Secret
27: Demi-Bride
Winners of the Wilderness
Sunset Derby
Sorrell and Son
The King of Kings
28: Rose Marie
Hell's Angels

28: Wife's Relations
Matinee Idol
Heart Trouble
Circus Kid PT
Roarin' Fires
29: From Headquarters PT
Unholy Night PT
Yellowback
Love Parade T
Redeeming Sin T
Stark Mad T
36: Mary of Scotland T

Alma Bennett
1922: Man's Size
Without Compromise
23: 3 Jumps Ahead
The Grail
Face on the Barroom Floor
24: Dawn of Tomorrow
26: Price of Success
Brooding Eyes
Silent Lover
27: Orchids and Ermine
Long Pants
28: Grain of Dust
Goodbye Kiss
Head of the Family
Squads Rights
29: My Lady's Past
New Orleans
Two Men and a Maid
Midnight Daddies
Woman Who was Forgotten PT

Belle Bennett (1891-1932)
1916: Sweet Kitty Bellairs
Judgment of the Guilty
17: Fuel of Life
Fires of Rebellion
The Charmer
The Hellcat of Alaska
The Devil Dodger
18: The Lonely Woman
A Soul in Trust
Bond of Fear
Ashes of Hope
Because of a Woman
The Last Rebel
19: The Mayor of Filbert
Reckoning Day
The Atom
22: Flesh and the Spirit
Your Best Friend
24: In Hollywood with Potash & Perlmutter
25: Stella Dallas
His Supreme Moment
26: Aloma of the South Seas
Reckless Lady
The Lily
4th Commandment
27: Wild Geese
Way of all Flesh
28: Power of Silence
Battle of the Sexes SSE
Mother Machree
Queen of Burlesque
Reputation
The Sporting Age
The Devil's Skipper
Patience
Moran of the Marines
Devil's Trade Mark
29: Iron Mask PT
Molly and Me PT
My Lady's Past PT
Their Own Desire T
30: Courage T
Recaptured Love T

Constance Bennett (1905-1965)
1920: Adam and Eve (1 reel short)
Clothes (1 reel short)
Men of the Force (1 reel short)
22: Reckless Youth
Evidence
What's Wrong With Women?
24: Cytherea
Into the Net
Code of the West
Her Own Free Will
25: Goose Hangs High
My Son
The Goose Woman
Sally, Irene, and Mary
Wandering Fires
My Wife and I
Stella Dallas
Married?
26: Pinch Hitter
Rich People
29: This Thing Called Love T

Enid Bennett (1894-1969)
1914: Wrath of the Gods
15: The Italian
16: The Aryan
Extravagance
17: Princess in the Dark
18: Fuss and Feathers
Vamp
Vive La France!
Carmen of the Klondike
A Desert Wooing
Keys of the Right House
Naughty Naughty
Biggest Show on Earth
Marriage Ring
19: What Every Woman Learns
The Haunted Bedroom
Happy Though Married
Stepping Out
Law of Men
When do we Eat?
Partners Three
20: Her Husband's Friend
The False Road
Woman in the Suitcase
Virtuous Thief
Hairpins
A Thousand to One
21: Silk Hosiery
Keeping Up With Lizzie
22: The Bootlegger's Daughter
Robin Hood
23: Your Friend and Mine
Strangers of the Night
Bad Man
Courtship of Miles Standish
24: Sea Hawk
Red Lily
Ambrose Appleby's Adventure
Good Medicine Skippy
26: A Woman's Heart
27: Wrong Mr. Wright
31: Skippy T
Waterloo Bridge T
Sooky T
39: Intermezzo T
Meet Dr. Christian T
40: Strike Up the Band T

Joseph Bennett
1917: Indiscreet Corrine

17: The Terror
18: Golden Fleece
Crown Jewels
Marked Cards
Limousine Life
19: Man's Desire
Rose of Hell
20: The Feud
21: Youth's Desire
The Gamesters
Their Mutual Child
Home Stretch
27: God's Great Wilderness
Somewhere in Sonora
Men of Daring
3 Miles Up
Valley of Hell
Straight Shootin'
Wolf's Trail
28: Shepherd of the Hills
29: The Lariat Kid
An Ace in the Hole

Richard Bennett (1873-1944)
1915: Damaged Goods
And the Law Says
Gilded Youth
21: Hell Diggers
23: Eternal City

Andre Beranger (1895-)
1914: Home Sweet Home
15: The Birth of a Nation
16: Intolerance
Half Breed
Good Bad Man
Flirting with Fate
Pillars of Society
Manhattan Madness
17: Mixed Blood
Those Without Sin
Sandy
19: Broken Blossoms
23: Dulcy
The Leopardess
Bright Shawl
Ashes of Vengeance
24: Beau Brummel
25: The Man in Blue
A Woman's Faith
Beauty and the Bad Man
Are Parents People?
Grounds for Divorce

26: The Bat
Grand Duchess and the Waiter
Lady of the Harem
Miss Brewster's Millions
Fig Leaves
So This is Paris
Eagle of the Sea
Popular Sin
27: Paradise for Two
Small Bachelor
If I Were Single
Altars of Desire
28: Powder My Back
Beware of Bachelors
5 and 10¢ Annie
Pay as You Enter
No Questions Asked
29: Strange Cargo T
Glad Rag Doll T

Milton Berle (1908-)
1914: Perils of Pauline (serial)
Tillie's Punctured Romance
16: Easy Street
17: Little Brother
20: Humoresque
Mark of Zorro
22: Divorce Coupons
25: Lena Rivers
26: Sparrows

Dorothy Bernard (1890-1955)
1908: A Smoked Husband
Mr. Jones at the Ball
An Awful Moment
09: Jonesy
Little Gypsy
Fine Feathers
Sporting Blood
Cricket on the Hearth
Jones and His Neighbor
Jones and the Lady Book Agent
Jones' Burglar
Mrs. Jones' Lover
The Girls and Daddy
Cord of Life
10: A Summer Idyll
12: Girl and Her Trust
Goddess of Sagebrush Gulch
One is Business, the Other is Crime
15: The District Attorney
16: A Man of Sorrow
18: Les Miserables
19: Little Women
21: Wild Goose
26: Unfair Sex

Sarah Bernhardt (1844-1923)
1900: Le Duel D'Hamlet
11: La Tosca
12: Adrienne Lecouvreur
La Dame Aux Camelias
Queen Elizabeth
15: Jeanne Dore
17: Mothers of France
23: Le Voyaole

Eugenie Besserer (d. 1934)
1912: Count of Monte Cristo
16: Crisis
Carpet from Bagdad
19: Turning the Tables
Little Orphan Annie
Auction of Souls
Scarlet Days
20: For the Soul of Rafael
45 Minutes from Broadway
The Gift Supreme
Sitting on the World
21: Light in the Clearing
What Happened to Rosa
Molly-O
Good Women
22: The Rosary
Sin of Martha Queed
Penrod
The Hands of Nara
June Madness
23: The Stranger's Banquet
24: Tess of the D'Ubervilles
26: Flesh and the Devil
27: The Fire Brigade
When a Man Loves
Captain Salvation
Slightly Used
The Jazz Singer PT
28: 2 Lovers
Yellow Lily
Lilac Time SSE
Lady of Chance
Drums of Love
29: Bridge of San Luis Rey T
Madame X T

29: Thunderbolt T
Whispering Winds T
Mr. Antonio T
7 Faces T
Fast Company T
Speedway T
Illusion T

Mathew Betz (d. 1938)

1921: Single Track
Burn 'em Up Barnes
22: My Old Kentucky Home
Boomerang Bill
23: Luck
24: Lighthouse by the Sea
Those Who Dance
26: Oh, What a Nurse!
Little Irish Girl
Shipwrecked
Flame of the Yukon
27: Broadway after Midnight
The Patent Leather Kid
28: Terror T
Wedding March
Big City
Crimson City
Exiles
Shepherd of the Hills
Sins of the Fathers
The Terror T
He Learned About Women
Telling the World
5 Aces
Iron Mike
29: Girls Gone Wild
Fugitives SSE
Girl in the Glass Case PT

Billy Bevan (1887-1957)

1919: Supporting roles in a number of Mack Sennett comedies
20: Let 'er Go
Quack Doctor
It's a Boy
My Goodness
Love Honor and Behave
A Fireside Brewer
21: A Small Town Idol
Be Reasonable
By Heck
Astray From the Steerage
22: Duck Hunter
22: On Patrol
Oh, Daddy!
Gymnasium Jim
Ma and Pa
When Summer Comes
23: Nip and Tuck
Inbad the Sailor
24: One Spooky Night
Wall Street Blues
Lizzies of the Field
Wandering Waistlines
Cannon Ball Express
25: Honeymoon Hardships
Giddap
The Lion's Whiskers
Skinners in Silk
Super-Hooper-Dyne Lizzies
Sneezing Breezers
Iron Nag
Butter Fingers
Over There-Abouts
From Rags to Britches
26: Whispering Whiskers
Trimmed in Gold
Circus Today
Wandering Willies
Hayfoot, Strawfoot!
Flight Night
Muscle Bound Music
Ice Cold Cocos
A Sea Dog's Tale
Hubby's Quiet Little Game
Hoboken to Hollywood
Masked Mamas
Divorce Dodger
Flirty Four-Flushers
27: Should Sleepwalkers Marry
Peaches and Plumbers
Small Town Princess
The Bull Fighter
Cured in the Excitement
The Gold Nut
Gold Digger of Weepah
Easy Pickings
28: The Beach Club
Best Man
Bicycle Flirt
His Unlucky Night
Mother Knows Best PT
Caught in the Kitchen
Motorboat Mamas
Motoring Mamas
Hubby's Latest Alibi

28: Hubby's Weekend Trip
The Lion's Roar T
His New Steno
Riley the Cop SSE
29: Button My Back
Calling Hubby's Bluff
Foolish Husbands
Pink Pajamas
High Voltage T
Don't Get Jealous
34: She Loves Me Not T

Buffalo Bill Jr.

1925: On the Go
Quicker'n Lightnin'
24: Rarin' to Go
Hard Hittin' Hamilton
Fast and Fearless
26: Deuce High
Trumpin' Trouble
Speedy Spurs
Saddle Cyclone
Desert Demon
A Streak of Luck
Rawhide
Bonanza Buckaroo
Final Reckoning
Pirates of Panama
27: Bad Man's Bluff
Gallopin' Gobs
Ridin' Howdy
Interferin' Gent
Obligin' Buckaroo
Pals in Peril
Roarin' Broncos
28: The Ballyhoo Buster
Valley of Hunted Men

Constance Binney (1900-)

1918: Sporting Life
Test of Honor
19: Erstwhile Susan
20: Something Different
Stolen Kiss
39 East
21: Such a Little Queen
Room and Board
First Love
The Magic Cup
22: The Case of Becky
The Sleep Walker
Bill of Divorcement
Midnight
23: 3 O'Clock in the Morning

Fair Binney

1918: Sporting Life
19: The Woman
Open Your Eyes
20: The Wonder Man
Here Comes the Bride
The Blue Pearl
Madonnas and Men
21: The Frontier of the Stars
A Man's Home
Girl from Porcupine
22: What Fools Men Are
24: Second Youth

Carlyle Blackwell (1884-1955)

1909: Uncle Tom's Cabin
10: A Dixie Mother
12: A Bell of Penance
Kentucky Girl
The Parasite
Indian Uprising at Santa Fe
13: Perils of the Sea
The Struggle
Battle for Freedom
The Invaders
14: The Man Who Could Not Lose
Such a Little Queen
The Spitfire
Key to Yesterday
15: The Secret Orchard
The Case of Becky
16: A Woman's Way
17: The Burglar
18: The Road to France
His Royal Highness
The Beloved Blackmailer
The Marriage Market
Mrs. Reynolds
The Way Out
Leap to Fame
The Cabaret
The Golden Wall
Stolen Orders
19: Hit or Miss
Love in a Hurry
Courage for Two
Three Green Eyes
By Hook or Crook
20: The Restless Sex
Third Woman

22: Virgin Queen
23: Bulldog Drummond
Hunchback of Notre Dame
24: Beloved Vagabond
25: Monte Carlo
26: She
28: Prodigals of Monte Carlo
29: The Wrecker

Sally Blane (1910-)
1927: Rolled Stockings
Casey at the Bat
Shootin' Irons
Her Summer Hero
28: Fools for Luck
The Vanishing Pioneer
Dead Man's Curve
King Cowboy
Horseman of the Plains
29: Outlawed
Wife Savers
Half Marriage T
The Very Idea T
Vagabond Lover T
Wolves of the City
Eyes of the Underworld

Holbrook Blinn (1872-1928
1914: The Boss
15: McTeague
The Butterfly on the Wheel
The Ivory Snuff Box
Madam of the Slums
The Family Cupboard
16: The Ballet Girl
The Weakness of Man
The Unpardonable Sin
Husband and Wife
The Hidden Scar
17: The Empress
Pride
The Prima Donn'a Husband
21: Power
23: Rosita
The Bad Man
24: Janice Meredith
25: Zander the Great
The New Commandment
26: The Unfair Sex
27: Telephone Girl
Masked Woman

Monte Blue (1890-1963)
1915: The Birth of a Nation
15: His Pal
Ghosts
The Man Behind
16: Intolerance
The Microscope Mystery
Prince of Power
17: Man from Painted Post
Wild and Wooly
Betsy's Burglar
Betrayed
Hands Up!
18: M'Liss
Squaw Man
Till I Come Back
Johanna Enlists
Goddess of Lost Lake
Romance of Tarzan
The Only Road
100% American
19: In Mizzoura
Everywoman
Come Back to Me
Rustling a Bride
Pettigrew's Girl
Told in the Hills
Romance and Arabella
20: The 13th Commandment
A Cumberland Romance
Something to Think About
The Jucklins
Too Much Johnson
21: The Kentuckians
A Perfect Crime
Affairs of Anatol
Peacock Alley
Moonlight and Honeysuckle
22: My Old Kentucky Home
Broadway Rose
Orphans of the Storm
23: Tents of Allah
Main Street
Brass
24: The Marriage Circle
Revelation
Love of Gamble
Lover of Camille
Loving Lies
Mademoiselle Midnight
The Dark Swan
Those Who Dance
25: Kiss Me Again
Hogan's Alley
The Limited Mail
Red Hot Tires

26: So This is Paris
Across the Pacific
The Man Upstairs
Other Women's Husbands
27: Wolf's Clothing
One Round Hogan
Black Diamond Express
Bitter Apples
Bush Leaguer
Brute
Brass Knuckles
28: Across the Atlantic
White Shadows of the South Sea
A Little Bit of Heaven
Under Sea Kingdom (serial)
29: Conquest T
Greyhound Limited T
No Defense T
From Headquarters PT
Skin Deep T

Betty Blythe (1893-)
1918: Over the Top
His Own People
Dust of Desire
Miss Ambition
A Game with Fate
Tangled Lives
All Man
19: Undercurrent
Charge It
Green God
20: Silver Horde
The Yellowback
Nomads of the North
The Third Generation
21: Queen of Sheba
Slander
22: Fair Lady
His Wife's Husband
How Men Love
23: Sinner or Saint
Darling of the Rich
Truth About Wives
24: In Hollywood with Potash & Perlmutter
25: Chu-Chin-Chow
Percy
26: She
His Wife's Relations
27: A Million Bid
Snowbound
Eager Lips
Girl from Gay Paree
28: Into No Man's Land
Sisters of Eve
Stolen Love
Glorious Betsy PTL
Daughter of Israel
Domestic Troubles SSE
??: Jacob's Well
Southern Love

Eleanor Boardman (1898-)
1923: Souls for Sale
Vanity Fair
The Stranger's Banquet
Gimme
Three Wise Fools
24: Wine of Youth
25: Wife of the Centaur
The Only Thing
Proud Flesh
26: Bardelys the Magnificent
Memory Lane
The Auction Block
27: Tell it to the Marines
28: The Crowd
Diamond Handcuffs
29: She Goes to War PT
30: Redemption

Eddie Boland (1885-)
1914: Lucille Love (serial)
The Mysterious Rose
16: Peg o' the Ring (serial)
20: June Madness
Queens Up
Mama's Boy
21: A Straight Crook
Prince Pistachio
The Love Lesson
22: Oliver Twist
23: Long Live the King
Within the Law
Face on the Barroom Floor
Star Comedies
24: Little Robinson Crusoe
Nobody's Business
Nothing Matters
27: Sunrise
28: Making the Varsity
29: Who's My Wife
Last Performance
??: Lady Raffles Series

Mary Boland (1882-1965)
1915: Edge of the Abyss
16: The Stepping Stone
Price of Happiness
Big John Garrity
18: The Prodigal Wife
19: A Woman's Experience
The Perfect Lover
20: His Temporary Wife (or, The Contrary Wife)

John Boles (1890-1969)
1927: The Loves of Sunya
Bride of the Night
Bride of the Colorado
28: We Americans
Man-Made Woman
Virgin Lips
Water Hole
Shepherd of the Hills
What Holds Men
Fazil
29: Last Warning PT
Romance of the Underworld SSE
She Goes to War PT
Scandal PT

Priscilla Bonner
1920: Homer Comes Home
Honest Hutch
Officer 666
21: The Man Who Had Everything
Bob Hampton of Placer
Son of the Wallingford
Home Stuff
23: April Showers
Little Church Around the Corner
The Fog Man
24: Tarnish
25: Drusilla with a Million
26: Red Kimono
Earth Woman
Strong Man
False Alarm
3 Bad Men
27: It
Long Pants
Paying the Price
Prince of Headwaiters
Broadway After Midnight
28: Outcast Souls
Golden Shackles
29: Girls Who Dare
Maud Muller

Olive Borden (1906-1947)
1926: Fig Leaves
The Yankee Senor
My Own Pal
3 Bad Men
Yellow Fingers
The Country Beyond
27: Monkey Talks
Joy Girl
Secret Studio
Pajamas
28: Come to My House
Virgin Lips
Gang War
Albany Night Boat
Sinners in Love
29: Eternal Woman
Stool Pigeon
Wedding Rings
Half Marriage
Love in the Desert PT
Dance Hall
30: Hello, Sister T
33: Hotel Variety T

Hobart Bosworth (1867-1943)
1909: The Sultan's Power
10: The Roman
11: The Profligate
12: The Count of Monte Cristo
Jackanapes
13: The Sea Wolf
Wise Old Elephant
14: The Country Mouse
John Barleycorn
15: An Odyssey of the North
Fatherhood
16: Joan the Woman
Oliver Twist
17: The Little American
The Woman God Forgot
19: Behind the Door
Border Legion
20: Below the Surface
Burning Daylight
21: Cup of Life
Blind Hearts
The Brute Master

21: His Own Law
A Thousand to One
22: The Sea Lion
White Hands
23: The Stranger's Banquet
Little Church Around the Corner
Man Alone
Vanity Fair
The Eternal Three
In the Palace of the King
King of the Mountain
Rupert of Hentzau
24: Captain January
Hearts of Oak
25: Zander the Great
Sundown
26: The Big Parade
The Far Cry
The Nervous Wreck
Steel Preferred
27: Blood Ship
Annie Laurie
Three Hours
My Best Girl
28: The Smart Set
After the Storm
Sawdust Paradise
Annapolis
Hangman's House
Freckles
29: Eternal Love
Woman of Affairs
King of the Bernina
General Crack T
30: DuBarry, Woman of Passion T

Wade Boteler (d. 1945)
1919: Crooked Straight
20: An Old-Fashioned Boy
Very Good Young Man
23-1/2 Hours Leave
Hard Proposition
Cup of Fury
Lahoma
She Couldn't Help It
Ducks and Drakes
Stranger than Fiction
The Home Stretch
Daughter of Mother McGuire
The Leatherneck PT
22: Deserted at the Altar
23: Alias the Night Wind
The Ghost Patrol
Ridin' Wild
While Satan Sleeps
27: Let it Rain
Soft Cushions
High School Hero
28: Sporting Goods
That's My Daddy
A Woman Against the World
Let 'em Go, Gallagher
Top Sgt. Mulligan
The Toilers SSE
Warming Up
Baby Cyclone
Just Married
The Wrecking Boss
Life's Like That
Gold Braid
The Crash

Clara Bow (1904-1965)
1922: Beyond the Rainbow
23: Down to the Sea in Ships
Enemies of Women
Maytime
Daring Years
24: Grit
Black Oxen
Poisoned Paradise
Painted People
Daughters of Pleasure
Empty Hearts
This Woman
Black Lightning
25: Capital Punishment
Helen's Babies
Adventurous Sex
My Lady's Lips
Parisian Love
Eve's Lover
Kiss Me Again
The Scarlet West
The Primrose Path
The Plastic Age
Keeper of the Bees
Free to Love
Best Bad Man
Lawful Cheaters
26: Ancient Mariner
My Lady of Whims

26: Dancing Mothers
Shadow of the Law
Two Can Play
The Runaway
Mantrap
Kid Boots
27: It
Children of Divorce
Rough House Rosie
Wings
Hula
Get Your Man
28: Red Hair
Ladies of the Mob
The Fleet's In
3 Weekends
29: The Wild Party T
Dangerous Curves T
Saturday Night Kid T
30: Paramount on Parade T
True to the Navy T
Love Among the Millionaires T
Her Wedding Night T
31: No Limit T
Kick In T
32: Call Her Savage T
33: Hoopla T

John Bowers (1891-1936)
1916: Hulda from Holland
17: Divorce Game
Betsy Ross
Darkest Russia
Maternity
A Self-Made Widow
18: Joan of the Woods
The Oldest Law
Spurs of Sybill
19: Day Dreams
Sis Hopkins
Daughter of Mine
The Pest
20: Woman in Room 13
Cumberland Romance
Madame X
21: Sky Pilot
Godless Men
Roads of Destiny
Bits of Life
Silent Call
Ace of Hearts
Poverty of Riches
21: Night Rose
Golden Gift
22: Lorna Doone
Voices of the City
Quincy Adams Sawyer
South of Suva
Bonded Woman
Affinities
23: Richard the Lion-Hearted
What a Wife Learned
Woman of Bronze
Desire
24: When a Man's a Man
25: Chickie
So Big
26: Rocking Moon
Danger Girl
Hearts and Fists
Whispering Smith
Dice Woman
Laddie
Pals in Paradise
27: Three Hours
Heart of the Yukon
Heroes in Blue
Opening Night
28: Ragtime
29: Say it with Songs T
Skin Deep T
31: Mounted Fury T

William "Bill" Boyd (1898-)
1918: New Loves for Old
Michael O'Halloran
Exit the Vamp
Money Mad
Old Wives for New
2 reelers
19: Why Change Your Wife?
21: Moonlight and Honeysuckle
Affairs of Anatol
22: Bobbed Hair
Young Rajah
23: Temple of Venus
24: Feet of Clay
Triumph
25: Midshipman
The Road to Yesterday
40 Winks
Lady of the Night
26: Volga Boatman
Her Man O'War
Eve's Leaves

26: The Last Frontier
Steel Preferred
Wolves of the Air
27: Jim the Conqueror
Yankee Clipper
The King Of Kings
2 Arabian Knights
Dress Parade
Thumbs Down
28: Night Flyer
Skyscraper
The Cop
Power
The Love Song
29: Leatherneck PT
Lady of the Pavements PT
Wolf Song PT
Flying Fool T
High Voltage T
30: His First Command T
Officer O'Brien
Locked Door
31: Painted Desert
War and Women T

Sidney Bracy (1882-1941)
1914: Million Dollar Myster (serial)
The Invisible Ray (serial)
Zudora (serial)
16: Social Buccaneers
Merely Mary Ann
Sporting Blood
Elusive Isabel
Temptation and the Man
Miser's Reversion
17: Crime and Punishment
The Deemster
The Long Trail
20: An Amateur Devil
Woman Outside
21: March Hare
Passion Fruit
Crazy to Marry
22: The Radio King (serial)
Midnight
Morals
Is Matrimony a Failure?
Dictator
The Miser's Revenge
23: Nobody's Bride
Social Buccaneer (serial)
24: Her Night of Romance

28: Snapshots SSE
Show People SSE
The Haunted House SSE
The Cameraman
Home, James
Man-Made Woman
The Wedding March
Queen Kelly (unreleased)
29: Sioux Blood
His Captive Woman PT

James Bradbury, Jr. (1894-)
1924: Classmates
27: The Circus Ace
Drop Kick
28: The Hawk's Nest
The Glorious Trail
Waterfront
29: In Old Arizona T
Night Stick
Smilin' Guns
Annie Against the World
Alibi T

James Bradbury, Sr. (1857-
1927: Blood Ship
Fair Co-Ed
28: Tide of the Empire
Skinner's Big Idea
Blockade PT
Waterfront SSE
Scarlet Seas
29: Woman from Hell

Alice Brady (1892-1939)
1914: As Ye Sow
15: The Boss
Cup of Chance
Lure of Woman
La Boheme
16: The Rack
Ballet Girl
Woman in 47
Then I'll Come Back to You
Tangled Fates
Miss Petticoats
Gilded Cage
Bought and Paid For
17: Woman Alone
Hungry Heart
The Danger's Peril
Darkest Russia

17: Maternity
Divorce Game
A Self-Made Widow
Betsy Ross
A Maid of Belgium
18: Her Silent Sacrifice
Womand and Wife
The Knife
Spurs of Sybil
At the Mercy of Men
The Trap
Whirlpool
Death Dance
Ordeal of Rosetta
Better Half
In the Hollow of Her Hand
Her Great Chance
19: Indestructible Wife
The World to Live in
Marie Ltd.
Redhead
His Bridal Night
20: Fear Market
Sinners
A Dark Lantern
New York Idea
21: Out of the Chorus
Land of Hope
Little Italy
Dawn of the East
Hush Money
22: Missing Millions
Anna Ascends
23: Leopardess
Snow Bride

Ed Brady (1889-)
1919: Out of the Shadow
Hedge of Heart's Desire
Fount of Courage
Almost a Husband
When Bearcat Went Dry
20: Kentucky Colonel
The False Code
21: The Light in the Clearing
Rough Diamond
The Silent Call
Old Dad
22: Boy Crazy
Over the Border
If you Believe It, It's So
The Siren Call
The Old Homestead
22: The Pride of Palomar
23: Racing Hearts
Trail of the Lonesome Pine
Who Pays? (series)
Neal of the Navy
28: Code of the Scarlet
Harold Teen
Bushranger
Do Your Duty

Sylvia Breamer (1896-)
1917: Cold Deck
Narrow Trail
Sudden Jim
Pinch Hitter
The Millionaire Vagrant
18: Family Skeleton
Missing
We Can't Have Everything
19: A House Divided
The Common Cause
My Husband's Other Wife
20: The Moonshine Trail
Dawn
Respectable by Proxy
The Blood Barrier
The Devil
My Lady's Garter
Unseen Forces
21: Doubling for Romeo
Not Guilty
22: Man Unconquerable
23: Bava
Girl of the Golden West
Lord of Thundergate
Flaming Youth
Her Temporary Husband
24: Lilies of the Field
26: Up in Mabel's Room
Lightning Reporter

Edmund Breese (1871-1935)
1914: Walls of Jericho
The Master Mind
15: Song of the Wage Slave
Early Bird
16: Spell of the Yukon
Lure of Heart's Desire
Weakness of Stength
19: Someone Must Pay
Temporary Wife
Common Level

19: Chains of Evidence
21: Burn 'Em Up, Barnes
A Man's Home
22: The Curse of Drink
Sure-Fire Flint
Beyond the Rainbow
23: Luck
Jacqueline of Blazing Barriers
Little Red School House
24: Shooting of Dan McGrew
Damaged Hearts
3 O'Clock in the Morning
25: Live Wire
26: Stepping Along
Womanhandled
Brown Derby
Highbinders
27: Paradise For Two
Home Made
Back to Liberty
28: Burning Daylight
Perfect Crime PT
Haunted House SSE
Finders Keepers
The Wright Idea
On Trial T
29: Port of Dreams
Conquest T
Sonny Boy T
Fancy Baggage T
From Headquarters PT
Girls Gone Wild SSE
The Gamblers T
Hottentot T
Girl Overboard PT
In the Headlines T

El Brendel (1898-1964)

1926: Campus Flirt
The Man of the Forest
You Never Know Women
What Price Glory?
Cross Pull
Jubilo
27: Too Many Crooks
Wings
Arizona Bound
29: Cock-Eyed World

Walter Brennan (1894-)

1928: Silks and Saddles
Smiling Guns

Evelyn Brent (1899-)

1916: The Lure of Heart's Desire
The Spell of the Yukon
The Soul Market
The Iron Woman
17: The Millionaire's Double
Who's Your Neighbor?
19: Other Men's Wives (or, The Other Man's Wife)
Help! Help! Police!
The Glorious Lady
Fool's Gold
Harbor Bar
20: Divine Law
Shuttle of Life
21: Why Men Forget
22: Spanish Jade
The Woman Who Came Back
Door That Has No Key
Loving Lies
23: Held to Answer
24: Silk Stocking Sal
25: Dangerous Flirt
Smooth as Silk
Lady Robinhood
Forbidden Cargo
Midnight Molly
3 Wise Crooks
26: The Jade Cup
Flame of the Argentine
Secret Orders
Queen of Diamonds
Love 'Em and Leave 'Em
Imposter
27: Underworld
Beau Sabreur
Blind Alleys
Women's Wares
28: The Last Command
Interference T
Law Divine
Night of Mystery
His Tiger Lady
Dragnet
Mating Call
Showdown
29: Darkened Rooms T
Fast Company T
Why Bring That Up? T
Broadway T

Mary Brian (1908-)

1925: Peter Pan
Air Mail
Little French Girl
Street of Forgotten Men
Regular Fellow

26: Enchanted Hill
Behind the Front
Beau Geste
Paris at Midnight
More Pay Less Work
Prince of Tempters
Stepping Along

27: Brown of Harvard
Knockout Reilly
Running Wild
Man Power
Two Flaming Youths
Her Father Said No
High Hat
Children of Divorce
Alias the Deacon

28: Harold Teen
Partners in Crime
Under the Tonto Rim
The Big Killing
Forgotten Faces
Varsity
Someone to Love

29: The Man I Love T
River of Romance T
Black Waters T
The Virginian T
Marriage Playground T
Kibitzer T

Gladys Brockwell (1893-1930)

1914: One of the Discard

15: Double Trouble

16: She-Devil
Sins of the Parents

17: One Touch of Sin
A Branded Soul
For Liberty

18: The Devil's Riddle
Strange Woman
The Moral Law (dual role)
The Scarlet Road
Bird of Prey
Conscience
Her One Mistake
The Devil's Wheel
The Strange Woman

19: Call of the Soul
The Divorce Trap
Pitfalls of a Big City
Chasing Rainbows
Broken Commandments
Flames of the Flesh
The Forbidden Room
Kultur
The Sneak

20: The Devil's Riddle
The Mother of His Children
White Lies
Sister to Salome
Rose of Nome
Continued Above
Thieves Again

21: Sage Hen

22: Paid Back
Oliver Twist
Double Stakes

23: Penrod and Sam
Hunchback of Notre Dame

25: So Big

26: Spangles
Stella Maris
Last Frontier
Twinkletoes
Carnival Girl

27: Seventh Heaven
Long Pants
Satan Woman
Man, Woman and Sin
Her Sacrifice

28: My Home Town
La Granga
Woman Disputed
Law and the Man
Lights of New York T
Home Towners T

29: From Headquarters T
Hardboiled Rose PT
Hottentot T
The Argyle Case T
The Drake Case T

Anna Brody (1894-)

1916: The Suspect

17: Princess of Park Row

18: The Yellow Ticket

19: Girl at Bay
Mrs. Wiggs of the Cabbage Patch

19:	The Perfect Lover	
	Who's Your Brother?	
	The Jewelled Hand (serial)	
20:	A Fool and His Money	
	Headin' Home	
21:	Shams of Society	
	Footlights	
23:	Lost in a Big City	
27:	Clancy's Kosher Wedding	
	Alias the Lone Wolf	
	Afraid to Love	
	Jake the Plumber	
	Why Girls Say No	
28:	My Man	PT
	Turn Back the Hours	
	Times Square	PT
	The Case of Lena Smith	

Betty Bronson (1906-)

1924:	Peter Pan	
25:	Are Parents People?	
	Little French Girl	
	Golden Princess	
26:	A Kiss for Cinderella	
	A Modern Sappho	
	Paradise	
	Not So Long Ago	
	Ben Hur	
	The Cat's Pajamas	
	Everybody's Acting	
	Grand Duchess and the Waiter	
27:	Paradise for Two	
	Ritzy	
	Open Range	
	Brass Knuckles	
28:	The Singing Fool	T
29:	The Bellamy Trial	T
	Sonny Boy	T
30:	Locked Door	T
	One Stolen Night	T
	Medicine Man	T
32:	Midnight Patrol	T
37:	Yodelin' Kid from Pine Ridge	T

Clive Brook (1891-)

1923:	Royal Oak	
	This Freedom	
24:	Christine of the Hungry Heart	
	Woman to Woman	
	Christie Johnstone	
	Daniel Deronda	
	Enticement	
24:	Mirage	
	White Shadow	
25:	Declassee	
	Woman Hater	
	The Home Maker	
	Pleasure Buyers	
	Compromise	
	Seven Sinners	
	Playing with Souls	
	If Marriage Fails	
26:	Three Faces East	
	When Love Grows Cold	
	Why Girls Go Back Home	
	You Never Know Women	
	For Alimony Only	
	Popular Sin	
27:	Afraid to Love	
	Barbed Wire	
	Underworld	
	Hula	
	French Dressing	
28:	Midnight Madness	
	Yellow Lily	
	Heliotrope	
	Interference	T
	Forgotten Faces	
	The Awakening	SSE
29:	Four Feathers	SSE
	Dangerous Woman	T
	Charming Sinners	T
	Return of Sherlock Holmes	T
30:	Laughing Lady	T
	Slightly Scarlet	T

Tyler Brooke

1927:	8 Van Bibber comedies	
	Stage Madness	
	Rich But Honest	
	Cradle Snatchers	
28:	Fazil	SSE
	A Night of Daze	
	The Kiss Doctor	
	Too Many Cookies	
	None But the Brave	
29:	Dynamite	

Van Dyke Brooke

1911:	Leading Lady
	My Old Dutch
12:	Ida's Christmas
	Billy's Burglar
13:	A Soul in Bondage
	O'Hara Helps Cupid

13: Wanted A Strong Hand
Moonshine Trail
The Stormy Petrel
Under the Daisies
The Doctor's Secret
Father's Hat Band
His Silver Bachelorhood
An Elopement at Home
Fanny's Conspiracy
The Honorable Algernon
His Little Page
Officer John Donovan
The Vavawert Ball
14: Old Reliable
Sawdust and Salome
The Helpful Sisterhood
Daughter of Israel
Cupid Vs. Money
Mr. Murray's Wedding Present
The Right of Way
John Rance-Gentleman
Politics and the Press
The Loan Shark King
A Question of Clothes
Under False Colors
Goodbye Summer
Sunshine and Shadow
Memories in Men's Souls
The Hidden Letters
Peacemaker
A Daughter of Israel
15: Barrier of Faith
A Daughter's Strange Inheritance
Janet of the Chorus
Elsa's Brother
Pillar of Flame
The Criminal
The Crown Prince's Double
20: The Fortune Hunter
21: Son of the Wallingford
The Passionate Pilgrim
Midnight Bell
The Crimson Cross

Louise Brooks (1906-)
1925: Street of Forgotten Men
26: American Venus
Show-Off
Love 'Em and Leave 'Em
A Social Celebrity
It's the Old Army Game
26: Just Another Blonde
27: Now We're in the Air
City Gone Wild
Rolled Stocks
Evening Clothes
28: A Girl in Every Port
Beggars of Life T
29: Canary Murder Case T
Too Many Women T
Windy Riley Goes to Hollywood T
Pandora's Box T
Diary of a Lost Girl T
30: Beauty Prize T
31: It Pays to Advertise T
Steel Highway T
God's Gift to Women T
Public Enemy T
36: Empty Saddles T
37: Hollywood Boulevard T
38: Overland Stage Raiders T

Robert Brower (1850-)
1919: Hawthorne of the U. S. A.
Beauty Market
20: Jack Straw
The Jucklins
Held by the Enemy
City Sparrow
A Cumberland Romance
21: Faith Healer
What Every Woman Knows
Lost Romance
22: Singed Wings
Harbinger of Peace
The Lying Truth
Fools First
The Little Minister
23: Long Live the King
25: 5th Avenue Models
26: Honeymoon Express
27: The Last Trail
28: The Gay Defender
Beggars of Life T

John E. Brown (1892-)
1928: Crooks Can't Win
Hit of the Show PT
The Circus Kid PT
Take Me Home
Queen of the Burlesque

Johnny Mack Brown (1904-)

1927: The Fair Co-ed
The Bugle Call
Varsity Girl
28: Our Dancing Daughters
Divine Woman
Little Angel
The Sport Girl
Square Crooks
Annapolis SSE
Angel Face
Soft Living
Play Girl
29: A Woman of Affairs
The Single Standard
Hurricane T
Lady of Chance PT
Coquette T
The Valiant T
Jazz Heaven

Tom Brown (1913-)

1924: Hoosier Schoolmaster
25: Wrongdoers
26: That Old Gang of Mine
Sons of the Legion
The Lady Lies

Kate Bruce

1908: An Awful Moment
09: At the Altar
Golden Louis
Choosing a Husband
The Girls and Daddy
In the Hamper Bag
10: A Romance of the Western Hills
The Rocky Road
Wilful Peggy
Exam Days at School
12: The Punishment
One is Business, The Other is Crime
The Informer
A Dash Through the Clouds
In Old Kentucky
Death's Marathon
The Would-Be Shriner
13: Battle of Elderbrush Gulch
My Hero
Just Gold
Look Up
A Tender-Hearted Boy
13: The Yaqui Cur
The Sheriff's Baby
14: Judith of Bethulia
16: Betty of Greystone
Suzan Rocks the Boat
Gretchan, the Greenhorn
The Microscope Mystery
17: Betsy's Burglar
18: Hearts of the World
The Hun Within
19: A Romance of Happy Valley
The Girl Who Stayed at Home
Scarlet Days
20: Mary Ellen Comes to Town
Flying Pat
The Idol Dancer
Jacqueline of the Blazing Barriers
Way Down East
21: The City of Silent Men
Star Dust
22: Orphans of the Storm

Fritzi Brunette (1894- 1943)

1917: The Jaguar's Claw
18: Playthings
The Velvet Hand
Whitewashed Walls
Who Shall Take My Life?
19: City of Purple Dreams?
Woman Under Cover
Sealed Envelope
Beware of Strangers
The Still Small Voice
Jacques of the Silver North
A Sporting Chance
20: The Lord Loves the Irish
Live Sparks
$30,000
The Dream Cheater
No. 99
The Green Flame
The House of Whispers
The Coast of Opportunity
The Woman Thou Gavest Me
21: The Devil to Pay
Sure Fire
Tiger True
22: Bells of San Juan
Boss of Camp 4
While Satan Sleeps

22: The Man From Lost River
Give Me My Son
23: Footlight Ranger
28: Driftwood

Charles Bryant (1887-1948)
1916: War Brides
18: Revelation
Toys of Fate
Eye for Eye
19: Out of the Fog
Stronger Than Death
The Red Lantern
The Brat
20: Heart of a Child
Billions
22: A Doll's House
23: Salome

Winifred Bryson
1921: Her Face Value
22: South of Suva
The Great Night
23: Truxton King
Suzanna
Crashing Through
28: Adoration SSE

John Bunny (1863-1915)
1910: Cupid and the Motor Boat
11: Subduing of Mrs. Nag
The New Stenographer
Her Crowning Glory
The Politician's Dream
Vanity Fair
The Leading Lady
12: Her Hero
Ida's Christmas
Cure for Pokeritus
The Troublesome Step-Daughters
Leap Year Proposals
Chumps
Diamond Cut Diamond
The Honeymooners
Stenographers Wanted
13: Autocrat of Flapjack Junction
John Tobin's Sweetheart
There's Music in the Hair
The Pickwick Papers
1. The Honorable Event
2. The Advanture of the Westgate Seminary
3. The Adventure of Shooting Party
Bunny at the Derby
Bunny for the Cause
Bunny's Mistake
14: Bunny's Birthday
Love's Old Dream
Polishing Up
Bachelor Buttons
Bunny Attempts Suicide
15: Bunny in Bunnyland

Billie Burke (1885-1970
1915: My Wife
The Marquise
Truth Game
16: Peggy
Gloria's Romance (serial)
17: The Mysterious Miss Terry
The Land of Promise
Arms and the Girl
18: Good Gracious Annabel
The Make-Believe Wife
Eve's Daughter
Lets Get a Divorce
In Pursuit of Polly
19: Sadie Love
The Misleading Widow
20: Wanted: A Husband
Away Goes Prudence
21: The Frisky Mrs. Johnson
The Education of Elizabeth

Edmund Burns (1892-)
1918: Ordeal of Rosetta
19: Male and Female
The Love Burglar
20: Virgin of Stamboul
22: East is West
Green Temptation
Ruling Passion
23: Jazzmania
24: Humming Bird
26: Sunnyside Up
Made for Love
Million Dollar Handicap
Out of the Storm
Paris at Midnight
Forlorn River
Lady in the Wilderness
Whispering Wires
27: The Princess From Hoboken

27: The Shamrock and the Rose
28: Chinese Parrot
Phyllis of the Follies
Ransom
Poor Girls
29: She goes to War PT
Children of the Ritz PT
Black Cargo of the South Seas
Hard to Get
30: The Love Racket T
Tanned Legs T
31: Sea Devils T
32: Air Mail T
33: When a Man Rides Alone T
36: Hollywood Boulevard T

Neal Burns (1892-1962)

1917: Bucking Broadway
Ocean Swells
Be Yourself
18: Out of the Night
Wedding Blues
Shuffle the Queens
Sand Witches
Ouija Did It
Movie Mad
19: A Pair of Sixes
No Parking
Rambling Romeo
20: Mary's Ankle
22: Any Old Port
That Son of a Sheik
24: Hot Water
He Married His Wife
Rough and Western
25: A Dollar Down
28: Slick Slickers
Hot Scotch
Loose Change
Should Scotchmen Marry?
Darn That Stocking

Robert "Bobby" Burns

1916: The Tryout
Ups and Downs
This Way Out
Chickens
Frenzied Finance
Busted Hearts
17: The Little Yank
Captain of the Gray Horse Troop
17: Counterfeit Trail
22: Arabian Love

Clarence Burton (1882-)

1918: Sporting Life
19: Hawthorne of the U. S. A.
20: Conrad in Quest of His Youth
The 6 Best Cellars
Thou Art the Man
Fighting Chance
What's Your Hurry?
The Jucklins
21: Fool's Paradise
Miss Lulu Bett
Forbidden Fruit
Behold My Wife
The Love Special
Lost Romance
22: Law and the Woman
One Glorious Day
Her Husband's Trademark
Her Own Money
Crimson Challenge
Ordeal
Man Unconquerable
Impossible Mrs. Bellew
23: Mr. Billings Spends His Dime
The 10 Commandments
Nobody's Money
Adam's Rib
Garrison's Finish
Beautiful and Damned
24: Bluff
27: Rubber Tires
Angel of Broadway
The King of Kings
28: Stool Pigeon
Submarine
Square Brooks
Midnight Madness
29: Godless Girl SPT
Dynamite T
Barnum was Right T
30: The Love Racket

Mae Busch (1895-1944)

1912: The Agitator
15: A Favorite Fool
One Night Stand
Settled at the Seaside
The Rent Jumpers

15: A Rascal of Wolfish Ways
(or A Polished Villain)
16: Wife and Auto Trouble
Better Late Than Never
The Worst of Friends
Because He Loved Her
A Bath House Blunder
19: Grim Game
20: The Devil's Pass key
Her Husband's Friend
21: A Parisian Scandal
Love Charm
22: Foolish Wives
Her Own Money
Pardon My Nerve
Brothers Under the Skin
23: The Christian
Souls for Sale
24: Name the Man
Shooting of Dan McGrew
25: The Unholy Three
Time the Comedian
Bride of the Night
Kiss Me Again
26: The Miracle of Life
Fools of Fashion
Nut Cracker
27: Tongues of Scandal
Ruthful Sex
Beauty Shoppers
Perch of the Devil
San Francisco Nights
Love 'Em and Weep
Her Husband's Friend
Only a Shop Girl
28: Fazil SSE
Sisters of Eve
Perfect Alibi
Black Butterflies
While The City Sleeps
Nightstick
Racing Through
29: A Man's Man SSE
Alibi T
30: Young Desire T
Come Clean T
31: Wicked T
32: Rider of Death Valley T
Man Called Back T
Twice Two T
33: Sons of the Desert T
Lilly Turner T
35: Our Relations T
36: Bohemian Girl T

Francis X. Bushman, Jr. (1903-)

1926: Brown of Harvard
Midnight Faces
Dangerous Traffic
Eyes Right
27: The Understanding Heart
28: Four Sons
Marlie the Killer
Scarlet Arrow (serial)

Francis X. Bushman (1883-1966)

1911: Fate's Funny Frolic
Ladies' World
The Rosary
12: Neptune's Daughter
Virtue of Rags
A Good Catch
The Magic Wand
When Soul Meets Soul
13: The Spy's Defeat
The Voice of Conscience
14: One Wonderful Night
Blood Will Tell
Under Royal Patronage
15: Graustark
The Master Thief
Return of Richard Neal
The Silent Voice
Lost Years
Billy the Bear Tamer
16: The Great Secret (serial)
Romeo and Juliet
17: Red, White and Blue Blood
18: A Pair of Cupids
Social Quicksands
The Poor Rich Man
Their Compact
The Adopted Son
The Brass Check
Under Suspicion
With Neatness and Dispatch
Cyclone Higgins D. F.
19: Daring Hearts
20: Smiling all the Way
22: Making the Grade
According to Hoyle
The Scarlet Arrow
23: Modern Marriage
26: Ben Hur
The Marriage Clause
27: The 13th Juror
Lady in Ermine
28: Grip of the Yukon
Man Higher Up

28: Midnight Life
Say it with Sables
Charge of the Gauchos
30: Dude Wrangler T
Galloping Ghost T
Call of the Circus

David Butler (1894-)
1918: The Greatest Thing in Life
19: The Girl Who Stayed at Home
Upstairs and Down
Better Times
The Other Half
Nugget Nell
The Unpainted Woman
The Petal on the Current
Bonnie, Bonnie Lassie
Rush Hour
20: Don't Ever Marry
Fickle Women
The Triflers
Smiling all the way
21: The County Fair
Sky Pilot
22: The Wise Kid
The Milky Way
According to Hoyle
Bing Bang Boom!
Village Blacksmith
23: Temple of Venus
Conquering the Woman
Poor Men's Wives
The Hero
A Noise in Newboro
Hoodman Blind
24: Triflers
26: Blue Eagle
Quarterback
Meet the Prince
Oh, Lady!
Womanpower
27: Nobody's Widow
Seventh Heaven
28: Rush Hour

Fred Butler
1916: Ruth Meena's Romance
19: Nugget Nell
24: Bluff
In Hollywood with Potash & Perlmutter
25: Plastic Age

Orville Caldwell (1896-1967)
1919: silent color film produced by J. Searle Dawley
20: Ramon the Sailmaker
22: Lonesome Road
23: The Scarlet Lily
Crossed Wires
26: Wives of the Prophet
A Girl's Diary
27: The Harvester
Judgment of the Hills
The Flamingo
28: Little Yellow House
The Patsy

Alice Calhoun (1903-1966)
1918: The Dream Lady
19: The 13th Chair
Everybody's Business
A Bride in Bond
20: Sea Rider
21: Charming Deceiver
Closed Doors
Peggy Puts it Over
Princess Jones
22: Angel of Crooked Street
The Little Minister
Girl in His Room
Matrimonial Web
The Rainbow
A Girl's Desire
Little Wildcat
23: Midnight Alarm
One Stolen Night
Sea Riders
Masters of Men
Man Next Door
26: Other Woman's Story
Power of the Weak
Hero of the Big Snows
Tentacles of the North
27: Flying High
In the First Degree
The Trunk Mystery
The Down Grade
Hidden Aces
Isle of Forgotten Women
29: Bride of the Desert
The Man from Brodney's

Catherine Calvert
1917: Behind the Mask
18: A Romance of the Underworld

18: Out of the Night
Marriage
19: Career of Katherine Bush
Fires of Faith
A Marriage of Convenience
20: Dead Men Tell No Tales
21: Heart of Maryland
Moral Fibre
You Find it Everywhere
23: That Woman
Indian Love Lyrics

E. H. Calvert (1890-)
1911: The Love Test
12: From the Submerged
Tapped Wires
13: Into the North
14: One Wonderful Night-dir.
15: Affinities
A Daughter of the City
The Reaping
The Outer Edge
16: The Last Adventure
Money to Burn
Vultures of Society
17: Is Marriage Sacred? (series)
27: The First Auto
The Wizard
28: Prep and Pep
King Robert of Sicily
The Man Trail (dir.)
29: The Virginian T
Thunderbolt T

Eric Campbell (d. 1917)
1914: Between Showers
Cruel, Cruel Love
Mabel at the Wheel
Caught in a Cabaret
The Fatal Mallet
Her Friend the Bandit
The Knockout
15: His New Job
16: The Floorwalker
The Fireman
The Vagabond
Behind the Screen
The Rink
The Count
The Pawnshop
17: East Street
The Cure
17: The Adventure
The Immigrant

Frank Campeau (d. 1943)
1915: Jordan is a Hard Road
17: Reaching for the Moon
Man From Painted Post
18: Bound in Morocco
Light of the Western Stars
Headin' South
Arizona
A Modern Musketeer
Say, Young Fellow!
Down to Earth
Mr. Fixit
19: Knickerbocker Buckaroo
His Majesty the American
When the Clouds Roll By
20: Rio Grande
Life of the Party
21: The Killer
For Those We Love
The Kid
Small Town Idol
22: Sin of Martha Queed
False Kisses
The Lane that has no Turning
Crimson Challenge
The Trap
Just Tony
Skin Deep
Yosemite Trail
Three Who Paid
The Greater Duty
23: Quicksands
Isle of Lost Ships
The Spider and the Rose
To the Last Man
Those Who Dance
Hoodman Blind
North to Hudson Bay
26: The Three Bad Men
27: Let it Rain
Heart of the Yukon
First Auto
28: The Candy Kid
29: Sea Fury PT
Points West T
The Gamblers T
Frozen River PT

Eddie Cantor (1892-1964)
1926: Kid Boots
27: Special Delivery
1927 Follies
29: Glorifying the American Girl T

Yakima Canutt (1895-)
1921: The Vanishing West (serial)
24: Days of '49 (serial)
25: The Human Tornado
White Thunder
26: The Outlaw Breaker
Hellhounds of the Plains
Fighting Stallion
Desert Greed
28: The Vanishing West (serial)
29: 3 Outcasts
Bad Men's Money
Captain Cowboy
Riders of Storm Ranch

June Caprice (1899-1936)
1916: Caprice of the Mountains
17: Miss U. S. A.
Unknown 274
A Child of the Wild
Every Girl's Dream
Sunshine Maid
A Small Town Girl
A Modern Cinderella
18: Heart of Romance
A Camouflaged Kiss
Blue Eyed Mary
Miss Innocence
19: The Love Cheat
Oh Boy!
The Ragged Princess
20: In Walked Mary
A Damsel in Distress
Pirate Gold (serial)
21: Rogues and Romance
The Sky Rangers (serial)

Arthur Edmund Carew (1894-)
1919: World and Its Woman
20: Rio Grande
Palace of Darkened Windows
Breath of the Gods
21: The Easy Road
21: Sham
Something Money Can't Buy
22: Prodigal Judge
Children of Destiny
Trilby
Refuse
Daddy
25: Phantom of the Opera
27: Uncle Tom's Cabin
A Man's Past

Ora Carew (1893-1955)
1915: Martyrs of the Alamo
Her Painted Hero
16: Wings and Wheels
A Reckless Romeo
Dollars and Sense
17: Her Circus Knight
Skidding Hearts
Little Lady of the Big House
18: Too Many Millions
Go West, Young Man
19: Loot
Under Suspicion
Terror of the Range (serial)
20: The Peddler of Lies
21: Beyond the Crossroads
Big Town Round-Up
After Your Own Heart
Ladyfingers
Voice in the Dark
Little Fool
22: Sherlock Holmes
Smiles are Trumps
Girl from Rocky Point
Smudge
24: Paying the Limit
Three Days to Live
Waterfront Wolves
?? Love's Protege

Edwin Carewe (1883-1940)
1915: The Final Judgment
16: Snowbird
18: Trail to Yesterday
The Splendid Sinner
20: Rio Grande
21: Isobel
Playthings of Destiny
22: The Trail's End

22: Silver Wings
23: The Bad Man
Girl of the Golden West
24: Madonna of the Streets
25: My Son
The Lady Who Lied
Joanna
27: Resurrection
28: Ramona
Revenge
29: Evangeline
30: The Spoilers T
31: Resurrection T
34: Are We Civilized? T

Rita Carewe
1925: Joanna
26: High Steppers
27: Resurrection
28: Revenge
The Stronger Will (or, The Will of a Woman)

Harry Carey (1878-1947)
1911: The Informer
My Hero
12: A Cry for Help
Unseen Enemy
Musketeers of Pig Alley
In the Aisles of the Wild
13: Brothers
Three Friends
A Chance of Deception
Broken Ways
Hero of Little Italy
14: Judith of Bethulia
Love in an Apartment Hotel
Her Father's Silent Partner
15: Graft (serial)
17: The Soul Herder
Cheyenne's Pal
Straight Shooting
The Secret Man
Bucking Broadway
A Marked Man
18: Phantom Riders
The Hillbilly
Wild Women
Thieves' Gold
The Scarlet Drop
A Woman's Fool
Heart Beat
18: Three Mounted Men
Hell Bent
19: Riders of Vengeance
Outcasts of Poker Flat
Bare Fists
Riders of the Law
Marked Men
A Gun Fightin' Gentleman
Roped
A Fight for Love
Ace of the Saddle
Man Who Wouldn't Shoot
20: Blue Streak McCoy
West is West
Satan Town
Frontier Trail
Overland Red
Bullet Proof
Human Stuff
21: If Only Jim
Freeze-Out
The Wallop
The Fox
Desperate Trails
Love's Lariat
The Telephone Girl and the Lady
Sundown Slim
Hearts Up
The Sheriff's Baby
A Cry for Help
Hair Trigger Burk
Six Shootin' Justice
The Man Who Wouldn't Shoot
22: Man to Man
Night Riders
The Outlaw and the Lady
Kick-Back
Good Men and True
23: Canyon of the Fools
Crashin' Through
Desert Driven
Miracle Baby
24: Lightning Rider
Night Hawk
Man from Texas
Tiger Thompson
Roaring Rails
25: Beyond the Border
Soft Shoes
The Texas Trail
Silent Sanderson

25: The Bad Lands
Prairie Pirates
The Man from Red Gulch
The Wanderer
The Battle of Elderbush Gulsh
The Flaming '40s
26: The 7th Bandit
Driftin' Through
Satan Town
The Frontier Trail
27: Slide, Kelly, Slide
A Little Journey
28: Border Patrol
Burning Bridges
Trail of '98

Richard Carle (1871-1941)
1928: While the City Sleeps
The Fleet's In
29: It Can Be Done PT
Habeas Corpus

Richard Carlyle (1879-)
1919: Spotlight Sadie
Men Women Marry
20: The Copperhead
21: Out of the Chorus
Inside of the Cup
22: 10 Nights in a Bar Room
25: Bridge of Sighs
Purple Knight
Those Who Toil
Stolen Will
28: Brotherly Love
Baby Cyclone
29: Hearts in Dixie
Girl in the Show
Taking a Chance
The Valiant T
In Old California T
It Can Be Done PT
30: Playing Around T
Abraham Lincoln T
Kismet T
Tol'able David T
?? The Vow

Jewel Carmen
1916: Intolerance
Flirting with Fate
The Half-Breed
Manhattan Madness
16: American Aristocracy
The Matrimoniac
Children in the House
17: A Tale of Two Cities
The Conqueror
18: Les Miserables
Kingdom of Love
Girl with Champagne Eyes
The Bride of Fear
Confession
Fallen Angel
Lawless Love
21: Silver Lining
Nobody
23: You Can't Get Away With It
Rossmore Case
26: The Bat

Tulio Carminati (1894-)
1926: The Duchess of Buffalo
The Bag
27: Stage Madness
Honeymoon Hate
28: The Patriot SSE
Sybil
3 Sinners
1912-1926 all Italian films

Sue Carol (1908-)
1927: Is Zat So?
Slaves of Beauty
Soft Cushions
Win That Girl
28: Walking Back
Air Circus PT
Skyscraper
The Cohens and the Kellys in Paris
Captain Swagger SSE
Movietone Follies of '29 T
It Can Be Done PT
Beau Broadway
29: Girls Gone Wild SSE
Why Leave Home?
Chasing Through Europe SSE
Exalted Flapper SSE
30: She's My Weakness T
Big Party T
Dancing Sweeties T
Check and Double Check T

30:	Graft	T
	In Line of Duty	T
	The Lone Rider	T
34:	Straightaway	T

Mary Carr (1874-)

1918:	Beloved Rogue	
19:	Mrs. Wiggs of the Cabbage Patch	
20:	Over the Hill	
21:	Thunderclap	
	Great Adventure	
22:	Silver Wings	
23:	Custard Cup	
	You Are Guilty	
24:	3 Women	
26:	Flaming Waters	
	Stop, Look and Listen	
	King of the Turf	
	Night Patrol	
	Pleasures of the Rich	
	Wise Guy	
	4th Commandment	
	Frenzied Flames	
	Midnight Message	
	Regular Scout	
	False Alarm	
	Whom Shall I Marry?	
	Hidden Way	
27:	On Your Toes	
	Swelled Head	
	Paying the Price	
	Jesse James	
	Special Delivery	
	God's Great Wilderness	
	Blonde or Brunette	
	Show Girl	
28:	A Million for Love	
	Lights of New York	T
	Love Over Night	
29:	Sailor's Holliday	T
	Some Mother's Boy	T
30:	Paramount Novelties	
	Hot Curves	
32:	Pack Up Your Troubles	T
33:	Gun Law	T
	Police Call	T
36:	Friendly Persuasion	T

Nancy Carroll (1905-1965)

1927:	Ladies Must Dress	
28:	Abie's Irish Rose	SSE
	Easy Come, Easy Go	
	Chicken A La King	
	Mr. Romeo	
	Water Hole	
	Manhattan Cocktail	SSE
29:	Wolf of Wall Street	T
	Dance of Life	
	Shopworn Angel	T
	Close Harmony	T
	Illusion	T
	Sweetie	T

Mrs. Leslie Carter (1862-1937)

1914:	La DuBarry	
15:	The Heart of Maryland	
35:	Rocky Mountain Mystery	T

Enrico Caruso (1873-1921)

1919:	The Splendid Romance	
	My Cousin	
	Prince Ubaldo	

Kathryn Carver

1927:	Beware of Widows	
	Ladies for Service	
	Serenade	
28:	Outcast	
	His Private Life	
29:	No Defense	PT

Louise Carver (1875-1956)

1924:	The First 100 Years are the Worst	
26:	Shameless Behavior	
	4 Married Men	
28:	Tillie's Punctured Romance	
	Wolves of the City	
29:	The Redeeming Sin	PT
	Must We Marry?	
	The Sap	PT
30:	Big Trail	T

Dolores Cassinelli

1912:	When Soul Meets Soul	
18:	Lafayette, We Come	
19:	A Soul Adrift	
	Unknown Love	
20:	The Right to Lie	
	Tarnished Reputations	
	The Virtuous Model	
	Web of Deceit	
21:	The Hidden Light	

21: Forever (Peter Ibbetson)
22: The Challenge
Anne of Little Smoky
Do Dreams Come True?
The Greek Singer
Stars of Glory
The Web of Lies

Irene Castle (1893-1969)
1915: Whirl of Life
16: Patria (serial)
Arms and the Woman
17: The Girl from Bohemia
Stranded in Arcady
The Mark of Cain
Convict 993
Mystery of the Double Cross
18: Sylvia of the Secret Service
The Hillcrest Mystery (serial)
The First Law
Vengeance is Mine
19: The Mysterious Client
The Firing Line
Invisible Bond
20: Amateur Wife
22: French Heels
No Trespassing
Slim Shoulders

Barbara Castleton (1896-)
1916: Daughter of the Gods
War Brides
17: For the Freedom of the World
On Trial
18: Empty Pockets
Vengeance
Heart of a Girl
Heredity
Sins of Ambition
19: Just Sylvia
What Love Forgives
Dangerous Hours
The Silver King
Americanism
The Tower of Ivory
The Man Who Turned White
Peg o' my Heart
20: The Branding Iron
Out of the Storm
Dangerous Days
21: Sham
Shame of Society
Sheik of Araby
The Child Thou Gavest Me
22: Wild Honey
False Fronts
What's Wrong With Women?
My Friend the Devil
Streets of New York
The Net (Fair Lady)

Lina Cavalieri (1874-)
1914: Manon Lescaut
15: La Sposa Della Morte
18: The Eternal Temptress
Love's Conquest
19: Rose of Granada (The House of Granada)
The Temptress
Two Brides
21: Mad Love

Joseph Cawthorn (1867-1949)
1927: Two Girls Wanted
Silk Legs
Strictly Confidential
28: Hold 'Em, Yale!
29: Speakeasy T
Street Girl T
Jazz Heaven T
Dance Hall T
Taming of the Shrew T

Nora Cecil (1879-)
1919: Miss Crusoe
Woman, Woman
20: The Daughter Pays
The Town That Forgot God
Piccadilly Jim
21: Red Foam
Poor Dear Margaret Kirby
Footfalls
26: Passionate Quest
28: Too Many Crooks
Baby Cyclone
The Cavalier SSE
Driftwood
29: 7 Footprints to Satan SSE

Cyril Chadwick
1920: 3 Live Ghosts
His Wife's Money
Clothes
21: Misleading Lady
22: 30 Days
Men Women Marry
Till We Meet Again
23: The Christian
Rustle of Silk
The Stranger's Banquet
Little Church Around the Corner
Brass
Don't Marry for Money
Slander the Woman
24: The Iron Horse
Happiness
25: Peter Pan
Thank You
His Supreme Moment
26: Hold That Lion
27: Is Zat So?
Foreign Devils
28: The Actress
Excess Baggage
The Mating Call
29: Black Watch T
The 13th Chair T
Last of Mrs. Cheyney PT

Helene Chadwick (1897-1940)
1917: The Angel Factory
18: Naulahka
19: Girls
An Adventure in Hearts
Caleb Piper's Girl
Go Get 'Em, Garringer
Heartease
20: Godless Men
Solitary Sin
Long Arm of Mannister
21: The Cup of Fury
Scratch My Back
The Cow-Puncher
Sin Flood
Dangerous Curve Ahead
From the Ground Up
22: Yellow Men and Gold
Dust Flower
Brothers Under the Skin
23: Gimme
Quicksands
24: Her Own Free Will
The Border Legion
26: Pleasures of the Rich
Dancing Days
Still Warm
27: Getaway Kate (serial)
Bachelor Baby
Rose of Kildare
Stage Kisses
Hard Boiled Haggerty
28: Quicksands
Modern Mothers
Say it with Sables
Women Who Dare
29: Confessions of a Wife
Father and Son

George Chandler (1902-)
1928: Saps and Saddles
Dangerous Dude
Jackson Comes Home
A Clean Sweep
A Tenderfoot Hero
Riding Romeo
Two Gun Morgan
Red Romance
Go Get 'Em, Kid
A Close Call
29: The Kid's Clever
Tenderfoot Thrillers
Black Hills
Cloud Dodger

Lane Chandler (1899-)
1928: Love and Learn
Region of the Condemned
Red Hair
The Big Killing
First Kiss
29: The Single Standard
Wolf of Wall Street T

Lon Chaney (1883-1930)
1913: Poor Jake's Demise
The Sea Urchin
The Trap
Almost an Actress
Red Margaret Moonshiner
Bloodhounds of the North
14: The Lie
Honor of the Mounted
Remember Mary Magdalen
Discord and Harmony

14: Menace of Carlotta
Embezzler
The Lamb, The Woman, The Wolf
End of the Feud
Tragedy of Whispering Creek
Unlawful Trade
Forbidden Room
The Old Cobbler
A Ranch Romance
Her Grave Mistake
By the Sun's Ray
The Oubiette
A Miner's Romance
Her Bounty
Richelieu
Pipes of Pan
Virtue Its Own Reward
His Life's Story
Lights and Shadows
The Lion, The Lamb, The Man
A Night of Thrills
Her Escape

15: Sin of Olga Brandt
Star of the Sea
Measure of a Man
Threads of Fate
Where the Forest Ends
Outside the Gate
All for Peggy
The Desert Breed
Maid of the Mist
The Grind
Girl of the Night
An Idyll of the Hills
Steady Company
Bound on the Wheel
Mountain Justice
Two Mountains
The Pines Revenge
Fascination of the Fleur De Lis
Alas and Alack
A Mother's Atonement
Love of the Mountains
Millionaire Paupers
Under the Shadow
Father and Boys
Stronger Than Death
Stool Pigeon (director)
For Cash (director)
The Oyster Dredger (dir.)
The Violin Maker (dir.)
The Trust (dir.) (actor)
The Chimney's Secret (dir.) (actor)

16: Dolly's Scoop
Grip of Jealousy
Tangled Hearts
The Gilded Spider
Bobbie of the Ballet
Grasp of Greed
Mark of Cain
Place Beyond the Winds
Price of Silence
The Piper's Price

17: Hell Morgan's Girl
Girl in the Checked Coat
The Flashlight
A Doll's House
The Rescue
Vengeance of the West
Triumph
The Empty Gun
Any Way Once
Bondage
The Scarlet Car

18: Riddle Gawne
Grand Passion
The Girl Who Dared
Fast Company
A Broadway Scandal
The Kaiser--Beast of Berlin
That Devil, Batesse
Broadway Love

19: The Wicked Darling
A Man's Country
The Trap
Paid in Advance
False Faces
The Miracle Man
Victory
When Bearcat Went Dry

20: The Gift Supreme
Nomads of the North
Treasure Island
Daredevil Jack

21: The Penalty
Outside the Law
Bits of Life
For Those We Love
Ace of Hearts
Night Rose

22: Light in the Dark

22: Voices of the City
Flesh and Blood
Oliver Twist
Shadows
Quincy Adams Sawyer
23: A Blind Bargain
Shock
Hunchback of Notre Dame
While Paris Sleeps
All the Brothers were Valiant
24: He Who Gets Slapped
The Next Corner
25: Phantom of the Opera
Unholy Three
Tower of Lies
26: Black Bird
Road to Mandalay
The Monster
27: Mr. Wu
Unknown
Mockery
London After Midnight
Tell it to the Marines
28: Laugh, Clown, Laugh
While the City Sleeps
Big City
29: West of Zanzibar
Thunder
Where East is East
30: Unholy Three T

Charlie Chaplin (1889-)

1914: Making a Living
Kid Auto Races at Venice
Mabel's Strange Predicament
Between Showers
A Film Johnnie
Tango Tangles
His Favorite Pastime
Cruel, Cruel Love
The Star Boarder
Mabel at the Wheel
Twenty Minutes of Love
Caught in a Cabaret
Caught in the Rain
A Busy Day
The Fatal Mallet
Her Friend the Bandit
The Knockout
Mabel's Busy Day
Mabel's Married Life
14: Laughing Gas
The Property Man
The Face of the Bar-Room Floor
Recreation
The Masquerader
His New Profession
The Rounders
The New Janitor
Those Love Pangs
Dough and Dynamite
Gentlemen of Nerve
His Musical Career
His Trysting Place
Tillie's Punctured Romance
Getting Acquainted
His Prehistoric Past
15: His New Job
A Night Out
The Champion
In the Park
The Jitney Elopement
The Dog Catcher
The Baggage Smasher
The Tramp
By the Sea
Work
The Bank
Shanghaied
A Night in the Show
16: Police
Carmen
Triple Trouble
The Essanay-Chaplin Revue of 1916 (contained scenes from His New Job, A Night Out, the Tramp. A similar compilation entitled Chase Me, Charlie in 7 reels was released in England in May 1918 by George Kleine.)
The Floorwalker
The Fireman
The Vagabond
One A. M.
The Count
The Pawnshop
Behind the Screen
The Rink

17: Easy Street
The Cure
The Immigrant
The Adventurer
18: A Dog's Life
Shoulder Arms
The Bond (a split-reel was made by Chaplin for the war effort and was in distribution during the autumn of '18.)
19: Sunnyside
A Day's Pleasure
21: The Kid
The Idle Class
22: Pay Day
23: The Pilgrim
A Woman of Paris (Chaplin did not act, but wrote and directed)
25: The Gold Rush
28: The Circus
Show People (a cameo) also "Special Award" (an Oscar)
31: City Lights
36: Modern Times SSE
40: The Great Dictator T
47: Monsieur Verdoux T
53: Limelight T
57: King of New York T
67: The Countess from Hong Kong T

Sydney Chaplin (1885-1965)
1914: Keystone comedies
Fatty's Wine Party
15: Submarine Pirate
One Hundred Million
A Bit of Fluff
Gussle, the Golfer
Giddy, Gay, and Ticklish (or a Gay Lothario)
Gussle's Day of Rest
Gussle's Wayward Path
Gussle's Rival, Jonah
Gussle's Backward Way
Gussle Tied to Trouble
16: No One to Guide Him
18: A Dog's Life
Shoulder Arms
The Fortune Hunter
21: King, Queen, Joker
22: Pay Day
The Pilgrim
25: Charley's Aunt
Man on the Box
26: Oh! What a Nurse
Her Temporary Husband
The Better 'Ole
27: The Fortune Hunter
28: Skirts
The Wild Waiter
40: The Great Dictator T

Edythe Chapman (1863-1948)
1916: Public Opinion
Golden Chance
The Selfish Woman
17: Little Princess
The Evil Eye
18: Say, Young Fellow!
Whispering Chorus
Bound in Morocco
Alias Ladyfingers
19: Alias Mike Moran
Experimental Marriage
The Knickerbocker Buckaroo
The Hometown Girl
Secret Service
The Winning Girl
The Rescuing Angel
Everywoman
Flame of the Desert
20: Faith
Pinto
Little Shepherd of Kingdom Come
Out of the Storm
Double-Dyed Deceiver
Huckleberry Finn
21: Dangerous Curve Ahead
A Tailor Made Man
Bunty Pulls the Strings
Just out of College
County Fair
Tale of 2 Worlds
22: American Wife
Manslaughter
Saturday Night
Beyond the Rocks
23: The Girl I Loved
Ten Commandments
25: Learning to Love
Lightnin'

27: Student Prince
Naughty But Nice
Man Crazy
28: Shepherd of the Hills
The Count of Ten
Little Yellow House
Happiness Ahead
Heart Trouble
Sally's Shoulders
Three Week Ends
29: Synthetic Sin
Idle Rich T
Twin Beds T
30: Up the River T
Navy Blues T

Mary Charleson (1885-1968)
1915: Road's Strife (serial)
16: The Prince Chap
The Country That God Forgot
17: The Truant Soul
Little Shoes
The Saint's Adventure
18: His Robe of Honor
Humdrum Brown
With Hoops of Steel
19: A Long Lane's Turning
Upstairs and Down
20: Human Stuff

Charley Chase (1893-1940)
1914: His New Profession
Dough and Dynamite
Gentlemen of Nerve
Tillie's Punctured Romance
The Knock-out
Mabel's New Job
The Masquerader
The Rounders
Shot in the Excitement
Cursed by His Beauty
15: Only a Farmer's Daughter
Has House Mashers
The Home Breakers
Love in Armor
Settled at the Seaside
The Rent Jumpers
Love, Loot and Crash
His Father's Footsteps
The Hunt
16: A Versatile Villain
Paste and Waste
Long Flib the King
Public Ghost No. 1
The Panic is On
17: Her Torpedoed Love
Chased into Love
18: Hello Trouble
19: Ship Ahoy
20: Kids and Kids
24: Fluttering Hearts
Crazy Like a Fox
27: Call of the Cuckoo
28: The Family Group
Limousine Love
The Fight Pest
Midsummer Mush
Imagine My Embarrassment
All Parts
Is Everybody Happy?
Loud Speakers
The Booster
Chasing Husbands
You Can't Buy Love
29: Snappy Sneezer
Modern Love PT
Movie Night
34: Sons of the Desert T
36: Kelly the Second T

Emile Chautard (1881-1934)
1912: Mystery of the Yellow Room
L'Apprentie
13: L'Aiglon
Le Poison de L'Humanitie
16: Human Driftwood
17: Sapho
Magda
Eternal Temptress
Poppy
18: Hungry Heart
Marionettes
House of Glass
Under the Greenwood Tree
24: Untamed Youth
26: Bardelys the Magnificent
Flaming Forest
My Official Wife
27: Seventh Heaven
Blonde or Brunette
Now We're in the Air
Upstream

28: Lilac Time SSE
Adoration SSE
His Tiger Lady
Out of the Ruins
29: Marianne T
Times Square PT
South Sea Rose T
House of Horror PT
Tide of Empire

Jack Chefee
1928: Reward
Runaway Girls
29: Redeeming Sin PT
Tailor Made Romance
Veiled Woman
Marquis Preferred

Virginia Cherrill (1908-)
1931: City Lights
Girls Demand Excitement T
The Brat T
Delicious T

Naomi Childers (1892-1964)
1915: Anselo Lee
Island of Regeneration
Dust of Egypt
16: The Devil's Price
18: The Yellow Dog (or Dove)
19: Blind Man's Eyes
Shadows of Suspicion
Lord and Lady Algy
Gay Lord Quex
20: Street Called Straight
Earthbound
Duds
21: Hold your Horses
Courage
22: Mr. Barnes of New York
23: Success
29: Trial Marriage
34: White Head T

Ann Christy (1909-)
1927: Fire Brigade
The Kid Sister
Hell Wreckers
28: Water Hole
Speedy
The Love Charm

Ethlyne Clair (1908-)
1927: Hero on Horseback
Painted Ponies
28: Riding for Fame
Road to Eldorado
Battling Buckaroo
Hey, Rube!

Gertrude Claire
1913: The Boomerang
14: The Latent Spark
City of Darkness
Wells of Paradise
15: Honor Thy Name
Cup of Life
The Coward
16: Ramona
Wolf Woman
Peggy
17: Golden Rule Kate
18: A Nine O'Clock Town
His Mother's Boy
19: Romance and Arabella
Crimson Gardenia
Jinx
Hard Boiled
Little Comrade
Stepping Out
Widow by Proxy
Blind Man's Eyes
20: Brothers Divided
Paris Green
Cradle of Courage
Forbidden Thing
Money Changers
21: Society Secrets
22: Sins of Martha Queed
Human Hearts
Hail the Woman
What Are Daughters Doing?
27: Married Alive
We're All Gamblers

Marguerite Clark (1882-1940)
1914: Wildflower
The Crucible
15: Gretna Green
The Pretty Sister of Jose
The Prince and the Pauper (dual role)
Seven Sisters
Golden Bird
Still Waters

15: A Honeymoon for Three
Goose Girl
Helene of the North
16: Snow White
Miss George Washington
Out of the Drifts
Molly-Make-Believe
Mice and Men
Little Lady Eileen
Silks and Satins
17: The Seven Swans
Bab's Diary
Bab's Burglar
Bab's Matinee Idol
The Valentine Girl
The Amazons
Fortunes of Fifi
18: The Bluebird
Rich Man, Poor Man
Uncle Tom's Cabin
Little Miss Hoover
Out of a Clear Sky
Prunella
19: Mrs. Wiggs of the Cabbage Patch
Come Out of the Kitchen
Three Men and a Girl
Girls
Let's Elope
Widow by Proxy
Luck in Pawn
20: Easy to Get
A Girl Named Mary
All of a Sudden Peggy
23: Scrambled Wives

Ethel Clayton (1884-1966)
1914: The Lion and the Mouse
The Fortune Hunter
Mazie Puts One Over
15: The Great Divide
16: Husband and Wife
For the Defense
A Woman's Way
17: The Stolen Paradise
18: The Soul Without Windows
A Woman's Weapons
A Woman Beneath
Dormant Power
Easy Money
Stolen Hours
Witch Woman
Whims of Society
18: Journey's End
19: Pettigrew's Girl
Maggie Pepper
Men, Women and Money
The Woman Next Door
The Girl Who Came Back
A Sporting Chance
Mystery Girl
20: The 13th Commandment
A Lady in Love
The Ladder of Lies
The City Sparrow
More Deadly than the Male
Young Mrs. Winthrop
The Fortune Hunter
Dollars and the Woman
The Blessed Miracle
Crooked Streets
Sins of Rosanne
21: The Price of Possession
Sham
Wealth
22: Exit the Vamp
Her Own Money
The Cradle
If I Were Queen
For the Defense
23: Can A Woman Love Twice?
Remittance Woman
25: Wings of Youth
26: His New York Wife
Risky Business
The Bar C Mystery (serial)
Sunnyside Up
The Merry Widower
The Buccaneer
Cocoanut Grove
The Blessed Miracle
27: Princess of Broadway
28: Mother Machree SSE
Inspiration
Mad Hour
29: Hit the Deck T
32: Hotel Continental T
33: Secrets T
Private Jones T

Marguerite Clayton (1896-)
1912: When Love and Honor Called
14: The Promised Land
15: A Daughter of the City

17: The Clock Struck One
18: Hit-The-Trail Holiday
The Long Green Trail
Prince of Graustark
The Bronze Man
Inside the Lines
Bolshevist Burlesque
19: The New Moon
Bride 13
21: Pleasure Seekers
Inside the Cup
Dangerous Love
Forbidden Love (Women Who Wait)
Canyon of Fools
Man of the Desert
Stardust
22: Go Get 'Em, Hutch (serial)

Ruth Clifford (1900-)

1917: A Kentucky Cinderella
Desire of the Moth
The Door Between
Savage
Mysterious Mr. Tiller
18: The Kaiser--The Beast of Berlin
The Lure of Luxury
The Cabaret Girl
The Guilt of Silence
Midnight Madness
The Red, Red Heart
Mothers-In-Law
19: The Game's Up
The Millionaire Pirate
20: Fires of Youth
The Amazing Woman
The Invisible Ray
The Black Gate
21: Tropical Love
22: Eternal Love
My Dad
Home, James
23: Dangerous Age
The Face on the Barroom Floor
Truxton King
Daughters of the Rich
The Life of Abraham Lincoln
Ponjola
25: A Man's Desire
25: Her Husband's Secret
26: Brooding Eyes
27: Don Mike
28: Thrill Seekers
29: The Devil's Apple Tree

Elmer Clifton (1895-1947)

1914: The Sisters
15: The Missing Links
The Birth of a Nation
16: The Little School Ma'am
Intolerance
19: Nobody Home
22: Down to the Sea in Ships (dir.)
23: 6 Cylinder Love
27: The Wreck of the Hesperus
28: Virgin Lips
Tropical Nights
29: The Devil's Apple Tree
Maid to Order

Andy Clyde (1892-1967)

1924: His New Mama
26: A Sea Dog's Life
28: Blindfolded SSE
Ships of the Night
Hold 'er, Cowboy
The Branded Man
Head Man
A Taxi Scandal
Ladies Must Eat
The Case of Mary Brown
29: Midnight Daddies T
Should a Girl Marry? PT
?? Mack Sennett comedies:
The Lunkhead
The Golfers
Hollywood Star
Bulls and Bears
The New Half-Back
Uppercut O'Brien
Scotch
Sugar Plum
Match Play
Fat Wives for Thin
Campus Crushers
The Chumps
Goodbye Legs
Average Husband
Half Holiday
Shopping with Wifie
Heavens, My Husband!
Speed in the Gay '90s

Edmund Cobb (1892-)

1920: The Desert Scorpion
Wolves of the Street
21: Out of the Depths
Finders Keepers
23: Law Rustlers
Playing it Wild
Sting of the Scorpion
At Devil's Gorge
24: Western Yesterday
Rodeo Mixup
Range Blood
Days of '49 (serial)
The Danger Line
26: Fighting With Buffalo Bill (serial)
27: The Wolf's Trail
Fangs of Destiny
California in '49
28: The Lariat Kid
The Boundary Battle
Beyond the Smoke
The Danger Line
Perilous Paths
Rider of the Sierras
Dodging Danger
Just in Time
Call of the Heart
Four-Footed Ranger
Hound of Silver Creek
Fighting Redhead
29: A Final Reckoning (serial)
30: The Indians are Coming!

Joey Cobb (1917-)

1922-1929:
Our Gang Kid Comedies

Lew Cody (1884-1934)

1915: The Mating
Comrade John
17: A Branded Soul
18: Treasure of the Sea
The Demon
For Husbands Only
19: Don't Change Your Husband
The Beloved Cheater
Broken Butterfly
20: The Butterfly Man
Occasionally Yours
21: The Sign on the Door
Dangerous Pastime
22: Valley of Silent Men
Secrets of Paris
23: Lawful Larceny
Jacqueline
Souls for Sale
Rupert of Hentzau
Within the Law
24: Shooting of Dan McGrew
Reno
Revelation
Nellie the Beautiful Cloak Model
Three Women
25: So This Is Marriage?
Man and Maid
Slave of Fashion
Sporting Venus
Time for the Comedian
An Exchange of Wives
His Secretary
Tower of Lies
26: Monte Carlo
The Gay Deceiver
27: The Demi-Bride
Tea for Three
On Ze Boulevard
Adam and Evil
28: Man About Town
Baby Cyclone SSE
Wickedness Preferred
Beau Broadway
29: A Single Man
30: What a Widow T
31: Beyond Victory T
Divorce Among Friends T
Not Exactly Gentlemen T
Woman of Experience T
Sweepstakes T
Meet the Wife T
Three Girls Lost T
Dishonored T
Sporting Blood T
X Marks the Spot T
File 113 T
A Parisian Romance T
32: Undercover Man T
The Tenderfoot T
Madison Square Garden T
33: I Love That Man T
Sitting Pretty T

33: By Appointment Only T
Wine, Women, and Song T
34: Private Scandal T
Shoot the Works T

Junior Coghlan (1917-)
1921: Poverty of Riches
23: Garrison's Finish
The Fourth Musketeer
24: Cause for Divorce
25: Bobbed Hair
The Road to Yesterday
26: Mike
Skyrocket
Her Man O'War
Last Frontier
27: Slide, Kelly, Slide
The Yankee Clipper
The Country Doctor
Gallagher
28: Marked Money SSE
29: Square Shoulders

Nick Cogley (1869-)
1912: Mabel's Heros
13: Mother's Boy
15: Peanuts and Bullets
Saved by Wireless
16: Dizzy Heights and Daring Hearts and Sparks
A La Cabaret
Dollars and Sense
17: Her Circus Knight
Oriental Love
19: Sis Hopkins
Maid o' the Storm
Toby's Bow
20: Jes' Call Me Jim
Honest Hutch
21: Boys will be Boys
An Unwilling Hero

George M. Cohan (1878-1942)
1918: Seven Keys to Baldpate
Hit-The-Trail Holiday

Constance Collier (1878-1955)
1916: Code of Marcia Gray
Macbeth
Intolerance

William Collier, Jr. (1900-)
1916: The Bugle Call
19: The Servant Question
Taking the Count
20: The Soul of Youth
Everybody's Sweetheart
21: The Heart of Maryland
At the Stage Door
22: Cardigan
Good Provider
Secrets of Paris
23: Enemies of Women
Loyal Wives
24: The Sea Hawk
Wine of Youth
25: The Wanderer
Eve's Secret
Devil's Cargo
26: Lady of the Harem
The Rainmaker
God Gave Me 20¢
Lucky Lady
Just Another Blonde
27: Desired Woman
College Widow
Broken Gates
Convoy
Sunset Derby
Dearie
Back Stage
Stranded
28: Lion and the Mouse
The Broadway Sap
29: Red Sword
Beware of Bachelors PT
2 Men and a Maid T
Hard Boiled Rose PT
One Stolen Night PT

June Collyer (1907-1968)
1927: East Side West Side
Let's Make Whoopee
28: 4 Sons SSE
Hangman's House
Husbands are Liars
Me Gangster SSE
Woman Wise
29: Red Wine SSE
Not Quite Decent PT

Ronald Colman (1891-1958)
1919: The Toilers

19: Snow in the Desert (serial)
A Son of David
Anna the Adventuress
20: Black Spider
23: The White Sister
The Eternal City
$20 a Week
24: Romola
Heart Trouble
Tarnish
Her Night of Romance
25: Lady Windemere's Fan
His Supreme Moment
Her Sister from Paris
Sporting Venus
Dark Angel
A Thief in Paradise
26: Beau Geste
Stella Dallas
The Winning of Barbara Worth
Kiki
27: Magic Flame
Night of Love
28: Two Lovers
29: The Rescue SSE
Bulldog Drummond T
Condemned T

Betty Compson (1897-)
1915: Wanted: A Leading Lady
Their Quiet Honeymoon
Where the Heather Blooms
Love and a Savage
Some Chaperone
Jed's Trip to the Fair
Mingling Spirits
When the Losers Won
Her Steady Carfare
A Quiet Supper for 4
Her Friend the Doctor
When Lizzie Disappeared
Cupid Trims His Lordship
The Deacon's Waterloo
Love and Vaccination
He Almost Eloped
The Janitor's Busy Day
A Leap Year Tangle
Eddie's Night Out
The Newlyweds' Mix Up
Lem's College Career
Pott Bungles Again
He's a Devil

15: Wooing of Aunt Jamina
Her Celluloid Hero
All Over a Stocking
Almost a Widow
Wanted: A Husband
His Baby
The Making of Mother
A Brass Buttoned Romance
Some Kid
History at 6 o'clock
Cupid's Uppercut
Out for the Coin
Her Crooked Career
Her Friend the Chauffeur
Small Change
Hubby's Night Out
As Luck Would Have It
Suspended Sentence
His Last Pill
Those Wedding Bells
A Bold Bad Knight
Almost a Scandal
Down by the Sea
Won in a Cabaret
Crazy in Proxy
Betty's Big Idea
Love and Locksmiths
Almost a Bigamist
Almost Divorced
16-18: Betty Wakes Up
Their Seaside Tangle
Nearly a Papa
Cupid's Camouflage
Many a Slip
Whose Wife?
Betty's Adventure
All Dressed Up
Somebody's Baby
(and 17 other Christie Comedies totaling 78)
The Sheriff
Brother Raiders
The Prodigal Liar
Light of Victory
Little Diplomat
The Devil's Trail
19: The Miracle Man
Terror of the Range (serial)
21: Prisoners of Love
At the End of the World
Green Temptation

21: Bonded Woman
To Have and To Hold
Over the Border
For Those We Love
Ladies Must Live
22: Always the Woman
Law and the Woman
The Little Minister
23: Kick-In
White Flower
Woman with Four Faces
Rustle of Silk
Hollywood
Royal Oak
Pride's Fall
The Awakening
Eternal Survivor
24: Miami
Female
Woman to Woman
White Shadow
Ramshackle Hour
Garden of Weeds
The Stranger
The Enemy Sex
Fast Set
25: Beggar on Horseback
Eve's Secret
New Lives for Old
Paths to Paradise
Locked Door
Pony Express
26: Wise Guy
Palace of Pleasure
Belle of Broadway
Counsel for the Defense
27: Lady Bird
Say it with Diamonds
Cheating Cheaters
Temptations of a Shopgirl
Twelve Miles Out
28: Docks of New York
The Barker
Scarlet Seas
Miracle Girl
Desert Bride
Life's Mockery
Love Me and the World is Mine
Big City
Masked Angel
Court Martial
31: God's Country and the Man T

Jackie Condon (1923-)

1919: Daddy-Long-Legs
The Hoodlum
20: Pollyanna
21: Little Lord Fauntleroy
The Love Light
The Hallroom Boys Comedies
Our Gang Comedies

Charles "Heinie" Conklin (1880-1959)

1915: Mack Sennett Comedies (to 1920)
18: Battle Royal
19: Solome Vs. Shenandoah
20: Too Tough Tender Feet
East Lynn with Variations
Uncle Tom Without the Cabin
Married Life
Wet and Warmer
The Kick in High Life
Married 'N Everythin'
You Wouldn't Believe It
The Rainstorm
Tut Tut
Up in the Air
24: Beau Brummel
26: Fig Leaves
27: Ham and Eggs at the Front
Drums of the Desert
Silk Stockings
28: Air Circus
Man About Town
Beau Broadway
Beware of Widows
Feel My Pulse
29: Side Street T
Tiger Rose T
Show of Shows T

Chester Conklin (1886-)

1914: Keystone Comedies:
Those Love Pangs
Between Showers
Making a Living
Mabel's Strange Predicament
Tango Tangles
Mabel at the Wheel
20 Minutes of Love
Caught in a Cabaret

14: Mabel's Busy Day
The Face on the Bar Room Floor
Dough and Dynamite
Gentlemen of Nerve
Tillie's Punctured Romance
Back to Nature Girls
Her Private Husband
The Great Nickel Robbery
Those Dangerous Eyes
Home Rule
Soft Boiled Yegg
The Love Egg
Country Chickens
Rural Cinderella
Perfect Villain
False Alarm
Business is Business
Laughing Gas
The Piper
His Son's Wife
Step Lively, Please
The First Heir
15: A Woman
Bulldog Yale
The Pullman Bride
Bucking Society
The Love Thief
Shot in the Excitement
His Taking Ways
The Ham Artist
Wild West Love
Love Speed and Thrills
The Home Breakers
A Bird's a Bird
Hearts and Planets
Ambrose's Sour Grapes
One Night Stand
Droppington's Devilish Dream
Droppington's Family Tree
Do-Re-Me-Fa
A Hash House Fraud
The Cannon Ball (or The Dynamiter)
When Ambrose Dared Walrus
The Battle of Ambrose & Walrus
Saved by Wireless
The Best of Enemies
16: Dizzy Heights and Daring
Cinders of Love
16: Bucking Society
His First False Step
A Tugboat Romeo
17: Dodging His Doom
A Clever Dummy
A Pawnbroker's Heart
The Clever Dummy (and numerous other comedies in '17 and '18)
19: Uncle Tom's Cabin (burlesque)
20: Chicken A La Cabaret
24: Greed
Galloping Fish
25: A Woman of the World
One Year to Live
26: A Social Celebrity
Say it Again
We're In The Navy Now
Sybil
The Wilderness Woman
Duchess of Buffalo
The Nervous Wreck
Midnight Lover
27: A Kiss in the Taxi
Cabaret
Rubber Heels
Tell it to Sweeney
Two Flaming Youths
Beware of Widows
Silk Stocks
Ham and Eggs at the Front
Drums of the Desert
McFadden's Flats
28: Horseman of the Plains
Fools for Luck
Tillie's Punctured Romance
Varisty PT
The Big Noise
The Haunted House
House of Terror
Beau Broadway
Trick of Hearts
Feel My Pulse
Gentlemen Prefer Blondes
Bulldog Yale
29: Stairs of Sand
The Studio Murder Case T
Sunset Pass
The Virginian T
33: Hallelujah, I'm a Bum T

39: Hollywood Cavalcade T
40: The Great Dictator T
47: The Perils of Pauline T
49: The Beautiful Blonde From Bashful Bend T

William Conklin (1877-1935)
1917: The Price Mark
Love Letters
18: Flare-Up Sal
19: The Virtuous Thief
Hay Foot! Straw Foot!
20: Enfoldment
Woman in the Suitcase
Red Hot Dollars
Hairpins
Love Madness
The Brute Master
When Dawn Came
Sex
21: The Other Woman
24: 5th Avenue Models
The Goldfish
28: Divine Lady
Life's Crossroads

27: Slipping Wives
28: Show People SSE
He Loved the Ladies
Average Husband
Legion of the Condemned
Alex the Great
The Magnificent Flirt
Dry Martini SSE
Love Song T
Tempest
Stocks and Blondes
Plastered in Paris SSE
Green Grass Widows
Woman from Moscow
Love Me and the World is Mine
29: Captain Lash PT
Exalted Flapper SSE
Romance of the Underworld
Saturday's Children PT
Making the Grade PT
Jazz Heaven T
He Loved the Ladies T
Such Men are Dangerous T

Edward Connelly
1917: Rasputin, the Mad Monk
Fall of the Romanoffs
18: Toys of Fate
20: The Willow Tree
Shore Acres
Someone in the House
The Devil
21: Four Horsemen of the Apocalypse
Cinderella's Twin
The Saphead
27: The Show
Winners of the Wilderness
Lovers
Student Prince
28: Across to Singapore
Brotherly Love
War in the Dark
Forbidden Hours
Mysterious Lady

Albert Conti (1887-1967)
1922: Merry-Go-Round
25: The Merry Widow
The Eagle
26: Blonde Saint

Jackie Coogan (1914-)
1917: Skinner's Baby
19: A Day's Pleasure
21: The Kid
Peck's Bad Boy
22: Trouble
Oliver Twist
My Boy
23: Daddy
Circus Days
Long Live the King
24: A Boy of Flanders
Little Robinson Crusoe
25: The Rag Man
Old Clothes
27: Johnny Get Your Haircut
The Bugle Call
Buttons

Clyde Cook (1891-)
1917: Show Down
Southern Justice
The Greater Law
Up or Down
19: Soldiers of Fortune
The Toreador
The Chauffeur

19: The Eskimo
Lazy Bones
The Artist
20: Don't Tickle
24: He Who Gets Slapped
26: The Winning of Barbara Worth
27: White Gold
The Brute
Simple Sis
Barbed Wire
The Bush Leaguer
Good Time Charley
28: Docks of New York
Beware of Married Men
Pay as you Enter
Domestic Troubles
No Questions Asked
Miss Nobody
Celebrity
5 and 10¢ Annie
Through the Breakers
Beware of Bachelors PT
The Spieler PT
Interference
29: Captain Lash SSE
Strong Boy SSE
Dangerous Woman
Masquerade
Taming of the Shrew T
Jazz Heaven T
In the Headlines

Al Cooke
1927: Her Father Said No
Legionnaires in Paris
28: Rah! Rah! Rexie!
Too Many Hisses
Top Taps
My Kingdom for a Hearse
Are Husbands People?
Restless Bachelors
Silk Sock Harold
Almost a Gentleman
Jessie's James
Wages of Synthetic
You Just Know She Dares 'em
The Arabian Fights
Ruth is Stranger Than Fiction
Sweet Buy and Buy
Watch Your Pep!
28: Mild But She Satisfies
That Wild Irish Pose
The 6 Best Fellows
The Naughty '40s
Broadway Ladies
Come Meal

Hallam Cooley (1888-)
1919: One of the Finest
Upstairs
Girl from Outside
Happy though Married
Girl Dodger
More Deadly than the Male
20: Long Arm of Mannister
A Light Woman
Beware of the Bride
The Tom Boy
Helen & Warren series
O. Henry series
Leave it to Me
Trumpet Island
Pinto
An Old-Fashioned Boy
21: What Do Men Want?
$10 Raise
The Foolish Age
Playing with Fire
22: One Week of Love
Up and At 'Em
23: Are You a Failure?
Going Up
24: White Sin
Helen and Warren
the O. Henry series
25: Some Pun'kins
27: Naughty But Nice
Wedding Bills
28: Her Wild Oat
No Place to Go
Ladies Must Dress
29: Little Miss Wildcat PT
Fancy Baggage PT
Black Waters T
Stolen Kisses PT
Paris Bound T
Tonight at 12 T
30: Wedding Rings T
So Long Letty T

Gary Cooper (1901-1961)
1925: Poverty Row
The Vanishing American

25: The Lucky Horseshoe
Tricks
3 Pals
Lightning Justice
26: a bit with Hans Tissler (2 reels)
Winning of Barbara Worth
Old Ironsides (extra)
Enchanted Hill
27: It
Wings
Arizona Bound
Nevada
28: Legion of the Condemned
Beau Sabreur
Doomsday
Half a Bride
The First Kiss
Lilac Time SSE
29: Shopworn Angel PT
Wolf Song PT
Betrayal SSE
The Virginian T
The Patriot SSE
30: 7 Days' Leave

George Cooper (1891-)

1916: A Night Out
Hunted Woman
The Suspect
17: Her Secret
The Auction Block
18: Find the Woman
A Small Town Romance
The Veiled Mystery
19: The Dark Star
23: Susanna
Little Church Around the Corner
Daughter of Mother McGinn
Nth Commandment
Eternal Three
24: Claude Duval
25: Settled Out of Court
26: The Barrier
Red Dice
Wise Guy
Tin Hats
Pals First
27: The Lovelorn
Women Love Diamonds
Quicksands
28: The Barker T
Lilac Time SSE
Rose Marie
Hell's Angels ST
Diamond Handcuffs
Trail of '98
Mills of the Gods
29: The Devil's Apple Tree

Miriam Cooper (1894-)

1914: Their First Acquaintance
Home Sweet Home
The Odalisque
15: When Fate Frowned
The Birth of a Nation
16: Intolerance
17: The Honor System
The Innocent Sinner
The Silent Lie
Betrayed
Confederate Ironclad
18: The Prussion Cur
The Girl Who Came Back
Woman and the Law
19: Evangeline
Should a Husband Forgive?
20: Deep Purple
21: Serenade
The Oath
22: Kindred of the Dust
23: Her Accidental Husband
Is Money Everything?
Daughters of the Rich
Broken Wing

Virginia Lee Corbin (1912-)

1916: The Chorus Girl and the Kid
17: Jack and the Beanstalk
18: Aladdin and the Wonderful Lamp
Babes in the Woods
Treasure Island
19: Fan Fan
Enemies of Children
The Mikado
Ace High
Six Shooter Andy
24: The City That Never Sleeps
25: Headlines
The Forbidden Room
26: North Star
The Handsome Brute
The Whole Town's Talking

26: Hands Up
Ladies at Play
Honeymoon Express
27: Play Safe
Perfect Sap
Driven From Home
No Place to Go
28: Little Snob
Head of the Family
Bare Knees
Jazzland
29: Footlights and Fools T
31: Shotgun Pass T
Morals for Women T
32: Forgotten Women T
?? The White Dove

Marcelle Corday
1926: The Scarlet Letter
Into Her Kingdom
27: When a Man Loves
Quality Street
29: They Had to See Paris T
The Trespasser T

Anne Cornwall (1897-)
1918: The Knife
19: Indestructible Wife
The World to Live in
The Hollow of her Hand
Prunella
Quest of the Big'un
Firing Line
20: The Path She Chose
Girl in the Rain
The Copperhead
Everything but the Truth
La, La Lucille
22: To Have and to Hold
The Seventh Day
Her Gilded Cage
23: Dulcy
Only 38
26: Flaming Frontier
Under Western Skies
Splendid Crime
Fighting Fannie
27: Eyes of the Totem
Heart of the Yukon
College
28: Halfback Hannah
Love's Young Scream
30: Widow from Chicago T

Gino Corrado
1928: The Devil's Skipper
Hot News
Tide of Empire
Prowlers of the Sea
Gun Runner
Patience
29: The Rainbow
The Iron Mask PT
House of Scandal PT
One Woman Idea SSE

James Corrigan
1920: The Jack-Knife Man
21: Sky Pilot
Brewster's Millions
Peck's Bad Boy
Lavender and Old Lace
22: A Front Page Story

Richard Cortez (1899-)
1920: Hollywood
23: 60¢ an Hour
24: Feet of Clay
The Bedroom Window
A Society Scandal
Argentine Love
25: In the Name of Love
Children of Jazz
Pony Express
The Spaniard
Call of the Canyon
Gentlemen from America
26: The Torrent
Volcano
Sorrows of Satan
Eagle of the Sea
Not so Long Ago
The Swan
The Cat's Pajamas
27: By Whose Hands?
Private Life of Helen
of Troy
New York
Mockery
28: Grain of Dust
Gun Runner
Excess Baggage
Chicago
Prowlers of the Sea
Woman of Destiny
Ladies of the Night Club
29: Midstream PT

29: New Orleans PT
The Younger Generation PT
Phantom of the House
A Man's Man SSE
30: Lost Zeppelin T

Dolores Costello (1905-)
1908: Old San Francisco
11: The Geranium
(Mission of a Flower)
12: Ida's Christmas
13: The Hindu Charm
21: Heart of Maryland
25: Bobbed Hair
26: The Sea Beast
Bride of the Storm
Little Irish Girl
His Lady
Mannquin
27: A Million Bid
When a Man Loves
Old San Francisco
Heart of Maryland
Third Degree
College Widow
28: Glorious Betsy PT
Tenderloin PT
29: Noah's Ark PT
Redeeming Sin PT
Madonna of Avenue A PT
Glad Rag Doll T
Hearts in Exile T
Show of Shows T
30: Second Choice T

Helene Costello (1903-1957)
1911: The Geranium
(Mission of a Flower)
The Toymaker
12: The Night Before Christmas
Rip Van Winkle
13: Matrimonial Maneuvers
26: Don Juan
The Love Toy
Wet Paint
Honeymoon Express
While London Sleeps
27: Good Time Charley
Heart of Maryland
In Old Kentucky
Finger Prints
Ham and Eggs at the Front
Bronco Twister
28: Husbands for Rent
The Fortune Hunter
Lights of New York T
The Circus Kid PT
Midnight Taxi
Phantom of the Turf
Burning Up Broadway
Comrades
29: Broken Barriers
The Fatal Warning (serial)
When Dreams Come True
Show of Shows T

Maurice Costello (1877-1950)
1907: Dr. Le Fleur's Theory
10: The New Stenographer
The Tyrant is Dead
11: The First Violin
A Tale of Two Cities
My Old Dutch
12: As You Like It
Aunt's Romance
The Night Before Christmas
13: Extremities
The Sale of a Heart
14: Mr. Barnes of New York
The Mysterious Lodger
The Moonstone of Fez
15: Tried for his Own Murder
Altar of Love
The Man Who Couldn't Beat God
16: The Crimson Stain Mystery (serial)
The Crown Prince's Double
18: Cap'n Abe's Niece
The Captain's Captain
19: The Cambric Mask
Girl Woman
20: Deadlines at Eleven
Tower of Jewels
21: Conceit
What a Change of Clothes Did
22: Determination
23: None So Blind
Glimpses of the Moon
Man and Wife
Fogbound

23: The Man Who Won
24: Story Without a Name
Week End Husbands
The Law and the Lady
Let No Man Put Asunder
Virtuous Liars
Love of Woman
25: Mad Marriage
26: Wives of the Prophet
Wolves of the Air
Spider Web
27: Johnny Get Your Haircut
The Shamrock and the Rose
Camille
28: The Wagon Show
The Melody
Black Feather
Eagle of the Night (serial)
Jean and the Calico Dog
36: Hollywood Boulevard T
40: A Little Bit of Heaven T
41: Lady from Louisiana T

Lucy Cotton
1918: The Prodigal Wife
19: The Miracle of Love
The Broken Melody
20: The Invisible Foe
Misleading Lady
The Sin That was His
Blind Love
21: The Devil

Marguerite Courtot (1897-)
1913: The Octoroon
14: The Barefoot Boy
15: Ventures of Marguerite
16: Rolling Stones
17: Crime and Punishment
18: The Natural Law
The Unbeliever
Roaring Oaks (serial)
19: Bound and Gagged (serial)
Teeth of the Tiger
The Perfect Lover
20: Pirate Gold (serial)
Velvet Fingers (serial)
21: Yellow Arrow
Rogues and Romance
22: Rainbow
23: Down to the Sea in Ships
23: Outlaws of the Sea
Jacqueline of the Blazing Barriers

Blanche Craig (1878-)
1913: The Eagle's Nest
14: Cinderella
Dawn of Tomorrow
Behind the Scenes
16: Hulda of Holland
18: Come On In
I Want to Forget
21: The Magic Cup

Nell Craig
1920: The Triflers
The Peddler of Lies
Dangerous Hours
Passion's Playground
21: Her First Elopement
The Queen of Sheba

Ward Crane (d. 1928)
1919: The Dark Star
Soldiers of Fortune
20: Luck of the Irish
Heart of a Fool
Harriet and the Piper
21: The Scoffer
Frisky Mrs. Johnson
Something Different
22: French Heels
No Trespassing
Destiny's Isle
Broadway Rose
The Famous Mrs. Fair
24: The Mad Whirl
26: Upstage
Sporting Lover
Boy Friend
Risky Business
That Model from Paris
Million Dollar Handicap
Under Western Skies
Blind Goddess
Flaming Frontier
27: The Flag Maker
The Auctioneer
The Lady in Ermine
Down the Stretch
Rush Hour
Beauty Shoppers
28: Honeymoon Flats

Joan Crawford (1908-)
1925: Pretty Ladies
Old Clothes
The Only Thing
26: Sally, Irene and Mary
The Boob
Tramp, Tramp, Tramp
Paris
27: Taxi Driver
The Understanding Heart
Unknown
Twelve Miles Out
Spring Fever
Winners of the Wilderness
28: West Point
Rose Marie
Across to Singapore
Law of the Range
Four Walls
Our Dancing Daughters
Dream of Love

Donald Crisp (1880-)
1911: The Primal Call
13: By Man's Law
14: The Newer Woman
The Tavern of Tragedy
The Escape
The Mysterious Shot
Home Sweet Home
The Mountain Rat
15: The Birth of a Nation
16: Ramona
17: Countess Charming
Lost in Transit
18: Eyes of the World
Believe Me, Xantippe
Under the Top
19: Broken Blossoms
Love Insurance
A Very Good Young Man
Why Smith Left Home
It Pays to Advertise
20: Too Much Johnson
6 Best Cellars
Held by the Enemy
21: The Barbarians
Appearances
Princess of New York
The Bonnie Briar Bush
23: Ponjola (dir.)
24: The Navigator (asst. dir.)
25: Don Q. (dir.)
25: Son of Zorro (dir.)
26: The Black Pirate
Stand or Deliver (dir.)
Man Bait
Young April (dir.)
27: Dress Parade (dir.)
Nobody's Widow
Vanity
The Fighting Eagle
28: The Cop (dir.)
The Viking
The River Pirate SSE
29: The Pagan
Trent's Last Case
Return of Sherlock Holmes

Josephine Crowell (d. 1929)
1914: The Painted Lady
Home Sweet Home
15: Three Brothers
The Birth of a Nation
The Penitents
Pillars of Society
16: Old Folks at Home
Intolerance
The Little School Ma'am
17: Rebecca of Sunnybrook Farm
18: Betsy's Burglar
Hearts of the World
A Yankee from the West
19: Joselyn's Wife
House of Intrigue
Puppy Love
Peppy Polly
Flames of the Flesh
20: The Greatest Question
The 6 Best Cellars
Crooked Streets
Held by the Enemy
Dangerous to Men
White Lies
Half a Chance
21: Bunty Pulls the Strings
Don't Neglect Your Wife
The Snob
22: A Homespun Vamp
23: Nobody's Money
Rupert of Hentzau
Ashes of Vengeance
25: Merry Widow
Sporting Venus
27: The Man Who Laughs

29: Wrong Again

Dorothy Cummings

1920: Woman and the Puppet
Woman Who Understood
Idols of Clay
Notorious Mrs. Sands
Notorious Miss Lisle
The Thief
21: Ladies Must Live
Don't Tell Everything
22: The Man from Home
Manslaughter
24: The Female
25: Coast of Folly
26: Mlle. Modiste
Dancing Mothers
Butterflies in the Rain
27: King of Kings
In Old Kentucky
Lovelorn
Sally of our Alley
28: Divine Woman
Forbidden Hours
Our Dancing Daughters T
The Wind
29: Divine Lady SSE
Kitty
Applause T

Irving Cummings (1888-1959)

1912: The Faith Healer
Camille
13: The Bells
Ashes
Fight for the Right
14: Uncle Tom's Cabin
Jane Eyre
The Last Volunteer
Million Dollar Mystery (serial)
15: Diamond from the Sky (serial)
16: The Saleslady
The Gilded Cage
17: An American Widow
A Royal Romance
Rasputin the Black Monk
18: The Woman Who Gave
The Interloper
19: Don't Change Your Husband
Men Women and Money
Secret Service
19: Everywoman
Her Code of Honor
The Better Wife
Ladder of Lies
Mandarin's Gold
Unveiling Hand
What Every Woman Learns
20: The Round Up
Harriet and the Piper
The Scar
Beautifully Trimmed
21: Old Dad
The Saphead
22: Cameron of the Royal Mounties
Hell's River
Flesh and Blood
Paid Back
The Eternal Flame
Broad Day Light
The Jilt
Environment
23: East Side West Side
Rupert of Hentzau
Cameo Kirby
24: Behind that Curtain
25: As a Man Desires
26: The Country Beyond
The Johnstown Flood
In Every Woman's Life
Rustlin' for Cupid
28: Dressed to Kill
29: Romance of the Underworld SSE
In Old Arizona T
Not Quite Decent PT
30: On the Level T
A Devil with Women T
31: A Holy Terror T
The Cisco Kid T

Grace Cunard (1893-1967)

1913: The Favorite Son
14: Lucille Love (serial)
(Girl of Mystery)
The Mysterious Rose
The Phantom Violin
15: The Broken Coil (serial)
3 Bad Men and a Girl
The Hidden City
The Campbells are Coming
16: Peg o' the Ring (serial)
Brennon o' the Moor

16: Born of the People
Lady Raffles Returns
The Princely Bandit
The Lumber Yard Gang
The Bandit's Wager
17: Her Better Self
The Puzzle Woman
Unmasked
The Purple Mask (serial)
Her Western Adventure
The Man Hater
Return of the Riddle Rider (serial)
18: Society's Driftwood
19: After the War
20: A Dangerous Adventure
21: Daughter of the Law
27: Blake of Scotland Yard
28: The Masked Angel
Price of Fear
29: Eyes of the Underworld
Untamed T
31: Ex-Bad Boy T
33: Ladies They Talked About T
35: The Bride of Frankenstein T

Lester Cuneo (1888-)
1915: Graustark
16: Master 44
Big Tremaine
17: Under Handicap
Paradise Garden
Pidgin Island
The Haunted Pajamas
18: Blue Blazes
The Masked Avenger
Love Me for Myself Alone
20: Are All Men Alike?
The Terror
Food for Scandal
21: The Ranger and the Law
22: Blazing Arrows
26: Blue Blazes

Frank Currier (1857-1928)
1914: The Hidden Letters
15: Quality of Mercy
18: To Hell with the Kaiser
Revelation
Toys of Fate
19: The Red Lantern
Peggy Does Her Darndest
The Brat
Kingdom of Dreams
Easy to Make Money
It Pays to Advertise
Should a Woman Tell?
20: The Right of Way
The Cheater
Clothes
The Fatal Hour
Misleading Lady
21: Without Limit
Message from Mars
The Rookie's Return
Pleasure Seekers
Clay Dollars
22: Why Announce Your Marriage?
Reckless Youth
My Old Kentucky Home
The Woman Who Fooled Herself
23: Tents of Allah
Lights of New York
Go Getter
24: The Red Lily
25: Too Many Kisses
The Exquisite Sinner
26: La Boheme
Men of Steel
Ben Hur
27: Tell it to the Marines
Winners of the Wilderness
Rookies
California
The Callahans and the Murphys
Foreign Devils
28: The Enemy
Across to Singapore
Easy Come Easy Go
Telling the World
Riders of the Dark
Iron Mike

Jack Curtis
1917: Until They Get Me
18: Little Red Decides
Man's Desire
19: Brute Breaker
The Pest
20: The Servant in the House

20: The Gift Supreme
The Hell Ship
The Devil's Riddle
Courage of Marge O'Doone
Seeds of Vengeance
21: The Big Punch
The Torrent
Beach of Dreams
Steelheart
22: Western Speed
Caught Bluffing
The Long Chance
Flower of the North
The Silent Vow
Two Kinds of Women
The Sea Lion
His Back Against the Wall
23: Masters of Men
Canyon of the Fools
28: Scarlet Seas

Bob Custer (1898-)
1925: Flashing Spurs
The Range Terror
Texas Bearcat
That Man Jack
The Blood Hound
No Man's Law
A Man of Nerve
26: Beyond the Rockies
The Ridin' Streak
Man Rustlin'
The Fightin' Boob
Dude Cowboy
Border Whirlwind
Hair Trigger Baxter
The Deadline
Valley of Bravery
27: Cactus Trails
Bulldog Pluck
Fighting Hombre
Galloping Thunder
Terror of Bar X
28: Silent Trail
Arizona Days
Manhattan Cowboy
On the Divide
West of Santa Fe
29: Law of the Mounted
Texas Tommy
Headin' Westward
The Last Roundup
Riders of the Rio Grande

29: The Oklahoma Kid
The Fighting Terror

Lil Dagover (1894-)
1919: Kara-Kiri (Butterfly)
Cabinet of Dr. Caligari
20: Kabale Und Liebe
21: Destiny
25: Tartuffe
Chronicles of the Grushuus
26: Red and Black
(Der Geheime Kurier)
27: Discord
Bara En Danserka
28: Beyond the Wall
Love Makes Us Blind
Two Brothers
Across to Singapore
Monte Cristo
29: Hungarian Rhapsody
The Grand Passion
Melodie Des Herzens

Sidney D'Albrook
1916: The Gilded Cage
17: The Danger's Peril
18: Heart of the Wilds
19: 3 Men and a Girl
The Lost Battalion
20: Parlor Bedroom and Bath
Mutiny of the Elsinore
The Flaming Clue
21: Big Game
Son of Wallingford
The Chump
The Right Way
22: I Can Explain
Little Miss Smiles
West of Chicago
Yankee Doodle Jr.
Across the Continent
Over the Border
23: Bucking the Barrier
Making Good
28: Matinee Idol
29: Spirit of Youth

Dorothy Dalton (1893-)
1915: The Disciple
16: The Captive God
Vagabond Prince
The Jungle Child
The Weaker Sex

17: The Flame of the Yukon
Love Letters
Wild Winship's Widow
Taming of the Whirlwind
Back of the Man
18: Vive La France!
The Kaiser's Shadow
The Price Mark
Ten of Diamonds
Flare-Up Sal
Love Me
Unfaithful
Mating of Marcella
Tyrant Fear
Green Eyes
19: Hard Boiled
The Home Breaker
Market of Souls
L'Apache
Other Men's Wives
Black is White
Lady of Red Butte
Extravagance
Quicksands
20: Dark Mirror
Half an Hour
Vampire
His Wife's Friend
Guilty of Love
21: Fool's Paradise
Idol of the North
Romantic Adventuress
Behind the Masks
22: Woman Who Walked Alone
On the High Seas
Moran of the Lady Letty
Crimson Challenge
23: Fogbound
Dark Secrets
Law of the Lawless
24: Lone Wolf
Moral Sinner
26: Bigger Than Barnum

Hazel Daly

1917: Skinner's Dress Suit
Skinner's Bubble
Filling His Own Shoes
18: A Corner in Smith's
Tom Brown of Harvard
19: Little Rowdy
Gay Lord Quex
Stop Thief!

Viola Dana (1891-)

1913: The Squaw Man
14: Lena
15: The Blind Fiddler
16: The Poor Little Rich Girl
17: God's Law and Man's
Aladdin's Other Lamp
18: Blue Jeans
A Weaver of Dreams
The Night Rider
The Baby Devil
The Winding Trail
Breakers Ahead
Riders of the Night
The Only Road
Opportunity
Flower of the Dusk
19: Some Bride
Please Get Married
Satan Junior
Parisian Tigress
Jeanne of the Gutter
The Microbe
The Gold Cure
False Evidence
Diana Ardway
20: The Willow Tree
The Chorus Girl's Romance
Blackmail
Parlor Bedroom and Bath
Dangerous to Men
Oh, Annice
21: Cinderella's Twin
Off-Shore Pirate
Puppets of Fate
The Match Breaker
There Are No Villains
The 14th Lover
Home Stuff
Life's Darn Funny
22: Glass Houses
Seeing is Believing
They Like 'em Rough
The Five Dollar Baby
June Madness
Love in the Dark
The Siren Call
23: A Noise in Newboro
Her Fatal Millions
A Crinoline Romance
Rouged Lips
The Social Code
In Search of a Thrill

24: Open All Night
Revelation
Merton of the Movies
Stoning
Along Came Ruth
Don't Doubt Your Husband
Beauty Prize
Heart Bandit
25: As a Man Desires
Two Ghosts
The Devil of Alaska
26: Wild Oats Lane
Bigger than Barnum's
Kosher Kitty Kelly
The Silent Lover
The Ice Flood
Bred in Old Kentucky
27: Home Stretch
Naughty Nanette
Lure of the Night Club
Salvation Jane
28: That Certain Thing
29: Two Sisters
One Splendid Hour
Show of Shows T

Karl Dane (1886-1934)
1918: My Four Years in Germany
To Hell with the Kaiser
25: The Big Parade
26: The Scarlet Letter
La Boheme
Bardelys the Magnificent
Son of the Sheik
War Paint
Wyoming
27: The Red Mill
Rookies
Slide, Kelly, Slide
28: Circus Rookies
Brotherly Love
Trail of '98
Detectives
The Enemy
Baby Mine
29: Hollywood Revue of '29 T
Voice of the Storm
All at Sea
China Bound
Alias Jimmy Valentine PT
Speedway
30: Billy the Kid T
Navy Blues T
The Duke Steps Out T
The Big House T
32: Speak Easily T
33: Whispering Shadow (serial)

Bebe Daniels (1901-1971)
1917: Lonesome Luke comedies
Lonesome Luke Loses Patients
Bashful
We Never Sleep
All Aboard
Over the Fence
Stop! Luke! Listen!
Lonesome Luke's Wild Women
Lonesome Luke's Honey-Moon
Lonesome Luke from London to Laramie
15-19: made 172 Harold Lloyd Comedies
18: Step Lively
19: Bumping into Broadway
Just Neighbors
Captain Kidd's Kids
Male and Female
Everywoman
20: Why Change your Wife?
The Dancin' Fool
Sick Abed
The 14th Man
Oh Lady, Lady!
You Never Can Tell
21: Affairs of Anatol
2 Weeks With Pay
She Couldn't Help It
Ducks and Drakes
The March Hare
One Wild Week
The Speed Girl
22: Nancy from Nowhere
A Game Chicken
North to the Rio Grande
Nice People
Pink Gods
Singed Wings
23: The World's Applause
Glimpses of the Moon
The Exciters
His Children's Children

23: Sinners in Heaven
24: Unguarded Women
Daring Youth
Heritage of the Desert
Monsieur Beaucaire
Dangerous Money
Argentine Love
25: Miss Bluebeard
The Crowded Hour
Manicure Girl
Wild, Wild Susan
Lovers in Quarantine
The Splendid Crime
26: Miss Brewster's Millions
Volcano
Palm Beach Girl
Campus Flirt
Stranded in Paris
27: A Kiss in a Taxi
Senorita
Swim, Girl, Swim
28: She's a Sheik
The Fifty-Fifty Girl
Hot News
Feel My Pulse
Take Me Home
What a Night!
29: Rio Rita T

Roy D'Arcy (1894-1969)
1919: Oh Boy!
25: Merry Widow
Graustark
26: Beverly of Graustark
The Grey Hat
La Boheme
The Temptress
Valencia
Bardelys the Magnificent
His Night
Monte Carlo
27: On Ze Boulevard
Buttons
Winners of the Wilderness
Lovers
Adam and Evil
Road to Romance
Frisco Sally Levy
28: The Actress
Beware of Blondes
Beyond the Sierras
Riders of the Dark
The Masked Stranger

28: The Family Row
Forbidden Hours
Domestic Meddlers
29: Stolen Kisses PT
The Last Warning PT
Girls Gone Wild SSE
Woman from Hell
The Black Watch T

Grace Darling (1896-)
1916: Beatrice Fairfax (serial)
19: Virtuous Men
False Gods
20: The Discarded Woman
Amazing Lovers
Even as Eve
Common Sin
21: Every Man's Price
22: For Your Daughter's Sake

Jean Darling (1922-)
1925-1929 Our Gang Kids

Grace Darmond (1898-1963)
1916: The Shielding Shadow (serial)
18: The Gulf Between
The Seal of Silence
The Girl in His House
A Diplomatic Mission
19: Valley of the Giants
A Gentleman of Quality
The Highest Trump
What Every Woman Wants
20: The Hawk's Trail (serial)
Below the Surface
Invisible Divorce
So Long Letty
21: Hope Diamond Mystery (serial)
See My Lawyer
22: A Dangerous Adventure (serial)
Song of Life
Daytime Wives
Man from Ten Strike City
26: Marriage Clause
Night Patrol
27: Wide Open
Hour of Reckoning
28: Wages of Conscience

Frankie Darrow (1917-)

1923: The Signal Tower
25: Her Husband's Secret
26: Cowboy Cop
27: Flesh and the Devil
Lightning Lariats
Her Father Said No
Moulders of Men
Cyclone of the Range
Judgment of the Hills
Flying U Ranch
28: Little Mickey Grogan
Phantom of the Range
Texas Tornado
When the Law Rides
Terror Mountain
The Circus Kid PT
Tyrant of Red Gulch
Avenging Rider
Mystery Valley
Hearts and Hoofs
The Eagle's Talons
Road to Eldorado
Battling Buckaroo
29: Hearts and Spangles
Trail of the Horse Thieves
The Rainbow Man T
Gun Law
Red Sword
Idaho Red
Pride of the Pawnees
Blaze o' Glory

Jane Darwell (1880-1967)

1914: Rose of the Rancho
20: Master Mind
21: Brewster's Millions

Alice Davenport (1864-)

1912: Drummer's Vacation
13: The Telltale Light
Cohen's Outing
14: Making a Living
Mabel's Strange Predicament
The Star Boarder
Caught in a Cabaret
Caught in the Rain
Mabel's New Job
15: The Home Breakers
Ambrose's Fury
Fickle Fatty's Fall
Stolen Magic
16: The Worst of Friends
Perils of the Dark
Fido's Fate
Wife and Auto Trouble
A Love Riot
The Snow Cure
Pills of Peril
His Last Scent
17: Maggie's First False Step
Secrets of a Beauty Parlor
A Maiden's Trust

Dorothy Davenport (1895-)

1909: Her Indian Hero
11: The Best Man Wins
12: His Only Son
13: The Cracksman's Reformation
Fires of Fate
A Cracksman Santa Claus
Lightning Bolt
A Hopi Legend
14: The Intruder
Countess Betty's Mine
Wheel of Life
15: Fruit of Evil
16: Fires of Conscience
Greater Devotion
A Flash in the Dark
Breed of the Mountains
The Man Within
17: The Squaw Man's Son
19: Heart of the Hills
The Way of a Woman
20: Arms and the Gringo
The Fighting Chance
21: Every Woman's Problem
The Masked Avenger
22: The Test
23: Adam's Rib
Human Wreckage
24: Broken Laws
28: The Quack
The Siren
29: Linda
34: Road to Ruin T
Woman Condemned T
?? The Voice of Viola
The Spider and Her Web
The Mountaineer
Cupid Incognito
A Gypsy Romance
The Skeleton

??	Women and Roses	
	Spark of Manhood	
	Passing of the Beast	
	Love's Western Flight	
	A Wife on a Wager	
	'cross the Mexican Line	
	Den of Thieves	

Milla Davenport

1919:	The Brat	
	In Missoura	
	Daddy-Long-Legs	
20:	The Forbidden Woman	
	Stronger Than Death	
	You Never Can Tell	
	Leave it to Me	
	Faith	
21:	Don't Trust Your Husband	
	Rip Van Winkle	
29:	Sins of the Fathers	

John Davidson (1886-)

1915:	Sentimental Lady	
	Green Cloak	
	Caravan	
	Danger Signal	
16:	The Wall Between	
	Romeo and Juliet	
	A Million a Minute	
	Pawn of Fate	
18:	Spurs of Sybil	
19:	Through the Toils	
	The Genius Pierre	
	Black Circle	
	Forest Rivals	
20:	The Great Lover	
21:	No Woman Knows	
	The Idle Rich	
	A Fool's Paradise	
22:	Under Two Flags	
	The Woman Who Walked Alone	
	Saturday Night	
24:	Monsieur Beaucaire	
	Ramshackle House	
29:	The Rescue	SSE
	Queen of the Night Clubs	T
	Kid Gloves	PT
	Time, The Place and The Girl	T
29:	Skin Deep	T
	Thirteenth Chair	T

Max Davidson (1875-1946)

1916:	The Village Vampire	
18:	The Hun Within	
19:	The Hoodlum	
21:	No Woman Knows	
	The Idle Rich	
22:	Second Hand Rose	
	Right That Failed	
	Remembrance	
23:	Ghost Patrol	
26:	Izzy series of comedies	
	Puppets	
	The Doll Shop	
	Sunshine of Paradise Alley	
27:	Call of the Cuckoo	
	Hotel Imperial	
28:	Dumb Daddies	
	Came the Dawn	
	Should Women Drive?	
	That Night	
	Blow by Blow	
	All Parts	
	The Boy Friend	
	Do Gentlemen Snore?	
	Good Morning, Judge	
	Seed 'em and Weep	
29:	The Carnation Kid	PT

William B. Davidson (1888-1947)

1917:	White Raven	
	The Greatest Power	
	Persuasive Peggy	
18:	Friend Husband	
	Our Little Wife	
	Why I Would Not Marry	
19:	La Belle Russe	
	A Woman There Was	
	The Capitol	
	Impossible Catherine	
20:	Partners of the Night	
21:	Poor Dear Margaret Kirby	
28:	Good Morning, Judge	
29:	Queen of the Night Clubs	T
	The Carnation Kid	PT
	Woman Trap	T
	Blaze o' Glory	T

Marion Davies (1900-1961)

1917:	Runaway Romany	
18:	Cecilia of the Pink Roses	
	Burden of Proof	
19:	The Belle of New York	

19: The Dark Star
Getting Mary Married
20: The Cinema Murder
The Restless Sex
April Folly
21: Buried Treasure
The Bride of Kenmore
Enchantment
22: Beauty's Worth
Adam and Eva
When Knighthood was in Flower
23: Little Old New York
24: Janice Meredith
Yolanda
25: Zander the Great
Lights of Old Broadway
26: The Red Mill
Tillie the Toiler
Beverly of Graustark
27: Quality Street
The Fair Co-Ed
28: The Patsy
The Cardboard Lover
Show People SSE
29: Marianne T
Hollywood Revue of 1929 T
30: Not So Dumb T
The Bride of Kenmore T
33: Peg o' my Heart T

Mildred Davis (1903-1969)
1916: Marriage a la Carte
18: Weaver of Dreams
His Royal Slyness
19: All Wrong
21: I Do
The Sailor-Made Man
Never Weaken
Among Those Present
22: Grandma's Boy
Dr. Jack
23: Safety Last
Temporary Marriage
27: Too Many Crooks

Yola D'Avril (1907-)
1927: Hard Boiled Haggerty
28: Vamping Venus
Three Ring Marriage
Lady Be Good
The Awakening
28: She Goes to War
29: Love Parade T

Marjorie Daw (1902-)
1915: Carmen
The Chorus Lady
16: Joan the Woman
House with the Golden Windows
17: Rebecca of Sunnybrook Farm
The Americano
18: Arizona
He Comes Up Smiling
A Modern Musketeer
Headin' South
Say, Young Fellow
Mr. Fix-It
Bound in Morocco
19: Knickerbocker Buckaroo
His Majesty the American
Sunset Princess
20: The River's End
Don't Ever Marry
Dinty
Great Redeemer
21: The Butterfly Girl
Experience
22: Penrod
Love is an Awful Thing
The Long Chance
The Pride of Palomar
Lone Hand
Wandering Daughters
23: The Patsy
Going Up
Rupert of Hentzau
Call of the Canyon
Dangerous Maid
24: The Warrens of Virginia
Human Desires
25: East Lynne
26: The Highbinders
In Borrowed Plumes
Redheads Preferred
27: Outlaws of Red River
Home Made
Spoilers of the West
28: Victorious Defeat

Hazel Dawn (1891-)
1914: One of Our Girls
15: The Masqueraders

15: Niobe
16: The Saleslady
My Lady Incog
17: Under Cover
The Lone Wolf
21: Devotion
The Debutante
The Heart of Jennifer

Doris Dawson (1909-)
1928: Little Shepherd of Kingdom Come
Heart Trouble
Do Your Duty
Naughty Baby
29: Little Wildcat PT

Alice Day (1905-)
1923: Little Johnny Jones
24: Woman on the Jury
Secrets
Shangaied Lovers
Flickering Youth
The Cat's Meow
His New Mama
First 100 Years
Luck of the Foolish
26: Waiter from the Ritz
Spanking Breezes
Ghost of Folly
Puppy Lovetime
Alice Be Good
Her Actor Friend
His New York Wife
27: Night Life
The Gorilla
See You in Jail
28: Smart Set
Way of the Strong
Phyllis of the Follies
29: Red Hot Speed PT
Skin Deep
Times Square PT
Show of Shows PT
Drag T
Is Everybody Happy? T
30: Little Johnny Jones T
Viennese Nights T
The Love Racket T
?? Mack Sennett Bathing Beauty

Marceline Day (1907-)
1925: White Outlaw
26: The Barrier
That Model From Paris
Hell's 400
The Boy Friend
Gay Deceiver
College Days
Looking for Trouble
Fools of Fashion
27: The Beloved Rogue
Rookies
Captain Salvation
Road to Romance
London After Midnight
Red Clay
28: A Certain Young Man
Detectives
Driftwood
Under the Black Eagle
The Cameraman
Freedom of the Press
29: A Single Man
Snapshots
Stolen Love
Jazz Age
Restless Youth
Wild Party T
One Woman Idea SSE
Trent's Last Case
Show of Shows T

Julia Dean (1878-1953)
1914: Matrimony
15: Judge Not
How Molly Made Good
Rasputin the Black Monk
16: Ruling Passions
An Honorable Cad
The Ransom
17: The Black Monk

Priscilla Dean (1896-)
1917: The Gray Ghost
18: Kiss or Kill
Wildcat of Paris
Two Souled Woman
Brazen Beauty
Beautiful Beggar
Beloved Jim
Witch Woman
19: Pretty Smooth

19: Wicked Darling
Exquisite Thief
Silk Lined Burglar
She Hired a Husband
20: The Virgin of Stamboul
21: Outside the Law
Reputation
Conflict
Under Two Flags
22: Wild Honey
23: Flame of Life
Drifting
The White Tiger
24: A Cafe in Cairo
Storm Daughter
Siren of Seville
25: The Crimson Runner
Dice Woman
26: West of Broadway
Speeding Venus
Forbidden Waters
The Danger Girl
27: Birds of Prey
Jewels of Desire
Slipping Wives
28: The Aristocrat
How Do You Feel?

Hazel Deane
1916: Matrimoniacs
Son of Tarzan
Soft Boiled Yeggs
Monkey Movie Hero
White Winged Monkey
20: Soft Soap
Monkey Talks
That Darned Stocking
21: The Desert Within
South of the Northern Lights
3 Bill Jones Comedies

Nigel De Brulier (1878-1948)
1915: Ghosts
16: Intolerance
19: Sahara
Mystery of 13 (serial)
The Boomerang
Flames of the Flesh
20: The Dwelling Place of Light
The Virgin of Stamboul
4 Horsemen of the Apocalypse
20: Mother of His Children
His Pajama Girl
21: Three Musketeers
The Devil Within
22: A Doll's House
Omar the Tentmaker
Salome
23: Hunchback of Notre Dame
Rupert of Hentzau
26: Ben Hur
Don Juan
The Ancient Mariner
27: Beloved Rogue
The Gaucho
Romance of a Queen
Soft Cushions
Patent Leather Kid
Surrender
28: Two Lovers
Loves of an Actress SSE
The Divine Sinner
Me Gangster
Wings
The Iron Mask PT
29: The Wheel of Life
Noah's Ark T
Through Different Eyes T
30: The Green Goddess T
Golden Dawn T
Moby Dick T
Redemption T
31: Son of India T
32: Miss Pinkerton T

Pedro De Cordoba (1881-1950)
1915: Carmen
Temptation
16: Maria Rosa
17: Barbary Sheep
Runaway Romany
19: The New Moon
20: The World and His Wife
The Sin That Was His
The Inner Chamber
21: The Dark Mirror
22: Young Diana
When Knighthood was in Flower
23: Enemies of Women
24: Bandolero
Swords and the Woman
25: The New Commandment
Girl of the South

Adele De Garde

1913: The Lonely Villa
The Drunkard's Reformation

Sam De Grasse (1875-1953)

1915: Birth of a Nation
Martyrs of the Alamo
16: Intolerance
The Good, Bad Man
Half Breed
An Innocent Magdalene
Diane of the Follies
Children of the Feud
17: Wild and Woolly
Heart of the Hills
Her Official Fathers
Slippery
19: Silk Lined Burglar
Blind Husbands
The Hope Chest
20: Devil's Passkey
The Broken Gates
Unseen Forces
21: Courage
A Wife's Awakening
22: Robin Hood
King Tut
23: Slippy McGee
Forsaking All Others
The Spoilers
Courtship of Miles Standish
In the Palace of the King
25: One Year to Live
26: The Black Pirate
Her Second Change
Love's Blindness
27: King of Kings
When a Man Loves
Captain Salvation
The Fighting Eagle
Country Doctor
28: Our Dancing Daughters
The Man Who Laughs
Erick the Great
Wreck of the Hesperus
Honor Bound
29: The Last Performance
Silks and Saddles

Mr. & Mrs. Carter DeHaven (1896-)

1915: College Orphan (CDH alone)
16: From Broadway to a Throne (CDH alone)
17: The Losing Winner "
Rice and Old Shoes
Twin Husbands
Entertaining the Boss
Keep 'em Home
The Waggin' Tale
16: Timothy Dobbs (with Mrs. CDH)
That's Me "
19: In a Pinch "
21: Twin Beds "
Girl in the Taxi "
22: Marry the Poor Girl "
My Lady Friend "
23: Their First Vacation "
13 - 2 reelers for Goldwyn "
10 - 2 reelers for Paramount "
A Ringer for Dad

Mrs. Carter DeHaven (Flora Parker)

1916: The Mad Cap
Youth of Fortune
Excess Baggage
What Could be Sweeter?
Hoodooed
Teasing the Soil

Phillipe De Lacey (1917-)

1921: Without Benefit of Clergy
22: Is Matrimony a Failure?
A Doll's House
Thelma
Christmas
23: Why Do We Live?
Divorce
Wheel of Fortune
Wasted Lives
Rosita
25: Peter Pan
27: The Magic Garden
Is Zat So?
Student Prince
The Tigress
28: Love
Mother Machree SSE
Broken Mask
The 4 Devils T

28: Napoleon's Barber
29: Redeeming Sin PT
Square Shoulders PT
4 Feathers SSE
Marriage Playground SSE
Royal Rider PT

Marguerite De La Motte (1902-1950)
1918: Arizona
19: The Pagan God
For a Woman's Honor
Dangerous Waters
A Sagebrush Hamlet
In Wrong
20: Broken Gates
The Sagebrusher
The Hope
Trumpet Island
The U. P. Trail
The Mark of Zorro
21: The Nut
Three Musketeers
22: Shattered Idols
Shadows
Jilt
23: What a Wife Learned
Famous Mrs. Fair
Just Like a Woman
Scars of Jealousy
Man of Action
Richard the Lion-Hearted
Desire
The Talisman
Wandering Daughters
24: The Clean Heart
The Beloved Brute
25: The People Vs. Nancy Preston
Children of the Whirlwind
26: Red Rice
Fifth Avenue
Meet the Prince
Pals in Paradise
The Last Frontier
Hearts and Fists
Unknown Soldier
27: The Final Extra
Held by the Law
Kid Sister
Ragtime
28: Trailin' Back
29: Montmartre Rose
29: Iron Mask PT

Charles Delaney (1892-1959)
1926: College Days
Sky Pirate
The Cohens and the Kellys
Silent Power
27: The Silent Avenger
Outcast Souls
The Main Event
The Lovelorn
Frisco Sally Levy
The 13th Hour
The Adventurer
Mountains of Manhattan
28: After the Storm
The Branded Man
The Air Circus
Show Girl
The River Woman SSE
The Stool Pigeon
Do Your Duty
The Cohens and the Kellys in Paris
Women Who Dare
Home, James! PT
29: The Faker
Broadway Babies
Hard to Get
Girl From Woolworth's T

Dolores Del Rio (1905-)
1925: Joanna
26: What Price Glory?
High Steppers
Pals First
The Whole Town's Talking
27: Resurrection
The Loves of Carmen
28: Trail of '98
Ramona
Revenge
The Red Dance
The Dove
No Other Woman
Gateway of the Moon
29: Evangeline PT
30: The Bad One T
Hell's Harbor T
The Girl of Rio T

William Demarest (1892-)
1926: When the Wife's Away

26: Pa's Vacation
Amateur Night
27: Finger Prints
Gay Old Bird
Matinee Ladies
What Happened to Father
Bush Leaguer
A Reno Divorce
The Jazz Singer PT
28: Sharp Shooters
The Escape
5 and 10¢ Annie SSE
Pay as you Enter
The Butter and Egg Man
Wrecking Boss
The Crash
A Girl in Every Port
29: Broadway Melody T

Carol Dempster (1902-)
1916: Intolerance
19: Romance of Happy Valley
Hope Chest
The Girl Who Stayed at Home
Scarlet Days
20: The Love Flower
Way Down East (extra)
21: Dream Street
Black Beach
22: Sherlock Holmes
One Exciting Night
23: White Rose
24: America
Isn't Life Wonderful?
25: Sally of the Sawdust
26: That Royle Girl
Sorrows of Satan

Reginald Denny (1891-1967)
1919: Bringing up Betty
The Oakdale Affair
Experience
20: A Dark Lantern
39 East
21: The Price of Possession
Paying the Piper
Disraeli
Footlights
The Iron Trail
The Beggar Maid
22: Tropical Love
Never Let Go
22: The Kentucky Derby
The Leather Pushers
Jenny Lind
Romeo in Pajamas
Sherlock Holmes
23: The Abysmal Brute
Madame Butterfly
Sporting Youth
24: Oh, Doctor!
25: What Happened to Jones
I'll Show you the Town
California Straight Ahead
What Was I?
26: Skinner's Dress Suit
Take it from Me
Rolling Home
The Cheerful Fraud
27: On Your Toes
Fast and Furious
Out All Night
28: That's My Daddy!
Good Morning, Judge
Night Bird
29: Red Hot Speed PT
Clear the Decks PT
His Lucky Day PT
30: One Hysterical Night T
Embarrassing Moments T

Vernon Dent (d. 1963)
1924: Feet of Mud
His Marriage Wow
Plain Clothes
Remember When?
Lucky Stars
There He Goes
Saturday Afternoon
25: Bobbs in the Wood
27: His First Flame
28: Golf Widows
A Dumb Waiter
Ladies Must Eat
?? Hank Mann Comedies
A Harem Hero
An Eye for Figures
Broken Bubbles
A Depot Romance
A Gas Attack

Lya De Putti (1904-)
1925: Variety
The Phantom
26: Manon Lescaut

26: Sorrows of Satan
Prince of Tempters
God Gave Me 20¢
27: The Heart Thief
28: Buck Privates
Midnight Rose
Scarlet Lady
Jealously
Autumn Love

Ruby De Remer
1917: The Auction Block
Enlighten Thy Daughter
18: Pals First
19: Fires of Faith
Dust of Desire
Safe for Democracy
The Great Romance
20: His Temporary Wife
21: The Way Women Love
Luxury
The Passionate Pilgrim
Pilgrims of the Night
22: The Unconquered Woman
23: Don't Marry for Money
Glimpses of the Moon

Charles De Roche (1880-1952)
1908: Le Tango Rouge
12: La Masque D'Horreur
19: La Faute Des Autres
La Fille Du Peuple
20: Gigolette
22: L'Empereur Des Pauvres
L'Empire Des Diamants
Notre Dame D'Amour
Le Roi Du Camargue
The Spanish Jade
23: The Cheat
Law of the Lawless
The Marriage Maker
24: Shadows of Paris
The 10 Commandments
White Moth
Love and Glory
25: Madame Sans Gene
26: La Princesse Aux Clowns
31: La Croix Du Sud

Andres De Segurola (d. 1953)
1927: The Loves of Sunya
28: Bringing Up Father
Glorious Betsy PT
28: The Cardboard Lover
The Red Dance
29: My Man PT
Behind Closed Doors

William Desmond (1878-1949)
1915: Peggy
Peer Gynt
16: The Criminal
The Captive God
Not My Sister
17: Paws of the Bear
Flying Colors
Beyond the Shadow
A Sudden Gentleman
Fightin' Mad
Big Timber
18: The Honest Man
Fighting Back
Captain of His Soul
Sea Panther
Marriage Bubble
Society for Sale
Old Hartwell's Cub
Closin' In
Hell's End
Wild Life
19: Mints of Hell
Bare-Fisted Gallagher
Dangerous Waters
Her Code of Honor
Muffled Drums
The Pretender
A Sagebrush Hamlet
The Prodigal Liar
Life's Funny Proposition
Deuce Duncan
White-Washed Walls
20: Man From Make-Believe
The Prince and Betty
The Blue Bandanna
Broadway Cowboy
Sentenced to Soft Labor
21: Don't Leave Your Husband
The Parish Priest
Women Men Love
The Child Thou Gavest Me
22: Night Life in Hollywood
Perils of the Yukon (serial)
23: Around the World in 18
Days (serial)
The Phantom Fortune
(serial)

23: McQuire of the Mounted
Shadows of the North
Beasts of Paradise (serial)
24: The Riddle Rider (dual) (serial)
Breathless Moment
Measure of a Man
Sunset Trail
25: Ace of Spades (serial)
Perils of the Wild (serial)
The Meddler
Blood and Steel
The Burning Trail
26: Strings of Steel (serial)
The Winking Idol (serial)
Tongues of Steel
The Claw
27: Return of the Riddle Rider (serial)
Red Clay
28: The Mystery Rider (serial)
The Vanishing Rider (dual) (serial)
The Devil's Trade Mark
29: No Defense

Andy Devine (1905-)
1928: We Americans
Red Lips
29: Lonesome PT
29: Naughty Baby SSE
Hot Stuff T

Dorothy Devore (1901-)
1918: Law of the North
Fair Enough
Mile-A-Minute Mary
Let 'er Run
Babies Welcome
Hazel from Hollywood
19: Girl Dodger
20: 45 Minutes from Broadway
23: Winter Has Came
Movie Mad
The Magnificent Brute
Saving Sister Susie
One Stormy Night
24: The Narrow Street
25: Who Cares?
A Broadway Butterfly
How Baxter Butted In
26: Senor Daredevil
The Man Upstairs
26: The Social Highwayman
Mind Your Business
Money to Burn
The Midnight Flyer
The Gilded Highway
3 Weeks in Paris
Chop Suey
27: The First Night
Naughty Mary Brown
Mountains of Manhattan
28: No Babies Wanted
Cutie
30: Take the Heir
??: comedies with Lyon & Moran (15)

Elliott Dexter (1870-1941)
1915: The Masqueraders
16: The Heart of Nora Flynn
The Lash
Daphne and the Pirate
Diplomacy
Public Opinion
17: A Romance of the Redwoods
Castles for Two
The Rise of Jennie Cushing
Lost and Won
Tides of Barnegat
Sylvia of the Secret Service
18: Woman and Wife
Old Wives for New
The Whispering Chorus
The Girl Who Came Back
19: For Better, For Worse
Maggie Pepper
We Can't Have Everything
The Squaw Man
Don't Change your Husband
20: Something to Think About
Behold My Wife
21: The Affairs of Anatol
Forever
The Great Moment
The Witching Hour
Don't Tell Everything
22: Enter Madame
Her Husband's Trade Mark
Grand Larceny
Hands of Nara
23: Adam's Rib
Flaming Youth
Only 38
An Old Sweetheart of Mine

23: The Common Law
24: Age of Innocence
The Fast Set
25: Stella Maris
26: Capital Punishment
(Shadow of the Law)

29: Das Schippe Der Verlohenen Menschen
(The Ship of Lost Souls)
Liebesnachte
(Nightlife)
30: The Blue Angel
(Der Bleue Engel) T

Marlene Dietrich (1902-)

1923: Der Kleine Napoleon
(Little Napoleon)
Die Tragodie Der Liebe
(Tragedy of Love)
Der Mensch Am Wege
(The Man by the Roadside)
24: The Great Baritone
Der Sprung Ins Leben
(Leap into Life)
26: Die Freudlose Gasse
(Joyless Street)
The Street of Sorrows
Manon Lescaut
Ween Ein Weib Den Weg Verliert
Gefahren Der Brautzeit
(Dangers of the Engagement Period)
Kopf Hock, Charly!
(Heads Up, Charlie)
27: Madame Wunscht Keine Kinder
(Madame Doesn't Want Children)
Sein Grosster Bluff
(His Greatest Bluff)
Der Juxbaron
(The Imaginary Baron)
28: Eine Du Barry Von Heute
(A Modern DuBarry)
Die Frau Nach Der Man Sicht Sehnt
(The Woman One Longs For)
Cafe Electric
(When a Woman Loses Her Way)
29: Prinzessin Olala
(The Art of Love)
Ich Kusse Ihre Hand, Madame
(I Kiss Your Hand, Madame)
3 Loves

Eddie Dillon

1908: Ostler Joe
The Snow Man
11: Fisher Folks
12: The Would-Be Shriner
Look Up
The Banker's Daughter
Those Hicksville Boys
One Busy Hour
13: Almost a Man
Her Mother's Oath
Pa Pays
The Lady in Black
A Tender-Hearted Boy
The Wanderer
Love in an Apartment Hotel
The Sheriff's Baby
The Dutch Gold Mine
14: The Massacre
Home Sweet Home
15: Faithful to the Finish
16: Don Quixote
Sunshine Dad
18: Embarrassment of Riches
19: Luck and Pluck
20: Parlor Bedroom and Bath
A Heart to Let
23: Broadway Gold
24: Drums of Jeopardy
26: Danger Girl
The Deuce Woman
28: Lilac Time SSE

Rose Dione

1919: The World and Its Women
20: The Woman and the Puppet
The Great Lover
Suds
21: Silk Hosiery
The Blushing Bride
Silent Years
Little Lord Fauntleroy
22: Omar the Tentmaker

23: Salome
The French Doll
25: One Year to Live
26: Paris
The Duchess of Buffalo
27: Beloved Rogue
Polly of the Movies
Camille
28: The Mad Hour
Bringing up Father
His Tiger Lady
Out of the Ruins
Red Mark
Pants at any Price
Ragtime
29: Naughty Baby SSE
One Stolen Night PT
Hearts in Exile T

Richard Dix (1894-1949)

1921: Not Guilty
Poverty to Riches
Dangerous Curve Ahead
All's Fair in Love
The Sin Flood
22: The Glorious Fool
Yellow Men and Gold
Wall Flower
Fools First
Bonded Woman
23: Call of the Canyon
Racing Hearts
Quicksands
Souls for Sale
To the Last Man
The Christian
10 Commandments
Woman with 4 Faces
24: The Stranger
Unguarded Women
Sinners in Heaven
Icebound
Manhattan
25: A Man Must Live
Lucky Devil
Too Many Kisses
Shock Punch
Womanhandled
Men and Women
The Vanishing American
26: Let's Get Married
Say it Again
The Quarterback
27: Paradise for Two
Knockout Reilly
Manpower
Shanghai Bound
28: Sporting Goods
Warming Up
Easy Come, Easy Go
Moran of the Marines
Gay Defender
29: Redskin SSE

Billy Dooley (1893-)

?? Campus Cuties
A Gallant Gob
Sea Food
The Dizzy Diver
Oriental Hugs
A She-Going Sailor
Gobs of Love
Happy Heels

Johnny Dooley (1887-)

?? Johnny Dooley Comedies
Bobby, The Office Boy
Private Preserves
Pep
Beauty's Worth
When Knighthood was in Flower

Mlle. Doraldina

1912: Ten
15: Morals of Marcus
The White Pearl
16: The Heart of Nora Flynn
Oliver Twist
The Lash
Wood Nymph
Diplomacy
17: Castles for Two
Lost and Won
Heart's Desire
18: Naulahka
19: The Mysterious Princess
20: The Woman Untamed
Twelve-Ten
Beatrice
Midnight Gambols
21: Passion Flower
22: The Stronger Passion
24: Sally Bishop

Billie Dove (1904-)

1921: Get-Rich-Quick Wallingford
At the Stage Door
22: Polly of the Follies
Beyond the Rainbow
Youth to Youth
23: All the Brothers Were Valiant
Madness of Youth
The Thrill Chaser
Soft Boiled
Lone Star Ranger
24: Wanderer of the Wasteland
The Roughneck
Yankee Madness
25: Air Mail
The Fighting Heart
Wild Horse Mesa
Light of the Western Stars
Lucky Horseshoe
Ancient Highway
26: The Black Pirate
Marriage Clause
The Lone Wolf Returns
Kid Boots
27: An Affair of a Follies Girl
Sensation Seekers
The Tender Hour
An American Beauty
Stolen Bride
28: Heart of a Follies Girl
Yellow Lily
Adoration SSE
Night Watch
The Love Mart
29: Careers PT
Her Private Life T
Man and the Moment PT
30: Painted Angel T

Joseph Dowling (1850-)

1915: The Shoal Light
16: The Deserter
Home
17: Sudden Jim
The Pinch Hitter
18: A Law Unto Himself
Intelligence
Carmen of the Klondike
More Trouble
The Girl Who Came Back
Maid o' the Storm
Tidebrook
18: The Bells
19: The Joyous Liar
Riders of the Dawn
The Miracle Man
Midnight Stage
20: U. P. Trail
Life Sparks
Kentucky Colonel
House of Whispers
The Devil to Pay
21: The Spenders
The Turning Point
Lure of Egypt
Little Lord Fauntleroy
A Certain Rich Man
Fightin' Mad
The Other Woman
The Beautiful Liar
The Girl Who Ran Wild
22: Quincy Adams Sawyer
The Infidel
One Clear Call
The Half Breed
If You Believe It, It Is So
Pride of Palomar
Trail of the Ace
Danger Point
The Grim Comedian
The Sin of Martha Queed
23: Dollar Devils
The Christian
The Spider and the Rose
Barefoot Boy
Temporary Marriage
24: Tess of the D'Ubervilles
25: New Laws for Old
With Hoops of Steel
26: Little Irish Girl
2-Gun Man
The Rainmaker

Regina Doyle

1928: Beyond the Smoke
The Danger Line
Saps and Saddles
Ridin' Leather
Perilous Paths
Just in Time
A Clean Sweep

Louise Dresser (1879-1965)

1922: Enter Madame
The Glory of Clementina

23:	Ruggles of Red Gap	
	Prodigal Daughters	
25:	Percy	
	The Eagle	
	The Goose Woman	
26:	Padlocked	
	Blind Goddess	
	Broken Hearts of Hollywood	
	Gigolo	
	Everybody's Acting	
	5th Avenue	
27:	Mr. Wu	
	Third Degree	
	Lone Eagle	
	White Flannels	
28:	The Air Circus	PT
	Not Quite Decent	T
	Mother Knows Best	T
	A Ship Comes In	
	Garden of Eden	
29:	Madonna of Avenue A	T
30:	This Mad World	T

Marie Dressler (1869-1934)

1914:	Tillie's Punctured Romance	
15:	Tillie's Tomato Surprise	
17:	The Scrub Lady	
	Tillie Wakes Up	
27:	Breakfast at Sunrise	
	The Callahans and the Murphys	
	Joy Girl	
28:	Bringing up Father	
	The Patsy	
29:	Divine Lady	SSE
	Hollywood Revue of 1929	T
	Road Show	T
	Vagabond Lover	T

Roland Drew (1903-)

1926:	Fascinating Youth	
28:	Lady Raffles	
	Ramona	
29:	Broadway Forever	
	Evangeline	PT
30:	Racketeer	T
	Love Trader	T
31:	Ex-Flame	

Sidney & Lucille McVey Drew (1894-1919)

1913:	A Regiment of Two	
14:	Auntie's Portrait	
	When Two Hearts are Won	(SD soloed)
	Jerry's Uncle's Namesake	"
	Too Many Husbands	"
	A Model Young Man	"
	Mysterious Mr. Davey	"
	The Royal Wild West	"
	Never Again	"
15:	Wanted: A Nurse	
	Story of a Glove	"
	A Safe Investment	"
	Miss Sticky Moufit Kiss	"
	Good Gracious!	"
	Following the Scent	"
	Booble's Baby	"
	A Case of Eugenics	"
	Fox Trot Finesse	"
	The Home Cure	"
	The Honeymoon Baby	"
	Romantic Peggie	"
	When Two Play a Game	"
16:	Childhood's Happy Days	
	(Mr. and Mrs.)	
	(together up to 1919)	
	At the Count of Ten	
	At a Premium	
	Taking a Rest	
17:	The Hypochondriac	
	Cave Man's Bluff	
	His Perfect Day	
	The Pest	
	Blackmail	
	Her Obsession	
	Reliable Henry	
	Locked Out	
	High Cost of Living	
	Awakening of Helen Minor	
	Putting it Over on Henry	
	Handy Henry	
	One of the Family	
	Her Lesson	
	Nothing To Wear	
	Her Anniversaries	
	Tootsie	
	Too Much Henry	
	Wages No Object	
	The Spirit of Merry Xmas	
	The Unmarried Look	
	Shadowing Henry	
	Rubbing It In	

17: The Matchmakers
Lest We Forget
Mr. Parker - Hero
Henry's Ancestors
His Ear for Music
Her Economic Independence
Her First Game
The Patriot
Music Hath Charm
His Curiosity
The Joy of Freedom
Double Life
The Dentist
Hist... Spies!
12 Good Hens and True
His Deadly Calm
The Rebellion of Mr. Minor
As Others See Us
16: A Lady in the Library
Borrowing Trouble
Duplicity
Help
His Rival
Nobody Home
Number 1
Their First
Taking a Rest
A Close Resemblance
18: Before and After Taking
Gas Logic
His First Love
Special Today
Why Henry Left Home
19: Squared
Once a Man

Mrs. Sidney Drew (Lucille McVey) (1895-)
?? Once a Mason
The Amateur Liar
Harold, the Last of the Saxons
Bunkered
A Sisterly Scheme
Unconventional Maida
The Charming Mrs. Chase
Stimulating Mrs. Barton
Emotional Miss Vaughn
Cousin Kate
After Thirty

Nancy Drexel (1910-)
1927: Bronco Twister
28: Fangs of the Wild
Riding Renegade
Bantam Cowboy
The Escape
4 Devils T
Riley the Cop SSE
Prep and Pep SSE

Claire Du Brey (1893-)
1916: Peggy
18: Border Raiders
19: The Devil's Trail
When Fate Divides
Modern Husbands
What Every Woman Wants
The Old Maid's Baby
The Sawdust Doll
World Aflame
Man in the Open
Wishing Ring Man
Spite Bride
Dangerous Hours
20: Americanism
Walk-Offs
Heart of a Child
Green Flame
House of Whispers
Life's Twist
The Light Woman
21: That Girl Montana
My Lady's Latch Key
Hole in the Wall
22: Glass Houses
The Ordeal
When Love Comes
Only a Shop Girl
You Never Know
To Have and to Hold
23: Voice from the Minaret
25: The Exquisite Sinner
29: Two Sisters

Jack Duffy (1879-)
1928: Long Hose
Halfback Hannah
Love's Young Scream
Say Uncle
Harold Teen
Hot Scotch

28: Loose Change
Lay On, MacDuff
Should Scotchmen Marry?
Peg of the Ring
The Purple Mask
Farmers and Framers
Blackie's Redemption
Misfits and Matrimony

Tom Dugan (1889-1958)
1928: Midnight Taxi
Dressed to Kill
She Knew Men
Sharpshooters
Dead Line
Soft Living
Melody of Love
Shadows of the Night
The Barker T
29: Broadway Babies PT
Million Dollar Collar PT
Kid Gloves PT
Sonny Boy T
Drag T

Helen Dunbar
1915: Graustark
18: The Shuttle
19: The Squaw Man
Fighting Through
20: Young Mrs. Winthrop
City of Masks
Behold My Wife
You Never Can Tell
The Furnace
Man of Courage
21: Sacred and Profane Love
Her First Elopement
The Little Clown
House that Jazz Built
Her Winning Way
22: A Homespun Vamp
World's Champion
Beyond the Rocks
The Impossible Mrs. Bellew
30 Days
26: Fine Manners

Albert "Bud" Duncan (1886-1961)
1928: The Haunted Ship
Fixin' Father
Horse Play
28: Bee Cured
Have a Heart
Movie Mania
Rudolph's Revenge
Framing Youth
Soap and Water
Plastered
A Clean Sweep
Spooky Spooks
Bear Facts
Two Bad Men
Can-O-Bull Chief
Too Tired
Mabel's Mate
Gyping Gypsies
Sour Milk
Never Say Die
Happy Daze
Family Meal Ticket
Casper's Week End
Maggie Pepper
Mutt & Jeff
A Menagerie Mixup
The Onion Magnate's Revenge
Rival Romeos
Seaside Romeos
Twin Caddies

William Duncan (1880-1961)
1912: The Dynamiters
A Rough Ride with Nitroglycerine
13: Bill's Birthday Present
A Matrimonial Deluge
The Suffragette
Buck's Romance
An Embarrassed Bridegroom
The Good Indian
Sallie's Sure Shot
Religion and Gun Practice
How Betty Made Good
Taming a Tenderfoot
Silver Grindstone
Saved from the Vigilantes
The Taming of Texas Pete
Galloping Romeo
His Father's Deputy
Howlin' Jones
Jealousy of Miguel and Isabella
Stolen Moccasins

13: Juggling with Fate
Law and the Outlaw
Made a Coward
The Marshall's Capture
Rejected Lover's Luck
The Senorita's Repentance
The Cattle Thief's Escape
14: Marrying Gretchen
Marian the Holy Terror
Servant Question Out West
Romance of the Forest Reserve
16: The Last Man
17: The Tenderfoot
Dead Shot Baker
Money Magic
Aladdin from Broadway
Wolfville
18: The Fighting Trail (serial)
A Fight for Millions "
Vengeance and the Woman
19: Smashing Barriers (serial)
The Man of Might "
20: Silent Avenger "
Fighting Fate "
21: When Men are Men
Steelheart
No Defense
22: The Silent Vow
When Danger Smiles
The Fighting Guide
23: Steel Trail (serial)
Smashing Barriers (remake) "
Playing it Wild
24: The Fast Express (serial)
Wolves of the North "

Josephine Dunn (1906-)

1926: Everybody's Acting
Fascinating Youth
27: Love's Greatest Mistake
Swim, Girl, Swim
Fireman, Save My Child!
She's a Sheik
Get Your Man
28: The Americans
A Million for Love
The Singing Fool T
Excess Baggage
Heart of a Follies Girl
Air Patrol
29: Sin Sister SSE
29: All at Sea
Black Magic SSE
China Bound
A Man's Man SSE
Melody Lane T
Big Time T
Red Hot Rhythm T
A Most Immoral Lady

Miss DuPont

1921: False Kisses
Shattered Dreams
The Rage of Paris
22: Foolish Wives
The Golden Gallows
A Wonderful Wife
23: Brass
The Broken Wing
24: What Three Men Wanted
One Night in Rome
26: Good and Naughty
Mantrap
That Model from Paris

Minta Durfee (1889-)

1914: A Misplaced Foot
20 Minutes of Love
Leading Lizzie Astray
Fatty and Minnie He-Haw
Gentlemen of Nerve
His Trysting Place
Fatty's Jonah Day
Making a Living
A Film Johnnie
Caught in a Cabaret
The Knockout
The Masqueraders
Tillie's Punctured Romance
15: Dirty Work in a Laundry
Fickle Fatty's Fall
Mabel and Fatty and the Law
Love, Speed and Thrills
The Home Breakers
Hearts and Planets
Our Daredevil Chief
Court House Crooks
The Cabaret
The Sheriff
Bright Lights
Fickle Fatty's Romance
18: His Wife's Mistake
The Rounders

18: Mickey

George Duryea (Tom Keene) (1904-1963)

1928: Marked Money
29: The Godless Girl SSE
Tide of the Empire
Thunder
Honky Tonk T

Dorothy Dwan

1925: The Wizard of Oz
26: Dangerous Dude
Great K & A Train Robbery
Stop Look and Listen
Captain's Courage
Canyon of Light
27: McFadden's Flats
Hills of Kentucky
Princess of Broadway
Spuds
Land Beyond the Law
Tumbling River
Silver Valley
28: Virgin Queen
Square Crooks
Out with the Tide
Riders of the Dark
Obey Your Husband
29: The Peacock Fan
The Drifter
California Mail
30: Fighting Legion PT

Jeanne Eagels (1894-1929)

1916: Woman and the World
17: Under False Colors
27: Man Woman and Sin

Edna Earle

1925: Eagle
A Model's Confession

Edward Earle (1884-)

1916: The Innocence of Ruth
Gates of Eden
17: For France
18: The Blind Adventure
$1000
Transients in Arcadia
19: His Bridal Night
19: Miracle of Love
20: Law of the Yukon
21: Buried Treasure
East Lynne
Passion Fruit
25: The Splendid Road
26: Pals First
A Woman's Heart
The Captain's Courage
27: 12 Miles Out
Spring Fever
28: The Wind
29: Spite Marriage

Reeves Eason (1866-1956)

1920: Moon Riders (serial)
21: The Big Adventure
23: His Last Race
Around the World (serial)
24: Border Justice
25: Flaming Spurs
Ben Hur
The New Champion
Sign of the Claw
27: Prairie King
28: Flying Cowboy
Danger Rider
29: Winged Horseman

Helen Jerome Eddy (1897-)

1915: The Strange Unknown
16: Pasquale
19: Turn in the Road
20: Pollyanna
Life
House of Toys
Light Woman
City Sparrow
Forbidden Thing
First Born
The Trembling Hour
21: The County Fair
One Man in a Million
The Other Woman
22: The Flirt
When Love Comes
23: An Old Sweetheart of Mine
To the Ladies
26: Padlocked
27: Quality Street
Camille
28: Two Lovers
13 Washington Square

28: Chicago After Midnight
Speed Classic
Last Lap
29: Divine Lady
Blue Skies
Midstream PT

Robert Edeson (1868-1931)
1913: Where the Trail Divides
14: The Call of the North
The Absentees
15: Mortmain
The Cave Man
Man's Prerogative
16: The Light that Failed
Big Jim Garrity
The Public Defender
19: Sealed Hearts
21: Extravagance
22: Prisoner of Zenda
Sure Fire Flint
Foolish Wives
23: Luck
The Tie that Binds
Has the World Gone Mad?
You are Guilty!
The Spoilers
10 Commandments
24: Feet of Clay
Men
Triumph
The Bedroom Window
25: Locked Doors
The Golden Bed
Men and Women
26: The Blue Eagle
Volga Boatman
Eve's Leaves
Her Man of War
Braveheart
Whispering Smith
27: King of Kings
Night Bride
Altars of Desire
Rejuvenation of Aunt Mary
His Dog
28: Chicago
A Ship Comes In
10th Avenue
Beware of Blondes
Tomorrow
Power of the Press
Walking Back
28: Marriage by Contract
Home Towners
29: George Washington Cohen
Little Wildcat PT
The Doctor's Secret
Little Johnny Jones
Romance of the Rio Grande T
A Most Immoral Lady T
Marianne T
Dynamite T

Neely Edwards (1889-1965)
1920: You Never Can Tell
21: Brewster's Millions
The Little Clown
His Inheritance Taxi
Society Sailors
Taking Things Easy
A Shaky Family Tree
Easy to Cop
22: The Green Temptation
28: Excess Baggage
29: Show Boat
??: the Hallroom Boys comedies

Snitz Edwards (d. 1960)
1920: The City of Masks
Going Some
21: The Charm School
The Love Special
Cheated Love
No Woman Knows
Red Hot Romance
Ladies Must Live
22: Love is an Awful Thing
Rags to Riches
June Madness
The Ghost Breaker
Gray Dawn
Human Hearts
23: Rosita
Souls for Sale
Tiger Love
24: Thief of Bagdad
25: The Splendid Road
Phantom of the Opera
26: The General
Battling Butler
27: The Red Mill
Night Life
Old Shoes

27: College
28: The Mysterious Island
29: A Dangerous Woman

Jack Egan
1927: The Potters
28: Mad Hour
The Big Noise
Harold Teen
It Can Be Done

Sally Eilers (1908-)
1927: Slightly Used
The Cradle Snatchers
28: Dry Martini SSE
Goodbye Kiss SSE
Nize Baby
29: Trial Marriage
Broadway Daddies
Show of Shows T
Long, Long Trail T
Sailor's Holiday T

Maxine Elliott (1871-1940)
1918: Fighting Odds
19: The Eternal Magdalene

Robert Elliott
1917: Mary Moreland
Spirit of Lafayette
Unknown Love
18: Resurrection
19: Checkers
L'Apache
20: The Empire of Diamonds
28: Happiness Ahead
Romance of the Underworld SSE
Lights of New York T
Obey Your Husband
Headlines
29: Lone Wolf's Daughter PT
Protection SSE

Robert Ellis (1892-)
1919: Upstairs and Down
21: Ladies Must Live
22: The Woman Who Fooled Herself
Hurricane Girl
23: Flame of Life
24: For Sale
Montmartre
26: Brooding Eyes
The Devil's Dice
Whispering Canyon
The Girl from Montmartre
S. O. S.
Perils of the Sea
27: Lure of the Night Club
28: Law and the Man
Marry the Girl
Varsity
Freedom of the Press
The Law's Lash
Ragtime
29: Restless Youth
Night Parade

Julian Eltinge (1883-1941)
1914: Crinoline Girl
Cousin Lucy
An Adventuress
16: Isle of Love
17: The Charming Countess
Clever Mrs. Carfax
Her Grace the Vampire
18: Over the Rhine
25: Madame Behave
The Widow's Might
Fascinating Widow
40: If I Had My Way

June Elvidge (1893-)
1915: Lure of Woman
La Boheme
16: The Rack
18: The Marriage Market
Rasputin
Shall We Forgive Her?
The Tenth Case
Strong Way
Mrs. Reynolds
Broken Ties
The Way Out
The Oldest Law
Woman of Redemption
Joan of the Woods
Stolen Orders
19: The Bluffer
Moral Deadline
Zero Hour
Social Pirate
Coax Me
Love Defender
Love and the Woman

19: Appearance of Evil
Power and the Glory
Three Green Eyes
Poison Pen
His Father's Wife
The Quickening Flame
Woman of Lies
The Steel King
Call of the Yukon
21: Fine Feathers
22: The Man Who Saw Tomorrow
The Impossible Mrs. Bellew
23: Temptation
King Tut
Power of a Lie
Forsaking All Others

Alphonz Ethier
1919: Oh Johnny
Sandy Burke of the U-Bar-U
21: Frontier of the Stars
A Message from Mars
27: Alias the Lone Wolf
28: Say it with Sables
Shadows of the Night
Dead Line
Smoke Bellew
29: Hardboiled

Madge Evans (1909-)
1915: Zaza
Seven Sisters
16: Husband and Wife
Seventeen
Sudden Riches
17: Beloved Adventuress
The Burglar
Little Patriot
Web of Desire
Maternity
Little Duchess
The Volunteer
18: True Blue
Neighbors
Wanted: A Mother
Love Nest
Adventures of Carol
Gates of Gladness
Hilda
The Corner Grocer
18: Woman and Wife
The Golden Wall
Power and the Glory
Stolen Orders
19: Home Wanted
The Love Defender
23: On the Banks of the Wabash
24: Classmates

Bessie Eyton (1890-)
1912: God of Gold
13: A Wild Ride
Alone in the Jungles
The Long Ago
Story of Lavinia
3 Wise Men
14: The 5th Man
Salvation of Nance O'Shaughnessy
The Spoilers
16: The Crisis
17: Twisted Trails
Heart of Texas Ryan
The Smouldering Flame
Love of Madge O'Mara
The Sole Survivor
18: City of Purple Dreams
The Steel Alarm
Victor of the Plot
Law North of 65
19: Beware of Strangers
Who Shall Take My Life?
Way of a Man with a Maid
Man of Honor
The Usurper
20: A Lady in Love

Elinor Fair (1902-)
1916: End of the Trail
19: The Miracle Man
Words and Music
Be A Little Sport
Married in Haste
Love is Love
Vagabond Luck
20: Broadway and Home
Kismet
The Girl in Number 20
The Lost Princess
21: Through the Back Door
It Can't be Done
22: White Hands

23: Driven
Has the World Gone Mad?
The Eagle's Feather
25: Tin Pan Alley
26: Volga Boatman
Bachelor Brides
My Friend from India
27: Yankee Clipper
The Heart Thief
Jim the Conqueror
28: Let 'er Go, Gallagher
29: Sin Town

Douglas Fairbanks Jr. (1909-)
1923: Stephen Steps Out
25: Stella Dallas
26: Main Bait
Padlocked
Broken Hearts of Hollywood
27: Is Zat So?
Texas Steer
Brass Band
Women Love Diamonds
28: The Barker T
The Toilers SSE
Power of the Press
Dead Man's Curve
Modern Mothers
29: The Forward Pass T
Dance Hall
Our Modern Maidens
The Jazz Age
Woman of Affairs

Douglas Fairbanks (1884-1939)
1915: The Lamb
16: Double Trouble
His Picture in the Papers
Habit of Happiness
The Good Bad Man
Reggie Mixes In
Flirting with Fate
The Half Breed
Mystery of the Leaping Fish
Manhattan Madness
The Americano
American Aristocracy
Intolerance
The Matrimoniacs
Flames of '49
17: In Again Out Again
17: The Man From Painted Post
Wild and Woolly
Down to Earth
Reaching for the Moon
18: Mr. Fix-It
A Modern Musketeer
Headin' South
Say, Young Fellow
Bound in Morocco
He Comes Up Smiling
Arizona
19: Knickerbocker Buckaroo
His Majesty the American
When the Clouds Roll By
The Mollycoddle
20: Mark of Zorro
21: The Nut
Three Musketeers
22: Robin Hood
23: Stephen Steps Out
24: Thief of Bagdad
25: Don Q - Son of Zorro
26: The Black Pirate
27: The Gaucho
28: Show People (a cameo)
29: The Iron Mask PT
30: Taming of the Shrew T
32: Reaching for the Moon T
33: Around the World in 80 Minutes (doc.)
Mr. Robinson Crusoe T
Marco Polo in planning stage
34: Private Life of Don Juan T

William Fairbanks
1922: Hell's Border
Peaceful Peters
A Western Adventure
Western Demon
23: The Devil's Door Yard
Sheriff of Sun Dog
Spawn of the Desert
Law Rustlers
Sun Dog Trail
24: Do It Now
Border Women
25: Tainted Money
Speed Mad
The Great Sensation
26: Through Thick and Thin

26: The Winning Wallop
Mile-A-Minute Man
Fight to the Finish
New Champion
The Handsome Brute
Vanishing Millions (serial)
27: Flying High
One Chance in a Million
Catch as Catch Can
Down Grade
When Danger Calls
Spoilers of the West
28: Under the Black Eagle
Blue Washington
The Vanishing West (serial)
29: Burning the Wind
The Devil's Chaplain
The Donovan Affair
Handcuffed

Virginia Brown Faire (1904-)

1920: The Old-Fashioned Boy
Runnin' Straight
21: Doubling For Romeo
Without Benefit of Clergy
Fightin' Mad
22: Monte Cristo
Omar the Tentmaker
23: Storm Swept
Vengeance of the Deep
Cricket on the Hearth
24: Peter Pan
25: The Lost World
Friendly Enemies
26: The Temptress
Air Phantom
Chip of the Flying U
Racing Romance
Wolf Hunter
Frenzied Flames
Wings of the Storm
Man in the Saddle
27: White Flannels
Tracked by the Police
Hazardous Valleys
Gun Gospel
28: Canyon of Adventure
The Body Punch
The Chorus Kid
Danger Patrol
Queen of the Chorus
Undressed
The House of Shame
A Race for Life
Wagon Show
29: Sin Town
Untamed Justice

Dot Farley (1894-)

1910: Romantic Redskins
12: A Wife Wanted
Peril of the Plains
Raiders on the Mexican
Border
24: The Enemy Sex
The Signal Tower
25: So Big
26: Money Talks
King of Kings
So Big
Grand Duchess and the
Waiter
27: Nobody's Widow
Overland Stage
McFadden's Flats
The Lost Limited
The Shamrock and the Rose
All Aboard
His First Flame
28: Lady Be Good
Head Man
Code of the Scarlet
Celebrity
Black Feather
Bird in the Hand
29: Marquis Preferred
Why Leave Home?
Should a Girl Marry? T
Divorce Made Easy T

James Farley (1882-)

1917: Brute Force
For the Family Name
The Bride's Silence
19: Sue of the South
20: Girl in the Rain
The Fourteenth Man
Challenge of the Law
21: One Man Trail
4 Horsemen of the
Apocalypse
28: Mad Hour
Perfect Crime
The Mating Call

Dustin Farnum (1874-1929)

1914: The Squaw Man
The Virginian
Soldiers of Fortune
Rose of the Rancho
A Son of Erin
15: A Gentleman from Indiana
The Girl of the Golden West
Cameo Kirby
Captain Courtesy
16: David Garrick
Intrigue
The Iron Strain
The Parson of Panamint
Ben Blair
17: The Scarlet Pimpernel
The Spy
Durand of the Bad Lands
18: North of '53
19: The Corsican Brothers (dual role)
Light of the Western Stars
A Man's Fight
A Man in the Open
20: Big Happiness
21: Primal Law
The Devil Within
22: Strange Idols
Oathbound
Yosemite Trail
While Justice Waits
Three Who Paid
Trail of the Axe
Iron to Gold
23: The Buster
The Grail
The Man Who Won
Bucking the Barrier
24: Kentucky Days
25: Durand of the Bad Lands
26: Flaming Frontier

Franklyn Farnum (1883-1961)

1917: The Clock
Anything Once
18: Fighting Grin
In Judgment Of
20: The Struggle
Vanishing Trails (serial)
21: Fighting Stranger
The Galloping Devil
22: So This is Arizona
22: Last Chance
The Raiders
White Masks
Shackles of Gold
Gun Shy
Gold Grabbers
Trail's End
Smilin' Jim
23: Crossroads
The Two Gun Sap
The Firebrand
24: Battling Brewster (serial)
A Two Fisted Tenderfoot
Desperate Adventure
Calibre .45
25: The Gambling Fool
Drugstore Cowboy
Border Intrigue

William Farnum (1872-1953)

1914: Sign of the Cross
The Spoilers
15: The Plunderer
The Nigger
16: A Man of Sorrow
17: A Tale of Two Cities
The Conqueror
When a Man Sees Red
American Methods
18: Les Miserables
The Rainbow Trail
Heart of a Lion
True Blue
Riders of the Purple Sage
19: Last of the Duanes
Lone Star Ranger
Wolves of the Night
Jungle Trail
For Freedom
The Man Hunter
20: If I were King
The Adventurer
Drag Harlan
Heart Strings
The Orphan
Wings of the Morning
The Joyous Troublemaker
21: The Scuttlers
His Greatest Sacrifice
Perjury
22: Moonshine Valley
Without Compromise
Shackles of Gold

22: A Stage Romance
23: Brass Commandments
The Gunfighter
24: The Man Who Fights Alone

Geraldine Farrar (1882-1967)
1915: Carmen
Temptation
16: Joan the Woman
The Jaguar's Claws
Maria Rosa
17: The Woman God Forgot
The Devil Stone
18: Turn of the Wheel
The Hell Cat
19: The Stronger Vow
Shadows
The World and its Women
Flame of the Desert
20: The Woman and the Puppet
21: Riddle Woman

Charles Farrell (1902-)
1923: Rosita
24: The Man Who Came Back
25: Clash of Wolves
The Freshman
26: Old Ironsides
Sandy
Sunnyside Up
27: 7th Heaven
The Rough Riders
28: Street Angel
Fazil SSE
River PT
City Girl
Lucky Star
The Red Dance SSE

William Faversham (1868-1940)
1919: The Silver King
20: The Man Who Lost Himself
21: The Sin That Was His
25: The Man Who Found Himself

George Fawcett (1860-1939)
1912: Little Miss Rebellion
Such a Little Queen
16: The Crisis
Intolerance
The Habit of Happiness
17: The Cinderella Man
Panthea
18: The Great Love
Hearts of the World
The Hun Within
19: Romance of Happy Valley
The Hope Chest
The Girl Who Stayed at Home
Scarlet Days
The Railroaders
I'll Get Him Yet
Out of Luck
Turning the Tables
20: The Greatest Question
The Branded Woman
Dangerous Business
Idols of Clay
Deadline at 11
Two Weeks
Good References
Little Miss Rebellion
21: Lessons in Love
Paying the Piper
Sentimental Tommy
Moon Gold
Hush Money
Little Italy
Way of a Maid
Silas Marner
Burn 'em up Barnes
22: The Old Homestead
Ebb Tide
Manslaughter
Forever
Polly of the Follies
Chivalrous Charley
John Smith
Beyond the Rainbow
23: Java Head
Mr. Billings Spends His Dime
Only 38
Salomy Jane
Drums of Fate
Woman with 4 Faces
24: West of the Water Tower
The Mad Whirl
Bedroom Window
Tess of the D'Ubervilles
25: A Lost Lady
Merry Widow
Thank You
The Sporting Venus

25: Joanna
Some Pun'kins
Flaming Frontier
26: Son of the Sheik
Flesh and the Devil
Two can Play
Men of Steel
Under Western Skies
Man of the Forest
There You Are
27: Private Life of Helen of Troy
The Wedding March
See you in Jail
Duty's Reward
Tillie the Toiler
Painting the Town
Captain Salvation
Rich Men's Shoes
Riding to Fame
Snowbound
Hard Boiled Haggerty
Valley of the Giants
Little Firebrand
28: The Tempest
Prowlers of the Sea
The Enemy
Love
Honeymoon (not released)
29: Tide of Empire
Love Song T
His Captive Woman PT
Little Wildcat PT
Fancy Baggage PT
Lady of the Pavements PT
Innocents of Paris T
Four Feathers SSE
The Gamblers T
Wonder of Women T
Hot for Paris T
30: The Great Divide T
Hearts in Exile T

Julia Faye (1894-1966)
1915: Don Quixote
16: His Auto Ruination
His Last Laugh
A Lover's Might (or The Fire Chief)
17: The Woman God Forgot
18: Mrs. Leffingwell's Boots
Old Wives For New
19: Don't Change your Husband
19: Male and Female
20: Six Best Cellars
Something to Think About
Feet of Clay
Life of the Party
21: Forbidden Fruit
The Affairs of Anatol
The Great Moment
Fool's Paradise
The Snob
22: Nice People
Saturday Night
Manslaughter
23: Adam's Rib
Ten Commandments
Nobody's Money
24: Triumph
25: Road to Yesterday
The Golden Bed
26: The Volga Boatman
Martha
Corporal Kate
Bachelor Brides
Meet the Prince
27: King of Kings
The Main Event
28: Chicago
Turkish Delight
Condemned Woman
29: The Godless Girl SSE
Dynamite T
30: Not So Dumb T

Louise Fazenda (1895-1962)
1913: Mike and Jake at the Beach
14: Mack Sennett Comedies
Hubby's Cure
15: The Great Vacuum Robbery
A Versatile Villain
Wilful Ambrose
That Little Band of Gold (or, For Better or Worse)
Ambrose's Fury
Ambrose's Lofty Perch
A Bear Affair
Crossed Love and Swords
A Hash House Fraud
A Game Old Knight
16: His Hereafter
The Judge
A Love Riot
Her Marble Heart

16: Pills of Peril
A La Cabaret
The Feathered Nest
Maid Mad (or The Fortune Teller)
Bombs
17: Maggie's First False Step
Her Fame and Shame
Her Torpedoed Love
The Betrayal of Maggie
His Precious Life
18: The Village Smithy
The Kitchen Lady
Her Screen Idol
Her First Mistake
The Village Chestnut
Treatin' 'em Rough
Back to the Kitchen
It's a Boy
Fireside Brewer
Astray from Steerage
Wedding Bells out of Tune
20: Down on the Farm
Married Life
21: The Foolish Age
Hearts and Flowers
22: Quincy Adams Sawyer
The Beauty Shop
23: The Spoilers
The Gold Diggers
Main Street
Beautiful and Damned
The Fog
24: Lighthouse by the Sea
Lady of the Harem
26: The Bat
Footloose Widows
The Old Soak
Millionaires
Ladies at Play
The Passionate Quest
27: Cradle Snatchers
The Red Mill
Finger Prints
Gay Old Bird
Babe Comes Home
Simple Sis
Texas Steer
28: Tillie's Punctured Romance
It's All Greek to Me
5 and 10¢ Annie
Pay as You Enter
28: Heart to Heart
Riley the Cop
Outcast
Domestic Troubles
29: Noah's Ark PT
Stark Mad T
Hot Stuff T
Hard to Get PT
House of Horror T
Desert Song T
Show of Shows T
On With the Show PT

Fritz Feld (1900-)

1920: The Golem
28: His Country
Blindfold
The Case of Mary Brown
29: Black Magic SSE

Rockliffe Fellowes (1885-1950)

1915: Regeneration
17: The Web of Desire
The Easiest Way
The Bondage of Fear
The House Cat
19: Cup of Fury
20: Yes or No
Point of View
In Search of a Sinner
Pagan Love
21: Bits of Life
Price of Possession
22: Island Wives
23: The Stranger's Banquet
Penrod and Sam
The Spoilers
24: Borrowed Husbands
The Border Legion
Garden of Weeds
26: Road to Glory
Counsel for the Defense
Rocking Moon
Silence
Honesty is the Best Policy
Syncopation Sue
27: The Understanding Heart
The Third Degree
The Satan Woman
The Crystal Cup
Taxi Dancer
29: The Charlatan

Leslie Fenton (1902-)
1925: Havoc
26: What Price Glory?
The Shamrock Handicap
Black Paradise
The Road to Glory
Sandy
Going Crooked
28: Showdown
Dragnet
The First Kiss
Erick the Great
An Old Flame
Gateway of the Moon
29: Dynamite T
Girls Gone Wild SSE
Paris Bound T
Office Scandal T
Dangerous Woman T
The Man I Love T
Broadway T
Woman Trap T
The Last Performance PT

Al Ferguson
1921: The Lost City (serial)
Who Wins
Whiskey Runners
Miracle of the Jungle
Sunset Jones
28: Terror Mountain
Hearts and Hoofs
Hoofbeats of Vengeance
Headin' for Danger
Wolves of the City
Tarzan the Mighty (serial)
Vagabond Cub
Grit Wins
29: Smilin' Terror, The
A Clean Sweep
Outlaw
The Wagon Master PT

Casson Ferguson (1891-)
1916: Merely Mary Ann
18: How Could You, Jean?
Alias Mary Brown
The Shuttle
The Only Road
19: Secret Service
Johnny Get Your Gun
Flame of the Desert
Jane Goes A-Wooing
20: The Prince Chap
Madame X
Mutiny of the Elsinore
21: At the End of the World
An Unknown Wife
22: Law and the Woman
Manslaughter
Drums of Fate
Over the Border
A Virginia Courtship
23: A Gentleman of Leisure
Grumpy
Her Reputation
26: For Alimony Only
28: 10th Avenue

Elsie Ferguson (1883-1961)
1917: Barbary Sheep
Rise of Jennie Cushing
18: Rose of the World
Song of Songs
The Lie
A Doll's House
The Danger Mark
Heart of the Wilds
Under the Greenwood Tree
19: His Parisian Wife
The Marriage Price
Eyes of the Soul
The Avalanche
A Society Exile
Witness for the Defense
The Counterfeit
20: His House in Order
Lady Rose's Daughter
21: Sacred and Profane Love
Footlights
Forever
Such a Little Queen
22: Outcast
25: Unknown Lover
30: Scarlet Pages T

Helen Ferguson (1901-)
1917: Gift o' Gab
19: The Gamblers
20: Going Some
Shod with Fire
Just Pals
Straight from the Shoulder
Burning Daylight
The Crooked Dagger
(serial) (never released)

20: Challenge of the Law
21: Desert Blossoms
Call of the North
Miss Lulu Bett
Freeze-Out
Romance Promoters
22: The Flaming Hour
Hungry Hearts
23: The Famous Mrs. Fair
Brass
Within the Law
The Unknown Purple
25: Wild West (serial)
26: Casey of the Coast Guard (serial)
27: Fire Fighters (serial)
The Cheaters
Jaws of Steel
28: In Old California

Lew Fields (1867-1941)
1915: Old Dutch
18: The Corner Grocer
25: Friendly Enemies

W. C. Fields (1879-1946)
1915: Pool Sharks
His Lordship's Dilemma
24: Janice Meredith
25: Sally of the Sawdust
26: So's Your Old Man
That Royle Girl
It's the Old Army Game
27: Two Flaming Youths
The Potters
Running Wild
28: Tillie's Punctured Romance
Fools for Luck
shorts
30: The Golf Specialist T
32: The Dentist T
33: The Fatal Glass of Beer T
The Pharmacist T
The Barber Shop T

Romaine Fielding (1877-)
1920: A Woman's Man
27: 10 Modern Commandments
28: Shepherd of the Hills

Clyde Fillmore (1876-1948)
1919: Millionaire Pirate
Fire Flingers
20: The Devil's Passkey
Nurse Marjorie
The Soul of Youth
The City Sparrow
21: The Outside Woman
Sham
22: Real Adventure
23: Sundown Trail
The Midnight Guest
24: The Silent Accuser
Alimony

Flora Finch (1869-1940)
1909: Jones and the Lady Book Agent
10: The New Stenographer
11: Subduing Mrs. Nag
Strategy of Anne
The Politician's Dream
Polishing Up
12: Leap Year Proposals
Mr. Bullington Ran the House
A Cure for Pokeritus
Diamond Cut Diamond
13: Women Go on the War Path
Autocrat of Flapjack Junction
John Tobin's Sweetheart
There's Music in the Hair
14: The New Secretary
Love's Old Dream
15: Bunny in Bunnyland
The Lady of Shalott
The Starring of Flora Finchurch
War Prides
16: A Night Out
Prudence, the Pirate
19: Oh, Boy!
Unwelcome Guest
His Better Half
Dawn
21: Lessons in Love
The Great Adventure
22: When Knighthood was in Flower
Social Errors
Orphans of the Storm

23: Luck
25: Men and Women
26: The Scarlet Letter
Oh, Baby!
Brown Derby
27: Cat and the Canary
Quality Street
Captain Salvation
Rose of the Golden West
28: The Wife's Relations
5 and 10¢ Annie
The Haunted House SSE
29: Come Across PT
30: Sweet Kitty Bellairs T
36: Show Boat T

Jimmy Finlayson (1887-1953)
1915-20: Mack Sennett Comedies
20: Down on the Farm
Married Life
Great Scott
Don't Weaken
21: A Small Town Idol
26: Man About Town
45 Minutes from Hollywood
27: Love 'em and Weep (2 reels)
With Love and Hisses (2 reels)
Do Detectives Think? "
Flying Elephants "
Sugar Daddies "
The Second 100 Years "
Call of the Cuckoo "
28: Lady be Good
Show Girl
29: Hard to Get T
2 Weeks Off PT
A Bachelor's Paradise
Liberty
Big Business
Men o' War S-PT
Hoosegow T
30: Another Fine Mess T
?? One Horse Town
Crossroads of New York
Ma and Pa

Margarita Fisher (1893-)
1913: In Slavery Days
Uncle Tom's Cabin
14: The Primeval Test
15: The Peacock Feather Fan
15: Miracle of Life
16: Susie's New Shoes
The Quest
The Dragon
Pearl of Paradise
17: The Devil's Assistant
18: The Girl Who Couldn't Grow Up
Miss Jackie of the Navy
Molly Go Get 'em
Jilted Jane
Ann's Finish
Primitive Woman
A Square Deal
Impossible Susan
19: Tiger Lily
Charge it to Me
Trixie from Broadway
Mantle of Charity
Molly of the Follies
Money Isn't Everything
Put up your Hands!
20: Dangerous Talent
The Hellion
The 30th Piece of Silver
The Week End
21: The Gamester
Payment Guaranteed
Their Mutual Child
The Butterfly Girl
27: Uncle Tom's Cabin

Cissy Fitzgerald (1894-1941)
1913: The Accomplished Mrs. Thompson
14: The Winsome Widow (or The Winksome Widow)
How Cissy Made Good
Cissy's Innocent Wink
Curing Cissy
Cissy and Bertie
Cissy's Funnymoon
26: The High Flyer
The Love Thief
Her Big Night
Flames
Redheads Preferred
27: McFadden's Flats
Women Love Diamonds
Matinee Ladies
Fire and Steel
The Diplomat
Beauty Shoppers

27: Women's Wares
Arizona Wildcat
Two Flaming Youths
28: Ladies of the Night Club
Laugh, Clown, Laugh
No Babies Wanted
29: Seven Footprints to Satan SSE
His Lucky Day PT
30: The Painted Angel T

Emily Fitzroy (d. 1954)
1920: Deadline at Eleven
New York Idea
21: Out of the Chorus
Frisky Mrs. Johnson
Straight is the Way
Peacock Alley
Way Down East
22: Wife Against Wife
Find the Woman
Fascination
No Trespassing
23: Driven
Fury
The Lady
24: His Hour
Her Night of Romance
25: Bobbed Hair
Secrets
Learning to Love
26: The Bat
Bardelys the Magnificent
High Steppers
Don Juan
Marriage License
Hardboiled
The Cheerful Fraud
27: Love
One Increasing Purpose
Orchids and Ermine
The Sea Tiger
Married Alive
Mockery
Once and Forever
Foreign Devils
Strangers of the Night
28: Gentlemen Prefer Blondes
Trail of '98
Love Me and the World is Mine
No Babies Wanted
29: Bridge of San Luis Rey PT
The Case of Lena Smith
Show Boat PT

Paul Fix (1901-)
1926: Hoodoo Ranch
28: First Kiss
Third Night
The Tavern
Chicago
29: Trial Marriage
Sex
Shavings
Burlesque

Bess Flowers (1900-)
1926: Hands across the Border
Lone Hand Saunders
Glenister of the Royal Mounted
Laddie
28: Ladies Man
We Faw Down

Maurice Flynn (1876-1959)
1920: The Silver Horde
Going Some
The Great Accident
Officer 666
21: Bucking the Line
Dangerous Curve Ahead
Just out of College
Roads to Destiny
22: Omar the Tentmaker
The Last Trail
The Woman Who Walked Alone
Smiles are Trumps
23: The Snow Bridge
Salomy Jane
Drums of Fate
24: Open all Night
The No Gun Man
25: Breed of the Border
Speed Wild
High and Handsome
26: Traffic Cop
Sir Lumberjack
Smilin' at Trouble
The College Boob
Glenister of the Mounted
27: The Golden Stallion (serial)

Courtenay Foote

1915: Cross Currents
16: An International Marriage
Love's Law
19: His Parisian Wife
The Two Brides
20: The Star Rover
21: The Bronze Bell
The Passion Flower

Ralph Forbes (1896-1951)

1926: Beau Geste
27: Mr. Wu
The Enemy
28: The Actress
Comin' Through the Rye
Dog of War
Masks of the Devil
Trail of '98
The Whip
Restless Youth
Under the Black Eagle
The Latest From Paris
Submarine
29: The High Road

Francis Ford (1882-1953)

1913: Favorite Son
14: Lucille Love (serial)
The Phantom Violin
Be Neutral
The Mysterious Rose
15: The Broken Coil (serial)
Doorway of Destruction
3 Bad Men and a Girl
The Hidden City
16: The Bandit's Wager
Brennon o' the Moore
Lady Raffles Returns
Peg o' the Ring (serial) (dual)
Four from Nowhere
The Lumber Yard Gang
17: The Purple Mask (serial)
The Phantom Ship
The Isle of Intrigue
Chicken-Hearted Jim
The Puzzle Woman
Unmasked
18: The Silent Mystery (serial)
Thunderbolt Jack
Who was the Other Man?
John Ermine of Yellowstone
19: Mystery of 13 (serial)
20: The Caring
The Crimson Shoals
21: The Man from Nowhere
I am the Woman
Flower of the Range
The Heart of Lincoln
Action
The Great Reward (serial)
22: They're Off!
Another Man's Boots
The Trail's End
The Storm Girl
Gold Grabbers
The Lady from Longacre
The Village Blacksmith
23: 3 Jumps Ahead
Haunted Valley (serial)
The Fighting Skipper (serial) (dir.)
The Angel Citizens
24: Hearts of Oak
25: Perils of the Wild (dir.)
The Fighting Heart
26: Case of the Heart (dir.)
The Winking Idol (dir.)
27: The Wolf's Trail
Upstream
Men of Daring
The Heart of Maryland
The Devil's Saddle
Cruise of the Hellion
One Glorious Scrap
28: Wreck of the Hesperus
Four Footed Ranger
The Branded Sombrero
Sisters of Eve
The Chinatown Mystery (serial)
29: The Drake Case
Black Watch
The Lariat Kid

Harrison Ford (1892-1959)

1916: Mysterious Mrs. Musselwhite
17: Molly Entangled
Tides of Barnegat
18: Such a Little Pirate
The Gray Chiffon Veil
Goodnight Paul
Mrs. Leffingwell's Boots
Sauce for the Goose

18: A Lady's Name
Unclaimed Goods
19: A Pair of Stockings
Girls
The Lottery Man
The Third Kiss
Hawthorne of the U. S. A.
Who Cares?
Romance and Arabella
Experimental Marriage
The Veiled Adventure
Happiness A La Mode
20: A Lady in Love
Food for Scandal
Miss Hobbs
Oh Lady, Lady!
21: Wonderful Things
Wedding Bells
A Heart to Let
The Passion Flower
22: Smilin' Through
The Primitive Lover
Find the Woman
The Old Homestead
Shadows
When Love Comes
Her Gilded Cage
23: Vanity Fair
Little Old New York
24: Janice Meredith
25: Proud Flesh
Lovers in Quarantine
26: The Nervous Wreck
Up in Mabel's Room
Sandy
27: Rejuvenation of Aunt Mary
No Control
Rush Hour
Girl in the Pullman
Rubber Tires
Night Bride
28: Let 'er Go Gallagher
A Woman Against the World
Gold Widows
Just Married
Her Husband's Women
Three Week Ends
Blonde for a Night
Advice to Husbands
32: Love in High Gear T

Eugenie Forde
1915: The Diamond from the Sky (serial)
18: Fair Enough
19: Sis Hopkins
Strictly Confidential
20: The Road to Divorce
The Virgin of Stamboul
?? 7 Yrs. with Christie Comedies
Send Him Away with a Smile

Tom Forman (1893-1938)
1915: A Puppet Crown
Young Romance
The Governor's Lady
The Wild Goose Chase
16: Sweet Kitty Bellairs
The Ragamuffin
The Yellow Pawn
The $1000 Husband
Public Opinion
The Unprotected
17: A Kiss for Susie
Hashimura To Go
Trouble Buster
The Evil Eye
Those Without Sin
Tides of Barnegat
The American Consul
Her Strange Wedding
The Jaguar's Claws
Forbidden Paths
18: The Girl Who Came Back
19: For Better, for Worse
Heart of Youth
Louisiana
Told in the Hills
20: The Tree of Knowledge
The Round-Up
The Sea Wolf
The Ladder of Lies
Sins of Rosanne
21: Cappy Ricks
City of Silent Men
The Easy Road
22: Shadows (dir.)
White Shoulders
If You Believe It, It's So
23: Are You a Failure?
Money Money Money

28: Valley Beyond the Law
Yellow Contraband
Headin' for Danger
29: His Lucky Day
Saps and Saddles
Jackson Comes Home

Allan Forrest (1889-)
1915: The Captivating Mary Carstairs
18: Rosemary Climbs the Heights
19: A Bachelor's Wife
23: Long Live the King
The Man Between
Wandering Daughters
A Crinoline Romance
Noise in Newboro
24: Captain Blood
Dorothy Vernon of Haddon Hall
26: Two Can Play
The Prince of Pilsen
Phantom Bullet
Partners Again
5th Avenue
Carnival Girl
Summer Bachelors
27: Ankles Preferred
The Lovelorn
28: Wild West Show
Desert Bride
Sally of the Scandals
Riding for Fame
Black Feather
29: Winged Horseman

Ann Forrest (1897-)
1917: The Birth of Patriotism
18: The Midnight Man
The Tar Heel Warrior
19: The Grim Game
20: The Prince Chap
A Splendid Hazard
Dangerous Days
The Great Accident
Behold my Wife
21: The Faith Healer

Helen Foster (1907-)
1927: Naughty Nanette
28: 13 Washington Square
Won in the Clouds
Sweet Sixteen
The Mating Call
Hellship Bronson
Road to Ruin
29: Should a Girl Marry? PT
Harvest of Hate
Sky Skidder
Linda SSE
Circumstantial Evidence
Gentlemen of the Press T
Hoofbeats of Vengeance
Gold Diggers of Broadway T
30: So Long Letty T

Earle Foxe (1888-)
1914: Home Sweet Home
The Floor Above
16: Trail of the Lonesome Pine
Ashes of Embers
Public Opinion
17: The Honeymoon
The Love Mask
The Dream Girl
Alien Souls
The Fatal Ring (serial)
Panthea
Outwitted
18: The Studio Girl
From Two to Six
Peck's Bad Girl
21: The Black Panther's Cub
22: The Prodigal Judge
The Man She Brought Back
23: Vanity Fair
A Lady of Quality
24: The Last Man on Earth
The Ghost Talks
News Parade
River Pirate
The Case of Mary Brown
26: A Trip to Chinatown
The Man Upstairs
27: Upstream
Slaves of Beauty
Ladies must Dress
28: 4 Sons
Blindfold
Sailors' Wives
The Hangman's Horse
None but the Brave
29: Through Different Eyes PT

29: New Year's Eve SSE
Black Magic SSE
Fugitives SSE
?? The Escape

Alec B. Francis (1857-1934)
1911: Vanity Fair
12: Robin Hood
13: The Spectre Bridegroom
The Crimson Cross
14: Man of the Hour
15: Lola
16: The Gilded Cage
The Ballet Girl
Her Code of Honor
17: The Cinderella Man
A Hungry Heart
18: The Face in the Dark
Glorious Adventure
The Venus Model
The Marionettes
19: Day Dreams
The Crimson Gardenia
Probation Wife
City of Comrades
Heartease
World and Its Woman
Lord and Lady Algy
Flame of the Desert
20: Earthbound
21: Under the Lash
Godless Men
The Man Who Had Everything
Voice in the Dark
What's a Wife Worth
Courage
Her Great Moment
22: North of the Rio Grande
The Man Who Saw Tomorrow
A Virginia Courtship
Smilin' Through
Beyond the Rocks
23: The Gold Diggers
3 Wise Fools
24: The Mad Whirl
Beau Brummel
25: Charley's Aunt
The Coast of Folly
Thank You
26: The Return of Peter Grimm
26: The Terror
Vanishing Millions (serial)
Three Bad Men
Pals First
The Yankee Senor
Transcontinental Limited
Tramp Tramp Tramp
27: The Music Master
Camille
The Tender Hour
Sally of our Alley
28: Lion and the Mouse
Companionate Marriage
Life's Mockery
The Shepherd of the Hills
The Little Snob
Broadway Daddies
29: Evangeline
Fast Life T
Bishop Murder Case T
Evidence T
Mississippi Gambler T
The Sacred Flame T
30: Feet First T
32: Mata Hari T
33: His Private Secretary T
Oliver Twist T
34: The Cat's Paw T
Mystery of Mr. X T

Betty Francisco
1920: The Man from Make-Believe
A Broadway Cowboy
Furnace
Midsummer Madness
23: Ashes of Vengeance
26: Don Juan's 3 Nights
Man Bait
Exclusive Right
27: Long Pants
Uneasy Payments
Too Many Crooks
The Gingham Girl
Gay Retreat
Boy of the Streets
28: You Can't Beat the Law
Broadway Daddies
Queen of the Chorus
29: Spirit of Youth T

Robert Frazer (d. 1944)
1912: Robin Hood

16: The Ballet Girl
Feast of Life
Her Code of Honor
Bolshevism of Trial
Without Limit
22: Yellow Men and Gold
Fascination
As a Man Lives
23: Jazzmania
When the Desert Calls
24: Women Who Give
Men
25: Splendid Road
Keeper of the Bees
Why Women Love
The Charmer
26: Desert Gold
Dame Chance
Secret Riders
Other Woman's Story
27: Isle of Retribution
Speeding Venus
One Hour to Love
City
Sin Cargo
Back to God's Country
Silent Hero
Lightning
Not of the Past
28: Burning up Broadway
Scarlet Dove
Out of the Ruins
Black Butterflies
City of Purple Dreams
Little Snob SSE
29: Sioux Blood
The Woman I Love
Careers PT
The Drake Case
Frozen Justice PT

Blanche Frederici (d. 1933)
1928: Fleet Wings
Stolen Love

Pauline Frederick (1881-1938)
1915: The Eternal City
Sold
Zaza
16: Lydia Gilmore
The Spider
Audrey
The Moment Before
16: The World's Great Snare
Woman in the Case
Ashes of Embers
Nanette of the Wilds
17: Slave Market
Sleeping Fires
Love that Lives
Double Crossed
Hungry Heart
On Trial
18: Mrs. Dane's Defense
Madame Jealousy
La Tosca
Resurrection
Her Final Reckoning
Fedora
A Daughter of the Old South
19: Paid in Full
Woman on the Index
One Week of Life
Fear Women
Peace of Roaring River
Bonds of Love
Out of the Shadow
Sacred Flame
20: Loves of Letty
Paliser Case
Woman in Room 13
Madame X
A Slave of Vanity
21: Roads of Destiny
Mistress of Shenstone
Salvage
Sting of the Lash
Lure of Jade
22: Two Kinds of Women
Glory of Clementina
Woman Breed
Evidence
23: Bella Donna
24: Let No Man Put Asunder
Three Women
Smouldering Fires
Married Flirts
26: Her Honor the Governor
Devil's Island
Joselyn's Wife
27: The Nest
Mumsie
28: On Trial T
29: Evidence T
31: This Modern Age T

32:	Wayward	T
	Phantom of Crestwood	T
33:	Self Defense (reissued as My Mother)	T
34:	Social Register	T
36:	Ramona	T
	My Mother	T
37:	Thank You, Mr. Moto	T

Charles K. French

1909:	A True Indian's Heart
15:	The Coward
16:	A Corner in Colleen's
	The Honorable Clergy
	The Weaker Sex
	The Clodhopper
17:	The Lifted Veil
	Son of His Father
18:	Hired Man
	Playing the Game
	His Own Home Town
	Hermit Dr. of Garja
	Tiger Man
	That Hero Stuff
19:	Law of the North
	The Sheriff's Son
22:	The Unfoldment
	Smudge
23:	A Woman of Paris
	World's Applause
	Abysmal Brute
	Blanky
	Life of Abraham Lincoln
	Grumpy
24:	The Alaskan
25:	Girl of Gold
	Runaway Express
	Slow Down
26:	Under Western Skies
	Hands Up!
	Oh, What a Night!
	War Paint
	Winning Wallop
27:	Lost Limited
	Meddlin' Stranger
	Fast and Furious
	Good as Gold
	Ride 'em High
	Man, Woman and Sin
	One Chance in a Million
	Down Grade
	Cruise of the Hellion
	Adventurous Soul
28:	Cowboy Cavalier
	Big Hop
	Flying Buckaroo
	Night Watch
	Perfect Crime
29:	Divine Lady
	King of the Rodeo
	Last Warning PT

George B. French (1883-)

1918:	Tarzan of the Apes	
	Back to Nature	
	In and Out	
	Five Hundred or Bust	
	Sally's Blighted Career	
	His Pajama Girl	
	The Doctor and the Woman	
	Back to the Woods	
22:	Unfoldment	
	Reckless Sex	
	Winter Has Came	
	Women Wake Up	
28:	Sawdust Paradise	
	Won in the Clouds	
	Black Pearl	
30:	Street of Chance	T

Trixie Friganza

1923:	Mind Over Motor
28:	Thanks for the Buggy Ride
??	Motor Maniac

Dale Fuller (1897-)

1916:	An Oily Scoundrel
	Bath Tub Perils
	The Surf Girl
	The Scoundrel's Tale
17:	Dodging His Doom
21:	Foolish Wives
22:	Merry-Go-Round
23:	Six Days
	Greed
	Reno
	Souls for Sale
	One Wonderful Night
	Manslaughter
	Borderland
24:	Three Weeks
25:	Merry Widow
26:	Ben Hur
	Speeding Venus
	Canadian
	Her Second Chance

26: Midnight Lover
Shadow of the Law
27: Wedding March
Beauty Shoppers
28: Cossacks
29: Glad Rag Doll T
Sacred Flame T
The Man T
House of Terror
30: Office Wife T
32: Emma T
Law Against Law T
33: Cavalcade T
34: Twentieth Century T
We Live Again T

Mary Fuller (1893-)
1910: Elektra
11: Aida
12: Martin Chuzzlewit
Harbinger of Peace
The Convict's Parole
What Happened to Mary (serial)
13: Mercy Merrick
It's Never Too Late to Mend
With the Eyes of the Blind
Mary Stuart
Who Will Marry Mary? (serial)
14: Dolly of the Dailies (serial)
17: The Long Trail

Olive Fuller (1896-)
1916: Love's Lariat
The Devil's Own
A Woman's Eyes
22: Tess of the Storm Country
Committee on Credentials

Ray Gallagher (1889-1953)
1919: His Divorced Wife
20: The Phantom Melody
Go Get 'em
Crooked Trails
Secret Eyes
Dust
21: Guardians of the North
23: Around the Town
28: Trail of '98
Abie's Irish Rose SSE
28: Half a Bride
Nothing to Wear
Excess Baggage
29: Tide of Empire
The Argyle Case T

Richard "Skeets" Gallagher (1891-1955)
1927: The Potters
New York
For the Love of Mike
28: Three Ring Marriage
Alex the Great
Stocks and Blondes
The Racket
29: Dance of Life T

Tom Gallery
1920: Bright Skies
The Heart of Twenty
The Chorus Girl's Romance
Dinty
21: Bob Hampton of Placer
Glad Rags
The Son of Wallingford
A Parisian Scandal
22: Wall Flower
Grand Larceny
A Daughter of Luxury
27: Dog of the Regiment
Home Struck
One Round Hogan

Greta Garbo (1906-)
1921: Commercial films in Stockholm
22: Peter the Tramp
23: Luffar-Petter
24: Gosta Berling's Saga
25: Street of Sorrow
Die Freudlose Gasse
26: The Torrent
The Temptress
27: Flesh and the Devil
Love
28: The Divine Woman
Mysterious Lady
29: Wild Orchids
The Kiss
Single Standard
Woman of Affairs
War in the Dark
Joyless Street

Mary Garden (1875-1967)
1918: Thais
The Splendid Sinner

Pauline Garon (1901-1965)
1917: Good for Nothing
22: Reported Missing
The Power Within
23: Adam's Rib
The Man from Glengarry
You Can't Fool Your Wife
Children of the Dust
25: Compromise
Passionate Youth
Satan in Sables
26: Flaming Waters
Christine of the Big Tops
27: The Princess of Broadway
Eager Lips
Ladies at Ease
The College Hero
Temptations of a Shop Girl
Naughty
28: Sonny
Life's Mockery
The Devil's Cage
Dugan of the Dugout
Reilly of the Rainbow Division
The Girl He Didn't Buy
Heart of Broadway
The Candy Kid
29: The Gamblers T
Becky Sharp T
Must We Marry?
Show of Shows T
In the Headlines T

Anita Garvin (1907-)
1918: Old Wives for New
The Sport Girl
25: Play Girl
27: Bertha, the Sewing Machine Girl
29: Dynamite T
The Charlatan PT

Gene Gauntier (1891-)
1912: From the Manger to the Cross
A Prisoner of the Harem
Winning a Widow
13: Daughter of the Confederacy
17: Heart's Desire
??: The Girl Spy Series
Colleen Bawn
Tragedy of the Desert
Down through the Ages
In the Form of a Hypnotist

Janet Gaynor (1906-)
1926: The Return of Peter Grimm
The Johnstown Flood
The Blue Eagle
Pigs
27: Seventh Heaven
The Midnight Kiss
Sunrise
Two Girls Wanted
28: Street Angel
29: Christina T
The Four Devils T
Lucky Star
Sunny Side Up T

Clarence Geldert (1867-1936)
1915: Joan the Woman
16: Intolerance
18: The Fall of a Nation
20: Crooked Streets
Always Audacious
21: All Souls' Eve
The Affairs of Anatol
Sweetie Peach
The Great Moment
The Hell Diggers
23: Adam's Rib
Wasted Lives
Woman of Paris
26: Flaming Forest
27: Dress Parade
28: Humming Wives
29: The Ghost Talks
Unholy Night T
Thirteenth Chair T
Sioux Blood
Overland Telegraph

Gladys George (1904-1954)
1919: Red Hot Dollars
Woman in the Suitcase
20: Below the Surface
Homespun Folks
21: The Easy Road

21: Chickens
The House that Jazz Built

Maud George (1890-)
1916: Idle Wives
17: Even as You and I
18: Blue Blazes Rawden
The Marriage Ring
19: Shadows of Suspicion
A Rogue's Romance
The Midnight Stage
The Lamb and the Lion
The Devil's Pass Keys
20: Madame X
Heart Strings
21: Roads to Destiny
Foolish Wives
22: Merry-Go-Round
26: The Love Toy
27: The Wedding March
Altars of Desire
28: Honeymoon (not released)
After the Storm
The Woman from Moscow
Isle of Lost Men
Garden of Eden
29: The Veiled Woman

Carmelita Geraghty (1901-1966)
1922: To Have and to Hold
23: The Eternal Three
Daughter of Mother McGuire
Rosita
Bag and Baggage
25: My Lady of Whims
Pleasure Garden
26: The Great Gatsby
Canyon of Light
The Flying Mail
27: My Best Girl
The Last Trail
The Slaver
Venus of Venice
What Every Girl Should Know
28: The Good-Bye Kiss
Button My Back
South of Panama
29: Object--Alimony
Paris Bound
This Thing Called Love T
Mississippi Gambler T
30: Men Without Law T
Fightin' Through T
31: Fifty Million Frenchmen T
Texas Ranger T
Devil Plays T
32: Prestige T
Forgotten Women T
Escapade T
Malay Nights T
33: Flaming Signal T
35: Manhattan Butterfly T

Neva Gerber
1917: Voice on the Wire (serial)
The Awakening
The Great Secret
The Prodigal Widow
Like Wildfire
The Spindle of Life
The Mystery Ship (serial)
18: Caught in the Act
The Phantom Ship
Hell Bent
Three Mounted Men
19: Roped
The Trail of the Octopus
A Fight for Love
20: The Screaming Shadow (serial)
25: The Mystery Box (serial)
The Power of God (serial)
26: Officer 444 (serial)

Charles Gerrard (1887-)
1917: Little Miss Optimist
Double Standard
18: Hun Within
19: New Moon
The Isle of Conquest
Pettigrew's Girl
Something to Do
Counterfeit
Teeth of the Tiger
20: Blackbirds
World and His Wife
Whispers
Mary Ellen Comes to Town
21: The Passionate Pilgrim
You Can't Kill Love
Out of the Chorus
Conceit
Gilded Lily

22: When Knighthood was in Flower
Anna Ascends
Pawned
French Heels
Sure Fire Flint
Heroes and Husbands
23: Glimpses of the Moon
Lights of New York
The Darling of the Rich
The Dangerous Maid
24: Circe
25: California Straight Ahead
26: The Better 'ole
For Wives Only
27: Play Safe
The Heart Thief
Framed
Painting the Town
Home Made
28: Port of Missing Girls
Ladies of the Night Club
Romance of a Rogue
Caught in the Fog
29: Circumstantial Evidence
The Lone Wolf's Daughter PT
Light Fingers PT

Douglas Gerrard (1888-)
1914: The Merchant of Venice
Commanding Officer
15: The Dumb Girl of Portici
19: Lord and Lady Algy
22: A Tailor Made Man
Omar the Tentmaker
26: Footloose Widows
27: Wolf's Clothing
Dearie
College Widow
Ginsberg the Great
28: Ladies of the Night Club
5 and 10¢ Annie SSE
29: Glad Rag Doll
The Argyle Case
Madonna of Avenue A PT
30: General Crack T

Helen Gibson (1893-)
1915: Hazards of Helen (serial)
17: Fighting Mad
Peril of the Rails-2 reels
2 reels releases:
When Seconds Count
Border Watch Dogs
The Ghost of Canyon Diablo
The Robber of the Golden Star
Trail of the Rails
Tapped Wires
Girl of Gopher City
19: The Rustlers
The Gun Law
21: A Girl's Decision
No Man's Woman
The Wolverine
22: Thoroughbred
Why Worry
9 Points of the Law
28: The Vanishing West (serial)
The Dynamite Special
Man of God
The Run of the Yellow Mail
The Frustrated Holdup

Hoot Gibson (1892-1962)
1912: His Only Son
16: Hazards of Helen (serial)
A Knight in the Range
The Cactus Kid
A Daughter of Daring (serial)
17: Straight Shooting
Cheyenne's Pal
The Soul Herder
A Marked Man
The Voice on the Wire
19: The Double Holdup
Fighting Brothers
By Indian Post
The Rustlers
Gun Law
The Gun Packer
The Crow
Trail of the Holdup
The Jay Bird
20: The Sheriff's Oath
Roaring Dan
The Smilin' Kid
Saddle King
21: Action
Red Courage
22: Sure Fire
The Fire Eater
The Bearcat

22: Step on It
Trimmed
The Galloping Kid
Lone Hand
Ridin' Wild
23: Kindled Courage
The Gentlemen from America
Single Handed
Dead Game
Blinky
Double Dealing
Out of Luck
The Ramblin' Kid
Shootin' for Love
24: Hit and Run
Ride for your Life
The Sawdust Trail
Hook and Ladder
Broadway or Bust
40 Horses Hawkins
The Kid from Powder River
Fighting Fury
25: Taming the West
Spook Ranch
Saddle Hawk
The Hurricane Kid
Let 'er Buck!
Calgary Stampede
Arizona Sweepstakes
The Locked Door
26: The Man in the Saddle
Doubling for Trouble
The Flaming Frontier
Phantom Bullet
Chip of the Flying U
The Buckaroo Kid
The Texas Streak
27: King of the Rodeo
The Silent Rider
The Denver Dude
Hey, Hey, Cowboy!
The Prairie King
A Hero on Horseback
Painted Ponies
Galloping Fury
28: Silks and Saddles
Riding for Fame
The Rawhide Kid
Wild West Show
Clearing the Trail
Man with the Punch
Danger Rider
28: Flying Cowboy
Flying Fists
Man in the Saddle
On Sunset Range
Smiling Guns
29: Burning the Wind
The Lariat Kid
The Winged Horseman
Points West
The Long, Long Trail
Courtin' Wildcats
?? Should Husbands Mind Babies?
Pair of Twins
Shameless Salvation
Harmony Ranch

Billy Gilbert (1894-)
1928: A Simple Sap
Horse Play
Betwixt and Between
Movie Mania
Flaming Youth
29: Woman from Hell
Noisy Neighbors PT

Eugenia Gilbert
1927: Obey the Law
By Whose Hand?
6 years' experience

John Gilbert (1895-1936)
1915: The Mother Instinct
16: Hell's Hinges
17: Golden Rule Kate
The Millionaire Vagrant
The Devil Dodger
Apostle of Vengeance
Princess of the Dark
19: Heart of the Hills
The Busher
White Heather
20: Servant in the House
The Great Redeemer
The White Circle
Deep Waters
21: The Bait (dir.)
Love's Penalty (dir.)
Ladies Must Live
22: Gleam o' Dawn
The Yellow Stain
Honor First
Calvert's Valley

22: The Love Gambler
Arabian Love
Count of Monte Cristo
23: A California Romance
While Paris Sleeps
The Madness of Youth
Cameo Kirby
St. Elmo
The Exiles
24: The Wolf Man
Just Off Broadway
A Man's Mate
The Lone Chance
Wife of the Centaur
Romance Ranch
He Who Gets Slapped
His Hour
The Snob
25: Merry Widow
The Big Parade
26: La Boheme
Bardelys the Magnificent
27: Flesh and the Devil
Twelve Miles Out
The Show
28: Love
Man, Woman and Sin
The Cossacks
Masks of the Devil
Four Walls
Show People (a cameo)
29: Woman of Affairs
Desert Nights SSE
His Glorious Night T
Hollywood Revue of 1929 T
30: Redemption T
Way for a Sailor T
31: A Gentleman's Fate T
Phantom of Paris T
West of Broadway T
33: Downstairs T
Fast Workers T
Queen Christina T
34: The Captain Hates the Sea T
?? Glory of Love

William Gillespie (1894-)
1915: The Immigrant
22: Grandma's Boy
26: Exit Smiling
?? Now or Never
?? High and Dizzy
Easy Street
Horse Shy

William Gillette (1853-)
1916: Sherlock Holmes
19: Secret Service

Claude Gillingwater (1879-1939)
1921: Little Lord Fauntleroy
22: My Boy
Remembrance
The Dust Flower
Fools First
23: The Christian
The Stranger's Banquet
A Crinoline Romance
Alice Adams
A Chapter in her Life
Three Wise Fools
Dulcy
Tiger Rose
24: Daddies
How to Educate a Wife
A Madonna of the Streets
25: Idle Tongues
A Thief in Paradise
Cheaper to Marry
Winds of Chance
Wages of Wives
26: We Moderns
That's My Baby
Into Her Kingdom
27: For Wives Only
Barbed Wire
Fast and Furious
Naughty But Nice
The Gorilla
Ham and Eggs at the Front
28: Husbands for Rent
Little Shepherd of Kingdom Come
Women They Talk About T
Oh Kay! T
29: Stolen Kisses T
Stark Mad T
Glad Rag Doll T
Smiling Irish Eyes T
A Dangerous Woman T
30: The Great Divide T
So Long Letty T

Joseph Girard (1871-1949)
1916: 20,000 Leagues Under the Sea
17: Voice on the Air (serial)
19: Bare Fists
Two Souled Women
Kaiser--The Beast of Berlin
Loot
Paid in Advance
Midnight Man
Sign of the Rat
20: The Figurehead
The Branded Mystery
The Branded H (serial)
The Fatal Sign (serial)
The Screaming Shadow (serial)
21: Dangerous Paths
Mysteria
Sheriff of Hope Eternal
Blue Fox (serial)
The Crimson Lash (serial)
The Eagle's Talons (serial)
22: Step on It!
Nan of the North (serial)
Perils of the Yukon (serial)
23: One Wonderful Night
The Devil's Dooryard
24: Wolves of the North (serial)
In Hollywood with Potash and Perlmutter
27: Lady Bird
Whispering Sage
When Seconds Count
Silent Hero
Fireman, Save My Child!
28: Bullet Mark
Hello Cheyenne
Partners in Crime
King of the Rodeo
The Fleet's In
The Terror
Jazz Mad
29: Broken Barriers
Redskin SSE
The Leatherneck PT
Back from Shanghai
One Woman Idea SSE
From Headquarters PT
Girl from Havana T
29: Countin' Wildcats T

Dorothy Gish (1898-1968)
1912: An Unseen Enemy
Musketeers of Pig Alley
Gold and Glitter
The Informer
The New York Hat
My Hero
A Cry for Help
13: Oil and Water
The Wife
Perfidy of Mary
The Lady and the Mouse
Just Gold
Almost a Wild Man
Her Mother's Oath
Pa Says
The Vengeance of Galora
Those Little Flowers
The Widow's Kids
The Adopted Brother
The Lady in Black
The House of Discord
14: Her Old Teacher
Judith of Bethulia
Her Father's Silent Partner
The Mysterious Shot
The Floor Above
The Old Man
Rebellion of Kitty Belle
Liberty Belles
The Mountain Rat
Silent Sandy
The Newer Woman
Their First Acquaintance
Arms and the Gringo
The Suffragette's Battle
In Nutsyville
The City Beautiful
The Painted Lady
Home Sweet Home
The Tavern of Tragedy
Her Mother's Necklace
A Lesson in Mechanics
Granny
A Fair Rebel
Down the Road to Creditville
Sands of Fate
The Warning
Back to the Kitchen

14: The Availing Prayer
The Saving Grace
The Sisters
The Better Way
15: An Old-Fashioned Girl
The Nun
How Hazel Got Even
The Lost Lord Lowell
Minerva's Mission
Her Grandparents
Out of Bondage
Her Mother's Daughter
The Mountain Girl
The Little Catamount
Victorine
Bred in the Bone
Old Heidelberg
Jordan is a Hard Road
16: Betty of Graystone
Little Meena's Romance
Susan Rocks the Boat
Little School Ma'am
Gretchen the Greenhorn
The Best Bet
Katie Bauer
Atta-Boy's Last Race
That Colby Girl
Children of the Feud
17: The Little Yank
Stage Struck
Her Official Fathers
18: Hearts of the World
The Hun Within
Battling Jane
19: The Hope Chest
Boots
Peppy Polly
I'll Get Him
Nugget Nell
Out of Luck
Turning the Tables
20: Mary Ellen Comes to Town
Remodeling Her Husband
Little Miss Rebellion
Flying Pat
21: The Ghost in the Garret
Old Joe
22: Orphans of the Storm
The Country Flapper
23: Fury
Bright Shawl
24: Ramola
25: Night Life in New York
The Beautiful City
Clothes Make the Pirate
26: Nell Gwyn
27: London
Tip Toes
Madame Pompadour
30: Wolves T

Lillian Gish (1896-)

1912: The Test
An Unseen Enemy
Musketeers of Pig Alley
The New York Hat
In the Aisles of the Wild
Gold and Glitter
A Cry for Help
The Burglar's Dilemma
Two Daughters of Eve
My Baby
The One She Loved
13: Oil and Water
A Misunderstood Boy
An Indian's Loyalty
The Lady and the Mouse
The House of Darkness
Just Gold
The Mothering Heart
During the Round Up
So Runs the Way
The Left-Handed Man
A Timely Interception
Men and Muslin
The Madonna and Her Child
A Woman in Ultimate
A Modest Hero
The Battle of Elderbush Gulch
The Unwelcome Guest
The Conscience of Hassan Bey
14: Man's Enemy
Judith of Bethulia
The Sisters
Rebellion of Kitty Belle
The Hunchback
Angel of Contention
Home Sweet Home
The Battle of the Sexes
The Mountain Rat
The Green-Eyed Devil
Silent Sandy
Men and Women

14: Quicksands
The Wife
The Escape
The Tear that Burned
The Folly of Anne
Lord Chumley
15: The Birth of a Nation
Enoch Arden
The Lily and the Rose
Captain Macklin
The Lost House
16: Diane of the Follies
Intolerance
Sold for Marriage
Daphne and the Pirate
An Innocent Magdalene
17: Souls Triumphant
Life's Pathways
Flirting with Faith (guest)
The Children Pay
The House Built Upon Sand
18: Liberty Bond short
The Great Love
Hearts of the World
The Greatest Thing in Life
19: Remodeling Her Husband (dir.)
Romance of Happy Valley
Broken Blossoms
True Heart Susie
The Greatest Question
20: Way Down East
World Shadows (1/2 finished)
The Love Flower
22: Orphans of the Storm
23: The White Sister
24: Romola
26: The Scarlet Letter
27: Annie Laurie
La Boheme
28: The Enemy
The Wind
30: One Romantic Night T
33: His Double Life T

Gaston Glass (1899-1965)
1916: Behind Closed Doors
20: Humoresque
World and His Wife
The Foreigner
21: Her Winning Ways
There are no Villains
22: I am the Law
Cameron of the Royal Mounted
Rich Men's Wives
Little Miss Smiles
23: The Spider and the Rose
The Hero
Mothers-in-Law
Daughters of the Rich
24: After the Ball
26: Sweet Daddies
Subway Sadie
Romance of a Million Dollars
Exclusive Rights
Tentacles of the North
27: Her Sacrifice
The Show Girl
Sinews of Steel
The Gorilla
28: Easy Payments
A Woman's Justice
Wife's Relations
Name the Woman
My Home Town
Obey Your Husband
Red Mark
29: The Faker
Broken Barriers
Untamed Justice
Geraldine PT
Behind Closed Doors
Tiger Rose T

Louise Glaum (1894-)
1913: The Transgressor
The Quakeress
The Boomerang
14: Ike Gets a Goat
15: The Lure of Woman
The Iron Strain
Between Men
The Cup of Life
The Renegade
The Conversion of Frosty Blake
City of the Dead
16: Home
Hell's Hinges
Honor Thy Name
The Weaker Sex
The Aryan
The Wolf Woman

17: The Idolators
The Sweetheart of the Doomed
Love and Justice
Golden Rule Kate
18: An Alien Enemy
A Lass Unto Herself
Wedlock
19: Lone Wolf's Daughter
Sahara
Goddess of Lost Lake
20: Sex
The Leopard Woman
The Girl Who Dared
Love Madness
Love
21: I am Guilty
25: Fifty-Fifty

James Gleason (1886-1959)
1922: Polly of the Follies
27: The Count of Ten

Ernest Glendenning (1884-1936)
1922: When Knighthood was in Flower

J. Frank Glendon (1885-)
1920: Mid-Channel
21: Hush
What Do Men Want
Roman Candles
Tale of Two Worlds
?? Woman in the Web
Soul of Rafael

Dagmar Godowsky
1919: Lord and Lady Algy
The Trap
20: The Marriage Pit
The Hitchin' Posts
Honor Bound
Forced Bride
Stronger than Death
Peddler of Lies
The Path She Chose
22: The Altar Stairs
The Stranger's Banquet
The Rear Car
The Trap
23: The Cheat
Red Lights
The Common Law
24: Story Without a Name
Meddling Women
A Sainted Devil
Bands of Honor
26: In Borrowed Plumes
The Throwback

Harold Goodwin (1902-)
1915: Old Heidelberg
16: Dad's Out-Laws
20: Overland Red
The Family Honor
Suds
Sweet Lavender
You Never Can Tell
21: The Road Demon
Oliver Twist, Jr.
22: The Rosary
Man to Man
Tracked to Earth
The Bear Cat
Kissed
Seeing's Believing
23: Kindled Courage
Alice Adams
The Bootlegger's Daughter
26: Honeymoon Express
27: Tarzan and the Golden Lion
Snowbound
College
The Cheer Leader
Her Summer Hero
28: The Cameraman
Snapshots
29: Flight

Bruce Gordon
1920: House of the Tolling Bell
Forbidden Valley
Democracy
After Many Days
A Little Child Shall Lead Them
Sowing and Reaping
21: A Private Scandal
22: Toys
First Men in the Moon
Bring Him In
Riddle on the Range
The Timber Queen (serial)
23: Ruth of the Range (serial)
24: Battling Brewster (serial)
The 40th Door (serial)

26: Bucking the Truth
Born to the West
Moran of the Mounted
The Transcontinental Ltd.
Escape
Pals in Paradise
27: The Sonora Kid
The Outlaw Dog
Hands Off!
Blazing Days
Desert Dust
The Poor Nut
28: Mystery Rider
Partners in Crime
Life's Mockery
29: Clean-Up

Huntley Gordon (1897-1956)
1918: Our Mrs. McChesney
The Million Dollar Dollies
The Common Cause
19: The Glorious Lady
Too Many Crooks
The Unknown Quantity
Out Yonder
20: The Dark Mirror
Out of the Snow
21: The Girl from Nowhere
At the Stage Door
Red Foam
Society Snobs
Frisky Mrs. Johnson
22: Beyond the Rainbow
Tropical Love
Reckless Youth
His Wife's Husband
When the Desert Calls
What's Wrong with Women
23: Bluebeard's 8th Wife
The Famous Mrs. Fair
Your Friend and Mine
Her Fatal Millions
24: The Enemy Sex
Chastity
25: What Fools Men Are
26: The Gilded Butterfly
Her Second Chance
Silken Shackles
Lost at Sea
Other Women's Husbands
The Golden Web
27: Don't Tell the Wife
Sensation Seekers
27: The Truthful Sex
Name the Woman
28: Their Hour
A Certain Young Man
Sinners in Love
The Gypsy of the North
Our Dancing Daughters
Sally's Shoulders
Outcast
29: Scandal
Melody Lane T
Marriage Playground T

Julia Swayne Gordon (d. 1933)
1910: 12th Night
11: Lady Godiva
12: The Victoria Cross
Troublesome Step-Daughters
Lady of the Lake
Stenographer Wanted
13: Beau Brummel
Red and White Roses
The Tiger Lady
The Hidden Letters
14: Hamlet
Uncle Bill
A Bid
Two Women
17: Soldiers of Chance
The Soul Master
A Son of the Hills
Her Right to Live
The Message of the Mouse
The Hillman
18: Over the Top
Love Watches
The Soap Girl
19: The Moonshine Trail
The Captain's Captain
The Girl Problem
Miss Dulcie from Dixie
20: Heliotrope
Greater than Fame
Lifting Shadows
A Child for Sale
21: Passionate Pilgrim
The Silver Lining
Burn 'em Up Barnes
Why Girls Leave Home
Shams of Society
Handcuffs and Kisses
22: Road to Arcady
My Old Kentucky Home

22: What's Wrong with Women?
Wilderness of Youth
Till We Meet Again
When the Desert Calls
23: Darling of the Rich
Dark Secrets
The Tie that Binds
You Can't Fool Your Wife
Scaramouche
26: The Far Cry
27: Beloved Rogue
It
Heaven on Earth
Wings
Children of Divorce
28: 13 Washington Square
The Smart Sex
Hearts of Men
Scarlet Dove
Roadhouse
The Viking
Three Week Ends
Leif the Lucky
29: Eternal Woman
Younger Generation PT
Divine Lady
Girl in the Glass Cage PT
Gold Diggers of Broadway T
Is Everybody Happy? T

Kitty Gordon (1870-)
1916: As in a Looking Glass
18: Her Hour
Diamonds and Pearls
Divine Sacrifice
The Wasp
Purple Lily
Interloper
Tinsel
Merely Players
The Belgian
19: Adele
Playthings of Passion
Unveiling Hand
The Scar
Mandarin's Gold

Maude Turner Gordon (1870-)
1917: The Honeymoon
18: The Danger Mark
Making Her His Wife
19: Home
Bringing Up Betty
Oakdale Affair
21: Price of Possession
Enchantment
3 pictures with Marguerite Clark
3 pictures with Pauline Frederick

Robert Gordon
1917: The Varmint
Tom Sawyer
18: A Pair of Silk Stockings
Missing
Huck and Tom
19: My Husband's Other Wife
Captain Kidd, Jr.
5 films with Blackton-Pathé
20: Dollars and the Woman
Vice of Fools
21: If Women Only Knew
22: The Rosary
The Super Sex
23: Main Street
The Great Menace

Vera Gordon (1886-1948)
1920: Humoresque
Sorrows of Israel
The North Wind's Malice
21: Greatest Love
22: Your Best Friend
Good Provider
23: Potash and Perlmutter
24: In Hollywood with Potash and Perlmutter
26: The Cohens and the Kellys
Sweet Daddies
Millionaires
Kosher Kitty Kelly
Private Izzy Murphy
28: Four Walls
The Cohens and the Kellys in Paris
29: The Cohens and the Kellys in Atlantic City
Nize Baby

Jetta Goudal (1898-)
1923: The Bright Shawl
The Green Goddess
Forbidden Woman

24: Matador
25: The Spaniard
The Coming of Amos
The Road to Yesterday
Lady of the Night
26: Three Faces East
Paris at Midnight
Her Man o' War
27: Fighting Love
White Gold
Shipwrecked
28: The Cardboard Lover
Love Song
29: Lady of the Pavements
32: Business and Pleasure T
The Green Goddess T
Her Cardboard Lover T

John Gough (1897-)
1925: Smooth as Satin
Three Wise Crooks
Night Patrol
26: Flaming Waters
27: Judgment of the Hills
28: Air Legion
?? Half a Chance
Risky Business

Gibson Gowland (1882-)
1916: MacBeth
18: The Hawk
Blind Husbands
19: White Heather
20: The Right of Way
The Fighting Shepherdess
Behind the Door
21: Ladies Must Live
23: Shifting Sands
Harbor Lights
24: Greed
The Border Legion
27: Broken Gates
The First Auto
Topsy and Eva
Isle of Forgotten Women
28: Rose Marie
29: Mysterious Island PT

Ethel Grandin (1896-)
1911: Across the Plains
13: Traffic in Souls
14: The Dawn of a Romance
16: The Crimson Stain Mystery (serial)
22: A Tailor-Made Man

Greta Granstedt
1928: Excess Baggage
29: Behind Closed Doors
Mexicali Rose
Erik the Great
College Love T
Girl Troubles
Close Harmony T

Lawrence Grant (1898-)
1918: To Hell with the Kaiser!
20: Held in Trust
The Chorus Girl's Romance
Someone in the House
21: Extravagance
Great Impersonation
26: The Duchess of Buffalo
27: Service for Ladies
Serenade
A Gentleman of Paris
28: Doomsday
Red Hair
Woman from Moscow
Something Always Happens
His Hour
Hold 'em Yale!
29: The Case of Lena Smith

Valentine Grant
1914: A Mother of Men
The Melting Pot
16: Daughter of MacGregor
The Innocent Lie
17: The Belgian

Bertram Grassby (1880-)
1916: For the Defense
18: Battling Jane
19: The Hope Chest
Romance of Happy Valley
The Lone Wolf's Daughter
20: For the Soul of Rafael
Mid-Channel
The Fighting Chance
The Week End
21: Hush
Straight from Paris
Hold Your Horses
22: Borderland
50 Candles

23: Drums of Fate
The Tiger's Claw
King Tut

Ralph Graves (1900-)

1918: Tinsel
19: White Heather
I'll Get Him Yet
Sporting Life
Scarlet Days
The Home Town Girl
Out of Luck
20: Mary Ellen Comes to Town
Little Miss Rebellion
Polly with a Past
The Greatest Question
21: Dream Street
22: Come On Over
The Long Chance
The Jilt
23: Kindred of the Dust
Ghost Patrol
Prodigal Daughters
Out of Luck
Mind Over Motor
Just Like a Woman
24: Yolanda
25: Womanpower
The Country Beyond
Christine of the Big Tops
26: Blarney
27: Reno Divorce
Alias the Deacon
Rich Men's Sons
A Swelled Head
The Cheer Leader
28: Submarine
A Bachelor's Paradise
Silks and Saddles
Bitter Sweets
Gold Braid
That Certain Thing
29: Smilin' Guns
Eternal Woman
Song of Love T
Side Show
Fatal Warning (serial)
Glad Rag Doll T
Flight T
The Flying Fleet T

Cesare Gravina (1858-)

1914: Fricot E Le Uova
20: Scatch My Back
22: Foolish Wives
Merry-Go-Round
God's Country and the Law
23: Daddy
Circus Days
Greed
Hunchback of Notre Dame
26: Blonde Saint
27: Magic Garden
Cheating Cheaters
28: The Wedding March
The Man Who Laughs
Trail of '98
Honeymoon (not released)
Man in the Saddle
Divine Woman
How to Handle Women
29: Burning the Wind
30: Phantom of the Opera PT

Gilda Gray (1899-1959)

1919: A Virtuous Vamp
23: Lawful Larceny
26: Aloma of the South Seas
27: Devil Dancer
Passionate Island
29: Piccadilly SSE

Lawrence Gray (1898-1970)

1925: Stage Struck
Coast of Folly
26: Love 'em and Leave 'em
The American Venus
Untamed Lady
Palm Beach Girl
Kid Boots
Everybody's Acting
27: Convoy
After Midnight
Ankles Preferred
Telephone Girl
The Callahans and the Murphys
Pajamas
Ladies Must Dress
28: Love Hungry
Diamond Handcuffs
Dead Line
Marriage by Contract
Oh Kay
The Patsy
Shadows of the Night

28: Domestic Meddlers
29: The Rainbow
Tomorrow
The Family Row
Sin Sister SSE
Trent's Last Case
Marianne T
Imperfect Ladies

Kempton Greene (1890-)
1917: Brown of Harvard
18: Our Little Wife
Craig Kennedy (serial)
19: Fool's Gold
Fortune's Child
My Little Sister
Crook of Dreams
Forest Rivals
21: Sentimental Tommy
?? A Question of Right
The Man from the Sea

Winifred Greenwood
1915: The Two Orphans
16: Lying Lips
Reclamation
Dust
17: The Crystal Gazer
18: The Deciding Kiss
19: Come Again Smith
Maggie Pepper
Men, Women and Money
The Lottery Man
20: Sick-A-Bed
The Life of the Party
21: The Faith Healer
The Dollar a Year Man
Sacred and Profane Love
Jerry

Edna Gregory (1905-)
1925: Desert Flower
Her Favorite Hubby
?? 2 years with Bobby Vernon
9 years in leads

Ena Gregory
1928: The Bush Rangers
A Clean Sweep
29: Sioux Blood

Eddie Gribbon (1892-1965)
1919: In Keystone Kop Comedies
21: Love, Honor and Behave
The Speak Easy
Furnished Rooms
Heartbalm
Molly-O
Call a Cop
Among Those Present
Officer Cupid
A Small Town Idol
22: The Village Blacksmith
A Tailor-Made Man
Crossroads of New York
Alias Julius Caesar
Captain Fly-By-Night
23: Hoodman Blind
The Victor
Crossed Wires
The Poor Worm
Fourth Musketeer
24: Border Legion
26: The Bat
Tell it to the Marines
27: Convoy
The Callahans and the Murphys
Night Life
Cheating Cheaters
Streets of Shanghai
28: Buck Privates
Smart Set
The Clash
Nameless Men
Stop that Man!
United States Smith
A Bachelor's Paradise
Gang War
29: Fancy Baggage PT
Two Weeks Off PT
Twin Beds T
Two Men and a Maid T
From Headquarters PT
Tide of Empire
The Shakedown PT
Honeymoon
Mysterious Island PT
On with the Show PT
Midnight Daddies T
So Long Letty T

Harry Gribbon (1888-1960)
1915: Keystone Kop Comedies
Mabel, Fatty and the Law
Ye Olden Grafter

15: Ambrose's Sour Grapes
A Janitor's Wife's Temptation
16: The Great Pearl Tangle
Perils of the Park
Love Will Conquer
His Auto Ruination
His Wild Oats
A Lover's Might
Worst of Friends
A Dash of Courage
17: Stars and Bars
Pinched in the Finish
Two Crooks (or A Noble Crook)
18: Ladies First
20: Down on the Farm
Don't Blame the Stork
A Movie Bug
Slipping Feet
23: His Smothered Love
26: The Bat
27: Knockout Reilly
28: Snapshots
Gang War
Chinatown Charley
The Cameraman
Show People SSE

Corinne Griffith (1898-)

1918: Miss Ambition
The Love Doctor
I Will Repay
Who Goes There?
The Menace
Love Watches
The Clutch of Circumstances
19: Girl at Bay
Adventure Shop
The Last Man
Climbers
Girl of Today
The Bramble Bush
Girl Problem
Unknown Quality
Thin Ice
20: Tower of Jewels
Deadline at Eleven
The Garter Girl
Bab's Candidate
The Whisper Market
Human Collateral
21: Broadway Bubble
It Isn't Being Done This Season
What's Your Reputation Worth?
Moral Fibre
Single Track
22: Received Payment
Island Wives
A Virgin's Sacrifice
Divorce Coupons
23: Six Days
Black Oxen
The Common Law
24: Single Wives
Love's Wilderness
25: Declassee
The Marriage Whirl
Classified
26: Infatuation
Mlle. Modiste
Into Her Kingdom
Syncopating Sue
27: Lady in Ermine
Three Hours
28: Outcast
Garden of Weeds
29: Divine Lady SSE
Saturday's Children PT
Prisoners PT
Smiling Irish Eyes T
30: Back Pay T
Lilies of the Field T
32: Lily Christine T

David Wark Griffith (1875-1948)

1907: Rescued from an Eagle's Nest
Old Isaac, The Pawnbroker
Ostler Joe
At the Crossroads of Life
The Music Master
When Knights were Bold
The Stage Rustler
08: The Adventures of Dolly
For Love of Gold

Raymond Griffith (1890-1957)

1918: The Follies Girl
22: Crossroads of New York
Fools First
Minnie
23: Going Up

23: The Eternal Three
Red Lights
White Tiger
24: Poisoned Paradise
25: Night Club
Forty Winks
Lily of the Dust
Miss Bluebird
A Regular Fellow
26: Paths to Paradise
Hands Up
He's a Prince
Wet Paint
Sorrow of Satan
The Waiter from the Ritz
Silk Hat Harry
27: You'd Be Surprised
Wedding Bills
28: Time to Love
Rise and Shine
29: Trent's Last Case
30: All Quiet on the Western Front (a cameo) T
??: The Surf Girl
A Royal Rogue

Sybil Grove (1891-)
1927: An Angel of Broadway
Gaucho
28: My Friend from India
His Private Life
The Piano Next Door
Satan and the Woman
Someone to Love
Mother
The Black Pearl

Kit Guard (1894-1961)
1920: The Face at the Window
27: Her Father Said No
Dead Man's Curve
Legionnaires in Paris
28: Beau Broadway
Lingerie
Man About Town
29: The Racketeer T
Fighting Blood (serial)

Texas Guinan (1891-1933)
1917: Stainless Barrier
Fuel of Life
18: The Gun Woman
Love Brokers
18: She-Wolf
19: Little Miss Deputy
21: I Am the Woman
The Stampede
29: Queen of the Night Clubs T

Dorothy Gulliver (1913-)
1926: The Collegians (series)
27: Rambling Rangers
Dog of the Regiment
One Glorious Scrap
28: Shield of Honor
Wild West Show
Good Morning, Judge
Clearing the Trail
Honeymoon Flats
29: King of the Campus PT
College Love T
Night Parade T
Painted Faces T

George Hackathorne (1896-1940)
1917: Tom Sawyer
18: Amarilly of Clothesline Alley
Huck and Tom
19: Sue of the South
Shepherd of the Hills
Heart of Humanity
20: Last of the Mohicans
21: What Do Men Want?
Light in the Clearing
To Please One Woman
22: Sin of Martha Queed
Human Hearts
The Little Minister
Village Blacksmith
Gray Dawn
The Worldly Madonna
Notoriety
23: Merry-Go-Round
The Tip Off
Human Wreckage
La Marseillaise
College Racketeer
24: The Turmoil
When a Man's a Man
25: Night Life in New York
Wandering Fires
The Lady
Capital Punishment
26: Highbinders
Josselyn's Wife

27: Cheaters
Paying the Price
The Cabaret Kid
28: Sally's Shoulders
Sea Urchin
29: The Squall T
30: Tip Off T
Captain of the Clouds T
The Lonesome Trail T
Beyond the Law T
33: Self Defense T
Flaming Guns T
36: I Cover Chinatown T
39: Gone with the Wind T

Albert Hackett
1919: Ginger
Come out of the Kitchen
Anne of Green Gables
21: Oh Joe!
Molly O'
?? Poor Jimmy
Four Years
House Party
Boy Who Cried Wolf
Dope
The Grail

Frank Hagney
1920: The Gauntlet
21: The Ghost in the Garret
22: Anne of Little Smoky
Go Get 'em, Hutch (serial)
23: Backbone
26: The Fighting Marine (serial)
27: All Aboard
The Frontiersman
Rawhide Kid
One Round Hogan
28: The Fight Pest
Free Lips
Glorious Trail
Through the Breakers
On Your Toes
Midnight Madness
Vultures of the Sea (serial)
29: Captain Lash SSE
Oh Yeah? T
Broken Barriers

Rea Haines
20: Mary Ellen Comes to Town
Always Audacious
20: A Master Stroke
Smiling All the Way
21: Uncharted Seas

Robert T. Haines (1870-1943)
1917: The Victim
19: The Capitol
23: The Governor's Lady
Does it Pay?
26: Lew Tyler's Wives
Heart of New York
Secret Agent
28: The First Kiss
The Noose
Ladies of the Mob
Ten Minutes
Pomander Walk
The Foreigner
29: Careers PT
Shannons of Broadway T
Girl in the Glass Cage PT

William Haines (1900-)
1922: Brothers Under the Skin
23: Three Wise Fools
Souls for Sale
24: Circe
Wine of Youth
The Midnight Express
25: Tower of Lies
Little Miss Annie Rooney
I'll Tell the World
Wife of the Centaur
Sally, Irene and Mary
26: Brown of Harvard
Memory Lane
Lovey Mary
Mike
27: Tell it to the Marines
Spring Fever
Slide, Kelly, Slide
A Little Journey
28: Telling the World
West Point
Excess Baggage
The Smart Set
Show People SSE
Iron Mike
29: Alias Jimmy Valentine T
The Duke Steps Out T
Speedway
30: Navy Blues T

Alan Hale (1892-1950)

1913: The Prisoner of Zenda
By Man's Law
14: Strongheart
Men and Women
Masks and Faces
A Scrap of Paper
Martin Chuzzlewit
Cricket on the Hearth
15: Jane Eyre
16: Puddin' Head Wilson
Woman in the Case
The Scarlet Oath
17: The Price She Paid
The Lone Thief
One Hour
18: The Whirlpool
Moral Suicide
19: The Trap
21: Four Horsemen of the Apocalypse
The Great Impersonation
The Fox
Shirley of the Circus
The Wise Fool
Heart of a Woman
22: False Kisses
One Glorious Day
A Doll's House
The Dictator
Robin Hood
The Cowboy and the Lady
The Fighting Rev. Watts
Up and at 'em
23: Quicksands
Long Live the King
The Covered Wagon
Main Street
Hollywood
Cameo Kirby
24: Black Oxen
25: Rolling Stones
Stella Dallas
The Wedding Song (dir.)
Scarlet Honeymoon (dir.)
26: Forbidden Waters
27: Risky Business
Vanity
Wreck of the Hesperus
28: The Leopard Lady
Skyscraper
The Cop
Power
28: The Spieler PT
Oh Kay
29: Sal of Singapore PT
The Leatherneck PT
Sailor's Holiday T
The Sap PT
Red Hot Rhythm T

Creighton Hale (1882-1965)

1914: Million Dollar Mystery (serial)
15: Exploits of Elaine (serial)
The Three of Us
New Exploits of Elaine (serial)
The Romance of Elaine (serial)
16: Charity
The Iron Claw (serial)
17: Seven Pearls (serial)
18: The Woman the Germans Shot
Honor of His House
Wilson or the Kaiser
19: The Thirteenth Chair
Oh Boy!
A Damsel in Distress
Why Germany Must Pay
The Love Cheat
The Cavell Case
20: The Black Circle
The Idol Dancer
21: Way Down East
Child for Sale
Women Who Wait
22: Orphans of the Storm
Fascination
Her Majesty
23: Trilby
Three Wise Fools
Tea with a Kick
Dangerous Maid
24: The Marriage Circle
Wine of Youth
26: Shadow on the Wall
Should Men Walk Home?
Beverly of Graustark
The Midnight Message
Oh Baby!
Speeding Through
27: Thumbs Down
Cat and the Canary
Annie Laurie

28: Rose Marie
Sisters of Eve
House of Sham
Reilly of the Rainbow Division
29: Seven Footprints to Satan SSE
30: The Great Divide T

Georgia Hale (1906-)
1925: The Gold Rush
The Salvation Hunters
26: The Rainmaker
Man of the Forest
27: Hills of Peril
Wheel of Chance
28: The Rawhide Kid
The Last Moment
A Woman Against the World
Gypsy of the North
A Trick of Hearts
Floating College

Charlie Hall (Laurel & Hardy)
1927: Love 'em and Weep (Laurel & Hardy short)
Battle of the Century "
28: Crooks Can't Win "
You're Darn Tootin' "
Two Tars "
29: Berth Marks "
Men o' War "
They Go Boom "
Bacon Grabbers "
30: Below Zero T "
31: Laughing Gravy T "
Come Clean T "
32: The Music Box T "

Ella Hall (1896-)
1917: A Jewell in Pawn
The Little Orphan
Bitter Sweet
The Charmer
We are French
Green Magic
18: The Heart of Rachel
Three Mounted Men
The Spotted Lily
My Little Boy
New Love for Old
Beauty in Chains
18: Which Woman
19: Under the Top
The Gates of Doom (serial)

Evelyn Hall
1926: Men of Steel
27: My Best Girl
Hello Angel
29: Divine Lady SSE
She Goes to War PT
Children of the Ritz SSE
Nobody's Children
Pomander Walk

James Hall (1897-1940)
1926: The Campus Flirt
Stranded in Paris
27: Ritzy
Swim, Girl, Swim
Silk Legs
Hotel Imperial
Senorita
Love's Greatest Mistake
28: Hell's Angels
The Fifty-Fifty Girl
Just Married
The Fleet's In
Rolled Stockings
Four Sons SSE
29: This is Heaven PT
Saturday Night Kid T
The Case of Lena Smith
Smiling Irish Eyes T

Thurston Hall (1883-1959)
1917: Cleopatra
18: Tyrant Fear
We Can't Have Everything
19: The Squaw Man
The Weaker Vessel
The Unpainted Woman
20: Empty Arms

Winter Hall (1878-)
1917: The Primrose Ring
18: House of Silence
Till I Come Back to You
19: Captain Kidd, Jr.
City of Dim Faces
The Red Lantern
The Money Corral
20: The Tree of Knowledge
The Bleeders

20: Woman in the House
The Jucklins
Behold My Wife
What Every Woman Knows
21: The Witching Hour
The Little Clown
Affairs of Anatol
The Great Impersonation
Cheated Hearts
The Child Thou Gavest Me
22: Saturday Night
Burning Sands
On the High Seas
Her Social Value
East is West
Skin Deep
23: Her Reputation
Voice from the Minaret
Little Church Around the Corner
26: Ben Hur
29: Kitty PT
The Wrecker
Paradise
30: After the Verdict
Passion Flower T
31: Girls Demand Excitement T
32: Tomorrow and Tomorrow T

Ray Hallor (1900-)
1917: Amateur Orphan
20: Blackbirds
21: Plaything of Broadway
Dream Street
23: Courtship of Miles Standish
24: Inez from Hollywood
25: Learning to Love
Sally
26: Tongues of Scandal
27: Driven from Home
Quarantined Rivals
Haunted Ship
Man Crazy
28: Trail of '98
The Clash
Black Butterflies
Inside Prison Walls
Manhattan Knights
Green-Grass Widows
Thundergod
The Pearl Story
29: Noisy Neighbors PT
Circumstantial Evidence
Fast Life T

Harry Ham
1915: Father and the Boys
Tramp, Tramp, Tramp
A Gay Deceiver
His Wedded Wife
Kissing Sister
He Fell on the Beach
Down by the Sea
Crazy by Proxy
The Honeymooners
21: Skirts

Hale Hamilton (1880-1942)
1915: Her Painted Hero
18: The Winning of Beatrice
19: That's Good
The Four-Flusher
Johnny on the Spot
Five Thousand An Hour
Full of Pep
After His Own Heart
In His Brother's Place
26: The Great Gatsby
Tin Gods
Summer Bachelors
27: The Telephone Girl

Lloyd Hamilton (1891-1935)
1914: Ham and the Piano Mover
15: Ham and the Garbage Gentleman's Ball
24: His Darker Self
25: Rolling Stones
26: The Rainmaker
Poor Boy
The Speeder
The Educator
No Luck
Extra! Extra!
Uneasy Feet
28: Robinson Crusoe, Ltd.
The Greenhorn
The Vagrant
The Adviser
Papa's Boy
Always a Gentleman
"No Sale" Smitty
?? appeared in 134 releases
Mongrels

?? Son of a Hun
Roaring Lions and Wedding Bells
A Twilight Baby
Duck Inn
Dynamite
The Simp
Moonshine

Mahlon Hamilton (1885-1960)

1916: The Eternal Question
17: The Hidden Hand (serial)
18: The Danger Mark
The Death Dance
19: Daddy-Long-Legs
In Old Kentucky
20: The Deadlier Sex
Earthbound
Kingdom of Dreams
The Third Generation
Half a Chance
The Truant Husband
21: Ladies Must Live
That Girl Montana
I Am Guilty!
Under the Lash
The Lane that has no Turning
22: Green Temptation
A Fool There Was
Under Oath
Paid Back
23: Peg o' my Heart
The Christian
Little Old New York
The Heart Raider
The Midnight Guest
25: Idaho (serial)
The Wheel
26: The Other Woman's Story
27: What Price Love
28: The Aristocrat
Life's Crossroad
29: The Single Standard
Honky Tonk T

Neil Hamilton (1899-)

1921: Man and Woman
23: White Rose
24: America
Isn't Life Wonderful?
Side Show of Life
Three Weeks
25: Street of Forgotten Men
Little French Girl
New Brooms
The Splendid Crime
The Golden Princess
26: Desert Gold
Beau Geste
Diplomacy
The Great Gatsby
Old Ironsides
27: The Music Master
Joy Girl
Within the Law
Ten Modern Commandments
28: Something Always Happens
The Patriot
Mother Machree
Don't Marry
Hot News
Take Me Home
Three Week Ends
What a Night
Showdown
The Big Scoop
Shield of Honor
The Spotlight
Grip of the Yukon
Number Please
29: Why Be Good?
Dangerous Woman T
Darkened Rooms T
The Busybody T
Mysterious Dr. Fu Manchu T
The Studio Murder Case T
Kibitzer T
Love Trap PT

Elaine Hammerstein (1897-1948)

1917: Mad Lover
The Co-Respondent
The Argyle Case
18: Wanted for Murder
Accidental Honeymoon
Her Man
19: The Country Cousin
Love or Fame
20: Shadow of Rosalie Byrnes
Whispers
Greater than Fame
The Woman Game

20: Point of View
21: Pleasure Seekers
Miracle of Manhattan
Girl from Nowhere
Handcuffs and Kisses
The Way of a Maid
The Daughter Pays
Poor Dear Margaret Kirby
Remorseless Love
22: Why Announce Your Marriage?
Reckless Youth
Evidence
Under Oath
One Week of Love
23: Rupert of Hentzau
Broadway Gold
24: The Grand Guignol
The Foolish Virgin
Daring Love
Drums of Jeopardy
The Midnight Express
25: The Unwritten Law
30: Ladies of Leisure

Virginia Hammond
1919: The Battler
The Hand Invisible
Miss Crusoe
The World to Live in
20: A Manhattan Knight
28: The Crash

Hope Hampton (1901-)
1920: A Modern Salome
21: The Bait
Love's Penalty
Star Dust
22: Light in the Dark
23: The Gold Diggers
Lawful Larceny
Does it Pay?
24: Price of the Party
25: Lovers' Island
26: Unfair Sex
28: The Road to Reno T

Einar Hansen (d. 1927)
1926: Her Big Night
Into Her Kingdom
27: Masked Woman
Lady in Ermine
Fashions for Women
27: Children of Divorce
Streets of Sorrow
Barbed Wire
Woman on Trial

Juanita Hansen (1897-1961)
1915: Martyrs of the Alamo
16: Secrets of the Submarine (serial)
The Finishing Touch
His Pride and Shame
17: The Clever Dummy
Glory
(Mack Sennett Comedies)
A Royal Rogue
Dangers of a Bride
Whose Baby?
18: Broadway Love
Mating of Marcella
The Rough Lover
Fast Company
The Brass Bullet (serial)
19: The Sea Flower
A Midnight Romance
The Poppy Girl's Husband
Rough Riding Romance
Lombardi Limited
20: The Lost City (serial)
The Yellow Arm (serial)
The Phantom Foe (serial)
21: The Red Snow
22: Broadway Madonna
The Eternal Flame
23: Girl of the Golden West

Lars Hanson (1887-1965)
1923: Story of Gosta Berling
26: In Dalarna and Jerusalem
The Scarlet Letter
27: Captain Salvation
Flesh and the Devil
Buttons
28: Divine Woman
The Wind
29: Homecoming

Oliver Hardy (1892-1957)
1913: Outwitting Dad
14: Pokes and Jabs
15: The Paperhanger's Helper
Spaghetti A La Mode
Charley's Aunt
Artists and Models

15: The Tramps
Mother's Child
16: Back Stage
The Hero
The Millionaire
Doughnuts
The Scholar
The Try-Out
Ups and Downs
This Way Out
Chickens
Frenzied Finance
Busted Hearts
Plump and Runt (series)
17: He Winked and Won
series with Jimmy Aubrey
18: The Villain
The Artist
King Solomon
The Chief Cook
19: series at L-KO
2 or 3 films as "a heavy" in Earle Williams features
19-21: series with Jimmy Aubrey
21-25: The Fly Cop with Larry Semon
The Sawmill with L. Semon
Scars and Stripes with L. S.
Wizard of Oz with L. S.
Girl in the Limousine with L. S.
Kid Speed with L. S.
23: Playmates
Three Ages
26: Should Men Walk Home?
The Nickle Hopper
27: Lucky Dog
with Stan Laurel:
26: Slipping Wives
27: Putting the Pants on Phillip
With Love and Hisses
Sailors Beware
Do Detectives Think?
Flying Elephants
Sugar Daddies
Call of the Cuckoo
The Rap
Duck Soup
Eve's Love Letters
Love 'em and Weep
Why Girls Love Sailors
27: Hats Off!
Battle of the Century
The Second Hundred Years
Let George Do It!
The Way of the Pants
28: Double Whoopee
Big Business
Fourth of July
Leave 'em Laughing
From Soup to Nuts
You're Darn Tootin'
Their Purple Moment
Should Married Men Go Home?
Habeas Corpus
Two Tars
We Faw Down (or We Slip Up)
The Finishing Touch
Early to Bed
29: Liberty S-PT
Berth Marks S-PT
Men o' War S-PT
Unaccustomed as We Are T
A Perfect Day S-T
Bacon Grabbers S-T
They Go Boom S-T

Sam Hardy (1883-1935)
1921: Get-Rich-Quick Wallingford
23: Little Old New York
Mighty Lak' A Rose
26: The Savage
Great Deception
Prince of Tempters
Bluebeard's Seven Wives
When Love Grows Cold
27: High Hat
The Perfect Sap
Orchids and Ermine
Broadway Nights
Life of Riley
Texas Steer
28: Burning Up Broadway
Turn Back the Hours
The Big Noise
Diamond Handcuffs
Butter and Egg Man
Night Bird
Outcast
Give and Take

29:	Rainbow Man	T
	A Man's Man	SSE
	On With the Show	PT
	Dear Vivien	T
	Big News	T
	Fast Company	T
	Acquitted	T

Lumsden Hare (1874-1964)

1916:	Love's Crucible	
	Arms and the Woman	
17:	Barbary Sheep	
19:	The Avalanche	
	The Country Cousin	
20:	Mothers of Men	
	The Blue Pearl	
	No Children Allowed	
21:	Frisky Mrs. Johnson	
	Education of Elizabeth	
22:	Sherlock Holmes	
28:	False Colors	
29:	Black Watch	T
	Fugitives	SSE
	Girls Gone Wild	SSE
	Salute	T

Kenneth Harlan (1895-1967)

1917:	The Whim	
	A Man's Man	
	Betsy's Burglar	
	Cheerful Givers	
18:	The Wine Girl	
	Bread	
	The Model's Confession	
	Midnight Madness	
	The Turning Point	
	Lash of Power	
	Girl Who Came Back	
19:	The Hoodlum	
20:	Love, Honor and Obey	
	The Rossmore Case	
	Dangerous Business	
	The Penalty	
21:	Mama's Affair	
	Lessons in Love	
	Beauty and Brains	
	Nobody	
	Dawn of the East	
	Woman's Place	
	Wedding Bells	
22:	Polly of the Follies	
	I Am the Law	
	Primitive Lover	
	Married Flapper	
	The White Man	
23:	Toll of the Sea	
	The World's a Stage	
	Little Church Around the Corner	
	East Side, West Side	
	The Virginian	
	Broken Wing	
	Beautiful and Damned	
24:	Butterfly	
	Poisoned Paradise	
	For Another Woman	
25:	Bobbed Hair	
	The Fighter Ranger	
	Learning to Love	
	Marriage Whirl	
26:	Finders Keepers	
	Flame of the Yukon	
	The Sap	
	Ranger of the Big Pines	
	Stage Kisses	
	The Ice Flood	
	Fighting Edge	
	Twinkletoes	
27:	Easy Pickings	
	Down the Stretch	
	Cheating Cheaters	
	Streets of Shanghai	
28:	Fallen Angels	
	United States Smith	
	Code of the Air	
	Wilful Youth	
	Midnight Rose	
29:	Man, Woman and Wife	SSE
30:	Paradise Island	T

Otis Harlan (1865-1940)

1915:	Chronicles of Bloom Center	
21:	The Romance Promoters	
	Diamonds Adrift	
	When We Were Twenty-One	
	Keeping Up With Lizzie	
	A Black Sheep	
	Welcome Home	
22:	The Eternal Flame	
	The Girl in the Taxi	
23:	Voice from the Minaret	
	Truxton King	
	Main Street	
	The Spider and the Rose	
25:	Welcome Home	
	What Happened to Jones?	

25: 9 3-5 Seconds
Lightnin'
26: Three Bad Men
The Whole Town's Talking
The Cheerful Fraud
Silk Stockings
The Unknown Cavalier
Midnight Message
27: Student Prince
The Silent Rider
Don't Tell the Wife
Galloping Fury
28: Good Morning, Judge
Baby Mine
Shepherd of the Hills
Grip of the Yukon
Speed Classic
29: Silks and Saddles
Broadway
Embarrassing Moments
Girl Overboard PT
His Lucky Day PT
Barnum was Right T
Mississippi Gambler T
A Port of Dreams
Show Boat PT
Clear the Decks PT
?? A Stranger in New York
A Milk White Flag
A Temperance Town
Regeneration of Sam Packard
Everybody Loves a Fat Man

Jean Harlow (1911-1937)
1927: Laurel & Hardy comedies
28: Moran of the Marines
29: Hell's Angels
30: Hell's Angels (synchronized) T
31: City Lights

Pat Harmon (1890-)
1919: Speed Maniac
The Busher
20: Firebrand Trevison
23: Eternal Struggle
24: The Silent Watcher
When a Man's a Man
25: Nathan Hale
The Freshman
28: Court-Martial
Show Folks PT
28: Waterfront
29: The Warning PT
Sideshow
Weary River
The Duke Steps Out PT
Synthetic Sin
Homesick SSE
Sunset Pass

Mildred Harris (1901-1944)
1914: Wizard of Oz series
15: Enoch Arden
Quest of the Holy Grail
16: Intolerance
Old Folks at Home
Hoodoo Anne
17: The Price of a Good Time
18: For Husbands Only
The Doctor and the Woman
19: Home
Borrowed Clothes
When a Girl Loves
20: The Inferior Sex
Forbidden
Polly of the Storm Country
Woman in His House
21: Old Dad
Habit
A Prince There Was
22: A Fool's Paradise
The First Woman
23: The Daring Years
24: One Law for the Woman
Unmarried Wives
Village Prodigal
The Whim
K-The Unknown
The Man Who Dared God
Social Mockery
25: My Neighbor's Wife
26: The Cruise of the Jasper B
Isle of Retribution
Mystery Club
Wolf Hunters
One Hour of Love
27: Wolves of the Air
Out of the Past
The Melody Man
Side Street
Show Girl
Wandering Girls
Girl from Rio
Adventurous Souls

28: Lingerie
Melody of Love
Heart of a Follies Girl
Power of the Press
Hearts of Men
Speed Classic
The Last Lap
Out of the Past
29: Sea Fury PT
Side Street T
20: No, No, Nanette T
Ranch House Blues T
35: Lady Tubbs T

Jimmy Harrison
1917: The Bad Boy
Madame Bo-Beep
Kids and Kidlets
Reno, All Change
14 Christie Comedies
19: Nearly Newlyweds
21: Lessons in Love
Wedding Bells
A Heart to Let
22: The Barricade
Beyond the Rainbow
Why Announce Your Marriage?
25: Charley's Aunt
28: Wife's Relations
Long Hose
Halfback Hannah
Say... Uncle!
Stop Kidding
Nifty Numbers
Love's Young Scream

John Harron (1903-)
1918: Hearts of the World
23: Dulcy
24: The Supreme Test
25: Learning to Love
26: Bride of the Storm
The Night Cry
The Gilded Highway
Hell Bent for Heaven
Little Irish Girl
The Boy Friend
The False Alarm
Rose of the Tenements
27: Love Makes 'em Wild
Closed Gates
Silk Stockings
Once and Forever
Old Shoes
Night Life
Naughty
28: Finders Keepers
Their Hour
Green-Grass Widows
29: The Man in Hobble's
Street Girl T

Robert Harron (1894-1920)
1908: The Valet's Wife
The Test of Friendship
The Helping Hand
The Boy Detective
09: The Girls and Daddy
The Hindu Dagger
A Burglar's Mistake
A Sound Sleeper
Jones and the Lady Book Agent
Two Memories
The Message
Pranks
The Little Darling
In a Hempen Bag
10: A Child's Impulse
Another Story with a New Ending
Wilful Peggy
A Summer Idyll
Examination Day at School
The Banker's Daughter
11: Home Folks
White Rose of the Wilds
Enoch Arden
The Battle
12: Man's Genius
The New York Hat
The Girl and Her Trust
A Temporary Truce
Man's Lust for Gold
Those Hickville Boys
One Busy Hour
My Hero
The Informer
The Burglar's Dilemma
A Cry for Help
The Musketeers of Pig Alley
Unseen Enemy
13: Love in an Apartment Hotel

13: The Primitive Man
(War of the Primal Tribes)
Oil and Water
Broken Ways
Death's Marathon
The Coming of Angelo
The Sheriff's Baby
The Lady and the Mouse
Her Mother's Oath
The Adopted Brother
The Reformers
The Lost Art of Making Up One's Mind
Influence of the Unknown
The Yaqui Cur
The Tender-Hearted Boy
By Man's Law
The Battle of Elderbush Gulch
14: The Massacre
The Odalisque
The Newer Woman
Their First Acquaintance
Down by the Sounding Sea
Moonshine Molly
Home Sweet Home
The Escape
The Rebellion of Kitty Belle
Judith of Bethulia
Sands of Fate
15: The Birth of a Nation
Enoch Arden
For Those Unborn
Big James' Heart
The Missing Links
16: Intolerance
Wharf Rat
17: The Bad Boy
The Old-Fashioned Young Man
18: The Great Love
Hearts of the World
19: The Greatest Thing in Life
The Girl Who Stayed at Home
True Heart Susie
A Romance of Happy Valley
20: Way Down East (a bit)
21: Confidence

Neal Hart
1916: Liberty, A Daughter of the U.S.A. (serial)
18: Man from Montana
Quicksand
19: When the Desert Smiled
Bare Fisted Gallagher
The Element of Might
Black Sheep
The Lion's Claw (serial)
20: Skyfire
God's Gold
Danger Valley
Hell's Oasis
The Dead Line
The Square Shooter
Sands of the Desert
21: King Fisher's Roost
Rangeland
Tangled Trails
Lure of Gold
Heart of a Texas
Knight of the Western Land
22: Butterfly Range
Table Top Ranch
West of the Pecos
South of the Northern Lights
23: Salty Saunders
Squarin' It
24: Left Hand Brand
Tucker's Top Hand
27: The Scarlet Hound (serial)

Sunshine Hart (1886-)
1920: White Moll
Tiger Club
26: Lovey Mary
27: Red Mill
Student Prince
My Best Girl
Sound your A's
The Bride's Relations

William S. Hart (1870-1946)
1914: Jim Carmon's Wife
The Bargain
On the Night Stage (or The Bandit and the Preacher)
The Passing of Two Gun Hicks (or, Two Gun Hicks)

14: Mr. Silent Haskins
Scourge of the Desert
The Darkening Trail
15: His Hour of Manhood
The Sheriff's Streak of Yellow
The Fugitive (or, the Taking of Luke McVane)
The Ruse
Man from Nowhere
Cash Parrish's Pal
The Conversion of Frosty Blake (or, The Gentleman from Blue Gulch)
Grit
Bad Luck of Santa Ynez
The Grudge
Keno Bates the Liar
Tool of Providence
Golden Claw
Between Men
Pinto Ben
In Sagebrush Country
The Rough Neck
16: The Aryan
Return of Draw Egan
Apostle of Vengeance
Last Card
Hell's Hinges
The Primal Lure
The Captive God
The Devil's Double
Upholding the Law
The Sheriff
The Patriot
Dawnmaker
17: Silent Man
Narrow Trail
Cold Deck
Gun Fighter
Square Deal
Truthful Tulliver
Wolf Lowry
Desert Man
18: Wolves of the Trail
Tiger Man
Selfish Yates
Shark Monroe
Border Wireless
Narrow Trail
Riddle Gawne
19: Blue Blazes Rawden
Branding Broadway
19: Breed of Men
Money Corral
Square Deal Sanderson
Wagon Tracks
Poppy Girl's Husband
John Petticoats
20: Sand!
Cradle of Courage
The Toll Gate
The Testing Block
21: O'Malley of the Mounted
The Whistle
Three Word Brand
White Oak
22: Travelin' On
23: Wild Bill Hickok
24: Singer Jim McKee
25: Tumbleweeds (re-issued in 1929 with sound effects)
28: Show People (a cameo)

Gretchen Hartman (1897-)

1917: Mary Jane's Pa
Painted Madonna
18: Fantine
Les Miserables
19: House Without Children
Bandbox
20: Atonement
Bride 13 (serial)
29: Time, the Place and the Girl — T
She Goes to War — PT

Pat Hartigan (1881-)

1923: Down to the Sea in Ships
24: Find Your Man
28: Midnight Taxi
29: The Far Call — SSE
From Headquarters — PT

Lilian Harvey (1907-1968)

1923: Der Fluch
Die Liebeschaften Der Hella Von Gilsar
24: Du Sollst Nicht Stechten
25: Leidenschaft
26: Prinzessin Trulala
Adieu Mascott
Die Keusche Susanne
Die Kleine Von Bummel
27: Vater Werden Ist Nicht Schwer

27: Die Tolle Lola
28: Liebe Gert Seltsame Wege
29: Ihr Dundler Pinkt
Eine Nacht In London
Eheferien
Leise Kommt Das Gluck Zu Dir

Olive Hasbrouck (1907-)

1926: Border Sheriff
Rustler's Ranch
A Regular Scout
Two Gun Man
The Cohens and the Kellys
27: Tearin' into Trouble
Set Free
Ridin' Rowdy
Fighting Three
Shamrock and the Rose
Woman Who Did Not Care
White Pebbles
Interferin' Gent
Ride 'em High
Obligin' Buckaroo
28: Desperate Courage
Cowboy Cavalier
The Flying Cowboy
Flying Fists
Thou Shalt Not Kill
Charge of the Gauchos
29: Clear the Decks PT
Royal Rider

Raymond Hatton (1892-)

1914: The Circus Man
15: The Golden Chance
16: Joan the Woman
The Love Mask
Honorable Friend
Public Opinion
Oliver Twist
The Sowers
17: The Woman God Forgot
Nan of Music Mountain
The Devil Stone
Firefly of France
The Source
18: The Whispering Chorus
We Can't Have Everything
Arizona
19: Everywoman
The Dub
You're Fired!
19: The Love Burglar
Experimental Marriage
Male and Female
20: The Sea Wolf
Stop Thief!
Officer 666
The Dancin' Fool
Young Mrs. Winthrop
Jes' Call Me Jim
21: Bunty Pulls the Strings
Affairs of Anatol
Doubling for Romeo
Salvage
Lure of the Range
The Concert
Peck's Bad Boy
Ace of Hearts
Pilgrims of the Night
22: His Back Against the Wall
Head Over Heels
Manslaughter
Pink Gods
To Have and to Hold
Ebb Tide
The Hottentot
At Bay
Cornered
23: Java Head
Trimmed in Scarlet
The Tie that Binds
Hunchback of Notre Dame
Three Wise Fools
Barefoot Boy
Four Hearts
24: Mine with the Iron Door
Janice Meredith
Come On, Cowboys!
Western Fate
Whirlwind Ranger
The Rip Snorter
25: Thundering Herd
Big Brother
26: Silence
Behind the Front
Forlorn River
We're in the Navy Now
Born to the West
27: Fashions for Women
Fireman, Save My Child!
Now We're in the Air
28: Wife Savers
The Big Killing
Partners in Crime

29:	Trent's Last Case	
	Office Scandal	PT
	When Caesar ran a Newspaper	
	Hell's Heroes	T
30:	The Mighty	T

Ulrich Haupt (1887-1931)

1928:	Tempest	
	Captain Swagger	
	The Iron Mask	PT
29:	Far Call	SSE

Phyllis Haver (1899-1961)

1920:	Married Life	
21:	Never Too Old	
	The Foolish Age	
	Salome vs. Shenandoah	
	Love, Honor and Behave	
	A Small Town Idol	
	The Balloonatic	
	Hearts and Flowers	
	Among Those Present	
	His Last False Step	
23:	The Bolted Door	
	The Common Law	
	The Temple of Venus	
	The Christian	
24:	Singer Jim McKee	
25:	New Brooms	
	So Big	
	Her Husband's Secret	
26:	Don Juan	
	What Price Glory?	
	Little Adventuress	
	Other Women's Husbands	
	Fig Leaves	
	Hard Boiled	
	The Cave Man	
	3 Bad Men	
	Up in Mabel's Room	
	The Nervous Wreck	
27:	No Control	
	Rejuvenation of Aunt Mary	
	The Wise Wife	
	The Fighting Eagle	
	The Way of All Flesh	
	Nobody's Widow	
	Your Wife and Mine	
28:	Chicago	
	10th Avenue	
29:	Sal of Singapore	T
	Shady Lady	T
29:	Office Scandal	T
	Thunder	
??:	Appeared in Mack Sennet Comedies	

Ormi Hawley (1890-1942)

1915:	Insurrection
16:	Temptation
	Where Love Leads
17:	Runaway Romany
	The Antics of Ann
	Prince Ubaldo
18:	The Splendid Road
	The Ragged Earl
19:	The Road Called Straight
	(and 250 other films)

Wanda Hawley (1897-)

1917:	The Derelict
18:	The Gypsy Trail
	We Can't Have Everything
	A Pair of Silk Stockings
	Mr. Fix-It
	Old Wives for New
19:	Greased Lightning
	Everywoman
	For Better, For Worse
	Virtuous Sinners
	Pirates of the Sky
	You're Fired!
	The Lottery Man
	Peg o' My Heart (not released)
20:	Sick Abed
	The 6 Best Cellars
	Miss Hobbs
	Her Beloved Villain
	Her First Elopement
	The House that Jazz Built
	The Outside Woman
	The Snob
	Her Sturdy Oak
	The Tree of Knowledge
	Mrs. Temple's Telegram
	Held by the Enemy
	Food for Scandal
	Double Speed
	La Veglione
21:	The Affair of Anatol
	A Kiss in Time
	Her Face Value
	The Love Charm
22:	The Woman Who Walked Alone

22: Burning Sands
The Young Rajah
Too Much Wife
Thirty Days
The Truthful Liar
Bobbed Hair
23: Peg o' My Heart
24: Combat
25: America Pluck
Bobbed Hair
Secret Service
Fires of Fate
26: The Midnight Message
Men of the Night
Phantom of the Forest
Whom Shall I Marry?
Hearts and Spangles
The Smoke Eaters
27: Pirates of the Sky
Eyes of the Totem

Sessue Hayakawa (1889-)

1914: Typhoon
Wrath of the Gods
Last of the Line
The Ambassador's Envoy
15: The Cheat
Secret Sin
The Man Who Laughed Last
A Scarlet Sin
After Five Years
The Clue
16: Honorable Friend
Alien Souls
17: Bottle Imp
Each to His Own Kind
Daughter of the Dragon
The Jaguar's Claws
Forbidden Paths
Hashimura To Go
Call of the East
Secret Game
18: Hidden Pearls
Loyalty
Only a Nigger
Banzai
Honor of His House
White Man's Law
Temple of Dusk
Bravest Way
His Birthright
19: Gray Horizon
City of Dim Faces
19: Dragon Painter
Tong Man
His Highness-The Beggar
The Debt
A Heart in Pawn
Courageous Coward
Man Beneath
Bonds of Honor
Mysterious Prince
20: Li Ting Lang
An Arabian Knight
Beggar Prince
First Born
Brand of Lopez
The Devil's Claim
House of Intrigue
Illustrious Prince
21: Where Lights are Low
Black Roses
Street of the Flying Dragon
The Swamp
22: Five Days to Live
The Vermilion Pencil
Night Life in Hollywood
23: The Battalion
24: I Killed
Great Prince Shan
Sen Yan's Devotion

Richard Headrick (1917-)

1919: Should a Woman Tell?
20: The Toll Gate
21: The Child Thou Gavest Me
Playthings of Destiny
22: Retribution
Song of Life
Rich Men's Wives
White Shoulders
Hearts Aflame
Environment
23: Spider and the Rose
Woman in His House
The Grail
Stigma
Chicago Sal

Edward Hearne (1888-)

1915: White Scar
16: Her Bitter Cup
The Seekers
Idle Wives
Into the Night
17: Treason

18: Lure of Luxury
19: Undercurrent
Last of His People
20: Daredevil Jack (serial)
Down Home
The Coast of Opportunity
21: The Things Men Do
The Avenging Arrow (serial)
All Dolled Up
Keeping Up with Lizzie
22: Truthful Liar
Glory of Clementina
23: Patsy
24: Man Without a Country
25: One of the Bravest
26: The Lost Express
27: Hook and Ladder No. 9
Face of the World
28: Dog Justice
Yellow Cameo
Danger Line
Ned McCobb's Daughter SSE
29: One Man Dog
Donovan Affair T
Bachelor Girl PT

O. P. Heggie (1879-1936)

1928: The Letter
The Actress
29: Mysterious Dr. Fu Manchu T
30: The Mighty T
Wheel of Life T

Violet Heming (1893-)

1917: Turn of the Wheel
Judgment House
Danger Trail
19: Everywoman
Almost Married
Circumstances
20: Cost
When the Desert Calls

Del Henderson (1883-1956)

1910: A Child's Impulse
11: Making of a Man
12: The Crooked Way
Those Hicksville Boys
13: Comrades
14: The Massacre
16: Intolerance
17: The Runaway
17: The Beautiful Adventure
Please Help Emily
Outcast
18: Impostor
My Wife
The Road to France
19: Courage for Two
20: The Shark
21: Dynamite Allen
22: Broken Silence
23: Blazing Barriers
24: Gambling Wives
The Love Bandit
25: The Bad Lands
26: Pay Off
27: Rambling Rangers
The Crowd
Getting Gertie's Garter
28: The Patsy
Show People SSE
Power of the Press
Riley the Cop SSE
3 Ring Marriage
Iron Mike
Crowd
29: Is Everybody Happy? T
Condemned Woman
Hit the Deck T

Gale Henry (1893-)

1919: (5 years filmed 1 reel comedies)
21: The Hunch
22: Quincy Adams Sawyer
East is Worst
23: Night Life in Hollywood
25: New Lives for Old
28: Long Hose
All Parts
29: Love Doctor
Darkened Rooms T

Holmes Herbert (1882-1956)

1918: The Whirlpool
A Doll's House
19: White Heather
20: My Lady's Garter
His House in Order
Market of Souls
Black is White
The Right to Love
Lady Rose's Daughter
Dead Men Tell No Tales

21: The Inner Chamber
Divorce Coupons
The Family Closet
The Truth About Husbands
Wild Goose
22: Any Wife
A Stage Romance
Moonshine Valley
Evidence
A Woman's Woman
24: Sinners in Heaven
Enchanted Cottage
25: The Charlatan Mystery (serial)
26: The Honeymoon Express
The Passionate Quest
27: The Fire Brigade
One Increasing Purpose
When a Man Loves
Lovers
The Heart of Salome
Mr. Wu
Slaves of Beauty
The Gay Retreat
The Nest
East Side West Side
28: Gentlemen Prefer Blondes
Their Hour
This Sporting Age
The Terror
On Trial
Through the Breakers
29: The Charlatan PT
Madame X T
Say it with Songs T
Untamed T
The Kiss SSE
The 13th Chair T
The Careless Age T
30: The Ship from Shanghai T
Her Private Life T

Aggie Herring (d. 1938)
1916: Honor Thy Name
Home
17: The Millionaire Vagrant
19: Within the Cup
Cupid Forecloses
A Yankee Princess
A Man's Fight
The Hoodlum
20: The Lord Loves the Irish
The Sagebrusher
20: The Dream Cheater
The Dwelling Place of Light
Down Home
Little Shepherd of Kingdom Come
Big Happiness
Hairpins
21: The Rookie's Return
The Lure of Egypt
A Girl's Decision
Queenie
The Ragged Heiress
The Mysterious Rider
22: Heart's Haven
The Ninety and Nine
Oliver Twist
A Blind Bargain
23: Heroes of the Street
What a Wife Learned
Isle of Lost Ships
27: Loco Luck
McFadden's Flats
The Gorilla
Finnegan's Ball
28: That Certain Thing
Lady Be Good
Do Your Duty
Head of the Family
29: Children of the Ritz SSE
Smiling Irish Eyes T
Dark Streets

Jean Hersholt (1886-1956)
1916: Hell's Hinges
17: Soul Herder
21: Four Horsemen of the Apocalypse
22: Tess of the Storm Country
23: Greed
Quicksands
Jazzmania
Red Lights
Stranger's Banquet
24: Goldfish
Her Night of Romance
25: So Big
Stella Dallas
26: Don Q
It Must be Love
27: Student Prince
The Wrong Mr. Wright
Alias the Deacon
Secret Hour

28: Battle of the Sexes
Abie's Irish Rose SSE
Give and Take SSE
Jazz Mad
29: Girl on the Barge PT
Younger Generation PT
Modern Love PT

Herbert Heyes
1918: Heart of the Sunset
The Heart of Rachel
19: Deliverance
21: The Queen of Sheba
The Evil Half
Dangerous Moment

Ruth Hiatt (1908-)
1922: Extra! Extra!
For the Love of Tut
Captain Applesauce
26: Saturday Afternoon
Smith Family
27: Missing Link
Shanghai Road
Long Pants
His First Flame
29: Grass Skirts
30: Night Work T
?? The Speeder
No Luck
The Educator
Back Fire
Three Strikes

Howard Hickman (1880-1949)
1915: Jane
Matrimony
16: Civilization
Society Sinners
The First Command
18: Social Ambition
18: Alias Jimmy Valentine

Walter Hiers (1893-1933)
1916: Seventeen
18: The Lesson
19: It Pays to Advertise
Bill Henry
Hard Boiled
When Doctors Disagree
The Fear Woman
Spotlight Sadie
An Experimental Marriage
19: The Turning Point
20: What's Your Husband Doing
A City Sparrow
The Fourteenth Man
Mrs. Temple's Telegram
Oh, Lady, Lady
Going Some
Hunting Trouble
21: The Snob
Sham
22: Is Matrimony a Failure?
The Ghost Breaker
Jimmy
Bought and Paid For
Her Gilded Cage
23: Mr. Billings Spends His Dime
Sixty Cents an Hour
24: Fair Week
Flaming Barriers
Three O'Clock in the Morning
26: Hold That Lion!
27: Beware of Widows
Racing Romeo
Naughty
Blondes by Choice
Night Life
Hot Lemonade
28: A Woman Against the World

Doris Hill
1926: The Better 'ole
27: Rough House Rosie
Beauty Shoppers
Tell It To Sweeney
Figures Don't Lie
Casey at the Bat
28: Tillie's Punctured Romance
A Thief in the Dark
Take Me Home
Court Martial
Avalanche
Interference T
Fools For Luck
29: Studio Murder Mystery T
His Glorious Night T
Men are like That T
Darkened Rooms T

Ernest Hilliard (1886-1946)
1921: Silver Wings

21: A Little Child Shall Lead Them
22: Divorce Coupons
Matrimonial Web
Tropical Love
The Ruling Passion
Evidence
Married People
23: Man and Wife
Modern Marriage
24: Beloved Vagabond
26: White Mice
Forest Havoc
27: Wide Open
The Fighting Failure
Midnight Watch
Let it Rain
Modern Daughters
Smile, Brother, Smile
The Silent Hero
The Racing Fool
Broadway After Midnight
A Bowery Cinderella
28: Burning Up Broadway
The Matinee Idol
Lady Raffles
A Midnight Adventure
Dugan of the Dugout
Out with the Tide
Devil Dogs
Divine Sinners
The Big Hop
Sinners in Love
Husbands are Liars
29: When Dreams Come True
Big Diamond Robbery
Red Wine SSE
Red Hot Rhythm T

Harry Hilliard
1917: Every Girl's Dream
18: The Successful Adventure
A Romance of Rome
Cheating Herself
19: The Sneak
Little White Savage
The Little Rowdy
Destiny
20: The Dangerous Talent
The Girl in No. 29

Johnny Hines (1895-)
1914: Man of the Hour
14: As Ye Sow
16: Miss Petticoats
17: Tillie Wakes Up
The Dancer's Peril
18: Neighbors
The Studio Girl
19: Heart of Gold
Eastward Ho!
Just Sylvia
The Little Intruder
3 Green Eyes
20: Alias Jimmy Valentine
A Scrap of Paper
21: Burn 'em Up Barnes
22: Sure-Fire Flint
23: the Torchy Comedies
Torchy Turns Cupid
Torchy's Double Triumph
Torchy Mixes In
Torchy's Big Lead
Torchy in High
Torchy's Night Hood
Luck
Little Johnny Jones
24: The Speed Spook
Conductor 1492
25: The Crackerjack
The Early Bird
26: The Brown Derby
Rainbow Riley
Stepping Along
The Live Wire
27: Home Made
All Aboard
White Pants Willie
28: Chinatown Charlie

Raymond Hitchcock (1865-1929)
1915: My Valet
Stolen Magic
22: The Beauty Shop
26: Everybody's Acting
Redheads Preferred
27: Upstream
Monkey Talks

Otto Hoffman (1879-)
1918: String Beans
A 9 O'Clock Town
The Family Skeleton
His Own Home Town
Playing the Game
19: The Sheriff's Son

19: Home Town Girl
Egg Crate Wallop
The Busher
23-1/2 Hours Leave
City of Comrades
Greased Lightning
20: Paris Green
The Great Accident
Homer Comes Home
The Jailbird
21: The Sin Flood
Just out of College
Bunty Pulls the Strings
The Bronze Bell
22: The Glorious Fool
Mr. Barnes of New York
Very Truly Yours
The $5 Baby
Gas Oil and Water
23: Strangers of the Night
Human Wreckage
27: Beware of Widows
Painted Ponies
28: The Fourflusher
The Siren
Rinty of the Desert
Grain of Dust
The Terror
29: Desert Song T
The Hottentot T
On with the Show T
Madonna of Avenue A T
Is Everybody Happy? T
Acquitted T

Thomas Holding
1917: Redeeming Love
Daughters of Destiny
18: Vanity Pool
19: The Danger Zone
Lady of Red Butte
Tangled Threads
Beckoning Roads
Peace of Roaring River
Lone Wolf's Daughter
20: The Honey Bee
In Folly's Trail
Woman in his House
21: Sacred and Profane Love
Without Benefit of Clergy
Three Musketeers
23: Courtship of Miles Standish
23: Stranger's Banquet

Alice Hollister (1890-)
1912: From the Manger to the Cross
13: Vampire
The Destroyer
14: The Vampire's Trail
15: A Sister's Burden
Don Caesar De Bazan
The Kerry Gow
Yellow Sunbonnet
Lotus Woman
17: Her Better Self
18: The Knife
20: Milestones
The Great Lover
22: The Forgotten Law

Carol Holloway
1917: The Fighting Trail
The Tenderfoot
Vengeance and the Woman
The Iron Test
Perils of Thunder Mountain
21: Two Moons
Dangerous Love
The Saphead

Helen Holmes (1892-1950)
1914: The Hazards of Helen (serial)
15: The Girl and the Game (serial)
16: Medicine Bend
Whispering Smith
17: Danger Trail
The Lost Express (serial)
19: The Fatal Fortune (serial)
Railroad Raiders
A Desperate Deed
20: The Tiger Band (serial)
22: Ghost City
Hills of Missing Men
The Lone Hand
A Million in Jewels
23: Stormy Seas
24: Battling Brewster (serial)
25: Blood and Steel
26: Mistaken Orders
The Fast Freight
Crossed Signals

Stuart Holmes (1887-)

1911: How Mrs. Murray Saved the Army
14: In the Stretch
Life's Shop Window
Dust of Desire
Isle of Jewels
16: A Daughter of the Gods
17: The Scarlet Letter
The Wild Girl
18: Ghosts of Yesterday
When Men Betray
Poor Rich Man
19: Way of a Woman
New Moon
Little Intruder
Sins of the Children
Treason
The Other Man's Wife
20: A Dangerous Affair
Love, Honor and Behave
Body and Soul
Rich Men's Daughters
Trailed by Three (serial)
The Evil Eye (serial)
21: Four Horsemen of the Apocalypse
Passion Fruit
No Woman Knows
All's Fair in Love
22: Her Husband's Trade Mark
Prisoner of Zenda
Paid Back
Under Two Flags
23: Stranger's Banquet
Rip Tide
24: Tess of the D'Ubervilles
25: Salvation Hunters
Strongheart
26: Midnight Message
Everybody's Acting
Good and Naughty
North Star
27: Polly of the Movies
Your Wife and Mine
Should Tall Men Marry?
Beloved Brute
Between Friends
28: The Man Who Laughs
Burning Daylight
The Hawk's Nest
30: The Heroic Lover T

Taylor Holmes (1872-1959)

1917: Efficiency Edgar's Courtship
Fools for Luck
Two-Bit Seats
The Small Town Guy
Uneasy Money
18: Ruggles of Red Gap
$20 a Week
A Pair of Sixes
19: It's a Bear
Three Black Eyes
A Regular Fellow
Upside Down
Taxi
20: Nothing but the Truth
The Rainbow Chaser
The Very Idea
Nothing but Lies
25: The Crimson Runner
The Verdict
Borrowed Finery
27: One Hour of Love
King Harold
He did his Best
He Loved the Ladies

Jack Holt (1888-1951)

1915: A Cigarette-That's All
16: Liberty, Daughter of the U. S. A. (serial)
Joan the Woman
17: The Lone Wolf
The Little American
18: The Honor of His House
A Desert Wooing
The Marriage Ring
The Claw
19: The Life Line
The Woman Thou Gavest Me
The Squaw Man
Cheating Cheaters
A Midnight Romance
Kitty Kelly, M. D.
For Better, for Worse
Victory
20: Crooked Streets
Held by the Enemy
Midsummer Madness
21: The Lost Romance
After the Show
Call of the North

21: All Souls' Eve
Ducks and Drakes
22: While Satan Sleeps
Bought and Paid For
Man Unconquerable
On the High Seas
Making a Man
North of the Rio Grande
23: The Tiger's Claw
The Cheat
A Gentleman of Leisure
The Marriage Maker
Nobody's Money
24: Wanderer of the Wasteland
Empty Hands
Border Legion
Lone Wolf
25: Light of the Western Stars
Wild Horse Mesa
Enchanged Hill
Thundering Herd
North of '36
Eve's Secret
26: Born to the West
Sea Horses
Blind Goddess
Man of the Forest
Forlorn River
27: Tigress
Mysterious Rider
28: Submarine
Vanishing Pioneer
Water Hole
Avalanche
Sunset Legion
The Smart Set
Court Martial
29: Donovan Affair T
Flight T
Sunset Pass
Father and Son PT

Robert Homans
1928: Smiling Irish Eyes
Fury of the Wild
Blindfold
The Case of Mary Brown
29: Isle of Lost Ships

Gloria Hope (1901-)
1918: Naughty, Naughty!
Heart of Rachael
Law of the North
19: Outcasts of Poker Flat
Riders of the Law
Day She Paid
Hushed Hour
Burglar by Proxy
Gay Lord Quex
20: Great Lover
Too Much Johnson
Road to Divorce
The Third Woman
Seeds of Vengeance
Untamed
Prairie Trails
21: Colorado
The Texan
Woman Who Understood
Dangerous Hero

De Wolf Hopper (1858-1935)
1915: Don Quixote
16: Casey at the Bat
Sunshine Dad
19: A Rough Knight
Poor Papa
Girl and the Mummy
Puppets

Hedda Hopper (1891-1966)
1916: Battle of Hearts
Moriarity
17: Her Excellency the Governor
Seven Keys to Baldpate
19: Virtuous Wives
Third Degree
By Right of Purchase
Nearly Married
Isle of Conquest
Men Women Marry
20: The Man Who Lost Himself
The New York Idea
21: The Inner Chamber
Conceit
22: Sherlock Holmes
23: Free Love
24: Has the World Gone Mad?
Happiness
Miami
25: Zander the Great
26: Don Juan
The Silver Treasure
Adam and Evil
Pleasures of the Rich

26: Dance Madness
Obey the Law
Lew Tyler's Wives
The Cave Man
27: The Drop Kick
The Magic Garden
Matinee Ladies
Black Tears
The Cruel Touch
One Woman to Another
A Reno Divorce
Wings
Venus of Venice
Orchids and Ermine
Children of Divorce
28: Companionate Marriage
Mona Lisa
Love and Learn
The Chorus Kid
Harold Teen
Undressed
Green-Grass Widows
Runaway Girls
Port of Missing Girls
The Whip Woman
29: Girls Gone Wild SSE
The Last of Mrs. Cheyney PT
Half Marriage T
His Glorious Night T
30: The Racketeer T
Song of Kentucky T

Camilla Horn (1906-)
1926: Faust
27: Tempest
28: King of Berinia (or King of the Mountain)
Eternal Love
29: Eva and the Grasshopper
Happy Vineyard

Clara Horton (1904-)
1917: Tom Sawyer
18: Huck and Tom
19: Everywoman
In Wrong
Girl from Outside
20: Blind Youth
Fortune Hunter
Little Shepherd of Kingdom Come
It's a Great Life
20: Servant in the House
21: 19 and Phyllis
Action
Prisoners of Love
23: The Fighting Blade

Edward Everett Horton (1866-1970)
1920: Leave it to Me
22: The Ladder Jinx
Too Much Business
23: Ruggles of Red Gap
To the Ladies
A Front Page Story
25: Marry Me
The Beggar on Horseback
26: The Whole Town's Talking
The Nutcracker
Poker Faces
27: La Boheme
Taxi! Taxi!
28: The Terror
29: Sonny Boy T
The Hottentot T
The Sap T
The Aviator T

Harry Houdini (1873-1926)
1919: The Master Mystery (serial)
The Grim Game
20: Terror Island
22: The Man From Beyond
23: Haldane of the Secret Service
?? Deep Sea Loot
Adventures of Houdini

Arthur Housman (1890-1937)
1917: Brown of Harvard
Red, White and Blue Blood
18: All Woman
Back to the Woods
19: Bondage of Barbara
The Gay Lord Quex
Toby's Bow
20: The Blooming Angel
The Point of View
21: The County Fair
The Fighter
Clay Dollars
The Way of a Maid
Is Life Worth Living?
Worlds Apart
Road of Ambition

22: The Snitching Hour
Man Wanted
Shadows of the Sea
Why Announce Your Marriage?
Prophets Paradise
Love's Masquerade
Destiny's Isle
25: A Man Must Live
Night Life of New York
26: The Bat
Early to Wed
The Midnight Kiss
27: Ankles Preferred
Love Makes 'em Wild
Rough House Rosie
Publicity Madness
The Spotlight
Sunrise
28: Partners in Crime
Fools for Luck
Happiness Ahead
The Singing Fool T
29: Broadway T
Song of Love T
Times Square PT
Queen of the Night Clubs T
Fast Company T
Side Street T
Sins of the Fathers

Alice Howell (1892-)
1922 Balloonatics
?? Mother-in-Law
Honor of the Sawdust
Neptune's Naughty Daughter
Alice of the Sawdust
Her Horseshoe Obligation

Reed Howes (d. 1964)
1923: High Speed Lee
25: Youth's Gamble
Bobbed Hair
The Snob Buster
The Cyclone Cavalier
26: The Gentle Cyclone
Wings of the Storm
Racing Romance
Kentucky Handicap
The Self Starter
Night Owl
High Flyer
26: The Dangerous Dude
The Danger Quest
Moran of the Mounted
27: The Lost Limited
Rough House Rosie
The Royal American
The Racing Fool
The Scorcher
Romantic Rogue
28: Fashion Madness
Ladies' Night in a Turkish Bath
Hellship Bronson
A Million for Love
The Sky Ranger
Sawdust Paradise SSE
29: Stolen Kisses PT
Come Across PT
The Singing Fool T

Jobyna Howland (1880-1936)
1918: Her Only Way
What Might Have Been
19: Way of a Woman
23: The Gold Diggers

Hart Hoxie
1917: Nan of Music Mountain
18: Blue Blazes Rawden
19: Johnny Get Your Gun
The Iron Test (serial)
Fight for Millions (serial)
Valley of the Giants
Told in the Hills

Jack Hoxie (1885-1965)
1917: Nan of Music Mountain
19: Lightning Bryce (serial)
Valley of the Giants
Thunderbolt Jack
Riders of the Law
Gallopin' Through
20: Forbidden Trails
Man in the Raw
21: Dead or Alive
Man from Nowhere
Cyclone Bliss
22: Barbed Wire
Two-Fisted Jefferson
The Desert's Crucible
The Crow's Nest
23: Don Quickshot of the Rio Grande

23: The Double-O
Men in the Raw
Where is this West?
Red Warning
24: Galloping Ace
The Western Wallop
Daring Chances
Ridgeway of Montana
Fighting Fury
The Man from Wyoming
The Back Trail
Phantom Horseman
25: White Outlaw
Sign of the Cactus
Roaring Adventure
Ridin' Thunder
The Open Trail
Two-Fisted Jones
Hidden Loot
Don Daredevil
Bustin' Through
26: The Demon
The Border Sheriff
Looking for Trouble
The Fighting Peacemaker
Red Hot Leather
Wild Horse Stampede
A 6 Shootin' Romance
The Last Frontier
27: The Western Whirlwind
Rambling Rangers
Men of Daring
Grinning Guns
The Fighting Three
Rough and Ready
Heroes of the Wild (serial)
29: Forbidden Trail

Arthur Hoyt
1916: The Lash
Little Partner
17: Man Who Took a Chance
The Show-Down
Broadway Arizona
Bringing Home Father
Polly Ann
20: Trumpet Island
Slave of Vanity
21: In the Heart of a Fool
Don't Neglect Your Wife
Four Horsemen of the Apocalypse
22: Top of New York
22: Is Matrimony a Failure?
Love is an Awful Thing
23: White Flower
Stranger's Banquet
Souls for Sale
Love Piker
26: Dead Line
28: Just Married
My Man PT
29: Wheel of Life T
Protection SSE
Stolen Kisses PT

Louise Huff
1916: Seventeen
Great Expectation
17: The Varmint
Tom Sawyer
Bunker Bean
The Crook of Dreams
Jack and Jill
Freckles
What Money Can't Buy
18: Wild Youth
The Ghost House
Spirit of '17
19: Oh, You Women
Sea Waif
Little Intruder
Heart of Gold
T'Other Dear Charmer
20: What Women Want
21: Disraeli
Dangerous Paradise
22: The Seventh Day

Gareth Hughes (1894-1965)
1919: Eyes of Youth
Mrs. Wiggs of the Cabbage Patch
Red Viper
And the Children Pay
Ginger
Woman Under Oath
20: The Chorus Girl's Romance
Broken Hearts
Woman in his House
21: Sentimental Tommy
The Hunch
Whirlwind of Youth
Little Eva Ascends
Garments of Truth
The Lure of Youth

21: Life's Darn Funny
22: Penrod
Don't Write Letters
Forget-Me-Not
I Can Explain
Stay Home
23: Kick In
The Christian
Enemies of Women
Penrod and Sam
The Spanish Dancer
25: Midnight Girl
26: Men of the Night
27: The Auctioneer
Eyes of the Totem
Broadway After Midnight
In the First Degree
Heroes in Blue
28: Old Age Handicap
Better Days
Top Sergeant Mulligan
Sky Rider
Comrades
29: Silent Sentinel
Mister Antonio
Broken-Hearted
31: Scareheads T

Lloyd Hughes (1897-1960)
1918: Impossible Susan
19: The Haunted Bedroom
Turn in the Road
The Virtuous Thief
The Heart of Humanity
The Indestructible Wife
Satan, Jr.
18: Out of the Night
20: Homespun Folks
Dangerous Hours
The False Road
Below the Surface
21: Beau Revel
Love Never Dies
Mother O'Mine
22: Hail the Woman
Tess of the Storm Country
23: Scars of Jealousy
Her Reputation
Are You A Failure?
24: The Sea Hawk
Declassee
25: The Lost World
Sally
25: The Mysterious Island
26: Ladies at Play
Pals First
Irene
Ella Cinders
Forever After
Valencia
High Steppers
27: No Place to Go
The Stolen Bride
An Affair of the Follies
American Beauty
Too Many Crooks
28: Heart to Heart
Three Ring Marriage
Sailors' Wives
29: Where East is East
Acquitted
Mysterious Island PT

Gladys Hulette
1909: Hiawatha
14: Dolly of the Dailies
(serial)
The Stuff Dreams are
Made Of
17: Pots-And-Pans Peggy
The Candy Girl
The Streets of Illusion
The Last of the Carnabys
Miss Nobody
A Crooked Romance
The Cigarette Girl
Her New York
18: Over the Hill
Mrs. Slacker
For Sale
Annexing Bill
Waifs
20: High Speed
The Silent Barrier
Tomorrow
Young Mrs. Winthrop
21: Tol'able David
22: How Women Love
As a Man Lives
Secrets of Paris
23: Enemies of Women
24: Hoodman Blind
The Iron Horse
The Brass Bowl
26: Unknown Treasures
Then Came the Woman

26: The Warning Signal
The Skyrocket
27: A Bowery Cinderella
28: Faithless Lover
Making the Varsity
Life's Crossroads

Henry Hull (1890-)
1917: The Volunteer
22: One Exciting Night
24: The Man Who Came Back
For Woman's Favor

Glenn Hunter (1896-1945)
1921: The Case of Becky
22: Smilin' Through
The Cradle Buster
The Country Flapper
23: Second Fiddle
Youthful Cheaters
Puritan Passions
The Scarecrow
24: West of the Water Tower
Grit
Merton of the Movies
25: The Little Giant
His Buddy's Wife
26: The Pinch Hitter
Romance of a Million Dollars
The Broadway Boob

Madeline Hurlock
1924: His New Mama
The First 100 Years
Luck of the Foolish
25: From Rags to Britches
26: A Sea Dog's Tale
27: The Flirty Four-Flushers

Brandon Hurst (1866-1947)
1915: Via Wireless
20: Dr. Jekyll and Mr. Hyde
A Dark Lantern
23: The World's Applause
Hunchback of Notre Dame
26: The Shamrock Handicap
27: Seventh Heaven
High School Hero
Love
28: Interference T
The News Parade
The Man Who Laughs
28: The First Kiss
29: Wolf of Wall Street T
Voice of the Storm
Her Private Life T

Paul Hurst (1889-1953)
1917: A Champion of the Law
21: Behind the Mask
22: The Crow's Nest
Heart of a Texan
Table Top Ranch
24: Passing of Wolf MacLean
The Courageous Coward
25: The Rattler
The Fighting Cub
Gold Hunters
Haunted Ranch
26: Midnight Message
27: Buttons
Valley of the Giants
Red Raiders
28: The Cossacks
Tide of the Empire
29: California Mail
The Lawless Legion
Rainbow
Sailors' Holiday T
30: Lucky Larkin T
Racketeer T

Charles Hutchinson
1917: The Mystic Hour
The Golden God
Hidden Aces
18: The Hawk
19: The Great Gamble (serial)
20: The Whirlwind (serial)
21: Double Adventure (serial-dual)
Hurricane Hutch (serial)
22: Go-Get-'em Hutch (serial)
Speed (serial)
24: Ten After Ten
The Radio Flyer
The Fatal Plunge
The Law Demands
Fangs of the Wolf
The Surging Seas
Hutch of the U. S. A.
25: On Probation
Wolves of Kulture (serial)
27: Pirates of the Sky
The Trunk Mystery

??	Turned Up	
	Poison	

Leila Hyams (1905-)

1926:	Summer Bachelor	
	Kick-Off	
27:	White Pants Willie	
	The Brute	
	The Bush Leaguer	
	One Round Hogan	
	The Wizard	
28:	Branded Sombrero	
	Crimson City	
	Honor Bound	
	Land of the Silver Fox	
	Our Dancing Daughters	
	Foregoing Age	
29:	Spite Marriage	
	Alias Jimmy Valentine	PT
	Far Call	T
	Idle Rich	SSE
	Masquerade	T
	Wonder of Women	T
	The Thirteenth Chair	T

Peggy Hyland

1915:	Caste
	John Halifax-Gentleman
16:	The Chattel
	Official Chaperone
	Infidelity
	The Enemy
	Rose of the South
17:	Price of Silence
	Persuasive Peggy
	Sally Bishop
	Intrigue
18:	The Other Woman
	Debt of Honor
	Peg of the Pirates
	Other Men's Daughters
19:	Cowardice Court
	Rebellious Bride
	Marriages are Made
	Miss Adventure
	Bonnie Annie Laurie
	Girl with no Rights
	Caught in the Act
	Cheating Herself
20:	Faith
	Girl in Bohemia
	Merry-Go-Round
	Web of Chance
20:	Black Shadows
21:	Price of Silence
22:	Mr. Prim Passes By

Ralph Ince (1887-1937)

1911:	One Flag at Last
	Battle Hymn of the Republic
12:	The Lady and the Lake
	Lincoln's Gettysburg Address
	The Seventh Son
	The Serpents
13:	Regiment of Two
14:	He Danced Himself to Death
	413 (dir.)
	Uncle Bill (dir.)
15:	The Darkening Trail
	Shadow of the Past
19:	Virtuous Men
	Perfect Lover
20:	His Wife's Money
21:	Red Foam
	Justice
	Remorseless Love
	After Midnight
	A Man's Home
	Wet Gold
	The Highest Law
22:	A Wide Open Town
	Reckless Youth
	Channing of the Northwest
	The Referee
	Tropical Love
23:	Homeward Bound (dir.)
	Success
25:	Playing with Souls
26:	The Sea Wolf
	Hurricane
	Yellow Fingers
	Bigger than Barnum
	The Better Way
	Breed of the Sea
27:	Not for Publication
	Shanghaied
28:	Chicago After Midnight
	Wall Street
	Singapore Mutiny
	Danger Street
29:	The Dove

George Irving (1874-1961)

1924:	Wanderer of the Wasteland
25:	The American Father

25: Pigs
26: Three Bad Men
27: One Increasing Purpose
Fangs of Justice
Bronco Twister
Manpower
Drums of the Desert
Shanghai Bound
Two Flaming Youths
28: Erick the Great
Craig's Wife
Morgan of the Marines
Walking Back
Feel My Pulse
Partners in Crime
Napoleon and Josephine
Drag Net
Modern Mothers
Runaway Girls
Singapore Mutiny
Port of Missing Girls
Honor Bound
The Wright Idea
29: The Godless Girl PT
Dance of Life T
Thunderbolt T
Paris Bound T
Last Performance PT

Boyd Irwin (1880-1963)
1920: Eyes of the Eagle
Milestones
Lady in Love
A Gilded Dream
The Silken Sinner
21: Three Musketeers
Girl from God's Country
23: Ashes of Vengeance
Youth Triumphant

May Irwin (1862-)
1896: The Kiss from "Widow Jones"
1914: Mrs. Black is Back

Mary Ann Jackson (1923-)
?? Smith Family Comedies
When Greek Meets Greek
Our Gang Comedies

Peaches Jackson
1920: Rio Grande
Lahoma

20: The Prince Chap
When Dawn Came
21: Through the Back Door

Gardner James
1922: Sonny
The Headless Horseman
Fascination
26: The Passionate Quest
The Flaming Forest
27: Ladies at East
Eager Lips
28: Souls Aflame
Big Killing
Mating Call
Singapore Mutiny
29: Flying Feet SSE

Gladden James
1916: The Social Secretary
Mystery of the Double Cross
Hearts of Love
17: Scandal
Babbling Tongues
Runaway Romance
18: Heart of Wetona
19: Who's Your Brother?
20: The Midnight Bride
21: The Silver Lining
The Road to Ambition
Bucking the Tiger
His Brother's Keeper
22: Channing of the Northwest
The Faithless Sex
23: A Clouded Name
The Broken Violin
27: Temptations of a Shop Girl
28: The Look-Out Girl
Sweet Sixteen
The Adorable Cheat
29: The Peacock Fan
His Captive Woman

William "Bud" Jamison (1894-1943)
1915: A Night Out
The Tramp
By the Sea
27: Long Pants
His First Flame
Jake the Plumber

28: Heart Trouble
A Taxi Scandal
Buck Privates
The Chaser
?? 3 yrs. Lonesome Luke Series
L-Ko
Horse Sense
One Horse Town

Dorothy Janis (1910-)
1923: Fleetwing
28: Kit Carson
?? Humming Wires

Elsie Janis
1919: A Regular Girl
20: The Imp

Emil Jannings (1884-1950)
1914: Im Banne Der Leidenschaft
18: Eyes of the Mummy
20: Passion
Danton
Vendetta
Anne Boleyn
21: Deception
Loves of Pharaoh
All for a Woman
23: Othello
Peter the Great
24: NJU
25: The Last Laugh
Quo Vadis?
26: Faust
Vaudeville
Waxworks
DuBarry, Woman of Passion
Variety
27: Way of all Flesh (Oscar Award)
The Last Command
Tartuffe the Hypocrite
Husbands and Lovers
28: The Patriot
Street of Sin
29: Sins of the Fathers
The Betrayal
Three Wax Men
Fighting the White Slave Traffic
30: The Blue Angel T
31: Der Grosse Tenor T
32: The Tempest T
41: Ohm Kruger T
45: Wo Ist Her Belling T

Thomas Jefferson
1915: Sable Lorcha
The Fencing Master
Poor Gentleman
Beloved Liar
17: Hands Up
Paid to Love
18: Tarzan of the Apes
Romance of Tarzan
19: Lombardi Limited
Sis Hopkins
20: Splendid Hazard
White Youth
21: My Lady's Latch Key
Straight from Paris
The Spenders

DeWitt Jennings (1879-1937)
1915: At Bay
The Warrens of Virginia
16: Sporting Blood
18: The Hillcrest Mystery
20: Deep Purple
21: Nineteen and Phyllis
The Greater Claim
Three Sevens
The Invisible Power
Beating the Game
There are no Villains
From the Ground Up
Poverty of Riches
22: At Bay
Ladyfingers
The Right that Failed
The Face Between
Sherlock Brown
Flesh and Blood
Mixed Faces
23: Circus Days
Within the Law
Out of Luck
Blinky
24: Hit and Run
Gaiety Girl
Name the Man
26: Passionate Quest
27: The Fire Brigade

27: Two Arabian Knights
McFadden's Flats
The Great Mail Robbery
Home Made
The Unbroken Purple
28: Night Flyer
The Crash
Air Mail Pilot
Marry the Girl
The Wrecking Boss
Red Hot Speed
29: Seven Footprints to Satan SSE

Eulalie Jensen
1914: A Song of the Ghetto
16: Salvation Joan
The Tarantula
Strength of the Weak
17: Mary Jane's Pa
Tangled Lives
18: Wild Primrose
19: A Tempermental Wife
The Captain's Captain
The Girl Problem
Beating the Odds
20: Man and His Woman
The House of the Tolling Bell
Respectable by Proxy
The Whisper Market
In the Shadow of the Dome
21: The Passion Flower
The Iron Trail
22: Rags to Riches
When Husbands Deceive
Heroes and Husbands
23: Hunchback of Notre Dame
Sunshine Trail
Woman with Four Faces
24: Wine of Youth
25: Thundering Herd
27: Uncle Tom's Cabin
28: Freckles
Baggage Smashers
Little Shepherd of Kingdom Come
She Goes to War
Mother Machree
29: Strong Boy SSE

George Jessel (1898-)
1926: Private Izzy Murphy
27: Sailor Izzy Murphy
Ginsberg the Great
Comedy monologue
(At Peace with the World)
The Jazz Singer
28: The Ghetto
George Washington Cohen
29: Lucky Boy PT
Love, Live and Laugh T

Arthur Johnson (1876-1916)
1908: The Adventures of Dolly
The Taming of the Shrew
The Valet's Wife
The Test of Friendship
The Helping Hand
Balked at the Altar
09: The Song of the Shirt
Pippa Passes
Resurrection
The Gibson Goddess
A Drunkard's Reformation
The Way of a Man
The Girls and Daddy
A Sound Sleeper
Two Memories
Pranks
Confidence
The Little Darling
At the Altar
The Politician's Love Story
The Converts
The Mills of the Gods
10: The Unchanging Sea
In Old California
A Rich Revenge
All On Account of the Milk
The Day After
A Romance of the Western Hills
The Faithful
11: Her Two Sons
Her Awakening
12: Amateur Iceman
14: Beloved Adventurer

Edith Johnson (1895-)
1916: Behind the Lines
17: The Scarlet Car
For Love and Gold
Giant Powder
The Scarlet Crystal

17: The Franc Piece
In the Talons of the Eagle
Love and Honor (serial)
Steelheart (serial)
18: A Fight for Millions (serial)
19: Man of Might (serial)
Smashing Barriers (serial)
The Man of Fight (serial)
Fighting Fate (serial)
20: The Silent Avenger (serial)
21: Where Men are Men (serial)
Wolves of the North (ser.)
22: When Danger Smiles (ser.)
23: Steel Trail (serial)
Playing it Wild (serial)
24: The Fast Express (serial)

Martin Johnson Productions (1884-1937)
1908-12:
Jack London's Adventures in the South Seas
12: Cannibals of the South Seas
Captured by Cannibals
Borderland of Civilization
East of Suez
Martin Johnson's Voyage
23: Trailing African Wild Animals
Head Hunters of the South Seas
24-28: Simba
Camera Trails in Africa

Noble Johnson
1917: Red Ace (serial)
18: The Bull's Eye (serial)
19: Midnight Man (serial)
20: Under Crimson Skies
The Adorable Savage
Girl He Left Behind
The Leopard Woman
21: Four Horsemen of the Apocalypse
Serenade
The Wallop
23: Burning Words
Drums of Fate
Courtship of Miles Standish
Cameo Kirby
Ten Commandments
24: Adventures of Robinson Crusoe
27: Red Clay
Vanity
Topsy and Eva
28: Something Always Happens
The Black Ace
Yellow Contraband
The Yellow Cameo (serial)
Manhattan Knights
29: Redskin
Four Feathers SSE
Black Waters T

Julanne Johnston (1906-)
1917: Youth
19: Better Times
20: Sitting on the World
Seeing it Through
Miss Hobbs
24: Thief of Bagdad
26: Dangerous Virtue
Aloma of the South Seas
Dame Chance
Twinkletoes
27: Good Time Charley
Her Wild Oat
Venus of Venice
Captain Fearless
Garrangole
Pride's Fall
The Vision
28: The Whip Woman
Name the Woman
Black Ace
Oh Kay!
Olympic Hero
Prisoners
29: The Younger Generation PT
Synthetic Sin
Strictly Modern
Smiling Irish Eyes T
General Crack T
City of Temptation
30: Way of all Men T
Golden Dawn T

Justine Johnstone
1920: Nothing But Lies
21: Blackbirds
Plaything of Broadway
Sheltered Daughters
A Heart to Let
Moonlight and Honeysuckle

Rita Jolivet (1894-)

1914: Fata Morgana
15: Cuore Edarte
La Mano Di Fatma
The Unafraid
L'onore Di Morire
Monna Vanna
Zavni
16: An International Marriage
17: Quello Che Videro I Mici Occhi
18: Lest We Forget
One Law for Both
21: Theodora
22: The Bride's Confession
23: Messalina

Buck Jones (1889-1942)

1918: True Blue
Rainbow Trail
Riders of the Purple Sage
Western Blood
19: Speed Maniac
20: Last Straw
Just Pals
Straight from the Shoulder
Firebrand Trevision
Forbidden Trails
21: Square Shooter
Big Punch
Trail of Two Moons
One Man Trail
To a Finish
Bar Nothin'
Riding Speed
Get Your Man
Sunset Sprague
22: Rough Shod
The Fast Mail
Trooper O'Neill
West of Chicago
The Bells of San Juan
Boss of Camp 3
Western Speed
Riding with Death
Pardon My Nerve
23: The Footlight Ranger
Snowdrift
11th Hour
Hell's Hole
Skid Proof
Second Hand Love
Big Dan
23: Cupid's Fireman
24: Not a Drum was Heard
Vagabond Trail
Circus Cowboy
Western Luck
Against All Odds
Desert Outlaw
Winner Take All
25: Riders of the Purple Sage
The Man Who Played Square
Arizona Romeo
Gold and the Girl
Trail Rider
Hearts and Spurs
Timber Wolf
Durand of the Badlands
Lazybones
The Desert's Price
The Rainbow Trail
26: Fighting Buckaroo
A Man Four Square
The Flying Horseman
The Gentle Cyclone
Black Paradise
The Cowboy and the Countess
30 Below Zero
27: Desert Valley
War Horse
Good as Gold
Hills of Peril
The Whispering Sage
Chain Lightning
Blood will Tell
Black Jack
The Big Hop
28: The Branded Sombrero

Johnny Jones

1917: The Barrier
18: Shuttle
Walls of Jericho
the Edgar Series
19: Shepherd of the Hills
Salomy Jane

Leatrice Joy (1897-)

1917: A Girl's Folly
19: For Better, for Worse
A Man Hunter
20: Down Home
Just a Wife
A Dollar Bid

20: The Invisible Divorce
Smiling all the Way
21: Ladies Must Live
The Right Way
Bunty Pulls the Strings
Ace of Hearts
A Tale of Two Worlds
Saturday Night
Poverty to Riches
22: Manslaughter
Bachelor Daddy
Minnie
23: Java Head
10 Commandments
The Man Who Saw Tomorrow
You Can't Fool Your Wife
The Silent Partner
24: Triumph
The Dressmaker from Paris
The Marriage Cheat
25: The Wedding Song
26: Clinging Vine
For Alimony Only
Eve's Leaves
Made for Love
27: Vanity
Nobody's Widow
Angel of Broadway
28: The Blue Danube
A Man-Made Woman
Tropic Madness
Show People (a cameo)
29: A Most Immoral Lady
Strong Boy
The Bellamy Trial T
28: Of Human Hearts T
39: First Love T
40: The Old Swimmin' Hole T
51: The Love Nest T

Alice Joyce (1890-1955)
1910: The Engineer's Sweetheart
12: A Bell of Penance
13: The Shadow
Nina of the Theatre (serial)
An American Princess
An Unseen Terror
14: The Cabaret Dancer
A Celebrated Case
Mystery of the Sleeping Death
14: The Brand
The Vampire Trail
School for Scandal
Riddle of the Green Umbrella
17: Within the Law
Womanhood
18: A Woman Between Friends
Captain Abe's Niece
The Alabaster Box
The Fettered Woman
To the Highest Bidder
18: The Song of the Soul
The Business of Life
Triumph of the Weak
Find the Woman
19: The Cambric Mask
The Lion and the Mouse
The Captain's Captain
Everybody's Girl
Spark Divine
Third Degree
The Winchester Woman
20: The Sporting Duchess
The Desperate Heritage
Dollars and the Woman
The Prey
Vice of Fools
Slaves of Pride
Vengeance of Durand
21: Her Lord and Master
Cousin Kate
The Inner Chamber
The Scarab Ring
23: The Green Goddess
24: Passionate Adventurer
25: Stella Dallas
Little French Girl
Headlines
26: Beau Geste
Dancing Mothers
So's Your Old Man
Ace of Cads
Mannequin
27: Sorrell and Son
28: The Noose
13 Washington Square
29: The Squall
Song o' my Heart
The Green Goddess
30: He Knew Women
Midnight Mystery

Francis Joyner
1916: Less Than the Dust
18: Daybreak
The Brass Check
20: The Copperhead
21: The Kentuckians

Joyzelle
1926: Dance Madness
28: Out of the Past
Moran of the Marines
Souvenir
Bride of the Nile
Black Watch
29: Close Harmony T

Rupert Julian (1889-)
1914: The Merchant of Venice
15: The Dumb Girl of Portici
16: The Bugler of Algiers
17: A Kentucky Cinderella
23: Merry-Go-Round (dir.)

Armand Kaliz (1892-1941)
1919: A Tempermental Wife
26: Belle of Broadway
The Temptress
27: Say it with Diamonds
Fast and Furious
Stolen Bride
Temptations of a Shop Girl
28: Love Mart
That's My Daddy
Wife's Relations
The Virgin Queen
A Woman's Way
The Devil's Cage
Lingerie
29: Noah's Ark PT
Twin Beds T
Gold Diggers of Broadway T
Marriage Playground

Gail Kane (1892-)
1917: The Serpent's Tooth
Souls in Pawn
The Woman in Black
The Unafraid
For the Family Name
The Spectre of Suspicion
18: The Bride's Silence
18: Southern Pride
A Game of Wits
When Men Betray
19: Love's Law
20: The Daredevil
Someone Must Pay
Empty Arms
21: A Good Woman
Idle Hands
Wise Husbands
23: White Sister
27: Convoy

Boris Karloff (1887-1969)
1916: Dumb Girl of Portici
19: His Majesty, the American
The Prince and Betty
20: Deadlier Sex
Courage of Marge O'Doone
Last of the Mohicans
21: Without Benefit of Clergy
Cheated Hearts
Hope Diamond Mystery (serial)
22: Cave Girl
Man from Downing Street
The Infidel
The Altar Stairs
Omar the Tentmaker
23: A Woman Conquers
Prisoner
24: Dynamite Dan
25: Parisian Nights
Forbidden Cargo
Prairie Wife
Lady Robin Hood
Never the Twain Shall Meet
26: Greater Glory
Her Honor the Governor
Bells
Nickelhopper (unbilled)
Eagle of the Sea
Old Ironsides
Flames
Golden Web
Flaming Fury
Man in the Saddle
27: Tarzan and the Golden Lion
Let it Rain
Meddlin' Stranger
Phantom Buster
Soft Cushions

27: Two Arabian Knights
28: Love Mart
Burning the Wind
Vultures of the Sea (serial)
29: King of the Congo (serial)
The Fatal Warning (serial)
Yellowback
Behind that Curtain T
Little Wild Girl
Devil's Chaplain
Phantoms of the North
Two Sisters
Unholy Night T

Roscoe Karns (1893-1970)

1919: Poor Relations
20: The Life of the Party
The Family Honor
21: The Man Tamer
22: Too Much Married
Her Own Money
Afraid to Fight
The Trouper
Conquering the Woman
24: Bluff
25: Headlines
27: Ritzy
Win that Girl
Ten Modern Commandments
Wings
28: Eagles of the Fleet
Something Always Happens
Desert Bride
Beggars of Life PT
Moran of the Marines
Jazz Mad
Warming Up
Beau Sabreur
Object-Matrimony
Flying Ensign
29: Shopworn Angel PT
This Thing Called Love T

Raymond Keane

1926: Midnight Sun
April Fool
27: Lone Eagle
Magic Garden
28: Marriage of Tomorrow
Patience
Tomorrow
In a Persian Market
Marriage by Contract

Buster Keaton (1896-1966)

1917: The Butcher Boy
Rough House
His Wedding Night
Fatty at Coney Island
Oh, Doctor!
Out West
A Reckless Romeo
18: The Bell Boy
Goodnight Nurse
Moonshine
The Cook
19: A Desert Hero
The Hayseed
A Country Hero
The Garage
20: Round Up
The Saphead
One Week
Convict 13
The Scarecrow
Neighbors
21: High Sign
Haunted House
Hard Luck
The Goat
Electric House
The Playhouse
The Boat
Paleface
22: Cops
My Wife's Relations
The Blacksmith
The Frozen North
Electric House (2nd and complete version)
Daydreams
Balloonatics
23: The Three Ages
Our Hospitality
Love Nest
24: Sherlock Junior
The Navigator
25: Go West
Seven Chances
26: Battling Butler
The General
27: College
Steamboat Bill Jr.
28: The Cameraman
29: Spite Marriage

Cornelius Keefe (1902-)

1927: Poor Nut
Hook and Ladder No. 9
A Moment of Temptation
Three's a Crowd
A Light in the Window
28: You Can't Beat the Law
Hearts of Men
Adorable Cheat
Man from Headquarters
Satan and the Woman
29: Thunder God
Circumstantial Evidence
Devil's Chaplain
Thanksgiving Day
30: Brothers T
The Cohens and the Kellys in Atlantic City PT

Zeena Keefe (1896-)

1916: La Boheme
Hero of Submarine D-2
Perils of One Girl Reporter (serial)
17: Enlighten Thy Daughter
One Hour
18: Shame
19: The Challenge Accepted
Oh Boy!
The Woman that God Sent
20: Out of the Snow
Piccadilly Jim
His Wife's Money
Marooned Hearts
21: After Midnight
Red Foam
22: Broken Silence
Prejudice
When Love is Young
23: None So Blind
The Broken Violin

Frank Keenan (1868-1929)

1915: The Coward
16: Honor Thy Name
18: Bells
Loaded Dice
Ruler of the Road
More Trouble
19: Gates of Brass
World Aflame
The Silver Girl
Master Man
19: Todd of the Times
The Midnight Stage
20: Brothers Divided
Dollar for Dollar
The False Code
Smouldering Embers
22: The Thorobred
Night Stage
The Defender
Hearts Aflame
23: Lorna Doone
Scars of Jealously
Brass
25: Dixie Handicap
26: Gilded Butterfly

Donald Keith (1905-)

1925: The Plastic Age
27: Special Delivery
Whirlwind of Youth
Cruise of the Hellion
Wild Geese
28: Bare Knees
Comrades
The Devil's Cage
Top Sergeant Mulligan
29: Just Off Broadway
The Lone Wolf's Daughter PT
Phantoms of the North
Should a Girl Marry? PT

Ian Keith (1899-1960)

1924: Christina of the Hungry Heart
Manhandled
Her Love Story
Love's Wilderness
The Queen's Secret
25: Enticement
My Son
Tower of Lies
26: Prince of Tempters
27: Loves of Sunya
What Every Girl Should Know
Convoy
A Man's Past
Two Arabian Knights
28: Look-Out Girl
Street of Illusion
29: Divine Lady SSE
Prisoners PT

29: Light Fingers PT
30: The Great Divide T

Annette Kellerman (1887-)
1914: Neptune's Daughter
16: A Daughter of the Gods
Isle of Love
The Art of Diving (documentary)
18: Queen of the Sea
20: What Women Love
24: Venus of the South Sea

Paul Kelly (1899-1956)
1908: A Good Little Devil
14: Buddy's First Call
Buddy's Downfall
the "Buddy" Series
Jarr Family Series
Star Spangled Banner
17: Knights of the Square Table
18: Fit to Fight
19: Anne of Green Gables
21: Old Oaken Bucket
26: New Klondike

Fred Kelsey (1884-1961)
1914: Silent Sands
Arms and the Gringo
19: Light of Victory
20: Blackmail
21: Puppets of Fate
25: Paths to Paradise
28: Midnight Adventure
Ladies of the Mob
The Wright Idea
Harold Teen
Naughty Baby
Smiling Irish Eyes
The Donovan Affair
On Trial
The Tenderloin
29: The Faker
Last Warning PT

Mayme Kelso
1918: Old Wives for New
His Birthright
19: Men, Women and Money
Daughter of the Wolf
Peg o' my Heart
Don't Change your Husband
20: Jack Straw
The Week End
Simple Souls
The Hope
Never Get Married
Help Wanted: Male
The Furnace
21: Conrad in Quest of His Youth
The Lost Romance
Ducks and Drakes
The March Hare

Matty Kemp (1907-)
1928: Goodbye Kiss
Magnificent Flirt
29: Million Dollar Collar PT

Edgar Kennedy (1890-1948)
1914: Star Boarder
Twenty Minutes of Love
Caught in a Cabaret
The Knock-out
The Noise of Bombs
Getting Acquainted
15: The Village Scandal
A Game Old Knight
more Mack Sennett Comedies
The Great Vacuum Robbery
16: His Hereafter
His Bitter Pill
Madcap Ambrose
The Scoundrel's Tale
Bombs
Ambrose's Cup of Woe
17: Her Fame and Shame
Her Torpedoed Love
Oriental Love
The Lost Lady
The Toreador
26: My Old Dutch
27: Gay Old Bird
28: The Finishing Touch
The Family Group
Their Purple Moment
Limousine Love
The Fight Pest
Imagine My Embarrassment
Should Married Men Go Home?
All Parts
Seed 'em and Weep

28:	The Boy Friend	
	The Booster	
	Chasing Husbands	
	The Chinese Parrot	
	Two Tars	
	Leave 'em Laughing	
29:	Trent's Last Case	
	Liberty	S&PT
	Dad's Day	S&PT
	A Perfect Day	S&PT
	Bacon Grabbers	S&PT
	Angora Love	S&PT

Madge Kennedy (1892-)

1917:	Baby Mine	
	Nearly Married	
18:	The Kingdom of Youth	
	The Danger Game	
	Our Little Wife	
	The Fair Pretender	
	Service Star	
	Friend Husband	
	Venus Model	
	Wild Primrose	
19:	Leave it to Susan	
	Day Dreams	
	Daughter of Mine	
	Perfect Lady	
	Through the Wrong Door	
	Strictly Confidential	
20:	The Blooming Angel	
	Trimmed in Red	
	The Truth	
	Dollars & Sense	
21:	Girl with the Jazz Heart	
	The Highest Bidder	
	Oh Mary, Be Careful!	
	Help Yourself	
23:	Purple Highway	
24:	Three Miles Out	
25:	Bad Company	
	Primrose Path	
26:	Oh, Baby!	

Merna Kennedy (1908-1944)

1928:	The Circus	
29:	Broadway	T
	Barnum was Right	T
	Skinner Steps Out	T
30:	Embarrassing Moments	T

Tom Kennedy (1885-1965)

1916:	Village Blacksmith	
16:	Hearts and Sparks	
	Ambrose's Rapid Rise	
17:	Nick-of-Time Baby	
20:	Kismet	
21:	Roaring Lions on Parade	
	Skirts	
22:	Serenade	
	Our Leading Citizens	
	If you Believe it, It's So	
	Back Home and Broke	
	The Flaming Hour	
	Afraid to Fight	
	The Flirt	
26:	We're in the Navy Now	
	Mantrap	
	Behind the Front	
	Sir Lumberjack	
	Money Talks	
27:	Fireman, Save My Child!	
	Ham and Eggs at the Front	
28:	Hold 'em, Yale!	
	Tillie's Punctured Romance	
	Love Over Night	
	None but the Brave	
	The Cop	
	Wife Savers	
	Marked Money	
29:	The Cohens and the Kellys in Atlantic City	PT
	Glad Rag Doll	T
	Big News	T
	The Shannons of Broadway	T

Barbara Kent (1906-)

1927:	No Man's Law	
	Drop Kick	
	The Lone Eagle	
	Flesh and the Devil	
28:	That's My Daddy	
	Stop That Man!	
	Modern Mothers	
	Lonesome	PT
	Retribution	
29:	The Shakedown	PT
	Welcome Danger	
	Night Ride	
30:	Feet First	T

Charles Kent (1852-)

1910:	Uncle Tom's Cabin	
	Twelfth Night	
14:	The Old Flute Player	

15: Love's Way
On Her Wedding Night
Price for Folly
16: Tarantula
Rose of the South
Kennedy Square
The Supreme Temptation
Scarlet Runner
The Enemy
Whom the Gods Destroy
Daniel
Duplicity of Hargraves
17: Soldiers of Chance
18: White Lie
Dreams
19: Miss Dulcie from Dixie
Gamblers
20: Boy and Soul
Man and His Woman
Forbidden Valley

Crawford Kent (1881-1953)
1915: The Deep Purple
16: Dollars and the Woman
17: Broadway Jones
18: The Knife
The Trap
Kildare of the Storm
Ordeal of Rosetta
The Better Half
Song of Songs
The Danger Mark
Thais
19: Prince Cosmo
Good Gracious Annabelle
Career of Katherine Bush
Come Out of the Kitchen
Thou Shalt Not
20: Youthful Folly
Sinners
Other Men's Shoes
The Love Flower
21: The Plaything of Broadway
Shirley of the Circus
Silas Marner
Frozen Legion
23: Vanity Fair
27: Mother
The Missing Link
His Dog
Foreign Legion
See you in Jail
Pirates of the Sky
28: Show Folks
Blindfold
Man, Woman and Wife SSE
Show People SSE
Fallen Angels
Queen of the Chorus
Into No Man's Land
Forgotten Faces
Manhattan Knights
Wallflowers
Out With the Tide
29: The Charlatan T
Ace of Scotland Yard (ser.)
Seven Keys to Baldpate T
Wolf of Wall Street T
The Case of Mary Brown T
?? Mothers-In-Law

Larry Kent
1927: McFadden's Flats
Sea Tiger
Whirlwind of Youth
Women's Wares
Her Wild Oat
The Lovelorn
The Masked Menace (ser.)
28: Heart of a Follies Girl
Mad Hour
Hangman's House
The Head Man
The Haunted House
29: The Spirit of Youth
The Devil's Apple Tree
Midstream

Doris Kenyon (1897-)
1916: The Traveling Salesman
The Rack
The Ocean Waif
Strictly Business
17: The Hidden Hand (serial)
On Trial
The Great White Trail
18: Street of 7 Stars
19: Twilight
The Inn of the Blue Moon
Wild Honey
The Band Box
20: Burning Daylight
The Harvest Moon
Strictly Business
21: Get-Rich-Quick-Wallingford
Conquest of Canaan

22: Shadows of the Sea
The Ruling Passion
Sure-Fire Flint
23: You are Guilty
24: Born Rich
Monsieur Beaucaire
25: Thief in Paradise
26: The Blonde Saint
Mismates
Men of Steel
Ladies at Play
27: Valley of the Giants
28: Home Towners T
The Hawk's Nest
Interference T

J. Warren Kerrigan (1889-1947)
1910: The Hand of Uncle Sam
11: The Sheriff's Sister
12: The Stranger at Coyote
The Agitator
Calamity Anne's Inheritance
13: Her Big Story
Adventures of Jacques
In the Days of Trajan
For the Flag
The Wishing Seat
14: His Heart, His Hand and His Sword (serial)
Samson
15: The Adventures of Terrence O'Rourke
16: Landon's Secret Legacy
The Silent Battle
18: A Man's Man
Turn of a Card
One Dollar Bid
Burglar for a Night
19: A White Man's Chance
Prisoner of the Pines
End of the Game
3 X Gordon
The Drifters
Come Again Smith
The Best Man
20: Live Sparks
The Dream Cheater
The Green Flame
$30,000
The Joyous Liar
Number #99
The Lord Loves the Irish
21: The Coast of Six
House of Whispers
Coast of Opportunity
22: Night Life in Hollywood
23: The Covered Wagon
The Girl of the Golden West
The Man from Brodney's
24: Captain Blood
North of '36
Rory o' the Bogs
??: One Week End

Norman Kerry (1889-1956)
1916: Manhattan Madness
The Black Butterfly
17: Such a Little Princess
18: Amarilly of Clothesline Alley
The Dark Star
Rose of Paradise
Up the Road with Sally
Goodnight Paul
19: Soldiers of Fortune
Virtuous Sinners
20: Passion's Playground
Little Italy
A Splendid Hazard
21: Buried Treasure
Proxies
The Wild Goose
Get-Rich-Quick Wallingford
22: 3 Live Ghosts
Find the Woman
The Man from Home
Till We Meet Again
Brothers Under the Skin
Hunchback of Notre Dame
23: Is Money Everything?
Merry-Go-Round
24: Cytherea
Butterfly
25: Phantom of the Opera
The Spoilers
Fifth Avenue Model
Price of Pleasure
26: Mademoiselle Modiste
The Barrier
The Love Thief
Under Western Skies
27: The Claw
Annie Laurie
Unknown
Irresistible Lover

27: Body and Soul
28: Love Me and the World is Mine
Fallen Angels
Woman from Moscow
Foreign Legion
29: Man, Woman and Wife SSE
Trial Marriage
The Bondman
30: Ex-Flame T
31: Air Eagles T

Kathleen Key (1897-1954)
1922: Where is My Wandering Boy Tonight?
West of Chicago
Bells of San Juan
23: Beautiful and Damned
North of Hudson Bay
26: Ben Hur
27: Irish Hearts
28: Golf Widows

Joseph Kilgour (1864-1933)
1915: My Lady's Slipper
Thou Art the Man
16: The Writing on the Wall
17: The Easiest Way
The Divorcee
Runaway Romany
20: Hearts and Trumps
Love
The Leopard Woman
The Broken Gates
21: I am Guilty
At the End of the World
23: Woman with Four Faces
25: Percy
One Year to Live
26: Let's Get Married

Anita King (1880-)
1915: Snobs
18: The Girl Angle
19: Whatever the Cost
Mistaken Identity
One Against Many

Charles King (1898-1944)
1928: You Can't Beat the Law
Weary Winnie
Sisters of Eve
Phantom Fingers

Claude King (1879-1941)
1920: Idols of Clay
21: The Scarab Ring
23: Bella Donna
24: Behind that Curtain
25: Making of O'Malley
28: Red Hair
Night of Mystery
29: Black Watch
Strange Cargo T
Mysterious Dr. Fu Manchu

Emmett King
1919: In His Brother's Place
Please Get Married
The Fear Women
Reckoning Roads
20: Kismet
Billions
21: In the Heart of a Fool
Mistress of Shenstone
Lying Lips
Habit
O'Malley of the Mounted
24: Barbara Frietchie
28: Laugh, Clown, Laugh
On Trial
29: Noisy Neighbors PT
Shopworn Angel PT
When Dreams Come True

Molly King (1898-)
1916: The Summer Girl
17: Mystery of the Double Cross
Kick In (serial)
Seven Pearls (serial)
Blind Man's Luck
On-The-Square Girl
18: Human Clay
19: Suspense
20: Women Men Forget
21: Greater than Love
22: Suspicious Wives
Her Majesty

Florida Kingsley (1879-)
1917: The Turmoil
The Boy-Girl
The Iron Heart
18: Mrs. Slacker
19: Woman Under Oath
Sealed Hearts

19: Thou Shalt Not
Made in America
20: Love
Independence, B'Gosh!
Greater Than Fame
Dangerous Business
Annabel Lee

Muriel Kingston
1922: White Hell
Dawn of Revenge
23: Valley of Lost Souls
26: Subway Sadie
27: On Guard (serial)
Just Another Blonde
28: Masked Lover

Natalie Kingston
1924: Feet of Mud
25: His Marriage Wow
Remember When?
The Daredevil
Lucky Stars
26: The Silent Lover
Kid Boots
27: The Night of Love
Framed
Lost at the Front
The Harvester
Figures Don't Lie
Soldier Man
Long Pants
28: Tarzan the Mighty
Girl in Every Port
Port of Missing Girls
Street Angel
Painted Post
29: The River of Romance T
Tarzan, the Tiger SSE
(serial)
Pirate of Panama (serial)

Winifred Kingston (d. 1967)
1914: The Squaw Man
Where the Trail Divides
16: David Garrick
The Parson of Panamint
Davy Crockett
17: The Lifted Veil
The Scarlet Pimpernel
18: Light of the Western Stars
19: The Corsican Brothers
21: Beyond
22: Trail of the Axe
23: The Virginian

Kathleen Kirkham (1895-)
1918: Arizona
Tarzan of the Apes
19: Beloved Cheater
The Beauty Market
The Master of Men
He Comes Up Smiling
Upstairs and Down
The Third Kiss
20: Her Five Foot Highness
Dollar for Dollar
Parlor, Bedroom and Bath
When Damn Came
21: The Sky Pilot
Little 'fraid Lady
Nobody's Kid
Beau Revel
Pilgrims of the Night
22: A Homespun Vamp
The Innocent Cheat
Back to Yellow Jacket
One-Eighth Apache
Frivolous Wives
23: The Bolted Door

James Kirkwood (1883-1966)
1908: The Sioux
09: A Corner in Wheat
Comato the Sioux
The Mended Lute
The Message
The Gibson Goddess
At the Altar
Fools of Fate
Pippa Passes
12: Prince Charming
13: House of Discord
The Eagle's Mate
Behind the Scenes
14: Beating Back
The Mountain Rat
Home Sweet Home
Marriage of the Underworld
Rags
Men and Women (dir.)
Strongheart (dir.)
Ashes of the Past (dir.)
Soul of Honor (dir.)
15: The Foundling

16: Lost Bridegroom
17: The Struggle Everlasting
19: Back to God's Country
20: The Luck of the Irish
The Branding Iron
21: In the Heart of a Fool
The Scoffer
Love
Man-Woman Marriage
Bob Hampton of Placer
Great Impersonation (dual)
Sin Flood
22: The Man from Home
Pink Gods
Ebb Tide
Under Two Flags
23: You are Guilty
Human Wreckage
The Spoilers
Ponjola
The Eagle's Feather
24: Wandering Husbands
Another Man's Wife
25: Gerald Cranston's Lady
26: That Royale Girl
Lover's Island
Reckless Lady
The Wise Guy
27: Million Dollar Mystery
Butterflies in the Rain
28: Someone to Love
29: Hearts in Exile T
The Time, Place and Girl T
Black Waters T
30: The Spoilers T
The Devil's Holiday T
34: Hired Wife T
53: The Sun Shines Bright T
56: The Search for Bridey Murphy T
?? Eve's Daughter

Kithou (1904-)
1926: Mare Nostrum
La Puissance Du Pasaret
Parisette
L'Orpheline
Kithou

Lydia Knott (1873-)
1917: Crime and Punishment
Sudden Jim
18: His Mother's Boy
Home
19: The Clodhopper
The Pointing Finger
Heart of Youth
What Every Woman Learns
In Wrong
Should Women Tell
20: Blackmail
Dwelling Place of Light
Homespun Folks
Peaceful Valley
21: Lure of Youth
The Breaking Point
22: Turn to the Right
23: A Woman of Paris
24: Dynamite Smith
28: Two Lovers
Our Dancing Daughters
30: Guilty? T
Men Without Law T
The Conquering Horde T

Alice Knowland (1879-)
1919: Delicious Little Devil
Satan, Jr.
Rustling a Bride
20: Six Best Cellars
21: Parish Priest
All Souls' Eve
The Heart Line
Partners of the Tide

Fred Kohler (1889-1938)
1920: The Kentucky Colonel
A Thousand to One
21: Partners of the Tide
Cyclone Bliss
22: The Scrapper
Flame of Life
His Back Against the Wall
Yellow Men and Gold
Son of the Wolf
Three Who Paid
23: Trimmed
North of Hudson Bay
24: The Iron Horse
25: Thundering Herd
26: Old Ironsides
27: Blood Ship
Underworld
Shootin' Irons
Gay Defender

27: Open Range
City Gone Wild
The Loves of Carmen
Way of all Flesh
28: Showdown
Drag Net
Vanishing Pioneer
Chinatown Charlie
Forgotten Faces
The Spieler
Last Command
29: The Dummy
The Case of Lena Smith
Tide of the Empire PT
The Leatherneck PT
Sal of Singapore PT
Broadway Daddies
The Quitter
Stairs of Sand
Say it with Songs T
Thunderbolt T

Henry Kolker (1874-1947)
1919: Blackie's Redemption
Red Lantern
Her Purchase Price
20: Third Generation
Bright Skies
The Greatest Love
The Fighter
Bucking the Tiger
Man of Stone
Disraeli
23: Snow Bridge
The Leopardess
Purple Highway
I Will Repay
26: Hell's 400
Palace of Pleasure
27: Rough House Rosie
Silk Stockings
Kiss in a Taxi
28: Don't Marry
Red Hair
Pleasure Crazed
Charge of the Gauchos
29: The Valiant T

Leo Kolmar (1878-1946)
1920: Beautifully Trimmed
22: Orphans of the Storm
High Heels
Breaking Home Ties

22: The Secret Gift
29: The Kibitzer T

Tetsu Komai (1893-)
1928: Detectives
Moran of the Marines
Woman from Moscow
Chinatown Nights

Mary Kornman
1923: Hal Roach's "Our Gang Kids"

Theodore Kosloff (1882-1956)
1917: The Woman God Forgot
20: Something to Think About
Why Change Your Wife?
The Prince Chap
The City of Masks
21: Affairs of Anatol
A Fool's Paradise
Forbidden Fruit
22: Saturday Night
Green Temptation
The Dictator
To Have and to Hold
23: Adam's Rib
Law and the Lawless
Children of Jazz
The Lane that has no Turning
24: Feet of Clay
Triumph
25: The Golden Bed
Road to Yesterday
New Lives for Old
Beggar on Horseback
26: The Volga Boatman
27: King of Kings
Little Adventuress
28: Woman Wise
30: Madam Satan

Paul Kruger (1895-)
1927: First Auto
One Round Hogan
Non-Support
28: Fortune Hunter
29: Idle Rich T
The Rounders

Florence LaBadie (1893-1917)
1911: Enoch Arden

11: How She Triumphed
Blind Princess and the Poet
The Primal Call
12: Merchant of Venice
Lucile
Undine
Star of Bethlehem
13: Cymbeline
Snare of Fate
14: Million Dollar Mystery (serial)
15: The Country Girl

Frank Lackteen (1894-)

1924: The Fortieth Door (serial)
25: Sunken Silver (serial)
Pony Express
26: House without a Key (serial)
27: Warning
28: Prowlers of the Sea
Court Martial
The Tiger's Shadow
29: Hawk of the Hills (serial)

Ruby La Fayette (1844-)

19: In His Brother's Place
Toby's Bow
Big Bob
??: The Dragnet
Mother o' Mine

Roy Laidlaw

1918: His Robe of Honor
Honor's Cross
With Hoops of Steel
19: Back to God's Country
20: Live Sparks
The Weaker Sex
The Great Accident
21: The Cowpuncher

Alice Lake (1896-1967)

1912: Her Picture Idol
16: The Moonshiners
The Waiters' Ball
A Creampuff Romance (or His Alibi)
17: Her Mature Dance
The Late Lamented
His Wedding Night
Oh, Doctor!
Out West
18: The Bell Boy
Goodnight Nurse
Moonshine
The Cook
19: A Deserted Hero
Backstage
A Country Hero
The Garage
Red Lights
Matrimony
Chicago Sal
Should a Woman Tell?
20: Shore Acres
Body and Soul
The Misfit Wife
21: The Greater Claim
Uncharted Seas
Over the Wire
22: The Golden Gift
A Hole in the Wall
Kisses
Hate
I am the Law
More to be Pitied than Scorned
Environment
23: Spider and the Rose
Nobody's Bride
24: Fast Worker
Young Ideas
Dangerous Blonde
Excitement
26: Price of Success
Spider Webs
Broken Homes
27: Angel of Broadway
28: The Haunted House
Obey Your Husband
Air Circus
Watered Stock
Roarin' Fire
Runaway Girls
29: Untamed Justice
Twin Beds T
Circumstantial Evidence
Frozen Justice
30: Young Desire T
31: Wicked T
33: Skyway T
34: Wharf Angel T
Glamour T

Arthur Lake (1905-)

1917: Jack and the Beanstalk
24: When Love is Young
25: Skinner's Dress Suit
27: Cradle Snatchers
Irresistible Lover
28: Harold Teen
Count of Ten
Air Circus PT
Lilac Time SSE
Runaway Girls
29: On with the Show PT
Dance Hall T
Tanned Legs T

Barbara Lamarr (1897-1926)

1920: Harriet and the Piper
21: The Nut
Desperate Trails
Three Musketeers
Cinderella of the Hills
22: Arabian Love
Prisoner of Zenda
Trifling Women
Domestic Relations
Quincy Adams Sawyer
The Hero
23: Poor Men's Wives
Souls for Sale
Brass Bottle
St. Elmo
Strangers of the Night
The Eternal City
24: Thy Name is Woman
The Shooting of Dan McGrew
White Moth
Sandra
25: Heart of a Siren
White Monkey
26: The Girl from Montmartre

Cullen Landis (1895-)

1917: Who is Number One?
18: Beware of Blondes
19: Almost a Husband
The Outcasts of Poker Flat
Jinx
Girl from Outside
Where the West Begins
Upstairs
20: Going Some
Pinto
20: It's a Great Life
21: Bunty Pulls the Strings
Snow Blind
22: Watch your Step
Where is my Wandering Boy Tonight?
23: The Famous Mrs. Fair
Master of Men
The Fog
The Alibi
The Pioneer
The Midnight Alarm
24: Born Rich
The Fighting Coward (ser.)
25: The Midnight Flyer
Sweet Rosie O'Grady
26: The Dixie Flyer
Enemy of Men
My Old Dutch
Frenzied Flames
Then Came the Woman
Winning the Futurity
Perils of the Coast Guard
The Smoke Eaters
Davy Crockett at the Fall of the Alamo
Buffalo Bill on the U. P. Trail
Heroes of the Night
27: The Crimson Flash (serial)
The Fighting Fathers
We're All Gamblers
Broadway after Midnight
On to Reno
Finnigan's Ball
28: The Devil's Skipper
The Midnight Adventure
Out with the Tide
Say it with Flowers
Lights of New York T
Brown Mash
29: Little Wild Girl
30: Convict's Code T

Charles Lane (1899-)

1919: Wanted: A Husband
20: The Branded Woman
Dr. Jekyll and Mr. Hyde
The Restless Sex
Without Limit
The Great Adventure
Guilty of Love
Away Goes Prudence

22: Fascination
Broadway Rose
How Women Love
The Tents of Allah
23: Ruggles of Red Gap
Mrs. Black is Back
Man from Mexico
26: The Winning of Barbara Worth
27: The Music Master
Whirlwind of Youth
Barbed Wire
Service for Ladies
Married Alive
38: Sadie Thompson
29: The Canary Murder Case T
Saturday's Children PT

Lupino Lane (1892-1957)
1915: Nipper's Bank Holiday
Man in Possession
17: The Dummy
The Missing Link
18: Unexpected Treasure
22: The Broker
The Reporter
23: A Friendly Husband
25: The Fighting Dude
Isn't Life Wonderful?
27: Monty of the Mounted
28: Hello, Sailor
Sword Points
Pirates Beware
Be My King

Nora Lane
1927: Jesse James
Flying U Ranch
28: A Night of Mystery
Pioneer Scout
Texas Tornado
Kid Carson
The Gun Runner
The Cohens and the Kellys in Paris
29: Marquis Preferred
Sunset Pass
Lawless Legion
Masked Emotions SSE
30: One Hysterical Night T
Sally T

Harry Langdon (1884-1946)
1924: Picking Peaches
Smile Please
Shanghaied Lovers
Flickering Youth
The Cat's Meow
His New Mama
First 100 Years
Luck o' the Foolish
The Hansom Cabman
All Night Long
25: The Sea Squawk
Boobs in the Woods
His Marriage Wows
Plain Clothes
Remember When?
Horace Greeley Jr.
White Wing's Bride
Lucky Stars
There He Goes
26: Saturday Afternoon
Tramp, Tramp, Tramp
Strong Man
27: Fiddlesticks
Soldier Man
Ella Cinders
Long Pants
Three's a Crowd
28: The Chaser
Heart Trouble
29: Hotter than Hot
The Fighting Parson
Sky Boy
The Big Kick
Skirt Shy
33: The Hitch-Hiker
37: Wise Guys (dir.)
38: He Loved an Actress T
(Mad About Money)
40: There Goes My Heart (a cameo)

Lillian Langdon
1916: Diane of the Follies
Intolerance
19: Prudence on Broadway
A Regular Fellow
The Rebellious Bride
The Usurper
His Majesty, the American
20: The Hellion
Triflers

20: Water, Water, Everywhere
The Great Accident
Going Some
The Hope
Oh, Lady, Lady!
21: What's a Wife Worth?
The Highest Law - collaborated
24: The Price She Paid

Laura La Plante (1904-)
1921: The Old Swimmin' Hole
813
His Four Fathers
22: Perils of the Yukon (serial)
Wall Flower
23: Around the World in 18 Days (serial)
Dead Game
Shell Shocked
24: The Fast Worker
Butterfly
Young Ideas
Dangerous Blondes
Excitement
25: Skinner's Dress Suit
The Teaser
Dangerous Innocence
Smouldering Fires
Spring Reunion
26: The Midnight Sun
Poker Faces
Beware of Widows
Butterflies in the Rain
Her Big Night
The Beautiful Cheat
27: The Cat and the Canary
Love Thrill
Silk Stockings
28: Home James
Finders Keepers
Thanks for the Buggy Ride
29: Scandal
The Last Warning
Hold your Man
Show Boat PT
The Love Trap PT
30: King of Jazz T
31: The Sea Ghost T
Meet the Wife T
Too Many Women T
Lonely Wives T
32: Virtuous Wife T
32: Arizona T
33: Her Imaginary Lover T
Girl in Possession T
35: Man of the Moment T
36: God's Gift to Women T
46: Little Mister Jim T
57: Spring Reunion T

George Larkin (1889-)
1913: While Father Telephoned
14: The Trey of Hearts (serial)
18: Zongar
Hands Up! (serial)
Border Raiders
19: The Devil's Trail
The Tiger's Trail (serial)
Terror of the Range (serial)
Lurking Peril (serial)
Coming of the Law
The Unfortunate Sex
21: Terror Trail (serial)
Man Trackers
22: Barriers of Folly
Saved by Radio
Bulldog Courage
23: Way of the Transgressor
Her Reputation
Wolf Face (serial)
Flame of Passion
24: Yankee Madness
The Pell Street Mystery
25: The Right Man

Rod La Rocque (1896-1969)
1917: Efficiency Edgar's Courtship
18: A Perfect 36
Hidden Fires
The Kaiser Bride
The Venus Model
20: Easy to Get
Discarded Woman
Feet of Clay
The Garter Girl
21: Greater than Love
Paying the Piper
22: Suspicious Wives
Slim Shoulders
What's Wrong with Women?
For Your Daughter's Sake
A Woman's Woman
The Challenge

22: Notoriety
23: Jazzmania
Ten Commandments
The French Doll
24: Forbidden Paradise
Triumph
A Society Scandal
25: The Golden Bed
The Coming of Amos
Night Life of New York
26: The Cruise of the Jasper B
Braveheart
Brigadier General
Bachelor Brides
Gigolo
27: Resurrection
The Fighting Eagle
28: Hold 'em, Yale!
Stand and Deliver
Captain Swagger
The Love Pirate
Love Over Night
29: Man and the Moment PT
One Woman Idea SSE
Our Modern Maidens
This is Heaven PT
Delightful Rogue T
30: The Locked Door T
Beau Bandit T
One Romantic Night T
33: S. O. S. Iceberg T
36: Till We Meet Again T
The Previous Murder Mystery T
40: Beyond Tomorrow T
Dark Streets of Cairo T
41: Meet John Doe T

Francine Larrimore

1917: Somewhere in America
Royal Pauper
18: Resurrection
Devil's Darling

Fontaine LaRue

1917: The Lifted Veil
18: The Wildcat of Paris
19: Boots
The Woman Under Cover
20: The Sins of Rosanne
21: The Faith Healer
The Last Romance

Stan Laurel (1890-1965)

1917: Nuts in May
The Evolution of Fashion
18: Hoot Mon
Hickory Hiram
Whose Zoo
Huns and Hyphens
Just Rambling Along
No Place Like Jail
Bears and Bad Men
Frauds and Frenzies
Do You Love Your Wife?
Lucky Dog
It's Great to be Crazy
19: Mixed Nuts
Scars and Stripes
20: Wild Bill Hiccup
Rupert of Hee-Haw (or Colde Slaw)
21: The Rent Collector
22: When Knights Were Cold
The Egg
Weak End Party
Mud and Sand
The Pest
White Wings
23: The Handy Man
Noon Whistle
Under Two Jags
Pick and Shovel
Collars and Cuffs
Kill or Cure
Gas and Air
Oranges and Lemons
Short Orders
Man about Town
Roughest Africa
Frozen Hearts
The Whole Truth
Save the Ship!
The Soilers
Scorching Sands
Mother's Joy
24: The Smithy
Postage Due
Zeb Vs. Paprika
Brothers under the Chin
Near Dublin
Wide Open Spaces
Short Kilts
Mandarin Mix-Up
Detained

24: Monsieur Don't Care
West of Hot Dog
25: Somewhere in Wrong
Twins
Pie-Eyed
Snow Hawk
Navy Blue Days
The Sleuth
Dr. Pyckle and Mr. Pride
Half a Man
Cowboys Cry for it
26: Atta Boy!
On the Front Page
Get 'em Young
The Merry Widower (dir.)
45 Minutes from Hollywood

(with Oliver Hardy:)
27: Slipping Wives
Should Tall Men Marry?
Duck Soup
Eve's Love Letters
Love 'em and Weep
Why Girls Love Sailors
With Love and Hisses
Sailors Beware
Do Detectives Think?
Flying Elephants
Putting the Pants on Philip
Sugar Daddies
Call the Cuckoo
The Second 100 Years
Hats Off
The Battle of the Century
28: Leave 'em Laughing
The Finishing Touch
From Soup to Nuts
You're Darn Tootin'
Their Purple Moment
Should Married Men Go Home S-PT
Early to Bed
Two Tars
Habeas Corpus
We Faw Down
4th of July
29: Liberty ST
Wrong Again ST
That's My Wife
Big Business
Double Whoopee
Berth Marks ST
29: Men o' War ST
A Perfect Day ST
They Go Boom ST
Bacon Grabbers ST
Angora Love
Unaccustomed as we Are T

Lucille LaVerne (1869-1945)
1917: Polly of the Circus
22: Orphans of the Storm
23: Zaza
Among the Missing
White Rose
24: America
Her Darker Self
25: Sun Up
28: The Last Moment
30: Abraham Lincoln T

Dakota Lawrence (1902-)
??: When Big Dan Rides
The Hidden Pit
Danger Patrol
Across the Line
Where Peril Lurks
Code of the North
Fate's Chessboard
Heart of Big Dan

Florence Lawrence (1888-1938)
1908: Ingomar the Barbarian
Romeo and Juliet
The Valet's Wife
The Helping Hand
The Test of Friendship
An Awful Moment
09: The Mended Lute
The Song of the Shirt
The Slave
Resurrection
The Taming of the Shrew
The Ingrate
A Woman's Way
A Smoked Husband
(a Jones film)
The Girls and Daddy
Confidence
At the Altar
The Barbarian
10: The Angel of the Studio
11: A Good Turn
Flo's Discipline

11: Her Two Sons
Look Up
12: In Swift Waters
14: A Singular Cynic
20: The Enfoldment
Jane the Stranger
21: The Barbarian
The Dispatch Bearer
Betrayed by a Handprint
The Girl and the Outlaw
23: The Call of the Wild
The Zulu's Heart
24: Behind the Scenes
The Heart of Oyama
Concealing a Burglar
Romance of a Jewess
The Planter's Wife
The Vaquero's Vow

Rex Lease (1901-1966)
1927: Outlaw Dog
Moulders of Men
Not for Publication
Clancy's Kosher Wedding
Cancelled Debts
College Hero
28: Red Riders of Canada
Phantom of the Turf
Broadway Daddies
Law of the Range
Riders of the Dark
Queen of the Chorus
Speed Classic
Making the Varsity
The Candy Kid
29: The Younger Generation
Stolen Love
When Dreams Come True
Girls Who Dare
Two Sisters

Ivan Lebedeff (1895-1953)
1922: King Frederick
The Lucky Death
Soul of an Artist
600, 000 Francs Per Month
The Charming Prince
25: Burned Fingers
26: Sorrows of Satan
27: The Loves of Sunya
Angel of Broadway
The Forbidden Woman
28: Let 'er Go, Gallagher
Walking Back
29: Sin Town
The Veiled Woman
One Woman Idea SSE
Street Girl T
They Had to See Paris T

Gretchen Lederer (1891-1955)
1917: The House of Gloom
Greater Law
Little Orphan
Silent Lady
Kentucky Cinderella
18: Green Magic
Red, Red Heart
The Kaiser-Beast of Berlin
Wife or Country
The Model's Confession
19: The Rescue
The Pointing Finger
The Cruise of the Jolly Roger

Otto Lederer (1886-)
1917: Mr. Aladdin of Broadway
Captain of the Gray Horse Troop
By Right of Possession
Lady Sheriff
Red Prince
The Flaming Omen
Woman in the Web
Diplomat of Wolfville
18: Dead Shot Baker
Follow Me
19: Cupid Forecloses
Over the Garden Wall
20: The Dragon's Net (serial)
21: The Avenging Arrow (ser.)
22: White Eagle (serial)
Hungry Hearts
Forget-Me-Not
23: Your Friend and Mine
27: Trunk Mystery (The Shamrock and the Rose)
The Jazz Singer
Sailor Izzy Murphy
28: A Bit of Heaven
29: One Stolen Night
Man from Headquarters
The Cohens and the Kellys in Atlantic City PT
Prediction

29: Smiling Irish Eyes T

Dixie Lee
1919: The Law of Nature
Where Bonds are Loosed
20: Dad's Girl

Frances Lee (1908-)
1928: Sweeties
Bugs, My Dear
Hold 'er, Cowboy
Slick Slickers
Mr. Romeo
Chicken A La King
Stop Kidding
Skating Home
Picture My Astonishment
Believe It Or Not
Nifty Numbers
29: The Carnation Kid SSE
Confessions of a Chorus Girl
Little Snob PT
Divorce Made Easy T

Frankie Lee (1912-)
1916: Woman Who Dared
17: Field of Honor
Durand of the Bad Lands
18: Vive La France
19: Sheriff's Son
Daddy-Long-Legs
The Miracle Man
Ching
21: The Swamp
The Other Woman
The Killer
God's Crucible
A Christmas Carol
His Mother's People
22: Sin of Martha Queed

Gwen Lee (1904-)
1925: Pretty Ladies
26: There You Are
27: Orchids and Ermine
Women Love Diamonds
Twelve Miles Out
Heaven on Earth
Adam and Evil
After Midnight
Her Wild Oat
28: Sharpshooters
28: Diamond Handcuffs
Laugh, Clown, Laugh
The Actress
Baby Cyclone
Lady of Chance
Thief in the Dark
The Ghetto
Show Girl
Angel Face
29: Duke Steps Out PT
Lucky Boy PT
Man and the Moment T
Fast Company T
Hollywood Revue of 1929 T
Untamed T
Road Show T

Jane and Katherine Lee
(Jane 1912-1957)
1915: Soul of Broadway (J. alone)
The Master Hand (K. alone)
The Clemenceau Case
16: Circus Imps
Dixie Madcaps
Dicksville Terrors
A Pair of Aces
Double Trouble
Kids and Skids
The Spider and the Fly
A Daughter of the Gods
The Patsy
Two Little Imps
Love and Hate
18: Troublemakers
American Buds
We Should Worry
Doing Their Bit
19: Smiles
Swat the Spy
Tell it to the Marines

Lila Lee (1902-)
1918: Such a Little Pirate
The Cruise of the Make-Believe
19: A Daughter of the Wolf
Male and Female
Hawthorne of the U. S. A.
Heart of Youth
Cock o' the Walk
Rustling a Bride
Rose of the River

19: Puppy Love
The Secret Garden
20: The Prince Chap
Midsummer Madness
Love or Money
Terror Island
The Soul of Youth
21: The Charm School
The Easy Road
After the Show
If Women Only Knew
Dollar a Year Man
22: One Glorious Day
Is Matrimony a Failure?
The Dictator
Blood and Sand
Ebb Tide
Back Home and Broke
The Road to Arcady
Rent Free
The Ghost Breaker
23: The Ne'er-Do-Well
Homeward Bound
24: Those Who Dance
The New Klondike
Another Man's Wife
Wandering Husbands
25: The Unholy Three
Midnight Girl
26: Broken Hearts
27: One Increasing Purpose
Million Dollar Mystery
28: You Can't Beat the Law
Adorable Cheat
United States Smith
Top Sergeant Mulligan
Just Married
Black Butterflies
Thundergod
A Bit of Heaven
29: Hurdy Gurdy Man
The Man in Hobbles
The Little Wildcat T
Queen of the Night Clubs T
Black Pearl T
Honky Tonk T
Flight T
Sacred Flame T
The Argyle Case T
Drag T
Dark Streets T
Love, Live and Laugh T

Anna Lehr
1918: For Freedom
Men
My Own United States
Laughing Bill Hyde
19: The Jungle Trail
Upside Down
Home Wanted
Thunderbolts of Fate
The Open Door
20: Chains of Evidence
The Veiled Marriage
A Child for Sale
21: The Truth about Husbands
Cheated Hearts
22: The Cradle
Mr. Barnes of New York

Fritz Leiber (1882-1949)
1917: Cleopatra
20: If I Were King
The Song of the Soul
21: The Queen of Sheba

Frank Leigh
1918: Fedora
19: Lord and Lady Algy
20: Dangerous Days
Cup of Fury
The Mother of His Children
An Hour Before Dawn
Common Property
21: Bob Hampton of Placer
Light in the Clearing
22: Golden Dreams
24: Hill Billy
28: A Night of Mystery
The Devil's Skipper
Prowlers of the Sea
Drums of Araby
Love in the Desert
29: Below the Deadline

Lillian Leighton
1911: The Two Orphans
14: Cinderella
16: Other People's Money
17: Joan the Woman
Witchcraft
Freckles
The Devil's Stone
18: A Lady's Name
19: Secret Service

19: Louisiana
Poor Relations
20: All of a Sudden Peggy
The Jack Knife Man
30th Piece of Silver
House of Toys
21: Girl from God's Country
The Beloved Villain
Peck's Bad Boy
Crazy to Marry
Lost Romance
22: Is Matrimony a Failure?
23: The Grub Stake
Crinoline and Romance
Only 38
24: The Bedroom Window
Abraham Lincoln
25: Joanna
28: Blow by Blow
Fair and Muddy

Marion Leonard (1881-1956)
1908: At the Crossroads of Life
The Test of Friendship
The Awful Moment
09: Comato the Sioux
The Hindu Dagger
A Burglar's Mistake
Two Memories
Pranks
The Gibson Goddess
A Lonely Villa
Shadows of Doubt
09: The Cord of Life
The Golden Louis
At the Altar
Fools of Fate
The Converts
10: In Old California
The Day After
13: Carmen
15: The Dragon's Claw

Gladys Leslie (1899-)
1917: The Vicar of Wakefield
18: The Wooing of Princess Pat
His Own People
Little Miss No Account
The Soap Girl
Wild Primrose
19: Stitch in Time
Too Many Crooks
19: Miss Dulcie of Dixie
Fortune's Child
The Beloved Impostor
Nymph of the Woods
The Mating
The Girl Woman
20: Golden Shower
Mystery of Gray Towers
Midnight Bride
A Child for Sale
21: Straight is the Way
Jim the Penman
Elsie in New York
22: God's Country and the Law
Sisters
Timothy's Quest
The Snitching Hour
The Girl from Porcupine
23: The Darling of the Rich
If Winter Comes
Haldane of The Secret Service

Kate Lester
1916: A Coney Island Princess
17: Adventures of Carol
18: Little Women
The Unbeliever
20: Cup of Fury
Earthbound
Scratch My Back
Simple Souls
21: Dangerous Curve Ahead
Don't Neglect Your Wife
Made in Heaven
22: Remembrance
A Tailor-Made Man
The Hunted Man
The Glorious Fool
23: Hunchback of Notre Dame
Gimme
The 4th Musketeer

George Lewis
1925: His People
The Old Soak
13 Washington Square
28: We Americans
Give and Take SSE
The Collegiates
The Bookworm Hero
Honeymoon Flats
Four Flushers

29: College Love T
King of the Campus PT

Ida Lewis

1917: A Man's Man
Whither Thou Goest?
18: Maid o' the Storm
The Heart of Rachel
19: Dangerous Waters
20: Mary's Ankle
Paris Green
Peaceful Valley

28: The Way of the Strong
The Hawk's Nest
Docks of New York
Beau Sabreur
Out With the Tide
Speed Classic
29: Linda SSE
One Stolen Night PT
The Bridge of San Luis Rey T
Madame X T
Black Watch T

Mitchell Lewis (1880-1956)

1914: Million Dollar Mystery (serial)
17: The Barrier
Bar Sinister
18: The Sign Invisible
9/10th of the Law
19: Code of the Yukon
Children of Banishment
Jacques of the Silver North
Fool's Gold
Life's Greatest Problem
Sale for Democracy
20: Burning Daylight
Smoke Bellew
Faith of the Strong
A Daughter of the Snows
The Silent Barrier
The Last of his People
King Spruce
The Mutiny of the Elsinore
21: At the End of the World
22: Salome
The Siren Call
On the High Seas
The Bonded Woman
23: The Woman Conquers
Her Accidental Husband
The Spoilers
24: The Red Lily
25: Frivolous Sal
Tracked in the Snow Country
26: Eagle of the Sea
The Sea Wolf
Ben Hur
Tell it to the Marines
27: Hard Boiled Haggerty
Back to God's Country
28: Miss Nobody
The Tenderloin

Ralph Lewis (d. 1937)

1912: The Faith Healer
13: Gangsters of New York
14: The Avenging Conscience
Home Sweet Home
Her Awakening
The Floor Above
Big James' Heart
15: The Birth of a Nation
The Mountain Girl
The Little Catamount
Nectorine
Jordan is a Hard Road
16: Intolerance
The Flying Torpedo
Gretchen the Greenhorn
17: A Tale of Two Cities
Jack and the Beanstalk
18: Cheating the Public
Talk of the Town
19: The Hoodlum
Eyes of Youth
The Dub
The Valley of the Giants
20: Prisoners of Love
Sowing the Wind
Man-Woman-Marriage
When the Clouds Roll By
21: Salvage
The Sin Flood
A Private Scandal
The Conquering Pawn
22: The $5 Baby
In the Name of the Law
23: The Third Alarm
Westbound Limited
Vengeance of the Deep
The Fog
Desire
24: Dante's Inferno

26: Lady from Hell
The Million Dollar Handicap
The Silent Power
Bigger than Barnum's
Shadow of the Law
The False Alarm
The Block Signal
27: The Sunset Derby
Outcast Souls
Held by the Law
28: Casey Jones
Crooks Can't Win
Shield of Honor
29: The Girl in the Glass Cage PT

Sheldon Lewis (1869-1958)
1915: Exploits of Elaine (serial)
The Coward
Braga's Double
An Affair of 3 Nations
16: The Iron Claw (serial)
The Clutching Hand (ser.)
The King's Game
Charity
17: Warfare of the Flesh
The Hidden Hand
18: Wolves of Kultur (serial)
19: The Bishop's Emeralds
20: Dr. Jekyll and Mr. Hyde
Impossible Catherine
The Silent Barrier
22: Orphans of the Storm
23: The Darling of New York
24: Enemy Sex
The Dangerous Flirt
Honor Among Men
25: Top of the World
New Lives for Old
Super-Speed
Fighting the Flames
Silent Sanderson
The Sporting Chance
A Desperate Moment
26: Bride of the Storm
Señor Daredevil
Moran of the Mounted
Eagle of the Sea
Exclusive Rights
The Overland Stage
The Gilded Highway
The Sky Pirate
The Red Kimono
26: The Self Starter
Lightning Hutch (serial)
Vanishing Millions (serial)
27: The Cruise of the Hellion
Driven from Home
Burning Gold
The Life of an Actress
Lady Bird
Hazardous Valleys
28: Code of the Scarlet
Turn Back the Hours
The Sky Rider
Marlie the Killer
The River Woman
Top Sergeant Mulligan
The Chorus Kid
29: Untamed Justice
7 Footprints to Satan SSE
Black Magic SSE
Little Wild Girl
30: Terry of the Times (serial)

Vera Lewis (d. 1958)
1916: Intolerance
17: Lost in Transit
19: As the Sun Went Down
A Still Small Voice
Lombardi Ltd.
20: The Blooming Angel
Nurse Marjorie
The Devil's Riddle
21: She Couldn't Help It
22: Nancy from Nowhere
The Glorious Fool
23: Peg o' my Heart
25: Eve's Secret
26: King of the Pack
Up in Mabel's Room
The Gilded Butterfly
Ella Cinders
The Passionate Quest
27: The Broken Gate
What Happened to Father
Thumbs Down
Satan and the Woman
Resurrection
28: Something Always Happens
Ramona
Home Towners
29: The Iron Mask PT

Walter P. Lewis (1871-)
1919: A Woman Under Oath

19: Man Who Might Have Been
20: The Star Rover
The Daughter of Devil Dan
21: The Ghost in the Garret
The Black Sheep
23: Torchy
28: Leif the Lucky
Little Shepherd of Kingdom Come
Two Lovers

E. K. Lincoln

1918: For Freedom of the World
Lafayette, We Come
Stars of Glory
19: Fighting Through
Desert Gold
Virtuous Men
20: The Inner Voice
What is Love
21: The Woman God Changed
22: The Light in the Dark
Women Men Marry
23: Woman in Chains

Elmo Lincoln (1889-1952)

1915: Birth of a Nation
16: Intolerance
Children of the Feud
17: Betsy's Burglar
18: Treasure Island
The Kaiser-The Beast of Berlin
Tarzan of the Apes
The Romance of Tarzan (serial)
Desperation
19: Elmo the Mighty (serial)
20: Elmo the Fearless (serial)
The Return of Tarzan (serial)
The Flaming Disc (dual) (serial)
Under Crimson Skies
Man of Courage
21: Adventures of Tarzan (serial)
22: The Light in the Dark
Quincy Adams Sawyer
23: Rupert of Hentzau
45: The Man Who Walked Alone T
47: Rolling Home T
49: Tarzan's Magic Fountain T
51: Hollywood Story T

Max Linder (1882-1925)

1907: The Collegian's First Outing
The Legend of Polichinelle
Death of a Toreador
The Contrabanders
Poison
Whim of the Apaches
An Unexpected Meeting
The Collegian's First Cigar
Before and After the Wedding
A Graduation Celebration
An Evening at the Cinema
The Duel of Monsieur Myope
The Skater's Debut
Max Takes a Bath
Max in a Museum
Max and His Mother-in-Law's False Teeth
Max's Hanging
Max - Aeronaut
Max's New Landlord
Max - Photographer
10: Max in a Dilemma
Max is Absent-Minded
Max's Astigmatism
11: How Max Went Around the World
Max--Victim of Quinquina
Max in the Alps
Max Takes Up Sports
Max on Skis
Max - Toreador
Max, Jocky for Love
Max's Neighborly Neighbor
Max Embarrassed
Max is Forced to Work
An Escape of Gas
Max in the Movies
An American Marriage
Max Hypnotized
Marriage is a Puzzle
Max Searches for a Sweetheart
All's Well That Ends Well
I Want a Baby
The Cross Country Original
Max is Distraught

11: Max is Almost Married
Max Wears Tight Shoes
Max is Stuck Up
Max - Pedicurist
Max Teaches the Tango (or Too Much Mustard)
Max in the Arms of His Family (semi-documentary)
12: Max Virtuoso
Max Gets the Reward
Max's Vacation
Max's Marriage
Max's Honeymoon
Never Kiss the Maid
Max Makes a Conquest
Max is Jealous
Max Does Not Speak English
Max Makes Music
Max's Double
Max - Magician
Max's Duel
Boxing Match on Skates
Max and the Statue
Who Killed Max?
Max Creates A Fashion
12-14: Max and Jane Go to the Theatre
Max Plays in Drama
A Paris Original
Painter for Love
One Exciting Night
Entente Cordiale
Max Does Not Like Cats
My Dog Dick
The Little Roman
Max Attends an Inauguration
Marriage by Telephone
Flying by Hydroplane
The Billet Doux
Max's Hat
Max is Decorated
Max and Jane Make a Dessert
14: The Second of August (semi-doc.)
15: Max and the Clutching Hand
Max Between Fires
17: Max Comes Across
Max Wants a Divorce
Max and His Taxi
Max, the Heartbreaker (not filmed)
17: Max Plays Detective (not filmed)
19: The Little Cafe
20: Seven Years Bad Luck
Be My Wife
A Rustic Idyll
Max is Forced To Work
Max, the Headwaiter
22: The Three-Must-Get-Theres
23: 7 Years Bad Luck
24: Au Secours! (Help!)
25: King of the Circus

Ivan Linow
1921: Cappy Ricks
23: Enemies of Women
Fury
28: The Red Dance
The River PT
29: Black Magic SSE

Ann Little (1891-)
1914: The Black Box (serial)
The House of Bondage
For the Wearing of the Green
Paths of Genius
15: Damon and Pythias
16: That Girl of Burke's
17: Nan of Music Mountain
18: Rimrock Jones
The House of Silence
The Firefly of France
The Source
The Man from Funeral Range
The Silent Master
The Squaw Man
Believe Me, Xantippe
Less Than Kin
The Bear Trap
19: Alias Mike Moran
The Roaring Road
Told in the Hills
Lighting Bryce (serial)
Square Deal Sanderson
Service Stripes
20: Excuse My Dust
Life
Cradle of Courage
21: The Blue Fox (serial)
22: Nan of the North (serial)

22: Chain Lightning
Silent Shelby
23: The Eagle's Talons (serial)
25: Secret Service Saunders (serial)

Lucien Littlefield (1895-1960)
1915: Joan of Arc
The Miser
16: Blacklist
The Gutter Magdalene
17: The Golden Fetter
The Squaw Man's Son
The Hostage
19: Everywoman
20: Double Speed
Sick-Abed
The Fourteenth Man
The Round Up
The Furnace
Feet of Clay
Eyes of the Heart
Jack Straw
21: All Soul's Eve
Too Much Speed
The Hell Diggers
The Affairs of Anatol
Her First Elopement
The Little Clown
22: To Have and to Hold
Rent Free
Across the Continent
Our Leading Citizens
23: The French Doll
Joan of Arc
The Miser
In the Palace of the King
24: The Torrent
26: The Bachelor Bride
Small Bachelor
The Sheik
Charley's Aunt
Broadway Eyes
Twinkletoes
17: Uncle Tom's Cabin
My Best Girl
Taxi! Taxi!
Cat and the Canary
Cheating Cheaters
28: Heart to Heart
Making the Grade
Do Your Duty
Mothers Knows Best T
28: The Head Man
A Ship Comes In
Harold Teen
Blonde for a Night
Texas Steer
29: Drag
Girl in the Glass Cage PT
Great Divide PT
Saturday's Children T
This is Heaven PT
Clear the Decks
Wall Street
Big Ambition
Out for Game
Getting a Raise
The Potters at Home
The Potters Done in Oil
Pa Gets a Vacation
Big Money
The Man in Hobbles

Margaret Livingston (1902-)
1918: Within the Cup
19: All Wrong
The Busher
16: Billie's Fortune
When Johnny Comes Marching Home
Social Buccaneer
Leather Pushers
20: What's Your Husband Doing?
Water, Water, Everywhere!
Brute Master
21: Lying Lips
Colorado Pluck
House of a 1000 Candles
Chorus Lady
Wandering Husbands
23: Divorce
24: Alimony
25: Havoc
The Charlatan Mystery (serial)
After Marriage
26: The First Year
Hell's 300
A Trip to Chinatown
The Blue Eagle
Womanpower
The Yankee Señor
27: The Secret Studio
Slaves of Beauty
Married Alive

27: Lightning
American Beauty
Streets of Shanghai
Girl from Gay Paree
Sunrise
28: The Mad Hour
A Woman's Way
The Wheel of Chance
The Scarlet Dove
Say it with Sables
The Way of the Strong
Through the Breakers
No Questions Asked
His Private Life
Apache
Beware of Bachelors
29: The Last Warning PT
The Bellamy Trial PT
Office Scandal PT
The Charlatan PT
Innocents of Paris T
Tonight at 12 T
Acquitted T
7 Keys to Baldpate T

Doris Lloyd (1900-1968)
1927: The Auctioneer
The Bronco Twister
Is Zat So?
Lonesome Ladies
Two Girls Wanted
28: Come to My House
Trail of '98
29: The Drake Case T
Disraeli T
The Careless Age T

Harold Lloyd (1893-1971)
1912: Naked Yaqui (a bit)
14: Samson
Willie Work Comedies
(none released)
15: Once Every Ten Minutes
Spit Ball Sadie
Soaking the Clothes
Pressing His Suit
Terribly Stuck Up
A Mixup for Mazie
Some Baby
Fresh from the Farm
Giving Them Fits
Bughouse Bell Hops
Tinkering with Trouble
15: Great While It Lasted
Ragtime Snapshots
A Fozzle at a Tea Party
Ruses, Rhymes, Roughnecks
Peculiar Patients Pranks
Social Gangster
Phunphilms
16: Luke Leans to the Literary
Luke Lugs Luggage
Luke Rolls in Luxury
Luke the Candy Cut-Up
Luke Foils the Villain
Luke and the Rural Roughnecks
Luke Pipes the Pippins
Lonesome Luke, Circus King
Skylight Sleep
Luke's Double
Them Was the Happy Days
Trouble Enough
Luke and the Bomb Throwers
Reckless Wrestlers
Luke's Late Lunches
Ice
Luke Laughs Last
An Awful Romance
Luke's Fatal Flivver
Luke's Society Mixup
Luke's Wishful Waiting
Luke Rides Roughshod
Unfriendly Fruit
Luke, Crystal Gazer
A Matrimonial Mixup
Luke's Lost Lamb
Braver than the Bravest
Luke Does the Midway
Caught in a Jam
Luke Joins the Navy
Busting the Beanery
Luke and the Mermaids
Jailed
Luke's Speedy Club Life
Luke and the Bang-Tails
Luke, the Chauffeur
Luke's Preparedness Preparation
Luke, Gladiator
Luke, Patient Provider
Luke's Newsie Knockout
Luke's Movie Muddle

16: Luke's Fireworks Fizzle
Luke Locates the Loot
Luke's Shattered Sleep
17: Luke's Last Liberty
Luke's Busy Days
Drama's Dreadful Deal
Luke's Trolley Trouble
Lonesome Luke, Lawyer
Luke Wins Ye Ladye Faire
Lonesome Luke's Lively Rifle
Lonesome Luke in Tin Pan Alley
Lonesome Luke's Lively Life
Lonesome Luke's Honey-moon
Lonesome Luke, Plumber
Stop! Luke! Listen!
Lonesome Luke, Messenger
Lonesome Luke, Mechanic
Lonesome Luke's Wild Women
Over the Fence (Lloyd's first comedy using his new character with glasses alternated with the Luke comedies until Lloyd retired the Luke character at the end of the year.)
Lonesome Luke Loses Patients
Pinched
By the Sad Sea Waves
Bliss
Lonesome Luke from London to Laramie
Rainbow Island
Love, Laughs and Lather
The Flirt
Clubs are Trump
All Aboard
We Never Sleep
Bashful
The Tip
Step Lively
18: The Big Idea
The Lamb
Hit Him Again
Beat It
A Gasoline Wedding
Look Pleasant Please
18: Here Come the Girls
Let's Go!
On the Jump
Follow the Crowd
Pipe the Whiskers
It's a Wild Life
Hey There!
Kicked Out
The Non-Stop Kid
2 Gun-Gussie
Fireman, Save My Child!
The City Slicker
Sic'em Towser!
Somewhere in Turkey
Are Crooks Dishonest?
An Ozark Romance
Kicking the Germ Out of Germany
That's Him
Too Scrambled
Swing Your Partner
Why Pick on Me?
Nothing but Trouble
Hear 'em Rave
Take a Chance
She Loves Me Not
Bride and Groom
Bees in the Bonnet
19: From Italy's Shore
Captain Kidd's Kiddies
Just Neighbors
On the Fire
I'm on My Way
The Dutiful Dub
Wanted - $5000
Going! Going! Going!
Ask Father
Look Out Below
Next Aisle Over
A Sammy in Siberia
Just Dropped In
Crack Your Heels
Ring Up the Curtain
Young Mr. Jazz
Si, Señor
Before Breakfast
The Marathon
Back to the Woods
Pistols for Breakfast
Swat the Crook
Off the Trolley
Spring Fever
Billy Blazes, Esq.

19: At the Stage Door
Never Touched Me
A Jazzed Honeymoon
Count Your Change
Chop Suey & Co.
Heap Big Chief
Don't Shove!
Be My Wife
The Rajah
He Leads, Others Follow
Soft Money
Count the Votes
Pay Your Dues
Bumping into Broadway
From Hand to Mouth
His Royal Slyness
20: Haunted Spooks
An Eastern Westerner
High and Dizzy
Get Out and Get Under
Number, Please
21: Now or Never
Among Those Present
I Do
Never Weaken
A Tailor-Made Man
22: Grandma's Boy
Dr. Jack
23: Safety Last
Why Worry?
24: Girl Shy
Hot Water
25: The Freshman
26: For Heaven's Sake
27: The Kid Brother
28: Speedy
29: Welcome Danger T
30: Feet First T
32: Movie Crazy T
36: The Milky Way T
37: Hot Water T
38: Professor, Beware T

Harold Lockwood (1887-1919)
1908: Harbor Island
13: A Mansion of Mercy
Child of the Sea
14: The Unwelcome Mrs. Hatch
Wildflower
Tess of the Storm Country
Hearts Adrift
15: The Country Chairman
Shopgirls
16: The Secret Wire
The River of Romance
Big Tremaine
Life's Blind Alley
17: The Haunted Pajamas
The Promise
18: Broadway Bill
Under the Handicap
Paradise Green
The Square Deceiver
The Avenging Trail
The Landloper
Lend Me Your Name
19: Yankee Doodle in Berlin
Pals First
Shadows of Suspicion
The Great Romance
Man of Honor

Jeanette Loff (1906-)
1926: Young April
27: Uncle Tom's Cabin
My Friend from India
The Collegians
28: Hold 'em, Yale!
Black Aces
Man-Made Woman
Annapolis SSE
Love Over Night
Valley Beyond the Law
29: The Sophomore T
30: Racketeer T
32: 45 Calibre War

Jacqueline Logan (1900-)
1921: White and Unmarried
The Perfect Crime
22: Burning Sands
A Blind Bargain
A Tailor Made Man
Ebb Tide
23: Mr. Billings Spends his Dime
60¢ an Hour
Salomy Jane
The Light that Failed
Man Must Live
Java Head
Molly-O
24: Manhattan
The House of Youth
Playing with Souls
Gay and Devilish

24: Peacock Feathers
The Dawn of Tomorrow
Flaming Barriers
North of '36
Dynamite Smith
25: Thank You
A Man Must Live
Wages for Wives
26: The Outsider
Footloose Widows
Out of the Storm
Tony Runs Wild
27: The Wise Wife
The Blood Ship
King of Kings
One Hour of Love
For Ladies Only
28: Power
The Cop
The Leopard Lady
Midnight Madness
Stocks and Blondes
Nothing to Wear
The Lookout Girl
Broadway Daddies
Charge of the Gauchos
Ships of the Night
The River Woman SSE
29: Stark Mad T
Bachelor Girl PT
The Faker
King of the Congo (serial)
General Crack T
Show of Shows T

Carole Lombard (1909-1942)
1925: Hearts and Spurs
28: The Perfect Crime PT
Me Gangster SSE
Power
Divine Sinner
Ned McCobb's Daughter SSE
Show Folks PT
29: Dynamite T
?? Mack Sennett Comedies

Babe London (1901-)
1928: Tillie's Punctured Romance
Export Eloper
Too Many Burglars
When the Clouds Roll By
A Day's Pleasure
The Rent Diggers
28: A Parcel Post Husband
The Laundry
Merely Mary Ann
Sauce and Senoritas
When Romance Rides
Golden Dreams
Second Childhood
A Hula Honeymoon
Winter Has Came
Roll Along
30: Be Yourself T

Tom London (1882-1963)
1927: Long Loop on the Pecos
28: Yellow Contraband
The Yellow Cameo
Mysterious Rider
Eyes of the Underworld
29: The Border Wildcat
Lawless Legion
Harvest of Hate
Untamed Justice

Walter Long (1884-1952)
1915: Birth of a Nation
Nectorine
Out of Bondage
Jordan is a Hard Road
16: Intolerance
Unprotected
Years of the Locust
17: The Evil Eye
Joan the Woman
The Golden Fetter
The Woman God Forgot
Hashimura Togo
18: Queen of the Sea
19: The Poppy Girl's Husband
Chasing Rainbows
Scarlet Days
Desert Gold
20: What Women Love
Excuse My Dust
Held in Trust
21: The Sheik
The Fire Cat
White and Unmarried
22: Moran of the Lady Letty
Across the Continent
South of Suva
The Dictator
Blood and Sand
Shadows

22: To Have and to Hold
Omar the Tentmaker
23: Beautiful and Damned
Broken Wing
Kick In
My American Wife
The Last Hour
Little Church Around the Corner
Quicksands
Isle of Lost Ships
The Huntress
25: Shock Punch
Grass
26: Steel Preferred
Eve's Leaves
27: White Pants Willie
Back to God's Country
28: Gang War
Me Gangster
Thundergod
Forbidden Grass
29: Black Watch
Black Cargoes of the South Seas

Margaret Loomis
1919: Everywoman
Told in the Hills
Why Smith Left Home
20: What Happened to Jones?
Sins of St. Anthony
Always Audacious
Conrad in Quest of his Youth
Three Gold Coins

Lillian Lorraine (1892-1955)
1918: Playing the Game

Louise Lorraine (1901-)
1915: Should a Wife Forgive?
Neal of the Navy (serial)
20: Elmo the Fearless (serial)
The Flaming Disc (serial)
The American Gentleman
21: Adventures of Tarzan (serial)
The Fire Eater
22: Up in the Air About Mary
With Stanley in Africa (serial)
The Radio King (serial)
22: Headin' West (serial)
23: The Oregon Trail (serial)
25: Great Circus Mystery (serial)
26: The Silent Flyer (serial)
The Dead Line
27: Winners of the Wilderness
Rookies
Frontiersman
Legionnaires of Paris
Hard Fists
28: Chinatown Charlie
The Wright Idea
Baby Mine
Circus Rookies
Shadows of Night
29: A Final Reckoning (serial)
The Diamond Master (ser.)
30: The Lightning Express T (serial)

Frank Losee (d. 1937)
1915: Old Homestead
Helene of the North
The Eternal City
The Masqueraders
16: The Spider
Ashes of Embers
Hulda from Holland
17: The Valentine Girl
Here Comes the Bride
the Bab's Stories
18: La Tosca
Uncle Tom's Cabin
Song of Songs
19: Paid in Full
Good Gracious, Annabelle
Marie Limited
His Parisian Wife
The Firing Line
20: Kismet
The Right to Love
Civilian Clothes
Last of the Mohicans
The Fear Market
Sinners
His House in Order
Half an Hour
21: Dangerous Love
Disraeli
Broadway & Home
Don't Leave Your Husband
22: Orphans of the Storm

22: Wild Honey
The Seventh Day
Missing Million
False Fronts
As a Man Lives
The Man She Brought Back
Dangerous Trip
24: The Man Who Came Back
Unguarded Women

Willard Louis (1886-1926)
1919: Letty
20: Jubilo
Going Some
Unpainted Woman
The Scarlet Strain
The Great Accident
Madame X
A Slave of Vanity
21: The Highest Bidder
Roads of Destiny
22: Robin Hood
Only a Shop Girl
23: The Merry-Go-Round
Daddy
Vanity Fair
24: Three Women
Beau Brummell
26: The Passionate Quest
The Shamrock Handicap

Bessie Love (1891-)
1915: Birth of a Nation
16: The Flying Torpedo
The Aryan
The Good Bad Man
Stranded
Hell-To-Pay Austin
A Sister of Six
Intolerance
The Sawdust Ring
Acquitted
Reggie Mixes In
Quest of the Holy Grail
17: Wee Lady Betty
Persnickety Polly Ann
Nina the Flower Girl
Cheerful Givers
Mystery of the Leaping Fish
18: Great Adventure
Little Reformer
How Could You, Caroline?
18: Little Sister of Everybody
19: Dawn of Understanding
Carolyn of the Corners
Cupid Forecloses
Little Boss
The Yankee Princess
Over the Garden Wall
Enchanted Barn
20: Fighting Colleen
Pegeen
21: Bonnie May
Penny of Hilltop Trail
The Swamp
Sundown
The Living Dead
The Midlanders
22: The Sea Lion
Spirit of the Lake
The Vermilion Pencil
Forget-Me-Not
Deserted at the Altar
Village Blacksmith
Three Men to Pay
23: The Purple Dawn
St. Elmo
The Ghost Patrol
Human Wreckage
The Eternal Three
Slave of Desire
The Magic Skin
24: Those Who Dance
Sundown
Gentle Julia
Going Crooked
Torment
A Woman on the Jury
The Silent Watcher
Dynamite Smith
Tongues of Flame
25: The Lost World
A Son of His Father
King on Main Street
New Brooms
Soul Fire
26: Song and Dance Man
Young April
Meet the Prince
27: Dress Parade
A Harp in Hock
Rubber Tires
The Flag Maker
28: Matinee Idol
Has Anybody Seen Kelly?

28: Sally of the Scandals
29: The Road Show T
Hollywood Revue of 1929 T
Broadway Melody T
The Idle Rich T
30: Good News T
Girl in the Show T
Heiress of Coffee Dan's T
The Doll's Shop T
Chasing Rainbows T
Conspiracy T
Swellhead T
31: Morals for Women T
41: Atlantic Ferry T
46: Journey Together T
54: The Barefoot Contessa T
55: Touch and Go T
57: Story of Esther Costello T

Montagu Love (1887-1943)
1916: A Woman's Way
The Social Highwayman
The Gilded Cage
Bought and Paid For
17: Rasputin, the Black Monk
Hands Up
Night of Love
One Hour of Love
The Brand of Satan
18: The Cross Bearer
The Awakening
The Good for Nothing
Vengeance
Stolen Orders
19: The Hand Invisible
The Quickening Flame
The Steel King
Three Green Eyes
Through the Toils
To Him that Hath
Rough Neck
The Grouch
A Broadway Saint
20: The Place of the Honeymoons
World and His Wife
21: The Wrong Woman
Shams of Society
The Case of Becky
Forever (or, Peter Ibbetson)
22: Love's Redemption
22: What's Wrong with Women?
Secrets of Paris
The Beauty Shop
23: Darling of the Rich
The Leopardess
Little Old New York
The Eternal City
24: Sinners in Heaven
26: The Son of the Sheik
Don Juan
Out of the Storm
27: The King of Kings
The Tender Hour
Rose of the Golden West
Jesse James
Good Time Charley
28: The Haunted House SSE
The Wind
The Devil's Skipper
The Hawk's Nest
The Haunted Ship
The Noose
29: Divine Lady SSE
Her Private Life T
A Most Immoral Lady T
Mysterious Island PT
Charming Sinners T
Midstream PT
Bulldog Drummond T
Divine Love
Silks and Saddles
The Voice Within PT
The Last Warning PT
Synthetic Sin
The Condemned Woman
30: Love Comes Along T

Louise Lovely (1896-)
1916: Grasp of Greed
18: Sirens of the Sea
The Wolf and His Mate
Painted Lips
Nobody's Wife
The Girl Who Wouldn't Quit
A Rich Man's Darling
19: The Last of the Duanes
Wolves of the Night
Wings of the Morning
20: The Lone Star Ranger
The Butterfly Man
The Skywayman
The Third Woman

20: The Orphan
Twins of Suffering Creek
The Joyous Troublemaker
21: A Connecticut Yankee in King Arthur's Court
Partners of Fate
Heart of the North
Poverty of Riches
Little Grey Mouse
While the Devil Laughs
22: Shattered Idols
Life's Greatest Question

Edmund Lowe (1892-)

1918: Vive La France!
19: Eyes on Youth
20: The Woman Gives
Madonnas and Men
A Woman's Business
Someone in the House
My Lady's Latchkey
21: Peacock Alley
The Devil
Chicken in the Case
A Game of Graft
22: Living Lies
23: The Silent Command
In the Palace of the King
White Flower
24: Barbara Frietchie
The Brass Devil
Honor Among Men
25: The Fool
East Lynne
The Kiss Barrier
Marriage in Transit
Ports of Call
Greater than a Crown
26: What Price Glory?
Soul Mates
Palace of Pleasure
Siberia
Black Paradise
27: An Increasing Purpose
Is Zat So?
Publicity Madness
The Wizard
28: Dressed to Kill
Happiness Ahead
Baloo
A Girl in Every Port
Making the Grade
Outcast

Myrna Loy (1905-)

1923: Ten Commandments
24: Thief of Bagdad
25: Pretty Ladies
Satan in Sables
26: Ben Hur
Don Juan
Why Girls Go Back Home
The Cave Man
Across the Pacific
27: Heart of Maryland
Bitter Apples
Ham and Eggs at the Front
Girl from Chicago
The Jazz Singer
The Climbers
Simple Sis
28: If I Were Single
Beware of Married Men
Turn Back the Hours
The Crimson City
Pay as you Enter
State Street Sadie
Midnight Taxi PT
What Price Beauty?
29: Noah's Ark PT
Fancy Baggage PT
Desert Song T
Black Watch T
Hardboiled Rose PT
The Squall T
Show of Shows T
30: The Great Divide T
Bride of the Regiment T

Wilfred Lucas (d. 1940)

1909: The Girls and Daddy
Golden Louis
11: The Primal Call
The Rocky Road
Home Folks
His Trust Fulfilled
Enoch Arden
The Lonedale Operator
White Rose of the Wilds
The Fisher Folks
12: The Girl and Her Trust
A Sailor's Heart
Under Burning Skies
Man's Genesis
13: The Primitive Man
14: The Massacre

15: The Lily and the Rose
16: Acquitted
The Wood Nymph
Wild Girl of the Sierras
Intolerance
The Microscope Mystery
Macbeth
17: His Excellency, the Governor
Food Gamblers
The Judgment House
The Wild Cat
Sins of Ambition
18: The Return of Mary
Red Red Heart
19: Soldiers of Fortune
The Girl from Nowhere
The Hushed Hour
The Westerners
A Woman of Pleasure
21: The Breaking Point
The Beautiful Liar
Through the Back Door
The Fighting Breed
The Shadow of Lightning Ridge
The Better Man
22: Across the Deadline
The Kentucky Derby
Paid Back
The Barnstormer
Barriers of Folly
23: Heroes of the Street
Can a Woman Love Twice?
Jazzmania
27: Her Sacrifice
Burnt Fingers
The Nest
Flesh and Blood

Jack Luden (1902-)
1926: Fascinating Youth
It's the Old Army Game
The Jade Cup
Bill Grimm's Progress
Easy Payments
27: A Flame in the Sky
Shootin' Irons
Two Flaming Youths
Yours to Command
City of Shadows
The Last Outlaw
28: Partners in Crime
Under the Tonto Rim
28: Fools for Luck
Forgotten Faces
Sins of the Fathers
Woman from Moscow
29: Wild Party T
Wolf of Wall Street T
Innocents of Paris T
Dangerous Curves T
Tell it to Sweeney T
Why Bring That Up? T

Bela Lugosi (1883-1956)
1910: Nachenschnur Des Tot
14: Vad Izalmabogy
15: 2 Hungarian films
17: A Leopard
Az Elet Koralya
Tavaszi Vihar
Alarcosbal
Az Ezredes
18: Casanova
Kuzdelem A Letert
99
19: Der Tanz Auf Dem Vulken
Sklaven Fremder Willens
Hamlet
20: Die Frau In Delphin
Der Januskopf
Last of the Mohicans (Fr.)
Johann Hopkins De Dritte
Szineszno
23: Diadalmas Elet
Silent Command
24: Rejected Woman
25: Midnight Girl
Chadwick Bats
Daughters Who Pay
Prisoners
26: Arabesque
28: How to Handle Women (extra)
29: The 13th Chair
Veiled Woman
Prisoners PT

Paul Lukas (1891-)
1917: Sphynx
20: Sarga Arnyek
Maria Lazar
Little Fox
Nevtelen
Masamod
Olavi

20: Szineszno
21: New York Telegram
L'Amore Di Settecento Anni
La Dama Dal Vestito Grigio
Lady Violette
23: Diadalmas Elet
Egy Finnak A Fele
Samson and Dalilah
28: Two Lovers
3 Sinners
The Woman from Moscow
Hot News
Night Watch
Manhattan Cocktail
29: Wolf of Wall Street T
Shopworn Angel PT
Illusion T
Half Way to Heaven T

Alfred Lunt (1893-)
1923: Backbone
The Ragged Edge
24: Second Youth
25: Lovers in Quarantine
Sally of the Sawdust
The Man Who Found Himself

Anna Luther (1894-)
1918: Moral Suicide
The Marriage Bubble
Her Moment
19: Woman, Woman
The Jungle Trail
The Great Gamble
20: Neglected Wives
Her Father's Station
21: The Isle of Destiny

Helen Lynch (1904-)
1920: Honor Bound
21: What's a Wife Worth?
22: Minnie
The Other Side
Fools First
The Return of Gray Wolf
23: The Meanest Man in the World
Eternal Three
27: Cheaters
Avenging Fangs
Underworld
28: Love and Learn
Showdown
Ladies of the Mob
Husbands for Rent
Romance of the Underworld
Thundergod
29: Stolen Love
Speakeasy T
Why Bring That Up?
30: Behind the Makeup T

Sharon Lynn (1908-)
1927: Clancy's Kosher Wedding
The Coward
The Cherokee Kid
Jake the Plumber
Dad's Choice
A Flame in the Sky
28: None but the Brave
Son of the Golden West
Husbands and Liars
Give and Take
29: Trail of the Horse Thieves
Speakeasy T
Red Wine SSE
Fox Movietone Follies of 1929 T
One Woman Idea SSE
Sunny Side Up T

Ben Lyon (1901-)
1922: The Heart of Maryland
Ashes
23: The Custard Cup
24: The Wages of Virtue
The White Moth
Lily of the Dust
Wine of Youth
25: The New Commandment
So Big
26: Bluebeard's 7 Wives
Reckless Lady
The Savage
The Great Deception
The Prince of Tempters
27: For the Love of Mike
The Perfect Sap
High Hat
The Tender Hour
Dance Magic
28: The Air Legion
Hell's Angels
29: Dancing Vienna

29: The Quitter
The Flying Marine PT
Morgan's Raiders (or, Morgan's Last Raid)
The Transgressor
Conquest series

Eddie Lyons (1886-) & Lee Moran (1890-1960)

1913: Some Runner (Lyons alone)
15: Eddie's Little Love Affair (Eddie alone)
When the Mummy Cried for Help (Lyons alone)
Mrs. Plumb's Pudding (Lyons alone)
Co-starred with Moran in 52 (1 reel) Star Comedies such as:
1920: La, La, Lucille
Everything but the Truth
21: Fixed by George
Once a Plumber
A Shocking Night
How Do You Feel
Roman Romeos
?? The Rushin' Dancers
Dolls and Dollars
Too Much Women
Bad News
A Fire Escape Finish
There and Back
A Hasty Hazing
His Wife's Relatives
Place and Guest

Bert Lytell (1887-1954)
1917: The Lone Wolf
18: Empty Pockets
No Man's Land
Boston Blackie's Little Pal
The Trail to Yesterday
19: Unexpected Places
The Lion's Den
Hitting the High Spots
The Spender
Faith
Blackie's Redemption
Blindman's Eyes
One-Thing-At-A-Time o' Day
Easy to Make Money
20: Alias Jimmy Valentine
Lombardi, Ltd.
The Right of Way
Price of Redemption
21: The Man Who
A Message from Mars
The Misleading Lady
A Trip to Paradise
Ladyfingers
22: The Idle Rich
The Light that Failed
Sherlock Holmes
Mayflower
23: Kick In
Rupert of Hentzau
The Meanest Man in the World
The Eternal City
Temple of Dawn
24: Born Rich
25: Lady Windemere's Fan
26: Ship of Souls
The Gilded Butterfly
That Model from Paris
The Lone Wolf Returns
Obey the Law
The First Night
27: Alias the Lone Wolf
Women's Wares
28: On Trial
29: The Lone Wolf's Daughter PT
30: Brothers T
31: Single Sin T
37: Along Came Love T

Wilfred Lytell (1892-1954)
1916: The Destroyer
The Conflict
The Ninety and Nine
The Lily and the Rose
The Combat
18: Our Mrs. McChesney
20: Trailed by Three (serial)
Heliotrope
21: The Wrong Woman
The Kentuckians
Know Your Man
Isle of Jewels (serial)
22: The Trail of the Law
The Man Who Paid
The Wolf's Fangs
24: The Warrens of Virginia

Marc MacDermott (1880-1929)

1911: Aida
12: What Happened to Mary? (serial)
Martin Chuzzlewit
Lady Clare
An Old Appointment
The Convict's Parole
13: Mary Stuart
While John Bolt Slept
With the Eyes of the Blind
The Gauntlet of Washington
14: Colonel of the Red Hussars
The Man Who Disappeared (serial)
15: Ransom's Folly
17: Intrigue
An Alabaster Box
18: The Green God
The Girl of Today
Buchanan's Wife
19: The New Moon
Kathleen Mavourneen
Tony America
The 13th Chair
20: While New York Sleeps
21: Blind Wives
Footlights
22: The Amazing Lover
The Spanish Jade
23: Lights of New York
Hoodman Blind
24: He Who Gets Slapped
Dorothy Vernon of Haddon Hall
The Sea Hawk
25: Siege
Graustark
26: The Love Thief
The Temptress
Lucky Lady
Kiki
27: Flesh and the Devil
The Resurrection
The Taxi Dancer
California
The Road to Romance
Man, Woman, and Sin
28: The Whip
The Yellow Lily
Glorious Betsy
Under the Black Eagle
29: Mysterious Island PT

J. Farrell MacDonald (1875-1951)

1914: The Last Egyptian
15: The Heart of Maryland
Rags
Tides of Retribution
The Oz Features
17: Roped
19: Marked Men
A Fight for Love
The Outcasts of Poker Flat
20: Under Sentence
Hitchin' Post
21: The Freeze Out
Action
The Wallop
Bucking the Line
Little Miss Hawkshaw
Riding with Death
Trailin'
Sky High
22: Come on Over
The Bonded Woman
Over the Border
The Young Rajah
Tracks
While Satan Sleeps
23: Racing Hearts
Jazzmania
Quicksands
24: Western Luck
The Iron Horse
Brass Bowl
Kentucky Pride
25: Gerald Cranston's Lady
Scarlet Honeymoon
Trail Rider
Lightnin'
Thank You
Lucky Horseshoes
Kentucky Fair
The Fighting Heart
26: First Year
A Trip to Chinatown
Dixie Merchant
Shamrock Handicap
3 Bad Men
Last Frontier
The Family Upstairs
The Country Beyond
27: Bertha, the Sewing Machine Girl
Love Makes 'em Wild

27: Ankles Preferred
Cradle Snatchers
Rich But Honest
Colleen
Paid to Love
Sunrise
East Side, West Side
Outlaws of Red River
28: The Cohens and the Kellys in Paris
Bringing Up Father
Abie's Irish Rose SSE
The Four Devils T
Me Gangster SSE
None but the Brave
Riley the Cop SSE
Headlines
29: Masked Emotions SSE
The Painted Angel
In Old Arizona T
Strong Boy SSE
Masquerade

Katherine MacDonald (1894-1956)

1918: Headin' South
Riddle Gawne
Battling Jane
Shark Monroe
Mr. Fixit
His Own Home Town
19: The Squaw Man
The Woman Thou Gavest Me
The Beauty Market
20: The Notorious Miss Lisle
Passion's Playground
Curtain
The Turning Point
The Thunderbolt
21: My Lady's Latch Key
Trust Your Wife
Stranger than Fiction
22: Her Social Value
The Beautiful Liar
The Woman's Side
The Infidel
Domestic Relations
Heroes and Husbands
White Shoulders
Woman Conquers
23: Money, Money, Money
Lonely Road
Refuge
Scarlet Lily
23: Chastity
26: Old Loves and New

Wallace MacDonald (1891-)

1914: Mabel's Married Life
The Rounders
Dough and Dynamite
18: Madame Sphinx
19: Spotlight Sadie
20: Trumpet Island
Bright Lights
Who Shall Judge?
Breaking Through
22: A Poor Relation
The Understudy
A Fool There Was
Under Oath
Youth Must Have Love
Caught Bluffing
23: The Spoilers
The Day of Faith
Maytime
Angel Face Molly
24: The Sea Hawk
25: The Lady
New Lives for Old
Learning to Love
Lightnin'
26: Bar-C Mystery (serial)
Casey of the Coast Guard (serial)
Fighting with Buffalo Bill (serial)
Hell's 400
Your Wife and Mine
The Checkered Flag
Two Can Play
27: Drums of the Desert
His Foreign Wife
Tumbling River
Whispering Smith Rides (serial)
The Red Signal
28: Blockade
Free Lips
Tropical Nights
The Pearl Story
29: Darkened Rooms T
Sweetie
Fancy Baggage PT
Dark Skies T
Hit the Deck T

Fred Mace

1912: Cohen Collects a Debt
The Water Nymph
Riley and Schultz
The New Neighbor
The Beating He Needed
Pedro's Dilemma
Stolen Glory
Ambitious Butler
Mabel's Lovers
At It Again
The Deacon Trouble
A Tempermental Husband
Mr. Fix-It
A Desperate Lover
A Bear Escape
Pat's Day Off
A Family Mix-Up

13: Saving Mabel's Day
A Double Wedding
The Cure that Failed
Mabel's Adventures
Hoffmeyer's Legacy
Drummer's Vacation
Mabel's Stratagem
The Elite Ball
Just Brown's Luck
The Battle of Who Run
The Stolen Purse

14: Heinze's Resurrection
Mabel's Heros
The Professor's Daughter
A Red Hot Romance
The Sleuth's Last Stand
A Deaf Burglar
The Sleuth at the Floral Parade
The Rural 3rd Degree
Love and Pain
The Man Next Door
The Rube and the Baron
Jenny's Pearls
At 12 O'Clock
Her New Beau
Cupid in a Dental Parlour

15: My Valet
A Janitor's Wife's Temptation
Crooked to the End

16: Love Will Conquer
The Village Vampire
Bath Tub Perils
A Lover's Might

16: His Last Scent
An Oily Scoundrel
The Bangville Police
Algy on the Force
The Darktown Belle
Hubby's Job
The Foreman of the Jury
The Gangsters
The Tale of a Black Eye
The Firebugs

Charles Emmett Mack (d. 1927)

1921: Dream Street

23: Driven
The Daring Years

24: America

26: The Devil's Circus
The Unknown Soldier

27: The Rough Riders
Old San Francisco
The First Auto

Hughie Mack (1887-1952)

1914: Too Many Husbands
The Wink
Some Widow
The New Secretary

15: Desert of Egypt
Open Another Bottle
Make it Snappy
Fellow Romans
Rush Orders

20: Seeing It Through

22: Trifling Women

26: Mare Nostrum

27: Where Trails Begin
The Wedding March

28: 4 Sons

Marion Mack (1905-)

1922: Mary of the Movies

25: One of the Bravest

26: Alice in Movieland
Carnival Girl

27: The General

??: Mack Sennett Comedies
Mermaid Comedies
Fox Sunshine Comedies

Willard Mack (1873-1934)

1915: Aloha-Oe
The Corner
The Devil Decides

16: The Conqueror
18: Hellcat
19: Shadows
21: The Barbarian
Woman in the Index
23: Your Friend and Mine
28: Body Punch
Beauty and Bullets
Just in Time
Phantom Fingers
A Tenderfoot Hero
29: Voice of the City

Dorothy MacKaill (1903-)
20: A Face at the Window
21: The Lotus Eaters
Bits of Life
22: Isle of Doubt
A Woman's Woman
Streets of New York
The Inner Man
23: Mighty Lak' a Rose
The Broken Violin
The Fighting Blade
Wild Apples
His Children's Children
24: The Man Who Came Back
What Shall I Do?
25: Joanna
Shore Leave
One Year to Live
Chickie
26: The Dancer of Paris
Just Another Blonde
Ranson's Folly
27: Convoy
Subway Sadie
Smile, Brother, Smile
The Crystal Cup
A Lunatic at Large
Man Crazy
28: Waterfront
Stranded in Paradise
The Whip
The Barker T
Lady Be Good
Ladies Night in a Turkish Bath T
29: His Captive Woman PT
Hard to Get T
Children of the Ritz SSE
Two Weeks Off PT
30: The Love Racket T
30: The Great Divide T
??: The Torchy Series:
Torchy's Millions
Torchy Mixes In
Torchy's Promoter

Mary MacLaren (1896-)
1916: Idle Wives
Saving the Family Name
Shoes
The Mysterious Mrs. Musslewhite
18: The Model's Confession
Vanity Pool
The Brand
Bread
19: Bonnie Bonnie Lassie
A Petal on the Current
Creaking Stairs
The Amazing Wife
The Unpainted Woman
The Pointing Finger
The Secret Marriage
Weaker Vessels
20: The Forged Bride
Rouge and Riches
The Road to Divorce
21: The Wild Goose
The Three Musketeers
22: Across the Continent
The Face in the Fog
The Outcast
23: Under the Red Robe

Douglas MacLean (1894-1967)
1917: Souls in Pawn
18: As Ye Sow
Johanna Enlists
Fuss and Feathers
When Johnny Comes Marching Home
19: Happy Though Married
Captain Kidd, Jr.
The Home Breaker
The Hun Within
20: 23-1/2 Hours Leave
Mary's Ankle
What's Your Husband Doing?
Let's Be Fashionable
The Jailbird
One a Minute
21: Passing Through

21: Chickens
The Home Stretch
The Rookie's Return
22: The Hottentot
23: Bell Boy 13
A Man of Action
The Sunshine Trail
Going Up
24: The Yankee Consul
Never Say Die
25: Introduce Me
7 Keys to Baldpate
26: That's My Baby
Hold That Lion!
27: Let it Rain
Soft Cushions
29: Divorce Made Easy T
The Carnation Kid PT
31: Alugh and Get Rich (scenarist)
32: Full of Notions (sc.)
33: Mama Loves Papa (Producer)
Tillie and Guns (Producer)
34: Six of a Kind (sc.)
35: Accent on Youth (prod.)
So Red the Rose (prod.)
36: The Great Guy (prod.)
37: 23-1/2 Hours Leave (prod.)
41: New Wine (prod.)

Golda Madden (1894-)

1917: Fires of Rebellion
Flying Colors
18: Girl of My Dreams
Turn in the Road
Jilted Janet
Branded (serial)
20: Woman in Room 13
Mother of His Children

Cleo Madison (1882-1964)

1913: Heart of a Cracksman
Cross Purposes
14: The Trey of Hearts (serial)
15: Damon and Pythias
16: The Severed Hand
The Chalice of Sorrow
17: Black Orchids
18: Romance of Tarzan
19: Great Radium Mystery (serial)
20: Price of Redemption
21: Girl from Nowhere
Lure of Youth
Ladies Must Live
22: A Woman's Woman
Retribution
23: Dangerous Age

Charles Mailes (1870-1937)

1912: My Hero
Oil and Water
Just Gold
Those Hicksville Boys
A Temporary Truce
The Girl and Her Trust
Man's Genesis
A Young Patriot
Bittersweet
13: The Wanderer
Her Mother's Oath
The Primitive Man
Adopted Brother
Coming of Angelo
By Man's Law
The Reformers
14: Liberty Bells
The Massacre
17: The Lair of the Wolf
The Dynast
The Spotted Lily
The Girl Who Won Out
Beloved Jim
The Power
18: Talk of the Town
19: Full of Pep
Our Better Selves
The Speed Maniac
Outcasts of Poker Flat
20: Red Hot Dollars
Home Spun Folks
Go and Get It
The Mark of Zorro
21: Ten Dollar Raise
Courage
Chickens
The Home Stretch
22: Bond Boy
27: Play Safe
City Gone Wild
Manpower
Bitter Apples
28: Give and Take
Queen of the Chorus
The Big Scoop

28: What a Night!
Drums of Love
Charge of the Gauchos
Number, Please
29: Phantom City
The Faker
The Carnation Kid PT
The Bellamy Trial PT
One Stolen Night PT

Fred Malatesta (1889-)
1918: The Legion of Death
The Demon
The Other Side of Eden
The Wolf-Face Man (serial)
19: The Devil's Trail
The Greatest Thing in Life
Full of Pep
The Four-Flusher
20: The Best of Luck
Big Happiness
The Sins of Rozanne
The Challenge of the Law
Risky Business
21: The Mask
29: Peacock Fan

Molly Malone (1895-)
1916: The Red Stain
17: The Pullman Mystery
The Soul Herder
Straight Shooting
Bucking Broadway
18: Phantom Riders
Hill Billy
Wild Women
Thieves' Gold
The Scarlet Drop
A Woman's Fool
A Marked Man
19: The Garage
The Desert Hero
The Hayseed
20: Stop, Thief!
It's a Great Life
The Round Up
21: Made in Heaven
Just out of College
Sure Fire
Bucking the Line
Blazing Away
Not Guilty
Red Courage
22: A Poor Relation
Across the Dead Line
Trail of Fate
23: The Freshie
Mr. Parol and Company
27: Bad Man's Bluff
The Golden Stallion (serial)
28: Picture My Astonishment
?? Molly's Millions
Birds of a Feather
Come in the Kitchen
Molly's Mumps
Her Doctor's Dilemma
Back Stage

Leo Maloney (1888-1929)
1915: The Girl and the Game (serial)
16: A Flight for Millions
17: The Lost Express (serial)
Railroad Raiders (serial)
19: Partners Three
The Spitfire of Seville
The Wolverine
20: The Fatal Sign (serial)
21: No Man's Woman
His Own Law
Come and Get Me
The Bar Cross War
The Drifter
Deputized
22: Ghost City
24: The Perfect Alibi
Payable on Demand
Riding Double
Not Built for Running
King's Creek Law
Headin' Through
Huntin' Trouble
25: Across the Deadline
26: Win, Lose or Draw
The Outlaw Express
Luck and Sand
The High Hand
27: The Man from Hardpan
Long Loop on the Pecos
Don Desperado
Two Guns of Tumbleweed
Border Blackbirds
28: Apache Raider
Yellow Contraband
The Vanishing West (serial)
Boss of Rustler's Roost

28: Bronc Stomper
29: The Devil's Twin
Fire Detectives (serial)
Forty-Five Calibre War
Overland Bound

Hank Mann (1888-)
1914: The Fatal Mallet
Mabel's Strange Predicament
Caught in a Cabaret
The Knockout
Mabel's Married Life
Tillie's Punctured Romance
15: and other Keystone Comedies
16: A Modern Enoch Arden
Hearts and Sparks
17-19: more Mack Sennett Comedies
20: Dr. Jekyll and Mr. Hyde
22: The Village Blacksmith
Messenger
Harem Hero
Eye for Figures
Quincy Adams Sawyer
25: The Sporting Venus
Bon Bon Riot
His First Blow Out
The Fighting Heart
His Bread and Butter
26: Wings of the Storm
27: The Patent Leather Kid
Lady Bird
When Danger Calls
Broadway After Midnight
Paid to Love
Smile Brother Smile
28: Garden of Eden
Fazil SSE
29: The Donovan Affair T
Morgan's Last Raid
Should Women Drive?
Pants at any Price
Nize Baby
Fall of Eve T

Margaret Mann (1868-)
1919: Heart of Humanity
Right to Happiness
Once to Every Woman
20: Man-Woman-Marriage
The Girl and the Goose
21: The New Disciple
21: Black Beauty
22: Call of Home
28: Four Sons
??: Queen Victoria

Martha Mansfield (1899-1923)
1916: Max Comes Across
17: Max Wants a Divorce
Max in a Taxi
18: Broadway Bill
20: Dr. Jekyll and Mr. Hyde
Civilian Clothes
The Wonderful Chance
His Brother's Keeper
Mothers of Men
21: Society Snobs
Gilded Lies
Women Men Love
Man of Stone
22: Till We Meet Again
Queen of the Moulin Rouge
23: Is Money Everything?
Woman in Chains
Fog Bound

Edna Marion (1908-)
1926: Stern Bros. Comedies (2-1/2 years)
Christie Comedies
Hal Roach Comedies (7 years)
Still Alarm
28: Loud Speakers
From Soup to Nuts
The Family Group
Limousine Love
The Fight Pest
Should Married Men Go Home
29: Sinner's Paradise

George Marion (1860-1945)
1923: Anna Christie
The Girl I Loved
26: The Reckless Lady
The Wise Guy
29: Evangeline

Enid Markey (1895-)
1914: City of Darkness
The Fugitive
In the Tennessee Hills
Card Sharps

14: In the Cow Country
The Fortunes of War
Not of the Flock
The Friend
15: The Iron Strain
Between Men
Darkening Trail
Cup of Life
Spirit of the Bell
16: Civilization
The Devil's Double
Shell 43
The Aztec God
Jim Greenberg's Boy
War's Women
Aloha Oe
16: The Captive God
17: The Yankee Way
Responsibility
The Curse of Eve
18: Tarzan of the Apes
Cheating the Public
The Zeppelin's Last Raid
Romance of Tarzan
Mother, I Need You
45: Snafu T
48: The Naked City T

June Marlowe (1907-)
1925: The Clash of the Wolves
Man Without a Conscience
Below the Line
26: The Pleasure Buyers
The Night Cry
Don Juan
27: Fangs of Justice
Alias the Deacon
The Life of Riley
Wild Beauty
On the Stroke of Twelve
28: Their Hour
The Branded Man
Foreign Legion
Grip of the Yukon
Free Lips
Fighting Blood series (bits)
Code of the Air

Percy Marmont (1883-)
1914: Rose of the World
18: The Lie
In the Hollow of Her Hand
19: The Indestructible Wife
19: The Winchester Woman
Vengeance of Durand
The Climbers
Pride
20: The Sporting Duchess
Dead Men Tell No Tales
The Branded Woman
21: The Price
What's Your Reputation Worth?
Without Benefit of Clergy
22: Wife Against Wife
The First Woman
Married People
23: If Winter Comes
24: The Shooting of Dan McGrew
The Clean Heart
The Marriage Cheat
The Legend of Hollywood
The Enemy Sex
25: Street of Forgotten Men
Introspection
Lord Jim
Infatuation
26: Aloma of the South Seas
Mantrap
The Miracle of Life
28: The Stronger Will
San Francisco Nights
29: Silver King
30: Lady of the Lake
The Squealer T
Yellow Stockings T
Crossroads T
Rich and Strange T
The Blind Spot T
The Silver Greyhound T

Mae Marsh (1893-1968)
1911: Fighting Blood
Home Folks
12: The Sands of Dee
The New York Hat
Indian Uprising at Santa Fe
Man's Genesis
The Lesser Evil
A Temporary Truce
The Spirit Awakening
The Kentucky Girl
Brutality
The Parante
13: Lena and the Geese
Brute Force

13: The Telephone Girl and the Lady
The Primitive Man
The Perfidy of Mary
Broken Ways
Adventures in the Autumn Woods
The Tender-Hearted Boy
Brothers
Near to Earth
The Lady and the Mouse
The Wanderer
The Yaqui Cur
Her Mother's Oath
By Man's Law
Influence of the Unknown
The Reformers
Love in an Apartment Hotel
One Exciting Night
14: Judith of Bethulia
The Battle of Elderbush Gulch
The Escape
The Avenging Conscience
Down by the Sounding Sea
Big James' Heart
15: The Birth of a Nation
16: Wild Girl of the Sierras
A Child of the Paris Streets
Intolerance
Hoodoo Ann
The Marriage of Molly O'
Quest of the Holy Grail
Home Sweet Home
17: Polly of the Circus
The Wharf Rat
The Cinderella Man
Sunshine Alley
18: Beloved Traitor
The Face in the Dark
Glorious Adventure
All Woman
Hidden Fires
Money Mad
Fields of Honor
19: Spotlight Sadie
Bondage of Barbara
The Racing Strain
The Mother and the Law
21: The Little 'fraid Lady
Nobody's Kid
22: Till We Meet Again
23: White Rose
23: Paddy the Next Best Thing
24: The Rat
Arabella
A Woman's Secret
25: Daddies
Tides of Passion
28: Racing Through
The Little Liar
31: Over the Hill T

Marguerite Marsh (1892-)

1916: Little Meena's Romance
Mr. Goode, the Samaritan
18: Conquered Hearts
Fields of Honor
19: Royal Democrat
Eternal Magdalene
Fair Enough
The Master Mystery (serial)
The Carter Case (serial)
20: Phantom Honeymoon
Wits Vs. Wits
21: Women Men Love
Oh Mary, Be Careful
Idol of the North
22: Boomerang Bill
Iron to Gold
Face to Face
23: The Lion's Mouse

Tully Marshall (1864-1943)

1914: Paid in Full
15: Sable Lorcha
Let Katy Do It
16: A Child of the Paris Streets
The Devil's Needle
Oliver Twist
Intolerance
Martha's Vindication
17: Joan the Woman
The Golden Fetter
Romance of the Redwoods
Unconquered
The Devil's Stone
Countess Charming
18: A Modern Musketeer
The Whispering Chorus
The Thing We Love
M'Liss
Old Wives for New
We Can't Have Everything
Bound in Morocco

18: Arizona
Too Many Millions
The Man from Funeral Range
19: Cheating Cheaters
The Squaw Man
Maggie Pepper
The Girl Who Stayed at Home
Daughter of Mine
The Lady of Red Butte
Life Line
The Crimson Gardenia
The Grim Game
Her Kingdom of Dreams
Hawthorne of U. S. A.
Everywoman
20: Double Speed
Excuse My Dust
The Gift Supreme
The Dancin' Fool
Sick Abed
The Slim Princess
Honest Hutch
21: Her Beloved Villain
Little 'fraid Lady
What Happened to Rosa?
The Cup of Life
Three Musketeers
The Lotus Blossom
Silent Years
Mam'selle Jo
22: Hail the Woman
Penrod
Too Much Business
Is Matrimony a Failure?
The Lying Truth
Fools of Fortune
Deserted at the Altar
The Ladder Jinx
Without Compromise
The Village Blacksmith
Good Men and True
Super Sex
Only a Shopgirl
23: The Marriage Chance
The Covered Wagon
Temporary Marriage
Fools and Riches
Law of the Lawless
Broken Hearts of Broadway
The Brass Bottle
Hunchback of Notre Dame
23: Richard the Lion-Hearted
Let's Go!
Ponjola
The Barefoot Boy
Her Temporary Husband
Beautiful and Damned
The Dangerous Maid
24: Defying Destiny
Thundergate
The Stranger
Dangerous Trails
Hold Your Breath
For Sale
The Ridin' Kid from Powder River
Pagan Passions
Along Came Ruth
He Who Gets Slapped
Smouldering Fires
The Right of the Strongest
Reckless Romance
25: The Talker
Half-Way Girl
Merry Widow
The Pace that Thrills
Clothes Make the Pirate
26: Old Loves for New
Her Big Night
The Torrent
27: Twinkletoes
Jim the Conqueror
Beware of Widows
Cat and the Canary
The Gorilla
28: Dreams of Love
Queen Kelly (never released)
Trail of '98
The Mad Hour
The Perfect Crime
Alias Jimmy Valentine
29: Redskin SSE
Conquest T
The Bridge of San Luis Rey PT
Thunderbolt T
Skin Deep T
Mysterious Dr. Fu Manchu T

Vivian Martin (1893-)

1914: The Wishing Hour
15: Butterfly on the Wheel
16: The Stronger Love

16: A Modern Thelma
Her Father's Son
17: The Trouble Buster
Mary Gusta
Molly Entangled
Forbidden Paths
Little Miss Optimist
Molly Shawn
18: Her Country First
The Little Scrub Lady
The Sunset Trail
Fair Barrier
Petticoat Pilot
Unclaimed Goods
Viviette
19: Mirandy Smiles
The Third Kiss
Home Town Girl
Little Comrade
Louisiana
Jane Goes A-Wooing
You Never Saw Such a Girl
An Innocent Adventuress
20: His Official Wife
Husbands and Wives
21: Song of the Soul
Mother Eternal
22: Pardon My French

Edward Martindel (1876-1955)
1920: The Very Idea
The Misfit Wife
Captain Swift
The Furnace
You Never Can Tell
21: Forbidden Fruit
Ducks and Drakes
Athalie
Little Eva Ascends
Call of the North
22: Midnight
Manslaughter
The Glory of Clementine
Nice People
Clarence
Daughter of Luxury
Hail the Woman
23: White Flower
25: The Sporting Venus
Lady Windemere's Fan
26: We Americans
Tony Runs Wild
The Duchess of Buffalo
26: You'd Be Surprised
Everybody's Acting
The Dixie Merchant
27: Taxi! Taxi!
Lovers
Fashions for Women
Children of Divorce
Lonesome Ladies
The Woman Who Did Not Care
In Old Kentucky
Venus of Venice
28: The Garden of Eden
Desert Bride
On Trial
Companionate Marriage
29: The Devil's Apple Tree
Why Be Good?
Desert Song T
Hardboiled Rose PT
The Singing Fool T
Modern Love PT
The Aviator T
Footlights and Fools T

James Mason
1920: The Penalty
21: Godless Men
The Sage Hen
Two Weeks with Pay
The Mysterious Rider
25: Beggar on Horseback
27: Alias the Lone Wolf
28: Chicago After Midnight
Dead Man's Curve
Singapore Mutiny
Sally's Shoulders
The Big Killing
29: The Phantom City
Sunset Pass
The Long, Long, Trail T

Leroy Mason (1901-1947)
1927: Closed Gates
28: Avenging Shadow
The Law's Lash
Inside Prison Walls
Golden Shackles
The Hit of the Show PT
The Viking

Shirley Mason (1901-)
1915: Vanity Fair

17: The Apple Tree
The 7 Deadly Sins (series)
Envy - Sloth-- Pride -
Wrath - Greed - Passion -
the 7th Sin
Cy Whittaker's Ward
The Tell-Tale Step
The Awakening of Ruth
18: Come On In
Goodbye Bill
19: The Unwritten Code
The Final Close-up
The Wall Invisible
Gosh Darn the Kaiser
The Rescuing Angel
The Winning Girl
20: Treasure Island
Her Elephant Man
Molly and I
Girl of my Heart
Flame of Youth
Little Wanderer
Love's Harvest
21: Merely Mary Ann
Wing Toy
The Lamplighter
Ever Since Eve
Love Time
The Mother Heart
22: Jackie
Queenie
The Ragged Heiress
Very Truly Yours
Lights of the Desert
The New Teacher
Youth Must Have Love
Shirley of the Circus
Little Miss Smiles
23: Pawn Ticket # 210
The 11th Hour
Love Bound
South Sea Love
24: Love Letters
That French Lady
The Great Diamond Mystery
25: Curly Top
Scarlet Honeymoon
Scandal Proof
What Fools Men Are
Star Dust Trail
My Husband's Wives
26: So This is Paris
Desert Gold
26: Don Juan's Three Nights
Sweet Rosie O'Grady
Sin Cargo
Rose of the Tenements
27: Sally in our Alley
Stranded
Rich Men's Sons
The Wreck
Let It Rain
28: Runaway Girls
So This is Love
Vultures of the Sea (serial)
Wife's Relations
29: The Flying Marine
Anne Against the World
Dark Skies
Show of Shows T

Otto Matiesen (1893-)
1918: The Floor Below
22: Money to Burn
Sheriff of San Juan
23: West of Chicago
St. Elmo
Vanity Fair
Scaramouche
Dangerous Maid
Beloved Rogue
24: Napoleon and Josephine
The Dawn of Tomorrow
The Water Cross
25: Salvation Hunters
Happy Warrior
26: Bride of the Storm
While London Sleeps
27: Surrender
Too Many Crooks
Road to Romance
28: The Last Moment
The Tell-Tale Heart
The Woman from Moscow
Desert Bride
Scarlet Lady
The Missing Man
29: Strange Cargo
Napoleon's Barber
Behind Closed Doors
Prisoners PT
General Crack T
Show of Shows T

Martha Mattox (d. 1938)
1917: Polly Put the Kettle On

18: Wild Women
Scarlet Drop
Thieves' Gold
19: Scarlet Shadow
Eve in Exile
20: Huckleberry Finn
Old Lady 31
The Butterfly Man
Firebrand Trevison
Girl of My Heart
A Cumberland Romance
Everybody's Sweetheart
21: The Torrent
The Conflict
The Son of Wallingford
22: Rich Men's Wives
Hearts Aflame
Angel of Crooked Street
Restless Souls
The Married Flapper
Top o' the Morn
Hands of Nara
23: Penrod and Sam
Look Your Best
3 Wise Fools
The Hero
24: The Fast Worker
25: Dangerous Innocence
26: Shameful Behavior
Lovey Mary
Wolf Hunters
Yankee Señor
The Nut Cracker
Christine of the Big Tops
Forest Havoc
27: Cat and the Canary
Snowbound
Finger Prints
Her Wild Oats
28: Love Me and the World is Mine
Little Shepherd of Kingdom Come
The Head Man
A Bit of Heaven
Singapore Mutiny
The Naughty Duchess
29: The Big Diamond Robbery
Montmartre Rose
30: The Love Racket T
Night Work T
Misbehaving Ladies T
Extravagance T
31: Murder by the Clock T

Cyril Maude (1862-1951)
1913: House of Temperley
14: Beauty and the Barge
15: Peer Gynt
24: The Iron Horse
30: Grumpy T
32: These Charming People T
33: Counsel's Opinion T

Edwin Maxwell (d. 1948)
1927: The Jazz Singer PT
28: Easy Come, Easy Go
The Doctor's Dilemma
John Ferguson
29: Donovan Affair T

Doris May
1917: The Little American (doubled for Mary Pickford)
18: The Hired Man
Playing the Game
19: Twenty-Three and a Half Hour's Leave
What's Your Husband Doing
Let's Be Fashionable
20: Mary's Ankle
The Jailbird
21: Eden and Return
The Foolish Age
The Rookie's Return
Peck's Bad Boy
Foolish Matrons
22: Boy Crazy
Gay and Devilish
The Understudy
23: Tea With a Kick
The Common Law
Gunfighter
Why Do We Live?

Herschel Mayall
1914: Card Sharps
City of Darkness
The Heart of Rachel
15: Spirit of the Bell
The Renegade
City of the Dead
16: Civilization
18: Carmen of the Klondike
Seal of Death

19: Wings of the Morning
Kismet
21: The Queen of Sheba
29: Great Power

Ken Maynard (1895-)
1924: Janice Meredith
$50,000 Reward
25: The Demon Rider
The Haunted Ranch
Fighting Courage
26: North Star
Unknown Cavalier
Senor Daredevil
27: The Overland Stage
Somewhere in Sonora
Land Beyond the Law
The Devil's Saddle
Red Raiders
28: Wagon Show
The Glorious Trail
Canyon of Adventure
Upland Rider
Code of the Scarlet
29: Phantom City
Cheyenne
Lawless Legion
California Mail
Royal Rider
Wagon Master
Senor Americano

Tex Maynard
1925: The Ranger Fighter (serial)
27: Wild Born
Wanderer of the West
Ridin' Luck
Gun-Hand Garrison
Prince of the Plains

Edna Mayo (1893-)
1914: Key to Yesterday
15: Blinding Virtue
16: The Strange Case of Mary Page
Prince of Graustark
Salvation Joan
The Woman Hater
The Little Straw Wife
The Misleading Lady
The Return of Eve
The Chaperon
Hearts of Love

Frank Mayo (1886-1963)
1915: The Red Circle (serial)
A Little Brother of the Rich
The Hot Head
17: Glory
Betsy Ross
18: The Interloper
The Trap
Who Wins? (or the Price of Folly)
19: Mary Regan
The Brute Breaker
Evil of the Rich
20: Through the Eyes of Men
The Red Lane
Girl in 29
Burnt Wings
Hitchin' Posts
20: Peddler of Lies
21: The Shark Master
The Blazing Trail
Go Straight
The Magnificent Brute
Tiger True
Colorado
Honor Bound
The Marriage Pit
Fighting Lover
Dr. Jim
22: Across the Dead Line
Slippery Tongue
Tracked to Earth
The Man Who Married His Own Wife
Afraid to Fight
Out of the Silent North
Wolf Law
The Altar Stairs
Caught Bluffing
23: Souls for Sale
The Bolted Door
Six Days
Wild Oranges
Unknown Lover
First Degree
Flaming Hour
Legally Dead
26: Then Came the Woman
The Doughboys
Lew Tyler's Wives

Mary McAllister (1910-)

1917: The Kill-Joy
Pants
Do Children Count?
Sins of Ambition
On Trial
Young Mother Hubbard
Sadie Goes to Heaven
Borrowed Sunshine
Little Shoes
The Little Missionary
Where is My Mother?
The Uneven Road
Little White Savage
The Bride of Fancy
Whosoever Shall Offend
20: Half a Chance
23: Ashes of Vengeance
25: Ace of Spades (serial)
Simon the Jester
26: One Minute to Play
Waning Sex
Man in the Shadow
The Sap
27: The Midnight Watch
Fire and Steel
Singed
28: The Devil's Skipper
Loves of an Actress
Wickedness Preferred
Into No Man's Land

Paul McAllister (1875-)

1913: Scales of Justice
15: Via Wireless
Hearts in Exile
21: Forever
Sign on the Door
22: A Stage Romance
What's Wrong with Women?
23: You Can't Fool Your Wife
26: Winning of Barbara Worth
27: Beau Geste
Sorrell and Son
She's a Sheik
28: The Big Killing
29: Noah's Ark PT
Evangeline PT

May McAvoy (1901-)

1917: I'll Say
Hate
18: A Perfect Lady
18: To Hell with the Kaiser
19: Mrs. Wiggs of the Cabbage Patch
Woman Under Oath
My Husband's Other Wife
Hit or Miss
20: The Devil's Garden
House of the Tolling Bell
The Sporting Duchess
A Man and His Woman
Love Wins
21: Forbidden Valley
Everything for Sale
Sentimental Tommy
A Private Scandal
Truth About Husbands
22: Top of New York
Clarence
A Homespun Vamp
Morals
Through a Glass Window
A Virginia Courtship
23: The Kick In
Grumpy
Only 38
Her Reputation
Hollywood
24: Enchanted Cottage
Tarnished
West of the Water Tower
The Mad Whirl
The Bedroom Window
Three Women
Married Flirts
25: Lady Windemere's Fan
Tessie
26: Ben Hur
Road to Glory
Passionate Quest
The Fire Brigade
My Old Dutch
The Savage
27: Matinee Ladies
The Jazz Singer PT
Irish Hearts
Slightly Used
A Reno Divorce
28: If I Were Single
The Terror
A Little Snob
May McAvoy in Sunny California (Vitagraph 2239) T

28: The Lion and the Mouse PT
Caught in the Fog T
29: Stolen Kisses PT
No Defense PT

Gladys McConnell (1907-)
1927: Three's a Crowd
Riding to Fame
28: The Chaser
Code of Scarlet
The Perfect Crime
The Glorious Trail
Cheyenne
The Tiger's Shadow (serial)
29: Fire Detective (serial)

Clyde McCoy
1921: A Midnight Bell

Gertrude McCoy (1896-1967)
1915: Greater Than Art
The Auction Mart
Christine Johnstone
Chips
Through Turbulent Waters
On the Stroke of Twelve
What Could She Do?
June Friday
Friend Wilson's Daughter
26: The Last of Destiny
The Isle of Love
17: The Silent Witness
Madame Sherry
18: The Danger Mark
Men
The Blue Bird
The Working Girl
19: His Daughter Pays
21: Out of the Darkness
25: The Charlatan Mystery
??: Winsome Winnie (serial)

Harry McCoy (1894-)
1911: Joker Comedies
12: Keystone Comedies
13: Mike and Jake at the Beach
The Hoosier Romance
Twilight Baby
14: Mabel's Strange Predicament (or the Hotel Mix-up)
Mabel at the Wheel (or, Daredevil Queen)
14: Caught in a Cabaret (or, The Waiter)
Mabel's Busy Day
Mabel's Married Life
The Masquerader
Tillie's Punctured Romance
Getting Acquainted
15: One Night Stand
A Human Hound's Triumph
For Better, For Worse
Merely a Married Man
Saved by Wireless
The Village Scandal
16: Because He Loved Her
A Movie Star
Perils of the Park
Love Will Conquer
His Auto Ruination
Cinders of Love
She Loved a Sailor
His Last Laugh
Bubbles and Troubles
17: High and Dry
In Again - Out Again
19: The Garage
Fair Enough
False Roomers
20: His Wife's Friend
21: Skirts
28: Hearts of Men
31: Meet the Wife

Tim McCoy (1891-)
1923: The Covered Wagon
25: Thundering Herd
26: War Paint
27: Explorers of the West
Winners of the Wilderness
Spoilers of the West
The Frontiersman
28: The Masked Stranger
Foreign Devils
Wyoming
The Adventurer
Law of the Range
Riders of the Dark
Beyond the Sierras
29: The Bush Ranger
Morgan's Last Raid
Sioux Blood
Humming Wires
Overland Telegraph
Desert Rider

29: A Night on the Range
1 reel musical short T
30: The Indians are Coming
(serial) T

Philo McCullough (1893-)
1916: The Grip of Evil (serial)
The Red Circle (serial)
17: The Neglected Wife
20: A Dangerous Adventure
(serial)
21: The Primal Law
22: Strange Idols
West of Chicago
Calvert's Valley
The Right that Failed
Seein's Believing
The Married Flapper
More to be Pitied than
Scorned
23: The First Degree
Trimmed in Scarlet
Heroes of the Street
The 4th Musketeer
The Stranger's Banquet
25: Winds of Chance
Dick Turpin
26: The Savage
Mismates
The Bar C Mystery (serial)
27: Outlaw Dog
Easy Pickings
Fire and Steel
Smile, Brother, Smile
The Woman Who Did Not
Care
Silver Valley
We're All Gamblers
28: Warming Up
The Night Flyer
Power of the Press
The Painted Post
On Sunset Range
The Apache
Clearing the Trail
South of Panama
29: The Leatherneck PT
The Charlatan PT
The Million Dollar
Collar PT
Untamed Justice
Show of Shows T

Francis McDonald (1891-1968)
1915: A Bold Impersonation
17: The Voice on the Wire
(serial)
The Black Orchids
The Mansard Mystery
O'Connor's Mag
18: Gun Woman
19: Prudence on Broadway
20: The Kentucky Colonel
Nomads of the North
21: Puppets of Fate
Hearts and Masks
22: Trooper O'Neil
Monte Cristo
The Last Trail
Captain Fly-By-Night
23: Trilby
Going Up
24: Forbidden Paradise
26: The Desert's Toll
The Palace of Pleasure
The Temptress
Battling Butler
Puppets
The Yankee Senor
The Bar C Mystery (serial)
27: The Wreck
The Valley of Hell
The Notorious Lady
Outlaws of Red River
28: The Drag Net
Forgotten Faces
Forbidden Love
Legion of the Condemned
Girl in Every Port
The Carnation Kid
29: Port of Dreams
The Show Boat PT
Clean-Up
Girl Overboard PT
Blockade PT

Claire McDowell (1887-1967)
1910: A Mohawk Way
11: A Woman Scorned
Swords and Hearts
In the Days of '49
A Temporary Truce
The Primal Call
12: In the Aisles of the Wild
A Sailor's Heart
The God Within

12: A Cry for Help
Two Daughters of Eve
The Storm Woman
Everlasting Mercy
13: The Telephone Girl and the Lady
The Wanderer
14: The Massacre
Men and Women
Her Father's Silent Partner
17: The Gates of Doom
Heart of the Hills
The Ship of Doom
Fighting Back
18: The Follies Girl
20: The Mark of Zorro
The Jack Knife Man
Something to Think About
Midsummer Madness
The Feud
Woman in the Suitcase
The Devil's Riddle
Prisoners of Love
The Gift Supreme
21: What Every Woman Knows
A Ladies' Man
Love Never Dies
Mother O'Mine
Chickens
22: The Gray Dawn
Penrod
In the Name of the Law
Heart's Haven
Nice People
Quincy Adams Sawyer
Rent Free
23: Westbound Limited
Human Wreckage
25: The Big Parade
26: Ben Hur
The Show-Off
The Dixie Merchant
The Shamrock Handicap
The Midnight Flyer
The Unknown Soldier
27: The Taxi Dancer
Tillie the Toiler
The Black Diamond Express
The Little Journey
Cheaters
Almost Human
28: Tragedy of Youth
Don't Marry
28: Marriage by Contract
Gold Braid
The Viking
Tomorrow
The Girl Who Came Back
Shield of Honor
Winds of the Pampas
Silks and Saddles
29: The Quitter
The 4 Devils T
When Dreams Come True
Whispering Winds PT
30: Redemption T

J. P. McGowan (1880-1952)

1912: From the Manger to the Cross
15: The Hazards of Helen (serial-prod.)
20: King of the Circus (serial-prod.)
The White Horseman (serial-prod.)
21: Do or Die (serial-prod.)
22: The Hills of Missing Men
23: Stormy Seas
24: A Two-Fisted Tenderfoot
25: Blood and Steel
The Fighting Sheriff
26: The Ace of Clubs
The Lost Express
27: Tarzan and the Golden Lion
Red Signals
The Lost Limited
Royal American
Red Raiders
The Slaver
Gun Gospel
Whispering Smith Rides (serial)
28: Painted Trail
The Lightnin' Shot
Chinatown Mystery
Code of Scarlet
Dugan of the Dugouts
Devil Dogs
Black Ace
Two Outlaws
Old Code
Ships of the Night
Arizona Days
29: On the Divide
Silent Trail

29: West of Santa Fe
The Devil's Tower
Clean-Up
Plunging Hoofs
Lawless Legion
Heading Westward
Law of the Mounted
Bad Man's Money
Below the Deadline
Golden Bridle
Last Roundup
Texas Tommy
Phantom Rider SSE
The Invaders SSE
The Fighting Terror
Neath Western Skies
The Oklahoma Kid
Lone Horseman
30: Senor American T

Walter McGrail (1889-1970)
1914: The Perils of Pauline (serial)
16: The Scarlet Runner (serial)
17: Womanhood
Within the Law
18: Business of Life
Miss Ambition
The Black Secret
Song of the Soul
Trumpet of the Weak
19: Country Cousin
Black Secret (serial)
20: Greater than Fame
Life's Twist
Beware of the Bride
The Invisible Divorce
21: The Playthings of Destiny
The Breaking Point
Pilgrims of the Night
Habit
22: Her Mad Bargain
The Top of New York
The Yosemite Trail
The Kentucky Derby
23: Nobody's Money
Suzanna
Is Divorce a Failure?
Flaming Youth
The Bad Man
Lights Out
Wolf Fangs
The 11th Hour
24: Smouldering Fires
Unguarded Women
The Uninvited Guest
25: Her Husband's Secret
Havoc
26: Combat
Prisoners of the Storm
The City
Forbidden Waters
Marriage License
Across the Pacific
27: Old San Francisco
American Beauty
Man Crazy
The Secret Studio
28: Play Girl
Stop That Man!
Midnight Madness
Blockade
Old Code
Hey Rube!
29: One Splendid Hour
Confessions of a Wife
The Sport Girl
The Veiled Woman
River of Romance T

Malcolm McGregor (1892-1945)
1922: Prisoner of Zenda
Broken Chains
Greater Glory
23: A Noise in Newboro
All the Brothers Were Valiant
Can a Woman Love Twice?
Danger of the Nile
King Tut
24: Smouldering Fires
The Bedroom Window
25: Headlines
The Vanishing American
26: Infatuation
Flaming Waters
The Gay Deception
It Must Be Love
Don Juan's Three Nights
Money to Burn
27: The Silent Flyer (serial)
The Silver Streak (serial)
A Million Bid
The Wreck
Lady Bird
Matinee Ladies

27: The Place of Honor
The Kid Sister
Girl from Gay Paree
28: Lingerie
Stormy Waters
The Pearl Story
The Girl Who Came Back
Buck Privates
Freedom of the Press
Port of Missing Girls
Tropical Nights
29: Girl on the Barge PT
30: Murder Will Out T

Kathryn McGuire (1897-)

1921: Bucking the Line
The Silent Call
Playing with Fire
22: Crossroads of New York
23: The Shriek of Araby
Flame of Life
Woman of Bronze
24: The Printer's Devil
Sherlock Jr.
The Navigator
27: Naughty But Nice
Girl in the Pullman
28: Lilac Time SSE
29: Children of the Ritz SSE
Synthetic Sin
Big Diamond Robbery
Border Wildcat
The Long Long Trail T

Mickey McGuire (Mickey Rooney) (1922-)

1928: Mickey in Love
Mickey's Wild West
Mickey's Triumph
Mickey's Movies
Mickey's Rivals
Mickey the Detective
Mickey's Big Game Hunt
Mickey, I Love You
Orchids and Ermine

Burr McIntosh (1862-1942)

1915: Adventures of Wallingford (serial)
16: My Partner
20: Cynthia of the Minute
Way Down East
22: Driven
23: The Exciters
25: The Green Archer (serial)
26: Dangerous Friends
The Buckaroo Kid
Wilderness Woman
27: Taxi! Taxi!
See You in Jail
Fire and Steel
Naughty But Nice
Silk Stockings
Hazardous Valleys
Breakfast at Sunrise
Once and Forever
A Hero for a Night
The Golden Stallion (serial)
28: Moran of the Marines
Sailor's Wives
Fourflusher
Adorable Cheat
Across the Atlantic
That Certain Thing
Grip of the Yukon
Lilac Time SSE
Me Gangster
29: Fancy Baggage PT
Last Warning PT
Skinner Steps Out T

Lafe McKee (1872-)

1928: Saddle Mates
Upland Rider
Reilly of the Rainbow Division
29: California Mail
The Amazing Vagabond
Manhattan Cowboy
On the Divide
Trail Riders

Raymond McKee

1917: Kidnapped
18: Heart of the Hills
The Unbeliever
19: Kathleen Mavourneen
Captain Kidd, Jr.
20: The Fortune Teller
Love's Harvest
The Little Wanderer
Girl o' My Heart
Flame of Youth
Wing Toy
The Little Mother
21: The Lamplighter

21: Blind Hearts
22: The Jilt
Through a Glass Window
23: In the Fog
Down to the Sea in Ships
A Blind Bargain
the Burr Comedies
24: Three Women
25: Compromise
26: Speed Limit
Oh, What a Night!
Exclusive Rights
28: Heart to Heart
29: Frozen River
King of the Herd
Campus Knights

Robert McKim (1887-)

1915: Edge of the Abyss
The Disciple
16: The Primal Lure
The Stepping Stone
The Weaker Sex
17: The Silent Man
Son of His Father
Law of the Land
18: Claws of the Hun
Love Me
The Marriage Ring
The Vamp
Law of the North
Green Eyes
Playing the Game
19: Greased Lightning
20: The Mark of Zorro
The Silver Horde
Woman in Room 13
The Dwelling Place of Light
The U. P. Trail
The Money Changers
Devil to Pay
21: Man of the Forest
Lure of Egypt
22: White Hands
Monte Cristo
Without Compromise
23: The Spoilers
All the Brothers were Valiant
Mr. Billings Spends His Dime
Spider and the Rose
Dead Game
23: Ambrose Applejohn's Adventure
Strangers of the Night
24: Flaming Barriers
25: Percy
Spook Ranch
A Regular Scout
26: The Bat
The Dead Line
Strong Man
Wolf Hunters
Tough Guy
Pay Off
Winning of Barbara Worth
27: Show Girl SSE
A Flame in the Sky
28: Thrill Seeker

Victor McLaglen (1883-1959)

1920: Call of the Road
21: The Gary Corinthian
22: The Glorious Adventure
24: The Beloved Brute
25: Percy
Unholy Three
The Fighting Heart
The Hunted Woman
Winds of Chance
26: Beau Geste
It's the Old Army Game
Isle of Retribution
Men of Steel
27: Loves of Carmen
Rough and Ready
28: A Girl in Every Port
Mother Machree SSE
Hangman's House
29: Strong Boy SSE
Hot for Paris T
Black Watch T
Captain Lash

George Meeker (1904-)

1928: The Escape
The Thief in the Dark
Mr. Romeo
Chicken A La King
Girl Shy Cowboy
4 Sons

Thomas Meighan (1879-1936)

1915: The Secret Sin
Kindling

16: Puddin' Head Wilson
The Sowers
The Dupe
The Storm
Trail of the Lonesome Pine
17: The Land of Promise
The Mysterious Miss Terry
The Silent Partner
18: The Fighting Hope
M'Liss
Out of a Clear Sky
Missing
Heart of the Hills
The Heart of Wetona
19: Male and Female
The Miracle Man
The Prince Chap
Frontier of the Stars
For Better, For Worse
20: Why Change Your Wife?
Conrad in Quest of His Youth
21: The Easy Road
City of Silent Men
White and Unmarried
If You Believe It, It's So
A Prince There Was
The Man Who Saw Tomorrow
Civilian Clothes
Conquest of Canaan
22: The Bachelor Daddy
Our Leading Citizen
Manslaughter
Back Home and Broke
23: Homeward Bound
Woman Proof
The Ne'er-Do-Well
24: The Alaskan
Pied Piper Malone
Tongues of Flame
The Confidence Man
25: Irish Luck
Coming Through
The Man Who Found Himself
Old Home Week
26: The New Klondike
Tin Gods
The Canadian
27: We're All Gamblers
The City Gone Wild
Blind Alleys
27: Cappy Ricks
28: The Racket
The Mating Call
Two Arabian Knights
29: The Argyle Case T
31: Young Sinners T
34: Peck's Bad Boy T

Adolphe Menjou (1890-1963)

1916: The Blue Envelope Mystery
A Parisian Romance
17: The Moth
The Amazons
The Valentine Girl
18: Bella Donna
Rupert of Hentzau
21: The Kiss
Courage
Through the Back Door
Three Musketeers
The Sheik
The Faith Healer
22: Is Matrimony a Failure?
The Fast Mail
Eternal Flame
Pink Gods
Clarence
Singed Wings
Head Over Heels
23: The World's Applause
A Woman of Paris
The Spanish Dancer
24: The Marriage Circle
For Sale
Broadway After Dark
Sinners in Silk
Forbidden Paradise
The Fast Set
25: Are Parents People?
King of Main Street
A Gentleman of Paris
The Swan
A Kiss in the Dark
Lost a Wife
26: The Grand Duchess and the Waiter
Social Celebrity
Ace of Cads
Sorrows of Satan
27: Serenade
Service for Ladies
10 Months
Blonde or Brunette

27: Evening Clothes
28: A Night of Mystery
His Private Life
His Tiger Lady
29: Marquis Preferred
Fashions in Love
The Kiss SSE
Bachelor Girl PT

Charles Meredith (1890-1964)
1917: The Family Honor
19: Luck in Pawn
20: The Perfect Woman
Simple Souls
Judy of Rogue's Harbor
The Ladder of Lies
The Romantic Adventuress
21: The Beautiful Liar
Little 'Fraid Lady
That Something
Beyond
22: The Cradle
Hail the Woman
Cave Girl
Woman, Wake Up!
24: In Hollywood with Potash and Perlmutter

Violet Mesereau (1894-)
1908: Test of Friendship
09: Cricket of the Hearth
17: Little Miss Nobody
Girl by the Roadside
Princess Tatters
The Wild Cat
The Ragged Queen
Souls United
18: Together
19: The Nature Girl
20: Love Wins
21: Finders Keepers
Thunderclap
22: Nero
Luck
23: The Shepherd King

Buddy Messenger (1909-)
1916: Gloriana
The Street Urchin
17: Fighting Joe
Jack and the Beanstalk
Aladdin
Babes in the Wood
18: Treasure Island
19: The Hoodlum
Edgar's Little Saw
21: The Old Nest
28: Undressed
Angel Face
29: A Lady of Chance PT
Hot Stuff T
The Jazz Age

Gertrude Messenger (1911-)
1917: Aladdin and His Wonderful Lamp
18: Ali Baba and the Forty Thieves
29: The Jazz Age
Two Weeks Off PT
The Duke Steps Out PT
?? Civilization's Back Yard

Harry Mestayer
1915: The House of a Thousand Candles
The Gold Ship
18: The Atom
High Tide
19: Wife or Country
20: Stop Thief!
The Millionaire Baby

Earl Metcalf (1889-1928)
1916: Perils of our Girl Reporter (serial)
Insurrection
The Phantom Happiness
19: World to Live In
The Battler
Coax Me
Woman of Lies
Poison Pen
20: The Face at Your Window
The Fortune Hunter
The Great Mystery
While New York Sleeps
21: The Mother Eternal
What Women Will Do
Eden and Return
22: White Eagle (serial)
The Great Night
Boomerang Justice
Back to Yellow Jacket
The New Teacher
While Justice Waits

23: Power of a Lie
Look Your Best
26: The Flaming Forest
The High Flyer
Ship of Souls
Remember
Atta Boy!
Sin Cargo
27: The Notorious Lady
The Devil's Saddle
Night Life
28: Air Mail Pilot
Eagle of the Night (serial)

Adolph Milar
1920: Silent Barrier
21: Something Different
Road of Ambition
27: Back to God's Country
28: The Michigan Kid
The Devil's Skipper
The Woman Disputed
Gateway of the Moon
Clothes Make the Woman
The Kiss Doctor

John Miljan (1899-1960)
1923: Love Letters
24: The Lone Wolf
Romance Ranch
The Painted Lady
Empty Hearts
On the Stroke of Three
25: Unholy Three
Sackcloth and Scarlet
26: Flaming Waters
The Devil's Circus
Brooding Eyes
Footloose Widows
Devil's Island
Almost a Lady
Unknown Treasures
Race Wild
Amateur Gentleman
My Official Wife
27: Lovers
Final Extra
Wolf's Clothing
Lady Bird
Quarantined Rivals
Rough House Rosie
Paying the Price
What Happened to Father
27: Satin Woman
Stranded
Desired Woman
Sailor Izzy Murphy
Slaver
Ham and Eggs at the Front
The Silver Slave
Yankee Clipper
Old San Francisco
Sailor's Sweetheart
28: Glorious Betsy PT
Tenderloin PT
Land of the Silver Fox
Women They Talk About PT
Terror T
The Home Towners T
Lady, Be Good
Crimson City SSE
Little Snob SSE
Husbands for Rent
29: Stark Mad T
Speedway
Voice of the City
Fashions in Love T
Innocents of Paris T
Untamed
Eternal Woman
Desert Song T
Hardboiled Rose PT
Unholy Night T
Devil May Care T

Patsy Ruth Miller (1904-)
1921: The Sheik
Camille
22: Omar the Tentmaker
Affairs of Anatol
The Fighting Streak
Remembrance
Watch Your Step
Where's My Wandering
Boy Tonight?
Handle with Care
For Big Stakes
Fortune's Mask
23: The Girl I Loved
Hunchback of Notre Dame
24: Yankee Consul
Fools in the Dark
25: Red Hot Tires
Rose of the World
Seven Sinners
Head Winds

26: So This is Paris?
Trimmed
White Black Sheep
Oh, What a Nurse!
Private Izzy Murphy
Broken Hearts of Hollywood
Why Girls Go Back Home
King of the Turf
Hell Bent for Heaven
27: Painting the Town
Hero for a Night
The Hypocrites
Wolf's Clothing
The First Auto
What Every Girl Should Know
Shanghaied
Once's For Ever
South Sea Love
28: Marriage by Contract
Tragedy of Youth
We Americans
Beautiful But Dumb
Leave It To Me
The Pearl Story
Tomorrow
Red Riders of Canada
Hot Heels
Tropical Nights
Gate Crasher
29: The Aviator T
The Girl Who Came Back T
Fall of Eve T
Twin Beds T
The Sap PT
Hottentot T
Whispering Winds PT
Show of Shows T
So Long Letty T
Night Beat T

Walter Miller (1892-1940)
1912: The Musketeers of Pig Alley
A Change of Heart
The Informer
A Cry for Help
So Near, Yet So Far
2 Daughters of Eve
13: Oil and Water
Love in an Apartment Hotel
Death's Marathon
13: The Coming of Angelo
Two Men on the Desert
The Perfidy of Mary
Adventures in the Autumn Woods
Near to Earth
The Yaqui Cur
Adopted Brother
16: The Marble Heart
17: The Slacker
Miss Robinson Crusoe
The Mothering Heart
Manhattan Nights
You Can't Win (serial)
18: Draft 258
The 11th Commandment
19: A Girl at Bay
Thin Ice
The Friendly Call
The Open Door
20: The Return of Tarzan
The Revenge of Tarzan
Prisoners of Love
The Stealers
21: The Way Women Love
Luxury
22: Beyond the Rainbow
The Bootleggers
The Unconquered Woman
Till We Meet Again
23: The Tie That Binds
24: 10 Scars Make a Man (Serial)
The Way of a Man (serial)
Leatherstocking (serial)
25: The Green Archer (serial)
Play Ball "
Sunken Silver "
26: The Fighting Marine "
The Unfair Sex
Snowed In "
House Without a Key "
27: Melting Millions "
Hawk of the Hills "
28: The Man Without a Face "
Terrible People "
Mysterious Airman "
Police Reporter "
Perilous Mission "
29: Queen of the North Woods "
The King of the Kongo "
The Black Book "

Mary Miles Minter (1902-)

1912: The Nurse
15: Barbara Frietchie
The Fairy and the Waif
17: Environment
Charity Castle
18: Rosemary Climbs the Heights
The Eyes of Julia Deep
Her Country Calls
Peggy Rebels
Annie for Spite
The Mate of Sally Ann
Beauty and the Rogue
A Bit of Jade
Peggy Leads the Way
Social Briars
The Ghost of Rosy Taylor
19: Anne of Green Gables
The Amazing Imposter
The Bachelor's Wife
Wives and Other Wives
The Intrusion of Isabel
Homespun
Yvonne from Paris
20: Judy of Rogue's Harbor
Jerry
A Cumberland Romance
Jenny Be Good
Nurse Marjorie
21: Moonlight and Honeysuckle
Little Clown
Don't Call Me Little Girl
Her Winning Way
All Souls' Eve
Eyes of the Heart
Sweet Lavender
22: Tillie
The Heart Specialist
South of Suva
The Cowboy and the Lady
23: The Trail of the Lonesome Pine
The Drums of Fate
25: Her Husband's Secret

Rhea Mitchell (1891-1957)

1918: The Goat
Honor's Cross
Unexpected Places
19: The Money Corral
The Hawk's Trail
20: The Devil's Claim
21: Good Women
The Scoffer
23: Ponjola
The Great Menace
28: Danger Patrol

Tom Mix (1880-1940)

1910: The Long Trail
Ranch Life in the Great Southwest (documentary)
11: Back to the Primitive
13: The Law and the Outlaw
The Child of the Prairie
The Escape of Jim Dolan
The Way of the Redman
The Moving Picture Cowboy
14: Why the Sheriff is a Bachelor
The Ranger's Romance
The Man from the East
The Sheriff's Reward
When the Cock Fell In
Chip of the Flying U
Forked Trails
Slim Higgins
Man from Texas
A Child of the Prairie
(2nd use of title)
The Stagecoach Driver and the Girl
15: The Heart of the Sheriff
A Lucky Deal
The Range Girl and the Cowboy
The Brave Deserve the Fair
The Stagecoach Guard
Making Good
Arizona Wooing
The Passing of Pete
Along the Border
The Sheriff's Duty
Crooked Trails
(or Twisted Trails)
Going West to Make Good
The Cowpuncher's Peril
Taking a Chance
Some Duel
16: A Western Masquerade
Roping a Sweetheart
Tom's Strategy
The Taming of Grouchy Bill
The Pony Express Rider
A Corner in Water

16:
- The Raiders
- The Canby Hill Outlaws
- A Mistake in Rustlers
- A Close Call
- Tom's Sacrifice
- The Sheriff's Blunder
- Hearts and Saddles
- A Roman Cowboy

17:
- Tom and Jerry Mix
- Six Cylinder Love
- A Soft Tenderfoot
- Durand of the Badlands

18:
- Cupid's Round Up
- Six Shooter Andy
- Treat 'Em Rough
- Fame and Fortune
- Western Blood
- Ace High
- Mr. Logan - U. S. A.

19:
- Hell Roarin' Reform
- The Coming of the Law
- Wilderness Trail
- The Speed Maniac

20:
- Rough Riding Romance
- The Feud
- 3 Gold Coins
- Fighting for Gold
- The Untamed
- The Cyclone
- Desert Love
- The Dare Devil
- Queen of Sheba
- Chasing the Moon
- The Terror

21:
- The Texan
- Prairie Trails
- Hands Off!
- The Road Demon
- After Your Own Heart
- Big Town Round Up
- A Ridin' Romeo
- The Night Horseman
- The Rough Diamond

22:
- Sky High
- Trailin'
- The Fighting Streak
- For Big Stakes
- Up and Going
- Do and Dare
- Just Tony
- Tom Mix in Arabia
- Catch My Smoke
- Romance Land

23:
- 3 Jumps Ahead
- Stepping Fast
- Soft Boiled
- North of Hudson Bay
- The Lone Star Ranger
- Mile-A-Minute Romeo

24:
- Eyes of the Forest
- Ladies to Board
- Oh You Tony!
- Yes, We Have No Temper
- Last of the Duanes
- The Heart Buster
- Teeth
- The Deadwood Coach

25:
- Riders of the Purple Sage
- Lucky Horseshoe
- The Everlasting Whisper
- The Rainbow Trail
- Dick Turpin
- The Best Bad Man

26:
- The Yankee Senor
- My Own Pal
- Tony Runs Wild
- Hard Boiled
- No Man's Gold

27:
- The Great K&A Train Robbery
- Canyon of Light
- The Last Trail
- The Bronco Twister
- The Circus Ace
- Tumbling River
- Outlaws of Red River
- The Silver Valley
- Painted Ponies

28:
- Arizona Wildcat
- Daredevil's Reward
- A Horseman of the Plains
- Drums of Araby
- Hills of Cheyenne
- Painted Post
- Hello Cheyenne!
- Son of the Golden West
- King Cowboy

29:
- The Drifter
- Outlawed
- The Big Diamond Robbery

31:
- Dude Ranch

32:
- Destry Rides Again T
- Riders of Death Valley T
- My Pal the King T
- The Fourth Horseman T

33:
- Hidden Gold T

33: Flaming Guns T
Terror Trail T
The Rustlers Roundup T
Pony Boy T
Texas Bad Man T
The Miracle Rider T
(serial)

William V. Mong (1875-1940)

1916: The Severed Hand
18: The Hopper
The Man Who Woke Up
19: The Turning Point
20: Luck of Geraldine Laird
Sowing the Wind
The Stain
Burning Daylight
Mutiny of the Elsinore
21: A $10 Raise
Why Girls Leave Home
The County Fair
Ladies Must Live
A Connecticut Yankee in
King Arthur's Court
Pilgrims of the Night
Playthings of Destiny
22: Shattered Idols
Monte Cristo
A Fool There Was
The Woman He Loved
23: All the Brothers Were
Valiant
Lost and Found
Penrod and Sam
Drifting
In the Palace of the King
24: Thy Name is Woman
Maker of Dreams
25: Off the Highway
Lights of Old Broadway
26: Steel Preferred
The Shadow on the Wall
Strong Man
What Price Glory?
5th Avenue
Shadow of the Law
Brooding Eyes
The Old Soak
The Silent Lover
27: Taxi! Taxi!
The Magic Garden
The Price of Honor
Too Many Crooks
27: Alias the Lone Wolf
The Clown
28: Iron Mike
Ransom
Code of the Air
The Broken Mask
The Haunted House
Telling the World
The Devil's Trade-Mark
No Babies Wanted
29: Should a Girl Marry?
Dark Skies
Noah's Ark PT
7 Footprints to Satan SSE
House of Horror PT

Bull Montana (1887-1950)

1917: In Again, Out Again
18: He Comes Up Smiling
19: Victory
Go and Get It
Treasure Island
20: Girl in Number 29
What Women Love
Hearts are Trumps
21: The Foolish Age
One Wild Week
The 4 Horsemen of the
Apocalypse
Breaking Into Society
Snowed Under
22: Gay and Devilish
A Ladies' Man
3 Must-Get-Theres
The Punctured Prince
Glad Rags
Timber Queen (serial)
23: Rob 'em Good
Hollywood
The Two Twins (dual)
26: The Son of the Sheik
Vanishing Millions (serial)
28: How to Handle Women
Good Morning, Judge
Limousine Love
The Fight Pest
29: Show of Shows T
Tiger Rose T
35: Never Too Late T

Baby Peggy Montgomery (1918-)

1922: Grandma's Girl
The Senorita

23: Hansel and Gretel
The Darling of New York
24: Captain January
The Family Secret
The Law Forbids
Helen's Babies
The Flower Girl
Whose Baby Are You?
Edith's Burglar
Jack and the Beanstalk
25: There He Goes
26: Saturday Afternoon
Prisoners of the Storm
27: Sensation Seekers
Fighting Failure
The Sonora Kid
2 Guns of Tumbleweeds
28: Saddle Mates
Desert of the Lost
Silent Trail
On the Divide
29: Bad Man's Money
Arizona Days
West of Santa Fe

Colleen Moore (1900-)
1916: Intolerance
17: Hands Up!
The Bad Boy
The Old-Fashioned Young Man
18: A Hoosier Romance
That's a Bad Girl
19: The Wilderness Trail
Little Orphan Annie
The Busher
Hearts of the World (bit cut out)
The Egg-Crate Wallop
The Man in the Moonlight
20: So Long Letty
Dinty
Gym
The Cyclone
Common Property
A Roman Scandal
Her Bridal Nightmare
The Devil's Claim
When Dawn Came
21: The Lotus Eater
Sky Pilot
22: His Nibs
Affinities
22: Come On Over
The Ninety and Nine
The Wallflower
23: Broken Chains
Slippery McGee
Forsaking All Others
Look Your Best
The Nth Commandment
The Huntress
Flaming Youth
April Showers
24: Painted People
The Perfect Flapper
Flirting with Love
Through the Dark
25: So Big
Sally
Desert Flower
We Moderns
26: Ella Cinders
It Must Be Love
Irene
Twinkletoes
27: Her Wild Oat
Naughty But Nice
Small Bachelor
28: Lilac Time
Orchids and Ermine
Happiness Ahead
Oh Kay!
Burning Daylights
29: Synthetic Sin
Why Be Good?
Smiling Irish Eyes T
Footlights and Fools T
Paris Bound T
33: Power and the Glory T
Social Register T
34: Success at any Price T
The Scarlet Letter T

Matt Moore (1888-1960)
1913: Traffic in Souls
14: A Singular Cynic
16: 20,000 Leagues Under the Sea
17: Pride of the Clan
Runaway Romany
18: Heart of the Hills
Sport of Kings
Heart of the Wilds
19: The Dark Star
Unpardonable Sin

19: Sahara
A Regular Fellow
The Glorious Lady
Getting Mary Married
20: Don't Ever Marry
Madness of Manhattan
Love Madness
Hairpins
Everybody's Sweetheart
21: The Passionate Pilgrim
Straight is the Way
A Man's Home
22: Back Pay
Sisters
The Storm
The Jilt
Minnie
No More Women
23: Drifting
White Tiger
Strangers of the Night
24: Fools in the Dark
25: How Baxter Butted In
The Unholy Three
A Lost Lady
Narrow Street
26: His Jazz Bride
The First Year
The Cave Man
3 Weeks in Paris
Early to Wed
Mystery Club
Summer Bachelors
Diplomacy
27: Married Alive
Tillie the Toiler
Ambrose Applejohn's Adventure
28: Beware of Blondes
Phyllis of the Follies
Dry Martini
Coquette T
29: Side Street T

Owen Moore (1886-1930)
1908: The Valet's Wife
09: The Burglar's Mistake
Two Memories
Golden Louis
Pippa Passes
A Lonely Villa
The Cricket of the Hearth
Resurrection
09: The Violin Maker of Cremona
In Old Kentucky
Shadows of Doubt
Stolen Love
10: The First Misunderstanding
11: Flo's Discipline
The Courting of Mary
12: In Swift Waters
The Lesser Evil
13: Caprice
14: Battle of the Sexes
Home Sweet Home
Cinderella
15: The Escape
Mistress Nell
Pretty Mrs. Smith
Nearly a Lady
My Valet
Jordan is a Hard Road
16: A Coney Island Princess
Betty of Graystone
Little Meena's Romance
Suzan Rocks the Boat
17: Under Cover
The Little Boy Scout
A Girl Like That
Thing
19: The Crimson Gardenia
20: Piccadilly Jim
Who's Who
Dangerous Hero
Stop That Man!
The Poor Simp
Sooner or Later
The Desperate Hero
21: A Divorce of Convenience
Chicken in the Case
False Pride
22: Oh, Mabel, Behave
Reported Missing
Love is an Awful Thing
23: Modern Matrimony
Her Temporary Husband
Torment
24: Thundergate
The Silent Partner
East of Broadway
Camille of the Barbary Coast
Go Straight
25: Code of the West
The Parasite

25: Married?
26: Black Bird
Road to Mandalay
The Skyrocket
Money Talks
The Red Mill
False Pride
27: Taxi Dancer
Women Love Diamonds
Becky
Tea for Three
Husbands for Rent
28: Stolen Love
The Actress
The Condemned Woman
29: Side Street T
High Voltage T
30: What a Widow T
Outside the Law T
Extravagance T
Hush Money T
32: As You Desire Me T
33: She Done Him Wrong T
37: A Star is Born T

Tom Moore (1885-1955)
1913: Nina of the Theatre
An American Princess
14: An Unseen Terror
The Barefoot Boy
The Vampire's Trail
Mystery of the Sleeping Death
The Brand
16: Who's Guilty? (serial)
17: Brown of Harvard
The Cinderella Man
18: 30 a Week
The Lesson
19: Lord and Lady Algy
Just for Tonight
A Man and His Money
Go West, Young Man
One of the Finest
Heartease
Toby's Bow
City of Comrades
20: Dubs
Stop, Thief!
The Great Accident
Officer 666
Cyclone Hickey
The Gay Lord Quex
21: Hold Your Horses
Made in Heaven
Beating the Game
22: From the Ground Up
Over the Border
The Cowboy and the Lady
Pawned
Rouged Lips
Mr. Barnes of New York
23: Marriage Morals
Harbour Lights
Big Brother
24: Manhandled
One Night in Rome
Dangerous Money
25: Trouble with Wives
Adventure
Pretty Ladies
On Thin Ice
26: Syncopating Sue
Good and Naughty
The Clinging Vine
A Kiss for Cinderella
Song and Dance Man
27: The Love Thrill
The Wise Wife
Cabaret
28: Anybody Here Seen Kelly?
The Siren
The Last Haul
29: Side Street T
30: The Woman Racket T
Second Fiddle T
The Costello Murder Case T

Victor Moore (1876-1962)
1915: The Best Man
Snobs
Chimmie Fadden series
16: The Clown
The Race
The Moneyless Honeymoon
The Cinderella Husbands
Camping
17: Bungalowing
Moving
Flivvering
Home Defense

Lee Moran (1889-1961)
1909: Lyons & Moran Comedies (10 years)
15: When the Mummy Cried for Help

17: Eddie's Little Love Affair
War Bridegrooms
Ducks Out of Water
Camping Out
Bullsheviks
Dog-Gone Shame
Whose Wife is Kate?
Robinson's Trousseau
P. D. Q.
The Straphanger
The Touch Down
Upper and Lower
3 Weeks Off
10 Seconds
Apartment Wanted
Some Family
Hello, Judge
20: La, La, Lucille
Fixed by George
21: Once a Plumber
Blue Sunday
Roman Romeos
A Shocking Night
How Do You Feel?
Everything But the Truth
24: 5th Avenue Models
25: Tessie
26: Alimony Annie
Syncopating Sue
Her Big Night
My Lady of Whims
The Little Irish Girl
27: Fast and Furious
The Irresistible Lover
Rose of Kildare
Spring Fever
28: Thrill Seeker
Thanks for the Buggy Ride
Woman Against the World
The Lookout Girl
Show Girl
Outcast
29: Children of the Ritz SSE
On with the Show PT
Glad Rag Doll T
Gold Diggers of Broadway T
Madonna of Avenue A PT
Show of Shows T
Dance Hall T
The Aviator T

Lois Moran (1909-)

1924: La Galerie Des Monstres
25: Feu-Mathies Pascal
Stella Dallas
26: Just Suppose
Reckless Lady
Prince of Tempters
Padlocked
God Gave Me Twenty Cents
27: Whirlwind of Youth
Road to Mandalay
Irresistible Lover
The Music Master
Publicity Madness
28: Sharpshooters
Love Hungry
Don't Marry
River Pirate
Blindfold
False Colors
Beyond the Sierras
29: Making the Grade PT
Joy Street SSE
Behind That Curtain T
True Heaven
Words and Music T
The Case of Mary Brown
Song of Kentucky
30: Not Damaged T
The Dancers T
Under Suspicion T
Mammy T
31: Transatlantic T
The Spider T
West of Broadway T
Men of Her Life T

Polly Moran (1884-1952)

1914: The Janitor
15: A Favorite Fool
Sheriff Nell's Come Back
Their Social Splash
Those College Girls (or His Better Half)
Her Painted Hero
16: Love Will Conquer
The Village Blacksmith
By Stork Delivery
His Wild Oats
A Bath House Blunder
Madcap Ambrose
Vampire Ambrose

17: Her Fame and Shame
His Uncle Dudley
His Naughty Thought
Cactus Nell
She Needed a Doctor
The Pullman Bride
Roping Her Romeo
In Again, Out Again
High and Dry
21: Affairs of Anatol
Skirts
23: Luck
27: The Callahans and the Murphys
London After Midnight
Buttons
28: The Enemy
Rose Marie
Divine Woman
Show People
Beyond the Sierras
Shadows of the Night
While the City Sleeps
Trail of '98
Bring Up Father
Telling the World
29: Honeymoon
China Bound
Dangerous Females
Came the Dawn
Chasing Rainbows
Margin Mugs
That Night
Iron Mike
The Masked Stranger
Deadline
Hollywood Revue of 1929 T
Speedway
Unholy Night
So This is College? T
Road Show T
Hot for Paris T
Saucy Madeline T

Milburn Morante (1888-1964)
1929: Freckled rascal
Little Savage
?? 15 Gale Henry comedies
Also many Keystone comedies

Antonio Moreno (1887-1967)
1912: Voice of the Million
The Invisible Man
Two Daughters of Eve
So Near, Yet So Far
Musketeers of Pig Alley
13: House of Discord
No Place for Father
By Man's Law
14: In the Latin Quarter
Strongheart
Anselo Lee
John Rance, Gentleman
His Father's House
Our Mutual Girl
Too Many Husbands
The Accomplished Mrs. Thompson
The Persistent Mr. Prince
Song of the Ghetto
Memories in Men's Souls
The Hidden Letters
Politics and the Press
The Loan Shark King
The Peacemaker
Under False Colors
Goodbye Summer
The Old Flute Player
15: The Island of Regeneration
The Quality of Mercy
The Park Honeymooners
Love's Way
On Her Wedding Night
Dust of Egypt
Youth
The Gypsy Trail
A Model Wife
The Price of Folly
The Birth of a Nation
16: The Supreme Temptation
Susie, the Sleuth
She Won the Prize
Rose of the South
Kennedy Square
17: The Angel Factory
The Magnificent Meddler
Aladdin from Broadway
Her Right to Live
Money Magic
The Captain of the Gray Horse Troop
A Son of the Hills

17: By Right of Possession
The Mark of Cain
18: House of Hate (serial)
The Iron Test (serial)
777
The First Law
The House of a 1000 Candles
The Naulahka (or the Jewelled Girdle)
19: Perils of Thunder Mountain (serial)
20: The Invisible Hand (serial)
The Veiled Mystery (serial)
21: Secret of the Hills
22: A Guilty Conscience
23: Lost and Found in a South Sea Island
My American Wife
Trail of the Lonesome Pine
Look Your Best
The Spanish Dancer
The Exciters
24: The Story Without a Name
Border Legion
Tiger Love
Flaming Barriers
Bluff
25: One Year to Live
Her Husband's Secret
Learning to Love
26: Mare Nostrum
The Temptress
Beverly of Graustark
The Flaming Forest
Love's Blindness
27: It
Madam Pompadour
Venus of Venice
In the Land of the Sun
Come to My House
28: Nameless Men
Adoration
Midnight Taxi
The Whip Woman
The Clash
Synthetic Sin
The Air Legion
29: Romance of the Rio Grande PT
Careers PT

Harry T. Morey (1879-1936)
1912: As You Like It
12: Indian Romeo and Juliet
Lady of the Lake
Aunty's Romance
13: The Deerslayer
The Wreck
14: The Battle of the Weak
A Million Bid
Shadow of the Past
My Official Wife
15: A Price for Folly
16: Salvation Joan
Casey at the Bat
17: Within the Law
18: The Golden Goal
Who Goes There?
His Own People
The Other Man
A Desired Woman
A Bachelor's Children
A Game with Fate
Tangled Lives
All Man
Playing with Fate
19: Silent Strength
King of Diamonds
Hoarded Assets
The Gamble
The Man Who Won
The Green God
Fighting Destiny
Beauty Proof
Beating the Odds
20: The Gauntlet
In Honor's Web
The Flaming Clue
The Birth of a Soul
The Sea Rider
The Darkest Hour
21: A Man's Home
22: Beyond the Rainbow
The Curse of Drink
Wildness of Youth
23: Where the Pavement Ends
The Green Goddess
25: Headlines
26: Aloma of the South Seas
28: Under the Tonto Rim
Forgotten Faces
The Fifty-Fifty Girl
None but the Brave
29: Return of Sherlock Holmes

Frank Morgan (1890-1949)
1917: A Modern Cinderella
Sight in Darkness
Baby Mine
Who's Your Neighbor?
18: At the Mercy of Men
19: Gray Towers of Mystery
The Golden Shower

James Morrison (1888-)
1911: Saving an Audience
A Tale of Two Cities
12: As You Like It
15: The Battle Cry of Peace
16: Redemption of Dave Darcey
Hero of Submarine D-2
The Enemy
17: Babbling Tongues
Life Against Honor
18: Over the Top
Moral Suicide
19: Womanhood
Sacred Silence
20: Sowing the Wind
Love Without Question
21: Black Beauty
Seepore Rebellion
When We Were Twenty-One
23: Ten Commandments
On the Banks of the Wabash
24: Captain Blood
Wine of Youth

Charles Morton (1904-)
1927: Rich But Honest
Colleen
28: Four Sons
None but the Brave
Four Devils PT
Street Fair
29: Christina PT
New Year's Eve SSE
Far Call SSE
30: Cameo Kirby T
33: Check and Double Check T
36: Hollywood Boulevard T
39: Stunt Pilot T
44: Lumberjack

Maria Mosquini (1899-)
1926: Looking for Trouble
It's a Hard Life
Floor Below
26: His Royal Shyness
His Best Girl
Make it Snappy
Rush Orders
No Children

Edward Moulton
1928: The Big Killing
Grit Wins
A Double Cross

Jack Mower (1890- 1965)
1918: The Primitive Woman
Money Isn't Everything
Mantle of Charity
19: Molly of the Follies
Island of Intrigue
The Beloved Cheater
20: Bubbles
A Cowboy Ace
The Third Eye (serial)
The Tiger Band
21: Cotton and Cattle
The Beautiful Gambler
22: Manslaughter
Saturday Night
23: Days of Daniel Boone (serial)
24: 10 Scars Make a Man (serial)
25: Perils of the Wild (serial)
26: Officer 444 (serial)
The Radio Detective (serial)
Melodies
The Ghetto Shamrock
False Friends
Her Own Story
27: Trail of the Tiger (serial)
Pretty Clothes
Uncle Tom's Cabin
28: Sailors' Wives
Air Patrol
Water Hole
Sinners' Parade
29: Ships of the Night
Anne Against the World

Jack Mulhall (1891-)
1913: House of Discord
15: Tides of Retribution
17: Madam Spy
18: The Brass Bullet (serial)
Wild Youth
Sirens of the Sea
Mickey

19: The Midnight Man (serial)
The Solitary Sin
Whom the Gods Destroy
20: All of a Sudden Peggy
The Hope
High Speed
Three Women of France
Should a Woman Tell?
Boss of Powderville
The Ne'er To Return Road
21: The Offshore Pirate
The Little Clown
Two Weeks With Pay
Molly-O
Turn to the Right
The 14th Lover
22: Midnight
The Sleep Walker
Dusk to Dawn
Broad Daylight
White and Yellow
The Forgotten Law
Flesh and Blood
23: Heroes of the Street
Within the Law
Dulcy
The Bad Man
Cold Cash
Social Buccaneer (serial)
Call of the Wild
24: The Goldfish
The Mad Whirl
Into the Net (serial)
25: Friendly Enemies
Joanna
26: Subway Sadie
Just Another Blonde
The Dixie Merchant
Pleasures for the Rich
Silence
Sweet Daddies
God Gave Me Twenty Cents
27: Man Crazy
The Crystal Cup
The Poor Nut
Orchids and Ermine
Far Cry
See Me In Jail
Smile, Brother, Smile
28: Lady Be Good
Butter and Egg Man
Ladies' Night in a Turkish Bath
28: Waterfront
Sunset Legion
Hearts of Men
29: Naughty Baby T
Children of the Ritz SSE
Dark Streets T
Twin Beds T
Two Weeks Off PT
Show of Shows

Ann Murdock (1890-)

1916: Captain Jinks of the Horse Marines
17: The Beautiful Adventure
Please Help Emily
Seven Deadly Sins (Envy seq.)
Outcast
My Wife
The Richest Girl

Edna Murphy (1904-)

1920: Fantomas
Branded Woman
Over the Hill to the Poorhouse
The North Wind's Malice
21: What Love Will Do
Dynamite Allen
Play Square
22: The Jolt
Extra! Extra!
The Ordeal
Don't Shoot
The Galloping Kid
Caught Bluffing
Ridin' Wild
23: Nobody's Bride
Her Dangerous Path
24: Into the Net (serial)
King of the Wild Horses
Leatherstocking (serial)
25: A Man Must Live
Clothes Make the Pirate
26: Ermine and Rhinestones
Oh, What a Night!
Obey the Law
27: McFadden's Flats
Tarzan and the Golden Lion
All Aboard
Silver Comes Through
Modern Daughters
Valley of Hell

27: Burnt Fingers
Black Diamond Express
Silent Hero
Cruise of the Hellion
His Foreign Wife
28: Willful Youth
Across the Atlantic
Sunset Legion
The Midnight Adventure
Bachelor's Club
29: My Man PT
Greyhound Limited PT
Stolen Kisses PT
Kid Gloves PT
The Sap PT
30: Little Johnny Jones T
Show of Shows T

Charlie Murray (1872-1941)
1913: Almost a Man
other Keystone Comedies
14: The Passing of Izzy
A Fatal Flirtation
Her Friend the Bandit
Soldiers of Misfortune
Such a Crook (or the Bungling Burglars)
The Masquerader
Stout Hearts But Weak Knees
Cursed by his Beauty
The Noise of Bombs
His Halted Career
The Plumber
15: A Game Old Knight
The Great Vacuum Robbery
Hogan's Wild Oats
Hogan's Annual Spree
His Second Childhood
Hogan's Mussy Job
From Patches to Plenty
Their Social Splash
The Beauty Bunglers
Those College Girls (or His Better Half)
Her Painted Hero
16: His Hereafter (or Murray's Mix-Up)
Hogan the Porter
Hogan's Romance Upset
The Judge
Her Marble Heart
Pills of Peril
Bombs
16: Fido's Fate
A Love Riot
The Feathered Nest
Maid Mad (or the Fortune Teller)
17: Maggie's First False Step
Her Fame and Shame
Betrayal of Maggie
The Precious Life
A Bedroom Blunder
18: Watch Your Neighbor
19: Never Too Old
Reilly's Wash Day
Trying to Get Along
Up in Alf's Place
The Speak-Easy
21: A Small Town Idol
Love Honor and Behave
22: Cross Roads of New York
Faint Hearts
Social Errors
The Fatal Photo
The Nuisance
The Pill Pounder
Luck
24: The Pilgrim
25: My Son
26: The Cohens and the Kellys
Irene
Steel Preferred
Mike
Reckless Lady
Second Chance
The Boob
Sweet Daddies
Subway Sadie
Silent Lover
Mismates
Paradise
27: Masked Woman
The Poor Nut
Life of Riley
Lost at the Front
The Gorilla
28: Flying Romeos
The Head Man
Do Your Duty
It's All Greek to Me
Vamping Venus
?? Her Blighted Love
The Dentist
Great Scott
Don't Weaken

?? The Unhappy Finish

James Murray (1901- 1937)

1925:	Percy	
27:	In Old Kentucky	
	The Lovelorn	
28:	Rose Marie	
	The Crowd	
	Big City	
29:	Little Wildcat	PT
	The Shakedown	PT
	Thunder	T
	Shanghai Lady	T

Mae Murray (1889-1965)

1916:	To Have and to Hold	
	Sweet Kitty Bellairs	
	Dream Girl	
	Big Sister	
	Plow Girl	
17:	Morman Maid	
	Primrose Ring	
	At First Sight	
	Princess Virtue	
18:	Face Value	
	High Stakes	
	Bride's Awakening	
	Her Body in Bond	
	Danger-Go Slow	
	Modern Love	
19:	Scarlet Shadow	
	What Am I Bid?	
	Girl for Sale	
	Twin Pawns	
	Big Little Person	
20:	Delicious Little Devil	
	On With the Dance	
	Right to Love	
	Idols of Clay	
	ABCs of Love	
21:	Gilded Lily	
	Peacock Alley	
	Bachelor Apartment	
22:	Fascination	
	Broadway Rose	
23:	French Doll	
	Jazzmania	
	Fashion Row (dual role)	
24:	Mademoiselle Midnight	
	Circe the Adventuress	
25:	Merry Widow	
	Masked Bride	
26:	Valencia	
27:	Altars of Desire	
30:	Peacock Alley	T
31:	High Stakes	T

Carmel Myers (1899-1966)

1916:	Intolerance
	Haunted Pajamas
	The Matrimaniac
17:	Stage Struck
	Might and the Man
	Sirens of the Sea
	My Unmarried Wife
	The Heart of a Jewess
	Marriage Lie
18:	A Broadway Scandal
	My Dream Lady
	City of Tears
	The Wife He Brought Back
	Girl in the Dark
	The Wine Girl
	All Night
	A Society Sensation
19:	Little White Savage
	Who Will Marry Me?
20:	In Folly's Trail
	The Mad Marriage
	The Dangerous Moment
	Breaking Through (serial)
	Gilded Dream
	Beautifully Trimmed
	Cheated Love
	The Kiss
	Daughter of the Law
22:	Love Gambler
23:	Last Hour
	Goodbye Girls
	The Famous Mrs. Fair
	Dancer of the Nile
	Slave of Desire
	The Law Against the Law
	You Are in Danger
	King Tut
	The Little Girl Next Door
24:	Beau Brummell
	Song of Love
26:	Ben Hur
	Tell it to the Marines
27:	The Demi-Bride
	The Understanding Heart
	Sorrell and Son
	Girl from Rio
28:	A Certain Young Man
	Prowlers of the Sea

28:	4 Walls	
	Dream of Love	
29:	Ghost Talks	T
	Careers	PT
	Careless Age	T
	Red Sword	
	Broadway Scandals	T
	He Did His Best	T
30:	The Ship from Shanghai	T
	A Lady Surrenders	T
31:	Svengali	T
	Nice Women	T
34:	The Countess of Monte Cristo	T

Harry C. Myers (1882-1938)

1909:	The Jonesy films
11:	Her Two Sons
13:	When the Earth Trembled
14:	Baby
16:	Housekeeping
20:	Notorious Mrs. Sands
	Peaceful Valley
	45 Minutes from Broadway
21:	A Connecticut Yankee in King Arthur's Court
	Oh Mary, Be Careful!
	Nobody's Fool
	R. S. V. P.
	Turn to the Right
	On the High Card
	The March Hare
22:	Handle with Care
	Boy Crazy
	Kisses
	The Beautiful and Damned
	Adventures of Robinson Crusoe (serial)
	Top o' the Morning
23:	Brass
	Stephen Steps Out
	Main Street
	The Bad Man
	The Marriage Circle
24:	Daddies
26:	Up in Mabel's Room
	Exit Smiling
	The Beautiful Cheat
	The Nut Cracker
27:	Getting Gertie's Garter
	Girl in the Pullman
	The Bachelor's Baby
	The First Night
28:	The Dove
	Street of Illusion
	The Dream of Love
29:	City Lights
	The Clean-Up
	Montmartre Rose
	Wonder of Women T

Conrad Nagel (1896-1970)

1919:	Little Women
	Redhead
20:	Midsummer Madness
	The Fighting Chance
	Unseen Forces
21:	What Every Woman Knows
	Sacred and Profane Love
	Fool's Paradise
	The Lost Romance
22:	Saturday Night
	Nice People
	The Impossible Mrs. Bellew
	Romance of a Queen
	Pink Gods
23:	Grumpy
	Lawful Larceny
	Bella Donna
	Lion and the Mouse
	Rendezvous
	The Eternal Three
24	Three Weeks
	Tess of the D'Urbervilles
	The Snob
	So This is Marriage
25:	The Only Thing
	Pretty Ladies
	Lights of Old Broadway
	Sun Up
26:	The Waning Sex
	Tin Hats
	Exquisite Sinner
	Dance Madness
	Memory Lane
	Excuse Me
	There You Are
27:	Quality Street
	The Hypnotist
	Heaven on Earth
	Slightly Used
	The Girl from Chicago
	London After Midnight
28:	The Mysterious Lady
	The Michigan Kid
	Diamond Handcuffs

28: Husbands are Liars
War in the Dark
If I Were Single
Tenderloin PT
Glorious Betsy PT
State Street Sadie PT
Caught in the Fog PT
29: The 13th Chair T
Red Wine SSE
The Idle Rich T
Kid Gloves T
The Kiss SSE
Dynamite T
The Redeeming Sin PT
Hollywood Revue of 1929 T

Nita Naldi (1889-1961)
1920: Dr. Jekyll and Mr. Hyde
Life
21: Experience
22: Blood and Sand
Anna Ascends
The Man From Beyond
For Your Daughter's Sake
Channing of the Northwest
The Snitching Hour
Reported Missing
The 9th Commandment
23: Glimpses of the Moon
You Can't Fool Your Wife
Lawful Larceny
10 Commandments
24: The Sainted Devil
25: The Cobra
Clothes Make the Pirate
The Lady Who Died
The Marriage Whirl
26: The Unfair Sex
The Miracle of Life
The Mountain Eagle
The Pleasure Garden
Die Pratermizzi
La Femme Mie
28: What Price Beauty?
Model from Montmartre

Alla Nazimova (1879-1945)
1916: War Brides
18: Revelation
Toys of Fate
19: Red Lantern
Eye for Eye
Out of the Fog
19: The Brat
20: Stronger Than Death
Heart of a Child
Billions
21: Madame Peacock
Camille
22: A Doll's House
23: Salome
24: Madonna of the Streets
25: My Son
The Redeeming Sin
39: Zaza T
40: Escape T
41: Blood and Sand T
44: The Bridge of San Luis Rey T
Since You Went Away T
In Our Time T

Pola Negri (1894-)
1914: Niewolnica Zomyslow
15: Bestia
Czarna Ksiazeczka
Der Gelbe Schein
Pokoj Nr 13
16: Jego Ostatni Czyn
Studenci
Zona
Arabella
17: Love and Passion
Komtesse Doddy
18: Carmen
The Eyes of the Mummy
19: DuBarry
Kreuzigt Sie
20: Passion
One Arabian Night
Sumurun
Manja
Die Marchesa D'Arminiani
Das Martyrium
Arme Violetta
21: Gypsy Blood
Mad Love
Die Bergkatze
Camille
22: The Last Payment
The Red Peacock
The Devil's Pawn
Vendetta
Intrigue
The Spanish Dancer
Die Dame Im Glashave

22: Die Flamme
Die Geschlossene Kette
Sappho
23: Bella Donna
The Cheat
Montmartre
24: Men
Lily of the Dust
Shadows of Paris
The Passionate Journey
Forbidden Paradise
25: The Charmer
East of Suez
Flower of the Night
26: Crown of Lies
A Woman of the World
Hotel Imperial
Good and Naughty
27: Barbed Wire
Woman on Trial
28: Secret Hour
A Woman Commands
Loves of an Actress
Three Sinners
Woman from Moscow
29: The Woman He Scorned
Way of Lost Souls
30: Flame of Love T
32: A Woman Commands T
34: Fanatisme T
35: Mazurka T
36: Moskau-Shanghai T
37: Madame Bovary T
Tango Notturno T
38: Die Fromme Luge T
Die Nacht Der Entscheidung T
43: Hi Diddle Diddle T
64: The Moonspinners T

James Neill

1918: Say, Young Fellow
The Girl Who Came Back
His Official Fiancee
19: Men, Women, and Money
The Rescuing Angel
Everywoman
Romance and Arabella
Little Shepherd of Kingdom Come
20: The Double-Dyed Deceiver

Jack Nelson (1882-)

1917: The Man Trap
18: The Flash of Fate
Winner Takes All
19: The Girl Dodger
Twenty-Three and a Half Hours' Leave
The Long Chance
The Wilderness Trail
Rose of the West
Rough Riding Romance
20: Love Madness
21: The Rookie's Return
The Home Stretch
Chickens
I Am Guilty

Evelyn Nesbit (1885-1967)

1914: Threads of Destiny
15: Judge Not
17: Redemption
19: Woman, Woman
I Want to Forget
Her Mistake
My Little Sister
The Woman Who Gave
Thou Shalt Not
20: A Fallen Idol

George Nichols (1864-)

1917: Son of His Father
18: Keys of the Righteous
Battling Jane
Mickey
19: The Romance of Happy Valley
When Doctors Disagree
Bill Apperson's Boy
20: Pinto
The Greatest Question
The Iron Rider
21: Nineteen and Phyllis
Oliver Twist, Junior
Queen of Sheba
Deep Waters
Live and Let Live
22: The Flirt
The Barnstormer
Pride of Palomar
23: Ghost Patrol
28: Wedding March

Paul Nicholson

1926: The Johnstown Flood
Up in Mabel's Room
27: Bertha the Sewing Machine Girl
Bronco Twister
The Brute
29: Not Quite Decent

Anna Q. Nilsson (1893-)

1912: Siege of Petersburg
Under a Flag of Truce
15: A Sister's Burden
16: Who's Guilty? (serial)
17: Seven Keys to Baldpate
The Silent Master
18: Heart of the Sunset
Trail of Yesterday
No Man's Land
In Judgment Of
19: Way of the Strong
Soldiers of Fortune
The Love Burglar
Over There
20: Toll Gate
One Hour Before Dawn
The Fighting Chance
Luck of the Irish
21: The Lotus Eaters
Without Limit
Why Girls Leave Home
In the Heart of a Fool
What Women Will Do
22: The Man from Home
Pink Gods
The Man Who Came Back
Hearts Aflame
23: Three Live Ghosts
Isle of Lost Ships
Adam's Rib
The Spoilers
Rustle of Silk
Ponjola
24: Side Show of Life
Half a Dollar Bill
25: Inez from Hollywood
The Splendid Road
The Viennese Medley
Too Much Money
26: Miss Nobody
Midnight Lovers
Her Second Chance
Greater Glory
27: The Masked Woman
Easy Pickings
Babe Comes Home
Lonesome Ladies
Sorrell and Son
Thirteenth Juror
28: The Whip
The Blockade PT
33: The 13th Juror T
The World Changes T
34: School for Girls T
35: Wanderer of the Wasteland T
38: Prison Farm T
41: Riders of the Timberline T
42: Girls Town T
43: Headin' for God's Country T
47: The Farmer's Daughter T
Cynthia T
48: Fighting Father Dunne T
Every Girl Should Be Married T
50: Sunset Boulevard T
?? Molly Pitcher

Greta Nissen (1906-)

1923: Daarskat Dyd Og Driverter
25: In the Name of Love
The Wanderer
Lost - A Wife
Beggar on Horseback
26: The Love Thief
Lucky Lady
Lady of the Harem
27: The Popular Sin
Blind Alleys
Blonde or Brunette
The Swan
28: The Butter and Egg Man
Hell's Angels
The Tempest
Fazil SSE

Marian Nixon (1904-)

1923: Courtship of Miles Standish
Rosita
The Temple of Venus
Cupid's Fireman
Big Dan
24: Kentucky Days
A Vagabond's Trail

24: Just Off Broadway
Last of the Duanes
The Hurricane Kid
25: Riders of the Purple Sage
I'll Show You the Town
The Saddle Hawk
26: Spangles
Rolling Home
Cheerful Fraud
Devil's Island
Heroes of the Night
Hands Up!
27: Out All Night
The Chinese Parrot
The Auctioneer
Taxi! Taxi!
Down the Stretch
28: The Fourflusher
The Symphony
Out of the Ruins
Honeymoon Flats
How to Handle Women
Fallen Angles
Red Lips
Jazz Mad
Little Pal
Silk and Saddles
Man Woman and Wife SSE
29: Geraldine PT
General Crack T
Rainbow Man T
Red Sword T
Say it with Songs T
Young Nowheres T
Show of Shows T
In the Headlines T
30: Scarlet Pages T
??: Hallroom Boys Comedies
Lewis Sargent Comedies

Mary Nolan (1905-1948)
1925: Die Feuertanzerin
Die Panzergewalbe
26: Die Unberuhrte Frau
Wiener Herz
Viennese Lover
27: Taglich
Die Madchen Von Paris
Sorrel and Son
28: Good Morning, Judge
Foreign Legion
Thirst
West of Zanzibar
28: Uneasy Money
Silks and Saddles
29: Desert Nights SSE
Eleven Who Were Loyal
Charming Sinners T
Shanghai Lady T
30: Undertow T
Young Desire T
Outside the Law T
31: Enemies of the Law T
32: Docks of San Francisco T
Midnight Patrol T

Mabel Normand (1894-1930)
1911: Her Awakening
Saved By Himself
The Diving Girl
The Subduing of Mrs. Nag
12: Barney Oldfield's Race for Life
The Eternal Mother
Stolen Glory
Mender of Nets
A Dash Through the Clouds
13: Fatty's Flirtation
The Gusher
A Strange Revenge
Betty in the Lion's Den
Mabel's Dramatic Career
Brothers
Near to Earth
Zuzu the Band Leader
14: Mabel's Strange Predicament
Making a Living
Mabel at the Wheel
Caught in a Cabaret
The Fatal Mallet
Her Friend the Bandit
Mabel's Busy Day
Mabel's Married Life
Gentlemen of Nerve
His Trysting Place
Tillie's Punctured Romance
Getting Acquainted
15: The Misplaced Foot
My Valet
Fatty and Mabel
Fatty and Mabel Adrift
The Squaw's Love
A Mud Bath
Mabel's Stratagem
Mabel's Greatest Moment

15: Mabel and Fatty's Wash Day
Mabel, Fatty and the Law
Mabel and Fatty's Married Life
Mabel and Fatty Viewing the World's Fair
Mabel's Wilful Way
Mabel Lost and Won
Wished on Mabel
Mabel and Fatty at the San Diego Exposition
Mabel and Fatty's Simple Life
16: He Did and He Didn't
17: Mickey
18: The Floor Below
The Venus Model
Dodgin' a Million
Joan of Plattsburg
Back to the Woods
19: A Perfect 36
Upstairs
Mickey Gets Ready
Sis Hopkins
The Pest
When Doctors Disagree
Peck's Bad Girl
20: Pinto
Jinx
The Slim Princess
21: What Happened to Rosa?
Molly-O
22: Head Over Heels
Oh, Mabel, Behave
23: Suzanna
The Extra Girl
26: Raggety Rose
One Hour Married
The Nickel Hopper
Anything Once
Should Men Walk Home

Barry Norton (1905-1956)
1926: The Lily
What Price Glory?
27: Ankles Preferred
Heart of Salome
The Wizard
28: Legion of the Condemned
Fleet Wing T
Mother Knows Best T
29: The Four Devils T
Sins of the Fathers
29: Exalted Flapper SSE

Hedda Nova
1917: Woman in the Web (serial)
Bar Sinister
The Barrier
18: The Mask
19: The Crimson Gardenia
Spitfire of Seville
21: Shadows of the West

Eva Novak (1899-)
1919: The Speed Maniac
20: The Testing Block
The Daredevil
Desert Love
Silk Husbands and Calico Wives
Up in Mary's Attic
The Torrent
Wanted at Headquarters
21: Trailin'
Sky High
O'Malley of the Mounted
Chasing the Moon
The Smart Set
Society Secrets
Wolves of the North
The Rough Diamond
22: Making a Man
Hell's River
Up and Going
The Man Who Saw Yesterday
Barriers of Folly
23: Dollar Devils
A Noise in Newboro
The Tiger's Claw
Temptation
24: The Man Life Passed By
25: Sally
26: Irene
No Man's Gold
The Millionaire Policeman
The Dixie Flyer
30 Below Zero
27: The Romance of Runnibede
Red Signals
Duty's Reward
29: For the Term of His Natural Life

Jane Novak (1896-)

1914: From Italy's Shore
15: Just Nuts
Graft (serial)
18: Eyes of the World
The Tiger Man
Selfish Yates
Nine O'clock Town
String Beans
The Temple of Dusk
Claws of the Hun
19: Wagon Tracks
His Debt
20: The River's End
Behind the Door
Isobel
The Great Accident
21: The Barbarian
The Other Woman
3 Word Brand
Road of Destiny
Golden Trail
Kazan
22: Soul of a Woman
Belle of Alaska
The Rosary
Colleen of the Pines
Snowshoe Trail
Thelma
23: Divorce
Pride's Fall
24: The Man Who Life Passed By
Lullaby
25: Substitute Wife
26: Lure of the Wild
Dangerous Virtue
Whispering Canyon
Blackguard
Lost at Sea
27: One Increasing Purpose
Closed Gates
What Price Love?
28: Free Lips
29: Redskin SSE

Ramon Novarro (1899-1968)

1917: Little Princess
19: The Goat
21: A Small Town Idol
Four Horsemen of the Apocalypse (a bit)
22: Mr. Barnes of New York
22: Trifling Women
Prisoner of Zenda
Rubaiyat of Omar Khayyam
23: Scaramouche
Where the Pavement Ends
24: Thy Name is Woman
The Arab
Red Lily
25: Midshipman
A Lover's Oath
26: Ben Hur
Gold Braid
27: Student Prince
Road to Romance
Lovers
28: Forbidden Hours
Across to Singapore
29: The Flying Fleet
The Pagan SSE
Devil May Care T
Singer of Seville T
30: Call of the Flesh T

Wedgewood Nowell (1878-1957)

1916: The Deserter
20: 813
22: Enter Madame
Thelma
Eternal Flame
A Doll's House
When Knighthood was in Flower
23: A Wife's Romance
Adam's Rib
Little Heroes of the Street
24: Quo Vadis?
26: Ben Hur

Edward Nugent (1904-)

1928: Our Dancing Daughters
A Single Man
The First Kiss
Gold Braid
29: Bellamy Trial PT
Duke Steps Out PT
Man in Hobbles

Carroll Nye (1901-1968)

1925: Classified
26: The Imposter
Her Honor the Governor
27: What Every Girl Should Know

27: The Brute
Heart of Maryland
Kosher Kitty Kelly
Death Valley
The Silver Slave
Rose of Kildare
Girl from Chicago
28: Little Mickey Grogan
Race for Life
Sporting Age
Rinty of the Desert
Perfect Crime
Gold Braid
Confession
Powder My Back
Craig's Wife
While the City Sleeps
Jazzland
Land of the Silver Fox
29: The Flying Fleet SSE
Madame X T
Girl in the Glass Cage PT
The Squall T
Light Fingers PT

Jack Oakie (1903-)
1928: Finders Keepers
The Fleet's In
Someone to Love
29: Sin Town T
Hard to Get T
Chinatown Nights T
The Dummy T
Close Harmony T
Fast Company T
The Man I Love T
Sweetie T
The Wild Party T
Street Girl T

Vivian Oakland (1895-1958)
1924: Madonna of the Streets
26: Tell 'em Nothing
27: Love 'em and Weep
Uncle Tom's Cabin
Wedding Bells
28: Imagine My Embarrassment
29: The Man in Hobbles
Time the Place and the Girl T

Wheeler Oakman (1890-1949)
1913: The Long Ago
Three Wise Men
14: When the Cook Fell Ill
Story of the Blood Red Rose
Salvation of Nance O' Shaughnessy
The Spoilers
The Son of the Wolf
16: The Ne'er-Do-Well
Hell's Hinges
18: Face Value
20: The Virgin of Stamboul
22: The Half Breed
23: Slippery Magee (or Slippy McGee)
Outside the Law
26: In Borrowed Plumes
Heroes of the Night
27: Fangs of Justice
The Snarl of Hate
Out of the Night
Hey, Hey, Cowboy!
28: The Broken Mask
The Masked Angel
Power of the Press
The Miracle Girl
The Danger Patrol
While the City Sleeps
Heart of Broadway
Top Sergeant Mulligan
Lights of New York T
Number Please
Black Feather
What a Night!
29: The Devil's Chaplain
Handcuffed T
The Donovan Affair T
Father and Son PT
Shanghai Lady T
Morgan's Last Raid
Shakedown PT
Big Scoop T
On with the Show T
Show of Shows T
Girl from Woolworths T
Hurricane T
30: Little Johnny Jones T

Eugene O'Brien (1882-1966)
1915: Moonstone

16: Poor Little Peppina
The Scarlet Woman
Return of Eve
The Chaperon
17: Poppy
The Moth
Rebecca of Sunnybrook Farm
The Ghosts of Yesterday
Brown of Harvard
18: By Right of Purchase
De Luxe Annie
The Safety Curtain
A Romance of the Underworld
Her Only Way
Under the Greenwood Tree
Little Miss Hoover
19: Fires of Faith
Come Out of the Kitchen
The Broken Melody
The Perfect Lover
Sealed Hearts
20: A Fool and His Money
His Wife's Money
The Figurehead
Wonderful Chance (dual role)
The Thief
Broadway and Home
21: Worlds Apart
Gilded Lies
The Last Door
Is Life Worth Living?
Clay Dollars
Chivalrous Charlie
22: The Prophet's Paradise
Channing of the Northwest
John Smith
23: The Voice from the Minaret
24: Secrets
The Only Woman
25: Frivolous Sal
Dangerous Innocence
Graustark
Siege
Souls for Sables
Simon the Jester
26: Flames
Only the Brave
Fine Manners
27: The Romantic Age
28: The Faithless Lover

George O'Brien (1900-)

1922: White Hands
Moran of the Lady Letty
24: The Iron Horse
The Roughneck
Painted Lady
The Man Who Came Back
25: The Dancers
Thank You
Fighting Heart
26: Havoc
Three Bad Men
Fig Leaves
Silver Treasure
The Johnstown Flood
Rustlin' for Cupid
The Blue Eagle
27: Is Zat So?
East Side West Side
Paid to Love
Sunrise
Romantic Age
28: Honor Bound
Blindfold SSE
Sharpshooters
False Colors
The Case of Mary Brown
29: Noah's Ark PT
Masked Emotions SSE
Salute T
True Heaven

Pat O'Brien (1899-)

1929: Fury of the Wild
The Freckled Rascal
Married in Haste

Tom O'Brien (1898-)

1920: Sagebrusher
21: Scrap Iron
23: Abysmal Brute
The Scarlet Car
25: Big Parade
Gentleman from America
26: The Flaming Forest
Tin Hats
Runaway Express
Poker Faces
27: Fire Brigade
Winners of the Wilderness
Rookies
Is Zat So?
Annie Laurie

27: The Bugle Call
The Frontiersman
Private Life of Helen of Troy
28: The Chorus Kid
San Francisco Nights
That's My Daddy!
Anybody Here Seen Kelly?
29: Peacock Fan
It Can Be Done PT
Last Warning PT
Flying Fool T
Smiling Irish Eyes T
Untamed T
His Lucky Day T
Dark Skies T
Dance Hall T

Robert Emmett O'Connor (1885-1962)
1928: The Booster
Four Walls
Isle of Lost Ships
Freedom of the Press
29: Weary River T
Smiling Irish Eyes T

Peggy O'Dare
1917: In the Balance
20: The Vanishing Dagger (serial)
Kentuck's Ward
Blind Chance
?? For Life

Dawn O'Day (Anne Shirley) (1918-)
1928: Four Devils PT
Mother Knows Best T
29: Sins of the Fathers

Molly O'Day (1911-)
1927: Hard Boiled Haggerty
The Lovelorn
Patent Leather Kid
28: Little Shepherd of Kingdom Come

Spec O'Donnell (1911-)
1923: Main Street
Country Kid
Little Johnny Jones
Darling of New York
25: Little Annie Rooney
Devil's Cargo
25: Tomorrow's Love
Dressmaker of Paris
Headlines
26: Grand Parade
Sparrows
27: Casey at the Bat
We're All Gamblers
28: Vamping Venus
Dumb Daddies
It's All Greek to Me
Danger Street
Hot News
Do Gentlemen Snore?
29: The Sophomores T

Charles Ogle (1875-)
1911: How Mrs. Murray Saved the Army
12: Martin Chuzzlewit
13: Hard Cash
14: Dolly of the Dailies (serial)
17: Those Without Sin
18: The Thing We Love
Believe Me, Zantippe
Firefly of France
Less Than Kin
The Source
Too Many Millions
The Dub
19: Valley of the Giants
Alias Mike Moran
Capt. Hawthorne of the U. S. A.
Told in the Hills
20: What's Your Hurry?
The Prince Chap
The Jucklins
Rebecca of Sunnybrook Farm
Conrad in Quest of His Youth
Treasure Island
Jack Straw
21: Brewster's Millions
A Wise Fool
Miss Lulu Bett
The Affairs of Anatol
22: 30 Days
Is Matrimony a Failure?
Manslaughter
The Stage Door
Our Leading Citizens
The Young Rajah

23: The Covered Wagon
10 Commandments
Kick In
Grumpy
Salomy Jane
24: Garden of Weeds
The Bedroom Window
The Flaming Barriers
The Border Legion

Warner Oland (1880-1938)
1912: Pilgrim's Progress (dual role) (or The Life of John Bunyan)
15: Sin
16: Patria (serial)
The Eternal Question
The Serpent
Destruction
The Fool's Revenge
The Reapers
17: The Fatal Ring (serial)
The Cigarette Girl
The Yellow Ticket
The Mysterious Client
The Lightning Raider (serial)
Convict 993
18: The Naulahka
19: Mandarin's Gold
The Avalanche
Witness for the Defense
Twin Pawns
The Mad Talon
Roaring Oaks
20: The Phantom Foe (serial)
The Third Eye (serial)
21: The Yellow Arm (serial)
Hurricane Hutch (serial)
22: East is West
The Pride of Palomar
23: His Children's Children
24: One Night in Rome
The Throwback
The Fighting American
25: Curly Top
So This is Marriage
Don Q
Riders of the Purple Sage
The Winding Stair
26: The Marriage Clause
Don Juan
The Mystery Club
Infatuation
26: Twinkletoes
Tell it to the Marines
27: When a Man Loves
A Million Bid
What Happened to Father
Old San Francisco
The Jazz Singer PT
Good Time Charley
28: The Scarlet Lady
The Wheel of Chance
Stand and Deliver
Dream of Love
Tong War
29: The Faker
Chinatown Nights T
The Studio Murder Mystery T
Mysterious Dr. Fu Manchu T
30: The Mighty T

Edna May Oliver (1883-1942)
1924: Icebound
Manhattan
25: Lucky Devil
26: Let's Get Married
American Venus
29: Saturday Night Kid T

Guy Oliver (1875-)
1912: The Raven
Robin Hood
17: The Little Princess
The Golden Fetter
Nan of Music Mountain
The Little American
18: The Hidden Pearls
Rimrock Jones
Less Than Kin
The Whispering Chorus
19: The Roaring Road
Valley of the Giants
Hawthorne of the U. S. A.
Under the Top
The Heart of Youth
Told in the Hills
It Pays to Advertise
Male and Female
20: Double Speed
Excuse My Dust
Always Audacious
The Jucklins
Sins of Rosanne

20: The Round Up
21: Too Much Speed
The Affairs of Anatol
What Every Woman Knows
City of Silent Men
Moonlight and Honeysuckle
A Prince There Was
22: The World's Champion
Across the Continent
The Little Minister
A Virginia Courtship
A Homespun Vamp
Manslaughter
Our Leading Citizens
Pink Gods
The Cowboy and the Lady
23: The Covered Wagon
Woman with Four Faces
To the Last Man
Mr. Billings Spends His Dime
24: The Bedroom Window
25: The Vanishing American
26: The Blind Goddess
27: Old Ironsides
The Mysterious Rider
Drums of the Desert
Nevada
Shootin' Irons
Open Range
28: The Vanishing Pioneer
The Avalanche
3 Week Ends
Hot News
Beggars of Life
Easy Come Easy Go
Half a Bride
The Docks of New York
29: The Kibitzer T
Texas Tommy
Far Western Trails
The Fighting Terror
Stairs of Sand
The Studio Murder Case T
Sunset Pass
Woman Trap T
Half Way to Heaven T

Gertrude Olmstead (1897-)
1920: Tipped Off
21: The Big Adventure
Three in a 1000
22: The Lone Hand
22: Adventures of Robinson Crusoe (serial)
23: Cameo Kirby
Trilby
24: George Washington, Jr.
Fighting Fury
25: California Straight Ahead
26: The Torrent
Monte Carlo
Puppets
The Cheerful Fraud
Sweet Adeline
The Boob
27: Mr. Wu
Buttons
Becky
The Callahans and the Murphys
28: Cheer Leader
Hit of the Show
Sweet 16
Midnight Life
Green-Grass Widows
The Lone Wolf's Daughter
Bringing Up Father
Woman Against the World
Sporting Goods
29: Hey, Rube!
The Passion Song
Sonny Boy T
Time the Place and the Girl T
Show of Shows T
The Driftin' Kid
Kickaroo
A Key Too Many
Sweet Revenge

Pat O'Malley (1891-1966)
1919: Red Glove (serial)
False Evidence
20: Breath of the Gods
Blooming Angel
Sherry
Go and Get It
Dinty
21: The Breaking Point
Bob Hampton of Placer
The $10 Raise
22: False Kisses
The Game Chicken
My Wild Irish Rose
Brothers Under the Skin

23: The Last Hour
Brass
The Man from Brodney's
Wandering Daughters
24: Happiness
25: Proud Flesh
The Teaser
26: Spangles
My Old Dutch
The Midnight Sun
Watch your Wife
27: Rose of Kildare
Perch of the Devil
Cheaters
A Bowery Cinderella
The Slaver
28: Nightstick
A Woman's Law
House of Scandal
29: Alibi T
The Man I Love T

Nance O'Neil (1875-1965)
1915: The Kreutzer Sonata
17: The Fall of the Romanoffs
Hedda Gabler
Greed (The 7 Deadly Sins)
19: The Mad Woman
27: The Loves of Carmen
29: His Glorious Night T

Sally O'Neil (1910-1968)
1925: Sally Irene and Mary
26: Don't
The Auction Block
The Battling Butler
Mike
A Certain Young Man
27: Slide, Kelly, Slide
Becky
The Lovelorn
Frisco Sally Levy
The Callahans and the Murphys
28: The Mad Hour
A Bachelor's Paradise
Battle of the Sexes
The Floating College
On with the Show PT
The Sophomore T
Show of Shows T
Broadway Scandals T
Jazz Heaven T

29: Hardboiled
Broadway Fever
Girl on the Barge PT

William Orlamond (1867-)
1920: Stronger than Death
Madame Peacock
Body and Soul
27: Camille
28: Skinner's Big Idea
Little Yellow House
While the City Sleeps
Awakening SSE
29: Seven Keys to Baldpate T
House of Horror PT
Blue Skies SSE
Words and Music T

Louise Orth
1919: 3 Black Eyes
Mr. Shoestring in the Hole

Baby Marie Osborne (1911-)
1917: Joy and the Dragon
Little Mary Sunshine
When Baby Forgot
Baby Pulls the String
The Evidence
Baby's Diplomacy
18: Tears and Smiles
A Little Patriot
Daddy's Girl
Dolly Does Her Bit
A Daughter of the West
Voice of Destiny
Cupid by Proxy
Winning Grandma
19: Milady o' the Beanstalk
The Old Maid's Baby
Sawdust Doll
Dolly's Vacation
The Little Diplomat
Child of M'sieur
20: Baby Marie's Round Up
Miss Gingersnap

Miles "Bud" Osborne (1888-)
1923: Prairie Mystery
28: Bronc Stomper
Where the West Begins
Secrets of the Range
West of Santa Fe
On the Divide

28: Law of the Mounted
Cheyenne Trails
Forbidden Trails
The Mystery Rider
Texas Flash
Thrill Chaser
Valley Beyond the Law
Yellow Contraband
29: His Lucky Day PT
The Smiling Terror
Days of Daring
Riding Leather
A Fighting Tenderfoot
Texas Tommy
Far Western Trails
The Fighting Terror
Badman's Money
The Lariat Kid
The Last Roundup
West of Santa Fe
The Invaders

Vivienne Osborne (1900-)
1920: In Walked Mary
The Restless Sex
Over the Hill
The Foreigner
Love's Flame
21: Mother Eternal
The Right Way
22: Cameron of the Royal Mounted
A Good Provider

Muriel Ostriche (1897-)
1915: Mortmain
A Daughter of the Sea
16: Kennedy Square
A Circus Romance
By Whose Hand?
The Man She Married
17: A Square Deal
Moral Courage
The Dormant Power
18: Leap to Fame
Tinsel
19: What Love Forgives
The Bluffer
The Moral Deadline
The Hand Invisible
The Sacred Flame
Betty Sets the Pace
Betty's Green-Eyed Monster

"Our Gang" Comedies
"Our Gang" Kids
Mary Ann Jackson
Jean Darling
Joey Cobb
Harry Spear
Farina
Wheezer
Mickey Daniels
Mary Kornman
Stymie
Johnny Downs
Pete (the circle-eye dawg)
1922: One Terrible Day
Fire Fighters
Our Gang (with Snub Pollard)
Young Sherlocks
Saturday Morning
A Quiet Street
23: The Champeen
The Cobbler
The Big Show
A Pleasant Journey
Boys to Board
Giants Vs. Yanks
Back Stage
Dogs of War
Lodge Night
July Day
No Noise
Stage Fright
Derby Days
The Great Outdoors
Sunday Calm
24: Tire Trouble
Big Business
The Buccaneers
Seein' Things
Commencement Day
Craddle Robbers
Jubilo Jr.
It's a Bear
High Society
The Sun Down Limited
Every Man for Himself
Fast Company
The Mysterious Mystery
25: The Big Town
Circus Fever
Dog Days
The Love Bug
Shootin' Injuns

25: Ask Grandma
Official Officers
Boys will be Joys
Your Own Back Yard
Better Movies
One Wild Ride
26: Good Cheer
Buried Treasure
Monkey Business
Baby Clothes
Uncle Tom's Uncle
Thundering Fleas (with Charlie Chase)
Shivering Spooks
The Fourth Alarm
War Feathers
Telling Whoppers
27: Bring Home the Turkey
Seeing the World
Ten Years Ago
Love My Dog
The Tired Businessman
Baby Brother
The Glorious Fourth
Olympic Games
Chicken Feed
Yale Vs. Harvard
The Old Wallop
Heebee Jeebees
Dog Heaven
28: Playin' Hookey
The Smile Wins
Spook Spoofing
Rainy Days
Edison Marconi & Co.
Barnum & Ringling, Inc.
Fair and Muddy
Crazy House
Growing Pains
Ol' Gray Hoss
School Beings
The Spanking Age
29: Election Day
Noisy Noises (sound and silent)
Holy Terror
Wiggle Your Ears
Fast Freight
Small Talk s-s
Little Mother
Railroadin' s-s
Dad's Day s-s
Boxing Gloves s-s
29: Lazy Days
Cat Dog and Co.
Bouncing Babies
Saturday's Lesson
Moan and Groan, Inc.

Seena Owen (1895-1966)
1914: Out of the Air
15: The Fox Woman
A Yankee from the West
The Penitents
The Lamb
The Craven
An Old-Fashioned Girl
Bred in the Bone
16: Intolerance
Martha's Vindication
17: Madame Bo-Peep
18: Branding Broadway
19: Victory
The Sheriff's Son
Breed of Men
A Man and his Money
One of the Finest
City of Comrades
The Life Line
20: Price of Redemption
Sooner or Later
The Gift Supreme
The House of Toys
21: Lavender and Old Lace
The Woman God Changed
The Cheater Reformed
22: Back Pay
Sisters
At the Crossroads
23: The Go Getter
Unseeing Eyes
26: The Flame of the Yukon
Shipwrecked
28: The Rush Hour
The Blue Danube
Queen Kelly (unfinished)
Man-Made Woman
His Last Haul
29: Marriage Playground T

Charles Paddock
1925: 9 and 3/5 Seconds
26: The Campus Flirt
27: The High School Hero
The College Hero
28: The Olympic Hero

Anita Page (1910-)

1928: Telling the World
He Learned About Women
Our Dancing Daughters
While the City Sleeps
The Flying Ensign
Gold Braid
29: Protection SSE
The Flying Feet SSE

Alfred Paget

1910: A Romance of the Western Hills
The Banker's Daughter
11: Enoch Arden
Out from the Shadow
12: The Lesser Evil
Goddess of Sagebrush Gulch
The Girl and Her Trust
A Dash Through the Clouds
Man's Genesis
A Temporary Truce
13: Oil and Water
A Timely Interception
Just Gold
The Primitive Man
16: Intolerance
17: Big Timber
Nina the Flower Girl
Aladdin and the Wonderful Lamp
24: When a Girl Loves

Eugene Pallette (1889-1954)

1913: The Tattered Arm
When Jim Returned
Monroe
Broken Nose Bailey
14: The Peach Brand
The Burden
The Sheriff's Prisoner
On the Border
The Horse Wranglers
15: After 20 Years
How Hazel Got Even
The Story of a Story
The Spell of the Poppy
The Highbinders
The Emerald Broach
The Death Doll
The Birth of a Nation
The Penalty
The Ever Living Isles
15: When Love is Mocked
The Scarlet Lady
Isle of Content
16: Going Straight
Runaway Freight
Diamond in the Rough
Hell-To-Pay Austin
Intolerance
Sunshine Dad
Gretchen the Greenhorn
His Guardian Angel
Children in the House
17: The Purple Scar
The World Apart
The Marcellini Millions
The Handsome Chap
The Bond Between
The Winning of Sally Temple
The Victim
Each to His Kind
The Heir of the Ages
A Man's Man
The Ghost House
18: Madame Who
No Man's Land
His Robe of Honor
Turn of a Card
Tarzan of the Apes
Breakers Ahead
Vivette
19: Amateur Adventuress
Words and Music By...
Under Sea Loot
Fair and Warmer
20: Alias Jimmy Valentine
Parlor, Bedroom and Bath
Twin Beds
Terror Island
Santa Fe Trail
21: Fine Feathers
The Three Musketeers
22: Without Compromise
Two Kinds of Women
23: To the Last Man
The Wolf Man
North of Hudson Bay
24: Wandering Husbands
25: Light of the Western Stars
Ranger of the Big Pines
26: Fighting Edge
Rocking Moon
Yankee Señor

26: Mantrap
Should Men Walk Home?
27: Hell's Hero
Battle of the Century
The Light that Failed
Sugar Daddies
Call of the Cuckoo
The Second 100 Years
28: Chicago
Goodbye Kiss
Out of the Ruins
Men About Town
The Red Mark
His Private Life
Should Women Drive?
Loud Speakers
Fools for Luck
29: Lights of New York T
The Virginian T
31: Girls About Town T

Franklin Pangborn (1896-1958)

1927: The Night Bride
Cradle Snatchers
Watch Out
Rejuvenation of Aunt Mary
Getting Gertie's Garter
Girl in the Pullman
28: My Friend from India
Blonde for a Night
On Trial
29: The Sap PT
Lady of the Pavements PT
20: Not So Dumb T

Paul Panzer (1873-1958)

1904: A Curious Dream
08: Romeo and Juliet
09: The Life of Buffalo Bill
10: Sunshine in Poverty Row
13: The Governor's Double
The Cheapest Way
14: The Perils of Pauline (serial)
The Last Volunteer
17: The Clutching Hand (serial)
Jimmy Dale Alias The Grey Seal (serial)
19: Masked Rider (serial)
20: Mystery Mind (serial)
23: Enemies of Women
Jacqueline of the Blazing Barriers
23: Mighty Lak' a Rose
24: Son of the Sahara
25: Too Many Kisses
The Shock Punch
Thunder Mountain
26: The Ancient Mariner
Siberia
Johnstown Flood
30 Below Zero
27: Sally in our Alley
Wolf's Clothing
The Girl from Chicago
Brass Knuckles
Hawk of the Hills (serial)
The Mohican's Daughter
28: Rinty of the Desert
The Romance of a Rogue
Glorious Betsy PT
The Candy Kid
29: Black Book (serial)
Redskin SSE
George Washington Cohen

Kalla Pasha

1920: Married Life
21: Love, Honor and Behave
A Small Town Idol
22: 30 Days
The Dictator
Making a Man
23: Hollywood
Bella Donna
Racing Hearts
Children of Jazz
24: Shanghaied Lovers
The Cat's Meow
Yukon Jake
27: Tillie's Punctured Romance
Wolf's Clothing
28: West of Zanzibar
29: Seven Footprints to Satan SSE
Chasing Husbands
Midnight on the Barbary Coast
Show of Shows T
??: Mack Sennett Comedies

Elizabeth Patterson (1876-1966)

1926: Boy Friend
Mrs. Harper
Return of Peter Grimm
The Minister's Wife

Bill Patton
1920: Sand
21: Outlawed
24: Under Fire
26: Western Trails
The Last Chance
Lucky Spurs
Beyond the Trail
28: Yellow Contraband
The Lariat Kid
Orphan of the Sage
Below the Deadline
In Line of Duty
Vagabond Cub
The Freckled Rascal
Two Gun Morgan
One Man Dog

Doris Pawn (1896-)
1916: Trey of Hearts
Blue Blood and Red
17: The Book Agent
Some Boy
18: The Kid is Clever
19: The City of Dim Faces
Toby's Bow
20: Tower of Ivory
Li Ting Lang
Out of the Storm
The Strange Boarder
21: Guile of Women
Midnight Bell
What Happened to Rosa?

Virginia Pearson (1888-1958)
1914: The Stain
15: The Vital Question
16: Blazing Love
17: The Bitter Truth
A Royal Romance
18: The Liar
Queen of Hearts
Buchanan's Wife
The Firebrand
When False Tongues Speak
A Daughter of France
Thou Shalt Not Steal
Her Price
All for a Husband
Stolen Honor
19: The Bishop's Emerald
Love Auction
20: Impossible Catherine
22: Wildness of Youth
23: Sister Against Sister
25: Phantom of the Opera
26: Atta Boy!
Red Kimono
The Taxi Mystery
Silence
Lightning Hutch (serial)
28: The Actress
What Price Beauty?
Big City
Power of Silence
Smilin' Guns
29: Silks and Saddles
Patience

Ed Peil (1888-1958)
1916: The Stronger Love
18: Up the Road
Eyes of the World
19: Boots
Peppy Polly
I'll Get Him Yet
The Greatest Thing in Life
Broken Blossoms
20: The Money Changers
Servant in the House
Road to Divorce
21: Dream Street
That Girl Montana
22: Song of Life
Don't Doubt Your Wife
Dust Flower
23: Broken Chains
Purple Dawn
College Coquette
24: The Iron Horse
25: The Fighting Heart
28: Little Yellow House
Masked Emotions

Jack Pennick (1895-1964)
1928: Plastered in Paris SSE
Four Sons
Why Sailors Go Wrong
29: Strong Boy SSE

Ann Pennington (1895-)
1916: Susie Snowflakes
17: Little Boy Scout
Antics of Ann
18: Sunshine Nan
25: Madame Behave

25: Lucky Horseshoe
The Golden Strain
Hello Baby
The Mad Dancer
29: The Rainbow Man
Tanned Legs
Gold Diggers of Broadway T
Night Parade T
30: Happy Days T

Eileen Percy
1917: Down to Earth
The Man from Painted Post
Reaching for the Moon
Wild and Woolly
18: The Empty Cab
19: Some Liar
The Beloved Cheater
In Mizzoura
Where the West Begins
Brass Buttons
The Gray Horizon
Desperate Gold
20: The Third Eye (serial)
Her Honor, the Mayor
Beware of the Bride
The Man Who Dared
21: The Tomboy
The Blushing Bride
Little Miss Hawkshaw
Big Town Ideas
The Husband Hunter
Land of Jazz
Why Trust Your Husband
Maid of the West
Hickville Broadway
22: Pardon My Nerve
Elope If You Must
The Fast Mail
The Flirt
Whatever She Wants
23: The Prisoner
The 4th Musketeer
East Side, West Side
Within the Law
Children of Jazz
26: Lovey Mary
That Model from Paris
Shadow on the Wall
Phantom Bullet
Racewild
27: Burnt Fingers
27: 12 Miles Out
Backstage
Spring Fever
28: Telling the World
Iron Mike
30: Temptation T
31: Wicked T

Derelys Perdue
1928: Forbidden Range
The Mystery Rider
The Smiling Terror

George Periolat (d. 1960)
1915: The Diamond from the Sky (serial)
Adventures of Terence O'Rourke
16: Landon Legacy
17: Mate of the Sally Ann
18: The Ghost of Rory Taylor
19: Tiger Lily
20: Parlor, Bedroom and Bath
The Mark of Zorro
The Hellion
Life's Twist
21: Two Weeks with Pay
22: Blood and Sand
The Young Rajah
To Have and to Hold
23: Rosita
Barefoot Boy
24: Yankee Consul
27: The Prairie King
Secret Hour
Fangs of Destiny
28: Black Butterflies
The Night Watch SSE
29: One Splendid Hour
When Dreams Come True

Jack Perrin (1896-1967)
1917: Double Crossed
19: The Lion Man (serial)
Blind Husbands
20: Pink Tights
The Adorable Savage
Lahoma
21: The Torrent
The Trigger Trail
Big Bob
Coward of Covelo
The Outlaw

21: Partners of the Tide
The Match Breaker
22: Guttersnipe
Battle of Wits
The Phantom Terror
Dangerous Little Demon
The Trouper
Under Secret Orders
23: The Fighting Skipper (serial)
24: Riders of the Plains (serial)
25: Border Vengeance
26: Starlight's Revenge
The Grey Devil
A Ridin' Gent
The Man from Oklahoma
West of the Rainbow's End
Hi-Jacking Rustlers
Double Fisted
27: Code of the Range
Fire and Steel
Laffin' Fool
Thunderbolt's Tracks
Where the North Holds Sway
28: The Water Hole
Guardians of the Wild
Two Outlaws
The Vanishing West (serial)
29: Plunging Hoofs
Wild Blood
Harvest of Hate
Hoofbeats of Vengeance

Robert Perry

1928: The Deadline
The River Pirate
Me Gangster
Beggars of Life PT
No Picnic

House Peters (1888-1967)

1913: An Hour Before the Dawn
Leah Kleshna
Port of Doom
14: A Lady of Quality
The Brute
The Pride of Jennico
15: The Warrens of Virginia
The Unafraid
The Captive
The Winged Idol
15: Stolen Goods
19: Thunderbolts of Fate
Forfeit
You Never Know Your Luck
20: Clothes
The Leopard Woman
Isobel
Silk Husbands and Calico Wives
The Great Redeemer
The Invisible Power
Lying Lips
22: The Bishop's Carriage
The Man from Lost River
Human Hearts
Rich Men's Wives
The Storm
23: Salomy Jane
Mignon
Lost and Found
Held to Answer
Don't Marry for Money
24: The Tornado
25: The Great Divide
Raffles
Head Winds
The Storm Breaker
26: Counsel for the Defense
Combat
Prisoners of the Storm
28: Rose Marie

Olga Petrova (1886-)

1914: The Vampire
16: The Eternal Question
Black Butterfly
The Soul Market
The Orchid Lady
17: The Undying Flame
Law of the Land
The Soul of a Magdalen
Daughter of Destiny
Exile
Patience Sparhawk
The Silence Sellers
More Truth than Poetry
18: The Life Mask
The Light Within
Tempered Steel
19: The Panther Woman

Mary Philbin (1903-)

1921: The Blazing Trail

21: Danger Ahead
Red Courage
Sure Fire
22: Penrod
False Kisses
Human Hearts
The Trouper
Once to Every Boy
23: Merry-Go-Round
Penrod and Sam
Morality
The Temple of Venus
24: Fool's Highway
The Gaiety Girl
The Rose of Paris
25: Phantom of the Opera
5th Avenue Models
26: Stella Maris
27: Drums of Love
Surrender
28: The Man Who Laughs T
Footprints
Erick the Great
Love Me and the World is Mine
29: The Last Performance T
The Shannons of Broadway T
Girl Overboard PT
No Clothes to Guide Her
Port of Dreams

Carmen Phillips (1895-)
1917: Chased into Love
20: Right of Way
Mrs. Temple's Telegram
Always Audacious
There's Many a Fool
Forbidden Paths
The Cabaret Girl
The Pagan God
For a Woman's Honor
The Great Air Robbery
21: All Souls' Eve
The Fire Eater
The Sheik of Araby
22: Too Much Married
The Heart Specialist
30 Days
The Gentleman from America
23: Ashes of Vengeance

Dorothy Phillips (1892-)
1911: The Rosary
Fate's Funny Frolic
13: Into the North
16: Ambition
17: Hell Morgan's Girl
Triumph
Broadway Love
18: Talk of the Town
The Grand Passion
The Risky Road
A Soul for Sale
Mortgaged Wife
19: The Right to Happiness
Heart of Humanity
Destiny
20: Once to Every Woman
Man-Woman-Marriage
Paid in Advance
22: Hurricane's Gal
23: The World's a Stage
Slander the Woman
The Unknown Purple
26: Upstage
The Bar-C Mystery (serial)
The Gay Deceiver
Remember
27: Cradle Snatchers
Broken Gates
Women Love Diamonds
30: Jazz Cinderella T

Eddie Phillips
1921: The Love Light
29: Scandal PT
College Love T
His Lucky Day PT
King of the Campus PT

Jack Pickford (1896-1933)
1910: All on Account of the Milk
Exam Day at School
11: The Speed Demon
12: The New York Hat
With the Enemy's Help
The Would-Be Shriner
The Musketeers of Pig Alley
A Dash Through the Clouds
14: Home Sweet Home
Wildflower
The Massacre
The Mysterious Shot

14: Liberty Bells
15: The Pretty Sister of Jose
The Girl of Yesterday
16: Great Expectations
Seventeen
Jack and Jill
Poor Little Peppina
17: Tom Sawyer
The Varmint
The Girl at Home
What Money Can't Buy
Freckles
Sandy
The Dummy
The Ghost House
The Spirit of '17
18: His Majesty Bunker Bean
Mile-A-Minute Kendall
Huck and Tom
19: Bill Apperson's Boy
Burglar by Proxy
20: Huckleberry Finn
Little Shepherd of Kingdom Come
The Double-Dyed Deceiver
In Wrong
The Man Who Had Everything
21: Just Out of College
Little Lord Fauntleroy (asst. dir.)
Through the Back Door
22: Garrison's Finish
23: Valley of the Wolf
24: The Hill Billy
The End of the World
25: The Goose Woman
Waking Up the Town
My Son
26: The Bat
Brown of Harvard
Exit Smiling
28: Gang War
30: All Square T

Lottie Pickford (1895-1936)

1909: Two Memories
The Little Darling
10: A Summer Idyll
15: The Diamond from the Sky (serial)
16: Flying-A (serial)
18: The Man from Funeral Range
18: Mile-A-Minute Kendall
21: They Shall Pay
25: Don Q.

Mary Pickford (1893-)

1906: 1776
The Restoration
07: Jonesy
What Drink Did
Wedded But No Wife
The Gypsy Girl
They Would Elope
09: The Hessian Renegade
Lovers' Tryst
Going Straight
Pippa Passes
White Roses
Her First Biscuit
Shadows of Doubt
Retrospect (or, Sweet Memories)
The New York Hat
The Lonely Villa
In Old Kentucky
The Face on the Barroom Floor
To Save Her Soul
Getting Even
Two Memories
The Little Darling
Sweet and 20
His Wife's Visitors
The Indian Runner's Romance
The Awakening
The Savage Princess
10: Wilful Peggy
The Violin of Cremona
The Little Teacher
The Old Actor
Never Again
The Way of Man
Italian Barber
Exam Day at School
Simple Charity
The Englishman and the Girl
The Thread of Destiny
A Romance of the Western Hills
Ramona
The Face at the Window
What the Daisy Said

10: The Call to Arms
Sorrows of the Unfaithful
A Rich Revenge
A Lucky Toothache
The Masher
A Son's Return
Artful Kate
The Fisher Maid
All on Account of the Milk
The Narrow Road
11: Home Folks
A Decree of Destiny
The Courting of Mary
A Feud in the Kentucky Hills
In the Sultan's Garden
Little Red Riding Hood
The Informer
Science
Their First Misunderstanding
The Dream
Maid or Man
Her Darkest Hour
A Manly Man
In Old Madrid
For Her Brother's Sake
Her Awakening
A Lodging for the Night
12: When the Cat's Away
A Child's Impulse
The Old Actor
Song of the Wild Flute
Friends
The Mender of Nets
The One She Loved
An Arcadian Maid
Just Like a Woman
Fate's Interception
A Pueblo Legend
A Beast at Bay
So Near, Yet So Far
My Baby
The Inner Circle
Jola's Promise
With the Enemy's Help
Won By a Fish
13: Lena and the Geese
Caprice
A Good Little Devil
In the Bishop's Carriage
3 Friends
The Unwelcome Guest
13: When the Cat's Away
14: Tess of the Storm Country
Behind the Scenes
Hearts Adrift
The Eagle's Mate
Cinderella
Such a Little Queen
15: Rags
Girl of Yesterday
Esmeralda
A Dawn of Tomorrow
Fanchon the Cricket
Madam Butterfly
Mistress Nell
Little Pal
16: Ramona
Less than the Dust
The Foundling
Poor Little Peppina
Hulda from Holland
The Eternal Grind
17: Poor Little Rich Girl
Romance of the Redwoods
Pride of the Clan
Rebecca of Sunnybrook Farm
War Relief (behind the scenes)
The Light that Came
The Little American
The Little Princess
Molly Entangled
18: M'liss
Amarilly of Clothesline Alley
How Could You, Jean?
Johanna Enlists
19: Captain Kidd Jr.
Daddy Long Legs
Scraps
The Hoodlum
Heart of the Hills
20: Pollyanna
Suds
21: The Lovelight
Through the Back Door
Little Lord Fauntleroy
22: Tess of the Storm Country
Forever Yours
23: Rosita
24: Dorothy Vernon of Haddon Hall
25: Little Annie Rooney

26: Sparrows
27: My Best Girl
the "Virgin" in D. Fairbank's "The Gaucho"
29: Coquette (Oscar) T
The Taming of the Shrew T
32: Kiki T
33: Secrets T

Walter Pidgeon (1897-)
1926: Old Loves and New
Marriage License
Mannequin
The Outsider
Mlle. Modiste
Miss Nobody
27: The Heart of Salome
The Girl from Rio
The Gorilla
28: Gateway of the Moon
Woman Wise
Turn Back the Hours
Clothes Make the Woman
Melody of Love T
29: The Voice Within PT
A Most Immoral Lady T

Tempe Piggott (1884-1962)
1928: None But the Brave
29: 7 Days' Leave

Zasu Pitts (1898-1963)
1916: For the Defense
17: The Little Princess
Rebecca of Sunnybrook Farm
18: Modern Musketeers
How Could You, Jean?
19: Better Times
The Other Half
Poor Relations
As the Sun Went Down
Men, Women and Money
20: Bright Skies
Seeing it Through
The Heart of Twenty
22: Is Matrimony a Failure?
Youth to Youth
A Daughter of Luxury
23: Three Wise Fools
Patsy
Poor Men's Wives
The Girl Who Came Back
24: Greed
The Goldfish
Sunlight of Paris
West of the Water Tower
The Fast Set
26: Monte Carlo
Paris
The Mannequin
Early to Wed
Her Big Night
Risky Business
Sunnyside Up
27: Casey at the Bat
Old Shoes
Wife Savers
28: The Wedding March
Sins of the Fathers
The Honeymoon (not released)
13 Washington Square
Buck Privates
29: Her Private Life T
Twin Beds T
The Dummy T
The Squall T
The Argyle Case T
30: Oh Yeah! T
This Thing Called Love T
Locked Doors T
??: Behind the Footlights
Why They Left Home

Wellington Playter (1883-)
1919: Eagle's Eye (serial)
In Search of Arcady
Fool's Gold
Back to God's Country

Lon Poff (1870-)
1918: The Light of the Western Stars
19: The Shepherd of the Hills
20: Sand
Broken Gates
The Last Straw
21: Bonnie May
Bunty Pulls the Strings
The Night Horseman
The Old Swimmin' Hole
3 Musketeers
22: The Village Blacksmith
23: The Virginian
The Girl I Loved
Dulcy

23: Main Street
28: 2 Lovers
Greased Lightning
29: The Iron Mask PT
The Faker

Daphne Pollard (1894-)
1928: Sinners in Love
Ladies Must Eat
29: The Girl from Everywhere
Big Time T
30: South Sea Rose T
Sky Hawk T

Harry "Snub" Pollard (1886-1962)
1915: Great While it Lasted
Lonesome Luke's Double
Peculiar Patient's Prank
Lonesome Luke, Social Gangster
16: Luke Leans to the Literary
Luke Lugs Luggage
Luke Lolls in Luxury
Luke the Candy Cut-Up
Luke Foils the Villain
Rural Roughnecks
Luke Pipes the Pippins
Luke Laughs Last
Luke's Fatal Flivver
Luke's Society Mixup
Luke's Wishful Waiting
Luke Rides Roughshod
Luke Crystal Gazer
Luke's Lost Lamb
Luke Does the Midway
Luke Joins the Navy
Luke and the Mermaids
Luke's Speedy Club Life
17: Lonesome Luke in the Tin Can Alley
Lonesome Luke's Honeymoon
Lonesome Luke's Lively Life
Birds of a Feather
Love Laughs and Lather
Clubs are Trumps
We Never Sleep
Over the Fence
By the Sad Sea Waves
The Flirt
Bliss
All Aboard
17: Rainbow Island
Move On
Bashful
18: The Tip
The Big Idea
The Lamb
A Gasoline Wedding
The Non-Stop Kid
Nothing but Trouble
She Loves Me Not
19: On the Fire
Look Out Below
The Marathon
Pistols for Breakfast
Spring Fever
Chop Suey & Co.
The Rajah
His Only Father
Soft Money
His Royal Slyness
Heap Big Chief
Bumping Into Broadway
Captain Kid's Kiddies
Punch the Clock
Start Something
All at Sea
Call for Mr. Cave Man
Giving the Bride Away
Order in Court
It's a Hard Life
How Dry I Am
Looking for Trouble
Tough Luck
The Floor Below
20: Red Hot Hottentots
Why Go Home?
Slippery Slices
The Dippy Dentist
All Lit Up
Getting His Goat
Waltz Me Around
Raise the Rent
Find the Girl
Fresh Paint
Flat Broke
Cut the Cards
The Dining Hour
Cracked Wedding Bells
Speed to Spare
Shoot on Sight
Don't Weaken
Drink Hearty
Trotting Through Turkey

20: All Dressed Up
Grab the Ghost
All in a Day
Any Old Port
Don't Rock the Boat
The Home Stretch
Call a Taxi
Live and Learn
Run 'em Ragged
A London Bobby
Money to Burn
Go As You Please
Rock-A-By-Baby
Doing Time
Fellow Citizens
When the Wind Blows
Insulting the Sultan
The Dearly Departed
Cash Customers
Start Something
Park Your Car
21: The Morning After
Whirl o' the West
Open Another Bottle
His Best Girl
Make it Snappy
Fellow Romans
Rush Orders
Bubbling Over
No Children
Own Your Own Home
Big Game
Save Your Money
Blue Sunday
Where's the Fire
The High Rollers
You're Next
The Bike Bug
At the Ringside
No Stop-Over
What a Whopper
Teaching the Teacher
Spot Cash
Name the Day
The Jail Bird
Late Lodgers
Gone to the Country
Law and Order
15 Minutes
On Location
Hocus-Pocus
Penny-In-The-Slot
The Joy Rider

21: The Hustler
Sink or Swim
Shake 'em Up
Corner Pocket
22: Lose No Time
Call the Witness
Years to Come
Blow 'em Up
Stage Struck
Down and Out
Pardon Me
The Bow Wows
Hot Off the Press
The Anvil Chorus
Jump Your Job
Full o' Pep
Kill the Nerve
Days of Old
Light Showers
Do Me a Favor
In the Movies
Punch the Clock
Strictly Modern
Hale and Hearty
Some Baby
The Dumb Bell
Bed of Roses
The Stone Age
365 Days
The Old Sea Dog
Our Gang
Hook Line and Sinker
Nearly Rich
23: Dig Up
A Rough Winter
Before the Public
Where Am I?
California or Bust
Sold at Auction
Courtship of Miles Standish
Jack Frost
The Mystery Man
The Walkout
It's a Gift
Dear Ol' Pal
Join the Circus
Fully Insured
It's a Boy
24: The Big Idea
Why Marry?
Get Busy
25: Are Husbands Human?
26: Do Your Duty

26: The Old Warhorse
The Doughboy
The Yokel
The Fire
All Wet

Eddie Polo (1875-1961)
1915: The Hidden City
The Yellow Streak
The Broken Coin (serial)
16: Peg o' the Ring (serial)
For Liberty (serial)
Heritage of Hate
Captain Kidd
White Messenger
The Verdict
17: Money Madness
Cyclone Smith's Vow
A Ride for a Rancho
18: Lure of the Circus (serial)
The Thirteenth Hour (serial)
Ouda of the Orient
Gray Ghost
Bull's Eye
19: Cyclone Smith's Comeback
Cyclone Smith Plays Trumpet
Cyclone Smith's Partner
20: King of the Circus (serial)
The Vanishing Dagger (serial)
Return of Cyclone Smith
A Battle Against Odds
Square Deal Cyclone
21: Do or Die (serial)
The Secret Four (serial)
22: With Stanley in Africa (serial)
23: Knock on the Door
40: Son of Roaring Dan T
43: Between Us Girls T

Guy Bates Post (1876-1968)
1922: Omar the Tentmaker
The Masquerader
23: Gold Madness

Victor Potel (1889-1947)
1919: Amateur Adventuress
Slippery Slim Series
Full of Pep
In Mizzoura
Petal on the Current
19: Billy Fortune Series
One a Minute
Captain Kidd, Jr.
Outcasts of Poker Flat
20: The Heart of a Child
Billions
Mary's Ankle
21: Lavender and Old Lace
Bob Hampton of Placer
22: Quincy Adams Sawyer
A Tailor-Made Man
23: Meanest Man in the World
Refuge
27: Special Delivery
28: Little Shepherd of Kingdom Come
What Price Beauty
Captain Swagger SSE
Lingerie
29: The Virginian T

David Powell (1887-1923)
1915: Dawn of Tomorrow
16: Less than the Dust
Gloria's Romance (serial)
17: The Beautiful Adventure
Maternity
18: A Romance of the Underworld
The Unforeseen
The Make-Believe Wife
The Better Half
Under the Greenwood Tree
The Great Chances
The Lie
19: The Woman Under Oath
The Counterfeit
His Parisian Wife
The Firing Line
Teeth of the Tiger
20: On with the Dance
Idols of Clay
The Right to Love
Lady Rose's Daughter
21: The Mystery Road
The Princess of New York
22: Love's Boomerang
Her Gilded Cage
Anna Ascends
Outcast
Missing Millions
The Siren Call
23: The Hero

23: Glimpses of the Moon
The Green Goddess

William Powell (1892-)
1919: The Avalanche
A Society Exile
21: Sherlock Holmes
22: When Knighthood was in Flower
Moriarity
The Outcast
23: The Bright Shawl
24: Under the Red Robe
Romola
25: Too Many Kisses
The Beautiful City
26: The Great Gatsby
Dangerous Money
Aloma of the South Seas
The Runaway
Desert Gold
Sea Horses
White Mice
Beau Geste
Tin Gods
27: New York
Love's Greatest Mistake
Special Delivery
Time to Love
Senorita
She's a Sheik
Nevada
28: Beau Sabreur
The Last Command
Feel My Pulse
Partners in Crime
The Dragnet
The Vanishing Pioneer
Forgotten Faces
Interference T
29: Four Feathers SSE

Tyrone Power Sr. (1869-1931)
1915: A Texas Steer
16: John Needham's Double
Where Are My Children?
17: The Planter
The Lorelei, Siren of the Sea
20: The Great Shadow
21: Footfalls
The Black Panther's Club
Dream Street
23: Fury
Truth About Wives
24: The Story Without a Name
25: The Wanderer
26: Test of Donald Norton
Bride of the Storm
Out of the Storm
Braveheart
30: The Big Trail

Purnell Pratt (1882-1941)
1928: Nightstick
29: On with the Show PT
Alibi T

Arline Pretty (1893-)
1915: Crossed Currents
16: The Dawn of Freedom
The Woman in Gray (serial)
Where the Devil Drives
17: The Hidden Hand (serial)
The Secret Kingdom (serial)
The Surprises of an Empty Hotel
The 13th Girl
The Old Guard
In Again--Out Again
19: The Challenge of Chance
Scarlet Shadows
20: Life
The Valley of Doubt
22: Love in the Dark
23: Storm Swept
The White Flower
Bucking the Barriers
28: Virgin Lips

Marie Prevost (1898-1937)
1917: Secrets of a Beauty Parlor
2 Crooks (or, A Noble Crook)
The Ol' Swimmin' Hole
Mack Sennett Bathing Beauty
19: Uncle Tom's Cabin (burlesque)
East Lynn with Variations
Nature Dance
Sleuths

19: His Hidden Purpose
Never Too Old
Yankee Doodle in Berlin
Reilly's Wash Day
When Love is Blind
Love's False Faces
The Dentist
Salome Vs. Shenandoah
The Speak-Easy
20: Down on the Farm
21: A Small Town Idol
Love, Honor and Behave
22: Kissed
Her Night of Nights
The Married Flapper
The Beautiful and Damned
23: Nobody's Fool
Three Women
Don't Get Personal
The Dangerous Little Demon
Heroes of the Street
Brass
24: Red Lights
The Marriage Circle
Tarnish
The Dark Swan
Recompense
Cornered
The Butterfly
25: Kiss Me Again
Bobbed Hair
26: Up in Mabel's Room
Almost a Lady
For Wives Only
Man Bait
His Jazz Bride
The Cave Man
Other Women's Husbands
27: Getting Gertie's Garter
The Night Bride
Girl in the Pullman
The Rush Hour
On to Reno
28: Blonde for the Night
The Racket
Exodus of the New World
29: The Godless Girl PT
The Side Show
Divoce Made Easy T
The Flying Fool T
30: Ladies of Leisure T
War Nurse T
30: Within the Law T
Blonde Baby T
Slightly Married T
The Party Girl T
Sweethearts on Parade T
Paid T
31: Reckless Living T
Hell Divers T
Sporting Blood T
Lullaby T
Good Bad Girl T
Sin of Madelon Claudet T
32: 3 Wise Girls T
33: The 11th Commandment T
35: Hands Across the Table T
36: Tango T
13 Hours by Air T

Kate Price (1872-1943)

1908: Jack Fat and Jim Slim
11: Vanity Fair
12: As You Like It
How Mr. Billington Ran the House
Officer Kate
Fisherman Kate
Stenographers Wanted
O'Hara Helps Cupid
13: Sleuthing
Oracles and Omens
The Lady and Her Maid
A Dangerous Game
15: Spaghetti A La Mode
16: A Night Out
The Waiter's Ball
Mother's Child
Fat and Fickle
Week End Shopping
Casey at the Bat
18: Arizona
Perils of Thunder Mountain (serial)
Amarilly of Clothesline Alley
19: Put Up Your Hands
Tin Pan Alley
20: Bright Skies
The Figurehead
Dinty
The Girl of Gold
The Devil's Riddle
21: The Other Woman

21: Little Lord Fauntleroy
That Girl Montana
22: Guttersnipe
Come On Over
His Wife's Relations
The New Teacher
23: Her Fatal Millions
The Spoilers
A Dangerous Maid
24: The Sea Hawk
25: Wife of the Centaur
The Sporting Venus
Charley's Aunt
Artists and Models
The Tramps
The Lady of Shalott
26: Irene
The Cohens and the Kellys
Paradise
27: Frisco Sally Levy
Third Degree
Mountains of Manhattan
28: Show Girl
Anybody Here Seen Kelly?
The Mad Hour
The Cohens and the Kellys in Paris
Casey Jones
27: Quality Street
Orchids and Ermine
The Sea Tiger
29: Two Weeks Off PT
The Godless Girl PT
The Rainbow PT
The Cohens and the Kellys in Atlantic City PT
Linda
Mother Knows Best T
30: The Rogue Song T
The Cohens and the Kellys in Africa T
31: Ladies of the Jury T
34: Have a Heart T

Aileen Pringle (1895-)
1919: Redhead
22: Earthbound
23: My American Wife
The Tiger's Claw
The Stranger's Banquet
In the Palace of the King
Souls for Sale
The Christian
23: Don't Marry for Money
24: Three Weeks
His Hour
Romance of a Queen
25: Wife of the Centaur
One Year to Live
Wildfire
26: Tin Gods
The Great Deception
The Wilderness Woman
Soul Mates
27: Adam and Evil
Tea for Three
Body and Soul
28: Beau Broadway
Wall Street
Man About Town
Baby Cyclone
Wickedness Preferred
29: Dream of Love T
A Single Man T
Night Parade T
30: Prince of Diamonds T
Soliders and Women T
31: Convicted T
Son of Mine T
Are These Our Children? T
32: Phantom of Crestwood T
33: By Appointment Only T

Herbert Prior
1909: The Cricket on the Hearth
Mrs. George Washington
17: Great Expectations
Poor Little Rich Girl
The Model's Confession
18: A Burglar for a Night
20: Stronger than Death
Pollyanna
The House of Whispers
21: Little 'fraid Lady
Not Guilty
Made in Heaven
Garments of Truth
22: Dangerous Little Demon
Man from Downing Street
The Half Breed
Snowshoe Trail
23: Garrison's Finish
28: All at Sea

Lucien Prival (1900-)
1924: Hummingbird

26: The Great Deception
Just Another Blonde
Puppets
A Man of Quality
27: High Hat
American Beauty
The Next Room
28: Hell's Angels
The Racket
Adoration
29: Peacock Fan
30: Party Girl
The Lotus Lady
?? Sirocco
Die Kleptomaniac

Jed Prouty (1879-1956)
1925: The Sea Beast
The Knockout
26: Second Chance
Ella Cinders
27: Smile, Brother, Smile
Orchids and Ermine
28: The Siren
Grain of Dust
Name the Woman
29: His Captive Woman
Fall of Eve
Two Weeks Off PT

Frank Puglia (1894-1962)
1922: Orphans of the Storm
Fascination
23: White Sister
24: Romola
25: Beautiful City
Isn't Life Wonderful?
28: The Man Who Laughs

Edna Purviance (1894-1958)
1914: Between Showers
Cruel, Cruel Love
15: His New Job
The Champion
In the Park
The Tramp
By the Sea
Work
The Woman
The Bank
Shanghaied
A Night at the Show
A Night Out
15: Jitney Elopement
Perfect Lady
16: Carmen
The Floorwalker
The Fireman
The Vagabond
Behind the Screen
The Rink
Pawnshop
Police
Triple Trouble
The Count
17: Easy Street
The Cure
The Adventurer
The Immigrant
18: A Dog's Life
Shoulder Arms
19: Sunnyside
A Day's Pleasure
20: The Kid
21: The Idle Class
22: Pay Day
23: The Pilgrim
A Woman of Paris
26: The Sea Gull
Education of Prince
52: Limelight

Nena Quartaro (1911-)
1928: All Parts
Red Mark
29: Redeeming Sing PT
The Eternal Woman
One Stolen Night PT
Frozen River PT

Eddie Quillan (1907-)
1922: Up and At 'em
28: Show Folks
29: Noisy Neighbors PT
The Godless Girl PT
Geraldine PT
The Sophomore T
18 2-reel Sennett
Comedies

Margaret Quimby
1926: The Whole Town's Talking
27: Western Whirlwinds
New York
The World at Her Feet
28: The Ghetto

28: Squads Right
Tragedy of Youth
Sally of the Scandals
29: Lucky Boy
Two Men and a Maid

Billie Quirk
1909: They Would Elope
The Mended Lute
The Gibson Goddess
A Sound Sleeper
Franks
The Little Darling
Sweet and Twenty
His Wife's Visitors
1776 (or, the Hessian Renegades)
A Rich Revenge
14: Father's Timepiece
The Evolution of Percival
In Bridal Attire
The Egyptian Mummy
Forcing Dad's Consent
15: Billy's Wager
The Green Cat
The Young Man Who Figgered
A Stamp in Tramps
17: Master of His House
Boarding House Feud
The Vanishing Vault
Spades are Trumps
Bertisi Stratagem
Billy the Bear Tamer
21: At the Stage Door
22: My Old Kentucky Home
23: Broadway Broke
Salomy Jane

E. J. Radcliffe (1893-)
1920: Daughter of Two Worlds
The Discarded Woman
Love, Honor and Obey
Miss 139
21: Disraeli
Idol of the North
The Great Adventure
Every Man's Price
22: The Woman Who Walked Alone
Amazing Lovers
26: The Thrill Hunter
Rolling Home
26: The Fighting Buckaroo
Winning of Barbara Worth
27: Held by the Law
No Control
Framed
Prince of Headwaiters
Smile, Brother, Smile
Publicity Madness
Cheating Cheaters
28: Head Man
Floating College
Jazz Age
Four Feathers SSE
29: Show of Shows T
Sally T
Skinner Steps Out T
30: Wide Open T
The Cohens and the Kellys in Scotland Yard T
33: I Loved a Woman T

Esther Ralston (1902-)
1920: Huckleberry Finn
21: Whispering Devils
Under Secret Orders
Timberland Treachery
22: Oliver Twist
Remembrance
23: The Phantom Fortune (serial)
24: The Marriage Circle
Wolves of the North (serial)
25: Peter Pan
Beggar on Horseback
The Best People
The Goose Hangs High
Lucky Devil
Little French Girl
Trouble with Wives
26: American Venus
Womanhandled
The Quarterback
Blind Goddess
A Kiss for Cinderella
27: Children of Divorce
Fashions for Women
Ten Modern Commandments
Figures Don't Lie
Old Ironsides
28: The Spotlights
Love and Learn
Sawdust Paradise

28: Something Always Happens
Half a Bride
Power of the Press
29: The Case of Lena Smith
Betrayal
Wheel of Life T
30: The Mighty T
The Southerner T
31: Lonely Wives T
Prodigal T
Sheer Luck T

Jobyna Ralston (1902-1967)
1923: Why Worry?
24: Hot Water
Girl Shy
25: The Freshman
26: Gigolo
For Heaven's Sake
Sweet Daddies
27: Special Delivery
Count of Ten
Wings
Racing Romeo
Kid Brother
Pretty Clothes
Lightning
28: The Night Flyer
Little Mickey Grogan
The Toilers
Power of the Press
Black Butterflies
The Big Hop
29: Some Mother's Boy
College Coquette T
30: Rough Waters T
31: Sheer Luck T
?? Friday the Thirteenth
The Bride to Be
Face the Camera
Shiver and Shake
Take the Next Car
The Golf Bug
The Flivver
A While Blacksmith
Jailed and Bailed
The Three Must Get Theirs

Marjorie Rambeau (1889-)
1916: The Dazzling Miss Davison
17: The Debt
The Greater Woman
17: Mary Moreland
20: The Fortune Teller
26: Syncopating Sue
?? On Her Honor

Natacha Rambova (1897-1966)
1919: Woman in Chains
26: When Love Grows Cold

Sally Rand (1903-)
1925: Road to Yesterday
Dressmaker from Paris
26: Man Bait
Paris at Midnight
Grounds for Divorce
27: Night of Love
His Dog
Getting Gertie's Garter
Galloping Fury
Heroes in Blue
The Fighting Eagle
28: Crashing Through
A Girl in Every Port
Nameless Men
Golf Widows
Black Feather
Woman Against the World
The Clash
The Czarina's Secrets

Anders Randolf (1875-1930)
1914: Uncle Bill
16: Hero of Submarine D-2
17: Within the Law
Who's Your Neighbor?
The Belgian
The Price of Virtue
18: Splendid Sinner
Her Man
19: Erstwhile Susan
Lion and the Mouse
The Cinema Murder
The Black Beach
20: Madonnas and Men
21: Buried Treasure
Jim, The Penman
23: Bright Shawl
24: Dorothy Vernon of Haddon Hall
In Hollywood with Potash & Perlmutter
26: The Black Pirate
The Johnstown Flood

26: Womanpower
Ransom's Folly
The Silent Flyer (serial)
27: Slightly Used
The Tender Hour
Dearie
Old San Francisco
The Jazz Singer PT
College Widow
Sinews of Steel
A Reno Divorce
28: Me Gangster SSE
Three Sinners
The Big Killing
Patience
Gateway of the Moon
Women They Talk About
Power of Silence
Five Aces
29: Noah's Ark PT
The Viking
Four Devils T
Erick the Great
Sin Sister SSE
Dangerous Curves T
Young Nowheres
The Last Performance PT
Show of Shows T
Wrong Again
?? 413

Arthur Rankin (1900-)
1920: The Copperhead
The Amateur Wife
Romance
21: Truth About Husbands
Great Adventure
Jim, The Penman
24: Broken Laws
26: The Volga Boatman
27: Dearie
Riding to Fame
The Blood Ship
The Woman Who Did Not Care
Slightly Used
Adventurous Soul
28: Love and the Law
Making the Varsity
Companionate Marriage
Code of the Air
Say It With Sables
Runaway Girls

28: Submarine
Ships of the Night
29: Fall of Eve
Below the Deadline
Wild Party T

Doris Rankin
1920: The Copperhead
Devil's Garden
21: The Great Adventure
Jim, The Penman

Jules Raucourt (1890-)
1918: La Tosca
Frou-Frou
19: Prunella
27: Ranger of the North
28: His Tiger Lady
Glorious Betsy PT

Herbert Rawlinson (1885-1953)
1912: God of Gold
The Count of Monte Cristo
13: The Old Clerk
The Sea Wolf
14: On the Verge of War
Kid Regan's Hands
Flirting with Death
The High Sign
15: Damon and Pythias
The Black Box (serial)
17: Don't Shoot!
The Man Trap
18: Brace Up
Flesh of Fate
The Common Cause
The Sun Shining Through
Won in the Clouds
The Turn of the Wheel
Blind Fools
Smashing Through
19: The Carter Case (serial)
A Dangerous Affair
Kill or Be Killed
Charge It
Good Gracious, Annabelle!
House Divided
Craig Kennedy (serial)
Chief Flynn, Secret Service (series)
20: A Man and His Woman
Passers-By
21: Wealth

21: Conflict
The Wakefield Case
You Find It Everywhere
The Millionaire
Playthings of Destiny
22: The Scrapper
Confidence
Cheated Hearts
Another Man's Shoes
Man Under Cover
The Black Bag
23: Clean-Up
Railroaded
Millions to Burn
One Wonderful Night
The Scarlet Car
Nobody's Bride
Fools and Riches
The Prisoner
His Mystery Girl
24: The Victor
High Speed
The Dancing Cheat
Jack o' Clubs
Stolen Secrets
Dancing Stairways
25: My Neighbor's Wife
The Flame Fighter (serial)
Come Through
26: Trooper 77 (serial)
Gilded Butterfly
Men of the Night
Belle of Broadway
The Millionaire Policeman
27: Her Sacrifice
Burning Girl
Slipping Wives
The Bugle Call
Hour of Reckoning
28: Wages of Conscience

Allene Ray (1901-)
1920: Honeymoon Ranch
The High Card
21: West of the Rio Grande
Tex O'Reilly
22: Partners of the Sunset
23: Your Friend and Mine
Times Have Changed
24: The Fortieth Door (serial)
Galloping Hoofs (serial)
Ten Scars Make a Man (serial)
24: Way of a Man (serial)
25: The Green Archer (serial)
Play Ball (serial)
26: The House Without a Key (serial)
Snowed In (serial)
27: Melting Millions (serial)
Hawk of the Hills (serial)
28: The Man Without a Face (serial)
Terrible People (serial)
The Yellow Cameo (serial)
Perilous Mission (serial)
29: The Black Book (serial)
30: The Indians are Coming (serial)

Charles Ray (1891-1943)
1913: Favorite Son
Sharpshooter
Lost Dispatch
Sinews of War
Bread Cast Upon the Waters
A Slave's Devotion
The Boomerang
Transgressor
The Quakeress
The Bondsman
The Exoneration
Witch of Salem
Soul of the South
The Open Door
Eileen of Erin
14: A Military Judas
House of Bondage
For Her Brother's Sake
In the Tennessee Hills
Repaid
Desert Gold
For the Wearing of the Green
Path of Genius
Rightful Heir
Shorty's Sacrifice
The Card Sharps
In the Cow Country
Latent Spark
Curse of Humanity
The City
Red Mask
One of the Discard
Word of his People
Fortunes of War

14: City of Darkness
The Friend
Not of the Flock
Grey Sentinal
Gangsters and the Girl
15: The Grudge
Wells of Paradise
Cup of Life
Spirit of the Bell
Renegade
The Shoal Light
Conversion of Frosty Blake
Ace of Hearts
Painted Soul
Lure of Woman
16: Peggy
The Dividend
Deserter
Honor Thy Name
Home
A Corner in Colleen's
The Wolf Woman
Plain Jane
Honorable Algy
Weaker Sex
17: Back of the Man
Pinch Hitter
Millionaire Vagrant
Clodhopper
Sudden Jim
Son of His Father
Paddy O'Hara
18: His Mother's Boy
The Hired Man
Family Skeleton
Playing the Game
His Own Home Town
Claws of the Hun
String Beans
A Nine O'Clock Town
Law of the North
19: The Sheriff's Son
Greased Lightning
The Busher
Hay Foot! Straw Foot!
Bill Henry
Crooked Straight
Girl Dodger
Egg-Crate Wallop
20: Red Hot Dollars
Alarm Clock Andy
Paris Green
Gym
20: Forty-Five Minutes From Broadway
Village Sleuth
Peaceful Valley
Homer Comes Home
An Old-Fashioned Boy
21: Nineteen and Phyllis
Ol' Swimmin' Hole
Scrap Iron
A Midnight Bell
Two Minutes to Go
R. S. V. P.
22: The Barnstormer
Gas, Oil and Water
Deuce of Spades
Smudge
Alias Julius Caesar
Tailor-Made Man
23: The Girl I Loved
Courtship of Miles Standish
24: Dynamite Smith
25: Percy
Some Pun'kins
Wedding Song
Bright Lights
26: Sweet Adeline
Auction Block
Paris
Betty's a Lady
The Winner
27: Fire Brigade
The Flag Maker
Nobody's Widow
Getting Gertie's Garter
Vanity
28: Count of Ten
Garden of Eden
34: Ladies Should Listen T
School for Girls T
Ticket to a Crime T
35: Welcome Home T
36: Just My Luck T
Hollywood Boulevard T
40: A Little Bit of Heaven T
The Lady from Cheyenne T
41: Wild Geese Calling T
The Man Who Lost Himself T
A Yank in the R. A. F. T
42: The Magnificent Dope T

Florence Reed (1863-1967)
1915: The Dancing Girl

15: The Cowardly Way
16: New York
The Woman's Law
Lucretia Borgia
17: Today
The Eternal Sin
The Struggle Everlasting
18: Wives of Men
Call of the Heart
19: Woman Under Oath
Her Code of Honor
20: Her Game
The Eternal Mother
21: Black Panther's Cub
Indiscretion

Frank Reicher (1875-1965)
1926: Her Man O'War
27: Beau Sabreur
28: Masks of the Devil
Someone to Love
His Captive Woman
Sweet 16
Napoleon's Barber
4 Sons SSE
Blue Danube
29: Sins of the Fathers
Strange Cargo T
Mister Antonio T
Black Waters T

Wallace Reid (1892-1923)
1910: The Phoenix
11: The Reporter
The Leading Lady
Leather Stocking Tales
The Pathfinder
12: Jean Intervenes
Chumps
Indian Romeo and Juliet
The Telephone Girl
The Seventh Son
The Illumination
Brothers
The Victoria Cross (or, Charge of the Light Brigade)
The Hieroglyphic
Diamond Cut Diamond
Curfew Shall Not Ring Tonight
Kaintuck
Before The White Man Came
12: A Man's Duty
At Cripple Creek
His Only Son
Making Good
The Secret Service Man
Indian Raiders
Every Inch a Man
The Tribal Law
The Seepore Rebellion
13: Love and the Law
A Rose of Old Mexico
The Ways of Fate
The Picture of Dorian Gray
When Jim Returned
The Tattooed Arm
The Deerslayer
Youth and Jealousy
The Kiss
Her Innocent Marriage
His Mother's Son
A Modern Snare
When Luck Changes
Via Cabaret
The Spirit of the Flag
Hearts and Horses
In Love and War
Dead Man's Shoes
Pride of Lonesome
The Powder Flash of Death
A Foreign Spy
The Picket Guard
Mental Suicide
The Animal
The Harvest of Flame
Mystery of the Yellow Aster Mine
Gratitude of Wanda
The Wall of Money
The Heart of a Cracksman
The Cracksman's Reformation
Cross Purposes
The Fires of Fate
Retribution
A Cracksman Santa Claus
The Lightning Bolt
A Hopi Legend
14: Who So Diggeth a Pit
The Intruder
The Countess Betty's Mine
The Wheel of Life
Fires of Conscience
The Greater Devotion

14: A Flash in the Dark
Breed of the Mountains
Regeneration
Heart of the Hills
The Way of a Woman
The Voice of Viola
The Spider and Her Web
The Mountaineer
Cupid Incognito
A Gypsy Romance
The Skeleton
The Fruit of Evil
The Test
Women and Roses
The Quack
The Siren
The Man Within
The Spark of Manhood
Passing of the Beast
Love's Western Flight
A Wife on a Wager
Across the Mexican Line
Den of Thieves
Arms and the Gringo
Down by the Sounding Sea
Moonshine Molly
The City Beautiful
The Second Mrs. Roebuck
Sierra Jim's Reformation
Down the Road to Credit-ville
Her Awakening
For Her Father's Sins
A Mother's Influence
The Niggard
The Odalisque
The Little Country Mouse
Another Chance
At Dawn
Over the Ledge
Baby's Ride

15: The Craven
The Three Brothers
Birth of a Nation
The Lost House
Station Content
Enoch Arden
A Yankee from the West
The Chorus Lady
Old Heidelberg
Carmen
The Golden Chance

16: Intolerance
To Have and To Hold
The Love Mask
Maria Rosa
The Selfish Woman
The Golden Fetter
The Prison Without Walls
The World Apart
Big Timber
The Squaw Man's Son
The Hostage

17: The Woman God Forgot
Nan of Music Mountain

18: The Devil Stone
Rimrock Jones
The Thing We Love
The House of Silence
Believe Me, Xantippe
The Firefly of France
Less Than Kin
The Source
The Man from Funeral Range
Too Many Millions

19: The Dub
Alias Mike Moran
The Roaring Road
You're Fired!
The Love Burglar
Valley of the Giants
The Lottery Man
Hawthorne of the U. S. A.

20: Double Speed
Excuse My Dust
The Dancin' Fool
Sick Abed
What's Your Hurry?
Always Audacious

21: The Charm School
The Love Special
Too Much Speed
The Hell Diggers
The Affairs of Anatol
Don't Tell Everything
Forever (or, Peter Ibbetson)

22: Rent Free
The World's Champion
Clarence

23: Adam's Rib

Rennie Renfro

1928: Two of a Kind
And How!

Ruth Renick

1919: Hawthorne of the U. S. A.
20: White Dove
Conrad in Quest of His Youth
The Jucklins
21: She Couldn't Help It
The Witching Hour
What's a Wife Worth?
Parish Priest
The Molly Coddler

James Rennie (1889-1965)

1920: Flying Pat
Remodeling Her Husband
Moonlight and Honeysuckle
22: Stardust
23: Mighty Lak' A Rose
Dust Flower
His Children's Children
25: Clothes Make the Pirate

Dorothy Revier (1904-)

1926: Fate of a Flirt
Enemy of Men
Poker Faces
False Alarm
The Better Way
Stolen Pleasures
When the Wife's Away
27: Wandering Girls
The Price of Honor
Drop Kick
The Tigress
The Clown
Poor Girls
28: The Warning
The Siren
Submarine
Red Dance SSE
Beware of Blondes
Sinners' Parade
29: The Iron Mask PT
The Quitter
The Donovan Affair T
Father and Son PT
Dance of Life T
Light Fingers PT
Tanned Legs PT
The Man from God's Country
22: Broadway Madonna
30: Murder on the Roof T
Black Sheep T
The Mighty T
Hold Everything T

Rex (the horse)

1927: No Man's Law
Wild Beauty
28: Guardians of the Wind
Two Outlaws
29: Harvest of Hate
Wild Blood
Plunging Hoofs
Girl on the Barge
Hoofbeats of Vengeance

Vera Reynolds (1905-1962)

1921: Bedlam
A Saphead's Sacrifice
Dry and Thirsty
Parked in the Park
23: Hearts of Oak
Prodigal Daughters
24: Feet of Clay
Icebound
25: Road to Yesterday
The Limited Mail
The Golden Bed
26: Silence
Steel Preferred
The Million Dollar Handicap
Risky Business
Sunnyside Up
Corporal Kate
27: Main Event
Almost Human
Little Adventuress
28: Jazzland
Golf Widows
The Divine Sinner
29: Back from Shanghai
Tonight at 12
30: Last Dance T
31: The Lawless Woman T
Neck and Neck T
32: Dragnet Patrol T
Gorilla Ship T
Tangled Destinies T

Billie Rhodes (1906-)

1913: Perils of the Sea
16: A Seminary Scandal
17: Some Nurse

18: Beware of Blondes
Dad's Knockout
19: Lion and the Lamb
In Search of Arcady
Blue Bonnet
Hoop-La of the Circus
Girl of My Dreams
The Love Call
22: The Star Reporter
?? A 2 Cylinder Courtship
Bluffing Father
For Sweet Charity

Frank Rice (d. 1936)
1928: Headin' for Danger
The Lariat Kid
Orphan of the Sage
Rough Ridin' Red
Vagabond Cub
Humming Wires
Lawless Legion
Young Whirlwind
29: Overland Telegraph

Irene Rich (1894-)
1918: A Law Unto Herself
Stella Maris
Tale of Two Worlds
19: Todd of the Times
Blue Bonnet
Ropin' Fool
The Street Called Straight
Michael O'Halloran
Wolves of the Night
The Trap
20: Jes' Call Me Jim
The Godless Men
The Yosemite Trail
The Strange Boarder
Fruits of Faith
A Voice in the Dark
21: Just Out of College
Tough Proposition
Sunset Jones
The Invisible Power
Desperate Trails
One Man in a Million
Poverty of Riches
22: Strength of the Pines
One Clear Call
A Fool There Was
Brawn of the North
Lone Star Ranger
23: Main Street
The Gold Diggers
The Marriage Chance
Brass
Rosita
24: Cytherea
Beau Brummel
This Woman
25: Lady Windemere's Fan
A Lost Lady
Compromise
My Wife and I
26: So This is Paris
The Pleasure Buyers
My Official Wife
The Honeymoon Express
27: The Climbers
Don't Tell the Wife
Dearie
Desired Woman
28: Craig's Wife
Beware of Married Men
Powder My Back SSE
Women they Talk About PT
The Perfect Crime
Condemned Woman
29: Daughters of Desire
Ned McCobb's Daughter SSE
Shanghai Rose
Exalted Flapper SSE
30: They Had to See Paris T

Lillian Rich (1902-1954)
1913: The Ways of Fate
When Jim Returned
The Tattooed Arm
Youth and Jealousy
Her Innocent Marriage
A Modern Snare
When Luck Changes
Hearts and Horses
Dead Man's Shoes
A Foreign Spy
20: One Hour Before Dawn
Felix O'Day
Half a Chance
Dice of Destiny
The Red Lane
21: Blazing Trail
Go Straight
The Millionare
The Sage Hen

22: Her Social Value
Man to Man
The Bear Cat
Afraid to Fight
The Kentucky Derby
The Eternal Triangle
Catch My Smoke
23: One Wonderful Night
24: The Love Master
Never Say Die
25: The Golden Bed
26: Dancing Days
Isle of Retribution
Braveheart
Ship of Souls
A Silver Rosary
The Forger
High Seas
Stage Whispers
The Murdock Affair
Whispering Smith
On the Front Page
27: Woman's Law
Exclusive Rights
God's Great Wilderness
Snowbound
28: Old Code
Web of Fate
31: Once a Lady
Grief Street
The Devil Plays
32: Mark of the Spur
?? Behind Red Curtains

Viola Richard
1928: Dumb Daddies
Came the Dawn
Limousine Love
Blow by Blow
Should Married Men Go Home?

Jack Richardson (1883-)
1917: Man Above the Law
18: You Can't Believe Everything
The Painted Lily
His Enemy the Law
The Mayor of Filbert
19: Desert Law
Wife or Country
Dangerous Hours
20: The Toll Gate
20: Sting of the Lash
21: Fighter Mad
Too Much Speed
The Greater Love
22: A Dangerous Adventure
Silent Shelby
23: Souls for Sale
27: Snarl of Hate
The Sonora Kid
Avenging Fangs
Eager Lips
Polly of the Movies
28: Bally Hoo Buster
Wilful Youth
Women Who Dare
The Midnight Adventure
Speed Classic
Marked Money
Melody of Love
Trial Marriage
The Last Lap
Across the Plains
Partners in Crime
29: Midnight on the Barbary Coast
One Splendid Hour
Sailor's Holiday T

Charles Richman (1879-1940)
1915: The Battle Cry of Peace
16: The Hero of Submarine D-2
17: The Secret Kingdom (serial)
The Public Be Damned
The More Excellent Way
19: Over There
The Echo of Youth
The Hidden Truth
Everybody's Business
20: Half an Hour
Curtain
Harriet and the Piper
21: Trust Your Wife
22: My Friend the Devil
23: Has the World Gone Mad?

Warner Richmond (1895-1948)
1916: Betty of Graystone
18: Sporting Life
Woman
19: Eyes of Youth
As a Man Thinks
Little Miss Brown
Test of a Code

19: Gray Towers Mystery
20: Misleading Lady
A Woman's Business
My Lady's Garter
21: Tol'able David
The Mountain Woman
The Heart of Maryland
22: The Challenge
The Man from Glengarry
The Beast Within
Luck
23: Big Brother
Trail of the Lonesome Pine
25: Manhattan Madness
Fifty-Fifty
26: Good and Naughty
27: Slide, Kelly, Slide
The Fire Brigade
Finger Prints
Irish Hearts
White Flannels
Heart of Maryland
28: You Can't Beat the Law
Hearts of Men
The Dead Line
The Missing Man
The Crowd
Shadows of the Night
Fifty-Fifty
Big Brother
Stop That Man!
29: The Redeeming Sin PT
Apache
Strange Cargo T
Voice of the Storm
Stark Mad T
Big News T

Tom Ricketts (d. 1939)
1916: Other Side of the Door
17: The Single Code
A Daughter of the Well-Dressed Poor
20: Forbidden
The Counterfeit Soul
The Crime of the Hour
Sins of the World
The Great Lover
21: The Spenders
The Killer
Sham
Puppets of Fate
Wives of Men

22: Eternal Flame
Within the Law
Trifling Women
A Tailor Made Man
23: A Dangerous Maid
25: Bobbed Hair
27: Children of Divorce
Too Many Crooks
My Friend from India
28: Law and the Man
The Magnificent Flirt
Just Married
Interference T
5 and 10¢ Annie
Freedom of the Press
Dry Martini SSE
29: Red Hot Speed PT
Glad Rag Doll T
Light Fingers PT
?? The Great Question
The Buzzard's Shadow

Cleo Ridgely (1893-1962)
1915: The Chorus Lady
Stolen Goods
The Secret Orchard
The Golden Chance
16: The Love Mask
The Yellow Pawn
The Selfish Woman
The House with the Golden Windows
21: A Dangerous Pastime
22: The Law and the Woman
Sleep Walker
The Forgotten Law
23: Beautiful and Damned

Fritzie Ridgeway (1898-1960)
1917: The Soul Herder
Up or Down
19: The Danger Zone
Fire Flingers
Winning of a Bride
Ranger of Pike's Peak
Petal on the Current
20: Judy of Rogue's Harbor
The Fatal 30 (serial)
22: Bring Him In
The Hate Trail
Boomerang Justice
The Old Homestead
23: Ruggles of Red Gap

23: Trifling with Havoc
27: Nobody's Widow
Getting Gertie's Garter
Lonesome Ladies
Face Value
28: The Enemy
Flying Romeos
Son of the Golden West
The Rescue
29: Red Hot Speed PT
This is Heaven PT
Hell's Heroes T

Duncan Rinaldo (1904-)
(also Renaldo)
1928: The Gun Runner
The Naughty Duchess
Marcheta
The Devil's Skipper
Clothes Make the Woman
Romany Love
29: Bridge of San Luis Rey PT
Pals of the Prairie SSE
31: Trader Horn T

Rin-Tin-Tin (1916-1930)
1923: Where the North Begins
24: Find Your Man
Lighthouse by the Sea
25: Tracked in the Snow Country
The Clash of the Wolves
26: When London Sleeps
The Night Cry
Hero of the Big Snows
27: Jaws of Steel
A Dog of the Regiment
Hills of Kentucky
Tracked by the Police
28: Rinty of the Desert
Land of the Silver Fox
Race for Life
29: Tiger Rose T
Frozen River PT
Lightning Warrior
The Million Dollar Collar PT
Show of Shows T
30: The Man Hunter T
Rough Waters T
Lone Defender (serial) T
31: Lightning Warrior (serial) (Rinty Jr.)
33: Wolf Dog (serial) (Rinty Jr.)
34: Law of the Wild (serial) (Rinty Jr.)

Bert Roach (1891-)
1917: Fatty's Magic Pants
Cactus and Kate
Soapsuds and Sirens
19: Dirty's Daring Dash
• Yankee Doodle in Berlin
21: A Small Town Idol
The Millionaire
22: Marry the Poor Girl
The Black Bag
The Flirt
23: A Lady of Quality
26: Money Talks
Tin Hats
Don't Tell the Wife
The Flaming Forest
Excuse Me
27: The Taxi Dancer
12 Miles Out
Tillie the Toiler
28: The Crowd
The Latest from Paris
Iron Mike
Wickedness Preferred
Under the Black Eagle
Certain Young Man
Telling the World
Riders of the Dark
29: The Last Warning PT
Honeymoon
The Desert Rider
The Argyle Case T
Twin Beds T
The Time, Place and the Girl T
Young Nowheres T
The Aviator T
So Long Letty T
Show of Shows T

Jason Robards (1893-1963)
1926: Paris
The Cohens and the Kellys
Honeymoon Express
Stella Maris
27: Wild Geese
Polly of the Movies
Jaws of Steel

27: A Bird in the Hand
The Streets of Shanghai
The Third Degree
White Flannels
The Heart of Maryland
Hills of Kentucky
Tracked by the Police
Irish Hearts
28: Casey Jones
On Trial
29: Trial Marriage
The Flying Marine PT
Isle of Lost Ships T
Some Mother's Boy
The Gamblers T

Edith Roberts (1901-1935)
1918: The Deciding Kiss
The Love Swindle
Cherries are Ripe
The Brazen Beauty
19: Lasca
A Taste of Life
Set Free
Sue of the South
Beans
Bill Henry
The Lost Appetite
Jilted in Jail
A Burglar by Request
Her City Beau
The War Bridegroom
5 Little Widows
Seeing Things
O'Connor's Mag
Madame Spy
20: The Adorable Savage
Alias Miss Dodd
Bill Henry
Her Five Foot Highness
The Triflers
21: Open Shutters
The Fire Cat
The Unknown Wife
White Youth
Thunder Island
Living Lips
In Society
22: Saturday Night
Son of the Wolf
Flesh and Blood
Thorns and Orange Blossoms
Pawned
22: A Front Page Story
23: The Dangerous Age
Backbone
Big Brother
24: Age of Innocence
25: 7 Keys to Baldpate
On Thin Ice
Speed Mad
The Great Sensation
26: There You Are
New Champion
The Taxi Mystery
The Mystery Club
The Jazz Girl
The Road to Broadway
Shameful Behavior
28: The Man from Headquarters
Dreary House
29: Phantoms of the North
Black Cargoes of the South Seas
Wagon Master PT

Theodore Roberts (1861-1928)
1910: Uncle Tom
14: The Circus Man
The Ghost Breaker
Where the Trail Divides
Ready Money
15: Girl of the Golden West
The Captive
Stolen Goods
The Secret Orchard
The Case of Becky
16: Puddin' Head Wilson
The Sowers
Trail of the Lonesome Pine
The Storm
The Unprotected
17: Joan the Woman
Nan of Music Mountain
War Relief
18: M'liss
War Relief (propaganda film)
Wild Youth
Say Young Fellow
The Squaw Man
Arizona
The Source
Believe Me, Xantippe
Old Wives for New
19: The Wild Goose Chase

19: The Roaring Road
Male and Female
Everywoman
Don't Change Your Husband
You're Fired!
Hawthorne of the U. S. A.
20: Something to Think About
Judy of Rogue's Harbor
Double Speed
Excuse My Dust
Sweet Lavender
The Furnace
21: Forbidden Fruit
The Love Special
The Affairs of Anatol
Sham
Miss Lulu Bett
Too Much Speed
22: Across the Continent
Hail the Woman
Saturday Night
The Old Homestead
Exit the Vamp
Night Life in Hollywood
Our Leading Citizens
If You Believe It, It's So
The Man Who Saw Tomorrow
23: Ten Commandments
Prodigal Daughters
Grumpy
Stephen Steps Out
25: Locked Doors
26: The Cat's Pajamas
28: Masks of the Devil
Ned McCobb's Daughter
29: Noisy Neighbors PT

May Robson (1865-1942)
1918: A Night Out
19: A Broadway Saint
His Bridal Night
The Lost Battalion
26: Pals in Paradise
27: The Rejuvenation of Aunt Mary
The Angel of Broadway
Harp in Hock
28: Blue Danube
Chicago
Turkish Delight

John Roche (1896-1952)
1922: Rainbow
The Good Provider
23: Bag and Baggage
25: Kiss Me Again
Bobbed Hair
26: The Midnight Lovers
The Return of Peter Grimm
Her Big Night
The Man Upstairs
27: The Truthful Sex
Uncle Tom's Cabin
28: Their Hour
Diamond Handcuffs
29: The Dream Melody
The Donovan Affair T
The Unholy Night T
This Thing Called Love T
30: Monte Carlo T
32: Winner Takes All T
Prosperity T
33: Beauty for Sale T
35: Just My Luck T

Earle Rodney
1918: City of Tears
The Biggest Show on Earth
Naughty! Naughty!
Keys of the Righteous

Charles "Buddy" Rogers (1904-)
1926: Fascinating Youth
So's Your Old Man
Heads Up
More Pay Less Work
27: Wings
My Best Girl
Get Your Man
28: Abies Irish Rose SSE
Someone to Love
Varsity
Red Lips
29: Close Harmony PT
Here Comes the Bandwagon
Illusion T
The River of Romance T
Half Way to Heaven T
Man Must Fight T
30: Paramount on Parade T
Safety in Number T
Young Eagles T

30: Follow Through T
31: Along Came Youth T
The Movie Man T
The Ice Man T
The Lawyer's Secret T
Road to Reno T
Working Girls T
The Reckless Age T

Will Rogers (1879-1935)
1918: Jubilo
Laughing Bill Hyde
19: Almost a Husband
Water Water Everywhere
20: The Strange Boarder
Jes' Call Me Jim
Cupid, the Cowpuncher
Scratch My Back
Guile of Women
Fruits of Faith
21: Honest Hutch
Doubling for Romeo
Boys will be Boys
An Unwilling Hero
Connecticut Yankee in King Arthur's Court
22: One Glorious Day
The Headless Horseman
A Poor Relation
The Ropin' Fool
23: Jus' Passin' Through
Hustlin' Hank
Uncensored Movies
24: Two Wagons - Both Covered
Fruits of Faith
The Cowboy Sheik
The Cake Eater
Going to Congress-2 reels
Big Moments from Little Pictures
High Brow Stuff
No Parking Here (Don't Park There!)
A Truthful Liar
Our Congressman
26: Tip Toes
27: Texas Steer
29: They Had to See Paris T

Gilbert Roland (1905-)
1925: The Plastic Age
The Lady Who Lied
26: The Campus Flirt
The Blonde Saint
27: Camille
Rose of the Golden West
28: The Dove
The Woman Disputed
The Love Mart
The Cardboard Lover
29: New York Nights T
30: Monsieur the Fox T
Resurrection T
(Spanish version)

Ruth Roland (1892-1937)
1912: Hypnotic Nell
Ranch Girls on a Rampage
13: While Father Telephoned
14: Ham the Piano Mover
The Haunted Queen
15: Comrade John
Who Pays? (serial)
Ham at the Garbage Gentlemen's Ball
16: The Red Circle (serial)
Who Wins? (serial)
The Girl Detective (serial)
17: The Neglected Wife (serial)
Fringe of Society
18: Hands Up!
The Price of Folly (serial)
19: Adventures of Ruth (serial)
The Tiger's Trail (serial)
20: Ruth of the Rockies (serial)
What Would You Do? (serial)
21: The Avenging Arrow (serial)
The Riddle of the Range (serial)
22: White Eagle (serial)
Timber Queen (serial)
23: Haunted Valley (serial)
Ruth of the Range (serial)
Broadway Bob
27: The Masked Woman
29: Love and the Law
30: Reno

Buddy Roosevelt (1898-)
1925: Reckless Courage
Gold and Grit
26: Hoodoo Ranch
Tangled Herds
Thundering Through
Action Galore
Galloping Jinx

26: Twin Triggers
Easy Going
The Dangerous Dub
27: Between Dangers
The Fightin' Comeback
Code of Cow Country
The Phantom Buster
Ride 'em High
Bandit Buster
28: Cowboy Cavalier
The Lightnin' Shot
Mystery Valley
The Devil's Tower
Trailin' Back
Painted Trail
Trail Riders

Rosa Rosanova (1883-)
1922: Hungry Hearts
Blood and Sand
23: 10 Commandments
Trilby
28: Abie's Irish Rose SSE
Sonia
29: The Younger Generation PT
Lucky Boy PT

Albert Roscoe (1887-1931)
1916: The Last Card
17: Camille
Cleopatra
18: Salome
The She-Devil
When a Woman Sins
The Shuttle
19: A Siren's Song
Evangeline
The City of Comrades
Her Purchase Price
A Man's Country
20: Last of the Mohicans
Madame X
The Branding Iron
Her Unwilling Husband
22: No Trespassing
Burning Sands
The Man Who Saw Tomorrow
23: Java Head
The Spoilers
26: Tentacles of the North
27: Long Pants
Duty's Reward

31: Dirigible T

Bodil Rosing (d. 1942)
1928: The Big Noise
Wheel of Chance
Ladies of the Mob
The Woman from Moscow
Forgotten Faces
Out of the Ruins
King of the Rodeo
Pretty Lady
It Must Be Love
Sunrise
The Fleet's In
29: Why Be Good?
Betrayal
Broadway Daddies
Eternal Love SSE

Alma Rubens (1897-1931)
1916: Intolerance
Reggie Mixed In
Judith of the Cumberlands
The Half-Breed
Mystery of the Leaping Fish
17: Truthful Tolliver
The Americano
The Firefly of Tough Luck
Master of His Home
Regenerates
18: Blue Blood
Madame Sphinx
The Ghost Flower
The Answer
Gown of Destiny
I Love You
Love Brokers
The Painted Lily
False Ambition
19: A Man's Country
Restless Souls
Diana of the Green Van
20: Humoresque
World and His Wife
21: Thoughtless Women
Passion Flower
22: Valley of Silent Men
Find the Woman
23: Under the Red Robe
Unseeing Eyes
24: Cytherea
The Price She Paid

25: East Lynne
26: The Gilded Butterfly
Marriage License
Siberia
The Pelican
27: The Heart of Salome
One Increasing Purpose
28: Masks of the Devil
29: Show Boat PT
She Goes to War PT

Benny Rubin (1899-)
1928: Naughty Baby SSE
Football
Casino Gardens
Thanksgiving
Daisies Won't Tell

William Russell (1884-1929)
1909: The Slave
12: Lucile
The Star of Bethelehem
Merchant of Venice
Undine
13: Cymbeline
Robin Hood
14: The Cricket on the Hearth
The Straight Road
15: The Diamond from the Sky (serial)
The Garden of Lies
16: Signet of Sheba
17: Pride and the Man
Sands of Sacrifice
The Sea Master
Snap Judgment
New York Luck
18: The Midnight Trail
In Bad
Hearts or Diamonds?
Up Romance Road
All the World to Nothing
Hobbs in a Hurry
19: Brass Buttons
This Hero Stuff
When a Man Rides Alone
6 Feet 4
Some Liar
Where the West Begins
A Sporting Chance
20: Eastward Ho!
The Lincoln Highwayman
Sacred Silence
20: The Valley of Tomorrow
Leave It To Me
Shod with Fire
Slam Bang Jim
The Twins of Suffering Creek
The Man Who Dared
Slam the Law
The Iron Rider
Live Wire Hicks
21: The Singing River
The Cheater Reformed
Bare Knuckles
Colorado Pluck
Children of the Night
The Roof Tree
Challenge of the Law
22: Lady from Longacre
Desert Blossoms
Money to Burn
The Men of Zanzibar
A Self-Made Man
Mixed Faces
The Strength of the Pines
The Great Night
23: Anna Christie
The Crusader
Goodbye Girls
Boston Blackie
Alias the Night Wind
Times Have Changed
When Odds are Even
Man's Size
24: The Beloved Brute
25: Before Midnight
26: Still Alarm
The Blue Eagle
Wings of the Storm
27: Desired Woman
The Girl from Chicago
Brass Knuckles
28: The Escape
The Danger Patrol
The Head of the Family
Woman Size
State Street Sadie
The Midnight Taxi
29: Girls Gone Wild SSE
Madonna of Avenue A PT

Al St. John (1893-1963)
1913: In the Clutches of a Gang
14: Mabel's Strange Predicament

14: The Knockout
The Rounders
The New Janitor
Tillie's Punctured Romance
15: Fickle Fatty's Fall
A Village Scandal
Our Daredevil Chief
Fatty and the Broadway Stars
Dirty Work in a Laundry
16: The Waiters' Ball
Mabel and Fatty Adrift
The Other Man
He Did and He Didn't
Bright Lights
His Wife's Mistake
The Moonshiners
17: Fatty in Coney Island
The Rough House
The Butcher Boy
His Wedding Night
Oh, Doctor!
A Country Hero
A Reckless Romeo
The Sheriff (or, Out West)
18: Goodnight Nurse
Moonshine
The Bell Boy
The Cook
Camping Out
19: The Pullman Porter
Love
A Deserted Hero
Backstage
The Garage
The High Sign
Fool Days
20: Speed
Cleaning Up
21: Fast and Furious
The Simp
The Big Secret
The Hayseed
Ain't Love Grand
The Happy Pest
Small Town Stuff
22: The Studio Rube
The Village Sheik
The City Chap
The Alarm
Out of Place
Special Delivery
All Wet
23: Young and Dumb
The Salesman
The Author
Full Speed
The Tailor
Slow and Sure
A Tropical Romeo
24: Stupid but Brave
Lovemania
Garden of Weeds
25: Dynamite Doggie
Red Pepper
The Iron Mule
Fares, Please!
Fair Warning
Fire Away
26: Live Cowards
Hold Your Hat
Who Hit Me?
Pink Elephants
Flaming Romance
High Sea Blues
27: Listen, Lena!
Roped In
Jungle Heat
High Spots
American Beauty
28: Racing Mad
Casey Jones
Painted Post
Hello, Cheyenne!
Call Your Shots
Hot or Cold
29: The Dance of Life
She Goes to War PT
Hot Times

John Saint Polis (1887-1942)

1917: The Mark of Cain
20: The Great Lover
21: Old Dad
4 Horsemen of the Apocalypse
Cappy Ricks
The Wise Fool
22: Shadows
23: Held to Answer
The Untamable
The Hero
24: Three Weeks
25: Phantom of the Opera
26: The Lily
The Return of Peter Grimm

26: The Far Cry
27: Too Many Crooks
28: Green-Grass Widows
Romance of a Queen
Marriage by Contract
The Grain of Dust
Patience
The Gun Runner
Tomorrow
The Diplomat
Power of Silence
Woman's Way
29: Coquette T
Why Be Good?
Fast Life T
30: The Bad One T
In the Next Room T
Guilty T
Three Sisters T
Party Girl T
Melody Man T
Captain Thunder T
32: Alias the Doctor T
Gambling Sex T
Forbidden Company T
Kismet T
Doctors' Wives T
The Criminal Code T
Men of the Sky T
Transgression T
Heartbreak T
Lena Rivers T
Melody of Life T
33: The World Gone Mad T
Dangerous Business T
Sing, Sinner Sing T
Notorious But Nice T

Marin Sais (1888-)
1918: His Birthright
The Vanity Pool
Manya
Thunderbolt Jack
The Broken Spear
19: City of Dim Faces
Bonds of Honor
21: The Golden Hope
Dead or Alive
22: A Son of the Desert
28: Come and Get It
??: The American Girl
Girl from Frisco
Stingaree

Virginia Sale
1928: Say Uncle
The Crowd
Below the Deadline
Harold Teen
29: The Kid's Clever
The Cohens and the Kellys in Atlantic City PT
Fancy Baggage PT

Monroe Salisbury (1879-1935)
1913: The Squaw Man
14: Rose of the Rancho
15: The Goose Girl
16: Ramona
18: Hands Down
The Red Red Heart
The Guilt of Silence
The Eagle
Winner Takes All
The Devil Bat Sees
Zollenstein
Hugo the Mighty
Eyes of the World
The Devil Between
19: Man in the Moonlight
The Blinding Trail
The Sleeping Lion
Millionaire Pirate
Light of Victory
Sundown Trail
20: His Divorced Wife
The Phantom Melody
21: The Barbarian
That Devil Bateese
22: The Great Alone
30: The Jade Box (serial) T

Harry Salter
1908: When Knights Were Bold
The Slave
The Girls and Daddy
Balked at the Altar

Teddy Sampson (1895-)
1918: Our Little Wife
Her American Husband
19: Fighting for Gold
21: Chicken in the Case
??: Good Morning Judge
Are Honeymoons Happy?
Fox Woman

?? Sympathetic Sal
Child of the Surf
Big Jim's Heart
Fencing Master
Don't Blame the Stork

Tom Santschi (1882-1931)

1909: The Sultan's Power
12: Count of Monte Cristo
God of Gold
King of the Forest
13: Adventures of Kathlyn (serial)
A Wild Ride
Alone in the Jungle
Thor, Lord of the Jungle
In the Long Ago
Three Wise Men
The Hellcat
14: The Spoilers
The Test
15: The Millionaire Baby
16: The Crisis
17: Garden of Allah
18: Still Alarm
Who Shall Take My Life?
Beware of Strangers
City of Purple Dreams
19: Her Kingdom of Dreams
Mother o' Dreams
Lorraine of the Timberlands
Spirit of the Lake
A Guilty Cause
Shadows
Little Orphan Annie
Scarlet Shadow
Stronger Vow
Helgon the Mighty
Mother McGuire
22: Two Kinds of Women
23: Brass Commandments
Is Divorce a Failure?
Tipped Off
24: Street of Tears
Right of the Strongest
25: Paths to Paradise
26: Siberia
Three Bad Men
My Own Pal
Hands Across the Border
No Man's Gold
Her Honor the Governor
26: Forlorn River
The Desert's Toll
27: Jim the Conqueror
Third Degree
When a Man Loves
Old San Francisco
The Overland Stage
Hills of Kentucky
Eyes of the Totem
Land Beyond the Law
Shanghaied
Cruise of the Hellion
28: Honor Bound
Haunted Ship
Into No Man's Land
Isle of Lost Men
Adventurous Soul
Law and the Man
Crashing Through
Land of the Silver Fox
Vultures of the Sea (serial)
29: In Old Arizona T
Yellowback
The Shannons of Broadway T
Wagon Master PT

Lewis Sargent (1904-)

1919: The Soul of Youth
20: Huckleberry Fin
22: Just Around the Corner
23: 15 1-reelers for U.
24: Oliver Twist
26: Racing Blood
28: 12 Racing Blood stories
A Million for Love
Jessie's James
You Just Know She Dares 'em
The Arabian Fights
Ruth is Stranger than Fiction
Sweet Buy and Buy
Watch your Rep
Mud But She Satisfies
The Six Best Fellows
That Wild Irish Pose
The Mighty Four Hundred
Broadway Ladies
The River Pirate SSE
Roadhouse
29: The Godless Girl PT
South of Panama

29: One Splendid Hour

Jackie Saunders (1893-)

1916: Shrine of Happiness
Betty Be Good
The Grip of Evil
17: The Checkmate
Bab the Fixer
A Bit of Kindling
19: Miracle of Love
Muggsy
20: Dad's Girl
The Flirting Bride
Drag Harlan
21: The Infamous Miss Revel
Puppets of Fate
The Man Behind
The Scuttlers
24: Alimony

Templer Saxe

1916: Strength of the Weak
17: Pride
18: Miss Ambition
19: Mind the Paint Girl
Lion and the Mouse
The Teeth of the Tiger
At the Barn
A Dangerous Paradise
20: Polly with a Past
21: Bucking the Tiger
Liquid Gold

Betty Schade

1919: Bonds of Love
Through the Wrong Door
Happiness A La Mode
A Girl in Bohemia
20: Shod with Fire
Soul of Youth
Prisoners of Love
Village Sleuth
Flame of Youth
21: Wing Toy

Joseph Schildkraut (1895-1964)

1920: Der Roman Und Der Kromtesse
22: Orphans of the Storm
23: Dust of Desire (or, The Song of Love)
25: Road to Yesterday
26: Shipwrecked
Meet the Prince
Young April
27: King of Kings
His Dog
Tenth Avenue
The Heart Thief
Forbidden Woman
Country Doctor
A Harp in Hock
Main Event
28: Blue Danube
29: Show Boat PT
Mississippi Gambler T
30: Cock of the Walk T
Night Ride T
Carnival T

Rudolph Schildkraut (1862-1930)

1914: Damon Und Mensch
Lache Bajazzo
Ivan Koschula
17: Es Werde Licht
20: Schlemihl
21: Der Fluch
25: Proud Heart
His People
26: Pals in Paradise
Young April
27: King of Kings
The Country Doctor
His Country
The Main Event
A Harp in Hock
28: Turkish Delight
A Ship Comes In
29: Christina PT

Violet Schram (1898-)

1916: Shoes
Saving the Family Name
Graft (serial)
Two Rebels
19: Toby's Bow
The Desert of Wheat
20: The Gray Wolf's Ghost
White Lies
The Walkoffs
Riders of the Dawn
Big Happiness
21: Out of the Darkness
The Woman with the Parakeets

Karla Schramm

1919: Broken Blossoms
His Majesty, The American
20: Revenge of Tarzan
21: Hearts and Masks
The Son of Tarzan

Ferdinand-Schumann-Heink (1893-1955)

1927: Gallant Fool
28: Broadway Sap
Awakening SSE
Riley the Cop
Gold

Harry Schumm

1914: The Girl of Mystery
The Mysterious Rose
15: The Doorway of Destruction
The Broken Coin (serial)

Mabel Julienna Scott (1898-)

1917: The Barrier
18: Reclaimed
Ashes of Love
The Sign Invisible
19: Sacred Silence
20: The Round Up
Behold My Wife
The Jucklins
The Sea Wolf
21: Don't Neglect Your Wife
Fanny Herself
No Woman Knows
The Concert
23: Power of a Lie
Times Have Changed
The Abysmal Brute
25: 7 Days
26: Stranded in Paris
27: Mother
28: Wallflowers
29: Dream Melody

Allan Sears

1914: Birth of a Nation
The Little Yank
16: Children of the Feud
Girl of the Timberlands
17: Madame Bo-Beep
18: The Red, Red Heart
Kaiser, the Beast of Berlin
18: Kate of Kentucky
Her Inspiration
19: The Amateur Adventuress
Destiny

Dorothy Sebastian (1904-1957)

1924: Sackcloth and Scarlet
25: Winds of Chance
26: You'd Be Surprised
27: The Demi-Bride
California
On Ze Boulevard
12 Miles Out
The Show
28: Love
The Gallant Gringo
Haunted Ship
Isle of Forgotten Women
Arizona Wildcat
The Adventurer
Their Hour
Wyoming
House of Scandal
Our Dancing Daughters
29: The Rainbow
Woman of Affairs
The Spirit of Youth
The Devil's Apple Tree
Spite Marriage
Morgan's Last Raid
Single Standard
Unholy Night T
30: His First Command T

Rolfe Sedan (1896-)

1926: My Old Dutch
28: Chinatown Charlie
Ritzie Rosie
29: Making the Grade PT
The Iron Mask PT

Eileen Sedgwick (1897-)

1917: Man and Beast
No. #10 - Westbound
Dropped from the Clouds
18: Lure of the Circus (serial)
19: Great Radium Mystery (serial)
20: Love's Battle
21: The White Rider
The Diamond Queen (serial)
Terror Trail (serial)

22: False Brands
23: Beasts of Paradise (serial)
Days of Daniel Boone (serial)
24: The Riddle Rider (serial)
25: Poverty Row
The Fighting Ranger (serial)
26: Lure of the West
Beyond All Odds
Thundering Speed
Strings of Steel (serial)
The Winking Idol (serial)
27: When Danger Calls
28: The Vanishing West (serial)
30: The Jade Box (serial) T
Trail of No Return T

Josie Sedgwick (1900-)

1917: Boss of the Lazy Y
Maternal Spark
One Shot Ross
18: Lure of the Circus (serial)
Wolves of the Border
Wild Life
19: Jubilo
Camouflaged
20: Dare Devil Jack (serial)
21: The Double Adventure (serial)
Paying His Debt
Beyond the Shadow
Duke of Chimney Butte
22: Daddy
23: Sunshine Trail

George Seigmann (1884-1928)

1912: A Man's Duty
13: Wars of the Primal Tribes
14: Home Sweet Home
Avenging Conscience
At Dawn
A Yankee from the West
Saving Grace
Tell Tale Heart
Angel of Contention
15: Birth of a Nation
16: Intolerance
17: The Grafters
My Unmarried Wife
The Little Yank
18: Hearts of the World
The Great Love
19: Spitfire of Seville
19: Woman Under Cover
The Trembling Hour
20: The Hawk's Trail (serial)
Little Miss Rebellion
21: A Connecticut Yankee in King Arthur's Court
Mother Love and the Law
Shame
Three Musketeers
Queen of Sheba
The Big Punch
Desperate Trails
22: Monte Cristo
The Truthful Liar
Fools First
Hungry Hearts
Oliver Twist
23: A California Romance
Merry-Go-Round
Anna Christie
The Little Yank
Slander the Woman
24: Manhattan
Shooting of Dan McGrew
A Sainted Devil
25: Zander the Great
Never the Twain Shall Meet
26: The Midnight Sun
Palace of Pleasure
Hotel Imperial
Poker Faces
My Old Dutch
Carnival Girl
27: King of Kings
The Red Mill
Cat and the Canary
Uncle Tom's Cabin
28: The Man Who Laughs
Love Me and the World is Mine
Stop That Man!

Evelyn Selbie

1912: Bronco Billy Films
16: Pay Me
People Vs. John Doe
17: Mysterious Mrs. M.
Hand that Rocks the Cradle
20: Devil to Pay
Seeds of Vengeance
The Broken Gates
21: Without Benefit of Clergy

24: Name the Man
29: Mysterious Dr. Fu Manchu T
30: Love Comes Along T

Charles Sellon (1878-)
1923: The Bad Man
27: Mysterious Rider
Prairie King
Painted Ponies
28: Love Me and the World is Mine
Feel My Pulse
Count of Ten
Easy Come, Easy Go
Something Always Happens
Happiness Ahead
Number Please
What a Night!
Butter and Egg Man
The Big Scoop
Woman Proof
Alias Jimmy Valentine PT
29: Hot Stuff T
Bulldog Drummond T
The Gamblers T
Girl in the Glass Cage PT
Man and the Moment PT
Big News
Saturday Night Kid T
Vagabond Lover T
Sweetie T
Men are like That T

Clarissa Selwynne
1918: The Bride's Awakening
Smashing Through
The Talk of the Town
Tower of Ivory
19: Home
20: Black Gate
Dangerous Days
Cup of Fury
21: Straight from Paris
The Lure of Jade
The Marriage of William Ashe
Sacred and Profane Love
23: The Brass Bottle
24: Beau Brummel
27: Resurrection
Quarantined Rivals
Naughty But Nice
28: Devil Dancer
Heart of a Follies Girl
Broadway Daddies
Jazz Mad
Sinners' Parade
Baby Cyclone SSE
Glorious Betsy PT
My Man PT
29: Confessions of a Wife
Come Across PT
Hard to Get T
Love Trap PT
Isle of Lost Ships T

Larry Semon (1889-1928)
1916: The Man from Egypt
Losing Weight
A Jealous Guy
The Battler
Romance and Rough House
There and Back
A Villainous Villain
Loot and Love
Sands Scamp and Strategy
She Who Laughs Last
Tubby Turns the Tables
Rah! Rah! Rah!
More Money than Manners
Jumps and Jealousy
His Conscious Conscience
Help! Help! Help!
Hash and Havoc
Bullies and Bullets
17: Footlights and Fakers
Duds and Drygoods
Rips and Rushes
Cops and Cussedness
Hazards and Home Runs
Guff and Gunplay
Bombs and Blunders
He Never Touched Me
Jolts and Jewelry
Pests and Promises
Big Bluffs and Bowling Balls
Shells and Shivers
Masks and Mishaps
Flatheads and Flivvers
Worries and Wobbles
Boasts and Boldness
Chumps and Chances
Gall and Golf
Slips and Slackers

17: Risks and Roughnecks
Plans and Pajamas
Plagues and Puppy Love
Sports and Splashes
Tough Luck and Tin Lizzies
Rough Toughs and Rooftops
Spooks and Spasms
Noisy Naggers and Nosey Neighbors
18: Guns and Greasers
Babes and Boobs
Rooms and Rumors
Meddlers and Moonshine
Stripes and Stumbles
Rummies and Razors
Whistles and Windows
Spies and Spills
Romans and Rascals
Skids and Scalawags
Boodle and Bandits
Hindoos and Hazards
Bathing Beauties and Big Boobs
Dunces and Danger
Mutts and Motors
Huns and Hyphens
Bears and Bad Men
Frauds and Frenzies
Humbums and Husbands
Pluck and Plotters
19: Traps and Tangles
Scamps and Scandals
Soapsuds and Sapheads
Well, I'll Be....
Passing the Buck
The Star Boarder
His Home Sweet Home
The Simple Life
Between the Acts
Dull Care
Dew Drop Inn
The Headwaiter
20: The Grocery Clerk
The Fly Cop
School Days
Solid Concrete
The Stagehand
The Suitor
21: The Sportsman
The Hick
The Rent Collector
The Bakery
The Fall Guy
21: The Bell Hop
22: The Sawmill
The Show
A Pair of Kings
Golf
The Sleuth
The Counter Jumper
23: No Wedding Bells
The Barnyard
Midnight Cabaret
The Gown Shop
Lightning Love
Horseshoes
24: Trouble Brewing
Her Boy Friend
Kid Speed
The Girl in the Limousine
25: The Dome Doctor
The Cloudhopper
The Perfect Clown
The Wizard of Oz
26: Stop, Look and Listen
27: The Stuntman
Oh, What a Man!
Spuds
28: Dummies
A Simple Sap
Underworld

Mack Sennett (actor) (1880-1960)

1908: The Valet's Wife
The Test of Friendship
The Helping Hand
The Sculptor's Nightmare
An Awful Moment
Balked at the Altar
09: The Girls and Daddy
A Burglar's Mistake
A Sound Sleeper
Jones and the Lady Book Agent
Two Memories
The Little Darling
In a Hempen Bag
Cord of Life
Golden Louis
At the Altar
10: Exam Day at School
Faithful
11: Home Folks
Comrades
Their First Divorce Case
12: Those Hicksville Boys

12: One Busy Hour
The Politician's Love Story
The Fickle Spaniard
Their First Kidnaping Case
Pedro's Dilemma
At Coney Island
At It Again
Mabel's Lovers
A Desperate Lover
A Bear Escape
Pat's Day Off
A Family Mixup
Hoffmeyer's Legacy
The Duel
The Dutch Gold Mine
13: The Bangville Police
Mabel's Awful Mistake
Barney Oldfield's Race for Life
The Mistaken Masher
The Stolen Purse
Mabel's Heroes
The Elite Ball
The Sleuth's Last Stand
The Sleuth at the Floral Parade
A Strong Revenge
The Hanson Driver
Peeping Pete
His Crooked Career
For Love of Mabel
14: In the Clutches of the Gang
The Alarm
17: My Valet

Clarine Seymour (1900-1920)
1919: The Girl Who Stayed at Home
Scarlet Days
True Heart Susie
20: The Idol Dancer

Effie Shannon (1867-1954)
1914: After the Ball
21: Mama's Affair
22: The Man Who Played God
Secrets of Paris
Sure-Fire Flint
23: The Tie that Binds
Blazing Barriers (or, Jacqueline)
24: Three Weeks
25: Sally of the Sawdust
25: Soul Fire

Ethel Shannon
1919: Easy to Make Money
John Petticoats
20: The Master Stroke
An Old-Fashioned Boy
Birth of the Gods
Beware of the Bride
The Great Hope
Through Thick and Thin
26: Sign of the Claw
High Flyer
Buckaroo Kids
Oh, Baby!
Silent Power
27: Babe Comes Home

Montague Shaw (1884-1968)
1928: Water Hole
29: Morgan's Last Raid

Norma Shearer (1904-)
1920: The Flapper
Way Down East
The Stealers
The Restless Sex
22: The Bootleggers
Leather Pushers (serial)
Channing of the Northwest
The Man Who Paid
The Devil's Partner
23: Lucrezia Lombard
Man and Wife
The Clouded Name
Pleasure Mad
The Wanters
24: The Snob
He Who Gets Slapped
Empty Hands
Married Flirts
Broadway After Dark
Excuse Me
The Wolf Man
25: Tower of Lies
His Secretary
Lady of the Night
Waking Up the Town
Pretty Ladies
A Slave of Fashion
26: Upstage
The Waning Sex
The Devil's Circus

27: After Midnight
Student Prince
The Demi-Bride
28: The Actress
Angel Face
The Latest from Paris
A Lady of Chance
29: The Trial of Mary Dugan T
Last of Mrs. Cheyney T
Hollywood Revue of 1929 T
30: Their Own Desire T

Reginald Sheffield (1901-1957)
1928: Adorable Cheat
Sweet 16
Interference T

Lowell Sherman (1885-1934)
1920: Way Down East
The New York Idea
Yes or No
21: The Gilded Lily
What No Man Knows
Molly-O
22: Grand Larceny
The Face in the Fog
24: Monsieur Beaucaire
25: Satan in Sables
26: Reckless Lady
The Wilderness Woman
You Never Know Women
The Love Toy
Lost at Sea
27: Girl From Gay Paree
Convoy
28: The Whip
Divine Woman
A Lady of Chance
Garden of Eden
Scarlet Dove
The Mad Hour
Angel Face
Heart of a Follies Girl
Whip Woman
29: General Crack T
Nearly Divorced
Evidence T
30: Mammy T
He Knew Women T
Ladies of Leisure T
Midnight Mystery T
Lawful Larceny (dir.) T
Pay Off (dir.) T
31: O Sailor Behave! (dir.) T
Royal Bed (dir.) T
Bachelor Apartment (dir.) T
High Stakes (dir.) T
32: What Price Hollywood? (dir.) T
False Faces (dir.) T
Ladies of the Jury (dir.) T
Greeks Had a Word for Them (dir.) T
33: Morning Glory (dir.) T
She Done Him Wrong (dir.) T
Broadway Through a Keyhole (dir.) T
34: Born to be Bad (dir.) T
35: Night Life of the Gods (dir.) T

J. Barney Sherry (1874-)
1905: Raffles, Amateur Cracksman
09: 12 series of westerns
13: Soul of the South
Eileen of Erin
14: For Her Brother's Sake
Word of His People
The Latent Spark
15: Cup of Life
16: The Weaker Sex
17: Back of the Man
The Millionaire Vagrant
Flying Colors
Full of Life
18: Evidence
Who Killed Walton?
Her Decision
High Stakes
The Secret Code
Recording Day
19: Little Brother of the Rich
Mayor of Filbert
20: Breath of the Gods
The River's End
The Forged Bride
Dinty
Man-Woman-Marriage
Occasionally Yours
The Barbarian
23: White Sister

24: Born Rich
26: The Spider Web
28: Forgotten Faces
Victorious Defeat
29: Jazz Heaven T

Nell Shipman (1892-1970)
1916: Through the Wall
17: The Wild Strain
The Eighth Great Grand-Parent
18: Girl from Beyond
A Gentleman's Agreement
Baree, Son of Kazan
Cavanaugh of the Forest Range
The Home Trail
19: Tiger of the Sea
20: Back to God's Country
21: Girl from God's Country
23: Grub Stake
28: Golden Yukon

Lynn Shores
1928: Sally of the Scandals
Skinner's Big Idea
Sally's Shoulders
29: Stolen Love

Antrim Short
1917: Tom Sawyer
Pride and the Man
Jewel in Pawn
Poor Girl, Rich Girl?
18: The Yellow Dog
19: Please Get Married
Romance and Arabella
20: The Right of Way
Cressy
21: Son of Wallingford
Black Beauty
O'Malley of the Mounted
22: Beauty's Worth

Gertrude Short (1902-1968)
1913: Uncle Tom's Cabin
17: The Hostage
Little Angel of Canon Creek
19: Blackie's Redemption
Heart of Youth
The Mizzoura
20: You Never Can Tell
Sweet Lavender
21: Cinderella's Twin
She Couldn't Help It
22: Cowboy and the Lady
Rent Free
Boy Crazy
Beggar on Horseback
Tillie the Toiler
Youth to Youth
23: Gold Diggers
The Prisoner
25: Tessie
26: Sweet Adeline
27: The Show
Masked Woman
Ladies at Ease
Women's Wares
Polly of the Movies
Adam and Evil
28: None but the Brave
29: Trial Marriage

Hassard Short
1919: Way of a Woman
21: Woman's Place

Lew Short (1875-)
1920: Last of the Mohicans
Black Pearl
24: Leather Stockings
26: Blue Eagle
28: Big City
30: A Girl in the Show T

Marie Shotwell
1916: The Witching Hour
19: The Thirteenth Chair
20: Chains of Evidence
The Harvest Moon
The Evil Eye (serial)
Civilian Clothes
The Master Mind
Blackbirds
21: Her Lord and Master
22: Shackles of Gold
25: Sally of the Sawdust
27: Running Wild
One Woman to Another

Lee Shumway (1884-)
1917: The Phantom's Secret
Helen Grayson's Strategy
18: Bride of Fear
Bird of Prey

18: The Scarlet Road
The Siren's Song
19: A Girl in Bohemia
The Love Hunger
Eve in Exile
20: When the Dawn Came
Beggar in Purple
21: The Gamesters
To Please One Woman
The Torrent
Society Secrets
The Big Adventure
Conflict
The Alarm
Step on It
Lure of the Jade
The Speed Maniac
22: Over the Border
Brawn of the North
Hearts Aflame
26: The Bat
The Handsome Bride
Sign of the Claw
One Minute to Play
Whispering Canyon
Checkered Flag
Price of Success
27: Let it Rain
The Great Mail Robbery
Catch as Catch Can
His Foreign Wife
28: Valley of Haunted Men
House of Scandal
A Hit of the Show PT
A Million for Love
Son of the Golden West
29: The Leatherneck PT
Evangeline PT
So This is College? T
Night Parade T

George Sidney (1878-1945)
1923: Potash & Perlmutter
24: In Hollywood with Potash & Perlmutter
26: Partners Again
The Cohens and the Kellys
Prince of Pilsen
Sweet Daddies
Millionaires
27: The Auctioneer
Clancy's Kosher Wedding
For the Love of Mike
27: Lost at the Front
Life of Riley
28: The Cohens and the Kellys in Paris
The Latest from Paris
We Americans
Flying Romeos
Give and Take SSE
29: The Cohens and the Kellys in Atlantic City PT

Bernard Siegel
1917: The Maelstrom
18: The Green God
19: The Cambric Mask
20: Dead Men Tell No Tales
21: The Heart of Maryland
The Land of Hope
28: Laugh, Clown, Laugh
29: Sea Fury PT
The Rescue SSE
Redskin SSE

Milton Sills (1882-1930)
1915: The Deep Purple
16: Patria
The Wreck
Honor System
17: Married in Name Only
The Pit
Souls Adrift
The Struggle Everlasting
18: The Claw
Shadows
Yellow Ticket
Other Woman
Fringe of Society
The Savage Woman
The Mysterious Client
19: The Woman Thou Gavest Me
What Every Woman Learns
Eyes of Youth
The Stronger Vow
The Fear Woman
The Street Called Straight
The Hushed Hour
20: Behold My Wife
The Weekend
Dangerous Men
Sweet Lavender
The Furnace
21: The Little Fool

21: The Marriage Gamble
At the End of the World
The Faith Healer
The Great Moment
Miss Lulu Bett
22: Borderlands
Burning Sands
One Clear Call
Environment
Skin Deep
The Woman Who Walked Alone
23: Why Women Re-marry
The Last Hour
What a Wife Learned
The Marriage Chance
Isle of Lost Ships
The Spoilers
Adam's Rib
Flaming Youth
A Lady of Quality
Legally Dead
24: The Sea Hawk
Madonna of the Streets
Single Wives
The Heart Bandit
Flowing Gold
The Fire Patrol
25: The Making of O'Malley
I Want My Man
The Unguarded Hour
The Knockout
As a Man Desires
26: Paradise
The Silent Lover
Puppets
Men of Steel
27: Valley of the Giants
The Sea Tiger
Framed
Hard-Boiled Haggerty
28: The Crash
Circus Life
Burning Daylight
The Hawk's Nest
The Wrecking Boss
The Barker PT
29: His Captive Woman PT
Love and the Devil SSE
30: Man Trouble T
Sea Wolf T

Russell Simpson (1878-1959)

1916: Fate's Boomerang
17: The Barrier
18: Blue Jeans
19: Fighting Cressy
Our Teddy
20: The Brand
Bill Apperson's Boy
Lahoma
The Branding Iron
The Deadlier Sex
Out of the Dust
21: Snow Blind
Bunty Pulls the Strings
Under the Lash
Godless Men
22: Across the Dead Line
Human Hearts
Fools of Fortune
Rags to Riches
The Kingdom Within
Hearts Aflame
The Shadows of Conscience
23: Peg o' my Heart
Rip Tide
The Girl of the Golden West
Circus Days
The Hand Me Down
26: The Barrier
Rustling for Cupid
Lovey Mary
Ship of Souls
27: Wild Geese
Annie Laurie
God's Great Wilderness
First Auto
Heart of the Yukon
Old Shoes
Now We're in the Air
28: Trail of '98
Life's Mockery
The Bush Ranger
Tropical Midnights
29: The Kid's Clever
The Sap PT
Noisy Neighbors PT
My Lady's Past PT
Innocents of Paris T
The Virginian T

Vera Sisson (1895-)

1915: The Laurel of Tears
Trail of the Serpent
16: The Iron Woman
17: Paradise Garden
The Blackmailers
18: His Official Fiancee
The Marriage Blunder
19: The Veiled Adventure
Experimental Marriage
The Heart of Youth
20: The Married Virgin
21: The Man from Nowhere
23: The Bolted Door

Otis Skinner (1858-1942)

1919: Kismet
29: Mr. Antonio T

Martha Sleeper (1901-)

1923: The Mail Man
28: The Little Yellow House
Skinner's Big Idea
Danger Street
The Air Legion
29: Taxi 13 PT
Voice of the Storm

Phillips Smalley (1870-)

1913: The Picture of Dorian Grey
14: The Merchant of Venice
False Colors
The Spider and Her Web
Fatal Warning (serial)
Dumb Girl of Portici
15: A Cigarette - That's All
25: Charley's Aunt
26: Money Talks
The Taxi Mystery
Soul Mates
Queen of Diamonds
27: Sensation Seekers
Broken Gates
The Irresistible Lover
Man Crazy
Stage Kisses
28: Broadway Daddies
Sinners in Love
Honeymoon Flats
Border Patrol
Blindfold SSE
Too Many Crooks
The Case of Mary Brown
29: True Heaven T
High Voltage T
30: Peacock Alley T
Midnight Special T
Charley's Aunt T
31: Lawless Woman T
High Stakes T
Lady from Nowhere T
32: The Greeks Had a Word for Them T
Murder at Dawn T
Escapade T
13th Guest T
Midnight Warning T
33: Cocktail Hour T
34: Big Race T
Bolero T
Stolen Sweets T
35: Night Life of the Gods T
All the King's Horses T
Hold 'em, Yale! T
It's in the Air T
37: Hotel Haywire T

Marguerite Snow (1888-1958)

1911: She
12: Lucile
Undine
13: Carmen
14: Zudora (serial)
The Million Dollar Mystery (serial)
15: 20 Million Dollar Mystery (serial)
The Second in Command
Dora Thorne
The Silent Voice
16: Marble Heart
Notorious Gallagher
East Lynne
The Half Million Bride
17: Hunting of the Hawk
Broadway Jones
18: Eagle's Eye (serial)
The First Law
19: In His Brother's Place
20: Woman in Room 13
Felix O'Day
21: Lavender and Old Lace
22: Veiled Woman

Sojin (1891-1954)

1922: Thief of Bagdad

25: Soft Shoes
The Sea Beast
East of Suez
The Wanderer
26: The Rescue
Lady of the Harem
The Bat
Road to Mandalay
Lucky Lady
Diplomacy
Across the Pacific
Eve's Leaves
Telling the World
27: All Aboard
Streets of Shanghai
Haunted Ship
Foreign Devils
City of Sin
King of Kings
Old San Francisco
28: The Hawk's Nest
Chinese Parrot
Ships of the Night
Crimson City
Chinatown Charlie
Something Always Happens
Out With the Tide
The Devil Dancer
Man Without a Face (serial)
29: Careers PT
Seven Footprints to Satan SSE
Tropic Madness
China Slaver
Unholy Night T
Show of Shows T
30: Golden Dawn T
Dude Wrangler T
Back from Shanghai T

Slim Somerville (1892-)
(see Summerville p. 336)

Eve Southern (1898-)
1916: Intolerance
21: Rage of Paris
Golden Gallows
After the Show
22: Nice People
The Girl in His Room
Remembrance
23: Trimmed in Scarlet
Souls for Sale
27: Resurrection
The Gaucho
Wild Geese
28: Stormy Waters
Clothes Make the Woman
The Haunted House
The Girl Who Came Back
29: Voice Within
Whispering Winds

Sam Southern
1915: Two Orphans
19: Eyes of Youth
His Majesty, the American
20: Silk Husbands and Calico Wives
The Dream Cheater
21: Whispering Devils

Ned Sparks (1883-1957)
1919: A Virtuous Vamp
20: In Search of a Sinner
The Perfect Woman
Good References
22: A Wide Open Town
The Bond Boy
25: Bright Lights
27: The Secret Studio
Alias the Deacon
Alias the Lone Wolf
On to Reno
28: Big Noise
Magnificent Flirt
29: Strange Cargo T
Nothing but the Truth T
Street Girl T
30: Love Comes Along T
Canary Murder Case T

Harry Spear (1921-)
(see Our Gang Comedies)

Wyndham Standing (1880-)
1916: The Wolf Woman
Hypocrisy
17: Struggle Everlasting
18: Journey's End
Rose of the World
19: Paid in Full
Witness for the Defense
Eyes of the Soul
Miracle of Love
Port of Missing Girls

19: The Hushed Hour
The Marriage Price
A Tempermental Wife
Ave Maria
20: Earthbound
21: The Iron Trail
22: The Bride's Play
Smilin' Through
The Isle of Doubt
The Inner Man
23: The Lion's Mouse
24: Secrets
Women Who Give
25: Dark Angel
26: The Canadian
27: Thumbs Down
City Gone Wild
28: Hell's Angels
Widecombe Fair

Forrest Stanley (1889-)

1915: The Yankee Girl
Jane
Under Suspicion
Reform Candidate
16: Madame La Presidente
The Code of Marcia Gray
Kilkeny
Making of Madalena
The Heart of Paula
The Rug Maker's Daughter
18: His Official Fiancee
19: The Thunderbolt
30: The Triflers
21: Sacred and Profane Love
The House that Jazz Built
Enchantment
Forbidden Fruit
22: Beauty's Worth
The Young Diana
When Knighthood was in Flower
Her Accidental Husband
23: Tiger Rose
24: Up the Ladder
26: Forest Havoc
Dancing Days
The Fate of a Flirt
27: Cat and the Canary
Forbidden Fruit
Wheel of Destiny
28: Into the Night
The Virgin Queen

28: Bare Knees
Phantom of the Turf
Jazzland
29: The Drake Case
30: Love Kiss T
31: Men Are Like That (or, Arizona) T
32: Racing Youth T
Sin's Pay Day T
Rider of Death Valley T

Pauline Starke (1900-)

1916: Intolerance
Wharf Rat
Judith
17: Until They Get Me
18: The Shoes That Danced
Innocents' Progress
Alias Mary Brown
The Man Who Woke Up
Daughter Angele
The Atom
The Untamed
19: Eyes of Youth
The Life Line
Irish Eyes
Whom the Gods Destroy
Little Shepherd of Kingdom Come
Soldiers of Fortune
20: Seeds of Vengeance
Courage of Marge O'Doone
21: A Connecticut Yankee in King Arthur's Court
Salvation Bell
The Silent Years
The Forgotten Woman
22: My Wild Irish Rose
The Flower of the North
If You Believe It, It's So
The Kingdom Within
23: In the Palace of the King
Little Church Around the Corner
The Little Girl Next Door
Lost and Found
24: Hearts of Oak
Dante's Inferno
Forbidden Paradise
25: As No Man Has Loved
Devil's Cargo
Sun Up
Bright Lights

26: Love's Blindness
Honesty-The Best Policy
War Paint
27: The Perfect Sap
Women Love Diamonds
Captain Salvation
Dance Magic
Streets of Shanghai
The Man Without a Country
28: The Viking
Adventurer
Fallen Angels
Man, Woman, and Wife SSE
30: The Royal Romance T
What Men Want T

Vera Steadman (1900-1966)
1921: Scrap Iron
28: Campus Cuties
A Gallant Gob
Sea Food
Oriental Hugs
A She-Going Sailor
Gobs of Love
Happy Heels
?? Mack Sennett Bathing Beauty
Al Christie Comedies
Hula Hula Land
Tugboat Romeo
A Bedroom Blunder
A Pullman Bride
Are Waitresses Safe?
That Night
Why Men Go Wild
Watch Your Step, Mother
Oh, Doctor, Oh!
License Applied For
Papa by Proxy
Exit Quietly
The Chased Bride
Marry Me
Fit to Fight
Sand Witches
Wedding Blues

Lincoln Stedman (1900. 1941)
1920: Out of the Storm
Peaceful Valley
21: Nineteen and Phyllis
Two Minutes to Go
Under the Lash
Be My Wife
21: The Charm School
Old Swimmin' Hole
22: A Homespun Vamp
White Shoulder
Youth to Youth
23: The Meanest Man in the World
The Dangerous Age
The Freshie
The Prisoner
24: Captain January
27: Perch of the Devil
Let It Rain
Rookies
Little Firebrand
Prince of Headwaiters
28: Green-Grass Widows
The Devil's Cage
The Farmer's Daughter
Harold Teen
29: Why Be Good?
Wild Party T
Tanned Legs T
31: Woman Between T
33: Sailor, Be Good T

Myrtle Stedman (1887-1938)
1913: Valley of the Moon
14: It's No Laughing Matter
15: Peer Gynt
16: Soul of Kura San
17: The World Apart
The Prison Without Walls
18: The Hollow of Her Hand
Out of the Night
19: The Teeth of the Tiger
In Honor's Web
20: The Silver Horde
The Tiger's Coat
Sex
Harriet and the Piper
Bucko McAlister
21: Old Dad
The Concert
Black Roses
22: Nancy from Nowhere
Ashes
The Hands of Nara
Rich Men's Wives
23: The Dangerous Age
The Famous Mrs. Fair
Crashing Through
Flaming Youth

23: Temporary Marriage
24: The Mad Whirl
25: Tessie
26: The Far Cry
The Prince of Pilsen
Don Juan's Three Nights
Man in the Shadow
27: Alias the Deacon
Black Diamond Express
The Irresistible Lover
The Life of Riley
Women's Wares
No Place to Go
28: Their Hour
That's My Daddy
Sporting Goods
29: Jazz Age
Sin Sister SSE
Wheel of Life T
30: The Lummox T
Truth About Youth T
32: Widow in Scarlet T
Alias Mary Smith T
Forbidden Company T
Klondike T
34: Beggars in Ermine T
School for Girls T
36: Song of the Saddle T
The Green Light T

Bob Steele (1906-)
1920: Adventures of Bill and Bob
25: Bandit's Son
27: Mojave Kid
28: Man in the Rough
Driftin' Sands
Crooks Can't Win
Riding Renegades
Breed of the Sunsets
Captain Careless
Lighting Speed
Headin' for Danger
Trail of Courage
29: The Spirit of Youth
Come and Get It
Amazing Vagabond
Laughing at Death
The Invaders SSE
30: Breezy Bill

Larry Steers (1881-1951)
1918: A Pair of Silk Stockings
19: City of Dim Faces
Little Comrade
Heartease
20: Right of Way
Out of the Dust
21: The Fire Detectives (serial)
22: Elope If You Must
South of Suva
23: Haunted Valley (serial)
24: 10 Scars Make a Man (serial)
26: That's My Baby
27: The Claw
28: The Terrible People (serial)
The Phantom Flyer
Manhattan Cocktail SSE
29: The Wheel of Life T
Just Off Broadway
Redskin SSE

Ford Sterling (1883-1939)
1911: Abe Gets Even with Father
12: Cohen Collects a Debt
The Water Nymph
Riley and Schultz
The New Neighbor
The Beating he Needed
Pedro's Dilemma
The Ambitious Butler
The Flirting Husband
The Grocery Clerk's Romance
Stolen Glory
At It Again
A Bear Escape
Pat's Day Off
At Coney Island
The Deacon's Troubles
A Tempermental Husband
The Rivals
Mr. Fixit or Mr. Fixer
A Midnight Elopement
Mabel's Adventures
13: A Double Wedding
The Cure that Failed
How Hiram Won Out
The Mistaken Masher
The Elite Ball
Just Brown's Luck
The Battle of Who Run
The Stolen Purse
Heinze's Resurrection
The Professor's Daughter
The Sleuths at the Floral P-Rade

13: A Strong Revenge
The Two Widows
The Man Next Door
The Rube and the Baron
On His Wedding Day
A Poker Game
Murphy's I. O. U.
A Fishy Affair
The New Conductor
That Ragtime Band
His Ups and Downs
Barney Oldfield's Race for Life
The Handsome Driver
The Speed Queen
The Waiters' Picnic
Out and In
Peeping Pete
His Crooked Career
Safe in Jail
Love and Rubbish
The Peddler
Professor Bean's Removal
Cohen's Outing
A Game of Pool
The Firebugs
Baby Day
Mabel's Dramatic Career
The Bowling Match
Schnitz the Tailor
A Healthy Neighborhood
The Speed Kings
Love Sickness at Sea
Cohen Saves the Flag
The Gusher
Hoffmeyer's Legacy
The Deacon Outwitted
A Landlord's Trouble
A Red Hot Romance
The Land Salesman
Father's Choice
A Life in the Balance
The Faithful Taxicab
When Dreams Come True
Teddy Telzlaff and Earl Cooper--Speed Kings
A Small Time Act
A Muddy Romance (or, Muddled in Mud)
A Bad Game
Zuzu, The Band Leader
Some Nerve
14: Love and Dynamite
14: In the Clutches of the Gang
Between Showers
That Minstrel Man
Too Many Brides
Double Crossed
Raffles-Gentleman Burglar
Tango Tangles
15: Ambrose's Little Hatchet
Fatty and the Broadway Stars
That Little Band of Gold
Our Daredevil Chief
He Wouldn't Stay Down
Court House Crooks
Dirty Work in the Laundry
Only a Messenger Boy
His Father's Footsteps
The Hunt
16: His Pride and Shame
The Snow Cure
His Wild Oats
His Lying Heart
17: Stars and Bars
A Maiden's Trust
Her Torpedoed Love
18: Her Screen Idol
Beware of Boarders
19: Hearts and Flowers
Trying to Get Along
The Kaiser's Last Squeal
20: Married Life
Don't Weaken
His Youthful Fancy
Love, Honor and Behave
21: A Lady's Tailor
His Last False Step
Among Those Present
Uncle Tom Without the Cabin
The Unhappy Finish
23: Day of Faith
The Spoilers
Stranger's Banquet
The Brass Bottle
Guardian Angel
26: Stranded in Paris
Miss Brewster's Millions
Good and Naughty
Mike
American Venus
Road to Glory
Show-Off
Everybody's Acting

27: Casey at the Bat
The Little Widow
Hearts and Flowers
The Trunk Mystery
28: That's My Daddy
Mr. Romeo
Chicken A La King
Oh Kay!
Sporting Goods
29: Girl in the Show T
Fall of Eve T
33: Alice in Wonderland T
35: Behind the Green Lights T
Headline Woman T
Black Sheep T

Charles Stevens (1893-1964)
1916: The Americano
17: Mystery of the Leaping Fish
20: The Mollycoddle
21: Three Musketeers
22: Grandma's Boy
Captain Fly-By-Night
25: The Vanishing American
26: Don Q
The Black Pirate
27: The Gaucho
28: Diamond Handcuffs
Woman's Law
29: The Iron Mask PT
Mysterious Dr. Fu Manchu T
The Virginian T
30: Big Trail T
Tom Sawyer T
?? A Hickory Kick

Edwin Stevens
1916: Devil's Toy
19: The Squaw Man
Faith
Cheating Cheaters
Profiteers
Crimson Gardenia
Upstairs
Hawthorne of the U. S. A.
Lone Wolf's Daughter
Home Breaker
21: Charm School
What's Worth While?
Dollar-A-Year Man
Her First Elopement
21: Snob

Hayden Stevenson
1928: Red Lips
The Collegians
Bookworm Hero
Leather Pushers
King of the Campus PT
Diamond Master

Anita Stewart (1896-1962)
1912: The Wood Violet
Her Choice
The Godmother
Song of the Shell
13: The Classmates Frolic
Love Finds a Way (or, Love Laughs at Blacksmiths)
The Web
A Fighting Chance
Two's Company, Three's a Crowd
A Regiment of Two
The Forgotten Latchkey
The Song Bird of the North
Sweet Deception
The Moulding
The Prince of Evil
The Tiger
The Lost Millionaire
The Treasure of Desert Island
His Last Fight
Why I Am Here
The Wreck
The Swan Girl
His Second Wife
14: Diana's Dress Reform
The Right and the Wrong Of It
The Lucky Elopement
Lincoln the Lover
A Million Bid
Back to Broadway
The Girl from Prosperity
He Never Knew
Wife Wanted
The Shadow of the Past
Uncle Bill
The Painted World
Four Thirteen (413)
'Midst Woodland Shadows

14: Sins of the Mothers
15: Two Women
The Goddess (serial)
The Right Girl
From Headquarters
The Juggernaut
His Phantom Sweetheart
The Sort of a Girl Who Came From Heaven
The Awakening
Count 'em (or, The Counts)
16: My Lady's Slipper
The Suspect
The Daring of Diana
The Combat
17: The Girl Philippa
The Glory of Yolanda
The More Excellent Way
Clover's Rebellion
The Message of the Mouse
19: Virtuous Wives
The Mind-The-Paint Girl
Mary Regan
A Midnight Romance
Her Kingdom of Dreams
20: The Fighting Shepherdess
In Ole Kentucky
The Yellow Typhoon (dual roles)
Harriet and the Piper
Human Desire
21: Sowing the Wind
Playthings of Destiny
Her Mad Bargain
22: A Question of Honor
The Invisible Fear
The Woman He Married
Rose o' the Sea
23: The Love Piker
24: The Great White Way
25: The Boomerang
Baree, Son of Kazan
Never the Twain Shall Meet
26: The Prince of Pilsen
Rustling for Cupid
Whispering Wires
Lodge in the Wilderness
Morganson's Finish
27: Isle of Sunken Gold (serial)
Wild Geese
28: Name the Woman
Romance of a Rogue
28: Sisters of Eve

Lucille Lee Stewart (1894-)

1916: Conflict
His Wife's Good Name
The Ninety and Nine
18: Five Thousand an Hour
Our Mrs. McChesney
The Eleventh Commandment
19: The Perfect Lover
Sealed Hearts
20: Eastward Ho!
The Woman Gives
A Woman's Business

Roy Stewart (1884-1933)

1915: Just Nuts
16: The Fugitive
Desert of Wheat
Liberty, Daughter of the U. S. A. (serial)
17: The House Built Upon Sand
Daughter of the Poor
The Devil Dodger
The Bond of Fear
One Shot Ross
The Medicine Man
The Doll Shop
18: Boss of the Lazy Y
Faith Enduring
Wolves of the Border
A Red-Haired Cupid
Cactus Crandell
The Learnin' of Jim Benton
The Law's Outlaw
Keith of the Border
Paying His Debt
The Fly God
By Proxy
19: Untamed
The Silent Rider
The Westerners
20: The Lone Hand
Riders of the Dawn
Just a Wife
The Devil to Pay
The Sagebrusher
Prisoners of Love
Mistress of Shenstone
21: The Heart of the North
The Innocent Cheat

22: The Radio King (serial)
Back to the Yellow Jacket
One Eighth Apache
A Motion to Adjourn
Life's Greatest Question
The Snowshoe Trail
Social Value
Ridin' Wild
The Sage Brush Trail
23: The Burning Words
The Love Brand
Trimmed in Scarlet
Hearts of Oak
Under Secret Orders
Timberland Treachery
25: Sundown
26: The Lady from Hell
General Custer at Little Big Horn
Kit Carson Over the Great Divide
Buffalo Bill on the U. P. Trail
Daniel Boone Through the Wilderness
27: The Midnight Watch
One Woman to Another
28: Stormy Waters
Roarin' Fires
The Candy Kid
29: In Old Arizona T
Protection SSE
The Viking
30: The Great Divide T
Men Without Women T
Lone Star Ranger T
Rough Romance T
Born Reckless T
31: Fighting Caravans T
32: Mystery Ranch T
Come On, Tarzan! T
33: Zoo in Budapest T
Rustlers' Roundup T

Carl Stockdale (1874-1942)
1915: The Bank
16: Intolerance
The Americano
Atta Boy's Last Race
A Night in New York
Wanted A Home
The Crash
17: Peggy Leads the Way
18: The Lady of the Dugout
19: The Trembling Hour
The Fatal 30 (serial)
20: The Greatest Question
After Hours
Coast of Opportunity
21: Double Adventure (serial)
Bride of the Colorado
Society Secrets
22: Thorns and Orange Blossoms
Oliver Twist
23: Suzanna
Money Money Money
Brass Buttons
The Meanest Man in the World
26: While London Sleeps
28: My Home Town
The Terror T
The Shepherd of the Hills
29: Jazzland
China Bound
Broken Barriers
The Carnation Kid PT
The Black Pearl
The Love Parade

Edith Stockton
1921: Out of the Chorus
Keep to the Right
22: Through the Storm

Arthur Stone (1897-)
1927: Affair of the Follies
Sea Tiger
The Babe Comes Home
Patent Leather Kid
Hard Boiled Haggerty
Valley of the Giants
28: Burning Daylight
Chicken A La King
The Farmer's Daughter
29: Captain Lash SSE
Fugitives SSE
New Year's Eve SSE
Through Different Eyes T
Red Wine SSE
The Far Call SSE
Me Gangster SSE
Fox Movietone Follies T
Frozen Justice T
Husbands are Liars T

Fred Stone (1873-1959)

1918: The Goat
19: Under the Top
21: The Duke of Chimney Butte
22: Billy Jim

George E. Stone (1903-1967)

1916: Children of the Feud
The Little School Ma'am
Gretchen the Greenhorn
Going Straight
17: Sudden Jim
20: Just Pals
21: Desperate Trails
Jackie
The Whistle
White and Unmarried
Penny of Hilltop Trail
The Scoffer
23: The Fourth Musketeer
27: Seventh Heaven
Brass Knuckles
Two Men and a Maid
28: Walking Back
Turn Back the Hours
Clothes Make the Woman
The Racket
Beautiful but Dumb
State Street Sadie PT
Tenderloin PT
29: Naughty Baby SSE
The Redeeming Sin PT
The Girl in the Glass Cage PT
Weary River PT
Melody Lane T

Lewis Stone (1879-1953)

1915: Honour's Altar
16: The Havoc
18: Inside the Lines
The Man of Bronze
19: Two Brides
Man's Desire
Johnny Get Your Gun
20: Held by the Enemy
The River's End
Nomads of the North
Milestones
The Concert
21: Don't Neglect Your Wife
Beau Revel
The Child Thou Gavest Me
Pilgrims of the Night
The Golden Snare
Muffled Drum
22: Prisoner of Zenda
The Rosary
The White Mouse
A Fool There Was
Trifling Women
23: Scaramouche
The Dangerous Age
The World's Applause
You Can't Fool Your Wife
The Eternal City
24: Cytherea
The Stranger
25: The Lost World
Inez from Hollywood
Lady Who Lied
Cheaper to Marry
Confessions of a Queen
The Talker
26: Don Juan's 3 Nights
Too Much Money
Old Loves and New
Girl from Montmartre
Blonde Saint
Midnight Lover
27: Affair of the Follies
The Notorious Lady
Prince of Headwaiters
Lonesome Ladies
Private Life of Helen of Troy
28: Foreign Legion
Freedom of the Press
Woman of Affairs
The Patriot
29: Wild Orchids
Trial of Mary Dugan T

Ruth Stonehouse (1891-1940)

1911: The Papered Door
12: From the Submerged
13: In Convict Garb
The Spy's Defeat
14: Blood Will Tell
15: The Romance of an American
16: Peg o' the Ring (serial)
17: The Phantom Husband
The Edge of the Law
Daredevil Dan
The Heart of Mary Ann

17: Mary Ann in Society
A Limb of Satan
Puppy Love
The Stolen Actress
Tacky Sue's Romance
Dorothy Dares
19: The Master Mystery (serial)
The Masked Rider (serial)
The Four-Flusher
20: The Hope
Are All Men Alike?
Parlor, Bedroom and Bath
21: I am Guilty
Love Never Dies
23: Flame of Passion
The Cleanup
Lights Out
24: Broken Barriers
5th Avenue Models
26: Ermine and Rhinestones
27: Lady Bird
Satin Woman
28: The Devil's Cage

Edith Storey (1892-)
1911: Billy the Kid
12: The Troublesome Step-daughters
The Lady of the Lake
The Serpents
The Telephone Girl
The Victoria Cross
True Till Death
13: A Regiment of Two
14: The Old Flute Player
The Price of Folly
The Christian
The Scarlet Runner
15: The Island of Regeneration
Dust of Egypt
In the Latin Quarter
The Quality of Mercy
Love's Way
On Her Wedding Night
16: An Enemy to the King
Susie the Sleuth
She Won the Prize
Winifred the Shop Girl
The Tarantula
17: Mr. Aladdin from Broadway
Money Magic
Captain of the Grey Horse Troop
18: Revenge
Eyes of Mystery
The Claim
Treasure of the Sea
The Demon
The Legion of Death
19: As the Sun Went Down
The Silent Woman
20: Moon Madness
Beach of Dreams
21: Golden Hope
Greater Profit

William H. Strauss (1885-)
1920: North Wind's Malice
21: Magic Cup
Barricade
22: Solomon in Society
25: Skinner's Dress Suit
26: Private Izzy Murphy
27: Rubber Tires
Ankles Preferred
For Ladies Only
Sally in our Alley
Shamrock and the Rose
The Rawhide Kid
28: So This is Love?
The Ghetto
Abie's Irish Rose SSE
29: Do Your Duty
Lucky Boy

Strongheart (the dog)
1921: The Silent Call
22: Brawn of the North
27: Return of Boston Blackie
The Warning

Nipo (George) Strongheart (1891-1967)
1925: Road to Yesterday
26: A Brave Heart
The Last Frontier

Nick Stuart (1906-)
1927: Cradle Snatchers
High School Hero
28: Why Sailors Go Wrong
News Parade
River Pirate SSE
29: Girls Gone Wild SSE
Joy Street SSE
Chasing Through Europe SSE

29: Why Leave Home? T

Slim Summerville (1892-1946)

1914: The Knockout
Mabel's Busy Day
Laughing Gas
Dough and Dynamite
Gentlemen of Nerve
Tillie's Punctured Romance
Cursed by His Beauty
15: The Great Vacuum Robbery
Her Winning Punch
Home Breakers
Gussle's Day of Rest
Their Social Splash
Those College Girls (or, His Bitter Half)
Those Bitter Sweets
A Game Old Knight
Her Painted Hero
16: His Bread and Butter
Cinders of Love
His Busted Trust
The Three Slims
17: Villa of the Movies
Her Fame and Shame
Mary's Little Lobster
Hold the Line
Roping Her Romeo
A Dog Catcher's Love
Her Precious Life
Are Waitresses Safe?
It Pays to Exercise
The Kitchen Lady
High Diver's Last Kiss
Ten Nights Without a Barroom
27: Painted Ponies
Beloved Rogue
Hey, Hey, Cowboy
The Chinese Parrot
28: Wreck of the Hesperus
Riding for Fame
29: King of the Rodeo
Strong Boy SSE
The Shannons of Broadway T
Tiger Rose T
The Last Warning PT
?? Keystone Comedies

Valeska Suratt (1882-)

1915: The Immigrant
16: Jealousy

Eddie Sutherland (1897-)

1919: The Veiled Adventure
20: All of a Sudden Peggy
The Round Up
The Sea Wolf
Conrad in Search of His Youth
21: Dollar-A-Year Man
The Witching Hour
Just Outside the Door

Mack Swain (1876-1935)

1913-18: Keystone Comedies
14: The Fatal Mallet
Caught in the Rain
A Busy Day
The Knockout
Laughing Gas
Getting Acquainted
His Prehistoric Past
His Musical Career
His Trysting Place
Caught in a Cabaret
Mabel's Married Life
Sea Nymphs
Ambrose's First Falsehood
15: Tillie's Punctured Romance
Gussle, The Golfer
Love, Speed and Thrills
The Home Breakers
Ambrose's Sour Grapes
Wilful Ambrose
From Patches to Plenty
That Little Band of Gold (or, For Better, But Worse)
Ambrose's Fury
Ambrose's Lofty Perch
Ambrose's Nasty Temper
A Human Hound's Triumph
Our Daredevil Chief
Mabel Lost and Won
When Ambrose Dared Walrus
Battle of Ambrose and Walrus
Saved by Wireless
Best of Enemies
16: A Modern Enoch Arden
A Movie Star
Love Will Conquer
By Stork Delivery

16: His Wild Oats
Madcap Ambrose
Ambrose's Cup of Woe
Ambrose's Rapid Rise
Safety First Ambrose (or, Sheriff Ambrose)
His Bitter Pill
His Auto-Ruination
17: His Naughty Thought
Lost--A Cook
Danger Girl
The Pullman Bride
19: Ambrose's Day Off
Leading Lizzy Astray
The Schemers
Safety First Ambrose
Ambrose and the Lion-Hearted
21: The Idle Class
22: Pay Day
23: The Pilgrim
25: The Gold Rush
26: The Cohens and the Kellys
The Torrent
Whispering Wires
Hands Up!
27: Beloved Rogue
My Best Girl
See You in Jail
The Shamrock and the Rose
Mockery
Becky
Girl from Everywhere
Finnegan's Ball
28: Tillie's Punctured Romance
Caught in the Fog
Gentlemen Prefer Blondes
29: The Last Warning PT
Marianne T
The Cohens and the Kellys in Atlantic City T
30: Redemption T
The Sea Bat T
31: Finn and Hattie T
32: Midnight Patrol T
The Engineer's Daughter T

Gloria Swanson (1898-)
1915: At the End of a Perfect Day
Ambition of the Baron
15: His New Job
The Fable of Elvira and Farina and the Meal Ticket
Sweedie Goes to College
The Romance of an American Duchess
The Broken Pledge
16: A Dash of Courage
Hearts and Sparks
Whose Baby?
A Social Cub
The Danger Girl
Love on Skates
Haystacks and Steeples
17: Nick of Time Baby
Teddy at the Throttle
Baseball Madness
Dangers of a Bride
The Sultan's Wife
A Pullman Bride
18: Society for Sale
Her Decision
You Can't Believe Everything
Every Woman's Husband
Shifting Sands
Station Content
Secret Code
Wife or Country
19: Don't Change Your Husband
For Better, For Worse
Male and Female
20: Why Change Your Wife?
Something to Think About
The Great Moment
21: The Affairs of Anatol
Under the Lash
Don't Tell Everything
22: Her Husband's Trademark
Beyond the Rocks
Her Gilded Cage
The Impossible Mrs. Bellew
23: My American Wife
Prodigal Daughters
Bluebeard's 8th Wife
Zaza
24: The Humming Bird
A Society Scandal
Manhandled
Her Love Story
Wages of Virtue
25: Madame Sans-Gene

25: The Coast of Folly
Stage Struck
26: Untamed Lady
Fine Manners
27: The Love of Sunya
28: Sadie Thompson
Queen Kelly (unfinished)
29: The Trespasser T
30: What a Widow! T
31: Indiscreet T
Tonight or Never T
33: A Perfect Understanding T
34: Music in the Air T

Blanche Sweet (1895-)

1909: Choosing a Husband
A Man with Three Wives
A Corner in Wheat
The Day After
10: A Romance of the Western Hills
The Rocky Road
All On Account of the Milk
11: Country Lovers
Was He a Coward?
The Lonedale Operator
Home Folks
How She Triumphed
White Rose of the Wilds
A Smile of a Child
The Last Drop of Water
Out from the Shadow
The Blind Princess and the Poet
The Making of a Man
The Long Road
Love in the Hills
The Battle
Through Darkened Vales
A Woman Scorned
The Voice of a Child
The Primal Call
The Stuff Heroes Are Made Of
Fighting Blood
12: The Eternal Mother
For His Son
The Transformation of Mike
Under Burning Skies
The Goddess of Sagebrush Gulch
12: The Punishment
The Lesser Evil
One is Business, The Other Crime
An Outcast Among Outcasts
A Temporary Truce
The Spirit Awakened
Man's Lust for Gold
The Painted Lady
With the Enemy's Help
A Change of Spirit
Blind Love
The Chief's Blanket
A Sailor's Heart
The God Within
A Sister's Love
Cinderella Jane
13: Three Friends
Pirate Gold
Oil and Water
A Chance Deception
Broken Ways
The Hero of Little Italy
The Stolen Bride
Classmates
Love in an Apartment Hotel
If We Only Knew
Death's Marathon
The Coming of Angelo
The Mistake
Two Men on the Desert
The House of Discord
Near to Earth
The Vengeance of Galora
14: Her Wedding Bell
The Sentimental Sister
The Massacre
Strongheart
Men and Women
Ashes of the Past
The Soul of Honor
The Second Mrs. Roebuck
For Those Unborn
Her Awakening
For Her Father's Sins
The Tear That Burned
The Odalisque
The Little Country Mouse
The Old Maid
Judith of Bethulia
The Escape
Home Sweet Home

14: The Avenging Conscience
15: The Warrens of Virginia
The Captive
Stolen Goods
The Clue
The Secret Orchard
The Case of Becky
The Secret Sin
16: The Ragamuffin
Blacklist
The Sowers
$1000 Husband
The Dupe
Public Opinion
The Storm
Unprotected
17: The Evil Eye
Those Without Sin
The Tides of Barnegat
The Silent Partner
19: The Unpardonable Sin
The Hushed Hour
A Woman of Pleasure
Fighting Cressy
20: The Deadlier Sex
Simple Souls
The Girl in the Web
Help Wanted - Male
Her Unwilling Husband
21: That Girl Montana
22: Quincy Adams Sawyer
23: The Meanest Man in the World
Souls for Sale
Anna Christie
In the Palace of the King
24: Those Who Dance
Tess of the D'Ubervilles
25: The Sporting Venus
His Supreme Moment
Why Women Love
The New Commandment
26: Bluebeard's 7 Wives
The Far Cry
The Lady from Hell
Diplomacy
The Human Mill
For Those Unborn
27: Singed
28: Night Hostess
29: The Woman in White
Always Faithful
30: The Woman Racket T
30: Showgirl in Hollywood T
The Silver Horde T
Screen Snapshots T
Screen Fashions T

Josef Swickard (1867-1940)

1914: Laughing Gas
15: Home Breaking Hound
The Plumber
The Best of Enemies
16: Love Will Conquer
His Wild Oats
Haystacks and Steeples
Ambrose's Cup of Woe
The Village Vampire
17: Tale of Two Cities
18: Keys of the Righteous
19: A Woman of Pleasure
Last of His People
Trick of Fate
20: Blind Youth
Trumpet Island
Mothers-In-Law
Moon Madness
21: Sowing the Wind
Open Shutters
4 Horsemen of the Apocalypse
Serenade
No Woman Knows
Golden Gift
22: Across the Dead Line
Robinson Crusoe (serial)
The Storm
Another Man's Shoes
Pawned
23: My American Wife
Mr. Billings Spends His Dime
Daughters of the Rich
John of the Woods
Cricket on the Hearth
24: Men
Dante's Inferno
5th Avenue Models
26: Senor Daredevil
Hotel Imperial
Whispering Canyon
Don Juan
27: Old San Francisco
Senorita
Get Your Man
One Increasing Purpose

27: Time to Love
Golden Stallion (serial)
28: Sharp Shooters
Eagle of the Night (serial)
Comrades
Turn Back the Hours
29: Phantoms of the North
Street Corner
The Devil's Chaplain
The Eternal Woman
The Veiled Woman
Times Square
Frozen River PT
Bachelors' Club SSE
Dark Skies T
30: Mamba T
34: Cross Streets T
35: The Lost City T
A Dog of Flanders T
36: Caryl of the Mountains T
37: The Girl Says No T
38: You Can't Take It With You T

Richard Taber
1915: Eyes That See Not
Caught
When My Lady Smiles
19: Miss Crusoe
22: At Bay
23: Kick In
29: Lucky in Love

Edith Taliaferro
1920: Who Is Your Brother?

Mabel Taliaferro (1887-)
1914: Cinderella
15: The Three of Us
16: Dawn of Love
The Snowbird
The Great Price
The Sunbeam
17: The Jury of Fate
A Magdalene of the Hills
A Wife by Proxy
Peggy Leads the Way
The Barricade
18: Draft 258
19: The Battle for Billions
21: Sentimental Tommy

Constance Talmadge (1900-)
1914: Uncle Bill
Buddy's Call
Our Fairy Play
The Moonstone of Fez
Buddy's Downfall
The Mysterious Lodger
Father's Timepiece
The Peacemaker
The Evolution of Percival
In Bridal Attire
The Egyptian Mummy
Forcing Dad's Consent
15: The Missing Bank Notes
In the Latin Quarter
Billy's Wager
The Green Cat
The Young Man Who Figgered
A Study in Tramps
The Lady of Shalott
The Master of the House
The Boarding House Feud
The Vanishing Vault
Spades are Trump
Bertie's Stratagem
Billy the Bear Tamer
Captivating Mrs. Carstairs
Can You Beat It?
Beached and Bleached
The Missing Links
16: The She-Devil
The Microscope Mystery
The Matrimaniac
Intolerance
17: The Girl of the Timber Claims
Betsey's Burglar
The Honeymoon
Scandal
18: The Studio Girl
The Shuttle
The Lesson
Goodnight Paul
Up The Road With Sally
The Grey Chiffon Veil
Mrs. Leffingwell's Boots
Sauce for the Goose
A Pair of Silk Stockings
The Lady's Name
19: Experimental Marriage
Romance and Arabella
Happiness A La Mode

19: Who Cares?
Virtuous Vamp
A Tempermental Wife
20: In Search of a Sinner
The Love Expert
The Perfect Woman
Two Weeks
Good References
21: Dangerous Business
Lessons in Love
Wedding Bells
Mama's Affair
A Woman's Place
22: East is West
Polly of the Follies
Primitive Lover
Divorcee
23: Dulcy
The Dangerous Maid
24: Heart Trouble
The Goldfish
Her Night of Romance
25: Her Sister from Paris (dual role)
Learning to Love
26: Sybil
The Duchess of Buffalo
27: Venus of Venice
Breakfast at Sunrise
29: Venus

Natalie Talmadge (1898-1969)
1915: Civilization
16: Intolerance
18: The Bell Boy
A Tempermental Wife
19: The Isle of Conquest
20: The Love Expert
Yes or No
21: The Passion Flower
22: The Blacksmith
The Electric House
23: Our Hospitality

Norma Talmadge (1896-1957)
1910: Dixie Mother
The Household Pest
11: Paola and Francesca
In Neighboring Kingdoms
A Tale of Two Cities
Mrs. 'enry 'awkins
Casey at the Bat
O'Hara Helps Cupid
11: Wanted A Strong Hand
He Fell in Love with his Mother-In-Law
The Sky Pilot
The General's Daughter
12: The First Violin
The Troublesome Stepdaughters
Mr. Butler Buttles
Fortunes of a Composer
Omens and Oracles
The Midget's Revenge
The Lovesick Maidens of Cuddleton
Captain Barnacle's Messmates
Captain Barnacle's Waif
Captain Barnacle, Reformer
O'Hara-Squatter and Philosopher
The Extension Table
13: Just Show People
Extremities
His Official Appointment
Under the Daisies
The Doctor's Secret
Father's Conspiracy
His Silver Bachelorhood
An Elopement at Home
The Honorable Algernon
His Little Page
Officer John Donovan
The Sacrifice of Kathleen
Counsel for the Defense
The Silver Cigarette Case
'arriet's Baby
Country Barber
O'Hara as Guardian Angel
An Old Man's Love Story
The Tables Turned
Solitaires
14: Sawdust and Salome
The Vavasour Ball
The Helpful Sisterhood
Cupid Vs. Money
The Right of Way
John Rance - Gentleman
Under False Colors
Goodbye Summer
The Wooing of Myra May
Sunshine and Shadows
A Daughter of Israel
Miser Murphy's Wedding Present

14: The Hidden Letters
The Memories in Men's Souls
Politics and the Press
The Mill of Life
The Loan Shark King
The Peacemaker
A Wayward Daughter
A Question of Clothes
The Conspiracy
Fogg's Millions
15: A Daughter's Strange Inheritance
Janet of the Chorus
Pillar of Flame
The Criminal
The Missing Links
The Crown Prince's Double
The Barrier of Faith
Elsie's Brother
The Battle Cry of Peace
16: Children in the House
Martha's Vindication
Going Straight (or, Corruption)
The Devil's Needle
The Social Secretary
Fifty-Fifty
The Captivating Mary Carstairs
17: Panthea
Poppy
The Law of Compensation
The Honeymoon
The Moth
Missing Banknotes
18: The Secret of the Storm Country
By Right of Purchase
De Luxe Annie
Her Only Way
The Forbidden City
The Safety Curtain
The Heart of Wetona
Ghosts of Yesterday
19: The Probation Wife
The Way of a Woman
The New Moon
Isle of Conquest
20: She Loves and Lies
A Daughter of Two Worlds
Girl of Gold
The Woman Gives
20: Yes or No
The Branded Woman
21: The Sign on the Door
Wonderful Thing
The Passion Flower (or, Love or Hate)
Love's Redemption
22: Smilin' Through
The Eternal Flame
Voice from the Minaret
23: Within the Law
Ashes of Vengeance
Dust of Desire (or, Song of Love)
24: Secrets
The Only Woman
25: The Lady
Graustark
26: Kiki
27: Camille
28: The Dove
Woman Disputed
30: New York Nights
Du Barry, Woman of Passion T

Richard Talmadge (1898-)

1922: The Unknown
Watch Him Step
Taking Chances
The Cub Reporter
Wildcat Jordan
Putting It Over
23: Danger Ahead
Lucky Dan
The Speed King
Through the Flames
Let's Go!
24: American Manners
In Fast Company
Hail the Hero
25: Tearing Through
Youth and Adventure
Laughing at Danger
Jimmie's Millions
Fighting Demon
The Isle of Hope
Wall Street Whizz
27: The Prince of Pep
The Broadway Gallant
The Night Patrol
The Blue Streak
The Better Man

28: The Cavalier
29: The Bachelor's Club SSE

Rose Tapley (1883-)
1905: Wanted A Wife
11: Vanity Fair
12: As You Like It
14: The Christian
Money Kings
16: Susie the Sleuth
Rose of the South
The Victoria Cross
21: Rip Van Winkle
Memories That Haunt
23: Vanity Fair
Java Head
27: It
29: The Charlatan PT

Lilyan Tashman (1900. 1934)
1921: Experience
24: The Garden of Weeds
Ports of Call
Playing Around
25: Declassee
Bright Lights
Pretty Ladies
7 Days
26: Rocking Moon
Siberia
Whispering Smith
Love's Blindness
For Alimony Only
So This is Paris
Skyrocket
27: Don't Tell the Wife
Evening Clothes
Camille
The Prince of Headwaiters
The Woman Who Did Not Care
The Stolen Bride
The Texas Steer
28: French Dressing
Lady Raffles
Happiness Ahead
Craig's Wife
Take Me Home
Manhattan Cocktail
Phyllis of the Follies
29: Hardboiled
Trial of Mary Dugan T
Lone Wolf's Daughter PT
29: Bulldog Drummond T
The Marriage Play-ground T
New York Nights T
30: No No Nanette T
Playing Around T

Estelle Taylor (1899-1958)
1920: The Adventurer
While New York Sleeps
The Revenge of Tarzan
The Return of Tarzan
21: Blind Wives
Footballs
22: Monte Cristo
A Fool There Was
Thorns and Orange Blossoms
Only a Shop Girl
Peg O' My Heart
23: Lights of New York
The 10 Commandments
A California Romance
Desire
24: Dorothy Vernon of Haddon Hall
The Alaskan
Tiger Love
Happiness
One Night in Rome
25: Manhattan Madness
26: Don Juan
27: New York
28: The Singapore Mutiny
Lady Raffles
Honor Bound
Bavu
Pusher in the Face
The Whip Woman
Show People
29: Where East is East

Laurette Taylor (1884-1946)
1923: Peg O' My Heart
24: One Night in Rome
Happiness

Conway Tearle (1882-1938)
1914: The Nightingale
15: Seven Sisters
Helene of the North
16: The Common Law
Heart of the Hills

17: The Fall of the Romanoffs
18: Stella Maris
The Reason Why
19: A Virtuous Vamp
Way of a Woman
Virtuous Wives
Mind the Paint Girl
Her Game
Virtuous Sinners
20: Two Weeks
She Loves and Lies
21: The Oath
Bucking the Tiger
After Midnight
The Man of Stone
Marooned Hearts
Her Game
Road of Ambition
Society Snobs
Whispering Devils
The Fighter
22: Shadows of the Sea
Love's Masquerade
The Referee
The Eternal Flame
One Week of Love
The Wide Open Town
23: Bella Donna
Ashes of Vengeance
A Dangerous Maid
The Common Law
Rustle of Silk
24: Black Oxen
The White Moth
25: The Great Divide
The Viennese Medley
Learning to Love
26: Dancing Mothers
My Official Wife
Dancer of Paris
The Greater Glory
Sporting Lover
27: Moulders of Men
Altars of Desire
Isle of Forgotten Women
Venus of Venice
29: Smoke Bellew
Evidence T
Gold Diggers of Broadway T
30: Lost Zeppelin T
Truth About Youth T
31: Lady Who Dared T
Morals for Women T
Captivation T
32: Vanity Fair T
Man About Town T
False Idol T
Pleasure T
Her Mad Night T

Alma Tell (1892-1937)
1916: The Smugglers
20: On With the Dance
21: Paying the Piper
The Iron Trail
22: A Broadway Rose
29: Saturday's Children PT
30: Love Comes Along T
?? Right to Love

Olive Tell (1894-1951)
1913: The Girl and the Judge
16: The Smugglers
17: The Silent Master
18: Her Sister
To Hell with the Kaiser!
The Unforeseen
19: Secret Strings
The Trap
20: Love Without Question
Nothing a Year
A Woman's Business
21: Clothes
Worlds Apart
Wings of Pride
The Wrong Woman
25: Chickie
26: Prince of Tempters
Woman-Handled
Summer Bachelors
27: Slaves of Beauty
28: Sailors' Wives
Soft Living
29: Trial of Mary Dugan T
The Very Idea T
Hearts in Exile

Lou Tellegen (1881-1934)
1912: Queen Elizabeth
13: Adrienne Lecouvreur
La Dame Aux Camelias
15: The Unknown
16: The Victory of Conscience
What Money Can't Buy

16: The Victory Cross
17: The Long Trail
18: The Thing We Love
19: Flame of the Desert
World and Its Woman
20: Blind Youth
The Woman and the Puppet
24: Single Wives
Let No Man Put Asunder
Parisian Nights
Greater Than Marriage
25: Breath of Scandal
After Business Hours
The Sporting Chance
East Lynne
The Redeeming Sin
26: The Outsider
Siberia
Womanpower
Three Bad Men
Silver Treasure
27: Stage Madness
Princess from Hoboken
The Little Firebrand
Married Alive

Barbara Tennant

1916: The Price of Malice
The Closed Road
21: Wolves of the North
?? Dollar Mark
The Marked Woman

Alice Terry (1896-)

1915: The Bugle Call
16: The Clarion Call
A Corner in Colleen's
Not My Sister
17: The Bottom of the Well
18: Strictly Business
Love Watches
19: Thin Ice
The Love Burglar
Valley of the Giants
20: Hearts are Trumps
21: Four Horsemen of the Apocalypse
The Conquering Power
Turn to the Right
22: Prisoner of Zenda
23: Where the Pavement Ends
Scaramouche
24: The Arab
25: The Great Divide
26: Mare Nostrum
The Magician
27: Garden of Allah
Lovers
29: The 3 Passions

Ethel Grey Terry (1898-)

1914: Sign of the Cross
16: Intolerance
17: Arsene Lupin
19: Phil for Short
Craig Kennedy (serial)
The Carter Case (serial)
Mystery of the Yellow Room
The Snail
Denny from Ireland
20: Going Some
Food for Scandal
21: The Breaking Point
The White Mouse
Greater than Love
Habit
22: Oath Bound
Shattered Idols
Too Much Business
Crossroads of New York
The Kick Back
Under Two Flags
23: Garrison's Finish
Peg O' My Heart
Brass
The Self Made Wife
What Wives Want
Why Women Re-Marry
26: Hardboiled
The Love Toy
27: Canceled Debts
Old Shoes
28: Skinner's Big Idea
Modern Mothers
29: Confessions of a Wife
Object: Alimony
A Dumb Waiter
?? The Penalty

Rosemary Theby (1885-)

1910: The Wager
12: As You Like It
Reincarnation of Karma
The Illumination
13: The Web

13: Ashes
Fight for the Right
When the Earth Trembled
(or, The Strength of Love)
14: Baby
Too Much Women
15: The House of a 1000 Relations
16: Housekeeping
17: War Bridegroom
The Winged Mystery
18: Bright and Early
Boston Blackie's Little Pal
Unexpected Places
The Shooting of Sadie Rose
The Great Love
The Silent Mystery (serial)
19: The Mystery of 13 (serial)
The Hushed Hour
Love's Pay Day
Are You Legally Married?
When a Woman Strikes
20: Kismet
Rio Grande
A Splendid Hazard
The Dice of Destiny
21: A Connecticut Yankee in King Arthur's Court
Fightin' Mad
Good Woman
Partners of Fate
22: Yellow Men and Gold
More to be Pitied than Scorned
Rich Men's Wives
The Eternal Flame
Across the Divide
23: Long Live the King
Lost and Found
Rip Tide
Your Friend and Mine
Girl of the Golden West
Mill of the Gods
Weight of a Crown
14: Secrets of the Night
The Red Lily
5th Avenue Models
25: One Year to Live
So Big
26: The Truthful Sex
27: A Bowery Cinderella
28: Port of Missing Girls
Woman Against the World
29: Dream Melody
Peacock Fan
Trial Marriage
Girls Who Dare
Montmartre Rose
Midnight Daddies
31: 10 Nights in a Bar Room T
33: Fatal Glass of Beer (short)
35: Man on the Flying Trapeze
36: San Francisco
?? The Yankee

Olive Thomas (1898-1920)

1916: Beatrice Fairfax (serial)
17: Broadway Arizona
A Girl Like That
Madcap Madge
An Even Break
Frankly Chaste
18: Indiscreet Corinne
Betty Takes a Hand
Limousine Life
An Heiress for a Day
19: Follies Girl
Love's Prisoner
Upstairs and Down
Prudence of Broadway
Toto
The Spite Bride
20: Out Yonder
The Flapper
Footlights and Shadows
The Glorious Lady
Youthful Folly
Jennie
21: Everybody's Sweetheart
Darling Mine

Duane Thompson (1905-)

1927: Her Summer Hero
Silent Avenger
28: Flying Buckaroo
Phyllis of the Follies
The Kiss Doctor
Beauty and Bullets
Phantom Fingers
The Fighting Redhead
Price of Fear
Phantom of the Range
29: Born to the Saddle
Eyes of the Underworld
Slim Fingers
Frozen River

29: Voice of the City
Tip Off
37: Hollywood Hotel T

Lotus Thompson
1926: The Dangerous Dude
29: The Freckled Rascal
30: The Lone Rider T
Cowboy Pluck T
31: In Line of Duty T

Fred Thomson (1890-1928)
1921: The Love Light
23: The Eagle's Talons (serial)
Mask of Lopez
24: Silent Stranger
The Dangerous Coward
The Fighting Sap
Galloping Gallagher
North of Nevada
Thundering Hoofs
Quemado, That Devil
25: The Wild Bull's Lair
The Bandit's Baby
All Around the Frying Pan
Ridin' the Wind
26: Tough Guy
Two Gun Man
Lone Hand Sanders
A Regular Scout
Hands Across the Border
27: Don Mike
Silver Comes Through
Jesse James
28: The Sunset Legion
Pioneer Scout
Kit Carson
Into No Man's Land

Kenneth Thomson (1899-)
1927: White Gold
King of Kings
28: Secret Hour
29: Veiled Woman
Bellamy Trial PT
Broadway Melody T
Say It With Songs T
Careless Age T
Girl from Havana T
30: Faithful T
The Other Tomorrow T

Edith Thornton
1920: The Whirlwind
25: Fair Play
Was It Bigamy?
26: Lightnin' Hutch' (serial)
27: Little Firebrand

Mary Thurman (1894-1925)
1916: His First False Step
The Late Lamented
A Bedroom Blunder
Bombs
The Scoundrel's Tale
The Stone Age (or, Her Cave Man)
17: Mabel's First False Step
Pinched in the Finish
Danger Girl
Haystacks and Steeples
18: Watch Your Neighbor
Sunshine Dad
19: This Hero Stuff
The House of Betty
Spotlight Sadie
20: The Prince and Betty
Sand
21: In the Heart of a Fool
The Scoffer
The Primal Law
Should a Man Marry?
22: The Lady from Longacre
The Sin of Martha Queed
Green Temptation
The Bond Boy
23: Tents of Allah
Zaza
25: The Fool
Bare Knuckles
??: That Night
Valley of Yesterday

Zeffie Tilbury (1863-1945)
1920: Mothers of Men
Clothes
21: The Marriage of William Ashe
19: Single Standard

Fay Tincher
1914: Battle of the Sexes
15: Home Sweet Home
Faithful to the Finish

15: Don Quixote
16: A Rough Knight
Skirts
The French Milliner
The Two O'Clock Train
Bedelia's Bluff
The Lady Drummer
30: Dangerous Nan McGrew
?? Bill, The Office Boy Series
Rowdy Ann
Wild and Western
Go West, Young Woman

Lydia Yeamans Titus

1917: Aladdin
The Edge of the Law
18: All Night
19: World and Its Woman
Strictly Confidential
Little Marian's Triumph
Romance of Happy Valley
Happy Though Married
Yankee Princess
Peace of Roaring River
Gun Fightin' Gentleman
20: High Speed
The Prince of Avenue A
Nurse Marjorie
21: The Mad Marriage
The Freeze Out
All Dolled Up
The Marriage of William Ashe
The Concert
Beau Revel
Queenie
The Invisible Power
Nobody's Fool
22: His Nibs
Deep Waters
Beauty's Worth
The Married Flapper
A God's Desire
23: The Famous Mrs. Fair
Winter Has Came
Scaramouche
The Wanters
24: Tarnish
27: Upstream
Night Life
28: Two Lovers
While the City Sleeps
The Water Hole
28: Sweet Sixteen
29: Voice of the Storm

Lola Todd

1924: The Iron Man (serial)
26: The Scarlet Streak (serial)
Count of Luxembourg
27: Return of the Riddle Man (serial)
28: The Fifty-Fifty Girl
29: Taking a Chance

Thelma Todd (1908-1935)

1922: Fascination
23: Flaming Youth
26: Fascinating Youth
The Popular Sin
27: Nevada
The Gay Defender
28: Heart to Heart
The Wrecking Boss
Shield of Honor
The Noose
The Crash
The Haunted House SSE
Vamping Venus
29: Naughty Baby SSE
7 Footprints to Satan SSE
Trial Marriage
Bachelor Girl PT
Careers PT
House of Horror PT
Her Private Life T
30: Hell's Angels T
It's All Greek to Me T
?? The Sport Girl

Kate Toncray

1911: Fisher Folks
13: The Lady and the Mouse
Those Little Flowers
Love in an Apartment House
14: Liberty Bells
15: Old Heidelberg
16: Little Meena's Romance
17: The Little Yank
Stage Struck
Rebecca of Sunnybrook Farm
18: Battling Jane
19: The Hope Chest
Out of Luck

19: Turning the Tables
20: Prisoners of Love
21: The Charm School
The Failure
The Match Breaker
Silent Years
Mam'selle Jr.
Bing Bang Boom!

William Tooker (1875-)

1916: A Fool's Revenge
18: Woman the Germans Shot
20: The Stealers
Heliotrope
21: The Greatest Love
Worlds Apart
Proxies
The Lotus Eaters
22: God's Country and the Law
Power Within
26: The Scarlet Letter
White Black Sheep
27: Birds of Prey
Two Girls Wanted
Tell It To Sweeney
28: The Whip
Night Watch
Virgin Lips
Sweet Sixteen
Lookout Girl
Romance of a Rogue
A Romance of the Underworld
Fashion Madness
Woman Against the World
29: Love in the Desert PT
Why Girls Go Wrong
Protection SSE
No Defense PT
Bellamy Trial PT

David Torrence (1880-c1942)

1913: Tess of the D'Ubervilles
Prisoner of Zenda
21: Inside the Cup
Disraeli
22: Tess of the Storm Country
23: The Light that Failed
The Abysmal Brute
Power of a Lie
Trimmed in Scarlet
24: Drums of Jeopardy
Which Shall It Be?
Dawn of Tomorrow
Tiger Love
25: Her Husband's Secret
26: Oh, What a Nurse!
Brown of Harvard
The Auction Block
The Other Woman's Story
Isle of Retribution
Laddie
Racewild
Man in the Shadow
27: Annie Laurie
Third Degree
Midnight Watch
Mysterious Rider
Rolled Stockings
The World at Her Feet
Hazardous Valleys
28: On the Stroke of Twelve
Big Noise
City of Purple Dreams
King of the Khyber Rifles
The Cavalier
Undressed
Silks and Saddles
Little Shepherd of Kingdom Come
Steamboat Bill, Junior
29: Untamed Justice T
Black Watch T
Strong Boy T
Disraeli T
Hearts in Exile T

Ernest Torrence (1878-1933)

1921: Tol'able David
22: The Prodigal Judge
Broken Chains
23: Covered Wagon
Trail of the Lonesome Pine
The Brass Bottle
Hunchback of Notre Dame
Ruggles of Red Gap
Fighting Coward
24: North of '36
25: Side Show of Life
West of the Water Tower
Peter Pan
The Circle
Pony Express
Night Life of New York
26: Mantrap

26: The Blind Goddess
The Rainmaker
Lady of the Harem
27: King of Kings
Twelve Miles Out
Captain Salvation
28: The Cossacks
Steamboat Bill Junior
Across to Singapore
Undressed
Silks and Saddles
29: Bridge of San Luis Rey PT
Desert Nights T
Speedway T
Singer of Seville T
Untamed T
Unholy Night T

Raquel Torres (1908-)
1928: White Shadows of the South Seas
29: The Desert Rider
Bridge of San Luis Rey PT

Wayland Trask
1915: The Great Vacuum Robbery
16: His Hereafter
The Judge
A Love Riot
Pills of Peril
The Feathered Nest (or, Girl Guardian)
Maid Mad (or, A Fortune Teller)
Bombs
No One to Guide Him (or, Her Cave Man)
17: Dodging His Doom
A Maiden's Trust
Her Torpedoed Love
Cactus Nell
She Needed a Doctor
His Precious Life

Madalaine Travers (1875-1964)
1913: Leah Kleschna
14: Three Weeks
17: The Poor Little Rich Girl
Sins of Ambition
18: The Caillaux Case
19: The Danger Zone
Rose of the West
When Fate Decides
19: The Love That Dares
Gambling in Souls
The Splendid Sin
20: The Iron Heart
The Hell Ship
Lost Money
The Snares of Paris
The Tattlers
The Penalty
What Would You Do?
The Spirit of Good

Richard Travers (1890-)
1914: Romance of an American Duchess
16: Captain Jinks of the Horse Marines
Lost 24 Hours
Borrowed Sunshine
Phantom Buccaneer
19: House Without Children
The Love Nest
20: The White Moll
21: Among Those Present
The Hoodooed Story
The Mountain Woman
Rider of the King Log
22: Notoriety
Dawn of Revenge
23: The Acquitted
White Sister
In the Palace of the King
Covered Wagon
24: Rendezvous
The Broad Road
25: Lightnin'
26: The Dangerous Dude
29: Black Watch
?? The Egg

Hugh Trevor (1903-1933)
1928: Skinner's Big Idea
Red Lips
Man About Town
Beau Broadway
Wallflowers
Cream of the Earth
29: String
Taxi 13 PT
Dry Martini SSE
Hey, Rube!
Love in the Desert PT
The Very Idea T

29: Night Parade T

Norman Trevor (1877-1929)

1917: The Runaway
20: Romance
The Daughter Pays
21: Jane Eyre
The Black Panther's Cub
24: Wages of Virtue
25: The Man Who Found Himself
26: Dancing Mothers
Song and Dance Man
The Ace of Cads
Beau Geste
27: The Music Master
New York
The Coward
Afraid to Love
Sorrell and Son
The Wizard
28: Warning
The Siren
Love Trap PT
Tonight at Twelve T
The Mad Hour
29: Restless Youth

Maude Truax

1928: Midnight Adventure
No Picnic
No Sale
No Camping
No Vacation

Youcca Trubetzskoy (1905-)

1917: Hawk
25: Flower of Night
Peacock Feathers
26: Beautiful Cheat
29: Four Devils T
Road Show T
His Glorious Night T
30: Rogue Song T
?? Frou Frou
The Giants Pavement

Howard Truesdale (1870-)

1920: The Whisper Market
Youthful Folly
22: French Heels
No Thoroughfare
Van Bibber Comedies

28: Mating Call
The Tigress
Three-Ring Marriage
29: Lawless Legion

Ernest Truex (1889-)

1913: An American Citizen
14: The Bond Boy
A Good Little Devil
18: Come On In
Goodbye Bill
19: Oh, You Women
Stick Around
Too Good To Be True
Little But Oh My!
The Bashful Lover
23: Six Cylinder Love
?? Knight of the Dub

Glenn Tryon (1897-)

1924: White Sheep
Battling Orioles
17: The Poor Nut
Painting the Town
A Hero for a Night
Two Girls Wanted
28: How to Handle Women
Lonesome
Thanks for the Buggy Ride
Hot Heels
Gate Crasher
29: It Can Be Done PT
Broadway T
Kid's Clever
Barnum was Right T
Skinner Steps Out T
Leave It To Me
Half Marriage T
?? Hal Roach Comedies

Richard Tucker (1869-1942)

1915: While the Tide was Rising
Vanity Fair
20: The Branding Iron
Dollars and Sense
The Great Lover
Woman in Room 13
21: Roads of Destiny
Voice in the Dark
Everything for Sale
Don't Neglect Your Wife
What Love Will Do
22: Hearts Aflame

22: A Virginia Courtship
Yellow Men and Gold
Grand Larceny
Voices of the City
Remembrance
Strange Idols
Self Made Man
The Night Rose
The Worldly Madonna
When the Desire Drives
Rags to Riches
23: Cameo Kirby
Is Divorce a Failure?
The Broken Wing
Poor Men's Wives
The Dangerous Age
Her Accidental Husband
26: Devil's Island
Shameful Behavior
Lure of the Wild
That's My Baby
The Blind Goddess
The Lily
27: A Kiss in a Taxi
Matinee Ladies
World at Her Feet
Bush Leaguer
Women's Wares
Wings
Girl from Rio
Dearie
The Jazz Singer
28: Beware of Married Men
Thanks for the Buggy Ride
Crimson City SSE
On Trial
A Bit of Heaven
Love Over Night
Show Folks PT
Border Patrol
Loves of an Actress
The Grain of Dust
The Ghetto
Captain Swagger SSE
The Show Girl
29: Lucky Boy
My Man PT
The Dummy T
This is Heaven PT
Daughters of Desire
The Squall T
Half Marriage T
Unholy Night T

Florence Turner (1887-1946)

1910: How Champion Ships Are Won and Lost
Auld Robin Grey
A Dixie Mother
The New Stenographer
St. Elmo
Angel of the Studio
11: A Tale of Two Cities
The Deerslayer
Prejudice of Pierre Marie
12: Francesca Da Rimini
Aunty's Romance
How Mr. Bullington Ran the House
13: Rose of Surrey
Jean's Evidence
The Lucky Stone
14: The Murdock Trial
Through the Valley of Shadows
Creatures of Habit
Daisy's Doodad's Dial
Flotilla the Flirt
The Shepherd Lassie of Argyle
For Her People
15: Shopgirl
Alone in London
My Old Dutch
As Ye Repent
16: Far from the Madding Crowd
Doorsteps
Grim Justice
17: East is East
19: Fool's Gold
21: Passion Fruit
24: Janice Meredith
25: Never the Twain Shall Meet
The Dark Angel
26: The Gilded Highway
27: Canceled Debts
Sally in our Alley
Broken Gates
Stranded
College
28: Marry the Girl
The Chinese Parrot
The Law and the Man
Walking Back
The Road to Ruin

28: Jazzland
Jean and the Calico Doll
29: Kid's Clever
30: Rampant Age T
31: The Ridin' Fool T
?? A Welsh Singer

Ben Turpin (1874-1940)
1909: Midnight Disturbance
Keystone Comedies
15: A Night Out
His New Job
16: Carmen
When Papa Died
His Blowout (or, The Plumber)
The Delinquent Bridegroom
The Iron Mitt
Hired and Fired
(The Leading Man)
A Deep Sea Liar
(The Landlubber)
For Ten Thousand Bucks
Some Liars
The Stolen Booking
Doctoring a Leak
(A Total Loss)
Poultry A La Mode (or, The Harem)
Ducking a Discord
He Did and He Didn't
Picture Pirates
Shot in the Fracas
Jealous Jolts
The Wicked City
17: A Circus Cyclone
The Musical Marvels
The Butcher's Nightmare
His Bogus Roast (or, A Cheerful Liar)
A Studio Stampede
Frightened Flirts
Why Ben Bolted (or, He Looked Crooked)
Masked Mirth
Bucking the Tiger
Caught in the End
A Clever Dummy
Lost--A Crook
A Pawnbroker's Heart
Roping Her Romeo
Are Waitresses Safe?
Taming Target Center
18: Sheriff Nell's Tussle
Saucy Madeline
The Battle Royal
Two Tough Tenderfeet
She Loved Him Plenty
Hide and Seek - Detectives
19: Cupid's Day Off
East Lynne With Variations
When Love is Blind
No Mother to Guide Him
Yankee Doodle in Berlin
Uncle Tom with the Cabin
Sleuths
Whose Little Wife Are You?
Salome Vs. Shenandoah
20: The Star Boarder
Down on the Farm
Married Life
Countess Bloggie
Bloggie's Vacation
Snakeville Hen Medic
Snakeville's Champion
Snakeville Debutantes
21: A Small Town Idol
Love's Outcast
Love and Doughnuts
22: Bright Eyes
Step Forward
Home Made Movies
23: The Shriek of Araby
Where's My Wandering Boy Tonight?
Pitfalls of a Big City
Asleep at the Switch
24: The Daredevil
Ten Dollars or Ten Days
The Hollywood Kid
Yukon Jake
Romeo and Juliet
3 Foolish Weeks
The Reel Virginian
25: Wild Goose Chaser
Raspberry Romance
The Marriage Circus
26: When a Man's a Prince
A Prodigal Bridegroom
A Harem Knight
A Blonde's Revenge
27: A Hollywood Hero
The Jolly Jilter
Broke in China
Pride of Pikeville
Love's Languid Lure

27: Daddy's Boy
28: Hogan's Alley
Steel Preferred
College Hero
Wife's Relations
29: Show of Shows T
The Love Parade T
30: Swing High T
32: Make Me a Star T
Million Dollar Legs T
Hypnotized T

Tom Tyler (1903-1954)
1926: The Cowboy Cop
Mystery Valley
The Masquerade Bandit
The Cowboy Musketeer
Born to Battle
The Arizona Streak
Red Hot Hoofs
Out of the West
Wild to Go
27: Lightning Lariats
The Sonora Kid
Cyclone of the Range
The Flying U Ranch
The Cherokee Kid
Desperate Pirate
Splitting the Breeze
28: Phantom of the Range
Texas Tornado
When the Law Rides
Avenging Rider
Tyrant of Red Gulch
Terror Mountain
Hearts and Hoofs
The Eagle's Talons (serial)
The Road to Eldorado
The Battling Buckaroo
Mystery Valley
29: Idaho Red SSE
The Phantom Rider
The Man from Nevada
Trail of Horse Thieves
Gun Law
Pride of the Pawnee
Neath Western Skies
Lone Horseman

Lenore Ulric (1892-)
1915: Capital Punishment
The Better Woman
Kilmeny
16: The Heart of Paula
Intrigue
The Road to Love
17: Her Own People
23: Tiger Rose
29: Frozen Justice T
South Sea Rose T

Vola Vale
1916: The Eagle's Wings
The Adventures of the Last Cigarette
The Woman He Feared
17: The Price of Silence
Each To His Kind
The Secret of Black Mountain
The Son of His Father
The Silent Man
18: The Bloodhound
Wolves of the Rail
19: The Hornet's Nest
Happy Though Married
Heart in Pawn
Hearts Asleep
Six Feet Four
20: Alias Jimmy Valentine
Someone in the House
A Master Stroke
The Iron Rider
22: Daughters of the Rich
Mothers-In-Law
23: The Man Between
Crashing Through
24: Alimony

Grace Valentine (1890-)
1915: New Adam and Eve
16: Dorian's Divorce
Brand of Cowardice
17: Babbling Tongues
Unchastened Woman

Rudolph Valentino (1895-1926)
1916: Isle of Love
Ambition
18: All Night (or, The Marriage Virgin)
A Society Sensation
19: Eyes of Youth
Alimony
The Big Little Person
Delicious Little Devil

19: The Rogue's Romance
Out of Luck
The Homebreaker
The Greatest Thing in Life
20: Once to Every Woman (or, The Scarlet Power)
Passion's Playground
Stolen Moments
An Adventuress
The Cheater
A Lady of Quality
The Wonderful Chance
The Married Virgin (re-issued as All Night)
21: The Great Moment
4 Horsemen of the Apocalypse
Uncharted Seas
Camille
The Conquering Power
The Sheik
22: Moran of the Lady Letty
Beyond the Rocks
Blood and Sand
The Young Rajah
Frivolous Wives (another title of The Married Virgin)
Isle of Love (re-issue of An Adventuress)
23: The Fog
24: Monsieur Beaucaire
The Sainted Devil
The Sheik's Physique
25: The Cobra
The Eagle
26: The Son of the Sheik

Virginia Valli (1895-1968)

1916: The Girl Next Door
17: Skinner's Dress Suit
Efficiency Edgar's Courtship
The Golden Idiot
The Fibbers
18: Uneasy Money
20: The Plunger
The Very Idea
Love's Penalty
21: Sentimental Tommy
A Trip to Paradise
The Idle Rich
The Man Who
22: The Black Bag
The Storm
For Your Daughter's Sake
The Village Blacksmith
23: In the Palace of the King
A Lady of Quality
The Shock
24: Signal Towers
Wild Oranges
K--the Unknown
25: Siege
Up the Ladder
The Man Who Found Himself
26: Watch Your Wife
The Family Upstairs
Flames
Pleasure Garden
Price of Pleasure
27: Ladies Must Dress
Stage Madness
Evening Clothes
East Side West Side
Marriage
Paid to Love
Judgment of the Hills
28: Street of Illusion
Escape
29: Isle of Lost Ships T
Mr. Antonio
Behind Closed Doors
30: Storm
The Lost Zeppelin T
??: The Silver Lining

Mabel Van Buren

1915: The Money Master
16: The Sowers
The Victoria Cross
17: The Silent Partner
The Jaguar's Claws
Unconquered
The Squaw Man's Son
Hashimuro Togo
Countess Charming
The House with the Golden Windows
19: Hearts of Men
20: Conrad in Quest of His Youth
21: Four Horsemen of the Apocalypse
28: Ramona

Truman Van Dyke (1897-)

1917: The Peddler
18: A Lady's Name
19: Wishing Ring Man
Over the Garden Wall
20: The Red Glove
Betty Reforms
21: The Mad Marriage

Harry Van Meter

1916: Beachcombers
17: Princess Virtue
A Man's Man
18: Beloved Rogues
Broadway Love
19: A Man's Fight
The Day She Paid
Out of the Ashes
20: Judah
Alias Miss Dodd
The Cheater
21: Reputation
The Beautiful Gambler
Dangerous Love

Victor Varconi (1896-1958)

1920: Feet of Clay
22: Sodom and Gomorrah
24: Triumph
Changing Husbands
25: The Dancers
26: Last Days of Pompeii
Volga Boatman
Silken Shackles
For Wives Only
27: King of Kings
Angel of Broadway
Fighting Love
Forbidden Woman
28: Chicago
Tenth Avenue
Sinners' Parade
Dance Fever
29: Divine Lady SSE
Eternal Love SSE
King of Bernina T
30: Captain Thunder T
31: Doctors' Wives T
Men in Her Life T
32: Doomed Battalion T
33: The Rebel T
The Song You Gave Me T

Alberta Vaughn (1906-)

1923: Fighting Blood (serial)
Flip Flops
24: Smile Please
Picking Peaches
Telephone Girl (serial)
26: Adventures of Mazie (serial)
Ain't Love Funny?
Adorable Deceiver
27: Drop Kick
Uneasy Payments
Sinews of Steel
Back Stage
Romantic Age
28: Forbidden Hours
The Broadway Sap
Jessie's James
Wages of Synthetic
You Just Know She Dares 'em
The Arabian Fights
Ruth is Stranger than Fiction
Sweet Buy and Buy
Watch your Pep
Mild But She Satisfies
Six Fellows
That Wild Irish Pose
The Naughty Forties
Broadway Ladies
Queen of Burlesque
Age of Old Handicap
29: Noisy Neighbors
Molly and Me
Show of Shows T
Points West
?? Mack Sennett Comedies

Michael Vavitch

1924: His Hour
26: My Official Wife
27: Two Arabian Knights
Devil Dancer
Venus of Venice
28: Glorious Betsy PT
The Dove
The Woman Disputed
A Thief in the Dark
29: Wolf Song PT
The Divine Lady SSE
Mysterious Island PT
The Bridge of San Luis Rey PT

Conrad Veidt (1892-1943)

1917: Das Rasel Von Bangalore
19: The Cabinet of Dr. Caligari
20: Danton
21: Affairs of Lady Hamilton
22: NJU
24: The Waxworks
25: Violinist of Florence
26: Student of Prague
27: The Beloved Rogue
A Man's Past
Magic Flame
Husbands and Lovers
28: Hands of Orlac
Lady Hamilton
Brothers Schellenberg
Prince Cuckoo
Henry IV (German)
The Man Who Laughs
Love Makes Us Blind
Mystic Mirror
Unwelcome Children
Life's Mockery
Two Brothers
29: The Man Who Cheated Life
In Dalarna and Jerusalem
Erick the Great
Lucretia Borgia
3 Wax Men
The Last Performance PT
The Black Hussar T

Lupe Velez (1909-1944)

1927: The Gaucho
Sailors Beware
28: Stand and Deliver
29: Masquerade
The Wolf Song PT
Lady of the Pavements PT
Where East is East
Tiger Rose T
Love Song T

Bobby Vernon (1895-1939)

1913: Mike and Jake at the Beach
15: Our Dare Devil Chief
Fickle Fatty's Fall
The Hunt
16: Papa by Proxy
Haystacks and Steeples
Hearts and Sparks
A Social Club
The Danger Girl
16: Love on Skates
His Pride and Shame
Save the Pieces
17: Nick of Time Baby
Teddy at the Throttle
Dangers of a Bride
The Sultan's Wife
24: Bright Lights
25: French Pastry
Don't Pinch!
Air Tight
Watch Out!
Great Guns
Slippery Feet
26: Wife Shy
Yes, Yes, Babette
Sure Fire
Broken China
Dummy Love
Hoot Mon!
Page Me
27: Jail Birdies
Dead Easy
28: Sweeties
Hey, Rube!
Bugs My Dear
Hold 'em, Cowboy!
Stop Kidding
The Sock Exchange
Hot Sparks
Foot Loose Widows
30: Bobby Vernon in Cry Baby
31: Sheer Luck
32: Make Me a Star
?? appeared in Christie Comedies and Mack Sennett Comedies
Pearls in a Peach
Bobby Comes Marching Home
Fair, But False
Watch Your Step, Mother
Why Wild Men Go Wild
Oh Doctor, Doctor!
Exit Quietly
Pure and Simple
Fresh from the Farm
Barnyard Cavalier
One Stormy Night
A Hickory Hick
'tis the Bull
Pardon My Glove
Choose Your Weapon

?? In Dutch
Second Childhood
Take Your Chance
Coming Through the Rye
Back from the Front
Wedding Blues

Florence Vidor (1895-)

1916: The Yellow Girl
17: American Methods
The Countess Charming
A Tale of 2 Cities
18: Old Wives for New
Turn in the Road
Till I Come Back to You
Tong War
Widow's Might
Honor of His House
White Man's Law
19: The Bravest Way
Poor Relations
The Other Half
Better Times
20: The Family Honor
The Jack Knife Man
21: Lying Lips
Beau Revel
22: Hail the Woman
Woman, Wake Up!
Dusk to Dawn
Skin Deep
Conquering the Woman
The Real Adventure
23: Alice Adams
Main Street
The Virginian
24: Barbara Frietchie
The Marriage Circle
Christine of the Hungry Heart
The Mirage
Borrowed Husbands
The Flaming '40s
25: Are Parents People?
Trouble with Wives
Marry Me
26: You Never Know Women
The Grand Duchess and the Waiter
Sea Horses
Eagle of the Sea
Enchanted Hill
27: The Popular Sin
27: Afraid to Love
The World at Her Feet
One Woman to Another
Honeymoon Hate
28: Doomsday
The Magnificent Flirt
29: Chinatown Nights

Michael Visaroff (1890-1951)

1925: The Swan
26: Paris
27: Two Arabian Knights
28: The Last Command
Ramona
Cactus Trail
The Adventurer
We Americans
The Four Devils
Plastered in Paris
The Night Bird
29: Marquis Preferred
Hungarian Rhapsody SSE
The Exalted Flapper SSE
House of Horror PT
Disraeli T
Illusion T

Theodore Von Eltz (1889-1964)

1919: Way of the Strong
21: One Woman to Another
The Speed Girl
The 14th Lover
22: The Glorious Fool
23: The Woman with 4 Faces
Lights Out
The Common Law
Tiger Rose
24: Hearts of Oak
25: Paint and Powder
The Sea Wolf
26: Red Kimono
Fools of Fashion
Queen of Diamonds
Laddie
His New York Wife
Redhead Preferred
27: No Man's Law
Perch of the Devil
The Great Mail Robbery
Should Tall Men Marry?
28: Life's Mockery
Nothing to Wear
Way of the Strong

28: Love and the Law
Locked Doors
29: The Rescue
Very Idea T
Voice of the Storm
The Awful Truth T
Four Feathers SSE

Carl Von Hartman
1928: The Woman Disputed
The Awakening
29: Hell's Angels

Gustav Von Seyffertitz (1863-1943)
1917: The Devil Stone
18: Rimrock Jones
Less Than Kin
20: Dead Men Tell No Tales
22: When Knighthood was in Flower
The Face in the Fog
The Inner Man
Sherlock Holmes
25: The Goose Woman
Moriarity
Sherlock Holmes
26: Sparrows
The Bells
Diplomacy
The Lone Wolf Returns
Danger Girl
Red Dice
The Unknown Treasures
Private Izzy Murphy
Going Crooked
27: Magic Flame
Student Prince
The Gaucho
The Wizard
Barbed Wire
My Best Girl
Price of Honor
Birds of Prey
Rose of the Golden West
28: The Yellow Lily
Me Gangster SSE
Little Shepherd of Kingdom Come
It's All Greek to Me
The Docks of New York
War in the Dark
Red Mark
Vamping Venus
28: Mysterious Lady
29: His Glorious Night T
Canary Murder Case T
The Case of Lena Smith
Come Across PT
Seven Faces T
Chasing Through Europe SSE
31: Dishonored

Erich Von Stroheim (1885-1957)
1914: Captain Macklin
15: Birth of a Nation
The Failure
Ghosts
A Bold Impersonation
Old Heidelberg
16: The Social Secretary
His Picture in the Papers
Macbeth
Intolerance
Less than the Dust
17: Panthea
In Again Out Again
For Fance
Reaching for the Moon
Front for a Hotel
18: Hearts of the World
The Hun Within
The Unbeliever
19: Blind Husbands
Hearts of Humanity
20: The Devil's Passkey
22: Foolish Wives
23: Merry-Go-Round (co-dir.)
24: Greed (or, McTigue) (dir.)
25: Merry Widow (dir.)
28: Wedding March
The Honeymoon (never released--Part II of Greed)
Queen Kelly (unfinished)
29: The Great Gabbo T
Farewell to Thee T
32: Walking Down Broadway
33: (or, Hello, Sister)

Harold Vosburgh
1916: The Smugglers
21: What Every Woman Knows
If Women Only Knew
??: House of Mystery

Marie Walcamp (1894-)

1914: The Jungle Master
16: For Liberty (serial)
Hop, The Devil's Brew
The Flirt
John Needham's Double
Onda of the Orient
17: The Red Ace (serial)
Patria (serial)
The Red Glove (serial)
The Silent Terror
The Quest of Virginia
The Indian's Lament
18: The Lion's Claw (serial)
19: The Red Robe (serial)
Tongues of Flame (serial)
20: The Dragon's Net (serial)
21: The Blot

Ethel Wales

1921: Miss Lulu Bett
22: The Bonded Woman
The Old Homestead
23: The Covered Wagon
The Fog
Unguarded Gate
Gigi (or, John of Wood)
The Grail
24: Icebound
The Bedroom Window
25: Beggar on Horseback
26: Made for Love
27: Cradle Snatchers
Satin Woman
Girl in the Pullman
My Friend from India
Almost Human
On to Reno
Stage Kisses
28: Wreck of the Hesperus
The Perfect Crime
10th Avenue
Masks of the Devil
Taxi 13
Craig's Wife
29: The Doctor's Secret T
The Donovan Affair T
Blue Skies SSE
Saturday Night Kid T
30: Girl in the Show T

Wally Wales

1926: Vanishing Hoofs
26: Tearin' Loose
Riding Rivals
Double Daring
Twisted Triggers
The Fighting Cheat
Roaring Rider
Galloping On
The Hurricane Horseman
27: Cyclone Cowboy
Tearin' Into Trouble
Meddlin' Stranger
Skedaddle Gold
White Pebbles
Soda Water Cowboy
28: Desperate Courage
Saddle Mates
Desert of the Lost
The Flying Buckaroo

Charlotte Walker (1878-1958)

1915: Kindling
Out of the Darkness
16: The Trail of the Lonesome Pine
17: 7 Deadly Sins (Sloth-series)
The Lone Wolf
18: Pardners
Just a Woman
Men
19: Every Mother's Son
Eve in Exile
24: The 6th Commandment
25: Midnight Girl
26: The Savage
29: Paris Bound T
South Sea Rose T

Johnnie Walker (1894-1949)

1918: The Knife
20: Fantomas (serial)
Over the Hill
21: Live Wires
Play Square
What Love Will Do
22: Extra! Extra!
Jolt
My Dad
In the Name of the Law
23: Captain Fly-By-Night
The 4th Musketeer
Shattered Reputations
The Third Alarm
Children of Dust

23: Red Lights
24: Stepping Lively
Galloping Hoofs (serial)
25: Lilies of the Street
26: Transcontinental Limited
The Earth Woman
Honesty - The Best Policy
Old Ironsides
Morganson's Finish
Lightning Reporter
Wolves of the Air
27: Held by the Law
Fangs of Justice
Snarl of Hate
Princess of Broadway
Where Trails Begin
Boys of the Streets
Cross Breed
A Swelled Head
Pretty Clothes
28: Vultures of the Sea (serial)
Bare Knees
So This is Love?
Matinee Idol

Lillian Walker (1888-)
1911: A Tale of Two Cities
12: How Mr. Bullington Ran the House
Reincarnation of Karma
The Troublesome Step-Daughters
Stenographers Wanted
The Unseen Enemy
13: The Carpenter
The Artist's Madonna
The Accomplished Mrs. Thompson
The Persistent Mr. Prince
14: Love Luck and Gasoline
The New Secretary
15: A Model Wife
16: The Blue Envelope
17: Kitty McKay
Princess of Park Row
The Star Gazer
The Lust of the Ages
18: The Grain of Dust
19: A Joyous Liar
The Better Wife
Embarrassment of Riches
The Love Hunger
The White Man's Chance
20: $1,000,000 Reward (serial)
33: Enlighten Thy Daughter T
??: You and I

Morgan Wallace (1885-1953)
1920: Flying Pat
21: Dream Street
22: Orphans of the Storm
One Exciting Night
23: A Dangerous Maid

George Walsh (1892-)
1915: Don Quixote
16: Intolerance
The Island of Desire
The Beast
17: The Book Agent
The Yankee Way
Some Boy
Honor System
18: I'll Say So
This is the Life
The Pride of New York
Jack Spurlock - Prodigal
Brave and Bold
The Kid is Clever
19: Putting One Over
The Winning Stroke
Luck and Pluck
The 7th Person
Help! Help! Police!
Never Say Quit
On the Jump
20: The Plunger
From Now On
The Shark
The Dead Line
A Manhattan Knight
21: Number 17
Dynamite Allen
Serenade
22: With Stanley in Africa (serial)
23: Vanity Fair
Rosita
Slave of Desire
25: American Pluck
26: The Count of Luxembourg
The Prince of Broadway
The Kick-Off
The Test of Donald Norton
A Man of Quality
Striving for Fortune

27: Broadway Drifter
Winning Oar
Back to Liberty
28: Inspiration

Raoul Walsh (1889-)
1914: Sands of Fate
The Availing Prayer
The Great Leap
The Dishonored Medal
The Mystery of the Hindu Image
Sierra Jim's Reformation
For His Master
The Double Knot
The Final Verdict
15: The Birth of a Nation
The Smuggler
A Man for All of That
The Greaser

Henry B. Walthall (1870-1936)
1906: The Strange Case of Mary Page
07: A Convict's Sacrifice
09: Pranks
Choosing a Husband
Pippa Passes
In Old Kentucky
A Corner in Wheat
10: The Cloister's Touch
In Old California
11: A Little Child
Home Folks
12: My Hero
The Burglar's Dilemma
Wilful Peggy
A Summer Idyll
The Banker's Daughter
A Change of Spirit
The God Within
The Informer
Two Daughters of Eve
13: The Sheriff's Baby
Influence of the Unknown
Gangsters of New York
3 Friends
Oil and Water
Broken Ways
Classmates
Love in an Apartment Hotel
If We Only Knew
Death's Marathon
13: The Mistake
Two Men on the Desert
The Escape
Phantom of the House
The Lady and the Mouse
The Wanderers
The Perfidy of Mary
Her Mother's Oath
The Vengeance of Galora
14: Judith of Bethulia
Strongheart
The Soul of Honor
The Odalisque
The Avenging Conscience
Home Sweet Home
Beating Back
The Mountain Rat
Parted Curtains
The Mysterious Shot
The Floor Above
The Old Man
15: The Raven
Birth of a Nation
Ghosts
16: The Sting of Victory
The Come Back
Misunderstood
18: The Robe of Honor
Great Love
With Hoops of Steel
Humdrum Brown
19: False Faces
The Confession
A Long Lane's Turning
The Boomerang
And a Still Small Voice
The Long Arm of Mannister
Modern Husbands
20: A Splendid Hazard
21: Parted Curtains
22: The Able-Minded Lady
Flower of the North
Kick Back (or, The Come Back)
One Clear Call
23: Gimme
The Face on the Bar Room Floor
The Unknown Purple
24: Single Wives
Mine with the Iron Door
25: Kentucky Pride
The Golden Bed

25: The Plastic Age
26: Everybody's Acting
The Scarlet Letter
The Barrier
The Road to Mandalay
Three Faces East
The Ice Flood
Kit Carson Over the Great Divide
The Unknown Soldier
17: Street Corners
The Fighting Love
Enchanted Island
Light in the Window
Rose of Kildare
London After Midnight
Wings
18: Freedom of the Press
The Little Colonel
Jazz Age
Love Me and the World is Mine
The Man from Headquarters
29: The Trespasser T
Black Magic SSE
Speakeasy T
The Bridge of San Luis Rey PT
River of Romance T
In Old California T
Stark Mad
30: Abraham Lincoln
Tol'able David
Temple Tower
Blaze O'Glory
Retribution
Pay Off
32: Police Cort
33: Laughing at Life
Dark Hazard
Sin of Nora Moran
34: Viva Villa!
Change of Heart
35: Dante's Inferno
36: China Clipper

Gladys Walton (1904-)

1920: Pink Tights
Rich Girl, Poor Girl
Risky Business
21: The Girl Who Ran Wild
All Dolled Up
Desperate Youth
21: Short Skirts
The Rowdy
The Man Tamer
22: The Gutter Snipe
Second Hand Rose
The Trouper
Top o' the Morning
A Dangerous Game
The Lavender Bath Lady
High Heels
Playing with Fire
The Wise Kid
23: Crossed Wires
Sawdust
Untamable
Wild Party
Near Lady
The Love Letter
Gossip
The Town Scandal
?? The Secret Light

Fannie Ward (1872-1952)

1915: The Cheat
The Marriage of Kitty
16: The Years of the Locust
Tennessee's Partner
17: The School for Husbands
The Crystal Gazer
On the Level
Betty to the Rescue
Her Strange Wedding
The Sunset Trail
The Winning of Sally Temple
18: The Yellow Ticket
A Japanese Nightingale
Innocent
The Narrow Path
19: Common Clay
Our Better Selves
Cry of the Weak
The Profiteers
La Rafale
The Secret of the Lone Star
21: She Played and Paid
22: The Hardest Way
?? The Lure of Crooning Waters

Helen Ware

1915: Cross Currents

16: The Revolt
The Price
Secret Love
19: Third Degree
The Escape
20: The Deep Purple
21: Colorado Pluck
?? Garden of Allah

H. B. Warner (1876-1958)
1914: Lost Paradise
The Ghost Breaker
Your Girl and Mine
15: House of a 1000 Candles
16: The Beggar of Cawnpore
The Vagabond Prince
17: The Danger Trail
7 Deadly Sins (1)
God's Man
19: The Man Who Turned White
Pagan God
20: One Hour Before Dawn
The White Dove
Fugitive from Matrimony
Haunting Shadows
For a Woman's Honor
Maruga
Unchartered Channels
Grey Wolf's Ghost
Dice of Destiny
Felix O'Day
21: When We Were Twenty-One
23: Zaza
24: The Lone Fighter
The Dark Swan
26: Whispering Smith
Silence
The Temptress
27: King of Kings
Sorrell and Son
French Dressing
28: Wedding Rings
The Naughty Duchess
Man-Made Woman
Romance of a Rogue
29: Divine Lady SSE
Stark Mad T
The Doctor's Secret T
Conquest T
Trial of Mary Dugan T
The Gamblers T
The Argyle Case T
29: Show of Shows T
Tiger Rose T

Robert Warwick (1878-1965)
1914: The Dollar Mark
Man of the Hour
15: The Face in the Moonlight
16: Human Driftwood
17: The Argyle Case
The Mad Lover
A Modern Othello
18: The Silent Master
An Accidental Honeymoon
19: Secret Service
Told in the Hills
In Mizzoura
20: Hunting Trouble
City of Masks
An Adventure in Hearts
Jack Straw
Tree of Knowledge
Thou Art the Man!
21: The Fourteenth Man
24: Huntin' Trouble
29: Unmasked

Bryant Washburn (1889-1963)
1912: Voice of Conscience
14: The Promise Land
One Wonderful Night
At the End of a Perfect Day
15: The Little Straw Wife
The Blindness of Virtue
The Prince of Graustark
16: The Man Who Was Afraid
The Havoc
Marriage A La Carte
17: Skinner's Dress Suit
Skinner's Bubble
Skinner's Baby
The Fibbers
Sparks of Fate
The Masked Wrestler
Under Royal Patronage
The Golden Idiot
The Final Fraud
18: Till I Come Back to You
The Gypsy Trail
Venus in the East
The Poor Snob
21
Kidder & Co.

18: Ghost of the Rancho
19: It Pays to Advertise
The Way of a Man With a Maid
Why Smith Left Home
A Very Young Man
Something to Do
All Wrong
Love Insurance
Putting It Over
Destiny
Our People
An Old Old Song
Tides That Meet
Try and Get It
20: Six Best Cellars
What Happened to Jones
Too Much Johnson
Mrs. Temple's Telegram
Wet Paint
Sins of St. Anthony
An Amateur Devil
Burglar Proof
Sick-A Bed
21: A Full House
Road to London
22: Hungry Hearts
Night Life in Hollywood
June Madness
23: Rupert of Hentzau
Meanest Man in the World
Mine to Keep
Temptation
25: Passionate Youth
Wizard of Oz
26: Meet the Prince
Wet Paint
Sitting Bull at Spirit Lake
27: Sky Pirates
Her Sacrifice (Massacre)
In the First Degree
Black Tears
Breakfast at Sunrise
Beware of Widows
Love Thrill
28: Skinner's Big Idea
Honeymoon Flats
Undressed
Nothing to Wear
The Chorus Kid
A Bit of Heaven
Watered Stock
Jazzland

Blue Washington

1927: Blood Ship
By Whose Hand?
28: Wyoming
Beggars of Life PT
Ransom
There It Is
Do Your Duty
29: Phantom City
Black Magic SSE

Paul Weigel

1917: DuBarry
18: The Light
She Devil
19: Smiles
Evangeline
Luck in Pawn
The Beachcombers
20: Kismet
Breath of the Gods
Bullets of Justice
Right or Wrong
The Master Stroke
Merely Mary Ann
The Red Lane
27: Hidden Aces
Broadway After Midnight
28: Marry the Girl
Wagon Show

Niles Welch (1888-)

1916: Miss George Washington
17: The Gulf Between
Secret of the Storm Country
One of Many
18: Her Boy
Reclaimed
19: Law of Men
The Virtuous Thief
Stepping Out
Beckoning Roads
Jane Goes A-Wooing
20: Luck of Geraldine Laird
Courage of Marge O'Doone
21: The Spenders
Reputation
Who Am I?
Remorseless Love
22: Sin of Martha Queed
23: What Wives Want
Sawdust
Why Do We Live?

26: Ermine and Rhinestones
In Borrowed Plumes
The Spider Web

Charles West (1886-)

1909: Message of the Violin
10: A Romance of the Western Hills
12: The Would-Be Shriner
One in Business The Other in Crime
The Lesser Evil
An Outcast Among Outcasts
The Old Actor
The Massacre
The Girl and Her Trust
A Temporary Truce
From Out the Shadows
A Child's Impulse
Goddess of Sagebrush Gulch
Lodging for the Night
13: Just Gold
14: A Fair Rebel
18: White Man's Law
The Girl Who Came Back
Flash of Fate
19: His Divorced Wife
20: The Phantom Melody
Page Tim O'Brien
21: The Witching Hour
Black Roses
Bob Hampton of Placer
One in a Thousand
Not Guilty
22: Manslaughter
23: The Eternal Three
Red Lights
Things Have Changed
27: Nobody's Widow
28: The Man from Headquarters
29: Handcuffed T

William H. (Billy) West (1888-)

1912: The Parasite
Kentucky Girl
Cupid's Rival
Buck Stage
The Pest
The Slave
The Hero
The Candy Kid
The Stranger
12: The Rogue
The Scrapper
Playmates
Why Marry
In Again
He Loves Her Still
Service Stripes
Stolen Love
Wife Wanted
The Sap
Sweethearts
The Best Man Wins
15: His Lordship's Dilemma
Bright and Early
Straight and Narrow
The Messenger
21: The Orderly

Winifred Westover (1890-)

1916: Intolerance
Watch Out, William
Gift of the Desert
The Microscopic Mystery
The Matrimaniac
18: This Hero Stuff
Hobbs in a Hurry
19: Marked Men
John Petticoats
20: All the World to Nothing
Forbidden Trails
Firebrand Trevision
The Village Sleuth
Bucking the Tiger
Love's Masquerade
22: Anne of Little Smoky
30: The Lummox T
31: Old Lady

Stanhope Wheatcroft (1888-)

1916: East Lynne
Under Two Flags
17: A Modern Cinderella
19: The Right to Happiness
The Amazing Wife
The Blue Bonnet
The Old Town Girl
Destiny
The Veiled Adventure
20: The Breath of the Gods
Harmony Ranch
Way Down East
House of Toys
A Beggar in Purple

21: Their Mutual Child
Cold Steel
Dr. Jim
22: Hottentot
Manslaughter
Blood and Sand
23: Blow Your Own Horn
24: The Iron Horse
25: Madam Behave

Wheezer (1925-)
1927: Our Gang Kid Comedies

Alice White (1907-)
1927: The Sea Tiger
Satin Woman
American Beauty
Breakfast at Sunrise
The Private Life of Helen of Troy
28: The Mad Hour
The Big Noise
Three Ring Marriage
Lingerie
Show Girl
Gentlemen Prefer Blondes
Harold Teen
Naughty Baby SSE
Hot Stuff
Broadway Daddies
Show of Shows T
Girl from Woolworth's T
30: Playing Around

Leo White (1887-1948)
1915: His New Job
A Night Out
The Champion
In the Park
The Jitney Elopement
The Tramp
Work
A Woman
The Bank
Shanghaied
A Night in the Show
16: Police
Carmen (Chaplin)
Triple Trouble
The Floorwalker
The Fireman
The Vagabond
The Count
16: Behind the Scene
17: Easy Street
20: The Devil's Passkey
21: Keeping Up With Lizzie
22: Blood and Sand
23: Rustle of Silk
A Lady of Quality
24: Sporting Youth
Wolves of the North (serial)
The Goldfish
25: One Year to Live
26: Ben Hur
The Truthful Sex
27: McFadden's Flats
Lady Bird
See You in Jail
Beauty Shoppers
Bowery Cinderella
The Slaver
Girl from Gay Paree
28: What Price Beauty
Thunder Riders
Manhattan Knights
Silks and Saddles
29: Smilin' Guns
Born to the Saddle
Campus Knights
?? You Never Can Tell

Pearl White (1889-1938)
1910: The New Magdalene
11: The Necklace
Home Sweet Home
The Angel of the Slums
For Honor of the Name
12: The Girl in the Next Room
The Gypsy Flirt
Bella's Beau
The Chorus Girl
The Mind Cure
13: A Dip Into Society
Heroic Harold
That Other Girl
Pearl as a Detective
The Girl Reporter
Pearl and the Tramp
Pearl's Hero
Oh, You Pearl!
Pearl and the Poet
Pearl's Mistake
Where Charity Begins
14: The Ring
Lizzie and the Ice Man

14: The Perils of Pauline (serial)
15: The Exploits of Elaine (serial)
The Romance of Elaine (serial)
New Exploits of Elaine (serial)
The Hidden Voice
The Floating Coffin
The Hooded Helper
New York Lights
16: The King's Game
The Blossom and the Bee (serial)
The Iron Claw (serial)
Pearl of the Army (serial)
Hazel Kirke
17: May Blossoms
The Fatal Ring (serial)
18: The House of Hate (serial)
Perils of Paris (serial)
19: The Black Secret (serial)
The Lightning Raider (serial)
20: The White Moll
21: Know Your Men
A Virgin Paradise
The Tiger's Cub
The Thief
The Mountain Woman
Know Your Men
Beyond Price
22: Without Fear
The Broadway Peacock
Any Wife
23: Plunder (serial)
Hands of the Strangler (serial)
24: Terror
25: Parisian Nights

1915: Exploits of Elaine - Romance of Elaine

1. The Clutching Hand
The Twilight Sleep
The Vanishing Jewels
The Frozen Safe
The Poisoned Room
The Vampire
The Double Trap
The Hidden Voice
The Life Current
10. No Title
The Hour of 3
The Blood Crystals
The Devil Worshippers
The Reckoning
The Serpent Sign
The Cryptic Ring
The Watching Eye
The Vengeance of Wu Fang
The Saving Circle
20. Spontaneous Combustion
The Ear in the Wall
The Opium Smugglers
The Tell-Tale Heart
Shadows of War
The Lost Torpedo
The Gray Friar
The Vanishing Man
The Submarine Harbor
The Conspirators
30. The Wireless Detective
The Death Cloud
The Searchlight
The Life Chain
The Flash
The Disappearing Helmet
36. The Triumph of Elaine

1916: The Iron Claw

1. The Vengeance of Legar
The House of Unhappiness
The Cognac Cask
The Name and the Game
The Intervention of Tito
The Spotted Warning
The Hooded Helper
The Stroke of 12
Arrows of Hate
10. The Living Dead
The Saving of Dan O'Mara
The Haunted Canvas
The Hidden Face
The Plunge for Life
The Double Resurrection
The Unmasking of Davy
The Vanishing Fakir
The Green-Eyed God
The Cave of Despair
20. The Triumph of the Laughing Mask

1916-1917: Pearl of the Army

1. The Traitor
Found Guilty
The Silent Menace

War Clouds
Somewhere in Grenada
Major Brent's Perfidy
For the Stars and Stripes
International Diplomacy
The Monroe Doctrine
10. The Silent Army
A Million Volunteers
The Foreign Alliance
Modern Buccaneers
The Flag Despoiler
15. The Colonel's Orderly

1917: The Fatal Ring
1. The Violet Diamond
The Crushing Walls
Borrowed Identity
The Warning on the Ring
Danger Underground
Rays of Death
The Signal Lantern
The Switch in the Safe
The Dice of Death
10. The Perilous Plunge
The Short Circuit
A Desperate Chance
A Dash of Arabia
The Painted Safe
The Dagger Duel
The Double Disguise
The Death Weight
The Subterfuge
20. The End of the Trail

1918: The House of Hate
1. The Hooded Terror
The Tiger's Eye
A Woman's Perfidy
Hooded Terror Pursues Man Who Would Reveal His Secret
American Outwits Spies
Liquid Fire Apparatus Tested
Deadly Germs Play a Part
The Untold Secret
Poisoned Darts
10. no title to 15
15. The False Signal
The Vial of Death
The Death Switch
Net Tightens About Mysterious Hooded Terror
Identity of Hooded Terror is Revealed
20. ?

1918-1919: The Lightning Raider
1. The Ebony Block
The Counterplot
Underworld Terrors
Through Doors of Steel
The Brass Key
The Mystic Box
Meshes of Evil
Cave of Dread
Falsely Accused
10. The Baited Trap
The Bars of Death
Hurled Into Space
The White Roses
Cleared of Guilt
15. Wu Fang Atones

1919: The Black Secret
1. The Great Secret
Marked of Death
The Gas Chamber
No Title
No Title
No Title
The Betrayal
A Crippled Hand
Woes of Deceit
10. The Inn of Dread
The Death Studio
The Chance Trail
13. ?
14. ?
15. ?

1922-1923: Plunder
1. The Bandaged Man
Held by the Enemy
The Hidden Thing
Ruin
To Beat a Knave
Heights of Hazard
Mocked from the Grave
The Human Target
Game Clear Through
10. Against Time
Spunk
Under the Floor
The Swamp of Lost Souls
The Madman

15. A King's Ransom

Lloyd Whitlock (1900-1962)

1917: A Gentle Ill Wind
The Edge of the Law
19: Lasca
Rouge and Riches
The Boomerang
The Love Call
Rose Marie
20: Scratch My Back
The Cowpuncher
21: One Man in a Million
See My Lawyer
The Love Special
White and Unmarried
Courage
26: New Champion
Man in the Saddle
Paradise
27: War Horn
Pretty Clothes
28: Hot Heels
Queen of the Chorus
The Michigan Kid
The Man from Headquarters
House of Shame
Kid's Clever
29: The Leatherneck PT

Alfred Whitman (1890-)

1916: Enchantment
Her Father's Son
17: Souls in Pawn
Tongues of Flame
Days of '49
Trick of Fate
End of the Game
The Best Man
Princess in the Dark
The Serpent's Tooth
18: Sunlight's Last Raid
When Men are Tempted
The Flaming Omen
The Wild Strain
Cavanaugh of the Forest Rangers
The Home Trail
The Girl from Beyond
Baree, The Son of Kazan
A Gentleman's Agreement
The Eighth Great-Grand Parent

Gayne Whitman

1926: Oh, What a Nurse!
The Love Toy
The Night Cry
His Jazz Bride
Hell-Bent for Heaven
A Woman's Heart
Exclusive Rights
Stolen Pleasures
Wolves of the Air
Sunshine of Paradise Alley
27: Back Stage
Too Many Crooks
Woman on Trial
28: The Adventurer
The Ghetto
29: Lucky Boy

Claire Whitney

1914: Life's Shop Window
15: The Nigger
16: Ruling Passions
17: The Victim
The New York Peacock
When False Tongues Speak
Thou Shalt Not Steal
Camille
Shirley Kane
18: The Better 'ole
The Man Who Stayed at Home
The Romance of Old Bill
19: The Kaiser's Finish
Career of Katherine Bush
Isle of Conquest
20: Mothers of Men
Love, Honor and Obey
The Passionate Pilgrim
21: Fine Feathers
22: The Leech
??: Neglected Wives

Crane Wilbur (1889-)

1911: For Massa's Sake
12: The Compact
A Nation's Peril
14: The Perils of Pauline (serial)
The Corsair
All Love Excelling
15: Road of Strife (serial)
17: The Blood of His Fathers
The Spite Husband

17: The Painted Lie
Unlucky Jim
The Morals of Men
The Eye of Envy
Heirs of Hate
19: Devil M' Care
Breezy Jim
Unto the End
Finger of Justice
Stripped for a Million
20: Something Different
21: Heart of Maryland

Earle Williams (1880-1927)
1910: The Wager
11: Saving an Audience
13: Happy-Go-Lucky
The Lady of the Lake
The Seventh Son
13: The Artist's Madonna
A Soul in Bondage
The Tiger Lady
The Carpenter
War
14: My Official Wife
Two Women
The Christian
15: The Goddess (serial)
The Awakening
The Juggernaut
16: My Lady's Slipper
The Scarlet Runner
17: Arsene Lupin
The Love Doctor
In the Balance
18: The Seal of Silence
The Grell Mystery
A Mother's Sin
An American Live Wire
The Girl in His House
19: A Rogue's Romance
The Man Who Wouldn't Tell
The Highest Trump
The Wolf
The Usurper
The Hornet's Nest
A Gentleman of Quality
A Diplomatic Mission
20: The Fortune Hunter
The Black Gate
When a Man Loves
21: A Master Stroke
21: Captain Swift
The Silver Case
The Purple Cipher
The Romance Promoters
Diamonds Adrift
It Can Be Done
22: The Man from Downing Street
Bring Him In
Restless Souls
Fortune's Mask
You Never Know
The Hillman
23: The Eternal Struggle
Jealous Fools
24: Borrowed Husbands
The Painted Lady
25: The Ancient Mariner
26: The Skyrocket
Diplomacy
You'd Be Surprised
27: Say It With Diamonds
??: My Official Wife

Guinn "Big Boy" Williams (1899-1962)
1919: Almost a Husband
22: Western Firebrands
Trail of Hate
Across the Border
Blaze Away
Rounding Up the Law
23: Freshie
End of the Rope
Cyclone Jones
24: King of the Wild Horses
25: Red Blood and Blue
Whistling Jim
Black Cyclone
26: Brown of Harvard
27: Slide, Kelly, Slide
Quarantined Rivals
Back Stage
Snowbound
Down Grade
Lightning
The College Widow
It's All Greek To Me
28: Vamping Venus
Ladies' Night in a Turkish Bath
Burning Daylight
29: Noah's Ark PT

29:	My Man	PT
	Man from Headquarters	PT
	The Forward Pass	T
	Lucky Star	T

Kathlyn Williams (1888-1960)

1908: Harbor Island
10: The Fire Chief's Daughter
Mazeppa
11: The Two Orphans
Back to the Primitive
Maude Miller
10 Nights in a Bar Room
12: The Last Dance
The Coming of Columbus
13: A Mansion of Misery
Wise Old Elephant
A Child of the Sea
The Adventures of Kathlyn (serial)
Lost in the Jungle (serial)
14: The Spoilers
Story of the Blood Red Rose
The Leopard's Foundling
Chip of the Flying U.
15: The Juggernaut
16: Sweet Lady Peggy
The Ne'er-Do-Well
17: Big Timber
Redeeming Love
Out of the Wreck
18: The Highway of Hope
The Things We Love
The Whispering Chorus
We Can't Have Everything
19: The Better Wife
20: Just a Wife
Conrad in Quest of His Youth
A Girl Named Mary
Tree of Knowledge
The Prince Chap
21: Forbidden Fruit
Hush
The U. P. Trail
A Man's Home
Everything for Sale
A Private Scandal
22: Clarence
A Virginia Courtship
Morals
23: The Spanish Dancer
Trimmed in Scarlet
The World's Applause
24: Single Wives
The City That Never Sleeps
The Wanderer of the Wasteland
27: Sally in our Alley
28: Honeymoon Flats
Locked Doors
We Americans
Our Dancing Daughters
29: The Single Standard
A Single Man
30: Wedding Rings T

1913: Adventures of Kathlyn (episodes)
1. The Unwelcome Throne
2. The Two Ordeals
3. In the Temple of the Lions
4. The Royal Slave
5. A Colonel in Chains
6. 3 Bags of Silver
7. The Garden of Birds
8. The Cruel Crown
9. The Spellbound Multitude
10. ?
11. The Forged Parchment
12. The King's Will
13. The Court of Death

Ben Wilson (1885-)

1911: Her Brother's Crime
14: When the Cartridges Failed
While the Tide was Rising
17: The Mystery Ship (serial)
Who Will Marry Mary? (serial)
Voice on the Wire
18: The Brass Bullet (serial)
Trail of the Octopus (serial)
The Screaming Shadow (serial)
26: Tonio, Son of the Sierras
The Baited Trap
West of the Law
The Sheriff's Girl
Wolves of the Desert
27: The Mystery Brand
Riders of the West
Range Riders
Yellow Streak
29: Bye, Bye, Buddy

29: Girls Who Dare
China Slaver
The Branded Four (serial)
The Man from Nowhere

Lois Wilson (1896-)

1916: The Dumb Girl of Portici
17: A Man's Man
18: Alimony
Turn of a Card
His Robe of Honor
One Dollar Bid
19: It Pays to Advertise
End of the Game
Love Insurance
Why Smith Left Home
20: What's Your Hurry?
Too Much Johnson
Thou Art the Man
City of Masks
A Full House
Midsummer's Madness
21: Miss Lulu Bett
What Every Woman Knows
City of Silent Men
Hell Diggers
22: Our Leading Citizens
The World's Champion
Manslaughter
Is Marriage a Failure?
Without Compromise
Broad Daylight
23: The Covered Wagon
Only 38
To the Last Man
Call of the Canyon
Bella Donna
24: Monsieur Beaucaire
Icebound
North of '36
The Border Legion
25: The Vanishing American
The Pony Express
Irish Luck
26: The Great Gatsby
Show-Off
Bluebeard's Seven Wives
Let's Get Married
27: New York
Broadway Nights
Gingham Girl
Alias the Lone Wolf
28: French Dressing
28: On Trial T
Sally's Shoulders
Coney Island
Ransom
29: The Gamblers T
Advice to Husbands
Bird in the Hand
Object: Alimony
Kid Gloves PT
Conquest T
Show of Shows T
30: Wedding Rings

Margery Wilson

1915: Bred in the Bone
The Mother Instinct
A Corner in Colleen's
The Honorable Algy
Double Trouble
16: Intolerance (dual role)
Eye of the Night
Return of Draw Egan
Upholding the Law
The Primal Lure
17: Mountain Dew
Wild Sumac
Without Honor
The Clodhopper
The Desert Man
Wolf Lowry
The Kentucky School
Master
Lupin Gal
Bearing her Cross
18: The Flames of Chance
The Hard Rock Breed
The Law of the Great
Northwest
The Hand at the Window
19: Desert Gold
Crooked Straight
20: The Blooming Angel
21: That Some Thing
22: The Offenders
Insinuation
23: Finger Prints
26: Old Love for New
Marked Cards

Tom Wilson (1880-1965

1915: The Birth of a Nation
16: Atta Boy's Last Race
Intolerance

17: The Americano
Wild and Woolly
18: Amarilly of Clothesline Alley
A Dog's Life
19: Shoulder Arms
A Day's Pleasure
Sunnyside
The Greatest Question
20: Isobel
21: Scrap Iron
2 Minutes To Go
The Kid
Don't Ever Marry
Dinty
22: Minnie
Reported Missing
Alias Julius Caesar
23: Quicksands
My Wife's Relations
The Remittance Woman
The Courtship of Miles Standish
25: California Straight Ahead
26: Battling Butler
When a Man Loves
27: Ham and Eggs at the Front
28: Riley the Cop
29: Strong Boy SSE

Claire Windsor (1897-)
1916: The Heart of a Fool
19: Luck of the Irish
20: To Please One Woman
21: The Blot
What Do Men Want?
What's Worth While?
To Wise Wives
22: Fools First
One Clear Call
The Eternal Flame
Rich Men's Wives
Grand Larceny
Broken Chains
Brothers Under the Skin
23: The Stranger's Banquet
Rupert of Hentzau
Little Church Around the Corner
The Acquittal
24: Born Rich
For Sale
Son of the Sahara
24: The Beautiful Cloak Model
25: The Lady Who Lied
Souls for Sables
The White Desert
26: Dance Madness
Tin Hats
Money Talks
27: Foreign Devils
The Bugle Call
A Little Journey
The Claw
The Frontiersman
Blondes by Choice
Opening Night
28: Satan and the Woman
The Clash
The Grain of Dust
The Family Row
Fashion Madness
Nameless Men
Domestic Meddlers
29: Captain Lash SSE
Midstream PT

Dick Winslow (1915-)
1928: Avalanche
29: Sweetie T
The Virginian T
Marianne T
30: Sarah and Son T
Not One to Fail T

Laska Winters
1926: Rocking Moon
27: Night of Love
The Tender Hour
Satin Woman
28: Fashion Madness
The Rescue
Seven Footprints to Satan SSE
Mysterious Dr. Fu Manchu T
Frozen Justice T

Jane Winton (1905-1959)
1926: Don Juan
Across the Pacific
Why Girls Go Back Home
Honeymoon Express
The Passionate Quest
27: Perch of the Devil
Upstream

27: Monkey Talks
Beloved Rogue
Gay Old Bird
The Poor Nut
Lonesome Ladies
Sunrise
Fair Co-Ed
28: Bare Knees
Burning Daylight
The Patsy
The Yellow Lily
Melody of Love
Honeymoon Flats
Nothing to Wear
29: Captain Lash SSE
The Bridge of San Luis Rey PT
Scandal PT

Grant Withers (1904-1959)
1927: Final Extra
Upstream
28: Bringing Up Father
Golden Shackles
Tillie's Punctured Romance
The Road to Ruin
Nothing to Wear
Life's Like That
29: Greyhound Limited PT
Saturday's Children PT
Madonna of Avenue A PT
The Time, Place, and the Girl T
Show of Shows T
Hearts in Exile T
Tiger Rose T
In the Headlines T
30: So Long Letty T

Louis Wolheim (1880-1931)
1920: Dr. Jekyll and Mr. Hyde
A Manhattan Knight
21: Number #17
22: The Face in the Fog
Orphans of the Storm
Sherlock Holmes
23: Little Old New York
Unseeing Eyes
Enemies of Women
24: The Story Without a Name
America
26: Lover's Island
27: Two Arabian Knights
Sorrell and Son
28: The Racket
Tempest
The Awakening
29: Wolf Song PT
Shady Lady PT
Square Shoulders PT
Condemned T
Frozen Justice T
30: Ship from Shanghai T

Anna May Wong (1907-1961)
1920: Dinty
21: Bits of Life
Shame
22: Toll of the Sea
24: The Thief of Bagdad
The 40th Door (serial)
25: Peter Pan
40 Winks
His Supreme Moment
26: 5th Avenue
The Desert's Toll
A Trip to Chinatown
27: Old San Francisco
Mr. Wu
The Chinese Parrot
Driven from Home
Streets of Shanghai
28: Across to Singapore
Show Life
Chinatown Charlie
Devil Dancer
Crimson City
29: Piccadilly SSE
My Souvenirs T

Bert Woodruff (1856-)
1916: Jim Bludson
17: A Love Sublime
Men of the Desert
19: The Busher
Greased Lightning
Bill Henry
20: Paris Green
Homer Comes Home
The Jailbird
21: See My Lawyer
Eighty Dollars
Two Minutes To Go
22: Making a Man
The Rosary
Watch Your Step

22: The Grim Comedian
23: A Noise in Newboro
Children of Dust
Isle of Lost Ships
25: The Fighting Heart
26: The Barrier
27: Fire Brigade
Spring Fever
28: Speedy
The Awakening
Manhattan Cocktail
Marked Money SSE
?? Veteran Sinners
Flaming Gold

Harry Woods (1889-1968)
1927: Silver Comes Through
Jesse James
28: Red Riders of Canada
Sunset Legion
When the Law Rides
The Candy Kid
Mystery Valley
The Battling Buckaroo
Love and the Law
29: Gun Law
Desert Rider
China Bound
Phantom Rider
The Viking
Neath Western Skies

Barbara Worth
1927: Prairie King
Fast and Furious
28: Fearless Rider
On Your Toes

Helen Lee Worthing
1924: Janice Meredith
25: Night Life of New York
26: The Other Woman's Story
Watch Your Wife
27: Vanity
Thumbs Down

William Worthington (d. 1941)
1915: The Grail
In Search of a Wife
On the Level
17: The Devil's Pay Day
22: Grand to Fight
Out of the Silent North
23: Red Lights
The Green Goddess
26: Her Honor, the Governor
28: Happiness Ahead
Good Morning, Judge
Half a Bride

Fay Wray (1907-)
1923: Gasoline Love
26: Wild Horse Stampede
27: Loco Luck
One Man Game
28: Legion of the Condemned
Street of Sin
First Kiss
Wedding March
Honeymoon (unreleased)
29: Four Feathers SSE
Thunderbolt T
Pointed Heels T
30: Behind the Makeup T

Edith Yorke (1872-)
1920: Homespun Folks
The False Road
Below the Surface
21: Chickens
Lying Lips
Passing Through
22: A Daughter of Luxury
Step On It
One Clear Call
23: Slippery McGee
Souls for Sale
The Fourth Musketeer
Don't Marry for Money
Merry-Go-Round
25: Phantom of the Opera
26: His New York Wife
Rustlers Ranch
Belle of Broadway
Heart of a Coward
27: Timid Terror
Sensation Seekers
28: Satan and the Woman
Port of Missing Girls
Making the Varsity
29: Fugitives SSE
The Valiant T
Seven Keys to Baldpate T

Clara Kimball Young (1900-1960)
1912: The Little Minister

12: Beau Brummel
Cardinal Wolsey
Happy-Go-Lucky
Anne Boleyn
13: Women Go On The Warpath
14: Lola
Hamlet
The Violin of M'sieur
Good Gracious
Feast of Life
My Official Wife
Yellow Passport
Fates and Flora Fourflush
Ten Billion Dollar Vitagraph Mystery (serial)
15: Hearts in Exile
Heart of the Blueridge
The Deep Purple
Camille
Trilby
The Foolish Virgin
16: Rise of Susan
La Rubia
17: The Easiest Way
Magda
Shirley Kaye
She Paid the Price
The Marionettes
18: The Claw
The Savage Woman
Road Through the Dark
The Reason Why
Cheating Cheaters
19: Charge It
Eyes of Youth
The Better Wife
20: Forbidden Woman
Mid-Channel
For the Soul of Rafael
21: Hush
Straight from Paris
22: The Hands of Nara
Enter Madame
What No Man Knows
23: Cordelia the Magnificent
The Wife's Romance
24: The Woman of Bronze

Loretta Young (1914-)
1918: The Only Way
21: The Sheik
27: Naughty But Nice
28: Laugh, Clown, Laugh
28: The Head Man
Magnificent Flirt
Scarlet Seas SSE
Whip Woman
29: Girl in the Glass Cage PT
The Squall T
Fast Life T
Careless Age T
Forward Pass T
Show of Shows T

Polly Ann Young (1908-)
1928: Masks of the Devil

Tammany Young (d. 1935)
1917: The Amazons
18: The Service Star
The Racing Strain
19: Checkers
Lost Battalion
The Woman on the Index
A Regular Girl
20: The Imp
Our Gray Brothers
21: Bits of Life
The Right Way
22: The Seventh Day
Rainbow
John Smith
When the Desert Calls
Till We Meet Again

Vital Statistics

	Height	Weight	Hair	Eyes
Art Acord -	6'1"	185	br	lt bl
Spottiswoode Aitken -	6'2"		gr	bl
Ben Alexander-	4'7 1/2		bl	bl
Hugh Allan -	6'	160	blk	br
Don Alvarado -	5'11"	160	blk	br
Robert Ames -	5'10"	155	fair	bl
"Fatty" Arbuckle -	5'10"	245	lt br	bl gr
Richard Arlen -	5'11"	150	med br	bl
George Arliss -	5'9"	140	wh	br
Robert Armstrong -	5'10"	160	br	br
George K. Arthur -	5'6"	145	dk br	br
Johnny Arthur -	5'8"	140	br	br
Nils Asther	6' 1/2"	170	dk	br
Edwin August -	5'11"	155		
William Austin -	6'1"	170	br	bl
King Baggot -	6'	185	br	bl
George Bancroft -	6'2"	195	br	br
Monty Banks -	5'5"	120	blk	bl
Ben Bard -	5'11"	160	blk	br
T. Roy Barnes -	5'11"	172	br	bl
Nigel Barrie -	5'1"	175	br	bl
Wesley Barry -	5'6"		red	bl
John Barrymore -				
Lionel Barrymore -	5'11"	155	br	bl
Richard Barthelmess -	5'7"	135	blk	br
Warner Baxter -	5'11"	168	br	br
George Beban -	5'4"	130	br	br
Noah Beery -	6'1"	216	br	br
Wallace Beery -				
Rex Bell -	6'	134	fair	bl
Lionel Belmore -	5'11"	225	gr	haz
Joseph Bennett -	5'11"	162	dk br	bl
Richard Bennett -	5'10"	160	lt br	dk gr
Andre Beranger -	5'10"	150	dk br	br
Mathew Betz -	6'	180	dk br	bl
Billy Bevan -	5'7 1/2	170	br	br
Carlyle Blackwell -	5'11"	155	dk br	br
Monte Blue -	6'2"	185	dk br	br
John Boles	6'1"	185	br	gr-bl
Hobart Bosworth	6'	200	gr	bl
Wade Boteler -	6'	180	aub	bl
John Bowers	6'	175	br	br

Bill Boyd -	6'1"	170	br	bl
Sidney Bracy -	5'9"	138	br	dk br
Ed Brady -	5'10 1/2	165	br	br
Edmund Breese -	5'9 1/2		gr	bl
El Brendel -	5'9"	165	lt br	bl
Clive Brook -	5'11"	149	br	gr
Tyler Brooke -	5'8"	130	br	haz
Joe E. Brown -	5'7 1/2	149	dk br	bl
Johnny Mack Brown -	5'11"	175	blk	br
Otto Brower -	5'10"	158	dk	dk
Edmund Burns -	6'2"	170	blk	bl gr
Neal Burns -	5'6"	141	br	br
Clarence Burton -	5'11"	176	br	br
Francis X. Bushman -	5'11"	186	br	bl
David Butler -	6'	185	blk	bl
Walter Byron -	6'	163	br	lt bl
E. H. Calvert -	6'1"	200	br	br
Frank Campeau -	5'10"	158	dk br	gr
Eddie Cantor -	5'8"		blk	dk br
Harry Carey -	6'	180	lt br	bl
Richard Carle -	5'11 1/2	190	br	br
Richard Carlyle -	5'9"	145	br	bl
Georges Carpentier -	5'11 1/2	190	fair	bl
Joseph Cawthorn -	5'8 1/2	165	white	haz
George Chandler -	5'8"	140	br	br
Lane Chandler -	6'3"	188	aub	bl
Lon Chaney -	5'9"	155	blk	br
Charlie Chaplin -	5'6"	125	br	bl
Syd Chaplin -	5'7 1/2	165	blk	br
Charley Chase -	6'	155	br	bl
Berton Churchill -	5'11 1/2		white	bl
Frank Clark -	5'9"	170	fair	gr
Charles Clary -	6'	190	dk gr	haz
Elmer Clifton -	5'11"	170	br	br
Andy Clyde -			br	bl
Edmund Cobb -	6' 1/2	165	br	br
Joey Cobb -	4'10"	119	br	haz
Lew Cody -	5'11"	176	blk	br
Junior Coglan -	4'2"	63	br	br
Nick Cogley -	5'7 1/2	195	fair	bl
William Collier Jr. -	5'10"	155	blk	bl
Ronald Coleman -	5'11"	160	br	br
Jackie Condon -	5'3"	73	bl	bl
Chester Conklin -	5'5"	155	br	bl
Heinie Conklin -	5'6 1/2	150	blk	br
Albert Conti -	6'	150	br	br
Jackie Coogan -	6'		ltbr	br
Clyde Cook -	5'6"	142	br	bl
Hallam Cooley -	6'	167	dk br	haz
Gary Cooper -	6'2 1/2	178	dk br	bl
George Cooper -	5'9 1/2	162	br	br
Jackie Cooper -	4'3"	73	br	haz

Ricardo Cortez -	6'1"	175	blk	br
Maurice Costello -	5'10"	180	gr	bl gr
Ward Crane -	5'11"	175	dk br	br
Irving Cummings -	5'11"	170	blk	br
Frank Currier -	5'11"	180	gr	haz
Jack Curtis -	6'	200		
Sidney D'Albrook -	5'10"	155	blk	blk
Karl Dane -	6'3 1/2	205	brn	bl
Roy D'Arcy -	5'11"	158	br	gr
Max Davidson -	5'4"	130	blk	bl
William Davidson -	6'1"	195	dk	bl
Nigel De Brulier -	5'8"	128	blk	br
Sam De Grasse -	5'10"	150	dk br	br
Charles Delaney -	5'10 1/2	160	br	br
William Demarest -	5'11"	185	lt br	gr
C. B. DeMille -	5'11"	176	br	bl
William deMille -	5'9"	155	br	br
Reginald Denny -	6'	178	br	bl
Vernon Dent -	5'9"	250	br	bl
William Desmond -	5'11"	180	dk br	bl
Andy Devine -	6'	190	br	bl
Elliott Dexter -			blk	br
Richard Dix -	6'	180	br	br
Billy Dooley -	6'	145	bl	bl
Joseph Dowling -	6'1"	185	white	bl
Roland Drew -	6'	165	blk	br
Jack Duffy -	5'7"	132	br	bl
Tom Dugan -	5'8"	145	br	br
Bud Duncan -	4'11"	122	fair	bl
William Duncan -	5'10"	180	dk br	br
Edward Earle -	5'11 1/2	160	gr	bl
Robert Edeson -	6'	185	gr	haz
Neely Edwards -	5'5"	148	dk br	dk gr
Robert Elliott -	6'1 1/2	185	dk br	bl
Robert Ellis -	5'	170	br	bl
Julian Eltinge -	5'8"	165	br	gr
Douglas Fairbanks Jr. -	6'1"	170	br	bl
Douglas Fairbanks Sr. -	5'10"	165	br	br
William Fairbanks -	5'11	195	dk br	br
Farina -			blk	blk
James Farley -	5'11"	180	gr	dk br
Dustin Farnum -	6'	186	br	br
Franklyn Farnum -	5'11"	170	blk	br
William Farnum -	5'10"	195	br	bl
Charles Farrell -	6'2"	178	br	br
William Faversham -	6'1"	180	gr	bl
George Fawcett -	5'9"	180	gr	bl
Leslie Fenton -	6'	168	dk br	gr
Al Ferguson -	6'	185	br	br
Casson Ferguson -	5'11"	150	br	bl gr

W. C. Fields -	5'8"	160	gr	bl
Clyde Fillmore -	6'2"	195	br	gr
Paul Fix -	5'11"	145	br	br
Maurice Flynn -	6'2"	180	br	bl
Ralph Forbes -	5'11"	165	bl	dk bl
Harrison Ford -	5'10"	160	br	br
Tom Forman -			fair	bl
Allan Forrest -	6'	160	dk	dk
Norman Foster -	5'11"	170	blk	br
Earle Foxe -	6'2"	198	dk br	bl
Alec B. Francis -	5'11 1/2	160	gr	br
Robert Frazer -	6'	170	dk br	br
Douglas Gerrard -	5'10"	175	br	br
Hoot Gibson -	5'10"	160	bl	bl
Billy Gilbert -	5'11"	235	blk	br
John Gilbert -	5'11"	135	br	br
William Gillespie	5'11"	175	blk	gr
Claude Gillingwater -	6'2"	168	gr	br
Joseph Girard -	6'	198	gr	dk br
Gaston Glass -	5'10 1/2	160	dk br	br
James Gleason -	5'10"	150	gr	bl
Russell Gleason -	6'	150	lt br	bl
J. Frank Glendon -	6'	175	gr	br
Harold Goodwin -	6'2"	175	br	bl
C. Henry Gordon -	5'11"	165	dk br	br
Huntley Gordon -	6'	170	fair	bl
Gibson Gowland -	6'	196	br	bl
Lawrence Grant -	6'	175	gr	haz
Bertram Grassby -	6'	175	blk	blk
Ralph Graves -	6'2"	175	br	bl
Cesare Gravina -	5'	135	br	blk
Lawrence Gray -	5'10"	160	br	bl
Eddie Gribbon -	6'	190	br	bl
Harry Gribbon -	6'		dk br	bl
D. W. Griffith -	5'10"	190	br	gr
Raymond Griffith -	5'5 1/2	139	blk	bl gr
Kit Guard -	5' 8 1/2	150	lt br	bl
George Hackathorne -	5'7"	130	dk br	br
Frank Hagney -	6' 2 1/2	205	br	dk br
Robert T. Haines -	5'10"	174	dk	dk
William Haines-	6'	165	blk	br
Alan Hale -	6'	195	fair	bl
Creighton Hale -	5'9"	145	bl	bl
James Hall -	5'11"	158	lt br	bl
Winter Hall -	6'	180	gr	gr
Ray Hallor -	5'9 1/2	145	blk	gr
Lloyd Hamilton -	6'	200	lt br	bl
Mahlon Hamilton -	6'	185	lt br	bl
Neil Hamilton -	5'11"	155	br	br
Oliver Hardy -	6'1"	286	dk br	br
Sam Hardy -	6'3 1/2	195	br	br

Lumsden Hare -	6'	175	br	br
Kenneth Harlan -	6'1"	185	dk br	br
Otis Harlan -	5'5"	198	br	br
John Harron -	6'1 1/2	170	br	bl
Robert Harron -			br	br
Neal Hart -	5'9"	170	dk br	lt bl
William S. Hart -	6'1"	190	br	bl
Raymond Hatton -	5'7"	140	br	bl
Sessue Hayakawa -	5'7 1/2	157	blk	blk
Del Henderson -	6'1"	220	dk br	bl
Holmes Herbert -	5'11"	165	fair	gr
Jean Hersholt -	5'11"	185	br	br
Herbert Heyes -	6'1 1/2	190	br	br
Howard Hickman -	5'11"	175	gr	br
Walter Hiers -	5'10"	230	lt br	bl
Ernest Hilliard -	5'7"	160	br	br
Johnny Hines -	5'10"	155	blk	br
Otto Hoffman -	5'7 1/2	130	dk br	br
Thomas Holding -	6'	172	dk	bl
Stuart Holmes -	5'11"	180	gr	grn
Taylor Holmes -	5'8 1/2	150	dk br	br
Jack Holt -	6'	173	br	br
Edward Everett Horton -	5'11"	176	br	haz
Harry Houdini -	5'7"	179	blk	bl gr
Reed Howes -	6'		br	gr
Jack Hoxie -	6'2"	193	blk	bl
Gareth Hughes -	5'5"	125	br	bl
Lloyd Hughes -	6'	155	dk br	gr
Glenna Hunter -	6'	147	br	lt. bl
Charles Hutchison -	5'10"		br	br
John Ince -	5'10 1/2	185	gr	bl
George Irving -	6'	172	gr	gr
Boyd Irwin -	6'	170	br	bl
Bud Jameson -	6'	270	br	bl
Gardner James -	5'8"	139	lt br	dk br
Gladden James -	5'11"	160	lt br	bl
Emil Jannings -	6'2"	200	lt br	br
DeWitt Jennings -	6'	180	dk	haz
Al Jolson -	5'8"	150	dk	br
Buck Jones -	5'11 3/4	173	br	gr
Armond Kaliz -	5'10"	150	dk br	bl
Boris Karloff -	6'	175	dk br	br
Roscoe Karns -	5'10"	165	br	br
Buster Keaton -	5'5"	140	blk	br
Frank Keenan -	6' 1 1/2	170	lt br	bl
Donald Keith -	6'	168	br	bl
Ian Keith -	5'10"	155	blk	bl
Fred Kelsey -	5'11"	210	lt br	gr
Edgar Kennedy -	6'1"	210	br	br
Tom Kennedy -	6'2 1/2	215	blk	bl

Crawford Kent -	5'10 1/2	160	br	haz
Larry Kent -	5'11"	155	br	gr
J. Warren Kerrigan -	6'1 1/2	190	blk	haz
Norman Kerry -	6'2"	180	dk	haz
Guy Kibbee -	5'10"	200	br	
Joseph Kilgour -	4'11"	196	br	gr
Claude King -	5'11"	175	gr	dk br
James Kirkwood -	6	180	sandy	bl
Fred Kohler -	6'	200	lt br	bl
Henry Kolker -	5'10 1/2	168	br	dk
Tetsu Komai -	5'11"	175	blk	dk
Theodore Kosloff -	5'7"	140	br	br
Roy Laidlow -	5'10"	160	gr	bl
Arthur Lake -	6'	169	lt br	bl
Charles Lamont -	5'5"	145	br	bl
Cullen Landis -	5'6"	145	br	bl
Charles Lane -	6'1"	180	gr	br
Lupino Lane -	5'3"	135	dk br	br
Harry Langdon -			br	bl
George Larkin -	5'8 1/2	165	blk	br
Rod LaRocque -	6'3"	181	blk	dk br
Stan Laurel	5'8"	160	aub	bl
Frank Lawton -	5'10 1/2		dk	dk
Rex Lease -	5'10"	150	dk	grn
Ivan Lebedeff -	6'1"	157	blk	br
Otto Lederer -	5'10"	160	br	bl
Davy Lee -	3'	47	br	dk bl
Fritz Leiber -	6'1"	170	dk	dk br
Frank Leigh-	6'1"	184	dk	dk br
Dick L'Estrange -	6'4 1/2	185	bl	bl
George Lewis -	6'	175	br	br
Mitchell Lewis -	6'2"	195	blk	br
Ralph Lewis -	5'10"	180	blk gr	haz
Walter P. Lewis-	6'1"	180	fair	bl
Sheldon Lewis -	6'	177	dk	dk
E. K. Lincoln -	6'	185	blk	haz
Elmo Lincoln -	5'11"	200	br	bl
Max Linder -	5'4"	125	blk	br
Lucien Littlefield -	5'11"	145	lt br	grn
Harold Lloyd -	5'10 1/2	160	blk	bl
Harold Lockwood -	5'10 1/2	145	br	bl
John Loder -	6'3"	170	br	gr
Tom London -	6'1 1/2	190	br	dk bl
Walter Long -	5'11"	175	br	gr
Willard Louis -	5'10 1/2	250	br	br
Montague Love -	6'1"	195	aub	bl
Edmund Lowe -	6'	170	lt br	bl
Wilfred Lucas -	5'11"	178	br	br
Jack Luden -	6'	174	bl	br
Bela Lugosi -	5'1 1/2	177	br	gr
Paul Lukas -	6'1 1/2	186	br	br
Alfred Lunt -	6'1 1/2	177	dk br	br

Ben Lyon -	5'11"	160	br	bl
Eddie Lyons -	5-8"	143	br	grn
Bert Lytell -	5'10"	155	br	haz
Marc MacDermott -	6'	175	gr	br
J. Farrell MacDonald -	4'10"	185	dk br	bl
Wallace MacDonald -	5'11"	150	dk	br
Charles Emmett Mack -	5'11 1/2	185	br	gr
Kenneth MacKenna -	5'11 1/2	170	lt br	bl
Ian MacLaren -	6'	168	br	br
Douglas MacLean -	5'9"	140	br	br
Murdock MacQuarrie -	5'8"	150	br	gr
Charles Mailes -	6'	185	white	br
Fred Malatesta -	5'11"	188	dk	dk
Leo Maloney -	5'11"	170		
Hank Mann -	5'8"	165	br	br
Percy Marmont -	6'	150	bl	bl
Tully Marshall -	5'9 1/2	148	br gr	br
Edward Martindel -	6'1 1/2	190	br	bl
James Mason -	6'	174	br	br
Cyril Maude -	5'8 1/2	145	gr	bl
Herschel Mayall -	5'10"	185	dk br	dk gr
Ken Maynard -	6'	180	blk	gr
Frank Mayo	5'11 1/2	165	br	gr
Harry McCoy -	5'8 1/2	155	light	br
Tim McCoy -	5'11"	170	lt br	bl
Philo McCullough -	6'	180	br	bl
Francis McDonald -	5'9"	155	blk	dk
Frank McGlynn -	6' 1/2	160	br	gr
Walter McGrail -	6'	172	blk	bl
Malcolm McGregor -	5'11"	165	br	bl
Lafe McKee -	5'7 1/2	150	br	gr
Raymond McKee -	5'7"	155	br	bl gr
Robert McKim -	6'	175	br	bl
Victor McLaglen -	6'3 1/2	205	br	gr
George Meeker -	5'11"	155	br	br
Thomas Meighan	6'	170	br	br
Adolph Menjou -	5'10"	150	dk	bl
Buddy Messinger -	5'8 1/2	150	blk	haz
Earl Metcalf -	5'11"	170	br	bl
Charles Middleton -	6'	165	br	bl
John Miljan -	6'	168	br	br
Walter Miller	5'11"	165	dk br	br
Tom Mix -	5'11 1/2	175	dk br	blk
William V. Mong -	5'9"	140	dk br	br
Bull Montana -	5'8"	200	blk	dk
Matt Moore -	5'11"	160	aub	br
Owen Moore -	5'10"	140	blk	br
Tom Moore -	5'10 1/2	142	lt br	bl
Victor Moore -	5'7"	196	gr	br
Lee Moran -	5'10"	135	br	bl
Frank Morgan	5'11"	166	br	dk
Milburn Morante -	5'10 1/2	145	br	br

Antonio Moreno -	5'10"	175	br	blk
Harry T. Morey -	6'1"		br	bl
Chester Morris -	5'9"	150	blk	grn
Charles Morton -	6'	175	br	grn
Jack Mower -	6'	180	br	haz
Jack Mulhall -	5'11"	160	dk br	bl
Charlie Murray -	6'	200	aub	gr
James Murray -	5'11"	178	lt br	grn
Harry C. Myers -	5'11"	176	br	bl
Conrad Nagel -	6'	165	bl	bl
Jack Nelson -	5'10"	150	br	gr
George Nichols -	6'	242	gr	bl
Barry Norton -	5'11"	160	blk	br
Ramon Novarro-	5'10"	160	blk	dk br
Ivor Novello -	5'11"		blk	br
Wedgewood Nowell -	5'11 1/2	163	gr	br
Carroll Nye -	6'	160	dk br	br
Jack Oakie -	5'11"	170	blk	br
Wheeler Oakman -	5'11"	170	br	br
Eugene O'Brien -	6'	160	br	bl
George O'Brien -	6' 1/2"	180	br	dk br
Tom O'Brien -	5'10 1/2	185	dk br	bl
Charles Ogle -	6'2 1/2	200	dk br	br
Warner Oland -	5'11"	180	br	br
Guy Oliver -	5'11"	176	bt	gr
Pat O'Malley -	6'	160	br	bl
William Orlamond -	5'10 1/2	150	gr	bl
Eugene Pallette -	5'9 1/2	155	br	bl
Franklin Pangborn -	5'10 1/2	156	br	haz
Paul Panzer -	5'10 1/2	170	blk	br
Tom Patricola -	5'7"	170	br	br
Ed Peil -	5'10"	170	dk br	haz
Jack Pennick -	6'4"	195	lt br	bl
Esme Percy -	5'8 1/2		dk br	br
George Periolat -	5'10"	185	br gr	bl
House Peters -	6'1 1/2	190	br	haz
Eddie Phillips -	5'	160	blk	br
Jack Pickford -	5'7"	130	br	br
Walter Pidgeon -	6'2"	190	blk	bl
Lon Poff -	6'2 1/2	170	lt br	bl
Harry (Snub) Pollard -	5'6 1/2	148	br	br
Eddie Polo -	5'8 1/2	175	blk	blk
Guy Bates Post -	5'10"	165	br	gr
Victor Potel -	6'1 1/2	160	dk	dk
David Powell -	5'10"	169	dk br	br
William Powell -	6'	160	dk br	br
Herbert Prior -	6'	180	dk	gr
Lucien Prival -	6'	161	br	br

Eddie Quillan -	5'6"	140	br	br
Billie Quirk -	5'7"	147	dk bl	bl
Anders Randolf -	5'11 1/2	195	br gr	bl
Arthur Rankin -	5'10"	155	dk br	bl
Jules Raucourt -	5'11"	160	dk br	br
Herbert Rawlinson -	6'	165	br gr	bl
Charles Ray -	6' 1/2	170	dk br	br
Frank Reicher -	5'7"	148	dk br	br
Wallace Reid -	6'3 1/2	180	lt br	bl
Duncan Renaldo -	6'	175	dk br	dk
James Rennie -	5'10"	152	br	bl
Charles Richman -	6'1"	196	br	haz
Warner Richmond -	5'11"	165	br	bl
Tom Ricketts -	5'10"	150	white	bl
Bert Roach -	5'11"	220	br	dk
Theodore Roberts -	6'	195	gr	bl
John Roche -	6'1"	175	br	haz
Charles "Buddy" Rogers -	6'	175	blk	br
Will Rogers -	5'11"	170	dk	gr
Gilbert Roland -	5'11"	165	blk	br
Buddy Roosevelt -	5'11"	175	blk	br
Albert Roscoe -	6'	175	br	bl
Benny Rubin -	5'7"	142	blk	br
William Russell -	6'2"	206	br	br
Al St. John -	5'6 1/2	150	lt br	bl
John St. Polis -	5'10 1/2	170	gr	br
Tom Santschi -	6'2"	214	sandy	bl
Lewis Sargent -	5'9"	150	lt br	gr
Joseph Schildkraut -	5'10"	146	blk	blk
Harry Schumm -	5'11 1/2	175	dk br	br
George Seigmann -	6'2"	230	br	br
Charles Sellon -	5'11"	148	br	bl
Mack Sennett -			sandy	gr
Reginald Sheffield -	5'9"	150	lt br	dk bl
Lowell Sherman -	5'11"	150	br	br
J. Barney Sherry -	6'1 1/2	200	iron gr	gr
Antrim Short -	5'7 1/2	135	br	bl
Lee Shumway -	6'	180		
George Sidney -	5'3"	190	dk br	br
Bernard Siegel -	5'8"	140	gr	br
Milton Sills -	6'1 1/2	180	lt br	gr
Russell Simpson -	6'	175	med. br	bl
Phillips Smalley -	6'	180	br	br
Sojin -	5'8"	135	blk	br
Ned Sparks -	5'8 1/2	180	br	gr
Wyndham Standing -	6'1"	180	br	gr
Forrest Stanley -	5'11"	165	bl	bl
Lincoln Stedman -	5'11 1/2	210	dk br	haz
Bob Steele -	5'10	158	br	bl
Larry Steers -	6'	175	gr	br
Ford Sterling -	5'11"	180	blk	br

Charles Stevens -	5'10 1/2	150	blk	br
Edwin Stevens -	6'	200	br	bl
Hayden Stevenson -	5'11"	170	br	br
Roy Stewart -	6'2"	190	blk	br
Carl Stockdale -	5'11"	155	br	bl
Arthur Stone -	5'7 1/2	142	dk	br
Fred Stone -	5'9"	170	br	bl
George E. Stone -	5'3 1/2	130	br	br
Lewis Stone -	5'10 3/4	174	gr	haz
Nick Stuart -	5'9"	154	blk	br
Slim Summerville -	6'2"	164	br	br
Mack Swain -	6'2"	300	gr	grn
Josef Swickard -	5'10"	155	gr	dk gr
Richard Talmadge -	5'8"		br	dk br
Conway Tearle -	5'10 1/2	150	dk br	dk br
Lou Tellegen -	6'	175	dk	gr
Ernest Thesiger -	6'		fair	bl
Jameson Thomas -	5'11 1/2		blk	dk bl
Fred Thomson -	6'2"	200	br	bl
William Tooker -	5'11"	187	gr	dk bl
David Torrence -	6'1"	196	blk	haz
Ernest Torrence -	6'4"	210	br	br
Richard Travers -	6'1"	187	blk	br
Hugh Trevor -	6'1"	172	br	br
Ernest Truex -	5'2 1/2	120	lt br	bl
Glenn Tryon -	5'10"	165	blk	haz
Richard Tucker -	5'11 1/2	175	br	bl gr
Ben Turpin -	5'4"	125	blk	crossed
Tom Tyler -	6'1 1/2	190	blk	br
Rudolph Valentino -	5'11"	154	blk	brn
Truman Van Duke -	5'11"	155	dk red	br
Victor Varconi -	5'10"	180	br	br
Conrad Veidt -	6'4"	165	dk br	bl
Bobby Vernon -	5'2 1/2	145	lt br	bl
Michael Visaroff -	5'11"	210	gr	br
Theodore Von Eltz -	5'11"	160	br gr	gr
Erich Von Stroheim -	5'7"		br-shaved	br
Johnnie Walker -	5'11"	160	blk	br
George Walsh -	5'11"	180	dk	dk
Henry B. Walthall -	5'6"	135	dk br	br
H. B. Warner -	6' 1/2"	167	fair	bl
Robert Warwick -	6'	175	br	br
Bryant Washburn -	5'11"	155	dk br	br
Niles Welch -	6'	165	med br	bl
Charles West -	5'11"	150	lt br	dk br
Stanhope Wheatcroft -	5'11"	145	dk br	br
Wheezer -			lt br	bl
Leo White -	5'6"	132	br	bl
Lloyd Whitlock -	6'1 1/2	175	br	br
Crane Wilbur -	5'9"	169	br	gr

Earle Williams -	5'11"	176	blk	bl
Guinn "Big Boy" Williams -	6'2"	205	lt br	gr grn
Ben Wilson -	5'11 1/2	178	dk br	br
Tom Wilson -	6'2"	220	dk br	gr
Grant Withers -	6'3"	200	br	bl
Louis Wolheim -	5'10 1/2	160	br	br
Bert Woodruff -	5'7"	174	gr	bl
Roland Young -	6'	160	br	br

Vital Statistics - Women

	Height	Weight	Hair	Eyes
Jean Acker -	5'2 1/2	112	br	haz
Renee Adoree -	5'1"	105	br	bl
Mary Alden -	5'3 1/2		blk	bl
Phyllis Allen -	5'8"	170	reddish	bl
May Allison -	5'5"	125	golden	vio-bl
Tsuru Aoki -	5'1"		blk	dk
Julia Arthur -	5'4 1/2	125	dk	dk
Sylvia Ashton -	5'6"	140	bl	bl
Gertrude Astor -	5'7"	138	bl	gr
Mary Astor -	5'5"	120	aub	br
Agnes Ayres -	5'4 1/2	115	gold-br	bl
Baclanova -	5'4"	116	bl	bl
Mabel Ballin -	5'3"	120	br	br
Vilma Banky -	5'6"	125	bl	bl-grn
Bessie Barriscale -	5'2"	123	bl	br
Ethel Barrymore -	5'5"		br	bl
Theda Bara -	5'6"	135	dk br	blk
Lina Basquette -	5'3 1/2		blk	dk
Beverly Bayne	5'2"	125	dk br	br
Lucy Beaumont -	5'1"	113	br-gr	dk br
Barbara Bedford -	5'4"	130	dk br	bl
Madge Bellamy -	5'3"	110	dk br	bl
Alma Bennett -	5'4 1/2	118	blk	br
Belle Bennett -	5'2"	125	golden	gr
Constance Bennett -	5'4"	110	golden	bl
Enid Bennett -	5'3"	110	golden	haz
Constance Binney -	5' 1/2"	104	golden	gr
Fair Binney -	5'6"	106	br	br
Sally Blane -	5'4 1/2	119	lt br	haz
Betty Blythe -	5'7"	140	dk br	bl
Eleanor Boardman -	5'6"	125	dk br	grn
Mary Boland -	5'4"	125	bl	bl
Lillian Bond -	5'4 1/2	93	reddish	haz
Clara Bow -	5'3 1/2	110	fiery red	br
Alice Brady -	5'7"	108	dk br	br
Sylvia Breamer -	5'7"	135	dk br	br

Evelyn Brent -	5'4"	112	br	br
Mary Brian -	5'2"	105	br	haz
Ann Brody -	5'	170	dk br	br
Betty Bronson -	5'1"	98	chestnut	grn
Billie Burke -			bl	bl
Alice Calhoun -	5'4"	114	golden br	br
Ora Carew -	5'2 1/2	118	bl	br
Rita Carewe -	5'4 1/2	124	bl	bl
Sue Carol -	5'3"	108	br	br
Mary Carr -	5'2"	120	bl-gr	bl
Nancy Carroll -	5'4"	116	reddish	bl
Louise Carver -	5'9"	165	br	haz
Dolores Cassinelli -	5'7"	125	blk	haz
Helene Chadwick -	5'7"	130	bl	br
Edith Chapman -	5'1"	135	gr	bl
Virginia Cherrill -	5'4"	110	bl	bl
Ann Christy -	5'			
Gertrude Claire -	5'2"		gr	bl
Marguerite Clark -	4'10"	90	br	haz
Ethel Clayton -	5'5"	130	red gld	gr
Marguerite Clayton -	5'6"	116	bl	bl
Ruth Clifford -	5'3"	118	bl	bl
June Collyer -	5'5"	br	haz	
Betty Compson -	5'2 1/2	112	br	bl
Edna Mae Cooper	5'6 1/2	130	br	haz
Miriam Cooper -	4'10"		dk br	br
Virginia Lee Corbin -	5'5"	118	bl	bl
Marcella Corday	5'7 1/2	125	lt br	gr
Ann Cornwall -	4'10"	102	red br	dk
Dolores Costello -	5'4"	115	golden	bl
Helene Costello -	5'7"		lt br	br
Lucy Cotton -	5'6"	125	lt br	dk br
Marguerite Courtot -	5'2 1/2	110	golden br	grn
Nell Craig -	5'6"	124	blk	br
Joan Crawford -	5'4"	125	br	bl
Josephine Crowell -	5'5"	140	br	br
Dorothy Cummings -	5'7"	125	br	br
Grace Cunard -	5'4"	120	aub	gr
Frances Dade -	5'5"	110	br	bl
Lil Dagover -			br	grn
Lily Damita -	5'3"	114	ash bl	br
Viola Dana -	4'11 1/2	101	br	grn
Dorothy Dalton -	5'4 1/2	127	br	gr
Bebe Daniels -	5'3 1/2	120	blk	dk br
Jean Darling -	4'7"	46	bl	dk bl
Grace Darmond -	5'3 1/2	123	bl	gr
Alice Davenport -	5'2"	140	gr	haz
Dorothy Davenport -			lt br	
Milla Davenport -	5'6"	175	iron gr	gr
Marion Davies -	5'4 1/2	123	golden	bl
Mildred Davis -	5'2"	100	bl	bl

Yola D'Avril -	5'5"	120	br	gr bl
Marjorie Daw -	5'4 1/2	112	lt br	haz
Hazel Dawn -	5'4 1/2	135	bl	haz
Doris Dawson -	5'1"	103	reddish	bl
Alice Day -			br	bl
Marceline Day -	5'3"	106	br	bl
Priscilla Dean -	5'5"	130	dk br	br
Hazel Deane -	5'2 1/2	120	bl	gr
Marguerite De La Motte -	5' 1/2"	110	bl	haz
Claudia Dell -	5'5"	116	bl	haz
Dolores Del Rio -	5'3"	117	blk	br
Katherine DeMille -	5'3 3/4	115	dk br	br
Carol Dempster -	5'5"	114	chestnut	br
Lya De Putti -	5'2"	105	blk	br
Ruby De Remer -	5'6"	122	bl	bl
Florence Desmond -	5'3 1/2	105	bl	haz
Dorothy Devore -	5'2"	115	dk br	br
Marlene Dietrich -	5'5"	120	golden	bl
Rose Dione -	5'8"	158	blk	haz
Marie Doro -	5'4"	115	br	br
Billie Dove -	5'5"	115	br	haz
Louise Dressler -	5'7"	154	bl	bl
Marie Dressler -	5'5"	128	br	bl gr
Nancy Drexel -	5'2"	108	bl	br
Claire DuBrey -	5'7"	130	aub	br
Helen Dunbar -	5'6"		aub	br
Josephine Dunn -	5'3"	112	lt br	bl
Miss DuPont -	5'7"	135	bl	bl
Minta Durfee -	5'4"	130	reddish	bl
Dorothy Dwan -		120	br	bl
Jeanne Eagles -			lt br	bl
Helen Jerome Eddy -	5'7"	135	dk br	br
Sally Eilers -	5'2 1/2	110	golden	haz
Julian Eltinge (impersonator)	5'8"	165	br	gr
June Elvidge -	5'9"	135	br	br
Madge Evans -	5'4 1/2	116	bl	gr grn
Elinor Fair -	5'5"	125	br	br
Virginia Brown Faire -	5'1"	105	chestnut	haz
Dot Farley -	5'5"	138	bl	blk
Geraldine Farrar -	5'6"	135	blk	gr
Julia Faye -	5'2 1/2	115	br	br
Louise Fazenda -	5'4 1/2	135	lt br	haz
Edith Fellows -	5'	80	dk br	haz
Elsie Ferguson -	5'6"	125	lt br	bl
Helen Ferguson -	5'3"	125	br	br
Flora Finch -	5'5"	110	dk	bl gr
Margarita Fisher -	5'1"	117	blk	gr
Cissy Fitzgerald -	5'4 1/2		br	br
Emily Fitzroy -	5'6 1/2	160	dk br	haz
Bess Flowers -	5'8"	128	blk	br
Eugenie Forde -	5'6"	139	dk br	br

Ann Forrest -	5'2"	104	bl	bl
Helen Foster -	5'	98	bl	gr
Betty Francisco -	5'4 1/2	115	bl	haz
Pauline Frederick -	5'3 1/2	130	br	haz
Trixie Friganza -	5'4 1/2		white	gr bl
Dale Fuller -	5'3"	118	br	dk br
Greta Garbo -	5'6"	125	golden	bl
Pauline Garon -	5'1 1/2	96	bl	haz
Anita Garvin	5'6"	133	blk	grn
Gene Gauntier	5'3 1/2	130	dk br	amb
Janet Gaynor -	5'	100	aub	br
Maude George -	5'5 1/2	125	br	br
Carmelita Geraghty -	5'4 1/2	122	br	br
Neva Gerber -	5'2"	112	lt br	br
Helen Gibson -	5'6"	142	br	haz
Eugenia Gilbert -	5'4"	122	br	bl
Dorothy Gish -	5'2"	109	fair	bl
Lillian Gish -	5'4"	105	bl	bl
Louise Glaum -	5'5"	130	br	haz
Lucille Webster Gleason -	5'6"	140	lt br	bl
Paulette Goddard -	5'4"	110	bl	br
Dagmar Godowsky -	5'5 1/2	120	blk	haz
Maude Turner Gordon -	5'7 1/2	150	white	bl gr
Julia Swayne Gordon -	5'7"	135	br	bl
Vera Gordon -	5'5 1/2	165	blk	dk
Rosa Gore -	5'9"	135	dk gr	br
Jetta Goudal -	5'7"	128	br	br
Greta Granstedt -	5'1"	100	bl	grn
Valentine Grant -	5'4"	115	red	bl
Gilda Gray -	5'4"	122	bl	bl
Charlotte Greenwood -	5'9 1/2	140	bl	bl
Edna Gregory -	5'6"	124	br	br
Ena Gregory -	5'2"	107	bl	br
Corinne Griffith -	5'4"	118	br	bl
Texas Guinan -	5'6"	136	lt br	bl
Dorothy Gulliver -	5'2"	117	br	haz
Evelyn Hall -	5'6"	125	br	dk bl
Elaine Hammerstein -	5'4"	120	br	gr
Virginia Hammond -	5'6"	130	lt	bl
Hope Hampton -	5'3"	118	aub	dk bl
Juanita Hansen -	5'3"	130	bl	bl
Jean Harlow -	5'2 1/2	110	bl	bl
Mildred Harris -	5'4 1/2	118	golden	bl
Sunshine Hart -	5'6 1/4	245	aub	haz
Gretchen Hartman -	5'6"	135	br	br
Olive Hasbrouck -	5'3"	107	aub	haz
Phyllis Haver -	5'6"	126	bl	bl
Ormi Hawley -	5'3"	130	bl	gr
Wanda Hawley -	5'3"	110	bl	gr bl
Violet Heming -	5'4"	118	bl	bl
Gale Henry -	5'9"	128	dk	br

Aggie Herring -	5'4"	165	reddish	bl
Ruth Hiatt -	5'3"	120	bl	bl
Doris Hill -	5'2 1/2	100	aub	bl
Helen Holmes -	5'6"	135	br	br
Gloria Hope -	5'2"	106	aub	bl
Hedda Hopper -	5'7"	135	br	grn
Camilla Horn -	5'5"	120	bl	haz
Clara Horton -	5'2"	110	bl	bl
Alice Howell -			fair	haz
Jobyna Howland -	5'11"	150	aub	dk
Louise Huff -	5'	106	br	gr
Gladys Hulette -	5'4"	114	br	gr
Leila Hyams -	5'4 1/2	120	bl	grn
Mary Ann Jackson -			red br	bl gr
Dorothy Janis -	5'4"	94	dk br	br
Elsie Janis -	5'5 1/2	120	br	br
Eulalie Jensen -	5'8"	155	dk br	br
Zita Johann -	5'5"	105	dk br	dk
Edith Johnson -	5'3"	130	aub	bl
Julianne Johnston -	5'6"	120	br	grn
Leatrice Joy -	5'3"	125	blk	br
Alice Joyce -	5'7"	120	br	haz
Joyzelle -	5'5"	125	dk br	br
Kay Johnson -	5'4"		bl	bl
Gail Kane -	5'7"	142	dk br	br
Helen Kane -	5'2"		br	haz
Hazel Keener -	5'6"	128	chestnut	haz
Mayme Kelso -	5'6"	145	bl	bl
Madge Kennedy -	5'5"	120	br	br
Merna Kennedy -	5'2 1/2	107	aub	grn
Barbara Kent -	4'11"	104	br	bl
Doris Kenyon -	5'6"	125	bl	gr
Kathleen Key -	5'6"	128	blk	br
Natalie Kingston -	5'6"	126	br lt	br
Kathleen Kirkham -	5'8"	150	br	bl
Kithou -	5'5"	120	dk	dk
Evalyn Knapp -	5'4"	105	bl	bl
Lydia Knott -	5'4"	120	gr	bl
Mary Kornman -	5'3"	112	bl	br
Alice Lake -	5'2"	114	br	br
Barbara LaMarr -	5'3 1/2	123	blk	grn
Lola Lane -	5'3"	117	bl	bl
Nora Lane -	5'5"	125	br	bl
Laura LaPlante -	5'2"	112	bl	gr
Francine Larrimore -	5'1"		red gold	bl
Fontaine LaRue -	5'5"	130	lt br	dk br
Gretchen Lederer -	5'7"	140	br	br
Frances Lee -	5'	98	lt br	bl
Gwen Lee -	5'7"	135	bl	bl
Lila Lee -	5'3"	110	blk	haz

Anna Lehr -	5'8"	112	dk br	br
Lillian Leighton -	5'3 1/2	160	br	haz
Gladys Leslie -	5'	95	lt br	br
Ida Lewis -	5'5"	160	bl	bl
Vera Lewis -	5'8"	154	br	bl
Ann Little -	5'6"	112	blk	br
Margaret Livingston -	5'3 1/2	120	aub	br
Doris Lloyd -	5'5"	117	red br	bl
Jeanette Loff -	5'2"	105	bl	bl
Jacqueline Logan -	5'4"	115	aub	vio
Carole Lombard -	5'5 1/2	112	golden	bl
Babe London	5'7"	195	lt br	bl gr
Louise Lorraine -	5'1"	104	lt br	br
Bessie Love -	5'	100	lt br	br
Louise Lovely -	5'2"	128	fair	bl gr
Myrna Loy -	5'6"	125	titian	grn
Anna Luther -	5'5"	129	titian	bl
Helen Lynch -	5'3 1/2	120	bl	haz
Sharon Lynn -	5'4"	115	br	br
Katherine MacDonald -	5'8"	130	bl	bl
Dorothy MacKaill -	5'4 1/2	121	bl	haz
Mary MacLaren -	5'4"	120	bl	bl
Cleo Madison -	5'2"	125	aub	bl
Blanche Mahaffey -	5'2"	119	red	gr bl
Molly Malone -	5'	108	chestnut	br
Margaret Mann -	5'4 1/2	165	gr	gr
Martha Mansfield -	5'4"	122	dk br	br
Edna Marion	5'1"	107	bl	gr
Frances Marion -	5'3"	139	br	br
Enid Markey -	5'4"	119	dk br	dk br
June Marlowe -	5'5 1/2	116	br	br
Mae Marsh -	5'3"	110	aub	gr
Marguerite Marsh -	5'2"	120	aub	bl
Shirley Mason -	4'11"	94	br	gr
Martha Mattox -	5'7"	150	br	br
Edna Mayo -	5'3 1/2	112	ash bl	bl
Mary McAllister -	5'2 1/2	110	bl	br
May McAvoy -	4'11"	94	dk	bl
Gladys McConnell -	5'3 1/2	116	bl	bl
Claire McDowell -	5'4"	124	br	br
Kathryn McGuire -	5'4"	124	lt br	haz
Violet Mesereau -	5'4"	115	bl	bl
Gertrude Messenger -	5'3"	100	dk	bl
Marie Messenger -	5'3"	117	aub	bl
Patsy Ruth Miller -	5'2 1/2	108	br	br
Mary Miles Minter -	5'2"	110	bl	bl
Rhea Mitchell -	5'2"	110	bl	bl
De Sacia Mooers -	5'5"	131	ash bl	dk bl
Colleen Moore -	5'3"	105	dk br	br
Natalie Moorehead -	5'10 1/2		bl	bl
Lois Moran -	5'2"	108	bl	dk bl
Polly Moran -	5'4"	134	blk	dk br

Marie Mosquini -	5'4"	125	br	haz
Edna Murphy -	5'2"	118	bl	gr
Mae Murray -	5'3"	115	bl	bl gr
Carmel Myers -	5'3"	124	br	grn
Nita Naldi -	5'8"	136	blk	br
Alla Nazimova -	5'3"	116	blk	vio
Pola Negri -	5'4"	120	blk	haz
Evelyn Nesbit -	5'3 1/2	122	br	haz
Anna Q. Nilsson -	5'7"	135	bl	bl
Greta Nissen -	5'4 1/2	122	bl	bl
Marion Nixon -	5'1"	98	br	br
Mary Nolan -	5'3"	110	bl	bl
Mabel Normand -	5'		dk br	dk br
Hedda Nova -	5'6"	130	dk	br
Eva Novak -	5'5"	125	bl	gr
Jane Novak -	5'7"	135	bl	bl
Molly O'Day -	5'2 1/2	108	dk br	haz
Edna May Oliver -	5'7 1/2	138	br	bl
Gertrude Olmstead -	5'3"	114	chestnut	gr
Sally O'Neill -	5'2"	105	blk	dk bl
Vivienne Osborne -	5'4"	112	blk	br
Rafaela Ottiano -	5'5 1/2	126	br	br
Seena Owen -	5'8"	125	bl	bl
Anita Page -	5'2"	118	bl	bl
Elizabeth Patterson -	5'5"	115	dk br	dk bl
Virginia Pearson -	5'7 1/2	145	dk br	haz
Ann Pennington -	5'		dk br	br
Eileen Percy -	5'3"	118	bl	haz
Olga Petrova -	5'5"	130	titian	grn
Mary Philbin -	5'2"	96	br	haz
Carmen Phillips -	5'5"	130	br	blk
Dorothy Phillips -	5'3 1/2	123	br	gr
Sally Phipps -	5'2"	107	aub	br
Lottie Pickford -	5'5"		br	br
Mary Pickford -	5'	100	golden	haz
Zasu Pitts -	5'6"	115	br	bl
Daphne Pollard -	4'9"	100	bl	bl
Arline Pretty -	5'5 1/2	125	bl	bl
Marie Prevost -	5'4"	123	dk	bl
Kate Price -	5'6 1/2	210	dk br	gr grn
Aileen Pringle -	5'4"	119	dk br	gr grn
Edna Purviance -	5'4"	130	bl	gr
Esther Ralston -	5'5"	125	bl	gr bl
Sally Rand -	5'	114	bl	bl
Allene Ray -	5'3 1/2	114	golden	bl
Ruth Renick	5'1 1/2	110	titial	haz
Dorothy Revier -	5'4"	115	bl	bl gr
Vera Reynolds -	5'	101	bl	dk bl
Billie Rhodes -	5'	106	br	br

Irene Rich -	5'6"	138	dk br	br
Lillian Rich -	5'5"	119	dk br	bl
Lucille Ricksen -	5'2 1/2	112	br	br
Fritzie Ridgeway -	5'5"	120	br	bl
Allene Roberts -	5'1"	101	br	br
Edith Roberts -	5'1 1/2	105	br	br
May Robson -	5'2 1/2	105	dk br	bl gr
Ruth Roland -	5'4"	122	reddish br	bio
Ann Rork -	5'4 1/2	120	br	br
Rosa Rosanova -	5'5"	170	br	br
Bodil Rosing -			bl	bl
Alma Rubens -	5'7"	130	blk	dk
Virginia Sale -	5'6"	122	br	br
Teddy Sampson -	5'2"	110	blk	br
Jackie Saunders -	5'3"	115	bl	bl
Violet Schram -	5'3"	120	blk	dk br
Mabel Julienne Scott -	5'5 1/2	125	chestnut	haz
Dorothy Sebastian -	5'3"	109	br	haz
Eileen Sedgwick -	5'3"	120	bl	bl
Josie Sedgwick -	5'5"	132	br	bl gr
Evelyn Selbie	5'3 1/2	125	br	br
Clarissa Selwynne -	5'7"	150	dk br	dk br
Peggy Shannon -	5'4 1/2		reddish	bl gr
Norma Shearer -	5'1"	118	br	bl gr
Gertrude Short -	5'3"	103	bl	br
Marie Shotwell -	5'7 1/2	154	lt br	dk br
Martha Sleeper -	5'4"	118	med br	br
Marguerite Snow -	5'5"	105	br	haz
Vera Steadman -	5'3"	110	dk br	br
Myrtle Stedman -	5'7"	140	bl	haz
Anita Stewart -	5'5"	125	br	br
Ruth Stonehouse -	5'2"	112	lt br	br
June Storey -	5'4"	116	bl	bl
Gloria Swanson -	5'3 1/2	115	dk br	bl gr
Blanche Sweet -	5'4"	118	bl	bl
Constance Talmadge -	5'7"	120	golden	br
Natalie Talmadge -	5'2"	104	br	brn
Norma Talmadge -	5'4"	110	dk br	br
Rose Tapley -	5'6"	137	br	gr
Lilyan Tashman -	5'5"	112	bl	bl
Estelle Taylor -	5'4 1/2	129	dk br	br
Laurette Taylor -			br	haz
Ruth Taylor -	5'2"	104	bl	bl
Veree Teasdale -	5'6"	125	bl	bl
Olive Tell -	5'5 1/2	127	br	bl
Barbara Tennant -	5'5 1/2	124	aub	haz
Alice Terry -	5'1 1/2	115	bl	gr
Ethel Grey Terry -	5'6"	130	br	gr
Evelyn Thatcher -	5'7"	180	reddish	gr
Rosemary Theby -	5'5 1/2	124	dk br	haz
Olive Thomas -	5'3"	118	br	bl

Mary Thurman -	5'3 1/2	123	chestnut	gr
Lydia Yeamans Titus -	4'9"	140	br	bl
Lola Todd -	5'4 1/2	118	br	br
Thelma Todd -	5'4"	122	bl	bl gr
Raquel Torres -	5'2"	110	blk	dk br
Madalaine Travers -	5'9"	165	dk br	haz
Mary Treen -	5'8"		reddish	bl
Sophie Tucker -	5'6"	170	bl	bl
Florence Turner -	4'10"	102	blk	dk
Helen Twelvetrees -	5'3"	110	golden br	bl
Lenore Ulric -	5'3"	117	br	br
Viola Vale -	5'5"	122	br	br
Virginia Valli -	5'4"	122	dk br	bl
Alberta Vaughn -	5'2"	103	aub	br
Hilda Vaughn -	5'5"	120	br	grn
Mabel Van Buren -	5'3"	125	br	br
Lupe Velez -	5'5"	115	blk	br
Florence Vidor -	5'2"	125	br	br
Ethel Wales -	5'5 1/2	135	br	bl
Lillian Walker -	5'1 1/2	120	bl	bl
Gladys Walton -	5'1 1/2	113	br	haz
Fannie Ward -	5'1"	125	fair	bl
Jacqueline Wells -	5'3 1/2		br	haz
Winifred Westover -	5'3"	128	bl	dk bl
Alice White -	5'2"	110	bl	dk br
Pearl White -	5'6"	120	bl	bl
Claire Whitney -	5'4"	120	bl	br
Kathlyn Williams -	5'5"	128	bl	bl gr
Lois Wilson -	5'5 1/2	120	br	haz
Claire Windsor -	5'6 1/2	128	bl	bl gr
Laska Winters -	5'2"	115	br	blk
Jane Winton -	5'5 1/2	120	reddish	grn
Anna May Wong -	5'4 1/2	120	blk	brn
Barbara Worth -	5'4"	118	br	bl
Fay Wray -	5'3"	114	lt br	bl
Clara Kimball Young -	5'6"	135	dk	dk
Loretta Young -	5'3"	101	lt br	bl

PART II:

THE DIRECTORS AND PRODUCERS

Alphabetical List

A

John Adolfi
Del Andrews
Oscar Apfel
Roscoe Arbuckle
George Archainbaud
Dorothy Arzner
Charles Avery

B

Lloyd Bacon
Clarence Badger
King Baggott
Eddie Baker
George D. Baker
Reginald Barker
Rex Beach
William Beaudine
Harry Beaumont
Monta Bell
Spencer C. Bennet
George Beranger
Ludwig Berger
Paul Bern
William Bertram
Madame Alice Blache
Herbert Blache
J. Stuart Blackton
J. G. Blystone
Joseph C. Boyle
Frank Borzage
Charles J. Brabin
Bertram Bracken
Robert North Bradbury
Herbert Brenon
Howard Bretherton
Monte Brice
Otto Brower
Clarence Brown
Harry Joe Brown
Melville Brown
Tod Browning
Dimitri Buchowetzski
David Butler

C

W. Christy Cabanne
Colin Campbell
Albert Capellani
Frank Capra
Edwin Carewe
Charles Chaplin
Louis Chaudet
Emile Chautard
Benjamin Christiansen
Elmer Clifton
Eddie Cline
Bennett Cohn
Jack Conway
Meriam C. Cooper
William J. Craft
Donald Crisp
Alan Crosland
James Cruze
Irving Cummings
Michael Curtiz

D

J. Searle Dawley
Norman Dawn
Joseph De Grasse
Robert DeLacey
Hampton Del Ruth
Roy Del Ruth
Cecil B. DeMille
William deMille
Edward Dillon
Jack Dillon
William Duncan
Scott Dunlap
Allan Dwan

E

Reeves Eason
J. Gordon Edwards
Walter Edwards
John Emerson
Arthur Guy Empey
Ray Enright
Howard Estabrook

F

Jacques Feyder
Romaine Fielding
Dallas M. Fitzgerald
George Fitzmaurice
Victor Fleming
James Flood
Robert Florey
Emmett Flynn
Francis Ford
Hugh Ford
John Ford
Tom Forman
Wallace Fox
Chester M. Franklin
Sidney A. Franklin
William French

G

Harry Garson
Louis Gasnier
Howard Gaye
Douglas Gerrard
Charles Giblyn
Sven Glade
Alfred Goulding
Edmund Goulding
Frank J. Grandon
Alfred E. Green
Frank Griffin
David Wark Griffith
E. H. Griffith
Nicholas Grinde

H

Lloyd Hamilton
David M. Hartford
Pat Hartigan
Harry Harvey
Howard Hawks
Arch B. Heath
Victor Heerman
Thomas N. Heffron
Joseph Henabery
Del Henderson
Hobart Henley
George W. Hill
Robert F. Hill
Lambert Hillyer
Renaud Hoffman
James P. Hogan
Edwin L. Hollywood
George Holt
Allan Holubar
E. Mason Hopper
Charles Horan
James W. Horne
William K. Howard
Harry O. Hoyt
Rupert Hughes
Charles J. Hunt
T. Hayes Hunter
Paul C. Hurst
Charles Hutchinson

I

John Ince
Ralph Ince
Thomas Ince
Lloyd Ingraham
Rex Ingram
George Irving

J

Jacques Jaccard
Fred Jackman
Arthur V. Johnson
Martin Johnson
Tefft Johnson
F. Richard Jones
Edward Jose
Rupert Julian

K

Buster Keaton
Erle Kenton
Burton King
Henry King
Louis King
Charles Klein
Percy Knighton

L

Gregory La Cava
Edward Laemmle
Ernest Laemmle
Charles Lamont
Fritz Lang
Walter Lang
Harry Langan
Rowland V. Lee
Henry Lehrman
Paul Leni
Robert Z. Leonard
Melvyn LeRoy
Edward LeSaint
Edgar Lewis
Frank Lloyd
Del Lord
Ernst Lubitsch
Wilfred Lucas
The Lumiere Freres

M

Kenneth MacKenna
Jeanie MacPherson
Murdock MacQuarrie
Charles Maigne
Leo Maloney
Jay Marchant
Frances Marion
George Marshall
June Mathis
Frank S. Mattison
Archie Mayo
Leo McCarey
John P. McCarthy
Kenneth McDonald
Bernard McEveety
J. P. McGowan
Donald McKenzie
Henry McRae
Leo J. Meehan
George Melford
Georges Melies
Lothar Mendes
Lewis Milestone
Harry Millarde
Charles Miller
Bertram Millhauser
Bruce Mitchell
Howard Mitchell
Edmund Mortimer
F. W. Murnau

N

Marshall Neilan
H. William Neill
Alvin J. Neitz
Jack Nelson
Fred Newmeyer
Fred Niblo
William Nigh
John W. Noble
Mabel Norman
Wilfrid North

O

Frank O'Connor
Sidney Olcott
Henry Ott

P

Georg W. Pabst
Ida May Park
William Parke
Albert Parker
Stuart Paton
Scott Pembroke
Leonce Perret
Wray Physioc
Harry Joe Pollard
Edwin S. Porter
Frank Powell
Paul Powell

Q

Billy Quirk

R

Albert Ray
Charles Ray
Herman C. Raymaker
Luther Reed
Frank Reicher
Charles F. Reisner
Harry Revier
Lynn E. Reynolds
John Stuart Robertson
Albert Rogell
Philip Rosen
Arthur Rosson
Richard Rosson
Wesley H. Ruggles

S

Malcolm St. Clair
Al Santell
George Sargent
Paul Scardon
Victor Schertzinger
Ernest Schoedsack
Victor Seastrom
Edward Sedgwick
Lew Seiler
William S. Seiter
George B. Seitz
Larry Semon
Mack Sennett
Lowell Sherman
J. Barney Sherry
Scott Sidney
Paul Sloane
Edward Sloman
Ray C. Smallwood
Clifford Smith
David Smith
Noel Mason Smith
John Stahl
Penrhyn Stanlaws
Richard Stanton
Paul Stein
Ford Sterling
Mauritz Stiller
Benjamin Stoloff
Phil Stone
Jerome Storm
Frank Strayer
Rollin Sturgeon
Edward "Eddie" Sutherland
Charles Swickard

T

Norman Taurog
Charles Taylor
Ray Taylor
Sam Taylor
William Desmond Taylor
Tom Terriss
George Terwilliger
Robert T. Thornby
Richard Thorpe
Maurice Tourneur
Laurence Trimble
George Loane Tucker
Otis Turner
Frank Tuttle
Jacques Tyrol

V

Travers Vale
Wally Van
W. S. "Woody" Van Dyke
Perry Vekroff
Edward Venturini
King Vidor
Robert G. Vignola
Joseph Von Sternberg
Erich Von Stroheim

W

Richard Wallace
Raoul Walsh
Ernest Warde
John Waters
Harry Webb
Kenneth Webb
Millard Webb
Lois Weber
William Wellman
Alfred L. Werker

Roland West
Theodore & Leopold Wharton
Herbert Wilcox
Ted Wilde
Irvin Willat
Ben Wilson
Lawrence C. Windom
Chester Withey
William Wolbert
Sam Wood
Duke Worne
Wallace Worsley
William Worthington
John Griffith Wray
William Wyler

Y

James Young

Directors' Credits

John Adolfi (1888-)
1918: Heart of a Girl
Queen of the Sea
19: The Cavell Case
20: Wonder Man
Who's Your Brother?
21: Little 'fraid Lady
23: Darling of the Rich
Little Red School House
24: Chalk Marks
25: After Midnight
Scarlet West
Phantom Express
26: Big Pal
Checkered Flag
27: What Happened to Father
Husband Hunters
28: The Devil's Skipper
Prowlers of the Sea
Little Snob
Midnight Taxi
Sinners' Parade
29: Fancy Baggage PT
Evidence T
Show of Shows T
In the Headlines

Del Andrews (c1903)
1925: That Devil Quemado
Wild Bull's Lair
The Bandit's Baby
Ridin' the Wind
No Man's Law
26: Man Rustlin'
Ridin' Streak
Yellow Back
27: Ain't Love Funny
Is That Nice?
A Hero on Horseback
28: Rawhide Kid
Wild West Show

Oscar Apfel (d. 1938)
1915: A Soldier's Oath
16: Battle of Hearts
End of the Trail
Man of Sorrows
18: Interloper
Tinsel
Merely Players
Turn of a Card
19: To Him That Hath
Rough Neck
Phil-For-Short
Little Intruder
Mandarin's Gold
The Grouch
Squaw Man
Bringing Up Betty
Amateur Widow
Crooks of Dreams
Auction of Souls
20: Me and Captain Kidd
The Oakdale Affair
The Steel King
21: Blazed Trail
22: Ten Nights in a Bar Room
Trail of the Law
23: The Social Code
In Search of a Thrill
Lion's Mouse
Cameo Kirby
24: The Heart Bandit
The Man Who Paid
The Wolf's Fangs
Bulldog Drummond
25: Sporting Chance
Thoroughbred
Borrowed Finery
26: Midnight Limited
Somebody's Mother
Call of the Klondike
Last Alarm
Perils of the Coast Guard
Racewild
27: Cheaters
When Seconds Count
Code of the Cow Country

Roscoe "Fatty" Arbuckle (1887-1933)

1914: Barnyard Flirtations
Chicken Chaser
A Bath House Beauty
Where Hazel Met the Villain
A Suspended Ordeal
The Water Bug
The Alarm
Fatty and the Heiress
Fatty's Finish
The Sky Pirate
Those Happy Days
Fatty's Gift
Fatty's Debut (or, Fatty Butts In)
Fatty Again

15: Fickle Fatty's Fall
The Village Scandal
Fatty and the Broadway Stars
Fatty and Mabel Adrift
He Did and He Didn't (or, Love and Lobsters)
Bright Lights
His Wife's Mistakes
The Other Man
The Moonshiners
The Waiters' Ball
A Creampuff Romance

Roscoe "Fatty" Arbuckle under the assumed name of William Goodrich directed:

Keep Laughing
Moonlight and Cactus
Anybody's Goat
Smart Work
Hollywood Luck
Bridge Wives
Mother's Holiday
It's a Cinch

(No dates recorded, since unreleased to the public.)

George Archainbaud (1890-1959)

1918: Maid of Belgium
The Awakening
Diamonds and Pearls
Divine Sacrifice
The Cross-Bearer
The Trap
The Brand of Satan

19: Love Cheat

20: A Damsel in Distress
In Walked Mary
Shadow of Rosalie Byrne
What Women Want

21: Pleasure Seekers
Wonderful Chance
Marooned Hearts
Miracle of Manhattan
Girl from Nowhere
Handcuffs and Kisses

22: Evidence
Clay Dollars
Man of Stone
One Week of Love
Under Oath

23: The Common Law
Midnight Guest
Power of a Lie

24: The Flaming '40s
Christine of the Hungry Heart
For Sale
The Plunderer
Mirage
Shadows of the East
Single Wives
Storm Daughter

25: Necessary Evil
Enticement
Scarlet Saint
What Fools Men

26: Puppets
Men of Steel
Silent Lover

27: Easy Pickings
Night Life

28: Tragedy of Youth
Woman Against the World
Bachelor's Paradise
Ladies of the Night Club
Grain of Dust

29: Man in Hobbles
Two Men and a Maid
Voice Within PT
College Coquette T
Broadway Scandals T
George Washington Cohen

Dorothy Arzner (1900-)

1922: Blood and Sand (cutting)

23: Covered Wagon (cutting)
Wild Party (cutting)

27: Fashions for Women

27: Ten Modern Commandments
Get Your Man
Manhattan Cocktail
30: Anybody's Woman T

Charles Avery (1873-)
1915: Hogan's Wild Oats
Hogan's Mussy Job
Hogan's Romantic Upset
Hogan Out West
Gussle's Wayward Path
Gussle Rivals Jonah
Gussle's Backward Way
Gussle Tied to Trouble
A Lover's Lost Control
A Submarine Pirate
16: His Lying Heart
His Last Scent

Lloyd Bacon (1890-1955)
1926: Finger Prints
Private Izzy Murphy
Broken Hearts of Hollywood
27: Heart of Maryland
White Flannels
A Sailor's Sweetheart
Brass Knuckles
28: Pay As You Enter
Lion and the Mouse
Women Men Talk About
Singing Fool T
29: Stark Mad T
No Defense T
Honky Tonk T
Say it with a Song T
30: So Long Letty T

Clarence Badger (1880-)
1916: A Modern Enoch Arden
Gypsy Joe
His Wild Oats
A Social Cub
The Danger Girl
Haystacks and Steeples
17: Nick-Of-Time Baby
Teddy at the Throttle
Whose Baby?
The Sultan's Wife
18: The Floor Below
Venus Model
Friend Husband
19: Sis Hopkins
Kingdom of Youth
19: Leave It To Susan
Day Dreams
Daughter of Mine
Perfect Lady
Through the Wrong Door
20: Almost a Husband
Jes' Call Me Jim
Jubilo
The Strange Boarder
Water, Water, Everywhere
Strictly Confidential
Cupid, the Cowpuncher
21: Honest Hutch
Boys Will Be Boys
Guile of Women
An Unwilling Hero
22: A Poor Relation
Doubling for Romeo
Don't Get Personal
Dangerous Little Demon
Quincy Adams Sawyer
23: Potash and Perlmutter
Red Lights
Your Friend and Mine
24: Shooting of Dan McGrew
One Night in Rome
Painted People
25: Eve's Secret
New Lives for Old
Paths to Paradise
Golden Princess
26: Hands Up!
Miss Brewster's Millions
The Rainmaker
Campus Flirt
27: It
A Kiss in a Taxi
Senorita
Manpower
Swim, Girl, Swim
She's a Sheik
28: Red Hair
Fifty-Fifty Girl
Hot News
Three Week Ends
29: Paris Bound T

King Baggott (1880-1948)
1921: Cheated Love
Moonlight Follies
22: Human Hearts
Kissed
Nobody's Fool

22: Lavender Bath Lady
A Dangerous Game
Kentucky Derby
23: Crossed Wires
Gossip
Love Letter
Town Scandal
Darling of New York
25: Raffles
Home Maker
Tumbleweeds
26: Lovey Mary
27: Perch of the Devil
Notorious Lady
28: House of Scandal
Romance of a Rogue

Eddie Baker (1897-)

7 years Christie Comedies
2 1/2 years with Hal Roach
1925: French Pastry
28: Show People SSE
29: All at Sea
Carnation Kid PT
30: Oh Yeah!
?? Why Worry
Goofy Gab

George D. Baker

1915: The Dust of Egypt
16: The Price for Folly
The Shop Girl
Tarantula
A Night Out
The Wager
17: The White Raven
His Father's Son
Long Live the Queen
What Shall It Profit
Sowers and Reapers
18: In Judgment Of
Her Inspiration
Lifted Veil
A Sleeping Memory
Outwitted
The Shell Game
Revelation
Toys of Fate
The Demon
19: As the Sun Went Down
Unexpected Places
The Lion's Den
Castles in the Air
19: Peggy Does Her Darndest
Return of Mary
20: The Cinema Murder
The Man Who Lost Himself
21: Buried Treasure
Heliotrope
Proxies
Without Limit
22: Don't Write Letters
I Can Explain
The Hunch
Little Eva Ascends
Stay Home
23: Slave of Desire

Reginald Barker (1886-1936)

1914: The Bargain
15: The Coward
18: Madam Who?
Carmen of the Klondike
The One Woman
The Turn of the Wheel
The Hell-Cat
19: Shadows
The Stronger Vow
The Brand
The Crimson Gardenia
Girl from Outside
Bonds of Love
Flame of the Desert
20: Woman and the Puppet
Dangerous Days
The Branding Iron
21: Godless Men
The Old Nest
Poverty of Riches
22: Hearts Aflame
The Storm
23: Eternal Struggle
Pleasure Mad
24: Women Who Give
Broken Barriers
Biff Bang Buddy
25: The Great Divide
White Desert
Dixie Handicap
When the Door Opened
26: Flaming Forest
27: Body and Soul
Frontiersman
28: The Toilers
29: The Rainbow
New Orleans PT

29: Seven Keys to Baldpate T
30: The Great Divide T

Rex Beach (1877-)
1916: The Ne'er-Do-Well
The Net
17: The Barrier
The Auction Block
18: Heart of the Sunset
19: Rainbow's End
Crimson Gardenia
The Brand
Girl from Outside
20: The Silver Horde
North Wind's Malice
Going Some
21: The Iron Trail
23: The Spoilers

William Beaudine (1892-1970)
1922: Watch Your Step
Heroes of the Street
23: Her Fatal Millions
Catch My Smoke
Penrod and Sam
The Country Kid
The Printer's Devil
24: The Narrow Street
Daughters of Pleasure
Daring Youth
Cornered
Wandering Husbands
Boy of Mine
25: Broadway Butterfly
How Baxter Butted In
Little Annie Rooney
26: That's My Baby
The Social Highwayman
Sparrows
Hold That Lion
The Canadians
27: Frisco Sally Levy
Irresistible Lover
Life of Riley
28: The Cohens and the Kellys in Paris
Heart to Heart
Home, James
Do Your Duty
Give and Take SSE
29: Fugitives SSE
Two Weeks Off PT
Hard to Get T
29: Girl from Woolworth's T
Wedding Rings T
Homespun Hero
Hey Rube!
Seaside Siren
Seven Bald Pates
Movie Mad
Petticoats and Pants

Harry Beaumont (1888-1966)
1918: Brown of Harvard
19: Thirty a Week
Wild Goose Chase
Little Rowdy
Man and His Money
Go West, Young Man
One of the Finest
City of Comrades
Heartease
Lord and Lady Algy
20: Dollars and Sense
Toby's Bow
The Gay Lord Quex
The Great Accident
Going Some
Stop Thief!
Two Cents Worth of Humaneness
21: Officer 666
22: Lights of the Desert
The Ragged Heiress
Very Truly Yours
Seeing's Believing
They Like 'em Rough
Glass Houses
Fourteenth Lover
Five Dollar Baby
Love in the Dark
June Madness
23: Crinoline and Romance
Noise in Newboro
Gold Diggers
Main Street
24: Lost Lady
Lovers of Camille
Babbitt
Don't Doubt Your Husband
25: Recompense
His Majesty-Bunker Bean
Rose of the World
26: Sandy
Womanpower
27: One Increasing Purpose

27: The Secret Studio
28: Forbidden Hours
Our Dancing Daughters T
29: Broadway Melody T
Single Man
Speedway

Monta Bell (1891-1958)
1924: How to Educate a Wife
Broadway After Dark
The Snob
25: Lady of the Night
Pretty Ladies
Lights of Old Broadway
King of Main Street
26: The Torrent
Upstage
The Boy Friend
27: After Midnight
Man, Woman and Sin
29: The Bellamy Trial

Spencer G. Bennet (1893-)
1920: Phantom Foe (serial)
25: Sunken Silver (serial)
Play Ball (serial)
26: House Without a Key (serial)
Fighting Marine (serial)
Snowed In (serial)
27: Hawk of the Hills (serial)
Melting Millions (serial)
28: Man Without a Face (serial)
The Terrible People (serial)
The Tiger's Shadow (serial)
The Yellow Cameo (serial)
29: The Black Book (serial)
Fire Detective (serial)
Queen of the North Woods (serial)

George Beranger
1916: asst. on The Birth of a Nation
Half-Breed
Manhattan Madness
18: Find the Woman
19: Broken Blossoms (asst.)
20: A Manhattan Knight
Uncle Sam of Freedom Ridge

1921: Number 17
?? Flirting with Fate

Ludwig Berger
1926: The Waltz Dream
27: Woman from Moscow
Sins of the Fathers
The Coward
Fighting White Slave Traffic
?? The Judge from Zalamea
Story of Christine Herre
A Glass of Water
The Lost Shoe

Paul Bern (1889-1939)
1924: Open All Night
25: Dressmaker from Paris
Flower of the Night

William Bertram (1889-)
1917: The Neglected Wife (serial)
Who is Number One (serial)
18: Tears and Smiles
A Little Patriot
Daddy's Girl
Dolly Does Her Bit
A Daughter of the West
Voice of Destiny
Cupid by Proxy
Winning Grandma
19: Vacation
The Arizona Cat Claw
His Obligation
The Idol
The Mighty Hold
High Cost of Flirting
Madonna of the Night
The Owl Witch
Milady o' the Beanstalk
The Old Maid's Baby
Sawdust Doll
Dolly's Vacation
20: Hidden Dangers (serial)
Baby Marie's Roundup
Miss Gingersnap
21: The Purple Riders (serial)
The Wolverine
22: Alias Phil Kennedy
Ghost City
26: Ace of Action

26: Tangled Herds
Hoodoo Ranch
27: The Phantom Buster
Gold from Weepah

Madame Alice Blaché (1878-)
1910: The Pit and the Pendulum
The Rogues of Paris
The Dream Woman
17: The Empress
18: Sea Waif
House of Cards
When You and I Were Young
A Soul Adrift
Behind the Mask
The Great Adventure
20: Tarnished Reputations

Herbert Blaché
1919: Loaded Dice
A Man's World
The Uplifters
Fools and their Money
The Man Who Stayed at Home
Jeanne of the Gutter
Parisian Tigress
Satan Junior
The Divorce
The Brat
20: The Walk-Offs
Stronger than Death
Hope
21: The New York Idea
Out of the Chorus
Saphead
23: Fools and Riches
Nobody's Bride
Untamable
Wild Party
The War Lady
24: High Speed
25: Head Winds
Secrets of the Night
Calgary Stampede
26: The Mystery Club

J. Stuart Blackton (1875-1946)
1897-1911 (numerous quickies)
1898: Burglar on the Roof
Tearing Down the Spanish Flag
04: A Curious Dream
04: A Gentleman of France
Raffles, Amateur Crackman
06: Humorous Phases of Funny Faces (animated)
09: Life of Moses
Les Miserables
A Midsummer Night's Dream
12: The Two Portraits
14: Love, Luck and Gasoline
Goodness Gracious
The Honeymooners
The Winksome Widow
The Christian
15: The Park Honeymooners
The Juggernaut
The Battle Cry of Peace
The Island of Regeneration
16: An Enemy of the King
Whom the Gods Destroy
17: The Message of the Mouse
Judgment House
Womanhood, The Glory of the Nation
The Diary of a Puppy
The Fairy Godfather
The Collie Market
A Spring Idyll
Satin and Calico
The Little Strategist
18: Missing
The Common Cause
Safe for Democracy
Wild Youth
The World for Sale
19: The Littlest Scout
The House Divided
The Moonshine Trail
Life's Greatest Problem
My Husband's Other Wife
20: Dawn
Man and Woman
Respectable by Proxy
Passers-By
The Blood Barrier
21: House of the Tolling Bell
Forbidden Valley
22: The Glorious Adventure
A Gypsy Cavalier
23: The Virgin Queen
On the Banks of the Wabash
24: Let Not Man Put Asunder
Beloved Brute

24: Clean Heart
Behold This Woman
Between Friends
25: Happy Warrior
Tides of Passion
Redeeming Sin
26: Bride of the Storm
Hell Bent for Heaven
Gilded Highway
Passionate Quest
?? Richard III
Macbeth
King Lear

J. G. Blystone (1892-1938)
1922: Balloonatics
A Surf Scandal
Love Behind Bars
Virtuous Husbands
Yellow Dog Catcher
The Naughty Wink
The Quack Duck Hunter
23: Our Hospitality
25: Dick Turpin
The Last Man on Earth
The Lucky Horseshoe
Everlasting Whisper
The Best Bad Man
26: Wings of the Storm
The Family Upstairs
My Own Pal
Hardboiled
27: Ankles Preferred
Slaves of Beauty
Pajamas
28: The Sharpshooters
Mother Knows Best PT
29: Captain Lash SSE
Through Different Eyes T

Joseph C. Boyle (1890-)
1927: Convoy
Broadway Nights
28: The Whip Woman
The Mad Hour
The Man Higher Up
Through the Breakers
Head of the Family
29: Times Square

Frank Borzage (1893-1962)
1918: Flying Colors
Until They Get Me
The Gun Woman
18: Billy Jim
Shoes That Danced
Innocent's Progress
Society for Sale
An Honest Man
Who Is To Blame?
The Ghost Flower
The Curse of Iku
19: Toton
Prudence of Broadway
Whom the Gods Destroy
20: Humoresque
21: The Duke of Chimney Butte
22: Get Rich-Quick Wallingford
Back Pay
Silent Shelby
Billy Jim
Good Provider
Valley of Silent Men
Pride of Palomar
23: Children of Dust
The Nth Commandment
Song of Love
24: Age of Desire
Secrets
25: The Lady
Daddy's Gone A-Hunting
Wages for Wives
The Circle
Lazybones
26: Marriage License
The First Year
Dixie Merchant
Early to Wed
27: Seventh Heaven
28: Street Angel
29: The River PT
Lucky Star
They Had to See Paris T
True Heaven
30: Song o' My Heart T
Devil with Women T
Liliom T

Charles J. Brabin (1883-1959)
1914: The Man Who Disappeared (serial)
15: The Raven
16: The Price of Fame
17: Mary Jane's Pa
The Sixteenth Wife
The Secret Kingdom (serial)

18: Adopted Son
Red, White and Blue Blood
Breakers Ahead
Social Quicksands
A Pair of Cupids
Persuasive Peggy
19: His Bonded Wife
Thou Shalt Not
The Poor, Rich Man
Buchanan's Wife
20: La Belle Russe
Kathleen Mavourneen
While New York Sleeps
21: Blind Wives
Foot Falls
22: A Broadway Peacock
Driven
23: Lights of New York
Six Days
24: So Big
26: Stella Maris
Mismates
Twinkletoes
27: Framed
Valley of the Giants
Hard Boiled Haggerty
28: Burning Daylight
Whip
29: Bridge of San Luis Rey PT
30: Ship from Shanghai T

Bertram Bracken

1916: The Eternal Sappho
East Lynne
18: The Understudy
Conscience
A Branded Soul
For Liberty
Moral Law
19: The Boomerang
And a Still Small Voice
Code of the Yukon
20: Long Arm of Mannister
The Confession
21: Harriet and the Piper
Parted Curtains
Kazan
The Mask
24: Passion's Pathway
25: Heartless Husbands
26: Speeding Through
27: Duty's Reward
Rose of the Bowery

27: Fire and Steel

Robert North Bradbury

1916: The Harvest of Gold
To Have and To Hold
The False Prophet
18: The Iron Test (serial)
The Resurrection of Gold Bar
19: Perils of Thunder Mountain (serial)
Faith of the Strong
Last of His People
Into the Light
20: Courage of Marge O'Doone
The Death Trap
The Vanishing Dagger (serial)
25: Riders of Mystery
In High Gear
Hidden Loot
The Speed Demon
26: Looking for Trouble
The Border Sheriff
Davy Crockett at the Fall of the Alamo
Sitting Bull at the Spirit Lake Massacre
Daniel Boone Through the Wilderness
27: The Mojave Kid
28: Lighting Speed
Headin' for Danger
29: Forbidden Trail

Herbert Brenon (1880-1958)

1913: Ivanhoe
Absinthe
14: Neptune's Daughter
15: Across the Atlantic
16: A Daughter of the Gods
War Brides
17: Lone Wolf
The Fall of the Romanoffs
18: Passing of the Third Floor Back
Empty Pockets
19: Twelve Ten
20: Chains of Evidence
21: Passion Flower
The Sign on the Door
Garden of Allah
Wonderful Thing

22: A Stage Romance
Moonshine Valley
Any Wife
Shackles of Gold
Stronger Passion
23: Rustle of Silk
The Custard Cup
Woman with Four Faces
The Spanish Dancer
24: Peter Pan
Shadows of Paris
The Lone Wolf
Side Show of Life
The Alaskan
Breaking Point
25: A Kiss for Cinderella
Little French Girl
Secret of Forgotten Men
26: Beau Geste
The Great Gatsby
God Gave Me Twenty Cents
Dancing Mothers
Song and Dance Man
27: Sorrell and Son
Telephone Girl
Garden of Allah
28: Laugh, Clown, Laugh
29: The Rescue SSE
Case of Sergeant Grischa

Howard Bretherton (1896-)
1927: Slave Ship
Hills of Kentucky
Black Diamond Express
The Bush Leaguer
One Round Hogan
28: Turn Back the Hours
The Chorus Kid
Across the Atlantic
Caught in the Fog
29: Redeeming Sin PT
Greyhound Limited PT
The Man from Headquarters
The Argyle Case T
Time, The Place and the Girl T

Monte Brice (1895-)
1926: Behind the Front (wr., dir.)
We're in the Navy Now wr., dir.)
27: Casey at the Bat
28: Hot News (wr.)
The Fleet's In (wr.)

Otto Brower
1927: Shootin' Irons
28: Avalanche
29: Sunset Pass
Stairs of Sand

Clarence Brown (1890-)
1920: The Great Redeemer
Last of the Mohicans
21: Foolish Matrons
22: Light in the Dark
23: Robin Hood
Don't Marry for Money
The Acquittal
24: Signal Towers
Butterfly
25: The Goose Woman
The Eagle
26: Kiki
27: Flesh and the Devil
28: The Trail of '98
A Woman of Affairs T
29: Wonder of Women T
30: Navy Blues T

Harry Joe Brown (1890-)
1925: The Bashful Buccaneer
26: Windjammer
Fighting Thoroughbreds
Danger Quest
Broadway Billy
Racing Romance
High Flyer
Self Starter
The Dangerous Dude
One Punch o' Day
Kentucky Handicap
The Winner
Stick to Your Story
Rapid Fire Romance
Night Owl
Moran of the Mounted
27: Land Beyond the Law
The Scorcher
Red Raiders
Royal American
The Racing Fool
Overland Stage
Gun Gospel
Romantic Rogue

28: Wagon Show
Code of Scarlet
Sky Ranger
The Cloud Pistol
Air Derby
29: Lawless Legion
Royal Rider
Wagon Master
Palomino Entry
Kettle Creek
Golden Bridle
30: Señor American T
Fighting Legion PT
Parade of the West PT

Melville Brown
1926: Her Big Night
28: Red Lips
Oh, Geraldine
13 Washington Square
Buck Privates
29: Jazz Heaven T
Love Doctor T
Dance Hall T
I Love You T

Tod Browning (1880-1962)
1918: Which Woman
The Deciding Kiss
Eyes of Mystery
Revenge
Legion of Death
The House in the Mist
19: The Unpainted Woman
The Wicked Darling
An Exquisite Thief
Set Free
The Brazen Beauty
Petal on the Current
20: Virgin of Stamboul
Bonnie, Bonnie Lassie
21: Outside the Law
No Woman Knows
22: The Wise Kid
Man Under Cover
Under Two Flags
23: Drifting
White Tiger
Day of Faith
24: Dangerous Flirt
25: The Beautiful Beggar
Unholy Three
The Mystic
25: Dollar Down
Silk Stocking Sal
26: Road to Mandalay
Black Bird
27: The Snow
Unknown
London After Midnight
28: Big City
29: East is East
Thirteenth Chair T

Dimitri Buchowetzski (1895-)
1925: The Swan
Graustark
26: Crown of Lies
Midnight Sun
Valencia

David Butler (1895-)
1926: Quarterback
Meet the Prince
Oh, Lady!
Womanpower
27: Nobody's Widow
Seventh Heaven
Rush Hour
Night School Hero
28: News Parade
Win That Girl
Prep and Pep
29: Masked Emotions
Movietone Follies T
Chasing Through Europe SSE
Salute T
Sunny Side Up T

W. Christy Cabanne (1888-)
1915: Enoch Arden
Double Trouble
16: Reggie Mixes In
17: One of Many
The Slacker
The Great Secret (serial)
18: Draft 258
Cyclone Higgins, D. D.
19: The Pest
A Regular Fellow
Mayor of Filbert
Fighting Through
God's Outlaw
20: The Triflers
Burnt Wings

20: The Notorious Mrs. Sands
The Beloved Cheater
Life's Twist
21: Live and Let Live
The Stealers
What's a Wife Worth
22: Beyond the Rainbow
Barricade
At the Stage Door
Till We Meet Again
Reckless Youth
24: Is Love Everything?
Lend Me Your Husband
The Spitfire
Youth for Sale
The Sixth Commandment
Average Woman
25: Midshipman
Masked Bride
26: Monte Carlo
27: Altars of Desire
28: Nameless Men
Driftwood
Annapolis SSE
29: Restless Youth

Colin Campbell (1888-1966)
1916: The Crisis
18: A Hoosier Romance
The Still Alarm
19: Beauty Market
Tongues of Flame
Who Shall Take My Life?
Sea Flower
Railroaders
Little Orphan Annie
Beware of Strangers
City of Purple Dreams
20: Big Happiness
The First Born
Black Roses
When Dawn Came
Where Lights are Low
21: The Corsican Brothers
Thunderbolt
Moon Madness
22: The Swamp
Lure of Jade
Two Kinds of Women
Monte Cristo
The Rosary
Ne'er-Do-Well
23: The Spoilers
The Buster
Grail
Bucking the Barrier
Three Who Paid
World's a Stage
24: Bowery Bishop
Pagan Passions
27: Garden of Allah
?? Law North of 65
Love of Madge O'Mara
In the Carquinez Woods

Albert Capellani (1874-)
1918: American Made
Daybreak
The Richest Girl
Social Hypocrites
House of Mirth
19: Oh Boy
Out of the Fog
Red Lantern
Eye for Eye
20: Inside of the Cup
The Wild Goose
21: The Fortune Teller
The Virtuous Model
22: Sisters
Young Diana

Frank Capra (1897-)
1926: Strong Man
27: Long Pants
For the Love of Mike
28: So This is Love
Matinee Idol
That Certain Thing
Say It With Sables
Way of the Strong
Submarine
Power of the Press
29: Younger Generation PT
Donovan Affair T
Flight T

Edwin Carewe (1883-1940)
1915: Final Judgment
16: Snowbird
God's Half Acre
18: Splendid Sinner
Their Compact
Voice of Conscience
Trail to Yesterday
House of Gold

19: Pals First
False Evidence
Way of the Strong
Shadows of Suspicion
Easy to Make Money
20: Isobel
Habit
Playthings of Destiny
My Lady's Latch Key
21: Rio Grande
The Right to Lie
22: Trail's End
A Question of Honor
Invisible Fear
Her Mad Bargain
I Am the Law
Silver Wings
23: Bad Man
Girl of the Golden West
Mighty Lak' a Rose
24: A Son of the Sahara
Madonna of the Streets
25: My Son
The Lady Who Lied
Barriers Aflame
26: Joanna
High Steppers
Pals First
27: Resurrection
28: Ramona
29: Evangeline PT

Charlie Chaplin (1889-)

1914: Making a Living (or, A Busted Johnny, or, Doing His Best)
Kid Auto Races at Venice
Mabel's Strange Predicament (or, The Hotel Mix-Up)
Between Showers (or, The Flirts, or, In Wrong, or, Charlie and the Umbrella)
A Film Johnnie (or, The Movie Nut, or, The Million Dollar Job)
Tango Tangles (or, Charlie's Recreation or, The Music Hall)
His Favorite Pastime (or, The Bonehead)
Cruel, Cruel Love (or, Lord Help Us)
The Star Boarder (or, The Hash-House Hero)
Mabel at the Wheel (or, His Daredevil Queen, or, A Hot Finish)
Twenty Minutes of Love (or, He Loved Her So, or, Cops and Watches, or, The Love-Friend)
Caught in a Cabaret (or, The Waiter, or, The Jazz Waiter, or, Faking with Society)
Caught in the Rain (or, At It Again, or, Who Got Stung? or, In the Park)
A Busy Day (or, The Militant Suffragette)
The Fatal Mallet (or, The Pile Driver)
Her Friend the Bandit (or, Mabel's Flirtation)
The Knockout (or, Counted Out, or, The Pugilist)
Mabel's Busy Day (or, Charlie and the Sausages, or, Love and Lunch, or, Hot Dogs)
Laughing Gas (or, Turning His Ivories, or, The Dentist, or, Down and Out)
The Property Man (or, The Roustabout, or, Getting His Goat)
The Face on the Barroom Floor (or, The Ham Artist)
The Masquerader (or, Putting One Over, or, The Picnic, or, The Female Impersonator, or, The New Janitor)
Recreation (or, Spring Fever)
His New Profession (or, The Good-For-Nothing, or, Helping Himself)
The Rounders (or, Revelry, or, Two of a Kind, or, Oh, What a Night!)
The New Janitor (or, The

14: Porter, or The Blundering Boob)
Those Love Pangs (or, The Rival Mashers, or, Busted Hearts)
Dough and Dynamite (or, The Doughnut Designer, or, The Cook)
Gentlemen of Nerve (or, Some Nerve)
His Musical Career (or, The Piano Movers, or, Musical Tramps)
His Trysting Place (or, The Family House)
Tillie's Punctured Romance
Getting Acquainted (or, A Fair Exchange)
His Prehistoric Past (or, A Dream)
15: His New Job
A Night Out
The Champion
In the Park
The Jitney Elopement
The Tramp
By the Sea
Work (or, The Paper-hanger)
A Woman (or, The Perfect Lady)
The Bank (or, Charlie at the Bank)
Shanghaied
A Night in the Show
The Baggage Smasher
The Dog Catcher
16: Police
Carmen
Triple Trouble
The Essanay-Chaplin Revue of 1916
The Floorwalker
The Fireman
The Vagabond
One A. M.
The Count
The Pawnshop
Behind the Screen
The Rink
17: Easy Street
The Cure
The Immigrant
17: The Adventurer
18: A Dog's Life
Shoulder Arms
The Bond (for war effort)
19: Sunnyside
A Day's Pleasure
21: The Kid
The Idle Class
22: Pay Day
23: The Pilgrim
A Woman of Paris (dir., wr., prod.)
25: The Gold Rush
28: The Circus
Show People (cameo)
31: City Lights
36: Modern Times
40: The Great Dictator T
47: Monsieur Verdoux T
53: Limelight T
57: The King of New York T
67: The Countess from Hong Kong(bit) T

Louis Chaudet (1884-)

1918: Edge of the Law
Society's Driftwood
19: Long Lane's Turning
The Love Call
The Girl of My Dreams
The Blue Bonnet
20: Common Sense
22: The Pillagers
King Fisher's Roost
23: Defying Destiny
25: A Man of Nerve
26: Tentacles of the North
Eyes Right
27: Speeding Hoofs
Outcast Souls
33: Hoop-La
??: Merry Andrews

Emile Chautard (1892-1964)

1918: Magda
Eternal Temptress
Marionettes
House of Glass
Ordeal of Rosetta
Her Final Reckoning
Under False Colors
Heart of Ezra Greer
19: Marriage Price

19: Eyes of the Soul
Under the Greenwood Tree
Daughter of the South
Out of the Shadow
Paid in Full
20: Black Panther's Cub
21: Mystery of the Yellow Room
22: Living Lies
Whispering Shadows
Glory of Clementina
Youth to Youth
Forsaking All Others
23: Daytime Wives
24: Untamed Youth
26: Paris at Midnight
Times Square
Parisian Wife
Invisible Foe
28: Lilac Time SSE
Haunted House SSE
Love Mart
Adoration SSE
29: House of Horror PT
Marianne T

Benjamin Christiansen
1926: Devil's Circus
27: Mockery
28: Haunted House
Hawk's Nest
29: Seven Footprints to Satan SSE
House of Horror PT
Witchcraft Through the Ages

Elmer Clifton (1890-1949)
1918: The High Sign
A Stormy Knight
Flirting with Death
The Man Trap
The Flash of Fate
Brace Up
The Guilt of Silence
The Eagle
Smashing Through
Winner Takes All
19: Battling Jane
Boots
Safe for Democracy
Peppy Polly
Kiss or Kill
I'll Get Him Yet
19: The Hope Chest
Nugget Nell
Out of Luck
20: Mary Ellen Comes to Town
Turning the Tables
22: Down to Sea in Ships
23: Six Cylinder Love
24: Warrens of Virginia
Daughters of the Night
26: Wives at Auction
28: Wreck of the Hesperus
Let '34 Go Gallagher
Virgin Eyes
Beautiful Blue Danube
Tropical Nights
29: The Devil's Apple Tree

Eddie Cline (1892-)
1913: The Winning Punch
15: Sheriff Nell's Comeback
16: His Bread and Butter
Bubbles of Trouble
His Busted Trust
17: Villa of the Movies
A Dog Catcher's Love
The Pawnbroker's Heart
18: Those Athletic Girls
19: A School House Scandal
20: Training for Husbands
Ten Nights Without a Barroom
assistant director to Buster Keaton:
1920: The High Sign
One Week
Convict 13
The Scarecrow
Neighbors
21: The Haunted House
Hard Luck
The Boat
The Paleface
22: The Cops
My Wife's Relations
The Frozen North
The Electric House
Daydreams
Balloonatics
23: Circus Days
Three Ages
The Meanest Man in the World
When a Man's a Man
24: Helen's Babies

24: The Good Bad Boy
Captain January
Along Came Ruth
Little Robinson Crusoe
25: The Rag Man
Old Clothes
27: Let It Rain
Soft Cushions
Girl from Everywhere
28: Ladies' Night in a Turkish Bath
Head Man
Vamping Venus
The Chase
29: Broadway Fever
His Lucky Day PT
The Forward Pass T

Bennett Cohn (1894-)
1926: Hi-Jacking Rustlers
West of the Rainbow's End
A Ridin' Gent
Gray Devil
Dangerous Traffic
Midnight Faces
27: Laffin' Fool
Thunderbolt's Tracks
Where the North Holds Sway
Code of the Range
28: The Cop
Stand and Deliver

Jack Conway (1887-1952)
1917: Don't Shoot!
18: Bond of Fear
Because of a Woman
Doing Her Bit
Little Red Decides
Her Decision
You Can't Believe Everything
19: Diplomatic Mission
Desert Law
Lombardi, Limited
Lure of the Orient
20: Riders of the Dawn
21: The Killer
The Dwelling Place of Light
Money Changers
The Spenders
The U. P. Trail
21: The Kiss
A Daughter of the Law
22: Step on It!
Don't Shoot!
A Parisian Scandal
The Millionaire
Across the Deadline
Another Man's Shoes
Long Chance
Restless Souls
Judgment of the Guilty
A Jewel in Pawn
23: The Prisoner
Sawdust
Quicksands
What Wives Want
Trimmed in Scarlet
Lucretia Combard
24: Trouble Shooter
Heart Buster
25: Roughneck
Hunted Woman
The Only Thing
26: Brown of Harvard
Soul Mates
27: Understanding Heart
Twelve Miles Out
28: Quicksands
The Smart Set
Bringing Up Father
While the City Sleeps
29: Alias Jimmy Valentine PT
Our Modern Maidens T
Untamed T
?? Desert of Wheat
Bitter Sweet

Meriam C. Cooper (1893-)
1925: Grass
27: Chang
29: Four Feathers SSE
Beast
33: King Kong T

William J. Craft (1886-)
1914: Hazards of Helen (serial)
The Great Radial Mystery
20: White Riders
Sidewalks of New York
Way of the Law
Love's Battle
Sergeant Hammon of the R. C. M. P.

22: With Stanley in Africa (serial)
23: In the Days of Daniel Boone (serial)
Beasts of Paradise (serial)
24: The Riddle Rider (serial)
25: The Bloodhound
That Man Jack
Range Terror
Galloping Vengeance
26: Power of the Weak
King of the Saddle
Galloping Cowboy
The Silent Flyer (serial)
27: The Wreck
Arizona Whirlwind
Birds of Prey
The Clown
Poor Girls
Painting the Town
A Hero for a Night
28: Hot Heels
How to Handle Women
Gate Crasher
29: The Kid's Clever
Skinner Steps Out T
The Cohens and the Kellys in Atlantic City PT
30: Embarrassing Moments T

Donald Crisp (1880-)
1918: Eyes of the World
Lost in Transit
Countess Charming
Clever Mrs. Carfax
Jules of the Strong Heart
Rimrock Jones
House of Silence
Believe Me, Xantippe
Firefly of France
Less than Kin
19: The Goat
Something To Do
Putting It Over
Love Insurance
A Very Good Young Man
Under the Top
Venus in the East
Way of a Man With a Maid
Poor Boob
Johnny Get Your Gun
20: It Pays to Advertise
Miss Hobbs
Why Smith Left Home
The Six Best Cellars
Too Much Johnson
21: Held by the Enemy
The Barbarian
Appearances
Princess of New York
22: The Bonnie Briar Bush
24: The Navigator
25: Don Q
26: Man Bait
Sunnyside Up
Young April
27: Nobody's Widow
Vanity
The Fighting Eagle
Dress Parade
28: The Cop
Stand and Deliver
Ramona

Alan Crosland (1891-1936)
1917: Kidnapped
18: Apple Tree Girl
The Whirlpool
Unbeliever
19: The Country Cousin
20: Glorious South
The Flapper
Youthful Folly
Greater than Fame
Point of View
21: Worlds Apart
Broadway and Home
Is Life Worth Living?
Room and Board
22: Slim Shoulders
Why Announce Your Marriage?
The Prophet's Paradise
Shadows of the Sea
The Snitching Hour
Face in the Fog
23: Enemies of Women
Under the Red Robe
24: Unguarded Women
Miami
Sinners in Heaven
Three Weeks
25: Bobbed Hair
Contraband

25: Compromise
26: Don Juan
27: Beloved Rogue
When a Man Loves
Old San Francisco
The Jazz Singer PT
28: Glorious Betsy PT
The Scarlet Lady
29: On with the Show T
General Crack T
30: Song of the Flame T

James Cruze (1884-1942)

1911: A Boy of the Revolution (actor)
12: Lucille (actor)
14: Joseph in the Land of Egypt
The Million Dollar Mystery (serial - actor)
Zudora (serial - actor)
18: Too Many Millions (actor)
Less Than Kin (actor)
Believe Me, Xantippe (from here on... director:)
19: The City of Dim Faces
Johnny Get Your Gun
You're Fired!
Alias Mike Moran
The Roaring Road
Under the Top
The Love Burglar
Valley of the Giants
Too Many Millions
The Dub
Hawthorne of the U. S. A.
20: Terror Island
An Adventure in Hearts
The Lottery Man
Mrs. Temple's Telegram
What Happened to Jones
21: A Full House
Always Audacious
The Charm School
Food for Scandal
Crazy to Marry
The Dollar a Year Man
22: One Glorious Day
Is Matrimony a Failure?
The Dictator
The Old Homestead
30 Days
Rent Free
23: The Covered Wagon
Hollywood
City That Never Sleeps
To the Ladies
Ruggles of Red Gap
24: Merton of the Movies
The Fighting Coward
Garden of Weeds
The Enemy Sex
25: The Goose Hangs High
Marry Me
The Pony Express
Welcome Home
Beggar on Horseback
26: Mannequin
One Glorious Day
Old Ironsides
The Waiter from the Ritz
27: We're All Gamblers
City Gone Wild
28: Red Mark
On to Reno
Excess Baggage
The Mating Call
29: The Great Gabbo T

Irving Cummings (1888-1959)

1925: As Man Desires
The Desert Flower
One Year to Live
Just a Woman
26: Rustling for Cupid
The Johnstown Flood
Infatuation
The Country Beyond
27: Bertha the Sewing Machine Girl
The Brute
28: Port of Missing Girls
Dressed to Kill
Romance of the Underworld
29: In Old Arizona T
Behind That Curtain T
Not Quite Decent PT
?? The Freedom to Kiss

Michael Curtiz (1889-1962)

1927: The Third Degree
A Million Bid
Moon of Israel
The Desired Woman
Goodtime Charley
28: Tenderloin PT

29: Noah's Ark PT
Glad Rag Doll T
Madonna of Avenue A PT
Hearts in Exile T
The Gamblers T

J. Searle Dawley

1912: Treasure Island
The Charge of the Light Brigade
13: An American Citizen
On the Broad Stairway
An Hour Before Dawn
A Good Little Devil
The Daughter of the Hills
The Diamond Crown
14: Port of Doom
In the Name of the Prince
One of Millions
The Next Command
The Oath of a Viking
15: Four Feathers
A Daughter of the People
16: Mice and Men
Snow White
17: The Valentine Girl
The Mysterious Miss Terry
Bab's Matinee Idol
Bab's Diary
Bab's Burglar
18: The Seven Swans
Uncle Tom's Cabin
The Lie
Rich Man, Poor Man
The Death Dance
19: The Phantom Honeymoon
Everybody's Business
Twilight
20: Harvest Moon
21: A Virgin Paradise
Beyond Price
22: Who Are My Parents?
23: As a Man Lives
Has the World Gone Mad?
Broadway Broke

Norman Dawn (1887-)

1919: Eternal Triangle
20: Lasca
A Tokio Siren
Adorable Savage
21: Wolves of the North
Fire Cat
White Youth
Thunder Island
22: Five Days to Live
The Vermillion Pencil
Son of the Wolf
24: The Lure of the Yukon
Down by the Rio Grande
25: After Marriage
29: For the Term of His Natural Life
Black Cargoes of the South Seas
The Black Hills
?? Sinbad the Sailor
Two Men of Tinted Butte
Hermit Creek
Line Runners

Joseph De Grasse (d. 1940)

1916: Undertow
18: Anything Once
Winged Mystery
Scarlet Car
Fighting Grin
19: Wildcat of Paris
After the War
Heart of the Hills
20: Brand of Lopez
His Wife's Friend
L'Apache
Market of Souls
21: The Golden Hope
The Midlanders
Bonnie May
Nineteen and Phyllis
The Old Swimmin' Hole
45 Minutes from Broadway
22: Tailor Made Man
23: The Girl I Loved
Thundergate
24: Flowing Gold
26: The Hidden Way

Robert DeLacey

1925: Lets Go, Gallagher
The Wyoming Wildcat
26: The Masquerade Bandit
Wild To Go
The Cowboy Musketeer
The Arizona Streak
Born to Battle

26: Red Hot Hoofs
Out of the West
27: Lightning Lariats
The Sonora Kid
Cyclone of the Range
Splitting the Breeze
The Flying U Ranch
The Cherokee Kid
28: When the Law Rides
King Cowboy
Tyrant of Red Gulch
29: Trial of the Horse Thieves
The Drifter
Gun Law
Idaho Red
Pride of the Pawnee

Hampton Del Ruth (1888-)
1921: Skirts
22: The Marriage Chance
27: Naughty
Blondes by Choice

Roy Del Ruth (1895-1961)
1925: Eve's Lover
Hogan's Alley
26: 3 Weeks in Paris
The Man Upstairs
The Little Irish Girl
Footloose Widow
Across the Pacific
27: Wolf's Clothing
The First Auto
If I Were Single
Ham and Eggs at the Front
28: 5 and 10¢ Annie SSE
Powder My Back SSE
The Terror T
29: Beware of Bachelors PT
Conquest T
Desert Song T
The Hottentot T
Gold Diggers of Broadway T
The Aviator T

Cecil B. DeMille (1881-1959)
1913: The Squaw Man
14: The Virginian
The Call of the North
What's His Name
The Man from Home
14: Rose of the Rancho
15: The Girl of the Golden West
The Warrens of Virginia
The Unafraid
The Captive
The Wild Goose Chase
The Arab
Chimmie Fadden
Kindling
Carmen
Chimmie Fadden Out West
The Cheat
16: Maria Rosa
Temptation
The Golden Chance
The Trail of the Lonesome Pine
The Heart of Nora Flynn
The Dream Girl
17: Joan the Woman
Romance of the Redwoods
The Little American
The Woman God Forgot
The Devil Stone
18: The Whispering Chorus
Old Wives and New
We Can't Have Everything
Till I Come Back To You
The Squaw Man (revised)
19: Don't Change Your Husband
For Better, For Worse
Male and Female
20: Why Change Your Wife?
Something to Think About
21: Forbidden Fruit
The Affairs of Anatol
22: Fool's Paradise
Saturday Night
Manslaughter
23: Adam's Rib
Ten Commandments
24: Triumph
Feet of Clay
25: The Golden Bed
The Road to Yesterday
26: The Volga Boatman
27: The King of Kings
29: The Godless Girl PT
Dynamite T

William deMille (1878-1955)
1915: The Warrens of Virginia

15: The Wild Goose Chase
16: The Ragmuffin
Heir to the Hoorah
The Clown
The Blacklist
The Sowers
18: The Widow's Might
One More American
The Ghost House
The Secret Game
Honor of His House
19: For Better or for Worse
Why Change Your Wife?
Mirandy Smiles
The Mystery Girl
20: The Tree of Knowledge
The Prince Chap
Jack Straw
21: What Every Woman Knows
Conrad in Quest of His Youth
Midsummer's Madness
22: Miss Lulu Bett
The Lost Romance
After the Show
Bought and Paid For
Nice People
Clarence
23: Only 38
The World's Applause
Grumpy
The Marriage Maker
24: The Fast Set
Icebound
The Bedroom Window
Don't Call It Love
25: The Locked Doors
Men and Women
Lost: A Wife
New Brooms
26: The Splendid Crime
The Runaway
For Alimony Only
27: The Little Adventuress
28: 10th Avenue
Craig's Wife
29: The Doctor's Secret T
The Idle Rich T
30: This Mad World T
Passion Flower T
32: Two Kinds of Women T
33: Emperor Jones T
39: Captain Fury T

Edward Dillon
1918: Our Little Wife
Antics of Ann
Doll Shop
Might and the Man
19: Putting One Over
Never Say Quit
Luck and Pluck
Help! Help! Police!
Embarrassment of Riches
20: The Amateur Wife
The Winning Stroke
Parlor, Bedroom and Bath
21: The Education of Elizabeth
Frisky Mrs. Johnson
Sheltered Daughters
A Heart to Let
22: The Beauty Shop
Women Men Marry
23: Broadway Gold
24: Drums of Jeopardy
26: The Danger Girl
Bred in Old Kentucky
The Flame of the Argentine
The Dice Women

Jack Dillon (1887-)
1918: Indiscreet Corinne
Betty Takes Hand
Limousine Life
An Heiress for a Day
Nancy Comes Home
The Love Swindle
19: She Hired a Husband
Silk-Lined Burglar
Taste of Life
Love's Prisoner
Beans
Follies Girl
Burglar by Proxy
20: The Right of Way
Suds
Wanted--A Husband
21: Blackbirds
Playing on Broadway
22: The Cub Reporter
The Roof Tree
Gleam o' Dawn
The Yellow Stain
Man Wanted
Calvert's Valley
24: The Broken Violin
A Self-Made Wife

24: Flaming Youth
25: Chickie
If I Marry Again
The Half-Way Girl
We Moderns
One Way Street
26: Too Much Money
Love's Blindness
The Midnight Lovers
Don Juan's 3 Nights
27: The Sea Tiger
The Prince of Head-waiters
Smile, Brother, Smile
The Crystal Cup
Man Crazy
28: The Noose
Heart of a Follies Girl
Out of the Ruins
Scarlet Seas SSE
29: Children of the Ritz SSE
Careers PT
Fast Life T
Sally T
?? Hop o' My Thumb
Playthings of Ruin

William Duncan (1880-1961)
1917: The Fighting Trail (serial)
Vengeance and the Woman (serial)
18: A Fight for Millions (serial)
19: Man of Might (serial)
Smashing the Barriers (serial)
20: Silent Avenger (serial)
21: Fighting Fate (serial)
23: The Steel Trail (serial)
24: The Fast Express (serial)
Wolves of the North (serial)

Scott Dunlap (1892-)
1919: Words and Music
Be a Little Sport
Love is Love
20: Her Elephant Man
Would You Forgive
The Hell Ship
Forbidden Trails
The Lost Princess
20: Vagabond Luck
The Twins of Suffering Creek
21: Challenge of the Law
The Cheater Reformed
Iron Rider
22: Bluebeard Junior
Western Speed
Trooper O'Neil
Bells of San Juan
West of Chicago
23: The Footlight Ranger
Skid Proof
Snowdrift
Pawn Ticket # 210
Boston Blackie
24: Traffic in Hearts
25: Silent Sanderson
Beyond the Border
The Texas Trail
One Glorious Night
Wreckage
26: The 7th Bandit
The Frontier Trail
Driftin' Through
Blue Blood
The Better Man
27: Desert Valley
Good as Gold
The Whispering Sage
28: Midnight Life
29: Object: Alimony
Smoke Bellew
One Stolen Night PT

Allan Dwan (1885-)
1914: Wildflower
David Harum
15: The Girl of Yesterday
Jordan is a Hard Road
16: An Innocent Magdalene
Panthea
The Foundling
The Habit of Happiness
The Good Bad Man
The Half Breed
Manhattan Madness
17: Man Who Made Good
18: The Modern Musketeer
Headin' South
Bound in Morocco
Fighting Odds
Mr. Fix-It

19: He Comes Up Smiling
Getting Mary Married
Cheating Cheaters
The Dark Star
20: The Luck of the Irish
Soldiers of Fortune
21: The Forbidden Thing
The Splendid Hazard
The Perfect Crime
A Broken Doll
In the Heart of a Fool
The Scoffer
22: The Sin of Martha Queed
Superstition
23: Glimpses of the Moon
Lawful Larceny
Big Brother
Robin Hood
Zaza
24: Argentine Love
A Society Scandal
Manhandled
Her Love Story
25: Wages of Virtue
The Coast of Folly
Stage Struck
Night Life of New York
26: Sea Horses
Tin Gods
Padlocked
Summer Bachelors
27: The Music Master
The Joy Girl
East Side, West Side
28: French Dressing
The Big Noise
29: Far Call SSE
Tide of Empire
The Iron Mask PT
The Rainbow Man T
Frozen Justice T
South Sea Rose T

Reeves Eason (1891-1956)
1918: Nine-Tenths of the Law
20: Human Stuff
Blue Streak McCoy
Pink Tights
The Moon Riders (serial)
Two Kinds of Love
21: Colorado
Big Adventure
23: Around the World in 18 Days (serial)
25: The Texas Bearcat
Flashing Spurs
Fighting the Flames
26: A Fight to the Finish
Ben-Hur (chariot seq.)
The New Champion
The Shadow on the Walls
The Test of Donald Morton
Through Thick or Thin
The Sign of the Claw
Lone Hand Sanders
27: The Denver Dude
Johnny Get Your Haircut
The Prairie King
Painted Ponies
Galloping Fury
28: Trick of Hearts
Clearing the Trail
The Flying Cowboy
Riding for Fame
29: The Lariat Kid
Winged Horseman

J. Gordon Edwards (d. 1925)
1918: Camille
Cleopatra
The Rose of Blood
DuBarry
Under the Yoke
The Forbidden Path
Soul of Buddha
Salome
19: Last of the Duanes
When a Woman Sins
The Siren's Song
When Men Desire
Wolves of the Night
A Woman There Was
The Light
The Lone Star Ranger
20: Heart Strings
The Orphan
Wings of the Morning
The Adventurer
If I Were King
The Joyous Troublemaker
21: Drag Harlan
His Greatest Sacrifice
The Scuttlers
Queen of Sheba
22: Nero
23: The Silent Command
24: The Net

24: The Shepherd King
It Is The Law

Walter Edwards
1918: The Idolators
Ashes of Hope
Fuel of Life
I Love You
Evidence
Real Folks
The Marriage Bubble
Viviette
Goodnight Paul
A Pair of Silk Stockings
Sauce for the Goose
19: The Lady's Name
Veiled Adventure
Happiness A La Mode
Mrs. Leffingwell's Boot
Romance and Arabella
The Rescuing Angel
Final Clean-Up
Who Cares
Gypsy Trail
The Man From Funeral Range
Girls
20: A Girl Named Mary
All of a Sudden Peggy
Luck in Pawn
A Widow by Proxy
Easy to Get
Young Mrs. Winthrop
A Lady in Love

John Emerson (1874-)
producer and collatorator
1915: Old Heidelberg
16: The Americano
Macbeth
Social Secretary
17: In Again Out Again
Wild and Wooly
19: A Tempermental Wife
Virtuous Vamp
20: In Search of a Sinner
Love Expert
21: Red Hot Romance

Arthur Guy Empey (1883-1963)
1918: Over the Top
19: The Undercurrent
20: Liquid Gold
Millionaire for a Day

Ray Enright (1896-1965)
1927: Tracked by the Police
Jaws of Steel
Girl from Chicago
28: Domestic Troubles
Golden Dawn
Land of the Silver Fox
29: Little Wildcat PT
Stolen Kisses PT
Kid Gloves PT
Skin Deep T

Howard Estabrook (1884-)
1917: Giving Becky a Chance
Wild Girl
Aesop's Fables (cartoons)
18: Highway of Hope
20: Officer 666

Jacques Feyder (1894-)
1923: Cramquebella
26: Carmen
28: Therese Raquin
Shadows of Fear
Faces of Children
Mother of Mine
29: The Kiss SSE

Romaine Fielding
1915: Eagle Nest (asst. dir.)
16: In the Hour of Disaster (scenarist)
17: Moral Courage
Youth
18: For the Freedom of the World
20: Woman's Man
Rich Slave
??: Toll of Fear (asst. Dir.)
Garden of the Gods (sc.)
Valley of Lost Hope (sc.)

Dallas M. Fitzgerald
1920: Open Door
Chains of Evidence
21: Blackmail
Cinderella's Twin
Offshore Pirate
Puppets of Fate
Price of Redemption
Life's Darn Funny

21: Little Match Breaker
Big Game
22: The Guttersnipe
Mothers of Liberty
Playing with Fire
23: Her Accidental Husband
24: After the Ball
25: Passionate Youth
Tessie
26: My Lady of Whims
27: The Princess of Broadway
Woman's Law
Out of the Past
Rose of Kildare
28: Wilful Youth
Golden Shackles
The Girl He Didn't Buy
Lookout Girl
Web of Fate
29: Jazz Land

22: The Kick In
23: Bella Donna
The Cheat
The Eternal City
24: Cytherea
Tarnish
25: A Thief in Paradise
The Dark Angel
26: Son of the Sheik
27: The Night of Love
Tender Hour
Rose of the Golden West
28: Love Mart
Lilac Time SSE
The Barker T
29: The Captive Woman
The Man and the Moment PT
Tiger Rose T
30: The Locked Door T

George Fitzmaurice (1895-1940)

1916: Patria (serial)
17: Arms and the Woman
Sylvia of the Secret Service
Mark of Cain
Blind Man's Luck
On-The-Square Girl
Iron Heart
Recoil
18: The Hillcrest Mystery
Innocent
The Naulahka
19: Common Clay
Avalanche
City of the Weak
Our Better Selves
Witness for the Defense
The Narrow Path
Japanese Nightingale
A Society Exile
20: On With the Dance
The Right to Love
Counterfeit
21: Idols of Clay
Experience
Paying the Piper
22: The Man from Home
To Have and to Hold
Three Live Ghosts
Forever (or, Peter Ibbetson)

Victor Fleming (1883-1949)

1919: When the Clouds Roll By
20: The Mollycoddle
21: Mama's Affair
22: Anna Ascends
Women's Place
Red Hot Romance
The Lane That Had No Turning
23: Dark Secrets
Law of the Lawless
To the Last Man
Call of the Canyon
24: Empty Hands
Code of the Sea
25: The Devil's Cargo
A Son of His Father
Adventure
Lord Jim
26: The Blind Goddess
Mantrap
27: Rough Riders
Way of All Flesh
Hula
28: Abie's Irish Rose SSE
The Awakening SSE
29: The Wolf Song PT
The Virginian T

James Flood (1895-1953)

1923: Times Have Changed
When Odds Are Even

24: The Man Without a Conscience
The 10th Woman
25: The Wife Who Wasn't Wanted
Satan in Sables
26: Why Girls Go Back Home
The Honeymoon Express
27: The Lady in Ermine
3 Hours
28: The Count of Ten
Marriage by Contract SSE
Domestic Meddlers
29: Midstream PT
Whispering Winds PT
Mr. Antonio T

Robert Florey (1900-)
1927: The Romantic Age
Face Value
28: Night Club
Pusher in the Face
Hollywood Extra
Coffin Maker
29: Hole in the Wall T
The Cocoanuts T
Battle of Paris T

Emmett Flynn (1892-1937)
1918: Alimony
19: The Bachelor's Wife
Bondage of Barbara
Racing Strain
Virtuous Sinners
Yvonne from Paris
20: Eastward Ho
Leave It To Me
The Lincoln Highway Man
Shod with Fire
The Valley of Tomorrow
The Untamed
The Man Who Dared
A Connecticut Yankee in King Arthur's Court
Shame
21: The Last Trail
A Fool There Was
Without Compromise
Monte Cristo
23: Hell's Hole
In the Palace of the King
24: Nellie The Beautiful Cloak Model
24: The Man Who Came Back
25: The Dancers
Gerald Cranston's Lady
Wings of Youth
East Lynne
26: The Palace of Pleasure
The Yankee Señor
Yellow Fingers
27: Married Alive
28: The Veiled Woman
29: Hold Your Man T
The Shannons of Broadway T

Francis Ford (1882-1953)
1914: Lucille Love, Girl of Mystery (serial)
16: Adventures of Peg o' the Ring (serial)
The Broken Coin (serial)
The Purple Mask (serial)
18: The Silent Mystery (serial)
Who Was the Other Man
John Ermine of Yellowstone
19: The Mystery of 3 (serial)
The Craving
Riders of Vengeance
20: The Crimson Shoals
Thunderbolt Jack (serial)
21: The Man from Nowhere
Cyclone Bliss
Good Morning, Judge
Greatest Sacrifice
Phantom Ship
Berlin Via America
Isle of Intrigue
Gates of Doom (serial)
Flower of the Range
I am the Woman
The Heart of Lincoln (dir., act)
The Stampede
22: They're Off
So This is Arizona
The Angel Citizen
The Storm Girl
Thundering Hoofs
Gold Grabbers
23: The Fighting Skipper (serial)
25: Perils of the Wilds (serial)
26: The Winking Idol (serial)

26: Wolves of the Air
False Friends
The Ghetto Shamrock
Melodies
Her Own Story
27: The Wolf's Trail
28: Call of the Heart

Hugh Ford
1915: Prince and the Pauper
17: Sapho
18: Seven Keys to Baldpate
Mrs. Dane's Defense
Danger Mark
19: Mrs. Wiggs of the Cabbage Patch
The Secret Garden
Woman Thou Gavest Me
20: His House in Order
In Mizzoura
21: Price of Possession
Lady Rose's Daughter
Civilian Clothes
Great Day
Call of Youth
Such a Little Queen

John Ford (1895-)
1917: Cactus, My Pal
Joan of the Cattle Land
The Cattle War
The Round Up
The Range War
The Trail of Shadows
The Secret
The Scrapper
The Soul Herder
Straight Shooting
18: The Secret Man
Bucking Broadway
A Marked Man
Wild Women
Thieves' Gold
The Scarlet Drop
Hell Bent
A Woman's Fool
19: Three Mounted Men
Roped
A Fight for Love
Bare Fists
Riders of Vengeance
The Outcasts of Poker Flat
19: Ace of the Saddle
20: Rider of the Law
A Gun Fightin' Gentleman
Marked Men
The Prince of Avenue A
The Girl in Number 29
Hitchin' Posts
21: Just Pals
The Big Punch
The Freeze-Out
The Wallop
Desperate Trails
Action
22: Sure Fire
Jackie
Little Miss Smiles
Silver Wings
The Village Blacksmith
23: The Face on the Bar Room Floor
Three Jumps Ahead
Cameo Kirby
24: Hoodman Blind
North of Hudson Bay
The Iron Horse
Hearts of Oak
25: Lightnin'
Kentucky Pride
The Fighting Heart
26: Thank You
The Shamrock Handicap
The Blue Eagle
Three Bad Men
27: Mother Machree
Upstream
28: Four Sons SSE
Hangman's House
Napoleon's Barber
Riley the Cop SSE
29: Strong Boy SSE
The Black Watch T
Salute

Tom Forman (1893-1938)
1920: Ladder of Lies
21: Sins of Rosanne
City of Silent Men
White and Unmarried
22: A Prince There Was
Woman Conquers
If You Believe It, It's So
White Shoulders
Shadows

23: Money, Money, Money
Broken Wing
Are You a Failure?
The Girl Who Came Back
April Showers
The Virginian
24: Flattery
The Fighting American
Roaring Rails
25: The Crimson Runner
The People Vs. Nancy Preston
26: The Midnight Flyer
Whispering Canyon
The Devil's Dice

Wallace Fox (1895-)
1927: The Bandit's Son
Jake the Plumber
28: Ridin' Renegade
Driftin' Sands
Man in the Rough
Breed of the Sunsets
Avenging Rider
Trail of Courage
29: Come and Get It
The Amazing Vagabond
Laughing at Death

Chester M. Franklin (1890-)
1916: Sister of Six
17: Mikado
18: Ali Baba and the 40 Thieves
Babes in the Woods
Treasure Island
Aladdin and the Wonderful Lamp
Jack and the Beanstalk
Girl with the Champagne Eyes
21: You Never Can Tell
All Souls Eve
A Private Scandal
22: The Case of Becky
Nancy from Nowhere
A Game Chicken
Toll of the Sea
23: Where the North Begins
24: Behind the Curtain
The Silent Accuser
25: Wild Justice
27: The 13th Hour
28: The Detectives

Sidney A. Franklin (1893-)
1918: The Safety Curtain
Her Only Way
Babes in the Woods
6 Shooter Andy
Bride of Fear
Confession
19: Fan Fan
Probation Wife
Heart of Wetona
Forbidden City
Ali Baba and the 40 Thieves
20: Heart of the Hills
The Hoodlum
Two Weeks
Rogue's Romance (act.)
Sleeping Lion (act.)
Down Home
21: Not Guilty
Courage
Unseen Forces
22: Primitive Lover
Smilin' Through
Beautiful and Damned
East is West
23: Dulcy
Brass
Tiger Rose
24: Her Night of Romance
25: Learning to Love
Her Sister from Paris
26: Beverly of Graustark
Duchess of Buffalo
27: Quality Street
28: The Actress
29: Wild Orchids
Last of Mrs. Cheyney PT
Devil May Care T

William French (1885-)
1922: Power Within
New Minister
25: Down Upon the Swanee River
Shooting Stars

Harry Garson
1925: Speed Wild
Breed of the Border
O. U. West
High and Handsome

25: Heads Up!
26: Sir Lumberjack
The Traffic Cop
Smilin' at Trouble
Glenister of the Mounted
The College Boob

Louis Gasnier (1880-1963)
1905: La Premiere Sortie D'un Collegien
07: Le Pendu
Les Debuts D-un Patinateur
Tirez, S'il Vous Plait
10: Max Feut Du Ski
11: Max Et La Cinquine
14: The Perils of Pauline (serial)
15: Exploits of Elaine (serial)
New Exploits of Elaine (serial)
The Romance of Elaine (serial)
16: The Shielding Shadow (serial)
17: The Mystery of the Double Cross (serial)
The 7 Pearls (serial)
19: The Corsican Brothers
Hands Up (serial)
Tiger's Trail (serial)
Beloved Cheater
Butterfly Man
20: The Third Eye (serial)
Kismet
Good Woman
A Wife's Awakening
21: The Call of Home
Silent Years
Thorns and Orange Blossoms
Rich Men's Wives
The Hero
22: Mothers-In-Law
Daughters of the Rich
23: Poisoned Paradise
Poor Men's Wives
Maytime
24: The Triflers
The White Man
Wine
Breath of Scandal
25: Parasite
Boomerang
25: Parisian Love
Faint Perfume
26: Pleasures of the Rich
Out of the Storm
Sin Cargo
That Model from Paris
27: Lost at Sea
Beauty Shoppers
Streets of Shanghai
28: Fashion Madness
Dummy
29: Darkened Rooms T

Howard Gaye
1916: Diane of the Follies
Intolerance (asst. dir.)
17: Scarlet Pimpernel
Spy
By Super Strategy
19: Upstairs
20: Passion's Playground
A Slave of Vanity
21: My Lady's Latch Key
What's a Wife Worth?

Douglas Gerrard (1885-)
1918: $5000 Reward
Playthings
Velvet Hand
Better Half
19: Sealed Envelope
Should Women Tell?
His Divorced Wife
20: Phantom Melody
Sins of His Father

Charles Giblyn (d. 1933)
1916: Honor Thy Name
Vagabond Prince
Somewhere in France
18: Scandal
Honeymoon
The Studio Girl
The Lesson
Sunshine Nan
Let's Get a Divorce
19: Upstairs and Down
Perfect 36
Peck's Bad Girl
Just for Tonight
The Spite Bride
20: Dark Mirror
Black is White

21: Tiger's Cub
The Thief
Mountain Woman
Know Your Men
Singing River
22: A Woman's Woman
23: Loyal Lives
The Leavenworth Case
24: Price of a Party
25: Adventurous Sex
27: Ladies Beware

Sven Glade
1925: Fifth Avenue Models
Siege
Peacock Feathers
26: Watch Your Wife
Blonde Saint
Into Her Kingdom

Alfred Goulding
1916: 3-2 reel Fox Comedies
1-1/2 years Harold Lloyd Comedies
Cash Customers
Open Another Bottle
His Best Girl

Edmund Goulding (1891-1959)
1925: Sun-Up
Sally, Irene and Mary
26: Paris
27: Women Love Diamonds
28: Love
29: Trespassed T

Frank Grandon
1913: Adventures of Kathlyn (serial)
15: Cross Currents
Strathmore
17: Heart's Desire
Little Soldier Girl
Love's Law
The Dummy
Little Boy Scout
18: Wild Honey
Conquered Hearts
19: Lamb and the Lion
Modern Husbands
Price of the Prairie
20: Nobody's Girl

Alfred E. Green (1890-1960)
1920: Double-Dyed Deceiver
Silk Husbands and Calico Wives
Web of Chance
Little Lord Fauntleroy
21: Just Out of College
The Man Who Had Everything
Through the Back Door
22: Come On Over
Our Leading Citizens
Bachelor Daddy
Ghost Breaker
The Man Who Saw Yesterday
23: Back Home and Broke
Woman Proof
The Ne'er-Do-Well
24: Pied Piper Malone
In Hollywood with Potash and Perlmutter
25: Inez from Hollywood
The Talker
Sally
The Man Who Found Himself
26: Irene
Girl from Montmartre
Ella Cinders
Ladies at Play
It Must be Love
27: The Auctioneer
Is Zat So?
Two Girls Wanted
Come To My House
28: Honor Bound
29: Making the Grade PT
Disraeli T

Frank Griffin (1861-)
1916: Where Love Leads
Three Paces West
Her Private Husband
A Roaming Bathtub
Ship Ahoy!
The Aero-Nut
Half Angel
Mack Sennett Comedies
17: Blood Will Tell
His Wedding Day
Maggie's False Step

David Wark Griffith (1875-1948)

1907: Old Isaac, The Pawnbroker
The Stage Rustler
The Eagle's Nest

08: When Knights were Bold
At the Crossroads of Life
La Tosca
Ostler Joe
The Music Master
After Many Years
Call of the Wild
Song of the Shirt
Adventures of Dolly (serial)
The Stage Rustler
The Bandit's Waterloo
The Man and the Woman
Taming of the Shrew
A Smoked Husband
Confidence
Mr. Jones at the Ball
For the Love of Gold
Just Meat
Balked at the Altar
The Politician's Love Story
A Corner on Wheat
The Princess in the Vase
The Sculptor's Nightmare
At the French Ball
A Calamitous Elopement
Where the Breakers Roar
An Awful Moment
Saved from Himself
The Boy Detective
The Golden Louis
The Redman and the Child
Behind the Scenes
The Heart of Oyama
Money Mad
The Reckoning
The Barbarian
The Vaquero's Vow
Romance of a Jewess

09: At the Altar
The Cord of Life
The Girls and Daddy
Tragic Love
The Curtain Pole
A Fool's Revenge
The Resurrection
Cricket on the Hearth
Violin Maker of Cremona
The Lonely Villa

09: A Convict's Sacrifice
1776 (or, The Hessian Renegades)
Leather Stocking
Nursing a Viper
Pippa Passes
The Call
Restoration
The Drunkard's Reformation
Fools of Fate
Edgar Allan Poe
Comata, The Sioux
In Old Kentucky
Suicide Club
The Lover's Tale
Jones and His New Neighbor
Jones and The Lady Book Agent
Jones' Burglar
Her First Biscuits
The Way of a Man
Sweet and 20
They Would Elope
The Indian Runner's Romance
Getting Even
The Awakening
The Little Teacher
Mills of the Gods
Lines of White on a Sullen Sea
The Day After
Shadows of Doubt
Scarlet Days
Voice of the Violin
A Baby's Shoes
The Jilt
What Drink Did
The Necklace
The Country Doctor
The Cardinal's Conspiracy
The Renunciation
The Slave
A Strange Meeting
The Mended Lute
With Her Card
The Sealed Room
The Broken Locket
The Expiation
In the Watches of the Night
Two Women and a Man

09: The Open Gate
The Mountaineer's Honor
The Redman's View
To Save Her Soul
The Dancing Girl of Butte
On the Reef
Honor of His Family

10: One Night and Then
His Last Burglary
The Newlyweds
Faithful
In the Season of Buds
The Italian Barber
The Lily of the Tenements
The Battle
The Usurer
The Last Deal
Ramona
The Three King Fishers
In Old California
The Mohawk's Way
The Arcadian Maid
The Cloister's Touch
The Way of the World
The Englishman and the Girl
The Thread of Destiny
The Escape
All on Account of the Milk
The Twisted Trail
Gold Is Not All
An Unchanging Sea
Love Among the Roses
The Two Brothers
A Child of the Ghetto
On the Border States
The Face in the Window
A Call to Arms
The House with the Closed Shutters
The Sorrows of the Unfaithful
Wilful Peggy
Rose of Salem Town
Examination Day at School
The Broken Doll
Waiter #5
The Song of the Wildwood Flute
The Golden Supper
The Greaser's Gauntlet
The Muggsy Series
Over Silent Paths
The Gold Seekers
Unexpected Help
A Rich Revenge
As It Is In Life
What Daisy Said
The Romance of the Western Hills
The Converts

11: Rose of Kentucky
The Miser's Heart
Enoch Arden (Parts I and II)
The Lonedale Operator
A Terrible Discovery
Her Awakening
Knight of the Road
The New Dress
The Revenge Man and the Girl
Crossing the American Prairies in the Early '50s
The White Rose of the Wilds
Was He a Coward?
How She Triumphed
A Smile of a Child
The Last Drop of Water
Conscience
Swords and Hearts
In the Days of '49
Out from the Shadow
The Blind Princess and the Poet
The Making of a Man
The Long Road
Love in the Hills
The Battle
Through Darkened Vales
A Woman Scorned
Fighting Blood
The Corporal's Daughter
His Trust
His Trust Fulfilled
3 Sisters
A Decree of Destiny
Madame Rex
His Mother's Scarf
The Sunbeam
Bobby, The Coward
The Sorrowful Example
A Tale of the Wilderness

11: The Failure
12: A Plot in the 'Scutcheon
Billy's Stragem
The Mender of Nets
Iola's Promise
The Female of the Species
The Old Actor
A Lodging for the Night
A String of Pearls
A Beast at Bay
Home Folks
The Sands of Dee
A Pueblo Legend
Two Daughters of Eve
So Near, Yet So Far
A Feud in the Kentucky Hills
The One She Loved
Brutality
The Telephone Lady and the Girl
The Musketeers of Pig Alley
The New York Hat
The Girl and Her Trust
Man's Genesis
The Goddess of Sagebrush Gulch
The God Within
The Eternal Mother
For His Son
The Transformation of Mike
Under Burning Skies
The Punishment
One is Business? The Other Crime
The Lesser Evil
An Outcast Among Outcasts
A Temporary Truce
The Spirit Awakened
Man's Lust for Gold
With the Enemy's Help
A Change of Heart
Blind Love
The Chief's Blanket
A Dash Through the Clouds
In the Aisles of the Wild
13: Battle of the Sexes
The Mothering Heart
The Battle of Elderbush Gulch
13: Three Friends
Wars of the Primal Tribes
Oil and Water
Broken Ways
The Hero of Little Italy
The Stolen Bride
Love in an Apartment Hotel
If We Only Knew
Death's Marathon
The Coming of Angelo
The Mistake
Two Men on the Desert
The House of Discord (supervised)
The Sheriff's Baby
A Little Tease
The House of Darkness
The Yaqui Cur
The Reformers
14: The Massacre
The Mother and the Law
The Avenging Conscience
Judith of Bethulia
Olaf - The Atom
The Tell Tale Heart
The Hunchback
Life of Villa
Home Sweet Home
Escape
The Mountain Rat
Strong Heart (supervised)
Men and Women "
The Soul of Honor "
The Painted Lady "
The Second Mrs. Roebuck "
For Those Unborn "
Her Awakening "
For Her Father's Sins "
The Odalisque "
The Little Country Mouse "
The Old Maid "
15: Double Trouble
Martyrs of the Alamo
The Lily and the Rose
The Penitents
The Birth of a Nation
The Fatal Marriage
The Lamb
16: His Picture in the Papers
Wild Girl of the Sierras

16: An Innocent Magdalene
The Half Breed
The Marriage of Molly O'
Manhattan Madness
Old Folks at Home
A Sister of Six
The Americano
Macbeth
Intolerance
Hoodoo Ann
Sold for Marriage
17: Souls Triumphant
18: The Great Love
Hearts of the World
19: Romance of Happy Valley
The Greatest Thing in Life
Broken Blossoms
True Heart Susie
The Girl Who Stayed at Home
Fall of Babylon
Mother and the Law
20: The Greatest Question
Love Flower
The Idol Dancer
The Lesser Evil
Scarlet Days
21: Dream Street
Way Down East
22: Orphans of the Storm
One Exciting Night
23: White Rose
24: America
Isn't Life Wonderful?
25: Sally of the Sawdust
That Royal Girl
26: Sorrows of Satan
27: The Battle of the Sexes
28: Drums of Love
29: Lady of the Pavements PT
30: Abraham Lincoln T
31: The Struggle T

E. H. Griffith (1894-)
1917: One Touch of Nature
Billy and the Big Stick
18: The Awakening of Ruth
19: Fit to Win
20: The Garter Girl
Bab's Candidate
21: Vice of Fools
Scrambled Wives
If Women Only Knew
21: The Land of Hope
22: Dawn of the East
Free Air
23: The Go-Getter
Sea Raiders
Unseeing Eyes
24: Week End Husbands
Another Scandal
25: Bad Company
Headlines
26: White Mice
The Ultimate Good
Atta Boy!
27: The Price of Honor
Afraid to Love
Alias the Lone Wolf
Opening Night
28: Hold 'em Yale!
Captain Swagger
Love Over Night
29: Shady Lady PT
Paris Bound T

Nicholas Grinde (1894-)
1918: Desert Law
28: Beyond the Sierras
Riders of the Dark
29: Morgan's Last Raid
?? An Equal Chance

Lloyd Hamilton (1892-)
1917: Roaring Lions and Wedding Bells
18: Son of a Hun
A Tight Squeeze
?? Gallant Ghost Hounds
Seaside Romeos
Dudes for a Day
Mongrels
A Waster's Wasted Life

David M. Hartford (1876-)
1917: Bride of Hate
18: Inside the Lines
Madam Who?
Infernal Net
20: Back to God's Country
It Happened in Paris
21: Nomads of the North
The Golden Snare
22: Tess of the Storm Country
23: The Rapids

26: Then Came the Woman
Man in the Shadow
Jack o' Hearts
Dame Chance
Yellow Back
27: God's Great Wilderness

Pat Hartigan (1881-)
1917: The Planter
19: A Fallen Idol
20: The Adventurer
Wonder Man
??: I Love the Nurses
Life of Moses
Twelfth Night

Harry Harvey
1916: Grip of Evil (serial)
17: The Mystery Ship (serial)
18: The Lion's Claw (serial)

Howard Hawks (1896-)
1926: The Road to Glory
Fig Leaves
27: Cradle Snatchers
Paid to Love
28: Girl in Every Port
Fazil
Air Circus
29: Trent's Last Case

Arch B. Heath (1890-)
1927: The Crimson Flash (serial)
The Masked Menace (serial)
On Guard (serial)
28: Mark of the Frog (serial)

Victor Heerman (1893-)
1916: She Loved a Sailor
17: Stars and Bars
Two Crooks
18: Watch Your Neighbor
20: Are Waitresses Safe?
River's End
21: Chicken in the Case
Divorce of Convenience
25: Old Home Week
Irish Luck
26: For Wives Only
27: Rubber Heels
Ladies Must Dress
28: Love Hungry

Thomas N. Heffron (1872-)
1918: Mountain Dew
Stainless Barrier
The Planter
Sudden Gentlemen
The Hopper
Sea Panther
Who Killed Walton
The Lonely Woman
Old Hartwell's Cub
Madam Sphinx
Painted Lily
Price of Applause
19: Tony America
The Prodigal Liar
Mask of Riches
Life's a Funny Proposition
Deuce Duncan
Best Man
A Man's Fight
20: Thou Art the Man
Firebrand Trevison
City of Masks
21: Sham
Little Clown
Truant Husband
Sunset Sprague
A Kiss in Time
Her Sturdy Oak
22: Bobbed Hair
The Love Charm
Truthful Liar
Her Face Value
Too Much Wife
23: A Wife's Romance

Joseph Henabery (1888-)
1915: Birth of a Nation (acted)
16: Intolerance (actor)
18: Say Young Fellow (dir. from here on)
Man from Painted Post
19: His Majesty The American
20: Inferior Sex
Love Madness
21: Traveling Salesman
Life of the Party
Brewster's Millions
The Fourteenth Man
Don't Call Me Little Girl
Moonlight and Honeysuckle

21: Her Winning Way
22: Call of the North
While Satan Sleeps
Her Own Money
Missing Millions
Man Unconquerable
23: Sixty Cents An Hour
A Gentleman of Leisure
Making a Man
The Tiger's Claw
Stephen Steps Out
24: A Sainted Devil
The Stranger
The Guilty One
Tongues of Flame
25: Cobra
26: Broadway Boob
Shipwrecked
Pinch Hitter
Meet the Prince
27: Play Safe
See You in Jail
Lonesome Ladies
28: Sailors' Wives
Hellship Bronson
United States Smith
29: Red Hot Speed PT
Clear the Decks PT
River Woman SSE
The Quitter
Light Fingers PT

Del Henderson (1883-1946)
1915: Ambrose's Fury
Ambrose's Lofty Perch
A Janitor's Wife's Temptation
16: The Great Pearl Tangle
Because He Loved Her
Wife and Auto Trouble
A Bath House Blonde
Her Marble Heart
18: The Golden Wall
Beloved Blackmailer
The Outcast
The Runaway
The Beautiful Adventure
Please Help Emily
Her Second Husband
The Imposter
My Wife
19: By Hook or Crook
Courage for Two
19: Hit or Miss
Love in a Hurry
Road to France
Social Pirate
Three Green Eyes
20: The Deadline
The Shark
Servant Question
21: Dynamite Allen
The Plunger
22: Broken Silence
Sure-Fire Flint
Girl from Porcupine
Dead or Alive
23: Jacqueline (or, Blazing Barriers)
24: Gambling Wives
The Love Bandit
Battling Brewster (serial)
25: The Bad Lands
26: Accused
Defend Yourself
Pay Off
Pursued
27: Rambling Rangers

Hobart Henley (1886-1964)
1915: Graft (serial)
18: All Woman
Laughing Bill Hyde
Mrs. Slacker
Face in the Dark
Glorious Adventure
Money Mad
19: A Gay Old Dog
One Week of Life
Peace of Roaring River
Too Fat to Fight
Woman on the Index
20: Miracle of Money
Guilty of Love
21: Sin That Was His
Society Snobs
22: June Madness
Her Night of Nights
The Scrapper
Parentage
Cheated Hearts
Stardust
23: The Abysmal Brute
Flame of Life
The Flirt
24: Lady of Quality

24: So This is Marriage
Sinners in Silk
The Turmoil
25: A Slave of Fashion
The Denial
Exchange of Wives
His Secretary
26: A Certain Young Man
The Auction Block
27: Tillie the Toiler
28: His Tiger Lady
Wickedness Preferred
Roadhouse
29: The Lady Lies T
30: The Big Pond T
31: Bad Sister T
32: Night World T
34: Unknown Blonde T

George W. Hill (1895-1934)
1921: Get Your Man
While the Devil Laughs
23: The Hill Billy
24: Midnight Express
Through the Dark
Foolish Virgin
25: Zander the Great
The Limited Mail
26: Barrier
Tell It To The Marines
27: The Callahans and the Murphys
Buttons
28: The Cossacks
29: The Flying Fleet SSE

Robert F. Hill (1886-)
1919: Great Radium Mystery (serial)
20: The Flaming Disc (serial)
21: Adventures of Tarzan (serial)
22: Adventures of Robinson Crusoe (serial)
23: Social Buccaneer (serial)
Around the World in 18 Days (serial)
Shadows of the North
Crooked Alley
24: Breathless Moments
Jack o' Clubs
Dark Stairways
Young Ideas
Excitement
Dangerous Blonde
25: Idaho (serial)
Wild West (serial)
26: Bar C Mystery (serial)
27: Return of the Riddle Man (serial)
28: The Haunted Island (serial)
Life's Mockery (serial)
31: Spell of the Circus (serial) T

Lambert Hillyer (1893-)
1917: Sudden Jim
An Even Break
18: Narrow Trail
Riddle Gawne
19: Money Corral
Wagon Tracks
Square Deal Sanderson
20: John Petticoats
Toll Gate
Sand
21: Cradle of Courage
O'Malley of the Mounted
Testing Block
22: Travelin' On
Skin Deep
White Oak
Three Word Brand
White Hands
Caught Bluffing
The Super Sex
Altar Stairs
23: Shock
Fleetwing
The Spoilers
Scars of Jealously
Temporary Marriage
Lone Star Ranger
Mile-A-Minute Romeo
24: Those Who Dance
Barbara Frietchie
Eyes of the Forest
25: I Want My Man
Making of O'Malley
Unguarded Hour
The Knockout
26: Miss Nobody
Her Second Chance
27: War Horse
Hills of Peril
Chain Lightning
28: The Branded Sombrero

Renaud Hoffman (1900-)
1923: Not One to Spare
24: Legion of Hollywood
Women and Gold (producer)
Unmarried Wives (producer)
25: Overland Limited (producer)
One of the Bravest (producer)
Climax
Private Affairs
His Master's Voice
26: On the Threshold
Unknown Soldier
27: A Harp in Hock
28: Stool Pigeon
29: Blaze o' Glory
Speed Limit

James P. Hogan
1925: Mansion of Aching Hearts
My Lady's Lips
Jimmie's Millions
Women and Gold
26: S. O. S. Perils of the Sea
Steel Preferred
Isle of Retribution
King of the Turf
Flaming Fury
27: Final Extra
Mountains of Manhattan
Silent Avenger
Finnegan's Ball
28: Broken Mask
Hearts of Men
Top Sergeant Mulligan
Burning Bridges
Border Patrol
Code of the Air

Edwin L. Hollywood
1916: Sweet Kitty Bellaire
Thousand Dollar Husband
Less Than the Dust
17: Pride of the Clan
One Hour
Polly of the Circus
18: Challenge Accepted
19: The Immigrant
20: Birth of a Soul
Flaming Clue
Sea Rider
Gauntlet

George Holt
1917: Sacrifice
19: Little Shepherd of Kingdom Come
22: White Masks
Trail's End
Gold Grabbers
Traitor's Hour
Phantom Desperado
Boss of the Flying H
23: Cross Roads

Allan Holubar (1889-1925c)
1918: Siren of the Sea
Fear Not
A Soul for Sale
Mortgaged Wife
19: Talk of the Town
Heart of Humanity
Right to Happiness
20: Paid in Advance
Heart Strings
21: Once to Every Woman
Man, Woman, Marriage
22: Hurricane's Gal
23: Slander the Woman
Broken Chains

E. Mason Hopper (1885-1966)
1918: Tar Heel Warrior
Firefly of Tough Luck
Renegades
Without Honor
When Bearcat Went Dry
Edgar's Jonah Day
Her American Husband
The Answer
Love Brokers
Boston Blackie's Little Pet
19: As the Sun Went Down
Come Again Smith
Wife or Country
Mystic Face
Love's Pay Day
21: Hold Your Horses
It's a Great Life
Dangerous Curve Ahead
22: From the Ground Up
All's Fair in Love
The Glorious Fool
Hungry Hearts

22: Brothers Under the Skin
23: Daddy
The Love Piker
24: Janice Meredith
Great White Way
25: The Crowded Hour
26: Up in Mabel's Room
Paris at Midnight
Almost a Lady
27: Getting Gertie's Garter
Night Bride
Wise Wife
My Friend from India
Rush Hours
28: Blonde for a Night
29: The Carnation Kid PT
Square Shoulders PT
Their Own Desire T
Wise Girls T
Shop Girl T

Charles Horan
1918: Polly of the Circus
19: Three Black Eyes
20: A Man's Plaything
21: Young Find It Everywhere
Love, Hate and a Woman
22: The Splendid Lie
23: Does It Pay
24: No Mother to Guide Her
A Convert to Revenge

James W. Horne (1880-)
1918: Bull's Eye (serial)
Hands Up! (serial)
19: The Midnight Man (serial)
20: The Third Eye (serial)
21: Occasionally Yours
Dangerous Pastime
The Bronze Bell
22: Don't Doubt Your Wife
The Forgotten Law
23: Can a Woman Love Twice?
Hottentot
A Man of Action
The Sunshine Trail
Blow Your Own Horn
Itching Palms
Alimony
24: Hail the Hero
Stepping Lively
American Manners
In Fast Company
25: Laughing at Danger
Youth and Adventure
26: Kosher Kitty Kelly
Cruise of the Jasper B
27: College
28: Big Hop
Black Butterflies

William J. Howard (1899-1954)
1921: What Love Will Do
22: Extra! Extra!
Deserted at the Altar
Danger Ahead
23: Lucky Dan
Fourth Musketeer
Captain Fly-By-Night
Let's Go!
24: Border Legion
East of Broadway
The Torrent
25: Code of the West
Light of the Western Stars
Thundering Herd
26: Volcano
Red Dice
Bachelor Brides
Gigolo
27: White Gold
The Main Event
28: The Ship Comes In
River Pirate SSE
29: Christina PT
The Valiant T
Love, Live and Laugh T

Harry O. Hoyt (1880-1961)
1919: Through the Toils
Hand Invisible
Broadway Saint
20: Forest Rivals
21: Rider of King Log
22: Curse of Drink
24: The Lost World
Ten After Ten
The Radio Flyer
The Fatal Plunge
The Law Demands
Fangs of the Wolf
Woman on the Jury
25: Primrose Path
Unnamed Woman
26: When Love Grows Cold
Belle of Broadway

27: Bitter Apples
Return of Boston Blackie
29: Passion Song

Rupert Hughes (1872-1956)
1922: The Wallflower
Remembrance
23: Gimme
Look Your Best
Souls for Sale
24: True as Steel
Reno

Charles J. Hunt
1927: The Promise
Show Girl
Midnight Watch
Modern Daughters
Million Dollar Mystery
Boy of the Streets
On the Stroke of Twelve
28: Casey Jones
You Can't Beat the Law
Queen of the Chorus
Obey Your Husband
South of Panama
Thundergod

T. Hayes Hunter (1896-)
1916: Crimson Stain Mystery (serial)
18: Border Legion
19: Once to Every Man
Desert Gold
20: Cup of Fury
Earthbound
22: Light in the Clearing
24: Damaged Hearts
Trouping with Ellen
Recoil
25: Sky Raider
Wildfire
28: South Sea Bubble
29: Silver King
Triumph of the Scarlet Pimpernel
?? Fire and Sword
Puppet Jury
One of the Best

Paul C. Hurst (1889-1953)
1916: Lass of the Lumberlands (serial)
18: The Iron Test (serial)
A Woman in the Web (serial)
Rimrock Jones
19: Lightning Bryce (serial)
The Tiger's Trail (serial)
Frustrated Holdup
21: Shadows of the West
?? The Lone Claim
Return of Stingaree

Charles Hutchinson
1921: Hurricane Hutch (serial)
25: Red Blood and Blue
On Probation
Was It Bigamy?
26: The Winning Wallop
Lightning Hutch (serial)
27: Flying High
Little Firebrand
Catch as Catch Can
Down Grade
When Danger Calls
Hidden Aces
Pirates of the Sky
The Trunk Mystery
28: Dagger Street
Out with the Tide
Bitter Sweets

John Ince (1879-1947)
1915: Road of Strife (serial)
19: Secret Strings
One-Thing-At-A-Time o' Day
Blind Man's Eyes
Favor to a Friend
20: Should a Woman Tell
Please Get Married
Struggle
Sealed Lips
Old Lady 31
Held in Trust
21: Tempered Steel
Someone in the House
23: The Love Trap
24: Cheap Kisses
25: If Marriage Fails
Girl of Gold
26: Her Big Adventure
The Great Jewel Robbery
Hour of Reckoning
28: Wages of Conscience

28: Black Feather

Ralph Ince (1887-1937)

1915: The Goddess (serial)
18: Fields of Honor
The Eleventh Commandment
Her Man
The Lincoln series
The Co-Respondent
Our Mrs. McChesney
19: Virtuous Men
From Headquarters
Painted Woman
Stitch in Time
Too Many Crooks
Two Women
Perfect Lover
20: His Wife's Money
Out Yonder
Sealed Hearts
21: Out of the Snows
Red Foam
The Last Door
Justice
The Highest Law
Remorseless Love
After Midnight
A Man's Home
22: The Repeal
A Wide Open Town
Channing of the Northwest
Reckless Youth
Tropical Love
23: Homeward Bound
Counterfeit Love
Success
24: House of Youth
Chorus Lady
Uninvited Guest
Dynamite Smith
Mortal Sinner
25: Lady Robinhood
Alias Mary Flynn
Smooth as Satin
Playing with Souls
The Sea Wolf
26: Breed of the Sea
The Better Way
Bigger than Barnum
The Lone Wolf Returns
27: Home Struck
Wandering Girls
27: Moulders of Men
Not for Publication
Shanghaied
South Sea Love
28: Coney Island
Chicago After Midnight
Hit of the Show
Singapore Mutiny
Danger Street
29: Hardboiled
Hurricane T

Thomas Ince (1882-1924)

1908: Richard III (actor)
10: Their First Misunderstanding
11: The New Cook (dir.)
The Deserter
The Indian Massacre
Across the Plains
12: Shadow of the Past
Custer's Last Fight
13: Pride of the South
The Battle of Gettysburg
Favorite Son
City of Darkness
14: Wrath of the Gods
The Fugitive
Passing of Two Gun Hicks
The Typhoon
The Bargain
15: The Alien
The Coward
Primal Lure
Cup of Life
The Buster
The Disciple
The Last Card
On the Night Stage
The Darkening Trail
Between Men
Greed of the North
Forbidden Adventure
The Toast to Death
16: Extravagance
Hell's Hinges
Civilization
Nemesis
The Aryan
The Sheriff
The Captive God
The Devil's Trouble
The Patriot

17: The Narrow Trail
The Silent Man
Truthful Tulliver
The Gunfighter
Wolf Lowry
The Desert Man
Castigo
Ultimate Raid of the Zeppelin
Vive La France!
18: String Bean
Blue Blazes Rawden
19: The Busher
Greased Lightning
Hay Foot, Straw Foot
Behind the Door
Partners Three
Happy Though Married
20: Twenty-Three and a Half Hours Leave
What's Your Husband Doing?
Mary's Ankle
21: Lying Lips
Bronze Bell
22: Hail the Women
23: Hottentot
Soul of the Beast
Man of Action
24: Cup of Life
The Sea Lion
Idle Tongues

Lloyd Ingraham (1893-1956)
1915: The Sable Lercha
The Missing Links
16: Hoodoo Anne
American Aristocracy
Intolerance
17: Charity Castle
A Daughter of Joan
Her Country's Call
Peggy Leads the Way
Miss Jackie of the Army
18: Molly Go Get 'em
Jilted Janet
Ann's Finish
Primitive Woman
A Square Deal
Impossible Susan
The Eyes of Julia Deep
19: Man's Desire
19: The Amazing Imposter
Intrusion of Isabel
Rosemary Climbs the Heights
Wives and Other Wives
20: Mary's Ankle
What's Your Husband Doing?
Let's Be Fashionable
House of Intrigue
21: Keeping Up With Lizzie
Twin Beds
The Jailbird
Lavender and Old Lace
Girl in the Limousine
Old Dad
22: My Lady Friends
Marry the Poor Girl
Second Hand Rose
At the Sign of the Jack o'Lantern
The Veiled Woman
The Danger Point
23: Going Up
No More Woman
24: Beauty Prize
Lightning Rider
The Wise Virgin
25: Soft Shoes
Midnight Folly
26: The Nut Cracker
Hearts and Fists
Oh, What a Night!
27: Don Mike
Silver Comes Through
Jesse James
28: Pioneer Scout
Sunset Legion
29: Untamed T
So Long Letty T
30: Take the Heir T
33: The World Gone Mad T
35: The Cowboy T
36: Modern Times T
Captain Calamity T
45: Circumstantial Evidence T
48: Sixteen Fathoms Deep T

Rex Ingram (1892-1950)
1913: The Artist's Madonna
Blindness of Devotion
15: Song of Hate

15: Galley Slave
Cup of Bitterness
16: The Beachcomber
17: Black Orchids
Reward of the Faithless
Flower of Doom
Little Terror
18: His Robe of Honor
Humdrum Brown
19: The Great Problem
Chalice of Sorrow
Broken Fetters
20: Under Crimson Skies
Shoe Acres
The Day She Paid
21: Hearts are Trumps
Four Horsemen of the Apocalypse
The Conquering Power
22: Turn to the Right
Prisoner of Zenda
Trifling Women
23: Where the Pavement Ends
Scaramouche
24: The Arab
25: Mare Nostrum
26: The Magician
27: Garden of Allah
Siren of the Sea
29: Three Passions
32: Baroud T
33: Love in Morocco T

George Irving (1874-1961)
1916: Witching Hour
18: Back to the Woods
Her Boy
The Landloper
To Hell with the Kaiser!
Daughter of Destiny
Raffles
19: As a Man Thinks
Hidden Fires
Silver King
The Volcano
20: Glorious Lady
The Blue Pearl
The Capitol
21: Misleading Lady
The Wakefield Case
22: Her Majesty
23: Lost in a Big City
24: Floodgates

Jacques Jaccard (1885-)
1915: Diamond from the Sky (serial)
16: Adventures of Peg o' the Ring (serial)
Liberty, Daughter of the U. S. A. (serial)
Is Any Girl Safe? (wr., dir.)
17: Patria (serial)
The Red Ace (serial)
18: The Lion's Claw (serial)
20: Desert Love
The Terror
The Great Air Robbery
Under Northern Lights
21: If Only Jim
Honor Bound
22: The Great Alone
Riding With Death
24: Unseen Hands
Days of '49 (serial)
Riders of the Plains (serial)
25: Pony Express
26: Desert Greed
The Outlaw Breaker
27: California in '49
The Fighting Fighters (serial)
?? The Quest of Virginia (serial)
Cyclone Smith
Cassidy of the Air Lanes
The Scarlet Rider
Son of the North
Death Trap
Spur and Saddle Series

Fred Jackman (1881-)
1922: Timber Queen (serial)
White Eagle (serial)
23: Call of the Wild
24: King of the Beasts
25: Black Cyclone
26: Devil Horse
27: No Man's Law

Arthur V. Johnson (1876-1916)
1914: The Beloved Adventurer (serial)

Martin Johnson (1884-1937)
1921: Jungle Adventures
23: Headhunters of the South Seas
Trailing African Wild Animals

Tefft Johnson
1915: Turn of the Road
16: Writing on the Wall
Sonny Boy at the Bat
Sonny Boy in School Days
Sonny Boy and the Dog Show
19: Love Defender
Love Nest
Love and the Woman
Home Wanted

Richard Jones
1915: A Game Old Knight
Her Painted Hero
The Great Vacuum Robbery
16: His Hereafter
A Love Riot
Her Marble Heart
Pills of Peril
17: His Uncle Dudley
18: Mickey
19: Yankee Doodle in Berlin
21: Ghost in the Garret
Flying Pat
Oh Jo
22: Molly O
Cross Roads of New York
Country Flapper
23: The Extra Girl
Suzanna
The Shriek of Araby
27: The Gaucho
28: The Big Killing
Water Hole
Someone to Love
29: Bulldog Drummond T

Edward Jose
1916: Pearl of the Army (serial)
The Iron Claw (serial)
The Light That Failed
Poppy
18: The Moth
Her Silent Sacrifice
18: Woman and Wife
La Tosca
Resurrection
Love's Conquest
Fedora
19: Fires of Faith
My Cousin
Private Peat
Two Brides
Woman of Impulse
20: Fighting Shepherdess
Yellow Typhoon
Isle of Conquest
Mothers of Men
21: The Scarab Ring
What Women Will Do
The Riddle Woman
Her Lord and Master
The Inner Chamber
22: Prodigal Judge
The Rainbow
Matrimonial Bed
Girl in His House
Man from Downing Street
25: Perils of Paris
28: Daughter of Israel

Rupert Julian (1889-1943)
1914: Merchant of Venice (actor)
15: Dumb Girl of Portici (actor)
16: Bugler of Algiers (actor)
17: A Kentucky Cinderella (actor)
18: The Kaiser, Beast of Berlin (actor)
Mysterious Mr. Tiller (dir. from here on:)
Desire of the Moth
The Door Between
The Savage
Hands Down
Hungry Eyes
Midnight Madness
19: The Creaking Stairs
Sleeping Lion
Fire Flingers
Millionaire Pirate
20: The Honey Bee
22: The Girl Who Ran Wild
23: The Midnight Guest
Merry-Go-Round

24: Love and Glory
25: Phantom of the Opera
Hell's High Road
26: Silence
Three Faces East
27: Country Doctor
Yankee Clipper
28: Leopard Lady
Walking Back
30: Love Comes Along T

Buster Keaton (1896-1966)

1920: The High Sign
One Week
Convict 13
The Scarecrow
Neighbors
21: The Haunted House
Hard Luck
The Goat
The Electric House (1st vers. incomplete)
The Boat
The Paleface
22: The Cops
My Wife's Relations
The Frozen North
The Electric House (2nd Version, completed)
Daydreams
The Blacksmith
23: The Love Nest
The Three Ages
Our Hospitality
24: Sherlock Junior
The Navigator
25: Go West
26: Seven Chances
The General
Battling Butler
27: College
Steamboat Bill, Junior
28: The Cameraman
29: Spite Marriage
Hollywood Revue of 1929
30: Free and Easy

Erle Kenton (1896-)

1925: Red Hot Tires
Danger Signals
26: The Sap
Love Toy
Palm Beach Girl
Other Women's Husbands
27: Rejuvenation of Aunt Mary
Wedding Bills
Girl in the Pullman
28: Bare Knees
Name the Woman
Sporting Age
Golf Widows
Companionate Marriage
Street of Illusion
Nothing to Wear
Sideshow
29: Trial Marriage
Father and Son PT
Song of Love T

Burton King (1887-)

1916: Man and His Angel
Black Butterfly
17: Soul of a Magdalene
Seven Pearls
18: Silence Sellers
More Truth Than Poverty
Her Husband's Honor
19: Treason
Reckoning Day
Out of the Shadow
Font of Courage
Lost Battalion
Master Mystery (serial)
The Lurking Peril (serial)
20: Neglected Wives
Wit Wins
The Common Level
Discarded Woman
A Scream in the Night
Common Sin
Love is Money
21: Every Man's Price
22: The Man from Beyond
For Your Daughter's Sake
The Road to Arcady
Shylock of Wall Street
23: No Fair Cheat
None So Blind
Streets of New York
24: Man Without a Heart
The Masked Dancer
25: A Little Girl in a Big City
Police Patrol
Mad Dancer
Those Who Judge

26: Counsel for the Defense
Ermine and Rhinestones
27: Broadway Madness
Satan and the Woman
28: Adorable Cheat
Women Who Dare
House of Shame
Manhattan Knights
29: Broken Barriers
Dream Melody
Daughters of Leisure
One Splendid Hour
In Old California T

Henry King (1892-)
1918: Southern Pride
A Game of Wits
Mate of the Sally Ann
Beauty and the Rogue
Powers That Pray
Hearts or Diamonds
Up Romance Road
The Locked Heart
19: Where the West Begins
When a Man Rides Alone
Some Liar
Hobbs in a Hurry
Brass Buttons
All the World to Nothing
Sporting Chance
This Hero Stuff
6 Feet 4
20: A Fugitive from Matrimony
Haunting Shadows
23 1/2 Hours' Leave
Uncharted Channels
White Dove
One Hour Before Dawn
21: Mistress of Shenstone
Salvage
Help Wanted Male
Dice of Destiny
When We Were Twenty-One
Sting of the Lash
22: Sonny
Tol'able David
Bond Boy
23: Fury
White Sisters
25: Stella Dallas
Romola
Any Woman
Sackcloth and Scarlet
26: Partners Again
Winning of Barbara Worth
27: Magic Flame
28: Woman Disputed
29: She Goes to War PT

Louis King (1898-1962)
1927: Boy Rider
Slingshot Kid
28: Pinto Kid
Little Buckaroo
Bantam Cowboy
Young Whirlwind
Terror Mountain
Fighting Redhead
Rough Ridin' Red
Orphan of the Sage
29: Vagabond Cub
Freckled Rascal
Little Savage
Pals of the Prairie SSE

Charles Klein (1898-)
1926: Telltale Heart (prod.)
28: Blindfold SSE
White Silence
29: Sin Sister SSE
Pleasure Crazed T

Percy Knighton (1898-)
1925: The Only Thing
26: Riding Wild
Little Colonel
Sin Town
Red Dice
Her Man o' War
Volga Boatman

Gregory La Cava (1892-1952)
1925: Womanhandled
26: So's Your Old Man
Say It Again
Let's Get Married
27: Paradise for Two
Running Wild
Tell It To Sweeney
28: The Gay Defender
Feel My Pulse
Half a Bride
29: Saturday's Children
Big News
His First Command

Edward Laemmle (1887-)

1920: Shipwrecked Among the Cannibals
21: Winners of the West (serial)
Rim of the Desert
22: In the Days of Buffalo Bill (serial)
Top o' the Morning
23: The Oregon Trail (serial)
25: Spook Ranch
A Woman's Faith
Man in Blue
The Outlaw
26: The Still Alarm
The Whole Town's Talking
27: Held by the Law
Cheating Cheaters
Thirteenth Juror
28: Range Riders
Cowboy Editor
Pulpit Punch
29: Man, Woman and Wife
The Drake Case
?? Coward of Covelo
Under Blazing Skies

Ernst Laemmle (1900-)

1926: Prowlers of the Night
27: One Man's Game
Red Clay
Broncho Buster
Hands Off!
Range Courage
28: Grip of the Yukon
Phyllis of the Follies

Charles Lamont (1898-)

?? My Kid
Bachelor Babies
Navy Beans
Come to Papa
Companionate Service
Circus Blues
Brunettes Prefer Gentlemen
The Great Worker
Monty of the Mounted
Half Pint Hero
Live News
Wildcat Valley
Yankee Doodle Duke

Fritz Lang (1890-)

1921: Destiny
22: Dr. Mabuse
25: Siegfried
27: Metropolis
28: Beyond the Wall
Woman in the Moon
The Spy
Krumheld's Revenge
31: M T
32: Last Will of Dr. Mabuse T

Walter Lang (1898-)

1926: Red Kimono
Earth Woman
Golden Web
Money to Burn
27: Lady Bird
The Satin Woman
Sally in our Alley
College Hero
Elegy
Shadows of the Night
Clipped Wings
By Whose Hands
28: Night Flyer
Desert Bride
29: Spirit of Youth

John Langan (1902-)

1919: The Kibitzer T
Darkened Rooms T
30: Sarah and Son T
Light of the Western Stars T

Harry Langdon (1884-1944)

1927: Three's a Crowd
28: The Chaser
Heart Trouble

Rowland V. Lee

1925: As No Man Has Loved
In Love with Love
Havoc
26: The Silver Treasure
The Outrider
27: Whirlwind of Youth
Barbed Wire
The Secret Hour
28: Doomsday
Three Sinners

28: Loves of an Actress SSE
The First Kiss
29: Wolf of Wall Street T
Dangerous Woman T
Mysterious Dr. Fu Manchu T

Henry Lehrman (1886-)
1913: Her New Beau
Murphy's I. O. U.'s
A Dollar Did It
Cupid in a Dental Parlor
The Bangville Police
Algy on the Force
The Darktown Belle
Hubby's Job
Toplitsky & Co.
Passions, He Had 3
Help! Help! Hydrophobia!
Feeding Time
Out and In
For the Love of Mabel
Love and Rubbish
The Peddler
Love and Courage
Just Kids
Prof. Bean's Removal
A Chip Off the Old Block
The Abalone Industry
2 Old Tars
The Woman Haters
San Francisco Celebration
Protecting San Francisco from Fire
The Champion
14: Making a Living
Kid Auto Races at Venice
Between Showers
Raffles, Gentleman Burglar
A Rural Demon
18: Who's Your Father?
Wild Women and Tame Lions
A High Diver's Last Kiss
Mongrels
Fatal Marriage
21: The Kick in High Life
27: Ladies Only
Sailor Izzy Murphy
Husbands for Rent
28: Why Sailors Go Wrong
Chicken A La King
Homesick SSE
29: New Year's Eve SSE
?? A Tight Squeeze
Twilight Baby

Paul Leni (1885-)
1927: Cat and the Canary
Chinese Parrot
28: The Man Who Laughs
29: Last Warning PT
Three Wax Men

Robert Z. Leonard (1889-)
1907: The Vanishing Sex (actor)
Time and the Comedian "
Code of Honor "
13: Robinson Crusoe "
Diamond Makers "
In Slavery Days "
14: The Primeval Test "
The Master Key (serial) " director
16: Life's Pendulum
The Plow Girl
17: Princess Virtue
A Mormon Maid
Primrose Ring
18: Modern Love
The Bride's Awakening
Her Body in Bond
19: Delicious Little Devil
Miracle of Love
20: The Restless Sex
21: The Gilded Lily
Heedless Moths
Peacock Alley
22: Fascination
23: Broadway Rose
Jazzmania
French Doll
24: Circe, The Enchantress
Love's Wilderness
25: Time the Comedian
Cheaper To Marry
Bright Lights
26: The Vanishing Sex
Dance Madness
Mademoiselle Modiste
27: Little Journey
Adam and Evil
Tea for Three
The Demi-Bride
28: Baby Mine
The Cardboard Lover

29: Lady of Chance PT
Marianne T

Mervyn LeRoy (1900-)
1927: No Place To Go
28: Flying Romeos
Harold Teen
Oh Kay!
Broadway Daddies
29: Naughty Baby SSE
Hot Stuff T
30: Little Johnny Jones T

Edward Le Saint (1870-)
1916: Three Godfathers
18: The Devil's Wheel
Bird of Prey
Kultur
Strange Woman
19: Call of the Soul
Wilderness Trail
Speed Maniac
22: Long Chance

Edgar Lewis (1872-)
1915: The Great Divide
17: Barrier
Bar Sinister
18: The Sign Invincible
19: Calibre .38
20: Other Men's Shoes
Sherry
Lahoma
Beggar in Purple
21: Sage Hen
27: One Glorious Scrap
28: Fearless Rider
Stormy Waters
Arizona Cyclone
Put 'em Up!
Made-To-Order Hero
Gun Runner
Life's Crossroads
29: Unmasked Love T
At First Sight

Frank Lloyd (1889-1960)
actor
1914: Damon and Pythias
The Test
15: A Gentleman from Indiana
16: The Code of Marcia Gray
Sins of the Parents
director
17: The Price of Silence
A Tale of Two Cities
18: Les Miserables
When a Man Sees Red
American Methods
The Heart of a Lion
The Kingdom of Love
Blindness of Divorce
True Blue
19: The World and Its Women
The Man Hunter
For Freedom
Pitfalls of the Big City
Rainbow Trail
Riders of the Purple Sage
20: The Silver Horde
Madame X
The Great Lover
The Loves of Letty
The Woman in Room 13
21: A Tale of Two Worlds
Roads to Destiny
The Sin Flood
The Voice in the Dark
The Invisible Power
Judgment
22: The Man from Lost River
The Grim Comedian
The Eternal Flame
Oliver Twist
23: Within the Law
Voice from the Minaret
Ashes of Vengeance
24: The Sea Hawk
The Silent Watcher
Black Oxen
25: Winds of Chance
Her Husband's Secret
The Splendid Road
26: Wise Guy
Eagle of the Sea
27: Children of Divorce
28: Adoration SSE
29: Divine Lady SSE
Weary River T
Drag T
Dark Streets T
Young Nowheres T

Del Lord (1895-1970)
1927: Lost at the Front
Topsy and Eva

29: Barnum Was Right T

Ernst Lubitsch (1892-1947)

1918: Eyes of the Mummy
Carmen
19: The Oyster Princess
20: Danton
Passion (Du Barry)
Anne Boleyn
21: Affairs of Lady Hamilton
One Arabian Night
Gypsy Blood
Deception
22: Loves of Pharaoh
23: Souls for Sables
Rosita
24: The Marriage Circle
The Wildcat
The Doll
Montmartre
Three Women
Forbidden Paradise
25: Kiss Me Again
Lady Windemere's Fan
26: So This is Marriage
27: Student Prince
28: The Patriot
29: Eternal Love SSE
Love Parade T

Wilfred Lucas

1913: Get Rich Quick
Cohen's Outing
A Game of Pool
Fatty's Day Off
Los Angeles Harbor, Calif.
What Father Saw
Willie Minds the Dog
Billy Dodges Bulls
Across the Alley
Their Husbands
A Quiet Little Wedding
Making an Auto Tire
Milk We Drink
Rogues' Gallary
The Horse Thief
14: A Misplaced Foot
A Glimpse of Los Angeles

the Lumiere Brothers

August L. (1862-1954)
Louis (1864-1948)
1895: A Game of Cards
1895: Lunch Hour at the Lumiere Factory
Baby's Lunch
The Blacksmiths
Bathing Beach

Kenneth MacKenna (1899-)

1929: Pleasure Crazed T
Love, Live and Laugh
South Sea Rose T

Jeanie MacPherson (scenarist)

1909: A Corner in Wheat
11: Last Drop of Water
Out from the Shadow
Enoch Arden
15: The Captive
Carmen
16: The Golden Chance
Dream Girl
Joan the Woman
The Love Mask
17: The Woman God Forgot
Romance of the Redwoods
The Little American
The Devil Stone
18: Whispering Chorus
Old Wives for New
Till I Come Back To You
19: Male and Female
For Better For Worse
Don't Change Your Husband
20: Something To Think About
21: Affairs of Anatol
Fool's Paradise
22: Manslaughter
Saturday Night
23: Ten Commandments
Adam's Rib
24: Triumph
25: Road to Yesterday
The Golden Bed
26: Red Dice
Volga Boatman
Young April
Her Man o' War
27: King of Kings
29: Godless Girl PT
Dynamite T
30: Madame Satan T
35: The Crusades T
37: The Plainsman T
38: The Buccaneer T

40: Land of Liberty T
44: The Story of Dr. Wassell T

Murdock MacQuarrie

1913: Stain in the Blood
16: Nancy's Birthright
The Gambler's Last Love
17: Panthea
Humility
18: Loyalty
Justice
Twisted Souls
Keeper of Hell Gate

Charles Maigne (1881-)

1919: The Firing Line
Her Great Chance
Indestructible Wife
In the Hollow of Her Hand
Redhead
The World To Live In
20: The Copperhead
Invisible Bond
Fighting Chance
Cumberland Romance
21: Frontier of the Stars
The Kentuckians
22: Received Payment
Hush Money
Cowboy and the Lady
23: Trail of the Lonesome Pine
Drums of Fate
Silent Partner

Leo Maloney (1888-)

1925: The Loser's End
Across the Deadline
26: Win, Lose or Draw
Luck and Sand
Outlaw Express
High Hand
27: Long Loop on the Pecos
Man from Hardpan
Don Desperado
Two Guns of Tumbleweeds
Border Blackbirds
28: The Devil's Twin
Boss of Rustler's Roost
Apache Rider
Bronc Stomper
28: Black Ace
Yellow Contraband
29: Forty-Five Calibre War
Overland Bound T

Jay Marchant

1922: Perils of the Yukon (serial)
23: Ghost City (serial)
24: The Iron Man (serial)
25: The Fighting Ranger (serial)
Great Circus Mystery (serial)

Frances Marion (scenarist)

1915: A Daughter of the Sea
16: The Gilded Cage
17: Stolen Paradise
18: Temple of Dusk
Stella Maris
20: Humoresque
Pollyanna
24: Tarnish
Abraham Lincoln
Through the Dark
Secrets
25: The Dark Angel
Thank You
Lightnin'
Stella Dallas
His Supreme Moment
26: Winning of Barbara Worth
Son of the Sheik
Partners Again
Paris at Midnight
The Scarlet Letter
27: Red Mill
The Callahans and the Murphys
The Cossacks
Madame Pompadour
Love
28: Bringing Up Father
Masks of the Devil
Excess Baggage
The Wind

George Marshall (1891-)

1916: Liberty
Love's Lariat
18: The Man from Montana
19: Adventures of Ruth (serial)
20: Ruth of the Rockies (serial)

21: Why Trust Your Husband
Hands Off!
Prairie Trail
A Ridin' Romeo
After Your Heart
22: The Jolt
Lady from Longacre
Smiles are Trumps
23: Don Quickshot of the Rio Grande
Men in the Raw
Where is This West
Haunted Valley (serial)

June Mathis (scenarist) (d. 1927)

1918: Eye for Eye
19: Red Lantern
21: Four Horsemen of the Apocalypse
22: Blood and Sand
23: Young Rajah
Greed
24: Wild Oranges
25: Greater Glory
We Moderns
26: Ben Hur
27: The Magic Flame
28: Masked Woman

Frank S. Mattison (1890-)

1928: Old Age Handicap
29: Must We Marry?
Little Wild Girl
China Slaver
Girls Who Dare
Bye Bye Buddy PT
Broken Hearted PT
King of the Herd

Archie Mayo (1898-)

1926: Money Talks
Unknown Treasures
Christine of the Big Tops
27: Quarantined Rivals
Dearie
Slightly Used
College Widow
Johnnie Get Your Hair Cut
28: Beware of Married Men SSE
Crimson City SSE
State Street Sadie (or, The Great Manhunt) PT
28: On Trial T
29: My Man PT
Sonny Boy T
The Sap PT
Is Everybody Happy? T
The Sacred Flame T

Leo McCarey (1898-)

1918: Virgin of Stamboul (asst.)
Vengeance
Laurel & Hardy Comedies
Charley Chase Comedies
Joe College Comedies
29: The Sophomore T
Red Hot Rhythm T
30: Let's Go Native T

John P. McCarthy (1885-)

1926: Out of the Dust
Weakness of the Strong
Pals
Vanishing Hoofs
Border Whirlwind
27: Becky
His Foreign Wife
The Lovelorn
28: Diamond Handcuffs
29: Eternal Woman

Kenneth McDonald

1925: The Speed Demon
Coast Patrol
In High Gear
Sunshine of Paradise Alley
27: Avenging Fangs
28: Little Buckaroo

Bernard McEveety

1927: His Rise to Fame
Broadway Drifter
The Winning Oar
Bowery Cinderella
28: Stronger Will
Inspiration
Back to Liberty
29: Clean-Up

J. P. McGowan (1880-1952)

1914: Hazards of Helen (serial)
15: Girl and the Game (serial)
16: Lass of the Lumberlands (serial)

16: Whispering Smith
Medicine Bend
Diamond Runners
17: The Railroad Raiders (serial)
18: Lure of the Circus (serial)
19: The Red Glove (serial)
20: Elmo the Fearless (serial)
King of the Circus (serial)
21: Do or Die
Tiger True
Below the Deadline
Discontented Wives
Cold Steel (act., dir.)
Nerve of Nolan
22: Captain Kidd
Perils of the Yukon (serial)
Hills of Missing Men
Reckless Chances
Ruse of the Rattler
23: Stormy Seas
One Million in Jewels
Whipping Boss
24: Western Vengeance
Crossed Trails
A Desperate Adventure
A Two Fisted Tenderfoot
Baffled
Barriers of the Law
25: Blood and Steel
Border Intrigue
Outwitted
Fighting Sheriff
Peggy of the Secret Service
26: Lost Express
Seal of Satan (serial)
Silver Fingers
The Act of Clubs
Mistaken Orders
The Fast Freight
The Road Agent
Riding Romance
The Narrow Escape
Riding for Life
Red Blood
Buried Gold
The Iron Fist
Crossed Signals
The Desperate Chance
Fighting Luck
The Lost Express
27: Tarzan and the Golden Lion
27: The Outlaw Dog
The Lost Limited
City of Shadows
A Flame in the Sky
28: Trailin' Back
Trail Riders
The Painted Trail
West of Santa Fe
Manhattan Cowboy
On the Divide
Silent Trail
29: Law of the Mounted
Bad Men's Money
Texas Tommy
Below the Deadline
Arizona Days
Captain Cowboy
The Last Roundup
The Man from Nevada
Phantom Rider
The Invaders SSE
The Fighting Terror
Headin' Westward
Lone Horseman
'Neath Western Skies
The Oklahoma Kid
30: Riders of the Rio Grande

Donald McKenzie

1914: Perils of Pauline (serial)
16: The Shielding Shadow (serial)
17: 7 Pearls (serial)
19: The Carter Case (serial)
The Fatal Fortune (serial)
Terror of the Range (serial)

Henry McRae (1888-)

1916: Liberty, Daughter of the U.S.A. (serial)
Giant Powder
17: Man and Beast
Dropped from the Clouds
The Mystery Ship (serial)
19: Elmo the Mighty (serial)
20: The Dragon's Net (serial)
25: The Ace of Spades (serial)
26: The Scarlet Streak (serial)
Strings of Steel (serial)
27: Trail of the Tiger (serial)
Wild Beauty
28: Guardians of the Wild

28: Two Outlaws
Danger Rider
29: Wild Blood
King of the Rodeo
Harvest of Hate
Smilin' Guns
Plunging Hoofs
Burning the Wind
Hoofbeats of Vengeance
Tarzan the Tiger (ser.)SSE
Pirate of Panama (serial)
30: The Indians are Coming (serial) T
The Lightning Express (serial) T
Terry of the Times (serial) T
?? A Night with Whispering Smith
Range War

Leo J. Meehan
1927: Magic Garden
Mother
Naughty Nanette
Judgment of the Hills
The Harvester
28: Freckles
Little Mickey Grogan
Wildflowers
The Little Yellow House
The Devil's Trade Mark
29: Hunting Tigers in India

George Melford (1889-1961)
1913: The Struggle
The Boer War
15: Stolen Goods
17: The Evil Eye
The Hostage
18: The Cruise of the Make-Believe
The Crystal Gazer
On the Level
Sunset Trail
Call of the East
Nan of Music Mountain
Hidden Pearls
Wild Youth
The Bravest Way
Sandy
City of Dim Faces
The Source
19: The Young Romance
The Woman
21: The Marriage of Kitty
Good Gracious, Annabelle
Jane Goes A-Wooing
Men Women and Money
Pettigrew's Girl
Such a Little Pirate
Sporting Chance
Told in the Hills
20: Everywoman
The Sea Wolf
The Invisible Power
The Jucklins
Behold My Wife
The Faith Healer
A Wise Fool
The Round-Up
22: The Great Impersonation
The Sheik
The Woman Who Walked Alone
Burning Sands
Ebb Tide
Moran of the Lady Letty
23: You Can't Fool Your Wife
Salomy Jane
Java Head
The Light That Failed
24: Tiger Love
Sandra
Flaming Barriers
Dawn of Tomorrow
25: Top of the World
Friendly Enemies
Simon the Jester
Without Mercy
26: Whispering Smith
Rocking Moon
Flame of the Yukon
Going Crooked
27: A Man's Past
28: Freedom of the Press
Lingerie
Sinners in Love
29: Sea Fury PT
The Charlatan PT
Love in the Desert PT
The Woman I Love
32: East of Borneo T
33: The Cowboy Counsellor T
Man of Action T

34: Hired Wife T
35: East of Java T

George Melies (1861-1938)

1896: The Card Party
The Gardener Burning Weeds
Place De L'Opera
The Vanishing Lady
The Haunted Castle
In the Depth of the Sea
97: Peeping Tom at the Seaside
Dancing in a Harem
98: Blowing Up the Maine in Havana Harbor
99: Cleopatra, Svene Egyptienne
The Dreyfus Affair
Hallucinations of Baron Munchausen
1900: Cinderella
Joan of Arc
Christmas Dreams
01: Bluebeard
Red Riding Hood
A Maiden's Paradise
The Man with the Rubber Head
02: A Trip to the Moon
Eruption of Mt. Peles
Coronation of King Edward
04: Voyage à Travers L'Impossible
Off to Bloomingdale Asylum
08: Humanity Through the Ages
12: La Conquete Du Paole

Lothar Mendes (1894-)

1926: Prince of Tempters
27: Convoy
28: A Night of Mystery
Interference T
29: Four Feathers SSE
Dangerous Curves T
Illusion T
Marriage Playground T
The Children
?? Marriage Playground

Lewis Milestone (1895-)

1926: The Cave Man
Seven Sinners
26: The New Klondike
27: Two Arabian Knights
28: Garden of Eden
The Racket
29: Betrayal SSE
New York Nights T

Harry Millarde

1917: Every Girl's Dream
Sunshine Maid
18: Miss U. S. A.
Unknown 274
Heart of Romance
A Camouflage Kiss
Blue-Eyed Mary
Miss Innocence
19: Caught in the Act
Bonnie Annie Laurie
Gambling Souls
Girls with No Rights
Love That Dares
When Fate Decides
Rose of the West

Charles Miller

1917: Flame of the Yukon
18: The Little Reformer
Secret of the Storm Country
Wilson or the Kaiser
Ghosts of Yesterday
By Right of Purchase
Unfaithful
At the Mercy of Men
Fair Pretender
Service Star
19: Why Germany Must Pay
20: High Speed
Dangerous Affair
21: Law of the Yukon
22: The Man She Brought Back
26: On the Back Lot
Ship of Souls

Bertram Millhauser

1917: The Fatal Ring (serial)
18: House of Hate (serial)
19: The Lightning Raider (serial)
The Black Secret (serial)
Velvet Hawk (serial)
20: The Phantom Foe (serial)
21: The Yellow Arm (serial)

Bruce Mitchell (1882-)

1921: A Designing Husband
His Handsome Butler
27: Three Miles Up
Sky High Saunder
28: Air Patrol
Phantom Flyer
Won in the Clouds
Speed Classic
Cloud Dodger
The Last Lap
29: Sky Skidder
?? Captivating Mary
The Leper
The Night Before
Temptations
A Matrimonial Marathon

Howard Mitchell (1883-)

1918: Petticoat Politics
19: The Law That Divides
Splendid Sin
20: Molly and I
Snares of Paris
The Tattlers
Faith
Love's Harvest
The Girl in Bohemia
Black Shadows
The Little Wanderer
21: Flame of Youth
The Lamplighter
Wing Toy
Beware of the Bride
Husband Hunter
The Mother Heart
Ever Since Eve
Love Time
22: Queenie
Winning With Wits
Cinderella of the Hills
The Crusader
23: His Last Race
Man's Size
Forgive and Forget
24: The Lone Chance
Romance Ranch
26: Road to Broadway
Jazz Girl
27: Hidden Aces
Breed of Courage

Edmund Mortimer (1883-)

1918: The Savage Woman
19: Road Through the Dark
20: A Misfit Wife
23: Railroaded
The Exiles
24: A Man's Hate
That French Lady
The Desert Outlaw
The Wolf Man
Against All Odds
Just Off Broadway
25: Gold and the Girl
Scandal Proof
The Star Dust Trail
Arizona Romeo
The Prairie Pirate
The Man from Red Gulch
26: Satan Town
27: A Woman's Way

F. W. Murnau (1889-1931)

1920: Janus
22: Dr. Jekyll and Mr. Hyde (Ger. version)
The Burning Acre
The Phantom
Haunted Castle
Expulsion
Fiancee of the Grand Duke
25: The Last Laugh
26: Faust
27: Tartuffe The Hypercritic
Sunrise
Love's Mockery
28: The Four Devils T
29: Nosferatu, The Vampire
30: City Girl T
31: Tabu (documentary with Robert Flaherty)

Marshall Neilan (1891-1958)
actor

1912: Stranger at Coyote
13: Two Men on the Desert
Classmates
The House of Discord
The Powder Flash of Death
The Animal
The Harvest of Flame
The Wall of Money
14: The Sentimental Sister

14: Men and Women
15: Madame Butterfly
16: The Crisis
director
1916: Little Pal
Hulda from Holland
17: A Little Princess
The Bottle Imp
The Jaguar's Claw
Those Without Sin
The Tides of Barnegat
The Silent Partner
Rebecca of Sunnybrook Farm
18: M'liss
Stella Maris
Amarilly of Clothesline Alley
Hit-The-Trail Holliday
19: Daddy-Long-Legs
In Old Kentucky
Three Men and a Girl
Heart of the Wilds
The Unpardonable Sin
Out of a Clear Sky
20: River's End
Don't Ever Marry
Her Kingdom of Dreams
Go and Get It
21: Dinty
Bits of Life
The Lotus Eater
Bob Hampton of Placer
22: Penrod
Fools First
Minnie
23: The Stranger's Banquet
Fog
Rendez-Vous
Souls for Sale
The Eternal Three
24: Dorothy Vernon of Haddon Hall
Tess of the D'Ubervilles
25: The Sporting Venus
26: The Skyrocket
Diplomacy
Mike
Wild Oats Lane
Everybody's Acting
27: Venus of Venice
Her Wild Oat
28: Take Me Home
The Last Haul
Three Ring Marriage
29: Black Waters T
Taxi #13 PT
The Awful Truth T
Tanned Legs T
The Vagabond Lover T
Fog

R. William Neill (1892-)
1918: Price Mark
Love Letters
The Kaiser's Shadow
Flare Up Sal
Love Me
Tyrant Fear
Mating of Marcella
Green Eyes
19: Charge It To Me
Puppy Love
Trixie from Broadway
Vive Le France
Career of Katherine Bush
20: The Inner Voice
The Bandbox
The Woman Gives
Yes or No
21: Something Different
Idol of the North
Good References
Dangerous Business
Conquest of Canaan
22: The Iron Trail
What's Wrong with Women
23: Rodeo Mania
Toilers of the Sea
24: Broken Laws
By Divine Right
Vanity's Price
25: The Kiss Barrier
Percy
Marriage in Transit
Greater than a Crown
26: A Man Four Square
Black Paradise
The Fighting Buckaroo
The Cowboy and the Countess
The City
27: Marriage
Arizona Wildcat
28: San Francisco Nights
Lady Raffles

28: Olympic Hero
29: Behind Closed Doors
Wall Street

Alvin J. Neitz (1894-)
1925: The Reckless Sex
Warrior Gap
The Mystery Box (serial)
26: Beyond All Odds
Lure of the West
Thundering Speed
The Vanishing Millions (serial)
27: Bad Man's Bluff
Born to Battle
Hazardous Valleys
The Cheer Leader
28: The Silent Sentinel
Sky Rider

Jack Nelson (1882-)
1925: Wall Street Whizz
The Isle of Hope
26: The Fighting Boob
Mile-A-Minute Man
The Prince of Pep
Beyond the Rockies
Call of the Wilderness
The Dead Line
The Dude Cowboy
Hair Trigger Baxter
The Sunshine of Paradise
Two Gun Caballero
The Valley of Bravery
27: Say It With Diamonds
The Life of an Actress
Bulldog Pluck
The Fighting Hombre
The Shamrock and the Rose
Perils of the Jungle (serial)
28: Police Reporter (serial)
The Mysterious Rider (serial)
Tarzan the Mighty (serial)
29: The Diamond Master (serial)

Fred Newmeyer (1888-)
1922: Grandma's Boy
23: Safety Last
Never Weaken
23: Why Worry?
24: Girl Shy
25: The Freshman
7 Keys to Baldpate
26: The Perfect Clown
The Savage
The Quarterback
27: The Potters
Lunatic at Large
Too Many Crooks
On Your Toes
28: That's My Daddy
Warming Up
Night Bird
29: It Can Be Done
Rainbow Man
Sailor's Holiday
30: The Grand Parade
31: Scareheads T

Fred Niblo (1872-1948)
1918: The Marriage Ring
Fuss and Feathers
Hit-The-Trail Holliday
19: Happy Though Married
Daughters of Joy
Haunted Bedroom
When Do We Eat?
The Law of Men
Partners Three
The Virtuous Thief
20: Dangerous Hours
What Every Woman Learns
Sex
Stepping Out
Woman in the Suitcase
Hairpins
The False Road
Fortune Hunter
21: Mother o' Mine
Mark of Zorro
3 Musketeers
Her Husband's Friend
Silk Hosiery
22: The Woman He Married
Rose o'the Sea
Blood and Sand
23: The Famous Mrs. Fair
Strangers of the Night
24: Thy Name is Woman
The Red Lily
26: The Temptress
Ben Hur

27: Camille
The Devil Dancer
28: The Mysterious Lady
The Enemy
Two Lovers
29: Dream of Love
30: Redemption T

William Nigh (1881-)
1915: A Yellow Streak
16: Life's Shadows
Notorious Gallagher
17: Slave
18: Thou Shalt Not Steal
My Four Years in Germany
Sunshine Alley
My Own United States
Shame
19: The Fighting Roosevelts
Our Teddy
20: Democracy, The Vision Restored
21: Skinning Skinners
Why Girls Leave Home
22: Soul of Man
Your Best Friend
School Days
Notoriety
23: Marriage Morals
Salomy Jane
24: Born Rich
25: Fear Bound
The Little Giant
26: Fire Brigade
Casey of the Coast Guard (serial)
27: Mr. Wu
The Nest
28: Across to Singapore
Law of the Range
Four Walls
29: Desert Nights SSE
Thunder

John W. Noble (1880-)
1920: Footlights and Shadows
Gray Towers Mystery
The Golden Shower
21: Song of the Soul
Out of the House of Bondage
22: Cardigan
24: Stranger from the North
His Darker Self
26: Lightning Reporter
27: Burning Gold

Mabel Normand (1894-1930)
1914: Mabel's Strange Predicament
Love and Gasoline (or, The Skidding Joy Riders)
Mabel at the Wheel (or, His Daredevil Queen)
Caught in a Cabaret
Mabel's Nerve
Mabel's Busy Day
Mabel's Married Life (or, The Squarehead)

Wilfrid North
1916: Salvation Joan
Ordeal of Elizabeth
17: Kitty MacKay
18: Over There
Over the Top
19: Mind the Paint Girl
20: Undercurrent
The Kid
21: Get-Rich-Quick Wallingford

Frank O'Connor (1888-)
1925: Go Straight
One of the Bravest
Free to Love
26: Lawful Cheaters
Block Signal
Devil's Island
Exclusive Rights
Heroes of the Night
Hearts of Spangles
Speed Limit
Spangles
Silent Power
False Alarm
27: Sinews of Steel
Colleen
Your Wife and Mine
28: Masked Angel
29: Just Off Broadway

Sidney Olcott (1875-1949)
1906: Billy the Kid
07: Ben Hur (asst. dir.)
Wanted A Dog

08: Florida Crackers
09: Judgment
10: Love in the Everglades
Adventures of a Girl Spy
Another Hitch
11: Rory O'More
Arah-Na-Pogue
The Miser's Child
Indian Scout's Vengeance
Ireland the Oppressed
Colleen Bawn
Young Remember Allen
The O'Neil
12: A Daughter for the Confederacy
In the Power of a Hypnotist
From the Manger to the Cross
The Shaughraun
The Kerry Gow
15: Madame Butterfly
All for Old Ireland
Bold Emmett, Ireland's Martyr
The Irish in America
Nan o' the Backwoods
Seven Sisters
16: Poor Little Peppina
Daughter of MacGregor
17: The Belgian
19: Marriage for Convenience
20: Scratch My Back
Mothers of Men
21: The Right Way
22: God's Country and the Law
Pardon My French
Timothy's Quest
23: Little Old New York
The Green Goddess
24: The Only Woman
The Humming Bird
Monsieur Beaucaire
25: Charley's Aunt
The Charmer
Not So Long Ago
Salome of the Tenements
The Best People
26: Ransom's Folly
White Black Sheep
Amateur Gentleman
27: The Claw

Henry Otto

1916: River of Romance
Undine
Mr. 44
18: Lorelei of the Sea
Wild Life
19: The Microbe
Amateur Adventuress
Angel Child
The Great Romance
Island of Intrigue
Some Bride
20: The Cheater
Fair and Warmer
The Willow Tree
21: A Slave of Vanity
23: Love Bound
Temple of Venus
24: Dante's Inferno
25: Folly of Vanity
The Ancient Mariner

Georg Wilhelm Pabst (1885-)

1916: Crisis
Die Drei Groschen Oper
18: Westfront
Don't Play with Love
25: Joyless Street
26: Secrets of a Soul
27: Streets of Sorrow
28: Loves of Jeanne Ney
29: Pandora's Box
Tragedy of the Mine
Treasure
Diary of a Lost Girl
30: White Hell of Pitz Palu
31: Three-Penny Opera

Ida May Park

1917: Fires of Rebellion
18: Bondage
Broadway Love
Risky Road
The Model's Confession
Bread
19: The Amazing Wife
Vanity Pool
20: Butterfly Man
21: Bonnie May
The Midlanders

William Parke

1917: Mystery of the Double Cross

18: A Crooked Romance (serial)
Over the Hill
Sunshine Girl
Convict 993
Yellow Ticket
19: Key to Power
Tower of Ivory
20: Out of the Storm
The Paliser Case
21: Beach of Dreams
23: Legally Dead
Clean-Up
A Million to Burn
24: Ten Scars Make a Man (serial)

Albert Parker (1889-)

1918: The Haunted House
Man Hater
For Valour
The Other Woman
From Two to Six
Annexing Bill
Waifs
Shifting Sands
19: Arizona
Knickerbocker Buckaroo
Secret Code
20: Eyes of Youth
21: Branded Woman
22: Love's Redemption
Sherlock Holmes
24: Second Youth
Rejected Woman
26: Black Pirate
27: Love of Sunya

Stuart Paton (1885-)

1917: Gray Ghost (serial)
Voice on the Wire (serial)
18: Border Patrol
Beloved Jim
Girl in the Dark
The Wine Girl
Marriage Lie
19: Terror of the Range (serial)
Border Raiders
The Devil's Trail
Little Diplomat
20: The Fatal Sign (serial)
21: Hope Diamond Mystery (serial)
21: Reputation
Torrent
Wanted at Headquarters
22: Black Bag
Man Who Married His Own Wife
Conflict
Man to Man
Wolf Man
Married Flapper
23: The Scarlet Car
Love Brand
Bavu
Burning Words
26: Baited Trap
Lady from Hell
Frenzied Flames
Forest Havoc
Wolf Hunters
27: Fangs of Destiny
28: Bullet Mark
Four Footed Ranger
Hound of the Silver Creek

Scott Pembroke

1927: Cactus Trails
Terror of Bar X
For Ladies Only
Light in the Window
Ragtime
Galloping Thunder
Polly of the Movies
Law of the Man
28: Gypsy of the North
My Home Town
Sweet Sixteen
Divine Sinner
Sisters of Eve
29: Black Pearl
Shanghai Rose
Two Sisters
Should a Girl Marry? PT
30: Brothers T

Leonce Perret (1882-)

1918: Stars of Glory
Lest We Forget
The Million Dollar Dollies
19: Lafayette, We Come
Souls Adrift
Unknown Love
Thirteenth Chair
20: The A. B. C. 's of Love

20: The Twisted Man
Koenigsmark
Twin Pawns
Lifting Shadows
Modern Salome
21: Empire of Diamonds
Money Maniac
25: Madame Sans Gene
26: Secret Spring
28: Model from Montmartre
Morgane

Wray Physioc (1890-)
1922: The Blonde Vampire
24: Hearts of Oak
The Gulf Between
3 years with Biograph
producer of 8-reel
future in natural colors
for Technicolor

Harry Joe Pollard (1883-1934)
1915: Miracle of Life
The Quest
Girl from His Home Town
The Dragon
17: The Devil's Assistant
18: The Danger Game
Girl Who Couldn't Grow Up
20: The Invisible Ray (serial)
22: Trimmed
Confidence
Locked Doors
23: Trifling with Honor
24: Oh Doctor!
Sporting Youth
The Reckless Age
K-The Unknown
Ropes
Leather Pusher Series
25: I'll Show You the Town
California Straight Ahead
26: The Cohens and the Kellys
Poker Faces
27: Uncle Tom's Cabin
29: Show Boat PT
Tonight at Twelve T
Shanghai Lady T

Edwin S. Porter (1869-1941)
1902: Pres. McKinley's Inauguration
McKinley's Funeral Cortege
The Columbia and Shamrock Yacht Races
The Jeffries-Rublin Sparring Contest
The Galveston Cyclone
A Trip Through the Columbian Exposition
Grandma and Granpa Series
Happy Hooligan Series
Old Maid Series
Life of an American Fireman
03: Uncle Tom's Cabin
The Great Train Robbery
05: The Ex-Convict
06: Dream of Rarebit Fiend
The Kleptomaniac
White Caps
The Miller's Daughter
A River Tragedy
Desperate Encounter
Capture of the Yegg Bank Burglars
07: La Tosca
Rescued from an Eagle's Nest
A Night Before Christmas
12: The Prisoner of Zenda
13: Tess of the D'Ubervilles
The Count of Monte Cristo
The Near Wife
14: Tess of the Storm Country
Hearts Adrift
Sold
The Eternal City
15: Ex-Convict #61

Frank Powell
1918: Heart of the Desert
19: Forfeit
Unbroken Promise
20: Oficer 666
You Never Know Your Luck
22: A Fool There Was

Paul Powell
1915: The Lily and the Rose
16: The Marriage of Molly-O

16: The Wood Nymph
Little Meena's Romance
Wild Girl of the Sierras
The Matrimoniac
Susan Rocks the Boat
19: Blinding Trail
All Night
Little White Savage
Society of Sensation
Hell-To-Pay Austin
Girl of the Timberlands
Betsy's Burglar
The Weaker Vessel
Who Will Marry Me?
Man in the Moonlight
20: Common Property
Pollyanna
Crooked Street
Beggar in Purple
21: Eyes of the Heart
Sweet Lavender
Mystery Road
Dangerous Life
22: The Crimson Challenge
The Cradle
For the Defense
The Ordeal
Borderland
23: Daughter of Luxury
Racing Hearts
The Fog
25: The Awful Truth
Her Market Value
26: Prince of Pilsen
North Star
27: Death Valley
Jewels of Desire

Billy Quirk
1917: Winning an Heiress
19: The Devil's Trail
Arizona Cat Claw
The Old Maid's Baby
Sawdust Doll
?? Billy Joins the Band

Albert Ray (1883-)
1927: Love Makes 'em Wild
Rich But Honest
Publicity Madness
28: Woman Wise
None But the Brave
Thief in the Dark
29: Molly and Me PT
My Lady's Past PT

Charles Ray (1891-1943)
1921: Scrap Iron
Midnight Bell
22: Gas Oil or Water
Deuce of Spades
Alias Julius Caesar
R. S. V. P.
The Barnstormer
Two Minutes To Go
Smudge

Herman C. Raymaker (1893-1944)
1914: Entered films with Keystone
Directed Mack Sennett Comedies
Directed Hank Mann Comedies
Directed Monty Banks Comedies
Directed Hall Room Boys Series
16: Ambrose's Cup of Woe
A Dog's Own Tale
17: A Clever Dummy
His Precious Life
Innocent Sinner
A Hoodoo Hindu
Camera Cure
24: Racing Luck
25: Tracked in the Snow Country
Below the Line
The Love Hour
26: His Jazz Bride
Night Cry
Millionaires
Hero of the Big Snows
27: Gay Old Bird
Simple Sis
Flying Luck
28: Under the Tonto Rim
32: Tracking the Killer T
34: Adventure Girl T

Luther Reed (1888-1961)
1921: When Knighthood Was In Flower
23: Little Old New York
24: Janice Meredith
Yolanda

25: Zander the Great
Ace of Cads
27: New York
Evening Clothes
The World at Her Feet
Shanghai Bound
Honeymoon Hate
28: Sawdust Paradise SSE
29: Rio Rita T
Hit the Deck T
30: Hell's Angels T

Frank Reicher (1876-1965)
1916: Puddin' Head Wilson
Alien Souls
For the Defense
17: Inner Shrine
18: Trouble Buster
Eternal Mother
An American Widow
The Claim
Treasure of the Sea
The Only Road
19: Suspense
Prodigal Wife
The American Way
The Battler
The Trap
20: Black Circle
Empty Arms
21: Idle Hands
Behind Masks

Charles F. Reisner (1887-1962)
1917: Evil Men Do
Lust of the Ages
18: Romance of the Air
Unconditional Surrender
A Dog's Life (co-dir.)
19: His Puppy Love
The Greenhorn
Blue Ribbon Mutt
A Day's Pleasure
20: The Kid
25: The Man on the Box
26: Oh, What a Nurse!
The Better 'ole
27: What Every Girl Should Know
The Missing Link
The Fortune Hunter
28: Fools for Luck
Steamboat Bill Junior
Brotherly Love
29: Noisy Neighbors PT
China Bound
Hollywood Revue of 1929 T
Road Show T

Harry Revier (1889-)
1918: The Grain of Dust
19: What Shall We Do With Him?
Challenge of Chance
20: The Return of Tarzan
Son of Tarzan (serial)
21: Revenge of Tarzan
Heart of the North
22: Life's Greatest Question
The Broadway Madonna
27: What Price Love
The Slaver
28: The Thrill Seeker
The Mysterious Airman (serial)

Lynn E. Reynolds (1889-1927)
1918: Broadway Arizona
Up or Down
The Gown of Destiny
Fast Company
Western Blood
Ace High
19: Treat 'em Rough!
The Rebellious Bride
Mr. Logan U.S.A.
Miss Adventure
Forbidden Room
Fame and Fortune
Little Brother of the Rich
Brute Breaker
20: The Overland Red
Bullet Proof
The Red Lane
21: The Road Demon
The Texan
Big Town Roundup
22: The Night Horseman
Up and Going
Trailin'
Sky High
For Big Stakes
Just Tony
Tom Mix in Arabia
23: Brass Commandments

23: The Gun Fighter

John Stuart Robertson (1878-1964)

1917: Baby Mine
The Bottom of the Well
18: The Menace
Girl of Today
The Make-Believe Wife
19: Come Out of the Kitchen
Misleading Widow
Here Comes the Bride
Little Miss Hoover
The Test of Honor
Let's Elope
Erstwhile Susan
Sadie Love
The Better Half
20: Dr. Jekyll and Mr. Hyde
Away Goes Prudence
A Dark Lantern
21: 39 East
Sentimental Tommy
Footlights
The Magic Cup
22: The Spanish Jade
Love's Boomerang
Tess of the Storm Country
23: The Bright Shawl
The Fighting Blade
Twenty-One
24: The Enchanted Cottage
Classmates
25: Shore Leave
New Toys
Soul Fire
27: Captain Salvation
Annie Laurie
Road to Romance
29: The Single Standard
Shanghai Lady T
30: The Night Ride T

Albert Rogell (1901-)

1923: The Great Menace
The Mask of Lopez
Go Getter
24: Galloping Gallagher
North of Nevada
The Fighting Sap
The Dangerous Coward
The Silent Stranger
25: The Snob Buster
The Circus Cyclone
25: Easy Money
Super Speed
Youth's Gamble
The Crack o' Dawn
The Fear Fighter
The Wanderer
The Spaniard
26: Man from the West
Señor Daredevil
Fighting Fate
Red Hot Leather
Wild Horse Stampede
Men of the Night
What Price Glory?
Lucky Lady
Lady of the Harem
27: Overland Stage
Western Whirlwind
Somewhere in Sonora
Men of Daring
Grinning Guns
Two Arabian Knights
The Gorilla
Love Thrill
Cheating Cheaters
The Fighting Three
Sunset Derby
The Western Rover
The Devil's Saddle
The Red Raiders
Rough and Ready
28: Shepherd of the Hills
Canyon of Adventure
Upland Rider
The Glorious Trail
29: Phantom City
Cheyenne
The Lone Wolf's Daughter PT
The Flying Marine PT
California Mail
30: Painted Faces T

Philip Rosen (1888-)

1916: Beach Comber
17: Spreading Dawn
19: The Miracle Man
Little Brother of the Rich
Brute Breaker
The Double Hold Up
The Sheriff's Oath
20: The Road to Divorce
The Path She Chose

21: Are All Men Alike?
Extravagance
The Little Fool
Lure of Youth
22: The Young Rajah
The Bonded Woman
Handle with Care
Across the Continent
World's Champion
24: This Woman
Bridge of Sighs
A Wise Son
Lovers' Lane
Being Respectable
Abraham Lincoln
25: The Heart of a Siren
The White Monkey
Wandering Footsteps
26: A Woman's Heart
Stolen Pleasure
Rose of the Tenements
Adorable Deceiver
27: Closed Gates
Heaven on Earth
Salvation Jane
The Woman Who Did Not Care
Thumbs Down
The Cruel Truth
Stranded
Cancelled Debts
Pretty Clothes
28: Burning Up Broadway
Marry the Girl
Modern Mothers
Undressed
Apache
29: The Faker
Peacock Fan
The Phantom in the House

Arthur Rosson (1887-1960)
1918: Cassidy
100% American
Social Mockery
A Case of Law
Headin' South
19: Successful Failure
Sahara
Married in Haste
Coming of the Law
Rough Riding Romance
20: Polly of the Storm Country
21: Prisoners of Love
For Those We Love
22: The Fire Bride
Desert Blossoms
The Fighting Streak
Always the Woman
23: Little Johnny Jones
The Satin Girl
Garrison's Finish
24: Measure of a Woman
25: Ridin' Pretty
The Burning Trail
The Meddler
Taming the West
The Fighting Demon
Tearing Through
26: Wet Paint
You'd Be Surprised
Stranded in Paris
27: Set Free
The Last Outlaw
Silk Legs
The Wizard
28: Play Girl
The Farmer's Daughter
29: Points West
The Long, Long Trail T

Richard Rosson (1894-)
1922: Always the Woman
26: Fine Manners
27: Blonde or Brunette
Ritzy
Rolled Stockings
Dead Man's Curve
Shootin' Irons
28: The Escape
Roadhouse
29: The Very Idea

Wesley H. Ruggles (1889-)
1914: Keystone Comedies
15: Work
Hushing the Scandal
Shanghaied
Her Painted Hero
A Submarine Pirate
16: Carmen (Chaplin's burlesque)
No One to Guide Him
Police
17: For France
Captain Jinks In and Out

17: Bobby, Movie Director
Bobby, Philanthropist
Bobby, The Pacifist
Bobby's Bravery
He Had to Camouflage
18: The Blind Adventure
19: The Winchester Woman
The Agony Column
20: Piccadilly Jim
Sooner or Later
The Desperate Hero
21: Love
Uncharted Seas
Over the Wire
The Leopard Woman
The Greater Claim
Plans of Men
22: Slippery McGee
Wild Honey
If I Were Queen
23: Mr. Billings Spends His Dime
The Heater Raider
The Remittance Woman
24: The Age of Innocence
25: The Pacemakers (serial)
The Plastic Age
A Broadway Lady
26: Kick Off
A Man of Quality
The Collegians (serial)
27: Beware of Widows
Silk Stockings
28: The Fourflusher
Finders Keepers
29: Scandal PT
Girl Overboard PT
Street Girl T
Condemned T
30: Sea Bat T

Mal St. Clair (1897-1952)

1921: The Goat (asst. Buster Keaton)
The Electric House (asst. Buster Keaton) (1st version)
22: The Blacksmith (asst. Buster Keaton)
24: How Baxter Busted In
The Lighthouse By the Sea
Find Your Man
George Washington Junior
25: On Thin Ice
Are People Parents?
The Trouble with Wives
After Business Hours
26: The Grand Duchess and the Waiter
Good and Naughty
A Woman of the World
A Sound Celebrity
The Show-Off
The Popular Sin
27: Knockout Reilly
Breakfast at Sunrise
28: Gentlemen Prefer Blondes
Sporting Goods
Beau Broadway
The Fleet's In
29: The Canary Murder Case T
Side Street T
Night Parade T
Fighting Blood Series

Al Santell (1895-)

1921: It Might Happen To You
22: Wild Cat Jordan
23: Lights Out
24: Parisian Nights
Empty Hearts
Fools in the Dark
25: The Marriage Whirl
The Man Who Played Square
Classified
26: Sweet Daddies
Bluebeard's 7 Wives
The Dancer of Paris
Subway Sadie
Just Another Blonde
27: Orchids and Ermine
Patent Leather Kid
The Gorilla
28: The Little Shepherd of Kingdom Come
Wheel of Chance
Show Girl
29: This is Heaven PT
Twin Beds T
Romance of the Rio Grance T

George Sargent

1920: High Speed
The Prey
The Whisper Market

20: Broadway Bubble
21: His Brother's Keeper
It Isn't Being Done This Season
Charming Deceiver
24: Masked Dancer
Secret of the Submarine
Gilded Youth
?? Dollars and a Heart
Gentleman from Mississippi

Paul Scardon (1875-1954)
1917: Arsene Lupin
18: Soldiers of Chance
Love Doctor
Grell Mystery
In the Balance
The Other Man
Desired Woman
A Bachelor's Children
The Golden Goal
A Game with Fate
Tangled Lives
All Men
19: Beating the Odds
Beauty Proof
Fighting Destiny
The Green God
The Man Who Won
Hoarded Assets
King of Diamonds
Silent Strength
The Gamblers
20: Darkest Hour
In Honor's Web
Partners of the Night
Children Not Wanted
21: The Broken Gates
The Breaking Point
Her Unwilling Husband
Milestones
22: False Kisses
The Golden Gallows
Shattered Dreams
A Wonderful Wife
When the Devil Drives
24: Her Own Free Will

Victor Schertzinger (1889-1941)
1916: Civilization
17: Son of His Father
18: His Mother's Boy
Hired Man
Family Skeleton
Playing the Game
His Own Home Town
The Claws of the Hun
A Nine O'Clock Town
19: Quicksands
String Beans
Hard Boiled
The Home Breaker
Lady of Red Butte
Other Men's Wives
The Sheriff's Son
Extravagance
Upstairs
Peace of Roaring River
20: The Jinx
Pinto
The Blooming Angel
The Slim Princess
21: Made in Heaven
What Happened to Rosa
The Concert
Beating the Game
22: Mr. Barnes of New York
Head Over Heels
The Bootlegger's Daughter
23: The Lonely Road
Refuge
Dollar Devils
The Kingdom Within
The Scarlet Lily
The Man Next Door
Chastity
Long Live the King
The Man Life Passed By
24: Bread
A Boy of Flanders
25: Frivolous Sal
Man and Maid
The Wheel
Thunder Mountain
Also composed 31 scores for Thos. Ince productions
26: The Golden Strain
Return of Peter Grimm
Siberia
The Lily
27: Stage Madness
Heart of Salome
The Showdown
Forgotten Faces
29: Redskin SSE

29: Nothing But the Truth T
Wheel of Life T
Fashions in Love T
30: Laughing Lady T

Ernest Schoedsack (1893-)
1925: Grass
27: Chang
29: Four Feathers SSE
31: Rango T

Victor Seastrom (1879-1960)
1917: The Outlaw and His Wife (actor)
The Girl from the Marsh Croft (actor)
20: A Man There Was (dir.)
Thy Soul Shall Bear Witness
21: You and I
22: The Stroke of Midnight
Mortal Clay
23: Name the Man
24: He Who Gets Slapped
25: Tower of Lies
Confessions of a Queen
26: The Scarlet Letter
28: Divine Woman
Hell Ship
Masks of the Devil
The Wind
30: A Lady to Love

Edward Sedgwick (1892-1933?)
1917: The Yankee Way
20: Fantomas (serial)
21: Live Wires
22: Chasing the Moon
Do and Dare
The Rough Diamond
The Bear Cat
Bar Nothin'
Boomerang Justice
23: The Thrill Chasers
The Gentleman from America
Dead Game
Single Handed
Out of Luck
The First Degree
The Rambling Kid
The Flaming Hour
Romance Land
24: The Sawdust Trail
Ridin' Kid from Powder River
Hook and Ladder
Ride for your Life
Hit and Run
Broadway or Bust
25: The Saddle Hawk
Let 'er Buck!
The Hurricane Kid
2 Fisted Jones
Lorraine of the Lions
26: Under Western Skies
The Runaway Express
The Flaming Frontier
Tin Hats
There You Are
27: The Bugle Call
Slide, Kelly, Slide
Spring Fever
28: West Point
Circus Rookies
The Cameraman
29: The Spite Marriage
30: Free and Easy T

Lew Seiler
1926: No Man's Gold
The Great K & A Train Robbery
27: The Last Trail
Outlaws of Red River
Tumbling River
Wolf Fangs
28: Square Crooks
29: The Ghost Talks T
Girls Gone Wild SSE
Song of Kentucky T

William S. Seiter (1895-1964)
1919: Morning After
Tangled Threads
13 comedies for the Carter De Havens
21: Kentucky Colonel
Hearts and Masks
Passing Through
22: Boy Crazy
The Foolish Age
The Understudy
Gay and Devilish
Eden and Return
Up and at 'em

23: When Love Comes
Bell Boy 13
Little Church Around the Corner
24: The Mad Whirl
His Forgotten Wife
Daddies
The Family Secret
Listen, Lester!
The White Sin
The Fast Worker
25: The Teaser
Dangerous Innocence
Where Was I?
26: Skinner's Dress Suit
What Happened to Jones
Rolling Home
Take It From Me
The Cheerful Fraud
27: Out All Night
The Small Bachelor
28: Thanks for the Buggy Ride
Happiness Ahead
Good Morning, Judge
Waterfront
The Outcast
29: Synthetic Sin
Why Be Good?
Prisoners PT
Smiling Irish Eyes T
Footlights and Fools T
30: The Love Racket T

George B. Seitz (1883-1944)

1914: The Perils of Pauline (serial)
15: Exploits of Elaine "
The Clutching Hand "
New Exploits of Elaine "
Romance of Elaine "
Beloved Vagabond "
16: The Iron Claw "
Pearl of the Army "
17: The Fatal Ring "
The Shielding Shadow "
Nedra "
18: The House of Hate "
19: The Lightning Raider "
Black Secret "
Bound and Gagged "
20: Pirate Gold "
The Velvet Fingers "
21: Rogues and Romance "
Hurricane Hutch "
21: The Sky Rangers (serial)
Go-Get-'em Hutch "
Speed "
Plunder "
23: The Way of a Man "
24: The 40th Door "
Into the Net "
Leather Stockings "
25: Galloping Hoofs "
Sunken Silver
Wild Horse Mesa
The Vanishing American
26: Desert Gold
Pals in Paradise
The Last Frontier
Ice Flood
27: Jim the Conqueror
The Great Mail Robbery
Blood Ship
Tigress
The Warming
Isle of Forgotten Women
28: After the Storm
Ransom
Beware of Blondes
Circus Kid PT
Court Martial
Hey Rube!
Blockade PT
29: Black Magic SSE
30: Murder on the Roof T

Larry Semon (1889-1928)

1917: Plagues and Puppy Love
Rough Toughs and Rooftops
18: Huns and Hyphens
Pluck and Plotters
19: Traps and Tangles
Scamps and Scandals
The Head Waiter
20: The Grocery Clerk
Fly Cop (co-dir. with Norman Taurog)
School Days (co-dir. with Norman Taurog)
Solid Concrete (co-dir. with Norman Taurog)
The Stagehound (co-dir. with Norman Taurog)
The Suitor (co-dir. with Norman Taurog)
21: The Sportsman (co-dir. with Norman Taurog)

22: Golf (co-dir. with T. Buckingham)
23: Lightning Love (co-dir. with J. Davis)
Horseshoes (co-dir. with J. Davis)
24: Trouble Brewing (co-dir. with J. Davis)
Her Boy Friend (co-dir. with Noel Smith)
Kid Speed (co-dir. with Noel Smith)
Girl in the Limousine
25: The Wizard of Oz
26: Stop, Look, and Listen
27: Spuds
28: A Simple Sap

Mack Sennett (1880-1960)
1908: Balked at the Altar
Father Gets in the Game
09: A Corner in Wheat
Mr. Jones Has a Card Party
The Curtain Pole
The Politician's Love Story
The Hero
Nursing a Viper
The Song of the Shirt
The Slave
The Gibson Goddess
The Lonely Villa
10: All on Account of the Milk
The Dancing Girl of Butte
The Englishman and the Girl
The Call to Arms
An Arcadian Maid
A Midnight Cupid
Effecting a Cure
A Lucky Toothache
The Masher
11: The Italian Barber
Paradise Lost
The White Rose of the Wild
Man's Genesis
The Fatal Chocolate
A Spanish Dilemma
Tomboy Bessie
11: The Would-Be Shriner
Comrades
A Dutch Gold Mine
Their First Divorce Case
Country Lovers
12: One Round O'Brien
The Fickle Spaniard
A 10-Karat Hero
Their First Kidnaping Case
An Interrupted Elopement
The Speed Demon
Cohen at Coney Island (or, (Cohen Collects a Debt)
The Water Nymph
Riley and Schultze
The New Neighbor
The Beating He Needed
Pedro's Dilemma
Stolen Glory (or, Grand Army of the Republic)
The Flirting Husband
The Ambitious Butler
Grocery Clerk's Romance
At Coney Island
At It Again
Mabel's Lovers
The Deacon's Troubles
A Tempermental Husband
The Rivals
Mr. Fix-It
A Desperate Lover
A Bear Escape
Pat's Pay Day
Brown's Seance
A Family Mixup
A Midnight Elopement
Mabel's Adventure
Useful Sheep
Hoffmeyer's Legacy
The Drummer's Vacation
The Duel
Mabel's Stratagem
The New York Hat
13: Saving Mabel's Dad
A Double Wedding
The Cure That Failed
How Hiram Won Out
Sir Thomas Lipton Out West
For Lizzie's Sake
The Mistaken Masher
The Deacon Outwitted
The Battle Who Run

13: The Jealous Waiter
Mabel's Heroes
Her Birthday Present
A Landlord's Troubles
Forced Bravery
The Professor's Daughter
A Tangled Affair
Just Brown's Luck
The Elite Ball
Heinze's Resurrection
A Doctored Affair
A Red Hot Romance
The Sleuth's Last Stand
A Deaf Burglar
The Sleuth at the Floral Parade
A Rural Third Degree
A Strong Revenge
Jenny's Pearls
The Chief's Predicament
The Two Widows
Foiling Fickle Father
Love and Pain
The Man Next Door
A Wife Wanted
The Rube and the Baron
At 12 o'clock
Her New Beau
On His Wedding Day
The Land Salesman
Hide and Seek
Those Good Old Days
A Game of Poker
Father's Choice
A Life in the Balance
Murphy's I. O. U.
A Dollar Did It
The Bangville Police
Cupid in a Dental Parlor
A Fishy Affair
The New Conductor
His Chum the Baron
That Ragtime Band
A Darktown Belle
A Little Hero
Mabel's Awful Mistake
His Ups and Downs
Algie on the Force
Their First Execution
Hubby's Job
Betwixt Love and Fire
The Foreman on the Jury
Toplitsky & Co.

13: The Gangsters
Barney Oldfield's Race
Passions! He Had Three
Help! Help! Hydrophobia!
The Hansom Driver
The Speed Queen
The Waiters' Picnic
The Tale of a Black Eye
Out and In
A Bandit
Peeping Pete
His Crooked Career
The Largest Boat Ever Launched Sideways
For Love of Mabel
Rastus and the Game-Cock
Safe in Jail
The Telltale Light
Love and Rubbish
A Noise from the Deep
The Peddler
We Would A Hunting Go
Love and Courage
Get Rich Quick
Just Kids
Professor Bean's Removal
Cohen's Outing
The Riot
A Game of Pool
The Latest in Life-savings
A Chip Off the Old Block
The Firebugs
Baby Day
Fatty's Day Off
The Gypsy Queen
The New Baby
Mabel's Dramatic Career
Mother's Boy
The Bowling Match
When Dreams Come True
Los Angeles Harbor
The Faithful Taxicab
What Father Saw
Willie Minds the Dog
Louis' Sickness at Sea
Small Time Act
The Milk We Drink
Wine
Our Children
A Muddy Romance
Fatty Joins the Force
Cohen Saves the Flag
The Woman Haters

13: Rogues' Gallery Portola
A Ride for a Bride
The Horse Thief
San Francisco Celebration (doc.)
The Gusher
Fatty's Flirtation
Protecting San Francisco from Fire (documentary)
His Sister's Kids
A Bad Game
Some Nerve
The Champion
He Would A-Hunting Go

14: Zuzu the Band Leader
A Misplaced Foot
Glimpses of Los Angeles (doc.)
Love and Dynamite
In the Clutches of a Gang
Mabel's Stormy Love Affair
How Motion Pictures Are Made (doc.)
The Under Sheriff
A Flirt's Mistake
Too Many Brides
Won in a Closet
Rebecca's Wedding Day
Double Crossed
Little Billie's Triumph
Mabel's Bare Escape
Making a Living
Little Billy's Strategy
Kid Auto Races
Mabel's Strange Predicament
A Robust Romeo
Raffles--Gentlemen Burglar
A Thief Catcher
Love and Gasoline
'twixt Love and Fire
Billy's City Cousin
Between Showers
A Film Johnnie
A False Beauty
Olives and Their Oil (doc.)
The Rural Demon
Tango Tangles
His Favorite Pastime
Cruel, Cruel Love
Barnyard Flirtations

14: A Backyard Theatre
The Star Boarder
Mack At It Again
The Passing of Izzy
Bathhouse Beauty
Mabel at the Wheel
20 Minutes of Love
Caught in a Cabaret
Caught in the Rain
When Villaims Wait
A Busy Day
A Suspended Ordeal
Finnigan's Bomb
Down on the Farm
Across the Hall
Chicken Chaser
Fatal Hich C
Where Hazel Met the Villain
Bowery Boys
The Morning Papers
Mabel's Nerve
The Water Dog
When Reuben Fooled the Bandits
Acres of Alfalfa (doc.)
Of Large Birds (doc.)
The Fatal Flirtation
The Alarm
The Fatal Mallet
Her Friend the Bandit
Our Country Cousin
The Knockout
Mabel's Busy Day
A Gambling Rube
A Missing Bride
Mabel's Married Life
Laughing Gas
Among the Mourners
Cursed by his Beauty
The Property Man
Fatty and Minnie
He-Haw
The Face on the Bar-Room Floor
Recreation
The Yosemite (doc.)
The Fatal Bumping
Fatty's Magic Pants
The Masquerader
His New Profession
The Rounders
The New Janitor

14: Shot in the Excitement
Lovers' Post Office
Those Love Pangs
Curses! They Remarked
Dough and Dynamite
His Talented Wife
Gentlemen with Nerve
A Halted Career
Now Heroes are Made
His Musical Career
His Trysting Places
The Sea Nymphs
Leading Lizzie Astray
His Taking Ways
Fatty's Jonah Day
Fatty's Wine Party
Getting Acquainted
Gussie the Golfer
A Colored Girl's Love
His Prehistoric Past
Other People's Business
The Plumber
Shotguns That Kick
Hogan's Annual Spree
His Second Childhood
Fatty Again
Mabel's Latest Prank
Love and Salt Water
Hogan's Wild Oats
The Incompetent Hero
Gussle's Quiet Day
No One to Guide Him

15: A Submarine Pirate
Tillie's Punctured Romance
Wild West Love
Stout Hearts But Weak Knees
Melrose Tells His First Falsehood
The Sky Pilot
Mabel's Nerve
Caught in the Park
Hogan's Mussy Job
The Home Breakers
Hushing the Scandal
Love Speed and Thrills
Mabel and Fatty's Wash Day
Mabel, Fatty and the Law
Rum and Wallpaper
A Dark Lover's Play
Giddy, Gay and Ticklish
His House Masher
Her Winning Punch

15: Fatty and Mabel's Simple Life
Fatty and Mabel at the San Diego Exposition
Hogan the Porter
Hogan's Romance Upset
Fatty's New Role
Hearts and Planets
Hogan Out West
His Luckless Love
Hogan's Aristocratic Dream
Love in Armor
That Springtime Feeling
That Little Band of Gold
A One Night Stand
Settled at the Seaside
Fatty's Chance Acquaintance
Fatty's Faithful Fido
Fatty's Reckless Fling
From Patches to Plenty
A Glimpse of the San Diego Exposition (doc.)
Ye Olden Grafter
Gussle's Day of Rest
Love, Loot, and Crash
Mabel and Fatty Viewing the World's Fair at San Francisco
Their Social Splash
The Rent Jumpers
Do-Re-Mi-Boom!
Droppington's Devilish Deed
Droppington's Family Tree
Gussle's Wayward Path
He Wouldn't Stay Down
Gussle's Backward Pay
Our Dare Devil Chief
For Better, For Worse
Those College Girls
Gussle Tied to Trouble
A Hash House Fraud
Fatty's Plucky Pup
Those Bitter Sweets
Wilful Ambrose
A Versatile Villain
When Love Took Wings
Fatty's Tintype Tangle
Wished on Mabel
Viewing Sherman Institute for Indians at Riverside (doc.)
When Ambrose Dared Walrus

15: A Rural Demon
The Love Thief
His Busted Trust
A Scoundrel's Toll
Foiled By Fido
When Hazel Met the Villain
Only a Farmer's Daughter
Heroes are Made
Dirty Work in a Laundry
The Rivals
Saved by Wireless
A Favorite Fool
A Game Old Knight
Her Painted Hero
Fickle Fatty's Fall
My Valet
The Stolen Magic
The Village Scandal
Fatty and the Broadway Stars
Ambrose's Fury
Ambrose's Little Hatchet
A Bear Affair
A Human Hound's Triumph
Beauty Bunglers
His Father's Footsteps
The Hunt
A Home-Breaking Hound
The Little Teacher
A Night Out
Beating Hearts and Carpets
A Janitor's Temptation
Best of Enemies
A Lover's Lost Control
Mabel Lost and Won
Merely a Married Man
Bid's a Bird
Cannon Ball
Colored Villainy
Mabel's Wilful Way
Court House Crooks
Miss Fatty's Seaside Lovers
Crooked at the End
Crossed Love and Swords

16: Dizzy Heights and Daring Hearts
Fatty and Mabel
Fatty and Mabel Adrift
The Bitter Pill
A Seminary Scandal
The Great Pearl Tangle
The Worst of Friends

16: A Modern Enoch Arden
Because He Loved Her
Perils of the Park
A Movie Star
His Hereafter
Love and Lobsters
Love Will Conquer
He Did and He Didn't
His Pride and Shame
The Snow Cure
Better Late Than Never
Fido's Fate
Cinders of Love
The Judge
Gypsy Joe
A Village Vampire
The Bright Lights
Wife and Auto Trouble
The Village Blacksmith
A Bathhouse Blunder
Bathhouse Perils
Ambrose's Cup of Woe
His Wife's Mistake
Hearts and Sparks
Love's Getaway
Laundry Liz
Ambrose's Rapid Rise
Vampire Ambrose
The Winning Punch
His Lying Heart
Bedelia's Bluff
Willie's Wabbly Way
The Great Vacuum Robbery
By Stork Delivery
His Bread and Butter
An Oil Scoundrel
His Auto Ruination
His Last Laugh
A Love Riot
His First Step
Tugboat Romeos
The Lion and the Girl
A Dash of Courage
Beware of Boarders
Sunshine
Her First Beau
No One to Guide Him
The Waiters' Ball
His Wild Oats
The Fire Chief
Love on Skates
His Alibi
She Loved a Sailor

16: Love Comet
A La Cabaret
Haystacks and Steeples
A Scoundrel's Code
The Other Man
Wings and Wheels
17: Dollars and Sense
Skidding Hearts
Betrayal of Maggie
She Needed a Doctor
Lost a Cook
A Pawnbroker's Heart
Two Crooks
Shanghaied Jonah
Safety First Ambrose
The Nick of Time Baby
Villa of the Movies
Her Circus Knight
Her Fame and Shame
Pinched in the Finish
Her Nature Dance
Teddy at the Throttle
Secrets of a Beauty Parlor
A Maiden's Trust
His Naught Thought
Her Torpedoed Love
A Royal Rogue
Cactus Nell
His Precious Life
Hula Hula Land
The Late Lamented
The Sultan's Wife
Stars and Bars
Maggie's First False Step
Dodging His Doom
An Iceman's Bride
Taming Target Center
Roping Her Romeo
A Bedroom Blunder
Are Waitresses Safe?
The Pullman Bride
A Noble Crook
He Loves Her
Bombs
18: The Kitchen Lady
His Hidden Purpose
Watch Your Neighbor
It Pays to Exercise
Sheriff Nell's Tussle
Those Athletic Girls
Friend Husband
Saucy Madeline

18: His Smothered Love
Battle Royal
Love Loop the Loops
Two Tough Tenderfeet
Her Screen Idol
Ladies First
Her Blighted Love
That Night
She Loved Him Plenty
The Summer Girls
His Wife's Friend
Sleuths
Whose Little Wife Are You?
Her First Mistake
Hide and Seek Detectives
The Village Chestnut
Mickey
19: Cupid's Day Off
Never Too Old
Rip & Stitch Tailors
East Lynne with Variations
The Village Smithy
Reilly's Wash Day
The Foolish Age
The Little Widow
When Love is Blind
Love's False Faces
Hearts and Flowers
No Mother to Guide Him
Trying to Get Along
Among Those Present
Treating 'em Rough
1919 Comedy Revue
A Lady's Tailor
Uncle Tom Without the Cabin
Up in Alf's Place
Salome Vs. Shenandoah
His Last False Step
Love Honor and Behave
Down on the Farm
Yankee Doodle in Berlin (or The Kaiser's Last Squeal)
20: 10 Dollars or 10 Days
Gee Whiz!
Fresh From the City
The Gingham Girl
Let 'er Go!
By Golly!
You Wouldn't Believe It
The Quack Doctor

20: Great Scott
Don't Weaken
It's a Boy!
My Goodness
Movie Fans
Fickle Fancy
A Fireside Brewer
Dabbing in Art
Bungalow Troubles
Married Life
21: On a Summer's Day
The Unhappy Finish
Wedding Bells Out of Tune
Sweetheart Days
Officer Cupid
Astray from the Steerage
An International Sneak
Love and Doughnuts
It Pays to Advertise
Call a Cop
Hard Knocks and Love Taps
Home Talent
She Sighed by the Seaside
Love's Outcast
Molly-O
22: By Heck
Be Reasonable
Bright Eyes
The Duck Hunter
On Patrol
Step Forward
Gymnasium Jim
Home Made Movies
Bow Wow
When Summer Comes
Oh Mabel, Behave
Cross Roads of New York
23: Where is My Wandering Boy This Evening?
Nip and Tuck
Pitfalls of the Big City
Skylarking
Down to the Sea in Shoes
Asleep at the Switch
One Cylinder Love
The Dare Devil
Flip Flops
Inbad the Sailor
The Shriek of Araby
23: Suzanna
The Extra Girl
24: One Spooky Night
Picking Peaches
Smile Please
Scarem Much
Shanghaied Lovers
The Hollywood Kid
Flickering Youth
Black Oxfords
The Cat's Meow
Yukon Jake
The Lion and the Mouse
His New Mama
Romeo and Juliet
The First 100 Years
East of the Water Plug
The Luck of the Foolish
3 Foolish Weeks
Little Robinson Corkscrew
Riders of the Purple Cows
The Hansome Carman
The Reel Virginian
Galloping Bungalows
All Night Long
Loves Sweet Piffle
The Cannonball Express
Feed of Mud
Off His Trolley
Bulls and Sand
Lizzies of the Field
Wall Street Blues
Wandering Waist Lines
25: The Sea Squaw
The Wild Goose Chaser
There He Goes
Honeymoon Hardships
Boobs in the Wood
The Beloved Bozo
His Marriage Wow
Warer Wagons
A Raspberry Romance
Bashful Jim
Giddap
Plain Clothes
Breaking the Ice
The Lion's Whiskers
Remember When?
He Who Gets Smacked
The Marriage Circus
Good Morning, Nurse
Horace Greeley Junior
Super Hooper Dyne Lizzies

25: Butter Fingers
Cupid's Boots
Lucky Stars
The Iron Nag
Hurry, Doctor!
Don't Tell Dad
Isn't Love Cuckoo?
Cold Turkey
Over There-Abouts
A Rainy Knight
Tee for Two
Skinners in Silk
Sneering Beezers
Love and Kisses
A Sweet Pickle
Dangerous Curves Behind
Good Morning, Madam
Soap Suds Lady
Take Your Time
Window Dummy
From Rages to Britches
Hotsy Totsy
26: Gosh Darn Mortgage
Wide Open Faces
Hot Cakes for Two
Saturday Afternoon
Whispering Whiskers
Funny-Mooners
Trimmed in Gold
Gooseland
Circus Today
Spanking Breezes
Wandering Willies
Hooked at the Altar
Fight Night
Ghost of Folly
Hayfoot, Strawfoot
A Yankee Doodle Duke
Muscle Bound Music
Puppy Lovetime
A Sea Dog's Tale
Smith's Baby
Smith's Picnic
Soldier Man
Smith's Visitor
Alice Be Good
When a Man's a Prince
Hubby's Quiet Little Game
Her Actor Friend
Smith's Landlord
The Perils of Petersboro
Love's Last Laugh

26: The Prodigal Bridegroom
Should Husbands Marry
A Harem Knight
Smith's Uncle
The Divorce Dodge
Hesitating Horses
A Blonde's Revenge
A Bachelor Butt-In
A Dinner Jest
Fiddlesticks
His First Flame
Hoboken to Hollywood
Ice Cool Cocos
A Love Sundae
Masked Mammas
Meet my Girl
Oh, Uncle!
27: Kitty from Killarney
Flirty Four Flushers
Smith's Pets
Should Sleep Walkers Marry?
Pass the Dumplings
Smith's Customer
Peaches and Plumbers
A Hollywood Hero
The Plumber's Daughter
A Small Town Princess
A Dozen Socks
Smith's New Home
The Jolly Jilter
Broke in China
Smith's Surprise
Smith's Kindergarten
Crazy to Act
Smith's Fishing Trip
The Pride of Pikeville
Curled in the Excitement
Smith's Candy Shop
College Kiddo
Smith's Pony
A Gold Digger of Weepah
The Gold Nut
Daddy Boy
For Sale, a Bungalow
Smith's Cook
Smith's Cousin
The Bull Fighter
The Girl from Everywhere
Love in a Police Station
Smith's Modiste Shop
28: Smith's Holiday
Run, Girl Run!

28: The Beach Club
Love at First Flight
Smith's Army Life
The Best Man
The Swim Princess
Smith's Farm Days
The Bicycle Flirt
The Girl from Nowhere
Smith's Restaurant
His Unlucky Night
The Chicken
Smith's Baby's Birthday
The Campus Carmen
A Dumb Waiter
Smith's Catalina Rowboat Race
Hubby's Week End Trips
Motor Boat Mamas
A Taxi Scandal
Taxi Beauties
Taxi for Two
Taxi Spooks
Caught in the Kitchen
Pink Pajamas
His New Stenographer
Clinked on the Corner
A Jim Jam Janitor

29: Matchmaking Mama
Whirls and Girls
Night Watchman's Mistake
The Bride's Relations
Ladies Must Eat
Button My Back
Taxi Dolls
The Bees' Buzz
Broadway Blues
Calling Husband's Bluff
The Old Barn
A Close Shave
Caught in a Taxi
The Lion's Roar
A Finished Actor
Motoring Mamas
Girl Crazy
The Big Palooka
Lunkhead
Jazz Mamas
The Constable
A Hollywood Star
The Golfers
The New Halfback
Uppercut O'Brien
Clancy at the Bat

30: Bulls and Bears
Campus Crushes
The Chumps
Sugar Plum Papa
Radio Kisses
Scotch
Divorced Sweethearts
Fat Wives for Thin
Goodbye Legs
Match Play
Honeymoon Zeppelin
Hello Television
Vacation Loves
He Trumped Her Ace
Grandma's Girl
Don't Bite the Dentist
Racket Cheers
Average Husband
Rough Idea of Love

31: The Bluffer
A Hollywood Theme Song
One Yard To Go
Dance Hall Marge
The College Vamp
Ghost Parade
Hold 'er Sheriff
Monkey Business in Africa
A Poor Fish
Just a Bear
In Conference
Hollywood Happenings
Fainting Lover
I Surrender Dear
The Cannon Ball
The Dog Doctor
Movie-Town
Slide, Speedy, Slide
One More Chance
Poker Widows
Half Holiday
The Trail of the Swordfish
The World Flier
Wrestling Swordfish
Speed
Taxi Troubles

32: The Girl in the Tonneau
Shopping with Wifie
The Great Pie Mystery
Pottsville Palooka
Man-Eating Sharks (doc.)
Dream House
The Boudoir Butler

32: Sea Going Birds (doc.)
Heavens! My Husband!
Freaks of the Deep (doc.)
Speed in the Gay Nineties
The Flirty Sleepwalker
Alaska Love
Hatta Marri
His Royal Shyness
The Candid Camera
The Giddy Age
Young Onions
Playground of the Mammals (doc.)
33: Uncle Jake
Knockout Kisses
The Human Fish
The Fatal Glass of Beer
Blue of the Night
Sing, Bing, Sing
Singing Boxer

Lowell Sherman (1885-1933)
1930: Lawful Larceny T
Losing Game T
31: Royal Bed T
Bachelor Apartment T
High Stakes T
32: Ladies of the Jury T
The Greeks Had a Word For Them T

J. Barney Sherry (1874-1944)
1905: Raffles, Amateur Gentleman
09-12 series of westerns
14: Passing of Two Gun Hicks
16: Civilization
17: Full of Life
Flying Colors
Fanatics
18: Evidence
Real Folks
Who Killed Walton?
Her Decision
High Stakes
The Secret Code
Recording Day
19: Mayor of Filbert
The Lion Man (serial) (a)
20: River's End
Man Woman Marriage
21: The Lotus Eater
Terror Trail (serial) (a)
22: Back Pay
A Woman's Woman
Till We Meet Again
Notoriety
Secrets of Paris
Sure-Fire Flint
When the Desert Calls
23: The White Sister
24: The Warrens of Virginia
Galloping Hoofs (serial) (a)
Born Rich
25: What Fools Men Are
Play Ball (serial)
26: Brown Derby
Casey of the Coast Guard (serial)
27: The Crimson Flash (serial)
The Spider Web
28: Forgotten Faces
Zeppelin
Victorious Defeat
29: Jazz Heaven T
Broadway Scandals T

Scott Sidney
1916: Bullets and Brown Eyes
The Deserter
Road to Love
17: Her Own People
Go West, Young Woman
18: Tarzan of the Apes
21: 813
24: Hold Your Breath
Reckless Romance
25: Charley's Aunt
Stop Flirting
7 Days
Madame Behave
26: Christie Comedies
The Million Dollar Handicap
The Nervous Wreck
27: The Wrong Mr. Wright
No Control

Paul Sloane (1893-)
1925: Too Many Kisses
The Shock Punch
A Man Must Live
The Coming of Amos
26: Eve's Leaves
Made for Love

26: The Clinging Vine
Corporal Kate
27: Turkish Delight
28: Blue Danube T
29: Hearts in Dixie

Edward Sloman (1885-)

1916: Sequel to Diamond from the Sky (serial)
The Frame Up
A Night in New York
18: Sands of Sacrifice
The Sea Master
Snap Judgment
In Bad
New York Luck
The Midnight Trail
A Bit of Jade
Social Briars
The Ghost of Rosy Taylor
19: Fair Enough
Mantle of Charity
Molly of the Follies
Money Isn't Everything
Put Up Your Hands
Sandy Burke of the U-Bar-U
The Westerners
20: Slam Bang Jim
The Sagebrusher
Burning Daylight
The Luck of Geraldine Laird
Blind Youth
The Mutiny of the Elsinore
21: Marriage of William Ashe
The Other Woman
The $10 Raise
Star Rover
Pilgrims of the Night
22: Shattered Idols
Woman He Loved
23: Backbone
The Eagle's Feather
The Last Hour
25: Up the Ladder
The Price of Pleasure
His People
The Storm Breaker
26: The Beautiful Cheat
The Old Soak
Butterflies in the Rain
27: Alias the Deacon
Surrender
28: We Americans
The Foreign Legion
29: Girl on the Barge PT
The Kibitzer T

Ray C. Smallwood (1888-)

1920: The Heart of a Child
The Best of Luck
21: Billions
Madame Peacock
22: Queen of the Moulin Rouge
My Old Kentucky Home
When the Desert Calls
Fools of Fortune

Clifford Smith (d. 1937)

1918: Devil Dodger
One Shot Ross
The Medicine Man
The Learnin' of Jim Benton
The Law's Outlaw
Keith of the Border
Faith Endurin'
The Boss of Lazy Y
Paying His Debts
Wolves of the Border
A Red-Haired Cupid
The Fly God
By Proxy
Cactus Crandall
19: The Pretender
Silent Rider
Untamed
20: The Cyclone
The Lone Hand
3 Gold Coins
The Girl Who Dared
21: Western Hearts
Vanishing Maid
22: Crossing Trails
Daring Danger
My Dad
23: Wild Bill Hickock
24: Ridgeway of Montana
Singer Jim McKee
The Back Trail
Fighting Fury
Daring Chances
The Western Wallop
25: Roaring Adventure
Riding Thunder
The Sign of the Cactus

25: The Open Trail
The Scrappin' Kid
The Call of Courage
Arizona Sweepstakes
Bustin' Through
Don Daredevil
Flying Hoofs
26: The Set Up
The Demon
A Six Shootin' Romance
Phantom Bullet
Sky High Corral
Rustlers' Ranch
The Terror
The Riding Rascal
The Fighting Peacemaker
The Desert's Toll
27: Loco Luck
The Valley of Hell
Open Range
28: Spurs and Saddles
29: Three Outcasts

David Smith
1918: Woman in the Web (serial)
Baree, The Son of Kazan
A Gentleman's Agreement
The Changing Woman
19: By the World Forgot
The Enchanted Barn
Wishing Ring Man
Yankee Princess
Cupid Forecloses
Over the Garden Wall
20: The Fighting Colleen
The Courage of Marge O'Doone
Pageen
21: The Silver Car
Black Beauty
It Can Be Done
22: My Wild Irish Rose
Flower of the North
A Guilty Conscience
The Little Minister
23: Midnight Alarm
Masters of Men
The 90 and 9
Pioneer Trails
Red Roses
23: The Man from Brodney's
24: The Code of the Wilderness
Captain Blood
Borrowed Husbands
My Man

Noel Mason Smith
1920: My Goodness
Comedies for Sennett
Comedies for Lehrman
Fireside Brewer
21: Made in the Kitchen
24: Her Boy Friend (with L. Semon)
Kid Speed (with L. Semon)
27: Snarl of Hate
One Chance in a Million
Where Trails Begin
Cross Breed
28: Marlie, the Killer
The Law's Lash
Fangs of Fate

John Stahl (1886-1950)
1918: Wives of Men
19: Her Code of Honor
Suspicion
Woman Under Oath
Women Men Forget
Woman in His House
21: The Child Thou Gavest Me
Greater than Love
Sowing the Wind
22: The Song of Life
One Clear Call
Suspicious Wives
23: The Wanters
The Dangerous Age
24: Husbands and Lovers
Why Men Leave Home
25: Fine Clothes
26: The Gay Deceiver
27: Lovers
In Old Kentucky

Penrhyn Stanlaws (d. 1923)
1921: The Outside Woman
The House That Jazz Built
At the End of the World
22: Over the Border

22: The Law and the Woman
The Little Minister
Pink Gods
Singed Wings

Richard Stanton
1915: Graft (serial)
18: The Yankee Way
The Scarlet Pimpernel
The Spy
Cheating the Public
Stolen Honor
Rough and Ready
19: The Caillaux Case
Jungle Trail
Land of the Free
Why America Will Win
Why I Would Not Marry
Checkers
20: Bride Thirteen (serial)
21: Face at the Window
Thunder Clap
23: McGuire of the Mounted
25: Durand of the Badlands
Responsibility
Eyes of the Soul
26: The Love Thief
??: Aloha (producer)

Paul Stein (1892-)
1927: Don't Tell the Wife
The Climbers
Forbidden Woman
28: Man-Made Woman
Show Folks PT
29: Office Scandal PT
This Thing Called Love T

Ford Sterling (1883-1939)
1914: A Thief Catcher
A False Beauty (or, A Faded Vampire)
Across the Hall
15: His Father's Footsteps
The Hunt
16: His Lying Heart

Mauritz Stiller (1883-1928)
1922: Sir Arne's Treasure
In Self Defense
24: The Blizzard
27: Hotel Imperial
The Woman on Trial
28: Street of Sin
Legend of Gosta Berling

Benjamin Stoloff (1895-)
1927: Circus Ace
Gay Retreat
Silver Valley
28: Horsemen of the Plains
Plastered in Paris SSE
29: Speakeasy T
Protection SSE
Girl from Havana T

Phil Stone
1927: Snowbound
Back Stage
Once and Forever
Girl from Gay Paree
Wild Geese

Jerome Storm
1918: Keys of the Righteous
Naughty Naughty
The Biggest Show on Earth
Desert Wooing
The Vamp
19: The Busher
Girl Dodger
Greased Lightning
Hayfoot, Strawfoot
20: Alarm Clock Andy
Crooked Straight
Red Hot Dollars
Paris Green
The Egg Crate Wallop
Homer Comes Home
21: The Village Sleuth
An Old-Fashioned Boy
Peaceful Valley
22: The Rosary
Her Sound Value
Arabian Love
Honor First
23: The Madness of Youth
Truxton King
A California Romance
Goodbye Girls
Children of Jazz
St. Elmo
24: The Brass Bowl
The Goldfish
The Siren of Seville
25: Some Punkins

26: Sweet Adeline
27: Ladies at Ease
Ranger of the North
The Swift Shadow
28: Fangs of the Wild
Law of Fear
Dog of Justice
Dog Law
Captain Careless
Tracked
29: The Yellowback
Courtin' Wildcats

Frank Strayer (1891-1964)
1926: Steppin' Out
The Lure of the Wild
Enemy of Men
The Fate of a Flirt
When the Wife's Away
Sweet Rosie O'Grady
27: Rough House Rosie
Pleasure Before Business
Now We're in the Air
Bachelor's Baby
28: Partners in Crime
Just Married
Moran of the Marines
29: Fall of Eve T
Acquitted T

Rollin Sturgeon (d. 1925)
1916: Chalice of Courage
God's Country and the Woman
Through the Wall
18: The Bride's Silence
The Rainbow Girl
The Calendar Girl
Betty and the Buccaneers
The Shuttle
Petticoat Pilot
Unclaimed Goods
19: Destiny
Hugon the Mighty
Pretty Smooth
Sundown Trail
20: The Girl in the Rain
In Folly's Trail
Breath of the Gods
21: Gilded Dreams
Mad Marriage
All Dolled Up
Danger Ahead
22: North of the Rio Grande
23: West of the Water Tower
24: Daughters of Today

Edward (Eddie) Sutherland (1897-)
1920: Number, Please
25: Wild Wild Susan
Coming Through
A Regular Fellow
26: It's the Old Army Game
Behind the Front
We're in the Navy Now
27: Love's Greatest Mistake
Fireman, Save My Child!
Figures Don't Lie
28: Tillie's Punctured Romance
Baby Cyclone SSE
29: Close Harmony T
Dance of Life T
Fast Company T
The Saturday Night Kid T
Pointed Heels T
30: Burning Up T
??: Old Army Game

Charles Swickard
1919: Almost Married
Faith
Hitting the High Spots
Light of the Western Stars
The Spender
20: The Devil's Claim
The Third Woman
Li Ting Lang
An Arabian Night
21: Body and Soul

Norman Taurog (1899-)
1920: co-directed with L. Semon
Fly Cop
School Days
Solid Concrete
The Stagehand
The Suitor
21: The Sportsman
Lloyd Hamilton Comedies
28: The Farmer's Daughter
The Diplomats
29: Lucky Boy PT

Charles Taylor
1920: Through the Eyes of Men
22: Derby Mascott

?? King of the Opium Ring
Queen of the Highway
Yosemite
From Rags to Riches
Escape from the Harem
His Brother's Crime
White Tigress of Japan
Queen of the White Slaves
Female Detectives
Girl Engineer
Stolen by Gypsies
Child Wife
Held for Ransom
Tracked Around the World
Queen of the Jungle

Ray Taylor (1888-1950)
1926: Fighting with Buffalo Bill (serial)
27: Whispering Smith Rides (serial)
28: The Scarlet Arrow (serial)
The Vanishing Rider (serial)
29: Pirate of Panama (serial)
Ace of Scotland Yard PT (serial)
The Final Reckoning PT (serial)
30: The Jade Box (serial) T

Sam Taylor (1895-1958)
1922: The Mohican's Daughter
23: Why Worry
Safety Last
24: Hot Water
Girl Shy
25: The Freshman
26: For Heaven's Sake
Exit Smiling
27: My Best Girl
28: The Tempest
Woman Disputed
29: Coquette T
Taming of the Shrew T

William Desmond Taylor (1877-1922)
1915: Diamond from the Sky (serial)
18: North of '53
Jack and Jill
Tom Sawyer
Spirit of '17
Huck and Tom
18: Up the Road with Sally
His Majesty--Bunker Bean
Mile-A-Minute Kendall
19: How Could You, Jean?
Captain Kidd, Junior
Johanna Enlists
20: Judy of Rogue's Harbor
Anne of Green Gables
Jenny Be Good
Nurse Marjorie
Huckleberry Finn
Soul of Youth
21: The Witching Hour
Sacred and Profane Love
The Furnace
Wealth
22: Morals
The Top of New York
The Green Temptation

Tom Terriss (1887-)
1914: The Chimes
18: The Fettered Woman
A Woman Between Friends
The Song of the Soul
The Business of Life
Triumph of the Weak
Find the Woman
To the Highest Bidder
19: Third Degree
Spark Divine
The Lion and the Mouse
Everybody's Girl
The Cambric Mask
The Captain's Captain
20: The Fortune Hunter
The Climbers
Tower of Jewels
The Vengeance of Durand
Captain Swift
21: The Heart of Maryland
Dead Men Tell No Tales
Trumpet Island
22: Boomerang Bill
The Challenge
23: Harbor Lights
24: The Desert Sheik
The Bandolero
25: His Buddy's Wife
26: A Romance of a Million Dollars
27: The Girl from Rio
Temptations of a Shopgirl

28: Beyond London Lights
Clothes Make Women
The Naughty Duchess
35: Mystery of Edwin Drood

George Terwilliger (1882-)
1913: The Mothering Heart
15: The Nation's Peril
16: Perils of our Girl Reporter (serial)
20: The Price Woman Pays
Slaves of Pride
The Sporting Duchess
Dollars and Sense
21: The Fatal Hour
Little Italy
22: The Bride's Play
Misleading Lady
What Fools Men Are
24: Wife in Name Only
25: Daughters Who Pay
Married?
26: The Big Show
The Highbinders
?? The Battle
Cry of Blood

Robert T. Thornby (1889-)
1916: Broken Chains
Code of the Mountains
18: The Hostage
Molly Entangled
Fair Barbarian
Little Sister of Everybody
The Fallen Angel
Lawless Love
19: When My Ship Comes In
Are You Legally Married?
Carolyn of the Corners
Her Inspiration
20: The Deadlier Sex
Fighting Cressy
Simple Souls
The Prince and Betty
Girl in the Web
21: The Blazing Trail
The Magnificent Brute
That Girl Montana
Felix O'Day
Half a Chance
22: Ridin' Wild
The Fox
The Trap
22: Lorna Doone
23: Gold Madness
Stormswept
Drivin' Fool
26: West of Broadway
The Speeding Venus

Richard Thorpe (1896-)
1924: 3 o'clock in the Morning
Rough Ridin'
Battling Buddy
Rarin' To Go
Fast and Fearless
Hard Hittin' Hamilton
Walloping Wallace
Rip Roarin' Roberts
25: Bringing Home the Bacon
Thundering Romance
Fast Fightin'
Quicker'n Lightning
Gold and Grit
On the Go
Tearin' Loose
26: Double Action Daniels
Desert Demons
The Last Card
The Dangerous Dub
Twisted Triggers
Rawhide
The Fighting Cheat
Galloping On
The Roaring Rider
Bonanza Buckaroo
Comin' an' Goin'
College Days
Double Daring
Deuce High
Easy Going
Joselyn's Wife
The Saddle Cyclone
A Streak of Luck
Speedy Spurs
Twin Triggers
Riding Rivals
Trumpin' Trouble
27: Their First Night
Redheads Preferred
The Bandit Buster
The Roarin' Broncs
The Cyclone Cowboy
The Galloping Gobs
Between Dangers
Tearin' Into Trouble

27: The Ridin' Rowdy
Pals in Peril
The Meddlin' Stranger
Skedaddle Gold
White Pebbles
The Interferin' Gent
Soda Water Cowboy
Ride 'em High
The Obligin' Buckaroo
28: Desperate Courage
Ballyhoo Buster
Cowboy Cavalier
Valley of Hunted Men
Saddle Mates
The Flying Buckaroo
Pals in Peril
Desert of the Lost
The Vanishing West (serial)
Vultures of the Sea (serial)
29: King of the Congo (serial)
Fatal Warning (serial)
The Feminine Touch
Bachelor Girl PT

Maurice Tourneur (1876-1961)
1915: Trilby
17: The Whip
Poor Little Rich Girl
Barbary Sheep
18: The Blue Bird
A Doll's House
The Rise of Jennie Cushing
Rose of the World
Prunella
19: Sporting Life
Victory
The White Circle
The Pit
Mother
The Wishing Ring Man
Woman
My Lady's Garter
White Heather
20: Treasure Island
The Life Line
The Broken Butterfly
21: Foolish Matrons
22: Lorna Doone
Last of the Mohicans
Deep Waters
The Bait
The County Fair
23: The Christian
23: The Brass Bottle
While Paris Sleeps
Jealous Husbands
Isle of Lost Ships
24: Torment
The White Moth
25: Never the Twain Shall Meet
Sporting Life
Clothes Make the Pirate
26: Old Loves and New
Aloma of the South Seas
29: The Last Flight

Laurence Trimble (1885-1954)
1911: The Pathfinder
16: My Old Dutch
Doorsteps
East is East
The Saintly Show Girl
17: The Auction Block
18: Spreading Dawn
The Light Within
19: Fool's Gold
Spotlight Sadie
20: Going Some
Everybody's Sweetheart
The Woman God Sent
The Silver Horde
21: The Silent Call
Darling Mine
22: Brawn of the North
24: The Love Master
25: White Fang
26: My Old Dutch

George Loane Tucker (1872-1921)
1914: Trey of Hearts (serial)
18: A Man of His Word
The Cinderella Man
Mother
Dodging a Million
Joan of Plattsburg
Hypocrites
The Manx Man
19: Virtuous Wives
The Miracle Man
22: Ladies Must Live

Otis Turner
1914: Trey of Hearts (serial)

Frank Tuttle (1893-1963)

1924: Dangerous Money
25: A Kiss in the Dark
Miss Bluebeard
Manicure Girl
The Lucky Devil
Lovers in Quarantine
26: Untamed Lady
The American Venus
Love 'em and Leave 'em
Kid Boots
27: Blind Alleys
Time to Love
One Woman to Another
28: The Spotlight
Love and Learn
Easy Come, Easy Go
Something Always Happens
Varsity PT
His Private Life
29: Marquis Preferred
Studio Murder Mystery T
The Green Murder Case T
Sweetie T

Jacques Tyrol

1919: The Red Viper
Human Passions
And the Children Pay
20: Truth
The Hand
21: Out of the Darkness
Face in the Crowd

Travers Vale (1865-)

1917: A Self Made Widow
The Dancer's Peril
Darkest Russia
18: Vengeance
Betsy Ross
A Woman Beneath
The Dormant Power
Easy Money
Stolen Hours
Whims of Society
Spurs of Sybil
Witch Woman
Journey's End
Man Hunt
Woman of Redemption
Joan of the Woods
19: Heart of Gold
Zero Hour
19: Soul Without Windows
Quickening Flame
Moral Headlines
The Bluffer
Just Sylvia
21: Life
22: A Pasteboard Crown
26: Western Pluck

Wally Van (1885-)

1914: Man Behind the Door
Love Luck and Gasoline
15: Fates and Flora Fourflush (serial)
Ten Billion Dollar Mystery (serial)
16: The Scarlet Runner (serial)
19: False Gods
Trail of the Octopus (serial)
20: The Evil Eye

W. S. Van Dyke (1899-1943)

1918: Men of the Desert
Gift o' Gab
19: Lady of the Dugout
20: Daredevil Jack (serial)
The Hawk's Trail (serial)
21: The Avenging Arrow (serial)
Double Adventure (serial)
22: White Eagle (serial)
According to Hoyle
Boss of Camp 4
Forget Me Not
23: Little Girl Next Door
Miracle Makers
Loving Lies
You Are in Danger
24: Half a Dollar Bill
25: The Beautiful Sinner
Gold Heels
Hearts and Spurs
Trail Rider
Ranger of the Big Pines
Timber Wolf
Desert's Price
26: War Paint
The Gentle Cyclone
27: Winners of the Wilderness
California
Spoilers of the West
Heart of the Yukon
Eyes of the Totem

27: Explorers of the West
28: Foreign Devils
Wyoming
Under the Black Eagle
White Shadows of the South Seas
29: The Pagan SSE
31: Trader Horn T

Perry Vekroff
1914: Dust of Desire
Isle of Jewels (serial)
18: Man
A Woman's Experience
19: What Love Forgives
20: Cynthia of the Minute
Trailed by Three (serial)
21: The Secret 4 (serial)
22: Perils of the Yukon (serial)

Edward Venturini
1921: The Headless Horseman
24: The Old Fool

King Vidor (1894-)
1916: Intrigue
19: The Turn in the Road
Poor Relations
Better Times
The Other Half
20: The Jack Knife Man
The Family Honor
21: Sky Pilot
Love Never Dies
22: Conquering the Woman
Woman, Wake Up!
The Real Adventure
Dusk to Dawn
23: Peg o' My Heart
Woman of Bronze
Three Wise Fools
24: Wild Oranges
Happiness
Wine of Youth
His Hour
25: Wife of the Centaur
Proud Flesh
The Big Parade
26: Bardelys the Magnificent
La Boheme
28: The Crowd
The Patsy
Show People SSE
29: Hallelujah T
30: Not So Dumb T

Robert G. Vignola (1882-1953)
1911: Rory O'More (acted)
Arrah-Na-Pogue (asst. dir.)
13: Shenandoah
14: The Vampire's Trail
The Scorpion's Sting
The Barefoot Boy
16: Reward of Patience
Great Expectations
17: The Claw
Fortunes of Fifi
Her Better Self
Love that Lives
18: Girl Who Came Back
Hungry Hearts
The Knife
Madame Jealousy
The Reason Why
Double Crossed
19: Home Town Girl
You Never Saw Such a Girl
The Woman Next Door
The Winning Girl
An Innocent Adventuress
Women's Weapons
Louisiana
Experimental Marriage
The Heart of Youth
The Third Kiss
20: The 13th Commandment
More Deadly than the Male
The World and His Wife
His Official Fiancee
21: The Passionate Pilgrim
Straight is the Way
The Woman God Changed
22: Enchantment
Beauty's Worth
The Young Diana
When Knighthood was in Flower
23: Adam and Eva
24: Married Flirts
Yolanda
25: Declasse
The Way of a Girl
26: 5th Avenue
27: Cabaret

28: Tropical Madness
29: Red Sword

Josef Von Sternberg (1894-1969)
1925: Salvation Hunters
27: Underworld
28: The Last Command
Drag Net
Docks of New York
29: The Case of Lena Smith
Thunderbolt T

Erich Von Stroheim (1886-1957)
1922: Foolish Wives
Merry-Go-Round
24: Greed
Foolish Husbands
25: The Merry Widow
27: The Wedding March

Richard Wallace (1894-)
1926: Syncopating Sue
27: McFadden's Flats
The Poor Nut
American Beauty
The Texas Steer
28: Lady Be Good
The Butter and Egg Man
29: Shopworn Angel PT
Innocents of Paris T
River of Romance T
Man Must Fight
30: Seven Days' Leave T

Raoul Walsh (1892-)
1915: The Birth of a Nation (acted)
Carmen
17: Honor System
The Silent Lie
18: Betrayed
The Conqueror
This is the Life
The Pride of New York
Woman and the Law
The Prussion Cur
19: Every Mother's Son
On the Jump
Evangeline
20: Should a Husband Forgive
The Deep Purple
Headin' Home
21: From Now On
21: The Oath
The Serenade
22: Kindred of the Dust
24: Thief of Bagdad
25: The Wanderer
The Spaniard
East of Suez
26: What Price Glory?
Lady of the Harem
The Lucky Lady
27: Loves of Carmen
The Monkey Talks
28: The Red Dance SSE
Me Gangster SSE
29: In Old Arizona T
The Cock-Eyed World T
Sadie Thompson T

Ernest Warde (1874-)
1916: Silas Marner
Vicar of Wakefield
17: A Man Without a Country
18: Three X Gordon
Man's Man
Ruler of the Road
The Dollar Bid
More Trouble
Burglar for a Night
Woman and the Beast
19: Gates of Brass
The Bells
Man in the Open
The Master Man
The Midnight Stage
The World Flame
White Man's Chance
20: The Joyous Liar
Live Sparks
Number #99
$30,000
The False Code
The Lord Loves the Irish
The Green Flame
21: The Devil to Pay
Coast of Opportunity
House of Whispers
22: Trail of the Axe
23: Ruth of the Range (serial)

John Waters (1894-1962)
1926: Born to the West
Forlorn River
Man of the Forest

27: Mysterious Rider
Arizona Bound
Drums of the Desert
Nevada
Two Flaming Youths
28: Beau Sabreur
The Vanishing Pioneer
29: Overland Telegraph
Sioux Blood

Harry Webb
1927: The Golden Stallion (serial)
Heroes of the Wild (serial)
Isle of Sunken Gold (serial)

Kenneth Webb (1892-)
1918: $1,000
Sisters of the Golden Circle
Springtime A La Carte
Mammon and the Archer
Transients in Arcadia
Tobin's Palm
Ramble in Aphasia
19: Adventure Shop
Girl Problem
Marie Ltd.
His Bridal Night
20: The Fear Market
Sinners
Stolen Kiss
21: The Devil's Garden
The Great Adventure
Jim the Penman
The Master Mind
Truth About Husbands
Salvation Nell
Buried Treasure
Ghost of a Chance
22: Fair Lady
Without Fear
His Wife's Husband
How Women Love
Secrets of Paris
23: Daring Years
24: 3 o'clock in the Morning
25: The Beautiful City
26: Just Suppose
29: Lucky in Love T

Millard Webb (1893-)
1921: Not Guilty
22: Oliver Twist
Ishmael
25: My Wife and I
The Knockout Kid
26: The Sea Beast
The Golden Cocoon
27: An Affair of the Follies
The Love Thrill
Naughty But Nice
Drop Kick
Honeymoon Hate
28: Honeymoon Flats
29: Gentlemen of the Press T
Glorifying the American Girl T
30: The Painted Angel T

Lois Weber (1882-1939)
1916: The People Vs. John Doe
17: Even As You and I
The Hand that Rocks the Cradle
The Man Who Dared God
There's No Place Like Home
18: Hypocrites
Price of a Good Time
For Husbands Only
The Doctor and the Woman
19: Borrowed Clothes
Mary Regan
Midnight Romance
When a Girl Loves
Home
20: Forbidden
21: Two Wise Wives
What's Worth While
The Blot
To Please One Woman
22: What Do Men Want
23: A Chapter in Her Life
26: The Marriage Clause
27: Sensation Seekers
The Angel of Broadway

William Wellman (1896-)
1923: The Man Who Won
Second Hand Love
Big Dan
24: Vagabond Trail
Cupid's Fireman
Not a Drum Was Heard
Circus Cowboy
26: When Husbands Flirt
The Boob

26: The Cat's Pajamas
You Never Know Women
27: Wings
28: Legion of the Condemned
Ladies of the Mob
Beggars of Life T
29: Chinatown Nights T
The Man I Love T
Woman Trap T

Alfred L. Werker
1928: Sunset Legion
Pioneer Scout
Kit Carson
Jazz Cowboy

Roland West (1887-)
1925: The Monster
26: The Bat
27: The Dove
29: Alibi T

Theodore & Leopold Wharton
Theo. 1875 -
Leop. 1870 -
1916: Mysterious of Myra (serial)
Beatrice Fairfax (serial)
17: Patria
The Great White Trail
31: New Adventures of J. Rufus Wallingford
?? The Elusive Kiss
Memories
Besetting Sin

Herbert Wilcox (1890-)
1925: Chu Chin Chow
26: Nell Gwyn
The Only Way
London
27: Tip Toes
Madame Pompadour
28: Dawn
Decameron Nights
29: The Bondsman
Woman in White

Ted Wilde (1889-)
1922: Speedy
24: Battling Orioles
27: Kid Brother
Babe Comes Home

Irvin Willat (1892-)
1917: In Slumberland
18: Guilty Man
The Zeppelin's Last Raid
19: False Faces
Law of the North
Midnight Patrol
Rustling a Bride
The Grim Game
20: Behind the Door
Below the Surface
21: Down Home
Partners of the Tide
Face of the World
22: Fifty Candles
Yellow Men and Gold
The Siren Call
On the High Seas
Pawned
23: Fog Bound
All the Brothers Were Valiant
24: North of '36
Story Without a Name
Three Miles Out
Heritage of the Desert
Wanderer of the Wasteland
25: Rugged Water
The Air Mail
The Ancient Highway
26: Enchanted Hill
Paradise
27: Back to God's Country
28: The Michigan Kid
The Cavalier SSE
29: Isle of Lost Ships T

Ben Wilson
1918: The Brass Bullet (serial)
21: The Mysterious Pearl (serial)
24: Days of '49 (serial)
25: The Power God (serial)
White Thunder
Human Tornado
The Ridin' Comet
A Two Fisted Sheriff
Scar Hanan
A Daughter of the Sioux
Fort Frayne
26: Tonio, Son of the Sierras
West of the Law
The Sheriff's Girl

26: Wolves of the Desert
Fighting Stallion
Hellhounds of the Plains
Officer 444 (serial)
27: The Mystery Brand
Range Riders
Riders of the West
Saddle Jumpers
Western Courage
A Yellow Streak
28: Old Code

Lawrence C. Windom (1876-)
1916: Blind Justice
Chimney Sweep
Way of Patience
18: Efficiency Edgar's Courtship
Fools for Luck
Two Bit Seats
Small Town Guys
A Pair of Sixes
Ruggles of Red Gap
Uneasy Money
19: Appearances of Evil
The Grey Parasol
It's a Bear
Power and the Glory
Taxi
Upside Down
20: The Very Idea
Nothing But Lies
Wanted--A Husband
Human Collateral
The Truth
21: Girl with a Jazz Heart
Headin' Home
Truth About Wives
Solomon in Society
Modern Marriage
28: Faithless Loves

Chester Withey (1887-)
1916: Old Folks at Home
Wharf Rat
Mr. Goode--The Samaritan
The Village Prodigal
17: Madame Bo-Peep
18: An Alabaster Box
Nearly Married
In Pursuit of Polly
On the Quiet
19: The Hun Within
Maggie Pepper
New Moon
The Little Comrade
20: She Loves and Lies
Romance
The Teeth of the Tiger
Flying Pat
21: Coincidence
Lessons in Love
Wedding Bells
22: Domestic Relations
Heroes and Husbands
Outcast
23: Richard the Lion-Hearted
26: Secret Orders
The Queen of Diamonds
The Pleasure Buyer
The Imposter
Going the Limit
Her Honor the Governor
28: The Bushranger

William Wolbert
1918: Sunlight's Last Raid
The Flaming Omen
When Men are Tempted
The Wild Strain
Cavanaugh of the Forest Rangers
The Home Trail
The Girl from Beyond
That Devil Bateese
19: Light of Victory

Sam Wood (1883-1949)
1920: The Dancin' Fool
Double Speed
Excuse My Dust
Sick A-Bed
What's Your Hurry?
21: City Sparrow
Peck's Bad Boy
Her Beloved Villain
Her First Elopement
The Snob
The Great Moment
22: Beyond the Rocks
Her Husband's Trademark
Under the Lash
Don't Tell Everything
23: Bluebeard's 8th Wife
My American Wife
Prodigal Daughters

23: His Children's Children
Gilded Cage
24: Bluff
The Next Corner
25: The Re-creation of Brian Kent
The Mine with the Iron Door
The Female
26: Fascinating Youth
One Minute to Play
27: Rookies
Racing Romeo
The Fair Co-Ed
28: The Latest from Paris
Telling the World
29: So This is College? T
Imperfect Ladies T
It's a Great Life T

Duke Worne

1919: Trail of the Octopus (serial)
20: The Branded Four (serial)
The Screaming Shadow (serial)
21: The Blue Fox (serial)
22: Nan of the North (serial)
23: The Eagle's Talons (serial)
25: Too Much Youth
The Pride of the Force
Easy Going Gordon
Going the Limit
26: In search of a Hero
Speed Crazed
The Speed Cop
The Gallant Fool
The Heart of a Coward
Scotty of the Scouts (serial)
Trooper 77 (serial)
27: Fighting for Fame (serial)
The Boaster
Smiling Billy
The Silent Hero
The Cruise of the Hellion
Daring Deeds
Wheel of Destiny
Heroes in Blue
28: Phantom of the Turf
Danger Patrol
Heart of Broadway
Into the Night
28: City of Purple Dreams
Man from Headquarters
Isle of Lost Men
Ships of the Night
29: When Dreams Come True
Devil's Chaplain
Some Mother's Boy
Anne Against the World
Handcuffed T
Bride of the Desert T

Wallace Worsley (1880-1944)

1918: Honor's Cross
Social Ambition
An Alien Enemy
Shackled
Wedlocked
Law Unto Himself
Intelligence
19: Little Shepherd of Kingdome Come
Woman of Pleasure
Street Called Straight
Adele
20: Penalty
21: Highest Bidder
Don't Neglect Your Wife
22: Ace of Hearts
Beautiful Liar
Grand Larceny
Rags to Riches
When Husbands Deceive
Voice of the City
Enter Madame
23: Nobody's Money
Hunchback of Notre Dame
Is Divorce a Failure?
24: The Man Who Fights Alone
26: Shadow of the Law
28: Power of Silence

William Worthington (d. 1941)

1917: Devil's Pay Day
18: 21
Ghost of the Rancho
Beloved Traitor
His Birthright
Temple of Dusk
19: Gray Horizon
Man Beneath
All Wrong
Bonds of Honor

19: Courageous Coward
Heart in Pawn
His Debt
Illustrious Prince
Dragon Painter
20: The Tong Man
Beggar Prince
Silent Barrier
21: Unknown Wife
Beautiful Gambler
Greater Profit
Opened Shutters
22: Afraid to Fight
Dr. Jim
Go Straight
Out of the Silent North
Tracked to Earth
23: Kindled Courage
Bolted Door
Fashionable Fakirs
24: Girl on the Stairs

John Griffith Wray (1888-1940)
1921: Homespun
Bean Revel
Lying Lips
22: Hail the Woman
23: Human Wreckage
What a Wife Learned
Soul of the Beast
Anna Christie
Her Reputation
24: Marriage Cheat
25: Winding Stair
26: Gilded Butterfly
Hell's 400
27: Singed
29: Careless Age T
Most Immoral Lady T

William Wyler (1902-)
1926: Lazy Lighting
Stolen Ranch
27: Blazing Days
Hard Fists
Straight Shootin'
Border Cavalier
Desert Dust
28: Thunder Riders
Anybody Here Seen Kelly?
29: The Shakedown PT
Love Trap PT
Come Across T

James Young (1878-)
1918: White Man's Law
Rose of Paradise
Missing
Mickey
Hearts in Exile
19: Gentleman of Quality
Hornet's Nest
Dawn of Understanding
Temple of Dusk
Usurper
Highest Trump
Her Country First
Rogue's Romance
Goodness Gracious
The Man Who Wouldn't Tell
The Wolf
20: Daughter of Two Worlds
A Regular Girl
Notorious Miss Lisle
21: Curtain
The Devil
Without Benefit of Clergy
22: The Masquerader
The Infidel
Omar the Tentmaker
23: Ponjola
24: Welcome Stranger
26: The Unchastened Woman
The Bells
27: Driven from Home
28: Midnight Rose

PRODUCERS

Al Christie	1886-1951	London, Ont., Canada
Harry Cohn	1891-1958	New York, N. Y.
Walt Disney	1901-1968	Chicago, Ill.
Sam Goldwyn	1884-	Warsaw, Poland
Will H. Hays	1879-1954	Sullivan, Ind.
Howard Hughes	1904-	Houston, Texas
Martin E. Johnson	1884-1937	Rockford, Ill.
Carl Laemmle Sr.	1867-1939	Laupheim, Germany
Carl Laemmle Jr.	1908-	Chicago, Ill.
Jesse L. Lasky	1881-1958	San Francisco, Calif.
Louis B. Mayer	1885-1957	Minsk, Russia
Erich Pommer	1889-1966	Hildesheim, Germany
Hal Roach	1892-	Elmira, N. Y.
Joseph M. Schenck	1878-1961	Russia
B. P. Schulberg	1892-1957	Bridgeport, Conn.
David O. Selznick	1902-	Pittsburgh, Conn.
Mack Sennett	1884-1960	Denville, Que., Canada
Irving Thalberg	1899-1936	Brooklyn, N. Y.
Jack Warner	1892-	London, Ont., Canada
Darryl F. Zannuck	1902-	Wahoo, Nebr.
Adolph Zukor	1874-	Risce, Hungary

DIRECTORS

	Height	Weight	Hair	Eyes
Roscoe "Fatty" Arbuckle	5'10"	245	fair	bl
George Archainbaud	5'11"	182	br gr	br
Dorothy Arzner	5'4"	102	br	bl
Lloyd Bacon	5'10"	170	br	bl
King Baggott	6'	185	br	bl
William Beaudine	6'1 1/2	160	br	bl
Monte Bell	6'3"	175	br	bl
Paul Bern	5'6"	140	br	haz
J. G. Blystone	6'1"	195	br	gr-gry
Frank Borzage	5'10 1/2	175	br	haz
Herbert Brenon	5'8"	165	gry	bl
Harry Joe Brown	5'7 1/2	145	dk	bl
David Butler	6	225	blk	bl
Colin Campbell	5'4"	123	bl	bl
Charlie Chaplin	5'6"	125	br	bl
Emile Chautard	5'8"	150	gr	bl
Al Christie	6'1"	175	med. br.	bl
Irving Cummings	5'11"	170	blk	br
Michael Curtiz	6'	155	br	bl
Joseph De Grasse	5'9"	170	gry	br
Cecil B. DeMille	5'11"	176	br	bl
William deMille	5'9"	155	br	br
#Walt Disney	5'8"	155	br	br
William Duncan	5'10"	180	dk br	br
Allan Dwan	5'7 1/2	200	br	gry
Reeves Eason	5'8"		aub	bl
Victor Fleming	6'1"	180	red. br	bl
Robert Florey	6'4"	175	br	br
Francis Ford			dk br	lt bl
Sidney Franklin	5'6"	130	dk br	br
Alfred Goulding	5'9"	170	fair	bl
David Wark Griffith	5'10"	190	br	gry
Nicholas Grinde	6'	190	br	bl
William S. Hart	6'1"	190	blk	br
David M. Hartford	5'11"	160	gry	br
Howard Hawks	6'1"	175	gry	bl

Producer

#William Randolph Hearst	6'4"		gry	bl
Victor Heerman	5'8"	165	gry	bl
Del Henderson	6'1"	220	dk	bl
George W. Hill	6'3 1/2	210	dk	dk
Robert F. Hill	6 1/2"	200	white	blk
Renaud Hoffman	5'8"	140	br	br
John Ince	5'10 1/2	185	gry	bl
George Irving	6'	172	gry	gry
Buster Keaton	5'5"	140	blk	br
Henry King	6'	180	br	bl
Charles Klein	5'10"	160	gry	bl
#Carl Laemmle	5'2"	140	gry	br
Edward Laemmle	5'5 1/2	125	fair	bl
Charles Lamont	5'5"	145	br	bl
#Jesse L. Lasky			br	bl
Rowland V. Lee	5'10"	160	lt br	bl
Paul Leni	5'1"	230	blk	gr
Robert Z. Leonard	6'1"	210	aub	bl
Mervyn Leory	5'7 1/2	130	br	bl
Frank Lloyd	5'11 1/2	170	br	bl
Ernst Lubitsch	5'7"	142	blk	br
Wilfred Lucas	5'11"	178	br	br
Frank Mattison	6'	185	dk	bl-gry
Frances Marion	5'3"	139	br	br
Archie Mayo	5'8"	200	blk	bl
Norman Z. McLeod	5'8"	156	gry	gry
Lothar Mendes	5'7"	140	br	bl
Lewis Milestone	5'7 1/2	175	br	bl
Marshall Neilan	5'9 1/2	165	dk br	bl
Alvin J. Neitz	5'11 1/2	180	br	bl
Fred Niblo	6'	180	br	br
Mabel Normand			blk	br
Harry Joe Pollard	5'10"		blk gry	bl
Herman C. Raymaker	5'5 1/2	145	br	br
Frank Reicher	5'7"	148	dk br	br
Charles F. Riesner	5'11"	190	br	br
Stephen Roberts	5'6"	140	blk	br
John Stuart Robertson	6'	200	br	haz
Albert Rogell	5'10 1/2	170	dk	bl
Wesley H. Ruggles			dk	br
Malcolm St. Clair	6'3"	165	br	bl
Al Santell	5'7 1/2	163	blk	br
Victor Schertzinger	5'11"	189	br	br
Edward Sedgwick	6'	251	dk	bl
William S. Seiter	6'1"	195	blk	haz

George Seitz	5'5"	145	br	br
Edgar Selwyn	5'10"		blk	br
Mack Sennett			sandy	gr
J. Barney Sherry	6'	200	iron gry	gry
Paul Sloane	5'5"	155	br	br
John Stahl	5'10"	158	gry	gry
Paul Stein	5'10 1/2		br	bl
Benjamin Stoloff	5'8"		br	gry
Phil Stone	6'1"	200	br	haz
Frank Strayer	5'10 1/2	140	iron gry	gry
Eddie Sutherland	5'8"	160	br	haz
Charles Swickard	5'10"	155	dk gry	gry
Richard Thorpe	6'	178	blk	haz
Jim Tully	5'4"	170	aub	lt. bl
Frank Tuttle	6'	170	dk br	br
King Vidor	5'11 1/2	189	blk	bl
Josef Von Sternberg	5'5"	145	blk	gry
Erich Von Stroheim	5'7"		cropped	br
Richard Wallace	6'	170	br	bl
Raoul Walsh	5'11"	185	blk	bl
Irvin Willat	5'11"	170	br	bl
Sam Wood	6'	170	br	br
John Griffith Wray	5'8"	150	br	bl-gry
William Wyler	5'8"	145	blk	dk
# Adolph Zukor	5'3"		gry	bl

PART III:

SILENT FILM STUDIO CORPORATIONS AND DISTRIBUTORS

Silent Film Studio Corporations and Distrubutors

West Coast

Frank R. Adams Productions
Alco Films Corp.
W. F. Alder Exploitations Inc.
Alliance Films
All Star Films
Amalgamated Films Producing Co.
Ambassador Productions
American Films Co. - Santa Barbara
American Publishing Co.
American Releasing Corp.
Anchor Films Distributors
Angeles Pictures Inc.
Lou Anger Films
Approved Pictures Inc.
Arrow Pictures
Artclass Pictures Corp.
Artcraft Films
Artistic Dist. Co.
Artlee Pictures
Associated Arts Corp.
Associated Authors
Associated Distributors and Exhibitors
Associated First National Pictures Inc.
Associated Pictures Corp.
Associated Productions Corp.
Atmas Productions
Aywon Films Corp.

Bachman Studios - Glendale
Balboa Company - Long Beach
Balmac Educational Film Co.
Balshofer
Monty Banks Enterprises
Barsky Productions
Logan Baynham Productions
Rex Beach Productions
Beacon Distributing Co.
Bear State Films Co. Inc.
Beauty Comedies
Belasco Productions Inc. - San Francisco
Chester Bennett Productions
Bernstein Studios
Berwilla Films Corp.
Biograph Studios
Bison Company (101)
Bluebird Films
Blue Streak Westersn
Brentwood Studios
Broncho Films
Harry Joe Brown Productions
William Brush Productions
Bull's Eye Comedies
John Bunny Comedies

Fred Caldwell Productions
California Studios
Cameo Classics
Canyon Pictures
Capital Producing Export Co.
Edwin Carewe Productions
Carlos Production Inc.
Trem Carr Productions
Carson Films
C. C. Pictures
Centaur Company
Century Comedies
Century Films
Chadwick Pictures
Champion Films
Charlie Chaplin Studios
Chesterfield Motion Picture Corp.
Choice Productions Inc.
Choice Studios
Christie Comedies (Al & Charles)
Christie Film Co.
Chronicles of American Picture Corp.
Cinema Arts Company
M. Clevee Productions

Clune Laboratories
Clune Studio
Co-Artists Productions
Comet Films
Comique Films
Comstock Pictures
Corona Films
Cortland Productions
Cosmopolitan Pictures
Cosmos Art Studio
Court Street Studio
Creative Productions
Criterion Features
Crown Productions
Culver City Studios

D'Allesandro Productions
Darrell-Mounier Productions
Howard Davies Productions
Dearholt Productions
C. B. DeMille Studios - Culver City
Denver Dixon Productions
Dependable Pictures Corp.
Diamond Film Co.
Hugh Dierker Productions
Domino Brands
Doubleday Productions
Dyreda Films

E & R Jungle Film Co.
Eagle Producing and Financing Corp.
Eastlake Studio
Eclair Films
Eclectic Films
Educational Films
Educational Pictures Securities Corp.
Effenem Corp.
Elbee Pictures Corp.
C. S. Elfelt Productions
Arthur Guy Empey Co.
Encore Films
Equitable Motion Picture Corp.
Equity Films
Epoch Film Corp.
Ermine Production
Essanay Studios - Los Angeles branch
Excellent Films

F. B. O.
Famous Players
Famous Players-Lasky
Far East Film Corp.
Feature Picture Co.
Film Booking Offices
Film Guild Productions
Film Supply Co.
Fine Arts Studios
First Division
First National Productions
Fisher Productions
Emmett Flynn Productions
Francis Ford Studios
William Fox Company
Sidney Franklin Productions
Edwin Frazee Studios
Frothingham Productions

Helen Gardner Pictures Corp.
Harry Garson Productions
Gem Pictures
General Service Studios
Gerber Hatton Productions
Neva Gerber Productions
Paul Gerson Studios - San Francisco
Goebel-erb Productions
Golden State Film Co.
Golden West Studio
Phil Goldstone Productions
Sam Goldwyn Pictures
Goldwyn-Bray Comedies
Goodman Films
Goodman Productions
Good Will Pictures Inc.
John Gorman Productions
Gotham Productions
Graf Productions - San Francisco
Granada Productions
Grand-Asher Distributing Company
Grand Studio
Griffith Studios

H & B. Film Company
Hallroom Boys Comedies
Halperin Productions
Lloyd Hamilton Corp.
Hampton Production
Lawson Harris Productions
Neal Hart Productions

William S. Hart Productions
David Hartford Productions
Hearst-Pathe serials
Herald Pictures Corp.
Herbert Productions
Hercules Film Producing Co.
Herman Films Corp.
Historical Film Corp. of America
Renaud Hoffman Productions
Hollandia Film Corp.
Hollywood Enterprises
Hollywood Photoplay
Hollywood Studios
Robert J. Horner Productions
the Horsley Company
William Horsley Co.
William Horsley Laboratories
Roy Hughes Productions
Charles Hutchison Productions
Hurricane Film Co.
Hyperion Picture Corp.
Hysterical History Comedies

Ideal Pictures
Imp Co.
John S. Ince Productions
Thomas Ince Productions
Independent Motion Picture Co.
William Inglis Studios
International Films Service
International News Reel Corp.
Irving Productions

Arthur Jacobs Corp.
Jewel Film Co.
Emory Johnson Productions
Martin Johnson Film Co.
Jolly Comedies

Kid Kahn Comedies
Kalem Studios - Glendale
Kane & King Productions
Kay-Bee Films
Buster Keaton Productions Inc.
Kelley Color Films Inc.
Kellum Talking Pictures Co.
Kennedy Features
Keystone Comedies
Kinema Art Productions
Kinemart Productions
Kinetophone
King Bee Studios
Carlton King Productions & Super Features
Richard Kipling Enterprises
George Kleine Pictures
Roy H. Klumb

L. K. C. Producing Inc.
L-Ko Studios
Jesse Lasky Feature Plays
Stan Laurel Productions
Laval Productions
Jules Le Barron Productions
J. B. Leong Productions
Irving Lesser Productions
Al Lightman Co.
Frank Lloyd Productions
Harold Lloyd Corp.
Logan Productions
Logan Baynham Productions
Lone Star Studio
Lowell Productions
the Lubin Company - Highland Park
Ernst Lubitsch Productions
Lumas Films Corp.
Lumiere Films
Lux Films
Eddie Lyon Comedies

J. K. McDonald
Douglas MacLean Productions
McNamara Studio
A. B. Maescher Productions
Majestic Pictures
Maloford Productions
Mascot Films
Louis B. Mayer Studios Inc.
Mayer-Schulberg Studios
Mayflower Company
the Meglin Kid Comedies
Metro Picture Corp.
Metropolitan Studios and Productions
Mirror Studios
Mission Film Corporation
Mixville
Montague Studios - San Francisco
Bull Montana Comedies
Morosco Co.
Motion Picture Guild
Motion Picture Patent Co.
Motion Picture Utility Co.

Mowat Productions
Mustang Shorts (westerns)
Mutual Films Corp. - San Mateo

National Film Laboratories
National Studios
Marshall Neilan Studios
Alvin J. Neitz Productions
Nestor Co.
New Brunswick Films
New Era Productions
Fred Niblo Productions
Burr Nickle Productions
Norfleet Previews

Octagon Films
O. K. Picture Productions
101 Bison Company
Our Gang Comedies

Pacific Film Co.
Pacific Studios Corp. - San Mateo
Pallas Pictures (Bosworth)
Palmer Photoplay Productions
Paralta Films
Donald Parker Studios
Paramount Pictures (United Studios)
Pash Films Corp.
Pathe
Stuart Patosi Productions
C. W. Patton Productions
Photo Drama
Mary Pickford Co.
Pickford-Fairbanks Productions
Piermont Comedies
Pioneer Pictures
Pizor Studios
Playgoers Pictures
Plum Center Comedies
Popular Pictures
Gene Stratton Porter Productions
Powhatan Films
Preferred Pictures
Principal Distributing Corp.
Producers Distributing Corp.
Punch

Quality Pictures

Rah Art Films
Rapf Pictures
Charles Ray Producing Inc.
Rayart Syndicate Co.
R-C Pictures
Realart Films
Red Seal Picture Productions
Regal Pictures Inc.
Regent Films Co.
Reliable Pictures
Reliance Films Co.
Rellimeo Film Syndicate - San Francisco
Republic Studios
Resolute Films
Revillon Frères
Rex (Universal)
Ritz Carlton Pictures Inc.
Hal Roach Studios
Jess Robbins Productions
Robinson-Cole Picture Producing Inc.
Rocket-Lincoln Film Co.
Charles R. Rogers Productions
Ruth Roland serials
Sam E. Rork Productions
Rothacker-Aller Laboratories
Russell Producing Inc.
Russell Studios

S. A. Picture Corp.
S. L. Studios - San Diego
Sable Productions
Sacramento Picture Corp.
Sacred Films - Burbank
Samuelson Picture Corp.
Sanford Productions
Joseph M. Schenck Productions
B. R. Schulberg Productions
Screen Artists Production Associates
Screen Authors Productions
Second National
Select Pictures
Selig & Rork Productions
Selig-Polyscope Co.
Selig Studios - Edendale
Selig Zoo Films
Selwyn Studios
Selznick Films
Larry Semon Comedies
Mack Sennett Studios

Shadowland Producing Inc.
Sierra Pictures
Signal Film Co. (Helen Holmes serial)
Skyland Studio - Crestline
Smalley-Rex Co. (Universal)
Dave Smith Productions
Solax Films
Spectrum Pictures
Sphinx Serials
John Stahl Productions
Standard Films Laboratories
Star Production Inc.
Star Serial Corp.
State Rights
William Steiner Productions
Stereoscopic Films
Sterling Pictures
Hunt Stromberg Productions
Sturgeon-Hubbard Film Co.
Sultan Comedies
Sunset Productions
Sunshine Comedies
Super Pictures Inc.
Super Production Epics
Syracuse Motion Picture Co.

Richard Talmadge Productions
Tec-Art Studios
Technicolor Motion Picture Corp.
Tenneck Film Corp.
Paul Terry-Toons
Thanhouser Pictures
Theatre Owners Producing & Dist. Corp.
Richard Thomas Productions
Fred Thomson Productions
Tiger Films
Tiograph Productions
Maurice Tourneur Productions
Triangle Film Corp.
Trimble-Murfin Productions
Richard Tully Productions

United Artists Producers & Dist. Inc.
United Artists Studios
United Studios (Paramount)
Universal Film Mfg. Co.
Universal Films
Universal Studios
Usona Films - Glendale

Victory Distributing Co.
Vim Comedies
Vitagraph Pictures
Vital Pictures

Wade Productions
Waldorf Productions
Warner Brothers Pictures
Warner Brothers Studios
Lois Webber Productions
Billy West Comedies
Western Arts Studios
Western Feature Productions
Jack White Corp.
Pearl White serials
Ben Wilson Productions
Wistaria Films
Wolcott Studios
World Educational Films
World Pictures Corp.
Duke Worne Productions

Sam Zierler Photoplay Corp.

East Coast

Ivan Abramson Productions - N. Y.
Actophone Studio - N. Y.
Allied Producers & Distributing Co. - N. Y.
American Progressive Pictures Inc. N. Y.
Anderson Pictures Corp. - N. Y.
Ascher Features Inc. - N. Y.
Astra Studios - Long Island, N. Y.

Banner Productions - N. Y.
Whitman Bennett Productions - Riverdale, N. Y.
Biograph Studios - N. Y.
J. Stuart Blackton Films - Brooklyn, N. Y.
Bristol Photoplay Studios - N. Y.
British Gaumont - N. Y.

Centennial Picture Co. - N. Y.
Columbia-Metro Pictures - N. Y.

Crystal Films - N. Y.
Cosmopolitan Studios - N. Y.

Danish Great Northern Films - N. Y.
DeForrest Phonofilm Co. - N. Y.
Dillon Producing Inc. - N. Y.
Distinctive Productions - N. Y.

East Coast Productions - N. Y.
Eclair Films - N. Y.
Eclair-Fox Co. - Ft. Lee, N. J.
Edison Company - N. Y.
Edison Studios - N. Y.
Erbograph Co. - N. Y.
Howard Estabrook Productions - N. Y.
Estes Co. - N. Y.

Far East Film Co. - N. Y.
54th Street Studio - N. Y.
Film Development Corp. - Yonkers, N. Y.
Film Guild Inc. - N. Y.
Filmart Co. - N. Y.
A. H. Fisher Co. - New Rochelle, N. Y.
William Fox Film Co. - N. Y.
Fox Film Corp. - N. Y.
French Gaumont Pictures
Frohman Amusement Corp. - (Flushing, L. I., N. Y.)

Murray Garsson Inc. - N. Y.
Goldwyn-Cosmopolitan Dist. Corp. N. Y.
Daniel Carson Goodman Corp. - N. Y.
Gotham Pictures - N. Y.
Gotham Studios - N. Y.
Great Northern Film Co. - N. Y.
Griffith Productions
Griffith Studios

Hepworth Distributing Corp. - N. Y.
Hi-Mark Film Sales Co. - N. Y.
Historical Pictures Inc. - N. Y.
W. W. Hodkins Co. - N. Y.

Ideal Pictures - Hudson Hgts., N. J.
Independent Picture Corp. - N. Y.
Inspiration Pictures - N. Y.
International Pictures - N. Y.
Itala - N. Y.

Jackson Studios - Bronx
Jefferson Film Co. - N. Y.
Joan Film Sales Co. Inc. - N. Y.

Kalem Studios - Cliffside, N. J.
Kinogram Publishing Corp. - N. Y.

Lee-Bradford Corp. - N. Y.
Lincoln Pictures - Grantwood, N. J.
Loew's Enterprises
Loew's Incorporated
Long Island Cinema Corp. - N. Y.
Long Island Studios - Astoria, N. Y.
Lumiere Co. - N. Y.
Luxor Pictures Inc. - N. Y.

Madison Productions - N. Y.
Mastodon Film Inc. - N. Y.
Louis B. Mayer Productions - N. Y. (branch)
Melies Pictures - N. Y.
Metro Pictures Corp. - N. Y.
Monogram Pictures Corp. - N. Y.
Monopol - N. Y.
Mutual Films Corp. - N. Y.

New York Motion Picture Co.

Octagon Films

Paragon Co. - Ft. Lee, N. J.
Pathe - N. Y.
Peerless Pictures - Ft. Lee, N. J.
Playgoers - N. Y.
Plimpton - E. Yonkers, N. Y.
Popular Players and Plays - N. J.
Powers Picture Plays - Mt. Vernon, N. Y.
Principal Pictures - N. Y.

R-C Pictures Corp. - N. Y.
Renown Pictures - N. Y.
Richmount Pictures - N. Y.
Roamax Film Corp. - N. Y.

Screen Classics Films - N. Y.
Seeling Productions (Charles R.) - N. Y.
Selznick Distributing Corp. - N. Y.
Selznick Studios - Leonia, N. J.
S. G. Pictures Corp. - N. Y.
Star Light Studios - N. Y.
Sun Picture Corp. - N. J.

Tangier Studio - L. I., N. Y.
Tec-Art Studios - Bronx, N. Y.
Technicolor Motion Picture Corp. (Boston, Mass.)
Thanhouser Studios - New Rochelle, N. Y.
Tiffany Productions Inc. - N. Y.
Tilford Cinema Studios - N. Y.
Titanic Productions - N. Y.
Tri-Stone Pictures Inc. - N. Y.
Truart Film Corp. - N. Y.

Unexcelled Pictures - Yonkers, N. Y.
Union Hills Studios - N. J.
United Artists Corp. - N. Y.
United Pictures Corp. - N. Y.
Universal Pictures - Leonia, N. J.

Victor - N. Y.
Victory Distributing Co.

Warner Brothers Pictures Inc. - N. Y.
Warner Brothers Vitagraph - Brooklyn, N. Y.
Wharton Studios - N. Y.

Zenith Pictures Corp. - N. Y.

Mid-West

Alexander Film Co. - Denver Colorado
Colorado Pictures Corp. - Denver
Essanay Studios - Chicago, Ill.
Lyman H. Howe - Wilkes-Barre, Pa.
Independent Motion Picture Co. - Dayton, Ohio
Metropolitan Industrial Film Co. - Youngstown, Ohio
Motion Picture Producing Co. - Pittsburgh, Pa.
Rembrandt Studios - Omaha, Nebraska
Romell Motion Picture Inc. - Cincinnati, Ohio
Sinecraft Films Inc. - Pittsburgh, Pa.
Sun City Studios - Sun City, Florida

WAMPAS (Western Association of Motion Picture Advertisers)